Business Communication

Fifth Edition

A.C. "Buddy" Krizan
Murray State University

Patricia Merrier
University of Minnesota Duluth

Carol Larson Jones
California State University—Pomona

Australia · Canada · Mexico · Singapore · Spain · United Kingdom · United States

Business Communication 5e, by A. C. "Buddy" Krizan, Patricia Merrier, and Carol Larson Jones

Vice President: Dave Shaut
Acquisitions Editor: Pamela M. Person
Developmental Editor: Taney H. Wilkins
Marketing Manager: Marc Callahan
Production Editor: Anne Chimenti
Manufacturing Coordinator: Sandee Milewski
Design Manager: Michelle Kunkler
Internal Design: Meighan Depke Design
Cover Design: Grannan Graphic Design
Cover Photographer: © EyeWire, Inc. and © PhotoDisk, Inc.
Photo Manager: Cary Benbow
Photo Researcher: Charlotte Goldman
Production House: Pre-Press Company, Inc.
Printer: RR Donnelley & Sons Company

Printed in the United States of America
1 2 3 4 5 04 03 02 01

For more information contact South-Western College Publishing, 5101 Madison Road, Cincinnati, Ohio, 45227 or find us on the Internet at http://www.swcollege.com

Library of Congress Cataloging-in-Publication Data
Krizan, A.C.
Business communication / A.C. "Buddy" Krizan, Patricia Merrier, Carol Larson Jones.—5th ed.
p. cm.
Rev. ed. of: Business communication / A.C. "Buddy" Krizan . . . [et al.]. 4th ed. 1999.
Includes bibliographical references and index.
ISBN 0-324-03718-X (alk. paper)
1. Business communication. I. Merrier, Patricia. II. Jones, Carol Larson. III. Title.

HF5718.H288 2002
808'.06665—dc21 00-048486

Brief Contents

Contents

Preface

The ability to communicate effectively is essential to succeed in today's business environment. We are excited to share in your success as your students learn and succeed by using the techniques we offer in the fifth edition of *Business Communication* by Krizan, Merrier, and Jones. This product is designed to assist students in achieving academic and career goals through the development of strong communication skills. This revision is organized around the traditional content of an introductory business communication course, including principles of business communication, letters, memos, reports, career communications, oral communication, global and multicultural issues, legal and ethical situations, and technology in communication. Students learn traditional skills for long reports as well as the more commonly prepared short reports and proposals. Your students will understand and possess the skills needed to implement solid business communication skills through the use of this book.

New Features of the Book

- A new "Interpersonal Communication and Teamwork" chapter develops student skills for interacting in small-group settings and includes current topics such as conflict resolution, office politics, and giving and receiving criticism.
- Web exercises including discussion questions, application exercises, and an Internet problem for each chapter give students extra practice in the process of writing as they incorporate the use of technology. Students are challenged to use the Web to practice their business writing.
- Tips and Hints boxes throughout the chapters discuss handling on-the-spot situations such as working with a microphone during a presentation and creative ideas for solving workplace dilemmas.
- WebTutor, an interactive online learning aid, provides reinforcement that helps students grasp the concepts presented throughout *Business Communication,* 5e. WebTutor is much more than an electronic study guide offering customizable support; it is an easy-to-use system designed to help you organize your course, with powerful communication tools for greater interaction and involvement, and real-world, Web-savvy links for up-to-date information, including South-Western resource centers.
- Student Website at http://krizan.swcollege.com is an innovative and comprehensive student site that contains Web exercises for each chapter in the book, text links organized by chapter, and "E-mail it!" and "Click on It!" features.

Retained Hallmark Features

- Complete, up-to-date technology coverage throughout the book helps prepare students for competition in today's workplace. Students learn the implications of scannable and electronic resumes along with information on using the Web for job searches. This engaging feature serves as a reminder that real-world situations are right around the corner.

- End-of-chapter Message Analysis exercises give students practice in analyzing real business situations. These exercises ask students to analyze a message and respond to, improve, or develop a letter or memo.
- Margin notes summarize the text material to aid student comprehension. Each margin note is a summary of the concept being covered in that portion of the text. This feature will assist students in studying for tests and should be used as review and reinforcement of the chapter concepts.
- The Let's Talk Business section in each chapter features a businessperson relating information from the *real* world to the text materials. For example, Chapter Ten features David Alexander, Vice Chairman of Ernst & Young commenting on using persuasion in everyday operations.
- Informative and interesting Communication Notes steer students through the learning process. Items such as cellular phone etiquette, e-mail guidelines, and general workplace protocol and procedures are covered, thereby allowing students to get a glimpse of real, everyday workplace environments.
- Communication Quotes from experienced professionals as well as individuals beginning their careers help provide real-life application. For example, Ed Kruse, President of Blue Bell Creamery discusses the importance of being concise and accurate in business reports. This again brings students into close contact with the business world.
- The Business English Seminars and end-of-chapter Grammar Workshops provide complete and integrated coverage of business English. These features are increasingly important because they offer your students the opportunity to improve their writing ability and business English skills.
- A documentation appendix includes guidelines for APA and MLA, with guidelines documenting the Web, CD-ROM, and other technology sources; this appendix provides students with a valuable reference for citing an outside source in papers and reports.
- Business Cases illustrate how to communicate ethically and demonstrate how to comment on or correct unethical situations. Students are introduced to situations they may face in the real world and are challenged to react or respond to the ethical issue.
- Comparisons of well-written and poorly written messages provide students with models of positive and negative messages and reports. The Good/Needs Work examples do not instruct students to identify what is a well-devised message and what is a poorly devised message, but instead, teach students the differences through numerous examples in the text.
- Designated icons help students identify key areas and stay focused.

 Technology

 Ethics

 Collaboration

 Activity

 Global

Comprehensive Learning Package

INSTRUCTIONAL RESOURCES

Instructor's Manual (ISBN 0324037201) The Instructor's Manual provides resources to increase the teaching and learning value of *Business Communication*. This useful manual includes teaching tips, activities, and guidelines for classroom discussion. Also included in the Instructor's Manual is a full set of transparency masters.

Instructor's Resource CD-ROM (ISBN 0324111592) This wonderful instructor resource includes PowerPoint Slides, a great enhancement tool for stimulating classroom lectures; ExamView testing software, allowing instructors to create appropriate and challenging quizzes and tests; and the Instructor's Manual files, all in one easy to use CD.

Transparency Acetates (ISBN 0324037279) A full set of transparencies is provided for use in the classroom.

Printed Test Bank (ISBN 0324037252) The printed test bank is available for use in conjunction with, or in place of, the ExamView software. The combination allows for the most flexible testing system yet.

Web Site http://krizan.swcollege.com Online text resources in business communication are available at your fingertips.

STUDENT RESOURCES

Study Guide (ISBN 0324037236) The Study Guide provides supplementary questions and activities to prepare students for tests and writing exercises.

WebTutor for *Business Communication,* Fifth Edition. This online learning aid allows individual students or your class as a whole to practice in an online environment developed with your students in mind.

Student Website at http://krizan.swcollege.com The comprehensive new Website adds depth and challenges your students to do more than simply "surf" the Web.

PoWER Professional Writer's Electronic Resource (0538878959) by Mary Ellen Guffey, and James and Lyn Clark. This software serves as an online reference tool and electronic workbook. It references and reinforces business English skills—grammar, punctuation, usage—plus business communication skills—letter, memo, report, and resume writing.

Creating Dynamic Multimedia Presentation Using Microsoft® PowerPoint® (0324025378) by Carol Lehman. This brief book focuses on creating dynamic presentations using Microsoft PowerPoint. It goes beyond the traditional step-by-step manual by exploring specific design techniques that lead to superior PowerPoint presentations. Lessons and exercises are built around Microsoft PowerPoint 2000 to allow students the full benefit of the latest PowerPoint functionality and features, but it will also include explanations compatible with PowerPoint '97.

The Business Communicator: An Interactive CD Series (0324022344) by Michael Netzley. This series of interactive, technology-based learning tools focuses on key business communication issues that can be enhanced by CD-ROM delivery. This portion of the series consists of modules including message organization, document design, visual presentations, and financial information presentation. Technology-based delivery enhances understanding of the material through multimedia and highly interactive lessons, examples, and skill checks.

Presentation Success: A Step-by-Step Approach (0324100922) by Jackie Jankovich Hartman and Elaine LeMay. Presentation Success: A Step-by-Step Approach is divided into four phases. Each phase consists of building blocks that lead readers to success when making presentations. By using the checklists provided throughout the book, readers will avoid common mistakes made by others, as well as eliminate frantic moments and memorable disasters. The guidelines in this book are tried and true.

CaseNet http://www.casenet.thomson.com Visit our Web site and access relevant, leading-edge cases written by the top researchers in business communication.

About the Authors

Dr. A. C. "Buddy" Krizan is professor emeritus in the College of Business and Public Affairs at Murray State University. Formerly, he served as assistant dean, department chair, and professor in the College of Business and Public Affairs. He began teaching business communication courses, seminars, and workshops in 1977. He has conducted research on a variety of topics including basic business communication, resume content, visual aids, proposals, and written and oral messages. He has served in leadership positions for national, state, and local professional organizations. Buddy has made presentations at numerous professional conferences and has published in many professional journals.

Dr. Pat Merrier is Professor in the Finance and Management Information Sciences Department at the University of Minnesota Duluth. She has nearly 30 years of secondary and post-secondary teaching experience; business communication has been a part of her teaching assignment for almost 25 years. Pat has served in a variety of leadership roles within campus, community, and professional associations. Assistant Academic Vice Chancellor, Acting Athletic Director, union president, and NCBEA president are among the posts she has held. Dr. Merrier enjoys interdisciplinary and collaborative research and has been successful in having the results of her work presented at meetings or published in professional journals. Her current research interests include interpersonal communication, group leadership, and gender communication.

Dr. Carol Larson Jones is a Professor in the Management and Human Resources Department at California State Polytechnic University, Pomona, in Pomona, California. Carol has been instrumental in developing innovative approaches to teaching communication skills and principles of management at the high school, community college, and university levels for more than 25 years. Her current research, writing, and presentation areas include: international education, diversity in the workplace, women in development, internships, English-as-a-Second Language, and groupware. Carol has made presentations at numerous professional conferences and has been published in many professional journals. She has traveled, studied, and worked in China, Swaziland, Poland, Hong Kong, Vietnam, and various European countries. Carol has served in leadership positions for national, state, and local professional organizations.

Acknowledgments

We appreciate the support of the following individuals who have reviewed and offered creative and useful suggestions for improving *Business Communication*, Fifth Edition:

Anne Beebe
Lansing Community College

Janel Bloch
Iowa State University

Roosevelt D. Butler
The College of New Jersey

Elizabeth H. Campbell
Kettering University

William B. Chapel
Michigan Technological University

Ophelia Clark
City College San Francisco

Patricia A. LaRosa
California State University

Kenneth L. Mitchell
Southeastern Louisiana University

Jeffrey G. Phillips
Northwood University

Terry D. Roach
Arkansas State University

—Buddy Krizan

—Patricia Merrier

—Carol Larson Jones

PART 1

The Communication Environment

CHAPTER:

CHAPTER

1 Business Communication Foundations

Tara Benson, Buyer, Video Merchandising, Musicland Group, Inc.

LET'S TALK BUSINESS Communication is a vital part of life. I use it during most of my waking hours without really considering it, yet I am continually immersed in communication of one form or another. I use the media to determine how to dress for the day, to decide which roads to take to work, and to learn what's making headlines around the globe. I use oral and written communication to share ideas, knowledge, and messages with others at work and home. Nonverbal communication helps me display thoughts and emotions.

Communication is important because it is the foundation of my personal and professional relationships. Communicating forms bonds and creates trust between people. At Musicland, I use various forms and techniques of communication during the course of my day to negotiate business, inform coworkers,

(Continued)

[LEARNING OBJECTIVES]

[1] EXPLAIN WHY BUSINESS COMMUNICATION IS IMPORTANT TO INDIVIDUALS AND ORGANIZATIONS.

[2] LIST AND EXPLAIN THE GOALS OF BUSINESS COMMUNICATION.

[3] DESCRIBE THE PATTERNS OF BUSINESS COMMUNICATION.

[4] EXPLAIN THE COMMUNICATION PROCESS.

[5] IDENTIFY COMMUNICATION BARRIERS AND DESCRIBE WAYS TO REMOVE THEM.

and interact with colleagues. Keeping an open line of communication enables me to work effectively and make sound decisions.

Good communication skills are tools for achieving my goals and getting the results I want.

As Tara Benson notes in the Let's Talk Business section that opens this chapter, people spend the majority of their waking hours communicating. Because it is used so extensively, communication is one of the most important skills you can develop. How well you read, listen, speak, and write will affect the quality of your personal relationships and, as shown in Figure 1.1, help determine the progress you make in your career.

[NOTE 1.1]
Individuals spend most of their time communicating.

The Importance of Communicating Effectively

- **Getting Jobs You Want** Effective communication will make it possible for you to design a powerful resume, compose a persuasive application letter, interview with poise and confidence, and get the job you want.
- **Gaining Promotions** Moving ahead in your career depends on communicating your technical competence to others and maintaining effective relationships with them.
- **Providing Leadership** Your ability to motivate and help others achieve rests on your understanding of human nature and on mastering communication skills.
- **Being Productive on the Job** Work performance is enhanced by your ability to listen effectively, speak clearly, and write competently.
- **Relating Positively to Others** Successful business and personal realtionships depend on mutual trust and respect; communicating ethically, with concern and compassion, is essential.
- **Assuring the Success of Your Organization** Your organization will succeed only if it has the support of its constituencies—support that comes from effectively communicating with customers or clients about the organization's products or services.

Figure 1.1
Key Ways in Which Communicating Effectively Is Important to You

Learning Objective [1]
EXPLAIN WHY BUSINESS COMMUNICATION IS IMPORTANT TO INDIVIDUALS AND ORGANIZATIONS.

Research with business professionals reveals that effective communication ranks high among the skills necessary to succeed in business. The number and types of work-related communication activities in which a person engages depend on his or her field and level of responsibility. For example, telemarketers spend the majority of their work hours placing calls to prospective customers; entry-level tax accountants usually devote the majority of their time to entering and manipulating data; public relations specialists gather information and write news releases; and human resource managers attend meetings, train employees, and prepare reports.

[NOTE 1.2]
Communication is a necessary workplace skill.

Businesses must have effective internal and external communication in order to succeed.

Internal operations depend on the day-to-day exchange of information among employees. Performance objectives, job instructions, financial data, customer orders, inventory data, production problems and solutions, and employee production reports illustrate the range of *internal communication* exchanged in the course of business. Organizations accomplish long-range planning and strategic decision making by relying on research, reports, proposals, conferences, evaluations, and projections.

[NOTE 1.3]
How and when you communicate varies by field.

External communication builds goodwill, brings in orders, and ensures continued existence and growth. Day-to-day external communications include sales calls, product advertisements, news releases, employment notices, bank transactions, and periodic reports to governmental agencies. External communications that have a long-range impact include new product announcements, plant expansion plans, contributions to community activities, and annual reports.

As you can see from these examples, most business communication is ***transactional;*** it involves a give-and-take relationship between the sender and the receiver(s) in order to establish a common understanding. This interaction is the primary feature that distinguishes business writing from journalistic or creative writing.

COMMUNICATION NOTE

Definition of Business Communication

The word communication comes from the Latin word *communis,* which means common. When individuals communicate, they try to establish a common understanding between or among themselves. **Business communication** is the process of establishing a common understanding between or among people within a business environment.

[NOTE 1.4] Effective communication benefits you and the organization.

Effective communication is essential to both you and the organization for which you work. The material in this book is designed to help you improve your ability to communicate. This chapter focuses on the goals, patterns, and process of communication. It also addresses communication barriers and ways to remove them. Later chapters provide more details about meeting the challenges of communicating in a business environment.

Goals of Business Communication

Learning Objective [2] LIST AND EXPLAIN THE GOALS OF BUSINESS COMMUNICATION.

Effective business communication involves both the sender and the receiver. The four basic **goals of business communication** are

[NOTE 1.5] Business communication has four goals.

[1] Receiver understanding

[2] Receiver response

[3] Favorable relationship

[4] Organizational goodwill

[NOTE 1.6] The sender has primary responsibility for communication success.

The sender must take responsibility for achieving four goals of business communication. Keep these goals in mind and assume responsibility for accomplishing them every time you initiate or respond to a message.

RECEIVER UNDERSTANDING

[NOTE 1.7] First goal: Receiver understands message as sender intended.

The first goal of business communication, **receiver understanding,** is the most important. The message must be so clear that the receiver understands it *as the sender means it to be understood.* As illustrated in the following Communication Note, failure to achieve mutual understanding can be costly.

COMMUNICATION NOTE

Communication Errors Can Be Costly

In fall 1999, NASA lost a $125 million Mars Climate Orbiter because spacecraft engineers failed to achieve a mutual understanding about the type of measurements to be used. The navigation team at the Jet Propulsion Laboratory used the metric system of millimeters and meters; the firm that designed and built the spacecraft provided data in the English system of inches, feet, and pounds. None of the Laboratory's rigorous quality control procedures caught the error during the Orbiter's nine-month, 461-million mile flight to Mars.

Adapted from "Mars Probe Lost Due to Simple Math Error," Robert Lee Hotz, Los Angeles Times, *October 1, 1999, p. A1.*

For communication to be successful, the sender and receiver must achieve shared meaning. If a supervisor were to send an e-mail to a subordinate saying, "No one plans for a meeting like you do," should the worker react with pleasure or disappointment? Is the supervisor praising or criticizing the worker's attention to detail? The message is too vague to guarantee receiver understanding. If a worker says "I'll need time off to travel to my cousin's wedding," the sender and receiver might have different ideas about the length, type, and timing of the leave. The message would be clearer if the worker were to say, "I will be taking vacation August 5, 6, and 7." Company policy and the work relationship between the sender and receiver would dictate whether the sender included the reason for the absence as part of the written or spoken message.

It is a challenge for the sender to achieve the goal of receiver understanding. To develop a clear message, the sender must consider the following four issues, which are discussed in more detail later in this chapter:

[NOTE 1.8] Sending clear messages is challenging.

- Receiver characteristics
- Message form and content
- Receiver feedback
- Communication barriers

RECEIVER RESPONSE

The second goal of business communication is receiver response. The **receiver response** may be positive, neutral, or negative. It may be conveyed through words, actions, or both. The situation will determine what is appropriate. If the chair of a committee distributes a memo announcing the time and date of a meeting, those who receive the memo may act in any of four ways. They may (1) notify the chair that they will attend, (2) notify the chair that they will be unable to attend, (3) attend without having notified the chair in advance, or (4) miss the meeting without providing advance notice. The first three actions achieve the goal of receiver response; the fourth does not.

[NOTE 1.9] Second goal: Receiver provides necessary response.

Because this goal is achieved when the receiver demonstrates his or her understanding of the message by providing an appropriate response, a sender should assist the receiver to respond. The wording of the message should encourage response. In a face-to-face conversation, the sender (speaker) can ask the receiver (listener) if he or she understands the message. Further, the sender can ask directly for a specific response.

[NOTE 1.10] The sender should make it easy for the receiver to respond.

When written messages are used, the sender can encourage a response by asking questions, enclosing a reply envelope, asking the receiver to telephone, or using any one of many other possibilities. For example, suppose a publisher receives a mail order for a cookbook, but the customer does not specify hard or soft binding. To get the information needed to fill the order, the clerk could phone; send an e-mail message; or write an inquiry letter and enclose a postage-paid, self-addressed reply card on which the customer can simply check the type of binding desired.

FAVORABLE RELATIONSHIP

[NOTE 1.11] Third goal: Sender and receiver have a favorable relationship.

The third goal of business communication—**favorable relationship**—focuses on the people involved in the communication process. In order to establish a strong business relationship, the sender and the receiver should relate to each other in three important ways: positively, personally, and professionally. They must create and maintain a favorable relationship.

[NOTE 1.12] Good relationships are important to both sender and receiver.

Both the sender and the receiver will benefit from a favorable relationship. If the sender manufactures goods or provides services, a favorable relationship might mean job satisfaction, increased sales, and more profits. If the sender is a customer, a favorable relationship could lead to a continued source of supply, better prices, and assistance if problems develop.

The sender should assume primary responsibility for creating and maintaining a favorable relationship. Some of the ways the sender can do this include

- Using positive wording
- Stressing the receiver's interests and benefits
- Doing more than is expected

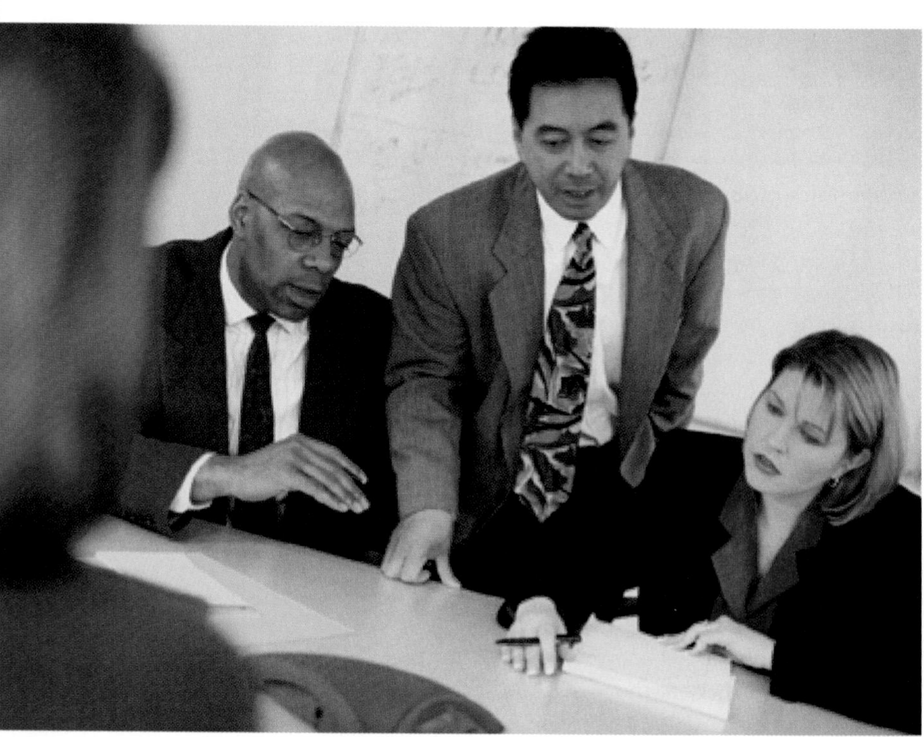

Communication helps foster positive relationships between people and the organizations they represent.

For example, suppose you have to refuse overtime work. If you simply say "No," you will do little to promote a favorable relationship with your supervisor. By finding someone who is willing to work, however, you will have helped your supervisor; you will have taken a positive approach and done more than was expected.

ORGANIZATIONAL GOODWILL

The fourth goal of business communication stresses benefit to the organization. The goodwill of customers or clients is essential to any business or organization. If a company has the goodwill of its customers, it has their confidence and often their continuing willingness to buy its products or services. The more goodwill a company has, the more successful it can be.

[NOTE 1.13]
Fourth goal: Organizational goodwill.

Senders of messages have a responsibility to try to increase goodwill for their organizations. They do so by ensuring that their communications reflect positively on the quality of the company's products, services, and personnel.

[NOTE 1.14]
Senders must help their organizations establish goodwill.

An example of an employee building goodwill for an organization is found in the handling of returned merchandise. If store policy dictates that employees should accept returned merchandise even when the customer doesn't have a receipt, the employee could say: "Would you prefer a refund or a replacement?" After the customer has chosen, the employee should complete the transaction quickly and courteously. Doing so might lead to repeat business for the company and enhance its reputation. This behavior allows the employee to generate goodwill for the store and achieve the fourth goal of business communication—**organizational goodwill.**

Learning Objective [3]
DESCRIBE THE PATTERNS OF BUSINESS COMMUNICATION.

Patterns of Business Communication

As communicators strive to achieve the four goals of business communication, they send and receive messages that are both internal and external to their organizations. Some of these messages are formal, some are informal. Some messages are work related, others are personal.

[NOTE 1.15]
Messages may be internal or external.

INTERNAL COMMUNICATION PATTERNS

Within an organization, communication can flow vertically, horizontally, or through a network. In **vertical** communication, messages flow upward or downward. Reports and proposals commonly follow the upward path; policy statements, plans, directives, and instructions typically flow downward. **Horizontal** message flow occurs when workers need to share data or coordinate efforts. These communications may occur within one unit or across two or more units. A **network** consists of a group of individuals who have some common bond. In network communication, messages flow freely between or among members.

[NOTE 1.16]
Organizational communication flows in all directions.

Figures 1.2 and 1.3 illustrate the difference between the traditional (vertical, horizontal) and network communication patterns. In the **traditional pattern,** vertical communication follows the chain of command and horizontal communication occurs between workers or units of comparable status. In **network communication,** information flow is not affected by unit or organizational level; therefore, communication can flow diagonally. In theory, all participants in network communication are viewed as equals; in reality, factors such as position, authority, and personality influence the way network members communicate with each other.

[NOTE 1.17]
Traditional and network communication have different flow patterns.

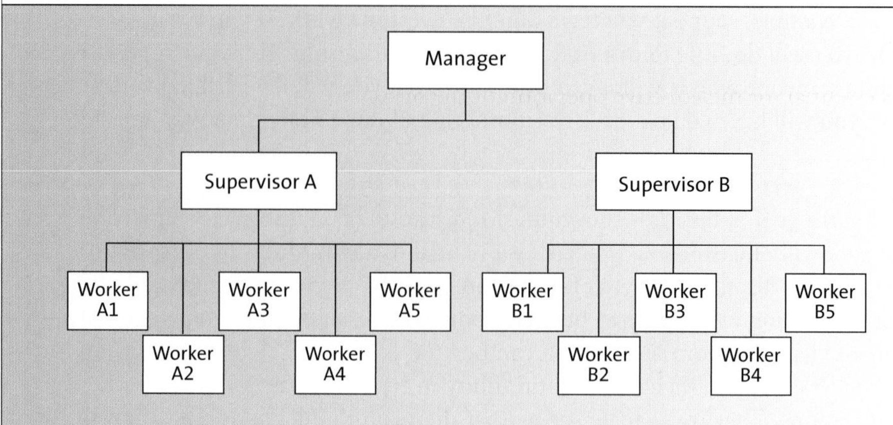

Figure 1.2
Traditional Patterns of Business Communication

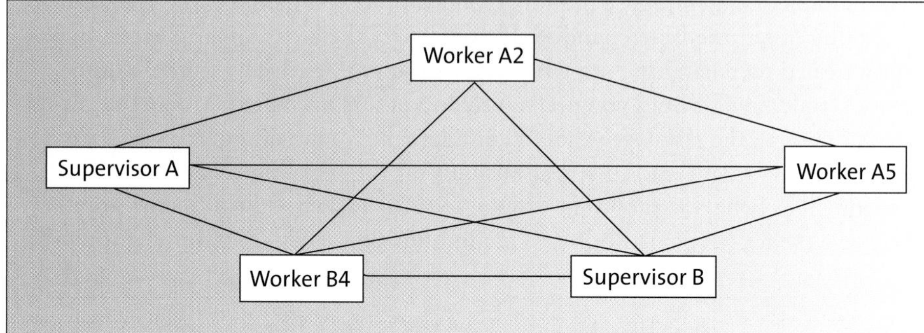

Figure 1.3
A Network

[NOTE 1.18]
Networks may be planned or unplanned.

A network may be a planned part of the business operation or it may arise from informal interactions. An example of a planned network is a project team formed to develop and market a new product. An informal network could consist of employees who share interests outside the workplace. They may eat lunch together or interact socially outside of work. Organization-based informal networks, such as company-sponsored softball teams, can be powerful. Members can discuss work-related issues outside the traditional communication structure and then combine efforts to influence the direction of the organization.

Networking extends beyond an organization and its employees into individuals' personal lives. For example, you currently participate in many different, possibly overlapping, networks. These networks consist of friends and relatives, classmates and faculty, current and former employers, and current and former coworkers. Networks are important sources of professional and personal support.

Regardless of the direction in which it flows, communication may have a formal, an informal, or a serial pattern. In this section, formal and informal refer to the nature of a communication, not the writing or speaking style used to convey a message. You'll learn more about communication style in later chapters.

[NOTE 1.19]
Formal communication is business related.

Formal Communication **Formal communication** is business related, possibly with some personal touches. It can be written (memo, report, policy) or oral (speech, meeting). Most organizations keep written records of formal oral communication—copies of speeches, minutes of meetings. Formal communication

- Is planned by the organization
- Flows in all directions
- Is essential for the effective operation of the business

Informal Communication **Informal communication**—sometimes referred to as a grapevine—consists of both business-related and personal information. Rumors about who is to become the new president of the company and a discussion of yesterday's baseball scores are two examples. Most informal communication is oral, but increased use of e-mail has made informal written communication more popular. Informal communication

[NOTE 1.20] Informal communication can be business related or personal.

- Is not planned by the organization
- Flows in all directions
- Develops and maintains positive human relationships

Serial Communication A great deal of the information flowing within an organization involves three or more individuals. Employee A will send a message to Employee B, who then sends that basic message to Employee C. The transmission chain may be longer and include more employees or groups of employees. This communication pattern is called **serial communication.**

[NOTE 1.21] Serial communication is chain transmission of information.

Serial communication is common in downward and upward flows of information. For example, job instructions are developed by managers and transmitted to the supervisors who report to them. The supervisors, in turn, transmit the instructions to the workers under their direction. Serial communication is usually oral, but it may be written as well. In serial communication, messages are usually changed—sometimes dramatically—as they are passed from one member of the chain to another. Each sender may omit, modify, or add details to the message as he or she relays it.

[NOTE 1.22] Serial communication may be oral or written.

Special precautions are necessary to maintain accuracy and achieve understanding in serial communication. Four techniques will assist in ensuring that the same meaning is transmitted.

[NOTE 1.23] Serial communication can be effective.

Senders should

- Keep the message simple
- Request feedback

Receivers should

- Take notes
- Repeat the message

E-mail has increased the amount of serial communication that occurs in writing. The ability to forward messages without paraphrasing them minimizes or eliminates the distortion customary in oral serial messages. This advantage is lost, however, when those who receive the message add to or comment on it before passing it along. Having to read the additional information can place a burden on the receiver.

EXTERNAL COMMUNICATION PATTERNS

External communication flows between a business organization and the entities with which it interacts. Companies have many external contacts such as customers, suppliers, competitors, the media, governmental agencies, and the general public. These contacts may be domestic or international. The information that flows

[NOTE 1.24] Organizations communicate with many external publics.

between a business and its external receivers can be either written or oral. Letters, reports, orders, invoices, and Web pages illustrate external written communication; telephone calls and advertisements broadcast over radio or television are examples of external oral communication.

[NOTE 1.25] External communication can be formal or informal.

Although external communication is typically formal, it may occur informally as well. Whenever an employee comments about work-related matters to someone not affiliated with the organization, informal external communication has occurred. The external audience could be a neighbor, a friend, someone to whom the worker has just been introduced at a party, or someone who accidentally overhears a conversation. Employees represent their organizations both on and off the job; therefore, they should demonstrate good communication skills in their professional and their social interactions.

Literally thousands of formal and informal communications take place every day. Individual and organizational success are enhanced only when communication is effective.

The Communication Process

Learning Objective [4] EXPLAIN THE COMMUNICATION PROCESS.

Studying the communication process can help you become a better communicator. The following sections focus on the components of the communication process model and ways to implement the model successfully.

A COMMUNICATION PROCESS MODEL

The best way to study the communication process is to analyze a model of it. An understanding of the communication process model shown in Figure 1.4 will strengthen your performance as a communicator.

Figure 1.4
A Communication Process Model

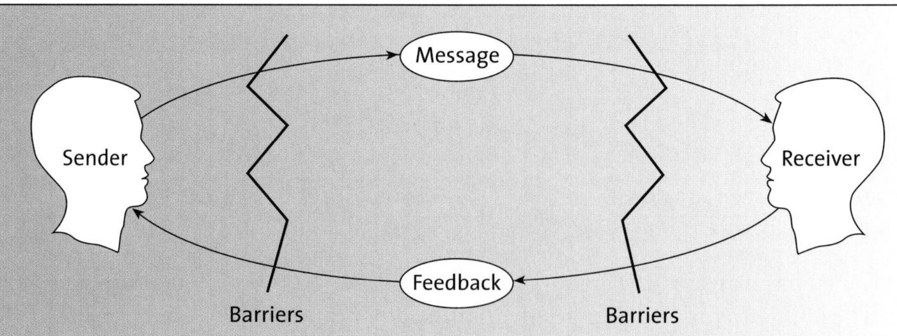

[NOTE 1.26] The communication process involves sender, receiver, message, feedback, and barriers.

The communication process model operates in an environment that includes the sender, the message, the receiver, feedback, and communication barriers. The **communication environment** includes all things perceived by the participants in that environment; namely, all things perceived by the senses—seeing, hearing, touching, smelling, and tasting.

[NOTE 1.27] Distractions must be minimized or eliminated.

The communication environment is complex and distracting. Overcoming distractions is necessary for the goals of business communication to be met. In addition, communicators must recognize that each organization has its own culture, a personality that affects the communication environment and the way the communication process is implemented. Leaders (past and present), traditions, attitudes, and philosophies determine each organization's culture. An organization may be formal, as indicated by conservative clothing, limited access to leaders, and a preference for written communication. On the other hand, an organization may be informal—casual dress, open-door policies, and a preference for oral communication. Other factors influencing the culture are the organization's values relating to diversity, seniority, friendliness, teamwork, individuality, and ethics. Effective business communicators adapt to and positively influence the development of their organizations' cultures.

[NOTE 1.28]
An organization's culture affects its communication environment.

SENDER'S AND RECEIVER'S ROLES

The sender and the receiver have important responsibilities in the communication process. If both fulfill their roles, the communication will be successful.

[NOTE 1.29]
Both sender and receiver have important roles.

Sender's Role In the communication process the sender initiates the message. The sender may be a writer, a speaker, or one who simply gestures. The **sender's role** in the communication process includes (1) selecting the type of message, (2) analyzing the receiver, (3) using the you–viewpoint, (4) encouraging feedback, and (5) removing communication barriers.

Receiver's Role The receiver is the listener, reader, or observer in the communication process. The **receiver's role** includes (1) listening or reading carefully, (2) being open to different types of senders and to new ideas, (3) making notes when necessary, (4) providing appropriate feedback to the sender, and (5) asking questions to clarify the message.

Remember, the sender has a greater responsibility for the success of communication than does the receiver. As Lisa Gutowsky notes in the Communication Quote, the sender uses words to make ideas come alive. How you can successfully fulfill your role as the initiator of the communication process is discussed in detail in the sections that follow.

[NOTE 1.30]
The sender has primary responsibility for the success of the communication.

COMMUNICATION QUOTE

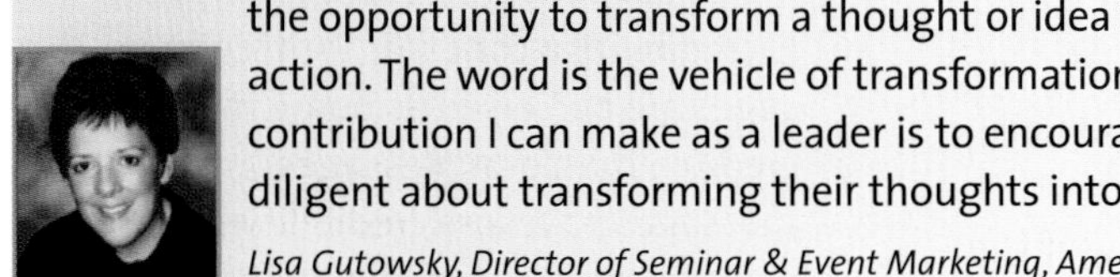

Every innovation, strategy, and concept is meaningless unless it is expressed in words. Saying the words—regardless of the medium—creates the opportunity to transform a thought or idea into possible action. The word is the vehicle of transformation. The greatest contribution I can make as a leader is to encourage others to be diligent about transforming their thoughts into words.

Lisa Gutowsky, Director of Seminar & Event Marketing, American Express.

COMMUNICATION TYPES AND CHANNELS

There are two types of communication: verbal and nonverbal. **Verbal** communication uses words; **nonverbal** communication does not. Verbal communication is commonly subdivided into two categories—written and oral.

[NOTE 1.31]
Messages may be
- Written
- Oral
- Nonverbal

All communications travel from their sender to their receiver(s) through **channels.** Written message channels include memos, letters, e-mail, notes, reports, telegrams, newsletters, and news releases. These items may include diagrams, drawings, charts, and tables. Oral message channels take many forms including face-to-face conversations, telephone conversations, voice mail, in-person conferences, video conferences, and speeches.

Senders must consider several things as they prepare to select the type of message they will send and the channel through which they will send it. Answering the questions listed in the following Tips and Hints will help you when you must make those choices.

Selecting Message Type and Channel

TIPS AND HINTS

When selecting the type of message to be used and the channel through which it will pass, ask yourself the following questions:

[1] **Do I need a permanent record of this communication?** If yes, choose a letter (external audience), a memo (internal audience), an e-mail message (either internal or external audience), or a report (either internal or external audience). Written messages can have historic and legal value.

[2] **Will my receiver(s) readily accept the message?** If yes, a written message is appropriate. If no, oral communication is preferred. The ability to convey emotion and to react to feedback make face-to-face oral communication the best format for persuading receivers or conveying bad news. The size of and distance from the audience must also be considered.

[3] **Where and how large is the audience for the message?** Face-to-face oral communication can be effective if the sender and receiver(s) are in the same location. A telephone call may work if the number of receivers is small. Written communication works best when it is impractical to bring receivers together or when the message doesn't warrant the personal touch of face-to-face communication.

[4] **Is the message long or complex?** If yes, select written communication. The writer can draft and revise the message before it is sent, and the receiver can refer to it as often as necessary to understand the message. Visual aids may supplement the written text.

[5] **Is timeliness a factor?** Do I need immediate feedback? Use face-to-face or telephone communication for urgent messages or when immediate feedback is important. In some circumstances, e-mail and fax may be viable alternatives. Letters or memos are often used to confirm messages conveyed orally.

[6] **Is credibility a concern?** Written messages are perceived as being more credible than oral messages. E-mail messages have less credibility than documents displayed on an organization's letterhead or presented as a report.

Nonverbal messages can be conveyed by both people and objects. The human channels through which these messages pass include gestures and facial expressions. Object-based nonverbal message channels include the appearance and layout of a document and the audio and visual clarity of a videotaped presentation. Nonverbal communication supplements verbal communication. Sometimes, it can be more powerful. When there is a conflict between a speaker's words and actions or between a document's contents and appearance, the receiver will most likely believe the nonverbal message.

[NOTE 1.32]
Nonverbal communication is powerful.

ANALYSIS OF THE RECEIVER FOR THE YOU–VIEWPOINT

The sender's most important task in the communication process is to analyze the receiver for the you–viewpoint. The **you–viewpoint** means that the sender gives primary consideration to the receiver's point of view when composing and sending messages. This is the most powerful concept in business communication, the key to achieving common understanding. To use the you–viewpoint, you must first analyze your receiver.

[NOTE 1.33]
The sender must analyze the receiver for the you–viewpoint.

Analyzing the Receiver No two receivers are alike. You must learn as much as possible about how a particular receiver or group of receivers thinks and feels, in general and with respect to the situation about which you will communicate. Specifically, you must analyze the receiver(s) in four areas—knowledge, interests, attitudes, and emotional reaction.

[NOTE 1.34]
Each receiver is unique.

Knowledge Begin the analysis with a review of each receiver's education and experience. Some of the questions you might ask are

[NOTE 1.35]
Analyze the receiver's knowledge.

- What is my receiver's highest level of education?
- Does my receiver have education specifically related to the topic of my message?
- How much work experience does my receiver have?
- How much of my receiver's work experience relates to the specific topic of my message?
- Does the receiver have prior experience interacting with me? with my organization?

Answers to these questions will help you decide the vocabulary level of your message, the extent to which you will be able to include technical terms, and the amount of detail the receiver will require.

Interests Second, analyze the receiver's interests. The sender will want to ask the following questions:

[NOTE 1.36]
Analyze the receiver's interests.

- What are the receiver's concerns? needs?
- Does the receiver have a particular motive? seek a particular outcome?

A receiver's position and level of authority may influence the nature of his or her interest in a situation. For example, an employee responsible for production will have a greater interest in the technical details of machine repair than will the manager to whom he or she reports. The manager's primary interests may be the timing and cost of the solution. A careful analysis of your receiver's interest will help you determine what content to include in your message and the approach you take in organizing it.

[NOTE 1.37]
Position and level of authority affect interests.

[NOTE 1.38] Analyze the receiver's attitudes.

Attitudes Third, examine the attitudes of the receiver. You'll want to ask the following questions:

- What values, beliefs, biases, and viewpoints does the receiver have?
- What words or symbols will make a positive impression on the receiver? a negative impression?
- What ideas can be used effectively to communicate with this receiver?

[NOTE 1.39] Status, personality, expectations, and culture affect attitudes.

Among the many attributes that can affect receiver attitudes are status, power, personality, expectations, nationality, and culture. Let us use the last attribute—culture—as an example. Generally speaking, Japanese prefer to communicate indirectly. Therefore, a person of Japanese heritage might use the phrase "very difficult" rather than say "No." Germans, on the other hand, favor directness; they tend to get to the point at the beginning of or very early in the message.

Culture can influence communications within a country as well as those that cross its borders. The population of the United States includes those with Hispanic, Asian, African, Native American, Polish, and many other heritages. Cultural diversity exists in other countries as well. Citizens of Canada, for example, have strong ties to the customs and traditions of England, Scotland, Ireland, France, India, Africa, Russia, and many other countries.

Knowing about a receiver's cultural heritage and nationality will help achieve the you–viewpoint in both verbal and nonverbal communication. The meaning of a gesture can vary dramatically from country to country and among cultures. An up/down nod of the head may be interpreted as *yes* in some cultures and as *no* in others. Using white paper as giftwrap will signal *joy* in some cultures, *death* in others. You will learn more about culture and communication in Chapter 2.

[NOTE 1.40] Anticipate the receiver's reaction to your message.

Emotional Reaction Finally, anticipate the receiver's emotional reaction to your message. Will the message make the receiver happy? make the receiver angry? leave the receiver unaffected? Your assessment will assist you in determining whether you should use a direct or an indirect approach. In most cultures, people will accept pleasant or neutral messages when you give the main point in your opening (direct approach). A message that could disappoint or anger a receiver, however, might gain greater acceptance if the sender offers an explanation, reason, or other supporting information before giving the main point (indirect approach).

Analyzing your receiver will assist you in every communication situation. It will enable you to make effective use of one of the most important concepts of business communication—the you–viewpoint—to achieve the goals of business communication.

[NOTE 1.41] Use the you–viewpoint to help achieve the goals of business communication.

Using the You–Viewpoint Using the you–viewpoint requires that you understand your receiver's point of view. It means that you will give your receiver's knowledge, interests, attitudes, and emotional reaction primary consideration as you develop and send your message. To achieve the goals of business communication—understanding, response, relationship, and goodwill—the sender should always use the you–viewpoint.

Your analysis of the receiver will enable use of the you–viewpoint. You can use your understanding of the receiver's knowledge to influence the ideas you include and the amount of explanation you give. In addition, you will be able to use words the receiver will understand and accept. You can design the message to address the receiver's concerns, needs, and motivations. Determining your receiver's opinions will assist you in avoiding or carefully handling negative situations. Finally, anticipating your receiver's emotional reaction will influence whether you use a direct or an indirect approach in your message.

If you are sending the same message to a group of receivers and you want to achieve the business communication goals with every member of that group, each individual in the group must be analyzed as fully as possible. Then, if the receivers are of equal importance to your goals, you must compose the message for the member(s) of the group with the least knowledge about, the least interest in, and the greatest emotional opposition to the subject.

[NOTE 1.42]
Members of a group of receivers must be individually analyzed.

The opposite of the you–viewpoint is the I–viewpoint, which includes the me–, my–, our–, and we–viewpoints. The **I–viewpoint** means the sender composes messages from his or her point of view instead of the receiver's point of view. Poor communicators use the I–viewpoint and choose message content based on their own knowledge, interests, attitudes, and emotional reaction. Only rarely will an I–viewpoint message achieve the goals of business communication.

[NOTE 1.43]
I–viewpoint messages are rarely effective.

Examine these contrasting examples of sentences from opposite viewpoints:

I–Viewpoint	You–Viewpoint
We've granted your request for a refund of your deposit.	Your deposit refund is enclosed.
We can sell each unit to you for $10 and you can charge your customers $15.	You can make a $5 profit on each unit when you buy them for $10 and sell them for $15 each.
I am really excited about your promotion.	Congratulations on being promoted!
We manufacture sunscreens with many different levels of protection.	You're sure to find a Summer Fun sunscreen with the protection factor just right for you.
You simply do not understand what I am saying.	Perhaps an example will help make the instructions more clear.

As these examples show, you–viewpoint messages respect and emphasize the receiver's perceptions and feelings. Note that *we* and *I* in many of the I–viewpoint examples have been changed to *you* and *your* in the you–viewpoint examples. This type of change seems obvious, but the you–viewpoint requires much more than simple word changes. It requires that the message be receiver-centered, not self-centered. It requires that you emphasize the receiver's interests and benefits rather than your own. When you use the you–viewpoint, the receiver is apt to respond positively to both you and the content of your message.

[NOTE 1.44]
Messages should be receiver centered.

The recommendation that you use the you–viewpoint in your messages does not suggest that you ignore basic values or compromise ethics. Honesty and forthrightness are basic to all successful business communication.

[NOTE 1.45]
Be honest and forthright when you communicate.

It will be helpful now to look at two examples of a message that the owners of a growing business wish to send to their prospective customers. The goals of the message are to inform the customers of the goods and services the business provides and to entice them to visit. Figure 1.5 is an example of a **poor** letter, one written from the I–viewpoint. Figure 1.6 is an example of a **good** letter, one written in the you–viewpoint—the receiver's viewpoint.

101 Court Square, Decatur, GA 30030-2523, 404-555-0549
Oak Tree Plaza, Decatur, GA 30030-2496, 404-555-0557

June 1, 2000

Dear Downtown Worker:

We'd like to take this opportunity to introduce ourselves. We're Kelly and Ben Antwon. We've just opened a coffee-centered gourmet shop on Court Square. We also have a shop in Oak Tree Plaza. We've been serving customers there for nearly a quarter of a century.

We invite you to visit us so we can show you our huge display of coffee and espresso machines. We also have specialty coffees, aromatic teas, thermos servers, and hundreds of cups and mugs. We also stock coffee and spice grinders, filters, and replacement carafes.

While you are in our shop, why not stop at our coffee bar for a real cup of coffee or an espresso drink . . . the best in town, people tell us.

Sincerely,

Kelly and Ben Antwon

Kelly and Ben Antwon
Owners

The opening focuses exclusively on the writers.

The invitation is overshadowed by product references.

Primary emphasis is on the writer.

Figure 1.5
Poor Letter to Prospective Customers, a Letter Written From the Sender's Viewpoint

PROVIDING FOR FEEDBACK

[NOTE 1.46]
The sender should encourage feedback from the receiver.

The sender's role in implementing the communication process includes providing for **feedback** from the receiver. Recall that appropriate receiver response is one of the goals of business communication. To achieve this goal, you can

- Ask directly or indirectly for the response
- Assist the receiver in giving the response

[NOTE 1.47]
Feedback is essential to confirm receiver understanding.

When a job applicant submits a letter and a resume to a company, he or she wants the receiver to respond by extending an invitation to interview for a job. To make it easier for the receiver to respond, the sender should be sure the message clearly asks for an interview and includes a telephone number and address where the sender can be reached easily. In a written sales message, the sender should ask for the order and provide a toll-free telephone number, an e-mail address, or an easy-to-use order form. If the communication is oral, the sender can tactfully ask

THE COFFEE CUP
A Specialty Shop and Coffee Bar

101 Court Square, Decatur, GA 30030-2523, 404-555-0549
Oak Tree Plaza, Decatur, GA 30030-2496, 404-555-0557

June 1, 2000

Dear Downtown Worker:

For nearly 25 years, The Coffee Cup has served coffee lovers in Decatur at its Oak Tree Plaza store. Now, you and others who love coffee have a chance to enjoy your favorite beverage at a new location—downtown, in the heart of Decatur's business district.

Conveniently located in Court Square, the new shop offers a huge display of coffee and espresso machines. You'll also find specialty coffees, aromatic teas, thermos servers, and hundreds of cups and mugs. Do you need filters or a replacement carafe? You'll find both here. When you need a gift for a coworker or client, consider selecting a coffee or spice grinder from among those we stock.

While you browse through our shop, why not stop at our coffee bar for a cup of great coffee or an espresso drink . . . customers tell us we serve the best in town!

The Coffee Cup is open from 9 to 5 Monday through Friday. Please stop in soon.

Sincerely,

Kelly and Ben Antwon

Kelly and Ben Antwon
Owners

Information is presented with a reader-benefit focus.

The reader-benefit theme continues.

Writer emphasis is minimized.

Additional information makes action easy.

Figure 1.6
Good *Letter to Prospective Customers, a Letter Written From the Receiver's Viewpoint*

whether the receiver understands the message or has any questions. In critical situations the sender might ask the receiver to repeat the message and explain his or her understanding of it. When speaking to a group, a sender can gain feedback by observing the audience, asking questions, or administering an evaluation instrument. Because the most important goal of business communication is that the receiver understand the message, feedback from the receiver to the sender is essential to confirm that understanding.

Communication Barriers

Learning Objective [5]
IDENTIFY COMMUNICATION BARRIERS AND DESCRIBE WAYS TO REMOVE THEM.

Although knowledge of the communication process and skill in implementing it are basic to effective communication, the sender must also deal with barriers that interfere with the communication process. A **communication barrier** is any factor that interferes with the success of the communication process (see Figure 1.4).

[NOTE 1.48]
Barriers interfere with the communication process.

These barriers may occur between any two of the communication process steps or may affect all the steps in the process. The most crucial barriers are discussed in the next sections.

WORD CHOICE

[NOTE 1.49] Communication Barrier 1: Poor word choice.

Choosing words that are too difficult, too technical, or too easy for your receiver can be a communication barrier. If words are too difficult or too technical, the receiver may not understand them; if they are too simple, the reader could become bored or be insulted. In either case, the message falls short of meeting its goals. As you will recall, analyzing the receiver will lead to determining the vocabulary level of the message. Therefore, senders must be careful to choose the correct words for their messages. Refer to Business English Seminar E for examples of many words that are easily confused or frequently misused.

Word choice is also a consideration when communicating with receivers for whom English is not the primary language. These receivers may not be familiar with *colloquial* English—the casual or informal way in which the language may be used.

DENOTATIVE VERSUS CONNOTATIVE MEANING

[NOTE 1.50] Communication Barrier 2: Differing connotation.

A receiver and a sender may attach different meanings to the words used in a message. A **denotation** is the specific dictionary definition for a word. A **connotation** is any other meaning a word suggests to a receiver based on his or her experiences, interests, opinions, and emotions. Connotative meanings can also be the result of slang or sarcasm. Senders should analyze their receivers as thoroughly as possible to determine what connotations those receivers might attach to specific words.

If you said to one of your subordinates, "Well, that certainly was fast work!" you may have meant the work was completed in less time than you expected. The receiver, however, may attach a different meaning to the statement. Based on what he or she is thinking and feeling at the moment, the receiver may think you meant the work was slow, was done too quickly, or was done improperly. Other specific examples of connotations versus denotations include the following:

Word	Possible Meanings	
assertive	energetic	pushy
compromise	adjust	give in
equitable	fair	equal
frugal	thrifty	cheap
funny	humorous	unusual

IMPLICATIONS AND INFERENCES

[NOTE 1.51] Communication Barrier 3: Inappropriate implications and inferences.

An **implication** is a meaning given through connotation rather than through specific details. An **inference** is a conclusion drawn from connotation rather than specific details. Although inferences and implications need not occur as a set, a speaker who *implies* something can cause a receiver to *infer* a meaning different from what was intended. For example, a person who says that his work is undervalued may mean to suggest that he doesn't get enough positive feedback from his supervisor. Without specific detail, however, the receiver of the message might infer that the speaker believes his salary isn't high enough. To guard against this communication barrier, senders should always use specific language and receivers should clarify meaning by asking questions. The following Communication Note describes a situation in which the sender's intent to imply humor was misunderstood.

COMMUNICATION NOTE

If It Was a Joke, Why Isn't Anyone Laughing?

If you saw an ad announcing a contest offering his-and-hers Mercedes Benzes as prizes for creating the best slogan for a convention, would you enter?

David Mears did, and his slogan "At the Top and Still Climbing" was selected as the best entry. When Nationwide Mutual Insurance Company tried to give him a gift certificate for dinner, however, Mr. Mears sued the company for breach of contract. The company, which says it meant the contest as a light-hearted invitation, maintained that readers should have recognized that a slogan wouldn't merit such expensive prizes.

The jury that decided the case awarded Mr. Mears $60,000, the approximate value of the two cars promised as a prize. The company appealed the case, but lost. In commenting about the result of the appellate court proceeding, a representative of the company noted that "you've got to be careful what you say."

Adapted from "Congratulations, Contest Winner! But Our Prize Offer Was a Joke," Arnold Ceballos, The Wall Street Journal, *September 6, 1996, p. B1.*

Implications may be made and inferences may be drawn from actions as well as words. For example, suppose that two employees laugh as their supervisor passes. The supervisor may infer that the workers are making fun of him or her. The workers, however, may have wanted to signal that their morale is high or, more likely, to signal nothing at all.

In spite of the problems they can cause, inferences and implications play a role in workplace communication. Intelligent and appropriate inferences are essential to initiative and follow-through on the job; implying rather than directly stating bad news can soften its impact on the receiver. The challenge is to ensure that inferences and implications are appropriate. Carefully analyzing the receiver and situation will help you to meet this challenge.

GRAMMAR, SPELLING, PUNCTUATION, AND SENTENCE STRUCTURE

Incorrect grammar and poor sentence structure could hinder the receiver's understanding of a spoken or written message. As Todd Fedora indicates in his Communication Quote, punctuation and spelling errors may create barriers to understanding a written message and may cause the sender to lose credibility. The errors suggest that the person who sent the message either does not know the basics of the language or was too careless to correct the problems. Neither explanation creates a positive impression of the person who sent the message.

[NOTE 1.52]
Communication Barrier 4: Incorrect grammar, spelling, punctuation, and sentence structure.

B.C.

COMMUNICATION QUOTE

New relationships are built on earning comfort, something that can only be achieved by projecting a positive and professional image. An integral part to supporting a positive and professional image is in the quality of its delivery. Correct grammar, and proofreading your marketing materials and correspondence, fuels the view that your present and prospective customers have about you.

Todd P. Fedora, Vice President, Senior Lending Officer, M&I Bank.

TYPE OF MESSAGE

[NOTE 1.53] Communication Barrier 5: Wrong type of message.

Selecting a message type appropriate to the situation is essential to communication success. For example, communicating complex job instructions orally will most likely fail because the receiver must rely solely on his or her memory of what was said—or perhaps memory plus sketchy notes. A written message to which the worker can refer as needed will achieve better results. An in-person oral message is desirable when resolving a conflict between employees. Both the sender and the receiver can take full advantage of the nonverbal cues that accompany the spoken words.

If the message is a report on an evaluation of alternative manufacturing processes, the type of message will depend on who will receive it. The report may be written or oral, long or short, technical or simple; graphic aids might be used to support verbal content. Often, more than one type of message can be used for the same communication situation.

Generally, the higher the level in an organization to which a message is sent, the more concise the message should be. Top managers view time as a precious commodity; therefore, a brief summary may be more suitable than a long, detailed report. Managers who have greater involvement with operating procedures may derive greater benefits from long, technical messages.

APPEARANCE OF THE MESSAGE

[NOTE 1.54] Communication Barrier 6: Poor appearance of written message.

The appearance of a message affects its readability and influences a receiver's acceptance of its content. Smudges, sloppy corrections, light print, wrinkled paper, and poor handwriting may distract the reader and become barriers to effective communication. Senders should examine every document before it is sent to ensure that its appearance does not interfere with its potential for success.

APPEARANCE OF THE SENDER

The credibility of an oral message can be reduced if the appearance of the sender is unattractive or unacceptable to the receiver. In addition, unintended nonverbal signals can distract a receiver and influence the way an oral message is received. For example, if you smile when you sympathetically give bad news, your motives may be suspect.

[NOTE 1.55]
Communication Barrier 7: Poor appearance of speaker.

If the credibility of the message is questioned, the quality of the receiver's understanding, acceptance, and response will be reduced. For success in oral business communication, senders should be sure that their dress, cleanliness, and facial and body movements are appropriate to their professions and to the communication situations they encounter. Wearing a tuxedo to a beach party is as inappropriate as wearing a swimsuit to the office.

ENVIRONMENTAL FACTORS

The environment in which communication occurs can interfere with the success of a message. One such example of a distracting environmental factor is a noisy machine in an area where a supervisor is trying to speak with an employee. When a supervisor's desk separates him or her from a worker during a meeting, the desk can intimidate the worker and limit his or her ability to respond to the message. Other examples of environmental factors that can serve as barriers to effective communication include room temperature, odor, light, color, and distance.

[NOTE 1.56]
Communication Barrier 8: Distracting environmental factors.

The sender has the responsibility to try to eliminate environmental factors that are communication barriers. If the room in which an oral presentation is to be given is too warm, the sender should try to get the thermostat turned down or to have the windows opened. If the receiver cannot see to read a message because of limited light, the sender should arrange for more light. Environmental barriers can usually be eliminated or reduced, often before communication begins.

RECEIVER'S CAPABILITY

If the receiver has a physical or mental disability that causes a communication barrier, the sender should recognize this in choosing message type and channel. The receiver may have a hearing impairment or a learning disability. The sender can remove or compensate for such barriers in the communication process by carefully selecting the form of the message and by providing for appropriate feedback mechanisms. Most of the solutions are clear choices. Increased volume, printed text, or a sign language interpreter can help overcome the potential barrier of a hearing impairment. When a visual impairment threatens the success of a written message, print can be enlarged or the message can be given orally.

[NOTE 1.57]
Communication Barrier 9: Receiver's limited capability.

In recent years considerable progress has been made in providing for full participation of persons with disabilities in all fields of human endeavor. Effective communicators will focus on their receivers' abilities and will work with receivers to ensure communication success.

LISTENING

Failure to listen is a common barrier to successful oral communication. Listening effectively is not easy. One reason listening is challenging is that most people speak 100 to 200 words a minute but are capable of listening to material of average

[NOTE 1.58]
Communication Barrier 10: Poor listening.

difficulty at 500 or more words a minute. This difference allows listeners' minds to wander to topics other than the message. In addition, listeners may tune out a speaker and begin thinking about how they will respond to the message. Listening is a skill that can and must be learned.

Senders can use several methods to overcome poor listening as a communication barrier. Receivers can be reminded to listen carefully, or they can be asked questions periodically to determine the extent of their comprehension. In some circumstances a poor listener may be encouraged to study and learn improved listening skills. One of the most effective ways to remove poor listening as a barrier to communication is to improve the quality of the message and the way in which it is conveyed. Thoroughly analyzing the audience before designing the message will help a sender plan, organize, and deliver an appropriate oral message.

OTHER COMMUNICATION BARRIERS

[NOTE 1.59] Several other important barriers exist.

Several of the most common communication barriers and ways to remove them have been discussed in the preceding sections. In attempting to improve your communication effectiveness, you must also eliminate other barriers. For example, some receiver-related communication barriers include lack of interest, lack of knowledge needed to understand, different cultural perceptions, language difficulty, emotional state, and bias. The sender must do everything possible to remove these receiver-related communication barriers. Information in the following Tips and Hints will help overcome barriers associated with cultural differences.

Enhance Your Multicultural Communication Skills

TIPS AND HINTS

Learn to enhance your multicultural communication skills by following these diversity action steps:

[1] Expect multicultural misunderstandings to occur sometimes.
[2] Recognize that our best intentions may be undermined by old assumptions.
[3] Catch ourselves in these assumptions in order to communicate more clearly and fairly.
[4] Learn about the cultural styles and values of different groups; understand and appreciate that individual differences exist within groups.
[5] Don't generalize about individuals because of their particular culture; many individual differences exist within groups.
[6] Avoid hot buttons or blunders like ethnic jokes, sexual expressions, racially based assumptions, inappropriate touching, and stereotyped job assignments.
[7] Use "we're all in this together" language to express trust and to foster a spirit of goodwill and partnership.
[8] Respond to the context and content of a person's words and deeds, rather than assumed motives.
[9] Don't be diverted by style, accent, grammar, or personal appearance; rather judge the merits of the statement or behavior.
[10] Consciously seek out new multicultural relationships and challenges.

From David P. Tulin, "Enhance Your Multi-cultural Communication Skills." Reprinted with permission from Tulin DiversiTeam Associates, Wyncote, PA.

Summary of Learning Objectives

Learning Objective [1]

Explain why business communication is important to individuals and organizations. Business communication is the process of establishing a common understanding between or among people within a business environment. Good communication skills will help individuals enhance their self-esteem, become effective employees, and advance in their careers. The quality of an organization's internal and external communications affects its success.

Learning Objective [2]

List and explain the goals of business communication. Business communication has four goals: (1) Receiver understanding—the receiver understands the message as the sender intended it to be understood. (2) Receiver response—the receiver demonstrates his or her understanding of a message by providing an appropriate response. (3) Favorable relationship—the people involved in the process relate to each other positively, personally, and professionally. (4) Organizational goodwill—the receiver has confidence in the sender's organization and is willing to continue the business relationship.

Learning Objective [3]

Describe the patterns of business communication. Business communication may be internal or external, formal or informal, work related or personal. Messages may flow vertically upward from workers, downward from managers, horizontally between or among workers who report to the same supervisor, or diagonally between or among workers regardless of unit or status. The diagonal pattern is known as a network.

Learning Objective [4]

Explain the communication process. Communication occurs in an open environment that includes the sender, the message, the receiver, feedback, and communication barriers. The sender will analyze the receiver and then design a message that reflects what was learned through that analysis. The message should focus on the receiver's interests, encourage feedback, and eliminate or minimize communication barriers. The receiver must listen or read carefully and be open to senders and to their ideas; making notes, asking questions, and providing feedback are also part of the receiver's role in the process.

Learning Objective [5]

Identify communication barriers and describe ways to remove them. The primary barrier to effective communication is failure to use the you–viewpoint. Other barriers include word choice; grammar, spelling, punctuation, and sentence structure; appearance of the sender or the message; environmental factors; type of message; receiver capability; and listening. Analyzing the receiver and taking the you–viewpoint will eliminate or minimize these and other communication barriers that might arise.

DISCUSSION QUESTIONS

1. Identify two ways in which communication is important to you and two ways in which it is important to an organization. (Objective 1)
2. Explain the difference between the business communication goals of a favorable relationship and organizational goodwill. (Objective 2)

3. What special precautions can be taken to ensure accuracy and understanding in serial communication? (Objective 3)

4. **Technology.** How have technologies such as e-mail and voice mail affected grapevine communication? (Objective 3)
5. Discuss the networks to which you belong. Identify the basis for the network—the thing the members have in common. (Objective 3)
6. How do formal and informal communication differ with respect to (a) planning, (b) directional flow, and (c) purpose? Give an example of each type of communication. (Objective 4)
7. Assume that you've just accepted a part-time job that will require you to work Tuesday and Thursday evenings, all day on Saturday, and from noon to closing on Sunday. The income from the job will enable you to remain in school. Analyze each of the following people to help you determine how to tell them your good news: (Objective 4)
   - **a.** Your parents, who expect you to attend your grandparents' 65th wedding anniversary celebration three weeks from Sunday.
   - **b.** Elena, your study partner, who works Monday, Wednesday, and Friday nights. You and she had planned to spend this Sunday studying for a major exam you'll both take at 8 a.m. on Monday. Elena hasn't pressed you to repay the $27 you borrowed two months ago.
   - **c.** Terry, your eight-year-old "buddy" in a mentoring program for disadvantaged youth. You've promised to be Terry's guest at the circus this Saturday afternoon; Terry earned the tickets in a school read-a-thon.
8. Describe a communication situation you have experienced or observed that succeeded because the sender and the receiver were successful in identifying and removing potential communication barriers. The situations need not be work related. (Objectives 4 and 5)

9. **Ethics.** Is it possible to use the you–viewpoint and transmit ethical messages? Discuss. (Objective 5)
10. How does each of the following sayings relate to communication? (Objectives 2, 3, and 5)
    - **a.** A picture is worth a thousand words.
    - **b.** Sticks and stones can break my bones, but words will never hurt me.
    - **c.** Seeing is believing.
    - **d.** Actions speak louder than words.

APPLICATION EXERCISES

1. **Internet.** Use the Internet or print resources in your library to locate a journal or magazine article related to communication, preferably in your career field. Summarize the article on a 3 × 5 index card. Be sure to include the complete citation and your reaction to the content of the article. (Objective 1)
2. Ask the following questions of your employer or another business professional in your community; share your findings with the class. (Objective 1)
   - **a.** How important is communication to the successful performance of your job?
   - **b.** What is an example of a successful communication experience you have had?
   - **c.** What is an example of an unsuccessful communication experience you have had?
   - **d.** What communication barriers do you commonly encounter?

e. What does organizational goodwill mean to you?

f. What recommendations do you have for someone who wants to improve his or her communication skills?

3. **Teamwork.** Form a four-person team. Have each team member select one of the business communication goals and prepare a one-minute presentation that explains and illustrates it. Practice, then join with another group and make the presentations to each other. (Objective 2)

4. Select an appropriate message type and channel for each of the following situations. Justify your choices. (Objective 3)
   - **a.** Effective the first of next month, the cost of dependent coverage under your company's group insurance policy will rise. Your task is to inform 300 employees who work at the three facilities in your state.
   - **b.** You want to invite the new manager in your division to have lunch with you today. The manager works on another floor of your building.
   - **c.** An employee you supervise has been named Volunteer of the Year in your community.
   - **d.** A sweater shown on page 6 of your company's fall catalog is no longer available in green. You want to persuade those who order the item to select another color.
   - **e.** The proposal you have written must reach your client's office by 3 p.m. today. Your offices are in the same community.

5. Analyze the receiver's knowledge, interests, attitudes, and emotional state in the following communication situation: (Objective 4)

You are a public accountant writing a letter to Wilson Brooks, a contractor who builds homes. Mr. Brooks prepares his own tax returns with occasional assistance from your firm. He has had last year's return, which he prepared himself, audited by the Internal Revenue Service (IRS). The IRS did not allow some of the deductions Mr. Brooks listed; therefore, he has been told he owes $3,750 in additional taxes. Mr. Brooks has sent you a copy of the IRS audit report. He asks you to review the report and advise him on what he should do.

6. Modify the following sentences to make them reflect the you–viewpoint. Be sure not to change the meaning of the sentences in your revised versions. (Objective 4)
   - **a.** The meeting time has been changed from 4 p.m. to 3 p.m.; don't be late.
   - **b.** I have enclosed a postage-paid reply card for you to use when ordering from us.
   - **c.** We have received your order and a check for the amount you owe for the merchandise.
   - **d.** I set extremely high standards for myself and for those who work for me; your work isn't meeting my standards.
   - **e.** What did you do to this CD player? I'll have to charge you at least $200 to repair it.
   - **f.** Be quiet and listen to these important instructions.
   - **g.** He always seems to interrupt while others are talking.
   - **h.** Your request for a promotion is denied. Talk to me again next month.
   - **i.** Don't be late again. Give the monthly reports to Amanda no later than the 20th of the month.
   - **j.** Make no mistakes. The report must be completely accurate.

7. For each of the following words give a denotative meaning and a possible connotative meaning: (a) reasonable, (b) trendy, (c) smart, (d) rare, (e) rich. (Objective 5)

8. **Cross-Cultural.** Select a culture other than your own. Gather information on that culture's values, attitudes, biases, and viewpoints. As your instructor directs, interview a student or faculty member from another culture or use Internet or library resources to conduct your research. Share your findings with the class. (Objective 5)
9. Observe a clerk, cafeteria worker, or custodial worker at your school. Record the number of nonverbal messages he/she conveys in five minutes. Identify each cue as positive or negative. (Objective 5)

10. **E-mail./Teamwork.** Think about a supervisor or teacher whom you would describe as your favorite.
    a. Make a list of the things that make him or her stand apart from others you have known (e.g., Is he or she a good listener? Does she or he respond to your verbal and nonverbal feedback?).
    b. Work with another member of the class. Exchange your lists; use e-mail if available. What items appear on both your and your partner's list? Which items relate to the ability to communicate well? What do your findings tell you about how the ability to communicate well influences someone's perception of you?
    c. Work alone. Summarize your findings and conclusions in an e-mail message to your instructor. Be sure your message is constructed using correct grammar, spelling, punctuation, and sentence structure. (Objectives 1, 2, and 5)

There are Web exercises at **http://krizan.swcollege.com** to accompany this chapter.

MESSAGE ANALYSIS

Correct the content and word choice errors in the following business memo:

TO: *Staff*

FROM: *Manager*

DATE: *June 1, 200–*

SUBJECT: *BUSINESS COMMUNICATION*

Yesterday, I attended a seminar on business communication. The speaker introduced me to some principals and techniques, and I want to pass some of his advise on to you. Specifically, pay attention to the items below:

- *Always analyze the situation. You'll get farther if you focus on yourself — use the You–Viewpoint!*
- *Use lots of technical words; readers are impressed by them.*
- *Long messages are better then brief ones because you may include more details.*
- *Don't waste time proofreading e-mail; its meant to be quick and dirty, and you can always send another one if you make a mistake.*

You may already have known these things, but a reminder never hurts. Discuss these items between yourselves, and let me know if you have any questions.

GRAMMAR WORKSHOP

Correct the grammar, spelling, punctuation, style, and word choice errors in the following sentences:

1. Sheridan's entire collection of mens' cardigans are also on sale.
2. Did Bill tell Bob whom would replace him on the Committee.
3. Max, a manager at Lugo Electronics said he would introduce the keynote speaker to Sybil and I after the luncheon.
4. The attornies tried to clearly explain the terms of the settlement to their client.
5. If you would like to order a subscription for a friend, record his name and address on the enclosed card and mail it to us now, we'll bill you later.
6. The meating sight has been changed form Sams' office too Conference room A, therefore, more people can attend.
7. The workshop was highlighted by the opportunity to learn and be refreshed by other managers through group discussions special presentations hands on seminars and social events.
8. While their outward appearance remains relatively unchanged designers note that lockers are larger more durable and can be customized for special purposes.
9. Any staff member who may come into contract with a biohazard during their duties, should have access to protective devices such as gloves masks and goggles.
10. The short term outlook is dim however long term projections are positive.

CHAPTER

2 International and Cross-Cultural Communication

Kent Nethery, Principal Consultant, SKOPOS Consulting, California

LET'S TALK BUSINESS As a principal of SKOPOS Consulting, I regularly consult with management teams in a variety of industries including health care–pharmaceutical, high technology, retail, and food service in North America, Europe, Asia, and the Middle East. When working with individuals from different cultures and different countries, I work at avoiding being ethnocentric—a person who believes that his or her own country and culture are superior. When I am working in our diverse and global society, I keep the following three things in mind: (1) First, I recognize that my natural instinct is to evaluate that person from an American cultural perspective and judge him or her based upon our customs, values, and beliefs. (2) Second,

(Continued)

[LEARNING OBJECTIVES]

[1] DESCRIBE THE CHALLENGES OF INTERNATIONAL AND CROSS-CULTURAL BUSINESS COMMUNICATION.

[2] DESCRIBE THE GOAL FOR EFFECTIVE CROSS-CULTURAL COMMUNICATION, AND EXPLAIN HOW THE GUIDELINES FOR CROSS-CULTURAL COMMUNICATION CAN BE USED.

[3] IDENTIFY CULTURAL ATTRIBUTES OF THE MAJOR TRADING PARTNERS OF THE UNITED STATES.

[4] LIST THE FIVE CORE DIMENSIONS OF HUMAN DIVERSITY, AND EXPLAIN THE IMPORTANCE OF UNDERSTANDING THESE DIMENSIONS.

[5] IDENTIFY KEY RESOURCES IN INTERNATIONAL, CROSS-CULTURAL, AND DIVERSITY IN BUSINESS FOR BUSINESS COMMUNICATION.

I remember that my American perspective may be based upon a viewpoint or a stereotype of that person's culture that may be incorrect. (3) Third, I recall that the other person is likely to have a stereotypical view of me based upon his or her own cultural background.

My awareness of these issues has helped me develop friends and successful business relationships both here and abroad. As you study the material in this chapter, keep in mind that there are many challenges to international and cross-cultural business communication and that our goal is to achieve normal business communication without cultural prejudice.

The rapidly increasing involvement of American (a term used worldwide to refer to citizens of the United States) businesses in international trade and the growing number of job opportunities in multinational businesses are reasons for you to develop skill in international and cross-cultural business communication. To succeed in the new millennium, American workers must receive the extensive cross-cultural training that employees in Europe and Japan receive.[1]

[NOTE 2.1]
International business opportunities are increasing.

The motivation for American firms to expand their involvement in world trade is increased profits. Businesses increase profits in their foreign operations by achieving increased productivity of high-quality products at lower costs. Also, American companies increase profit margins by exporting their products to other countries or importing products for sale in the United States.

[NOTE 2.2]
Increased profit is motivation for increased world trade.

Success in international and cross-cultural business communication depends on understanding other cultures and on skill in using the techniques of cross-cultural communication. The definitions of the following two terms will help you focus your study of this chapter. **International business communication** refers to the transmission of information between businesspeople from two different countries. **Cross-cultural business communication** refers to the transmission of information between businesspeople of two different cultures whether they reside in the same or different countries.

[NOTE 2.3]
International business success depends on effective cross-cultural communication.

A company and its employees can profit from a well-managed international business operation. Success in managing cultural diversity depends on the ability to communicate effectively. There is little doubt that most students studying this chapter will be involved in international and cross-cultural business communication at some point in their careers.

This chapter discusses the challenges of international and cross-cultural communication, ways to communicate successfully in international and cross-cultural business situations, and key resources in international and cross-cultural business communication.

[1] John Calvert Scott and Peter Whiteley, "The Necessity of Cross-Cultural Training for the International Marketplace," *Business Education Forum,* December 1999, pp. 37–40.

Learning Objective [1]
DESCRIBE THE CHALLENGES OF INTERNATIONAL AND CROSS-CULTURAL BUSINESS COMMUNICATION.

The Challenges of International and Cross-Cultural Business Communication

[NOTE 2.4]
Cultural variations create communication challenges.

The challenges of international and cross-cultural business communication are similar to the communication challenges within a culture—analyzing receivers and using the you–viewpoint—with one major difference. That difference is found in the striking variations among cultures throughout the world. Cultural variations exist in languages, values and attitudes, symbols and gestures, laws, religions, politics, educational levels, technological development, and social organizations.

[NOTE 2.5]
There are cultural differences within countries.

As many as 20,000 cultures exist in the world. The cultural diversity even within some countries is striking. This diversity, although possibly more subtle than that between two countries, must be considered when analyzing receivers.

Americans recognize that cultural differences exist within their own country. These include cultural differences such as pace of life and regional speech patterns which were found when comparing behaviors of people from New York City to people from Jackson, Mississippi.[2]

In Kentucky, for example, someone might say, "I would be proud to carry you to the office." For that person the word *proud* would mean "glad" and the word *carry* would mean "transport." In Tennessee a teacher who was a guest on a television game show stated to the audience that she wanted to perform well since her students were watching and she wanted to "do them proud." In North Carolina someone might say, "Please cut off the lights." For that person *cut off* would mean to "turn off." Although these statements would be readily understood by others from the same state, people from some other areas of the country could easily be confused.

[NOTE 2.6]
Great cultural differences are found among countries.

The amount of cultural diversity within the United States, however, is small in comparison with the cultural diversity throughout the world. A direct message composed in businesslike terms sent to a German businessperson may be extremely successful for you and your company. The same message sent to a Japanese businessperson—because of its directness—may fail miserably. The difference in the success of the two communications lies in the cultural differences of the two countries. The next sections describe examples of cultural differences and the challenges these differences present to the business communicator.

LANGUAGE DIFFERENCES

[NOTE 2.7]
There are more than 3,000 languages and 10,000 dialects in the world.

More than 3,000 different languages are spoken throughout the world. More than 200 different languages are spoken in India alone. Considering all the various dialects in the world, some linguists estimate that there are at least 10,000 variations of languages. If you are not skilled in the use of your receiver's primary language, you are facing your first major challenge in international business communication.

[NOTE 2.8]
Word choice can be a problem.

Many American companies have experienced great difficulties because of lack of knowledge of another culture's language. Pepsi Cola's slogan "Pepsi Comes Alive" was not received well in Taiwan since the Chinese translations means

[2] Lillian H. Chaney and Jeanette S. Martin, *Intercultural Business Communication,* Upper Saddle River, N.J.: Prentice Hall, 2000, p. 3.

"Pepsi Brings Your Ancestors Back from the Grave." In the Middle East an American company was marketing tomato paste, but learned that when "tomato paste" was translated into Arabic it meant "tomato glue." Chevrolet's Nova was not received well in Spanish-speaking countries. Its name sounded like *no va,* which in Spanish means "it doesn't go." In many countries the prefix "diet" cannot be used since it would require that the product be sold only in pharmacies.[3] As we communicate with individuals from other cultures and countries we must be mindful not only of translations but also of the products we sell. An excellent example is provided in the "McDiversity" Communication Note, which describes the various menus designed by McDonald's to address the needs of different countries and cultures.

COMMUNICATION NOTE

McDiversity

With 25,000 restaurants in 116 countries on six continents, McDonald's has developed menus that reflect specific regional tastes. It is, after all, more than a Big Mac-and-Fries world.

Mexico. McMuffin a la Mexicana: With cheese, peppers, and frijoles (beans), variation of the Egg McMuffin. McNifica: Burger with bacon, cheese, lettuce, mayo, and hot sauce.

Malaysia. McEgg: An Egg McMuffin with onions, cheese, and catsup on a toasted bun.

Puerto Rico. Western Criollo Sandwich: Fried egg, sausage, and cheese on Criollo bread.

United States. South: Biscuits and gravy. Kansas, Missouri, Wisconsin: Bratwurst. Maine, Rhode Island, New Hampshire, Massachusetts, Connecticut: Lobster sandwiches.

Uruguay. McHuevo: Burger topped with a poached egg.

Thailand. Samurai Pork Burger: Teriyaki-flavored pork sandwich.

Philippines. McSpaghetti: Pasta with tomato sauce and frankfurter bits.

New Zealand. Kiwi Burger: Burger with a fried egg and a slice of beet.

Japan. Chicken Tatsuta: Fried chicken sandwich spiced with ginger and soy sauce.

Austria. McCountry: Pork patty with onions and hot mustard on a bun.

Germany. McCroissant: Ham and cheese filled croissant. Frankfurters and beer.

France. Wine.

India. Maharaja Mac: Two lamb patties with lettuce, cheese, onions, and pickles.

As reported by Leilah Berstein in "SideTrips," Los Angeles Times Magazine, *October 17, 1999, p. 8.*

[3] Roger E. Axtell, *The Do's and Taboos of International Trade,* New York: John Wiley & Sons, Inc., 1994, pp. 217–222.

There are other examples of a word being appropriate in one country and not in another. A U.S. trade magazine promoting gift sales in Germany used the English word *gift* in its title. Unfortunately, the word gift in German means "poison." The trade magazine did not effectively achieve its objective of selling gifts in Germany. A foreign company inappropriately selected *EMU* for the name of its airline that flew to Australia. An emu is an Australian bird that cannot fly. Finally, *Esso* means "stalled car" in Japanese—hardly an appropriate name for gasoline and oil products that were being sold in Japan.

[NOTE 2.9] Languages are structured differently.

Even the way parts of speech are used in different languages varies culturally. In Japanese, the verb is at the end of a sentence. This enables the Japanese to begin to express a thought and watch the receiver's reaction. Depending on how the receiver is reacting to the message, the verb may be changed, thereby changing the whole meaning of the sentence. For example, a Japanese might start to say, "Please go away from me now," but end up saying "Please stay with me now" by changing the verb, which is said last.

[NOTE 2.10] The degree of formality will vary.

An American company caused itself considerable communication problems in Germany by insisting that all its employees call each other by their first names. This made Germans uncomfortable because they do not use first names with even close business associates with whom they have worked for years. In Germany, the use of first names is reserved for intimate friends and relatives. Forcing the Germans to adopt an American custom caused stress that seriously reduced the quality of communication in the German-based American operation.

NONVERBAL COMMUNICATION DIFFERENCES

[NOTE 2.11] Cultural differences in nonverbal signals are extensive.

A sender's nonverbal signals—facial expressions, body movements, and gestures—influence the receiver's understanding and acceptance of a message. In international and cross-cultural business communication, nonverbal signals vary as much as spoken languages do.

[NOTE 2.12] Acceptable greetings vary markedly.

The cultural diversity in nonverbal communication can be shown by an examination of worldwide differences in the way people greet each other. As can be noted in Figure 2.1, nonverbal greetings vary from a bow to a handshake, or from a hug to an upward flick of the eyebrows depending on the country and the culture involved.

[NOTE 2.13] Misunderstanding nonverbal messages can cause problems.

Not understanding cultural differences in nonverbal messages causes communication problems. For example, if in Germany an American were to signal *one* by holding up the index finger, it would be understood as *two*. Germans signal *one* by holding up the thumb and *two* by extending the thumb and index finger. An American ordering a train ticket in Germany by raising the index finger, therefore, would likely get two tickets instead of one. Using the index finger to point is considered rude in most Middle and Far Eastern countries. In most countries the "thumbs up" sign means "okay"; however, in Australia this gesture is considered rude.

Also in Germany, smiles are reserved mostly for close friends or relatives. The American who laughs often and smiles at everyone would overwhelm many Germans. Such unacceptable nonverbal behavior by an American would definitely interfere with any accompanying oral communication.

[NOTE 2.14] Some nonverbal signals are considered impolite or vulgar.

In Japan it is considered impolite or vulgar for people to cross their legs by placing one foot or ankle on the knee of the other leg. The preferred way of sitting in Japan is with both feet on the floor with knees held fairly close together. It is

Country	Nonverbal Method of Greeting
Argentina	Shaking hands while slightly nodding heads (After long absences, women kiss each other on the cheek and men may embrace.)
Australia	Warm handshake between men (A man shakes hands with a woman only if she extends her hand first.)
Belgium	Shaking hands with everyone, using a quick shake with light pressure
Chile	A handshake and a kiss to the right cheek
China	A nod or slight bow (In addition, a handshake is also acceptable.)
Fiji	A smile and an upward flick of the eyebrows (A handshake is also appropriate.)
France	A handshake (A firm, pumping American handshake is considered impolite.)
Greece	An embrace and a kiss on both cheeks or a handshake
India	The *namaste*—bending gently with palms together below chin
Japan	A bow followed by a handshake
Portugal	A warm, firm handshake for everyone
Russia	A handshake and sometimes, among older people, the traditional three kisses on the cheeks
Saudi Arabia	A handshake (Frequently, males will also extend the left hand to each other's right shoulders and then kiss the left and right cheeks.)
Thailand	The *wai*—placing both hands together in prayer position at chest and bowing slightly
United States	A warm, firm, pumping handshake
Zimbabwe	A handshake.

Figure 2.1
Cultural Differences in Greetings

acceptable to cross the legs by placing one knee directly over the other, or to cross the ankles.

In Italy a person waves goodbye by raising one hand with the palm facing the body and moving the hand back and forth to and from the body. In Korea, it is acceptable for men to hold hands in public, but it is frowned on to touch the opposite sex in public. In Lebanon, *yes* is signaled by nodding the head as Americans do, whereas *no* is indicated by an upward movement of the head or raised eyebrows.

[NOTE 2.15]
Other nonverbal signals are simply quite different.

In the Middle East, Latin America, France, and Italy direct eye contact with someone with whom you are speaking is appropriate. In most Asian countries, however, limited eye contact, with the eyes diverted most of the time, is more acceptable. The amount of physical space that people maintain between each other varies from country to country. People in the Middle East will stand as close as two or three inches from the person to whom they are talking, and if you back off, then they are insulted. A person involved in cross-cultural communication must be aware of the wide variation throughout the world in the meaning of nonverbal signals. These differences in nonverbal signals, however, are only illustrative of more important underlying cultural differences in the ways people think and feel.

OTHER CULTURAL DIFFERENCES

[NOTE 2.16]
The way people think and feel is the most important cultural difference.

Underlying the cultural variations in verbal and nonverbal communication are many other deep-seated cultural differences that affect communication. The most important differences are in the ways people in other cultures *think* and *feel*. These differences are grounded in such things as values, attitudes, religions, political systems, and social orders. Your understanding of other cultural differences is vital to your success in cross-cultural communication. If businesspeople are able to recognize differences as well as similarities, they can adjust their mode of communication to fit the individual culture.[4] A few examples will illustrate this point.

Roger E. Axtell, an author who has done extensive traveling and cross-cultural training, conducts a session that demonstrates built-in perceptions Americans have of other nationalities. When Axtell asked for the world's stereotypes of Americans, he was given the following one-word descriptors: arrogant, loud, friendly, impatient, monolingual, generous, and hard-working. At one of these seminars someone shouted "All of the above!"[5]

[NOTE 2.17] Most cultures are more reserved than the American culture.

The friendly, outgoing, competitive, informal American who primarily uses the direct plan for communicating may not be received well in Asian or some European countries. In most of these countries people are more reserved and less direct in their human relations than are Americans. Most Japanese, for example, need to build a personal relationship of trust and friendship before entering an important business relationship. On the other hand, most Americans are willing to do business with a limited or nonexistent personal relationship with their customers or vendors. In successfully relating to the Japanese, therefore, Americans must be willing to build the necessary personal relationships first. This requires more patience than most Americans normally need to use in their business dealings in the United States.

[NOTE 2.18] American businesswomen have special challenges in international business.

Deeply rooted cultural attitudes toward the appropriate roles of women vary markedly throughout the world. Although gender differences are de-emphasized in business in the United States, women—simply because they are women—find conducting business in some countries practically impossible.

COMMUNICATION QUOTE

How many times have you read or heard the term "global marketplace" recently? Commerce and trade is reshaping the world with a new wave of economic growth and development.

International business relationships are often much more demanding than what many of us are used to in America. For one thing, international relationships are based much more on personal relationships. In many countries, people won't buy your products unless they like you personally. So we have to be able to understand more than the language to be successful. We need to understand the culture and all the subtleties that go into it.

Tarja Bentgarde-Childers, CEO, Kemper International Corporation, reported in the The Kemper Partner, *July–August 1997, pp. 1, 6.*

Generally, developed nations are more accepting of women as equals in business, while opportunities for women in lesser developed nations are practically nonexistent. Businesswomen must analyze carefully cultural attitudes toward females in those

[4] Lillian H. Chaney and Jeanette S. Martin, *Intercultural Business Communication,* Upper Saddle River, N.J.: Prentice Hall, 2000, p. 8.

[5] Roger E. Axtell, *The Do's and Taboos of International Trade,* New York: John Wiley & Sons, Inc., 1994, pp. 75–77.

countries where they want to do business. Then adjustments in language and nonverbal behavior must be made. A less aggressive approach may be required. Indirectness may be essential. Women may even have to use men as intermediaries to do business in some countries.

Business office hours around the world vary considerably, making it difficult to transact business. For example, when it is 8 a.m. in New York City, it is 10 p.m. the next day in Beijing, China.

[NOTE 2.19]
Business hours and days limit contact time.

On a completely different level, a simple example of cultural diversity that affects business communication is business hours. You cannot, for instance, telephone a business if that business is not open. Figure 2.2 shows this variation. Note in Figure 2.2 that many countries in warmer climates tend to close their offices in the middle of the day; that time is used for the main meal and a rest. There is also, of course, variation in business hours due to time differences in international time zones. The six- to nine-hour difference in time between European or Asian countries and the United States allows little or no overlap in normal business hours.

[NOTE 2.20]
Days in the workweek vary.

It is also interesting to note that the days of the week that businesses operate vary around the world. In the United States most business offices operate Monday through Friday, with Saturday and Sunday off. In Korea the work week is Monday through Saturday, and possibly Sunday. In contrast, the workweek in Saudi Arabia and other Islamic countries is Saturday through Wednesday, with Thursday and Friday off. Friday is the Islamic day of rest and worship.

Countries also have different currencies. In addition, currency exchange rates change continuously. Differences in money are another factor that affects not only the international traveler but also the business person involved in trade. Figure 2.3 shows some of the major currencies in the world and their exchange rates on the referenced date against the U.S. dollar.

Figure 2.2
Common Business Office Hours Around the World

Country	Business Office Hours
Australia	8:30 a.m. to 5:30 p.m.
Brazil	8 a.m. to 12 noon; 2 p.m. to 6 p.m.
Canada	9 a.m. to 5 p.m., or 8 a.m. to 4 p.m.
China	8 a.m. to 12 noon; 1 p.m. to 5 p.m.
Germany	8 a.m. to 5 p.m. (banks may close at 4 p.m.)
Greece	8 a.m. to 1:30 p.m.; 5:30 p.m. to 8:30 p.m.
Hong Kong	9 a.m. to 5 p.m., weekdays; 9 a.m. to 1 p.m., Saturday
Northern Ireland	9 a.m. to 5 p.m.
Italy	8 or 9 a.m. to 1 p.m.; 3:30 or 4 p.m. to 7 or 8 p.m.
Japan	8 or 9 a.m. to 5 or 6 p.m.
Norway	8 a.m. to 4 p.m.
Mexico	9 a.m. to 6 or 7 p.m. (small towns may close between 2–4 p.m.)
Romania	7 a.m. to 3 or 4 p.m.
Spain	9 a.m. to 1:30 p.m.; 5 p.m. to 8 p.m.
Russia	8 a.m. to 5 p.m.
United States	8 a.m. to 5 p.m.
Zimbabwe	8 a.m. to 5 p.m.

Figure 2.3
Currency Exchange Rates Around the World

Currency Trading Denominations

Country	Currency	U.S. $ Equivalency
Argentina	Peso	.9998
Australia	Dollar	1.5718
Austria	Schilling	13.4522
Brazil	Real (Cruzeiro)	1.9230
Britain	Pound	.6156
Canada	Dollar	1.4740
Chile	Peso	545.9000
China	Yuan Renminbi	8.2371
Europe	Euro Dollar	.9776
France	Franc	6.4127
Germany	Mark	1.9120
Hong Kong	Dollar	7.7733
India	Rupee	43.3970
Japan	Yen	102.7300
Kuwait	Dinar	.3041
Mexico	Peso	9.4500
Norway	Kroner	7.9410
South Africa	Rand	6.1485
Spain	Peseta	162.6610
Zimbabwe	Dollar	38.7500

As cited on the Web, December 8, 1999. Address: **http://www.oanda.com/converter/classic.**

The cultural diversity described in this section is indicative of some of the challenges of international and cross-cultural business communication. Guidelines for meeting these and other cross-cultural communication challenges are given in the next section.

Guidelines for Successful Cross-Cultural Communication

Learning Objective [2]
DESCRIBE THE GOAL FOR EFFECTIVE CROSS-CULTURAL COMMUNICATION, AND EXPLAIN HOW THE GUIDELINES FOR CROSS-CULTURAL COMMUNICATION CAN BE USED.

You can be successful in cross-cultural communication if you follow proven guidelines. Use of the information given in Chapters 1 and 4 on business communication foundations and principles will be essential to your success. In addition, follow the special guidelines for international and cross-cultural business communication given in this section.

Your goal for effective cross-cultural communication is to achieve normal business communication without cultural prejudice. This means having the ability to communicate comfortably and naturally while eliminating barriers that might be caused by cultural differences.

[NOTE 2.21]
Goal: Communicate without cultural prejudice.

The guidelines for successful cross-cultural communication are presented in three groups. These consist of basic guidelines for cross-cultural communication, guidelines for cross-cultural communication in English, and guidelines for using an interpreter or translator.

The basic guidelines will assist you in gaining the necessary general information and perspective for cross-cultural communication in the international business environment. The guidelines for communicating cross-culturally in English are provided because most of the world's business is conducted in English. Finally, the guidelines for using an interpreter or translator cover those special situations where a bilingual person is employed to bridge the language barrier.

BASIC GUIDELINES FOR CROSS-CULTURAL COMMUNICATION

The basic guidelines presented in this section should be followed to prepare for cross-cultural communication in the international business environment.

Guideline 1: Review the Foundations and Principles of Business Communication
In any cross-cultural communication situation, the basic business communication knowledge you have already gained will apply. A review of that knowledge should be your first step in preparing to communicate in the international business environment.

[NOTE 2.22]
Use foundations and principles of business communication.

As you will recall, the goals of business communication given in Chapter 1 include receiver understanding, necessary receiver response, a favorable relationship between you and your receiver, and goodwill for your organization. These goals will be a part of your cross-cultural business communication effort.

In addition, the communication process will be the same—you need to analyze your receiver and use the you–viewpoint, select the appropriate form of message, provide for feedback, and remove communication barriers. Finally, application of the KISS principle of business communication (Keep It Short and Simple) will enhance your effectiveness in international and cross-cultural business communication.

Guideline 2: Analyze Your Own Culture A starting point in relating effectively to others is to know your own culture. Then, understanding how others view your culture is vital for success in cross-cultural communication. People throughout the world use comparisons, evaluations, and categories to assimilate and understand the messages they receive. This process, which helps give meaning to our understanding

[NOTE 2.23]
Understanding your own culture is essential.

of the world around us, is called **perception.** Understanding perception is crucial to understanding other cultures and coping with them.

People use **stereotypes,** a simplistic belief about the typical behaviors or characteristics of a particular group of people, to help them understand the messages those individuals are sending. Stereotypes should be used with extreme caution, however, since psychologists teach that stereotypes are perceptions and "perceptions are reality."[6]

To become an effective cross-cultural communicator it is essential to keep an open mind and learn as much as possible about one's own country, culture, and customs as well as the other country, culture, and customs. Although individuals within one culture may vary considerably, many have similar tastes in food and clothing. They may also hold common values and possess similar attitudes, opinions, and beliefs. To achieve effective cross-cultural communication, we must go beyond stereotypes and learn about the individuals with whom we are communicating and their cultures.

[NOTE 2.24] Cultural relativism refers to varying standards of right and wrong.

[NOTE 2.25] Ethnocentrism is the inherent belief that one's own group and culture are superior.

Cultural relativism is the term used to describe the fact that different cultures have somewhat different standards of right and wrong. **Ethnocentrism** is the inherent belief that one's own group and culture are superior. As people grow up, they tend to suppose that the ways they do things in their cultures are normal and that the ways of other cultures are not. The ways of others seem peculiar, strange, and even wrong. As you study other cultures, however, you may realize that there is not necessarily one right or wrong way to do something—merely many different, but equally correct, ways.

[NOTE 2.26] Americans tend to use the direct plan of communication.

Understanding the practices of your own culture will enable you to understand and relate more successfully to the practices of other cultures. The following is a limited analysis of the American culture; this stereotype can be helpful to you in cross-cultural communication. The American mainstream culture consists of people who prefer to communicate in the English language. According to the analysis, although Americans are inclined to use the direct plan of communication (versus the indirect plan), they tend to do so politely. Americans are generally friendly and informal. They are likely to greet you by your first name and shake your hand with a firm grip and pumping action. They tend to have a strong sense of humor and laugh and smile frequently.[7]

Americans are inclined to be time conscious, frank, and outspoken. Eye contact while conversing is a sign of strength and honesty to Americans. They tend to have a greater need for personal space than do some other cultures—at least two to three feet minimum distances between themselves and others. Americans tend to limit personal touching of each other in public. Americans tend to value highly an individual's freedom to achieve. Work, activity, and progress are valuable in their own right.

As you communicate with other cultures around the world, you will quickly note that while there is much in common, there are sharp differences in values, tastes, and attitudes. Remember that "one size does not fit all" as outlined in the Communication Note "Globalization Isn't a One-Size-Fits-All Answer."

[6] Roger E. Axtell, *The Do's and Taboos of International Trade,* New York: John Wiley & Sons, Inc., 1994, pp. 75–77.

[7] This cultural analysis was based on the following materials: *Culturgrams* © 1999; Lillian H. Chaney and Jeanette S. Martin, *Intercultural Business Communication,* 2000; Roger E. Axtell, *The Do's and Taboos Around the World,* 1993; Roger E. Axtell, *The Do's and Taboos of International Trade*, 1994.

COMMUNICATION NOTE

Globalization Isn't a One-Size-Fits-All Answer

The U.S. model of democracy may not apply to everyone. Don't go for 'one size fits all.' Try custom-made democracy for individual countries, taking into account their cultural differences, their lack of middle class, and their readiness for democracy. Apply your norms in a general way, but don't insist that everybody should follow the way you do things.

As reported by Tom Plate in, "Globalization Isn't a One-Size-Fits-All Answer." The Los Angeles Times, *December 1, 1999, p. B15.*

Guideline 3: Develop the Ability to Be Open to and Accepting of Other Cultures

[NOTE 2.27] Be open to and accepting of others' cultures.

As you think about your own culture, you begin to sense that it represents one way to believe and to do things. It is important to accept that this is not the only way. This understanding is essential in order to communicate successfully with people of other cultures who believe and do things differently. With your involvement in the international and cross-cultural business environment, you will want to adopt an open, accepting attitude toward the differences in others.

Cross-cultural involvement can be an exciting, new adventure. You may be (or have been) apprehensive the first time you meet with persons from another culture. You may feel inferior in some ways and superior in other ways. You will no doubt have many mixed emotions and you will no doubt experience culture shock. **Culture shock** is the confusion and discomfort people experience when they enter a culture that is different from their own. Many people traveling or working abroad experience culture shock since learning a different culture takes time and effort. Companies have found that offering training programs helps alleviate some of the frustrations found when adapting to a culture that is different from their own. The guideline that directs you to be open to and accepting of other cultures will serve you well in the international business environment.

[NOTE 2.28] Be open to and accepting of differences.

How can you be open and accepting? Be open to learning about the other culture with which you are interacting. Be open to different foods, to different ways of doing things, to different beliefs—beliefs, for example, about the value of time (a clock "runs" in the United States; it "walks" in Spanish-speaking Latin America). Be accepting of other people's needs for indirectness in communicating (as in Asia), and for the use of titles and last names instead of first names (as in Europe). Be open to and accepting of the different ways people of other cultures think and feel. Learn how to tolerate and cope with ambiguity. Understand that information can be interpreted in different ways.

Be patient, but do not be condescending. Be understanding of differences. Do not rush to an early judgment about the way a conversation or business deal is going. You may be misreading a communication situation because of cultural differences. Ask questions. Ask if you are being understood. Obtain feedback.

Your success in cross-cultural communication will depend largely on your ability to be open to and accepting of differences in others. Only in that way can you communicate in the you–viewpoint without cultural prejudice. The Communication Note "Learning to Feel at Home in Foreign-Based Firms" gives some valuable information on working abroad. The statement that "learning another language is not essential" is true; but, if you learn some of the common and useful phrases in the language of the country, you will be more successful.

COMMUNICATION NOTE

Learning to Feel at Home in Foreign-Based Firms

Fact: Increasing numbers of American managers are joining foreign-based companies that are doing business in the U.S. market.

Fact: Many of them don't know what they're getting into.

In foreign-based companies, career success often hinges on a keen understanding of the differences in culture and management style. In any guide to handling these differences, generalizations must be made, even though foreign companies and cultures also vary greatly from each other.

What kind of people do well in this foreign environment? Patient people, obviously. Also, foreign employers are "very concerned with personal integrity, reliability, and the ability to fit into the organization," says Mr. Foster of Foster Partners, an executive-search firm that does business with foreign-based firms. To be successful, you must be particularly careful about showing up early, meeting commitments, and being a dependable team player. Stamina can also be a valuable asset.

Here are some additional points to consider if you are planning to join a foreign-based company: Learn to interpret the subtleties of the company culture, be ready for big differences in management styles, and make sure you're being understood. Learning another language is not essential since English is often the second language of foreign executives.

As reported by Hal Lancaster in "Managing Your Career: How You Can Learn to Feel at Home in Foreign-Based Firms," The Wall Street Journal, *June 4, 1996, p. B1.*

Successful cross-cultural communication depends on the ability to be open and accepting of other cultures—their foods, beliefs, and ways of doing things.

Guideline 4: Learn All You Can About the Other Culture and Apply What You Learn This is the *key guideline* for effective cross-cultural communication. There is, of course, much to be learned about another culture. Do not let the volume of information overwhelm you. Anything you learn will be helpful and will strengthen your ability to communicate. "The Web of Culture" Web site is devoted to cross-cultural communications and may be accessed at: **http://www.webofculture.com/**.

[NOTE 2.29]
Learn about the other culture and use what you learn.

Culture is an abstract and complex concept whose elements are interrelated and intertwined. Since much of culture is hidden from view, cultural differences can be intricate, subtle, and difficult to learn. Cultural understanding consists of both factual knowledge and interpretive knowledge. This knowledge can be gained effectively only through personal experiences and personal insight.[8] Additionally, the last section of this chapter provides several good sources of information for learning about other cultures.

[NOTE 2.30]
Culture is an abstract and complex concept.

A basic recommendation in learning about another culture is to learn as much as you can of that culture's language. Ideally, you would be able to speak and write the other culture's language fluently. That may not be possible. In any case, learn as much as you can. Learn at least greetings, courtesy words, and the basic positive and negative signals. Learn the few basic phrases that represent typical words used in regard to the subject of your communication. For example, learn how to say "We want to do business with you," if that is appropriate.

You should not only learn as much as possible of the other culture's language, but you should also use what you know in your oral and written messages. Your receivers will appreciate your efforts. They will be understanding and accepting of any deficiencies in your use of their language.

A second aspect of learning about another culture is to learn as much as possible about the people of that culture. This aspect of learning includes a wide range of information from how the people think to the foods they eat. For example, there is considerable evidence that Americans think in an explicit, linear manner, while Asians think in an implicit, intuitive manner. Americans are more likely to think in terms of facts and dichotomies—black-white, right-wrong, good-evil, and true-false. Asians, in contrast, are likely to think in terms of feelings, relationships, and continuums.[9]

[NOTE 2.31]
Learn as much as possible about the people of another culture.

In addition to recognizing the ways people think, understanding other aspects of the culture you are studying is also important. You should try to learn about how the people relate to each other, what their preferences are in foods and how they eat, what their preferences are in apparel, what hours comprise their workday, how they negotiate, what their business ethics are, what topics of discussion are acceptable and what topics are unacceptable, and what gestures are acceptable and what gestures are unacceptable. The list goes on and on. You should try to learn about their religion, politics, educational system, economy, government, and history.

When you have acquired information about the other culture, analyze it in the following ways: How is it similar to your culture? How is it different? How can you best bridge these differences? By applying the information gained in this analysis—and with practice—you can become an effective cross-cultural communicator.

[NOTE 2.32]
You can become an effective cross-cultural communicator applying and practicing the information that you have gained.

[8] Sean Dwyer and Gene Johnson, "Cultural Simulation Training in the International Business Classroom," *Business Education Forum,* October 1999, pp. 36–38.

[9] Yukio Tsunda, *Language Inequality and Distortion in Intercultural Communication: A Critical Theory Approach,* Philadelphia: John Benjamin Publishing Company, 1987.

The preceding four basic guidelines are important for success in any cross-cultural communication in the business environment. There are two other categories of guidelines. The category to apply depends on whether your cross-cultural communication will be in English or in two languages.

GUIDELINES FOR CROSS-CULTURAL COMMUNICATION IN THE ENGLISH LANGUAGE

Fortunately for Americans, most cross-cultural business communication is conducted in the English language. This is true throughout the world.

[NOTE 2.33] Select topics carefully when conversing with members of another culture.

While the extensive use of English as the primary cross-cultural language is fortunate for Americans, it is important to recognize that for most people in the world, English is a second language. Non-Americans' facility with the English language and their understanding of its context will govern communication effectiveness. Choosing topics for discussion with members of another culture is extremely important. General guidelines are as follows:

- Avoid discussing politics or religion unless the other person initiates the discussion.
- Avoid highly personal questions including, "What do you do?"
- Keep the conversation positive. Avoid asking questions that would imply criticism.
- Avoid telling ethnic jokes because of the possibility of offending someone.[10]

Some Americans mistakenly equate a lack of ability to speak English fluently with a lack of intelligence in non-Americans. That serious error becomes a communication limitation for the Americans because they will analyze their receivers incorrectly. The next two guidelines will assist you in overcoming any such limitations.

[NOTE 2.34] Use the KISS principle in cross-cultural communication in English.

Guideline 5: Keep Your Message Short and Simple When Using English With Members of Another Culture This guideline reminds you to use the KISS principle of business communication (*Keep it Short and Simple*) when communicating in English with people from another culture. Use short words and short sentences. In addition, it is especially important to avoid jargon, slang, and colloquial expressions such as "back to square one," "piece of cake," "red tape," "ballpark figure," and "the bottom line." Most of your receivers will have learned only formal English in their schools. Except for the use of technical words appropriate for your receiver, the readability level of your message should be at about eighth- to tenth-grade level. Be sure to provide for feedback so that you can confirm receiver understanding of the message.

[NOTE 2.35] Pronounce words precisely.

Guideline 6: Enunciate Sounds and Pronounce Words Precisely If the communication in English is oral, be sure to enunciate sounds and pronounce words precisely. Try to overcome any accents or speech mannerisms that may be distracting and may create communication barriers. While you will not want the slowness to

[10] Letitia Baldrige (1993) in Lillian H. Chaney and Jeanette S. Martin, *Intercultural Business Communication,* Upper Saddle River, N.J.: Prentice Hall, 2000, p. 90.

appear exaggerated, speak somewhat more slowly. Be sure to speak at a normal conversational volume.

GUIDELINES FOR CROSS-CULTURAL COMMUNICATION USING AN INTERPRETER OR TRANSLATOR

If English is your only language and your receiver does not know English, then you must use an interpreter for oral communication and a translator for written communication. All previous guidelines apply when using an interpreter or a translator. The following four additional guidelines should be used as well.

Guideline 7: Use Short, Simple Phrases and Sentences When Using an Interpreter Avoid long introductory phrases, parenthetical elements, interjections, and complex and compound sentences. As you prepare to use an interpreter, give special attention to the parts of your message that may be difficult to convey. Develop clear illustrations of these difficult parts to help ensure your receiver's understanding.

[NOTE 2.36]
Use short, simple sentences when using an interpreter.

Avoid talking to your interpreter during your meeting. Talk directly to your receiver while keeping your interpreter in the corner of your eye. Permit your interpreter to explain your remarks if necessary, and encourage your receiver to ask questions if you sense you are not being understood clearly. Remain calm and poised. Concentrate on your receiver's interests and not on yourself or your interpreter.

[NOTE 2.37]
Avoid talking to the interpreter.

Guideline 8: Practice With Your Interpreter If possible, learn your interpreter's preferred ways of operating—in complete thought units, in short phrases, or word by word. You and your interpreter will be a team. Since practice improves any team effort, you will want to rehearse your cooperative effort with an interpreter.

[NOTE 2.38]
Practice using an interpreter.

Guideline 9: Select Only Translators Who Are Qualified to Translate the Type of Written Message You Are Sending Most people who have read instructions accompanying products manufactured overseas know the difficulty of translating from one language to another—generally, languages cannot be translated verbatim.

The translator must be both competent in the languages involved and qualified in the subject matter so that the *meaning* of the message is conveyed to the receiver, not just the words. As you will recall, insufficient knowledge resulted in using the Pepsi Cola slogan "Pepsi Comes Alive" in Taiwan and in naming an American car "Nova" in Spanish-speaking markets.

[NOTE 2.39]
Translators must know the subject matter.

Computerized language translation software can be of value when translating letters, memos, sales literature, and other business messages. Lernout & Hauspie (L&H), formerly "Globalink," offers speech recognition and translation software to customized documentation in any language. L&H provides the tools and services that help businesses large and small expand their horizons.

Guideline 10: Provide for Back Translation of Your Written Messages Check for translation errors; that is, have a second translator convert the message back into English for verification of its meaning. Back translation is a technique for obtaining essential feedback. Many translation errors have been caught this way.

[NOTE 2.40]
Back translation catches errors.

Communicating Successfully With Major Trading Partners of the United States

COMMUNICATION QUOTE

Having lived in Taiwan, Hong Kong, and the United States, I understand the value of being able to live and work with people with diverse cultural backgrounds. My position as a purchasing agent involves me in many aspects of my company's business with people from all over the world. My company appreciates my understanding of various cultures and regards this as a strength. To be successful in our global society, we must be able to conduct business with people from different backgrounds in a way that respects their traditions and business culture.

Nga Chan (Alan), Information Systems Analyst/Purchasing Agent, Golden Formosa International Enterprise Company Limited, Hong Kong and Taiwan.

Learning Objective [3]
IDENTIFY CULTURAL ATTRIBUTES OF THE MAJOR TRADING PARTNERS OF THE UNITED STATES.

[NOTE 2.41]
Examples from other cultures show how guidelines are used.

Brief examples of analyses of other cultures will help show the value of the previous guidelines. For these examples, the cultures of five major trading partners of the United States are examined—Japan, China, Germany, Canada, and Mexico.[11] Remember that information in the book *should only be used loosely* as a basis when conducting business abroad and that the only real way to be a good businessperson is to learn about the individuals with whom you are doing business. The suggestions for communicating successfully with businesspeople from various countries may be slightly stereotypical; however, as you prepare, recognize that variations do exist within cultures.

COMMUNICATING SUCCESSFULLY WITH JAPANESE BUSINESSPEOPLE

Japan consists of four main islands and has the second largest economy in the world. Japan's impressive level of economic and social organization is diminished by a high cost of living and the stress inherent in an emphasis on work and highly structured social institutions. Americans involved in international business can improve communication with the Japanese by taking into consideration Japanese cultural attributes. Remember that these are only stereotypes, and that individuals within cultures vary considerably.[12] Nonetheless, these guidelines can help Americans work more effectively with the Japanese in many business enterprises.

[11] This cultural analysis was based on the following materials: *Culturgrams* © 1999; Lillian H. Chaney and Jeanette S. Martin, *Intercultural Business Communication,* 2000; Roger E. Axtell, *The Do's and Taboos Around the World,* 1993; Roger E. Axtell, *The Do's and Taboos of International Trade*, 1994.

[12] This cultural analysis was based on the following materials: *Culturgrams* © 1999; Lillian H. Chaney and Jeanette S. Martin, *Intercultural Business Communication,* 2000; Roger E. Axtell, *The Do's and Taboos Around the World,* 1993; Roger E. Axtell, *The Do's and Taboos of International Trade*, 1994.

Japanese Cultural Attributes Japanese tend to be modest, respectful of superiors, loyal to their organizations, contemplative and holistic in their thinking, and traditional in terms of their society. They are achievement oriented. They value human relationships above business relationships and practice situational ethics; that is, moral judgments are based more on the merits of the situation than on some absolute ethical standard. Traditionally, most Japanese practice a combination of Buddhism and Shintoism. Their privacy is important to them, and direct questioning about their personal lives is resented. Never address a Japanese by his or her first name. To say Mr. Sakamoto, simply say Sakamoto *san*. "Losing face" is their worst catastrophe. The shame of losing face reflects not only on the individual but also on the family.

[NOTE 2.42]
Japanese are considered modest, respectful, and contemplative.

[NOTE 2.43]
Communicating with the Japanese calls for diplomacy.

Conducting Business With the Japanese When conducting business with the Japanese, American businesspeople should be gracious and diplomatic. In business meetings in Japan, bowing when greeting your hosts and then shaking hands are important gestures. Because status and hierarchy are important in Japan, an exchange of business cards upon meeting will be helpful to them in sorting out relationships. Business cards should be printed in English on one side and in Japanese on the other side. Business cards should be presented with both hands. The American belief in the equality of all does not prevail in Japan.

In business meetings in Japan, American businesspeople should bow when greeting their hosts and then shake hands.

Appointments should be arranged ahead of time. Punctuality is important for both business and social engagements. During meetings, confrontations should be avoided. The Japanese will prefer indirectness in approaching business transactions. They may seem to agree with you in order to avoid offending you. Do not let this courtesy mislead you into believing that the agreement is set. The agreement will not be finalized until it is in writing and signed. Japanese businesspeople will want to spend most of the meeting time clarifying the relationships of the trading partners and discussing the details of the business arrangement. Many times the actual terms will be agreed to during informal social gatherings.

[NOTE 2.44]
Primarily use the indirect organizational plan with the Japanese.

Being invited to a Japanese home is not the norm since most entertaining is done in Japanese restaurants. Tips are usually included in the bill. If you are invited to a private home, it is polite to take fruits or cakes. When giving a gift, present the gift with both hands. Remember to remove your shoes upon entering the home. Avoid excessive compliments on items in the home because that will embarrass the host. The traditional meal will be eaten from a bowl held at chest level. People eat most traditional food with chopsticks. Courtesy and humility should be an American's bywords in communicating with the Japanese.

COMMUNICATING SUCCESSFULLY WITH CHINESE BUSINESSPEOPLE

[NOTE 2.45] China is becoming a dominant force in the world economy.

China is rapidly becoming a dominant force in the world economy and could soon surpass the United States as the world's largest economic power. American businesspeople wishing to take advantage of the increasing consumer buying power in China must be adept in communicating with their Chinese counterparts. Consideration of Chinese cultural attributes is a key requirement for successful communication. Cultural attributes are stereotypical and may not apply to every individual within a culture.[13] Nevertheless, they are essential general guidelines for Americans who conduct business with the Chinese.

[NOTE 2.46] Chinese tend to be reserved and well mannered.

Chinese Cultural Attributes Chinese tend to be reserved and well mannered. They are superb hosts. Their attitudes are influenced by Confucianism. They take pride in their nation, its long history, and its influence on other countries. The Chinese have strong family ties and a loyalty to family members even though during the Cultural Revolution many families were separated by work assignments. The Chinese frequently display affection toward a member of the same sex by holding hands, but are discouraged from public displays of affection with members of the opposite sex. Chinese, however, do not like to be touched by people they do not know. A Chinese name is written with the one-syllable last name followed by a first name. For example, Ho Franklin would be addressed as Mr. Ho. "Losing face" remains a big concern among the Chinese. Great respect is afforded older Chinese.

[NOTE 2.47] Refer to the country as "People's Republic of China."

Conducting Business With the Chinese When communicating with the Chinese, American businesspeople should refer to the country as the "People's Republic of China" or simply "China." China regained possession of Hong Kong on July 1, 1997. China's relationship with Taiwan remains a sensitive political issue, and conversation regarding Taiwan should be avoided. In business meetings the Chinese are quite formal and use the full title of their guests when introducing them. A slight bow is appropriate when meeting someone and may be accompanied by a handshake. Business cards should be printed in English on one side and Chinese on the other side. Business cards should be presented with both hands. Business dress in the urban areas is very similar to the business dress in the United States.

Businesspeople traveling to China should have their appointments scheduled in advance and should arrive at meetings on time. It is customary for the Chinese to take a long time to make up their minds, so do not expect a quick business decision. Even after what appears to be a final decision, you should be prepared for a change in plans.

[NOTE 2.48] Tips and gifts are not expected.

If you are invited to an individual's home, it is polite to sample each of the dishes served. The food will be placed in the center of the table, and you will select the item you wish to eat with your chopsticks. You are expected to leave shortly after dinner. If you are invited out to a restaurant, the host will pay the bill. Again it is important that you sample all foods. The Chinese are very gracious and will make many toasts to friendship, thanks, and pleasure. Be prepared to at least take a sip of

[13] This cultural analysis was based on the following materials: *Culturgrams* © 1999; Lillian H. Chaney and Jeanette S. Martin, *Intercultural Business Communication,* 2000; Roger E. Axtell, *The Do's and Taboos Around the World,* 1993; Roger E. Axtell, *The Do's and Taboos of International Trade,* 1994.

your drink. Tips and gifts are not expected but with economic change are becoming more expected in the Guangdong and Fujian Provinces. Business is not discussed during meals; the Chinese use social occasions to get to know others and to build trusting relationships.

COMMUNICATING SUCCESSFULLY WITH GERMAN BUSINESSPEOPLE

Germany is one of the top five economic powers in the world and is preparing for the Economic and Monetary Union (EMU) within the European Union (EU). Germany assumed the EU presidency in January 1999 and provides leadership and generous financial support to the European Union. Overall, it has a high gross domestic product per capita, although it is far lower in the east due to the lingering effects of communist government. The German cultural attributes are quite distinctive. Remember, however, that the description that follows is a stereotype and may not apply to all Germans.[14]

German Cultural Attributes Compared with Americans, German businesspeople tend to be more formal, reserved, and restrained. Germans are likely to be inquisitive and want to hear the supporting evidence for a new idea or procedure. They enjoy vigorous discussion based on logical reasoning. They value intelligence and education. Like Americans, Germans value individualism and the success of the individual. While some Americans might think they are too outspoken or blunt, Germans would see their behavior as simple honesty.

[NOTE 2.49]
Germans tend to be more formal, reserved, and restrained.

Conducting Business With the Germans When communicating with German businesspeople, Americans should generally be formal, serious, impersonal, and thorough. Directness can be used effectively in communicating with German businesspeople in the same way that it can be used with Americans. Be businesslike, and focus on the agreed-upon goals of the meeting. In meeting with Germans, titles and last names should be used; and greetings should include firm handshakes with all those present.

[NOTE 2.50]
Communicating with Germans calls for formality and seriousness.

When traveling to Germany, make business appointments well in advance and arrive on time. Being on time for all business and social engagements is expected. Germans are basically conservative and prefer discipline and order to informality and change. They may seem to move slowly in their business operations, but they are strong and enduring. If you are presenting new information or a business proposal, be prepared to answer questions about it. Germans will demand supportive evidence based on solid research or logical reasoning. You may want to present your proposal privately to the top German executive for approval first. Then, that executive can either present the proposal to other Germans on your behalf or endorse your presentation after you have made it. This approach can increase the credibility of your proposal with other Germans and reduce the amount of time spent justifying it. Business cards are exchanged; English on one side and German on the other side. Business dress is similar but more conservative than the business dress in the United States.

[NOTE 2.51]
Make business appointments well in advance and arrive on time.

[14] This cultural analysis was based on the following materials: *Culturgrams* © 1999; Lillian H. Chaney and Jeanette S. Martin, *Intercultural Business Communication,* 2000; Roger E. Axtell, *The Do's and Taboos Around the World,* 1993; Roger E. Axtell, *The Do's and Taboos of International Trade,* 1994.

An invitation to a German's home is a special privilege. If you are invited, bring an odd number of flowers. These flowers should be unwrapped at the front door and then presented to the hostess. Avoid red roses which connote romance or carnations which connote mourning. Germans eat in the continental style, with the fork in the left hand and the knife in the right hand. Hands are kept above the table with the wrists resting on the edge. Dinner parties may last well into the night. If you eat at a restaurant, a service charge of 10 to 15 percent will be added to your bill so you do not need to leave an extra tip.

COMMUNICATING SUCCESSFULLY WITH CANADIAN BUSINESSPEOPLE

Canada is the United States' largest trading partner and has one of the strongest economies in the world. The North American Free Trade Agreement (NAFTA) eliminated all trade barriers between the two countries in 1999, so contact and communication with Canadians have increased for American businesspeople. The Canadian culture, while similar to the United States culture, has some diversity based on the origins of its citizens. Again, keep in mind that the following is a stereotype of the Canadian cultural attributes.[15]

[NOTE 2.52] Canada has two official languages.

Canadian Cultural Attributes Canadians generally tend to be more reserved and formal than the people of the United States. Most are friendly, kind, open, and polite. The Canadian people's ancestry is basically French and English, although some Canadians have their origins in Germany, the Netherlands, and Ireland. Canadians value their diversity. Both English and French are the official languages of Canada. Although French is the official language of Quebec, English is used in parts of Montreal, eastern Quebec, and throughout the rest of Canada. Western Canadians are likely to be less formal and reserved than eastern Canadians. When conversing, Canadians commonly stand about two feet apart; however, French Canadians often stand closer. When addressing a person in business, use the courtesy title and last name until told differently.

[NOTE 2.53] Dress is more conservative in Canada.

Conducting Business With the Canadians When conducting business with the Canadians, business people from the United States should be more formal and reserved than when dealing with those from the United States. Politeness and courtesy are essential. Greetings include a firm handshake and a sincere "hello." As in the United States, eye contact is important. Business cards are exchanged at the first meeting. If you are in the French-speaking area of Canada, business cards should be printed in English on one side and French on the other side. Your dress should be formal business attire.

[NOTE 2.54] Directness can be used in business negotiations in Canada.

Business people traveling to Canada should have their appointments scheduled in advance and should arrive at the meetings on time. Directness can be used, but the "hard sell" approach will not appeal to most Canadians. Be sincere, warm, and friendly. Negotiation practices are similar to those in the United States. Most busi-

[15] This cultural analysis was based on the following materials: *Culturgrams* © 1999; Lillian H. Chaney and Jeanette S. Martin, *Intercultural Business Communication,* 2000; Roger E. Axtell, *The Do's and Taboos Around the World,* 1993; Roger E. Axtell, *The Do's and Taboos of International Trade,* 1994.

ness entertainment is done in restaurants and clubs. In Canada the customary tip is 15 percent.

If you are invited to a private home, it would be polite to take or send candy, wine, or flowers. White lilies should be avoided since they are associated with funerals. Canadians are generally a little more formal in eating habits than the United States. The variety of foods found in Canada stems from the country's diversity. During conversations remember that Canadians are very proud of their history, clean cities, and diverse society. In conversation avoid making comparisons between the French-speaking and English-speaking provinces.

COMMUNICATING SUCCESSFULLY WITH MEXICAN BUSINESSPEOPLE

Mexico is recovering from its worst recession in more than 50 years. A U.S. loan package and restructuring has helped Mexico regain its footing. The North American Free Trade Agreement (NAFTA) with the United States and Canada has boosted Mexico's exports by lowering trade barriers and increasing the number of maquiladoras (border industries) where U.S. investment employs Mexican labor. The Mexican culture is quite different from that of the United States. Although the awareness of Mexican stereotype is extremely valuable, remember that individual Mexicans differ from one another.[16]

Mexican Cultural Attributes Mexicans tend to be warm, friendly, gracious people. They are good hosts. The Roman Catholic Church has greatly influenced the culture, attitudes, and history of Mexico. Mexicans are inclined to be patriotic and generally proud of their country. Family unity is important and the divorce rate is relatively low. Mexicans frequently stand very close while talking, possibly touching the other person or his or her clothing. Mexicans commonly have more than one given name and two surnames such as Jorge Juan Hernandez Gutierrez. The first surname comes from the father and the second from the mother. In this example, a business person would address him as Senor (Mr.) Hernandez (the first surname). They gain self-respect through the ways their friends treat and respect them. They generally trust only their friends.

[NOTE 2.55]
Mexicans tend to be warm, friendly, and gracious people.

Conducting Business With the Mexicans Developing a personal relationship is very important. Mexicans usually greet another person with a handshake. If a man is introduced to a woman, he will bow slightly and shake hands if she initiates it. Business cards are exchanged at the first meeting. One side of the card should be printed in English and the other side in Spanish. Business dress in the urban areas is very similar to the United States.

[NOTE 2.56]
Communicating with Mexicans calls for personal relationship development.

Businesspeople traveling to Mexico should make appointments in advance and arrive on time; however, remember that Mexicans tend to believe individuals are more important than schedules and may change a schedule at the last minute. Use indirectness in communicating with Mexican businesspeople. In your meetings, plan to visit socially first in order to accommodate their need for indirectness.

[NOTE 2.57]
Primarily use the indirect communication plan with Mexicans.

[16] This cultural analysis was based on the following materials: *Culturgrams* © 1999; Lillian H. Chaney and Jeanette S. Martin, *Intercultural Business Communication,* 2000; Roger E. Axtell, *The Do's and Taboos Around the World,* 1993; Roger E. Axtell, *The Do's and Taboos of International Trade,* 1994.

Typically, several meetings are held before a contract is signed, often during lunch. In Mexico, tipping is very important since wages tend to be lower. Since tipping amounts vary by regions, it is important to ask the hotel concierge or a local friend for advice on the rules of tipping.

If you are invited to an individual's home, it is polite to send flowers ahead of time. When sending flowers avoid marigolds, which are used to decorate cemeteries, and red flowers, which are used to cast spells. The standard food dishes are corn, beans, rice, and chiles which may be combined with meats or fish. Dinner may not be served until after 8 p.m., and guests are expected to relax and stay for conversation after the meal. It is expected that you sample the various dishes. While eating, Mexicans keep both hands above the table.

In many ways there are greater differences between the cultures of Mexico and the United States than there are between the United States and China, Japan, Germany, and Canada. Within the Communication Note "Doctors Learn to Bridge Cultural Gaps," information is given to doctors who are working with Latino and Asian patients. Remember that in business it is extremely important to be observant of the other people and to follow their lead.

COMMUNICATION NOTE

Doctors Learn to Bridge Cultural Gaps

Cal Optima, an Orange, California, HMO, offers training to doctors on working with Latino, Vietnamese, and Cambodian patients. Here are some pointers:

[1] **Seek** eye contact with Latino patients.

[2] **Forego** eye contact with some Asian patients.

[3] **Avoid** using patients' children as interpreters; family dynamics may make it difficult to get candid answers.

[4] **Reassure** Southeast Asian patients that blood, when drawn, is quickly regenerated.

[5] **Address** older patients in most nonwhite groups by surname and Mr. or Mrs.

As reported by George Anders in "Doctors Learn to Bridge Cultural Gaps," The Wall Street Journal, *September 4, 1997, p. Be.*

Communicating in a Diverse Workplace

Development of an organizational culture conducive to superior performance is the essence of concepts such as empowerment, involvement, continuous improvement, and total quality management. The common denominator of these prescriptions for improving organizational performance is the necessity to focus on the contribution of people. While the technical, conceptual, and administrative skills of managers continue to be of importance to superior results, human skills are what ultimately will make or break an organization. David Barclay, a former vice president of workforce diversity at Hughes, states his view on leadership in the following Communication Note.

COMMUNICATION NOTE

Leading Has Many Shades of Gray

"As the workforce becomes more diverse, a good leader is going to have to recognize that different people have different styles of getting things done" says David Barclay, a former vice president of workforce diversity at Hughes Electronics in Los Angeles.

As reported by Don Lee in "Leading Has Many Shades of Gray," The Los Angeles Times, *June 8, 1998, pp. 16–17.*

Diversity in the workplace is a reality that can be used to an organization's advantage. Diversity is good for business, and businesses have discovered that employee satisfaction and organizational success are linked. Because many organizations have become more aware of the relationship between valuing diversity and organizational performance, considerable attention is currently being devoted to managing diversity in the workplace.

[NOTE 2.58]
Diversity in the workplace is a reality that can be used to an organization's advantage.

Learning Objective [4]
LIST FIVE OF THE CORE DIMENSIONS OF HUMAN DIVERSITY, AND EXPLAIN THE IMPORTANCE OF UNDERSTANDING THESE DIMENSIONS.

When diversity is not understood and valued, discrimination often results. Analysis of the various dimensions of diversity helps the business communicator transmit messages that are more understandable and acceptable.

The dimensions defining differences between and among individuals are numerous. The following will focus on the core dimensions that may be considered relatively immutable or inborn. These are age, gender, physical challenges, ethnicity, and race.[17]

[NOTE 2.59]
There are five core dimensions of human diversity.

AGE

One in five Americans is 55 or older, compared to one in ten at the beginning of the century. The Census Bureau projects that by 2010 the number will be one in four. Age discrimination has increased with the aging of the workforce. The Equal Employment Opportunity Commission (EEOC) reports a 20 percent increase in age discrimination claims in 1991. To help convince American companies that there are advantages to hiring older workers, the American Association of Retired Persons (AARP) has begun research, education, and advocacy programs. The Communication Note "Job Prospects Look Hot for Boomers in 2020" reports that companies will be looking for ways to hire and retain older workers. When communicating with older workers, avoid phrases such as "deadwood," "resistant to change," "accident prone," "retired on the job," and "too old for the job."

[NOTE 2.60]
One in five Americans is 55 or older.

GENDER

Although many organizations have made significant progress in valuing and managing women in the workplace, many others have done very little. The workplace in 1990 was composed of approximately 68 percent of women. In the year 2000, approximately 80 percent of women between the ages of 25 and 54 worked full time. Sexual harassment is a form of discrimination predominately directed toward

[NOTE 2.61]
Sexual harassment is a form of discrimination predominately directed toward women.

[17] Marilyn Loden and Judy B. Rosener, *Workforce American!,* Homewood, Il.: Business One Irwin, 1991, p. 20.

COMMUNICATION NOTE

Job Prospects Look Hot for Boomers in 2020

Workplace: New study says employers will overhaul their employment practices to find ways to hire and retain older workers.

Older workers, often pushed out the door amid the corporate layoffs of the 1980s and 1990s, are likely to emerge in coming years as hot prospects in the job market.

That's one of the main conclusions of a new study by the Hudson Institute, an influential think tank focusing on major trends expected to shape the workforce through the year 2020.

Starting shortly after the current decade ends, "employers are going to have to make a 180-degree paradigm shift from the 1980s' downsizing mentality, when the urge was to slim down and collapse the managerial hierarchy," said Richard W. Judy, a coauthor of Hudson's *Workforce 2020* study.

Instead, said Judy, employers will overhaul their workplaces and employment practices to find ways to hire and retain aging baby boomers.

Adapted from article by Stuart Silverstein in "Job Prospects Look Hot . . . in 2020," Los Angeles Times, *April 27, 1997, p. D1.*

women.[18] Misunderstandings in business cost money as described within the "Styles of Communication" Communication Note. When communicating in a diverse workplace, avoid stereotypes such as women are not serious about careers and are emotionally out of control.

COMMUNICATION NOTE

Styles of Communication

When business was almost exclusively the domain of the white male, styles of communication were a nonissue. Most white men understood what other white men meant not necessarily by *what* they said but by *how* they said it. That has changed on the factory floor and in the management suite. Minorities and women bring their own styles of communicating and this proliferation of styles introduces a potential for misunderstanding. Misunderstandings cost money. Business can ill afford breakdowns in communication.

As reported in "Characteristics of Successful Programs," Good for Business: Making Use of the Nation's Human Capital: The Environmental Scan, *A Fact-Finding Report of the Federal Glass Ceiling Commission, Washington D.C., March 1995, p. 41.*

[18] Anne and Margaret Hennig, "The Last Barrier: Breaking Into the Boys' Club at the Top," *Working Woman,* pp. 130–134, 1990.

PHYSICAL CHALLENGES

Approximately 23 million Americans are physically challenged. The physically challenged frequently are patronized and judged based on ignorance and irrational fears and concerns. A major step toward removing these barriers was the passage of the Americans with Disabilities Act (ADA), intended to help prevent discrimination against qualified employees who are physically challenged and to make facilities accessible to the disabled. Avoid pitying or patronizing physically challenged employees when communicating in our diverse workplace.

ETHNICITY AND RACE

The Hudson Institute's *Workforce 2000* offered predictions about changes that would occur in the demographic composition of the U.S. population and workforce by the year 2000. This study, commissioned by the United States Department of Labor, made the following forecasts:

[NOTE 2.62]

The Hudson Institute's *Workforce 2000* offered predictions about changes in the workforce.

- White males will account for only 15 percent of the 25 million people who will join the workforce between the years 1985 and 2000.
- The remaining 85 percent joining the workforce will be white females; immigrants; and individuals (of both genders) of black, Hispanic, and Asian origins.
- The Hispanic and Asian populations will each grow by 48 percent; the black population will grow by 28 percent; and the white population will grow by only 5.6 percent.[19] The new Hudson report, as described in "Job Prospects Look Hot for Boomers in 2020," indicates the same increase in diversity in the workplace as shown in the following Communication Note.

COMMUNICATION NOTE

Job Prospects Look Hot for Boomers in 2020

The new Hudson report forecasts a continuing, albeit gradual, increase in women and minorities in the workplace. It predicts that the portion of the workforce consisting of minorities will edge up from 23% in 1994 to 26% in the year 2005. Likewise, the percentage of women is expected to inch up from 46% to 48% over the same period.

As reported by Stuart Silverstein in "Job Prospects Look Hot . . . in 2020," Los Angeles Times, *April 27, 1997, p. D1.*

In communicating in a diverse workplace, avoid stereotypes which are simplistic and often erroneous beliefs such as African-American men are good athletes and Hispanic women are subservient. Ineffective communication is due to the communicator's inaccurate assumptions about an individual's race or ethnicity. Effective communication can be achieved by focusing on an individual's actual behaviors, knowledge, skills, and abilities. Accurate perceptions contribute to effective communication.[20]

[19] William B. Johnston and Arnold H. Packer, *Workforce 2000,* Indianapolis: Hudson Institute, 1987.

The job of management is to achieve organizational goals and objectives in an effective and efficient manner through good communication skills with people. For people to be motivated and for them to put forth persistent effort in the direction of organizational goals requires job involvement and commitment. This in turn requires people to believe that they are valued and understood by the organization regardless of their age, gender, physical challenges, race, or ethnicity.

Management's challenge is to recognize the necessity of not only recruiting and retaining top talent but also marketing to the suppliers and customers who have become more diverse in our global society. To meet this challenge companies may use various strategies such as diversity training workshops to give employees the skills needed to function and communicate effectively in a diverse workplace.

[NOTE 2.63]
Management's challenge is to recognize the necessity of tapping into the potential of a diverse workforce.

As the guidelines for successful cross-cultural communication indicate, you must know yourself, be open, learn all you can about the other cultures and the dimensions of diversity, apply what you learn, and keep your message short and simple. When working in our diverse society, Lee Gardenswartz and Anita Rowe remind us that if individuals are treated with dignity and respect, they will be more likely to work with you. As business communicators, we must remember not to break this universal law of human relations.[21] The last section of this chapter provides sources of information for enhancing your understanding of the various cultures.

Sources of Business Communication Information for Understanding a Global and Diverse Society

Learning Objective [5]
IDENTIFY KEY RESOURCES IN INTERNATIONAL, CROSS-CULTURAL, AND DIVERSITY IN BUSINESS FOR BUSINESS COMMUNICATION.

This chapter presents basic information on the challenges of international and cross-cultural business communication and on communicating successfully in the international business environment and the diverse workplace. For more specific information on cross-cultural business communication or international business information, the following books and Web sites are suggested:

[NOTE 2.64]
Further information is available:
- In specialized books
- On Web sites
- From professional organizations

BOOKS

Axtell, Roger E. *The Do's and Taboos Around the World.* The Parker Pen Company. New York: John Wiley & Sons, 1993.

Axtell, Roger E. *The Do's and Taboos of International Trade,* New York: John Wiley & Sons, Inc., 1994.

Axtell, Roger E. and Fornwald, Mike (Illustrator). *Gestures: The Do's and Taboos of Body Language Around the World,* New York: John Wiley & Sons, January 1998.

[20] Gareth R. Jones, Jennifer M. George, and Charles W. L. Hill, *Contemporary Management,* Irwin, Il.: McGraw-Hill, 2000, p. 540.

[21] Lee Gardenswartz and Anita Rowe, *Managing Diversity: A Complete Reference Guide and Planning Guide,* Homewood, Il.: Business One Irwin, 1993, p. 96.

Chaney, Lillian H. and Martin, Jeanette S. *Intercultural Business Communication*, 2d ed. Upper Saddle River, N.J.: Prentice Hall, 2000.

Gardenswartz, Lee and Rowe, Anita. *Managing Diversity: A Complete Reference Guide and Planning Guide,* Homewood, Il.: Business One Irwin, 1993.

Kenton, Sherron B. and Valentine, Deborah. *CrossTalk: Communicating in a Multicultural Workplace.* New York: Prentice Hall, 1997.

Marx, Elisabeth. *Breaking Through Culture Shock.* London: Nicholas Brealey Publishing, 1999.

Morrison, Terri, et al. *Kiss, Bow, or Shake Hands: How to Do Business in 60 Countries.* Adams Media Corporation, April 1995.

Morrison, Terri, Conaway, Wayne A. and Douress, Joseph J. *Dun & Bradstreet's Guide to Doing Business Around the World,* Englewood Cliffs, N.J.: Prentice Hall, Inc., 1997.

Presner, Lewis. *The International Business Dictionary & Reference.* New York: John Wiley & Sons, September 1991.

Good for Business: Making Use of the Nation's Human Capital: The Environmental Scan. A Fact-Finding Report of the Federal Glass Ceiling Commission. Washington D.C., March 1995.

WEB SITES

Business Executive Resources Worldwide. **http://www.worldbiz.com** 2000. This Web site is a source of information on international business practices, international business protocol, international etiquette, cross-cultural communication, negotiating tactics, and country-specific data for 117 countries.

Gaining the Competitive Edge in International Markets. **http://www.iie.com/** 2000. This site is the home for the Institute for International Economics and offers current information on what is happening in today's global marketplace.

International Business Resources on the World Wide Web. **http://ciber.bus.msu.edu/busres.htm** 2000. This site has been designated as a national resource center in international business education by the U.S. Department of Education.

The Web of Culture. **http://www.webofculture.com/** 2000. This site is a source for conducting corporate research and providing information on culture topics.

The following organizations are good sources of information on communication generally and international and cross-cultural business communication specifically:

Association for Business Communication
Baruch College—C.U.N.Y.
Department of Speech
17 Lexington Avenue
New York, NY 10010

International Association of Business Communicators
870 Market Street, Suite 940
San Francisco, CA 94102

A key to success in cross-cultural communication is learning all that you can about the other culture. A good source of extensive publications on other cultures and how to relate effectively to them is the following center:

Culturgrams
1305 North Research Way
Orem, UT 84097-6200
Telephone: (800) 528-6279

You may locate the Web site **http://www.culturgram.com** for a catalog listing of available books and culturgrams for over 170 countries.

Summary of Learning Objectives

Learning Objective [1]

Describe the challenges of international and cross-cultural business communication. The challenges of international and cross-cultural business communication are similar to the communication challenges within a culture—analyzing receivers and using the you–viewpoint—with one major difference. That difference is found in the striking variations among cultures throughout the world. Cultural variations exist in languages, values and attitudes, symbols and gestures, laws, religions, politics, educational levels, technological development, and social organizations.

Learning Objective [2]

Describe the goal for effective cross-cultural communication, and explain how the guidelines for cross-cultural communication can be used. The goal for effective cross-cultural communication is to achieve normal business communication without prejudice. This means having the ability to communicate comfortably and naturally while eliminating barriers that might be caused by cultural differences.

Learning Objective [3]

Identify cultural attributes of the major trading partners of the United States. Japanese are considered modest, respectful, and contemplative. Germans are generally reserved, inquisitive, and conservative. Canadians are somewhat more reserved, formal, and conservative than are U.S. citizens. Mexicans are considered warm, gracious, and people oriented. Chinese tend to be reserved, well mannered, and patriotic.

Learning Objective [4]

List five of the core dimensions of human diversity, and explain the importance of understanding these dimensions. The five core dimensions of diversity are as follows: age, gender, physical challenges, ethnicity, and race. Analysis of the various dimensions of diversity helps the business communicator transmit messages that are more understandable and acceptable to the members of that dimension of diversity.

Learning Objective [5]

Identify key resources in international, cross-cultural, and diversity in business for business communication. Basic to your study should be a review of one or more of the several good international business textbooks now on the market. You may also access Web sites for current information.

DISCUSSION QUESTIONS

1. Why should students study international and cross-cultural business communication? (Objective 1)
2. Define international business communication and cross-cultural business communication. (Objective 1)
3. Explain how you would greet a person from Canada, China, Germany, Japan, and Mexico. (Objective 1)
4. Describe what is meant by the statement, "The most important differences are in the ways people in other cultures think and feel." (Objective 1)
5. What is the goal of cross-cultural communication? Discuss the meaning of this goal. (Objective 2)
6. Give one example of a culture difference for each of the following categories: behaviors, values, business hours, and workdays. (Objective 2)
7. Explain the terms stereotype, cultural relativism, and ethnocentrism. (Objective 2)
8. List five features of the Chinese culture that are distinctively different from the American culture. (Objective 3)
9. List the five core dimensions of diversity and explain them. Why is understanding the five core dimensions of diversity important to business communication? (Objective 4)
10. List resources for the business communicator in a global and diverse society as specified in the following items: (a) two books, (b) one professional association, (c) two Web sites, and (d) one government publication. (Objective 5)

APPLICATION EXERCISES

1. **Global/Cross-Cultural.** Gather information at the library that will enable you to analyze a culture other than the cultures (American, Japanese, Chinese, German, Canadian, and Mexican) analyzed in this chapter. Give particular attention in your analysis to the way the people of the culture think and how that would affect their communication with Americans. Report your findings as directed by your instructor. (Objectives 1–4)
2. **Global/Cross-Cultural.** Interview a student or businessperson from another culture who is currently residing in your area and ask the following questions: (Objectives 1–2)
   a. How do the people of your country perceive Americans?
   b. What was the most difficult adjustment you had to make when you moved into this culture?
   c. What advice would you give to someone going to your country to live and work?

   Write a report that contains the answers to your interview questions.

3. **Global/Cross-Cultural.** Visit the international center or talk with a foreign language instructor and obtain information on a study abroad or work abroad program. Develop and present your findings to your class. (Objectives 1–2)

4. **Teamwork. Global/Cross-Cultural. Ethics.** Form groups of four to seven students each. Assign each group a specific culture from among the following: American, Canadian, German, Japanese, Mexican, Chinese. Each group is responsible for describing its assigned culture by answering these questions. (Objectives 1–3 and 5)

For your assigned culture, how important is/are

a. Time?

b. Groups versus individuals?

c. Eye contact?

d. Rank and authority?

e. Personal relationships?

f. Standards of business ethics?

Write a report of your findings.

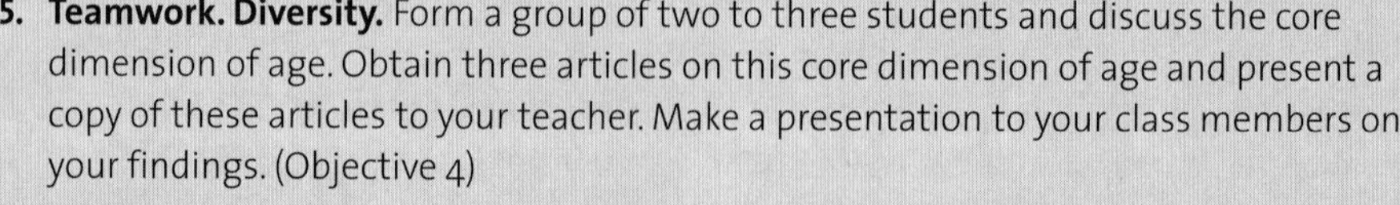

5. Teamwork. Diversity. Form a group of two to three students and discuss the core dimension of age. Obtain three articles on this core dimension of age and present a copy of these articles to your teacher. Make a presentation to your class members on your findings. (Objective 4)

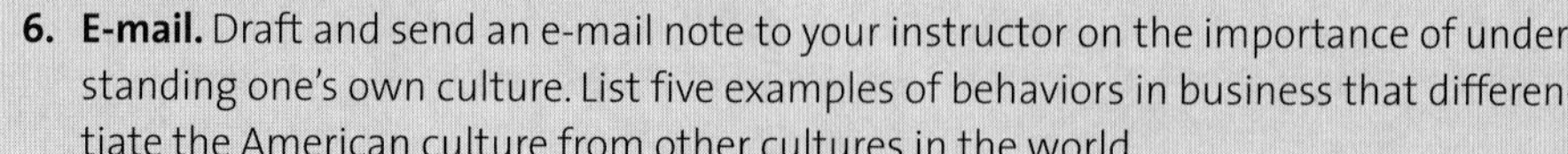

6. E-mail. Draft and send an e-mail note to your instructor on the importance of understanding one's own culture. List five examples of behaviors in business that differentiate the American culture from other cultures in the world.

7. Diversity BusinessLink Video. *Diversity in Business: A Study of Hudson's.* Target Corp., formerly known as The Dayton-Hudson Corporation, with headquarters in Minneapolis, is the fourth largest general merchandise retailer in the United States. The corporation consists of Target, an upscale discount chain; Mervyn's, a middle-market promotional department store; and the Department Store Division, consisting of Dayton's, Hudson's, and Marshall Field's, all upscale department stores. Hudson's is committed to developing a diverse workforce that can effectively serve its diverse customer population.

After viewing the video *Diversity in Business: A Study of Hudson's*, complete the following and submit a memo to your instructor outlining your answers and recommendations.

a. List the two major goals of the Dayton-Hudson Corporation.

b. Explain why Hudson's is committed to diversity. Develop a list of the benefits for a company that is committed to diversity.

c. Form a group and design a one-day event you could hold in your class to promote diversity awareness.

There are Web exercises at **http://krizan.swcollege.com** to accompany this chapter.

MESSAGE ANALYSIS

Global/Cross Cultural. Correct the following message that has been written to Mei Su, a high school junior born and living in Arizona, who has been accepted as an American Field Service (AFS) student to study in Spain.

Dear Mei Su:

Congradulations! You have been accepted to participate in the Short homestay Summer program departing in 2002. After we here back from the staff in spain, we will contact you immediately with the name' of you're host family.

If you havent' applyed for your Pass Port, you should apply now. Please make sure you're Pass Port will be valid for the intire duration of your AFS program. If you're Pass Port expires wild you are abroad you may have difficulty returning in the United States.

If you have any questions please call you're local ASF voolunteer or a member of the Student admissions' team at (800) 555-2300. We look foreward to providing you with the experience of a life time!

Sincerely,

(Your name)

Afs Regional Cordinator

GRAMMAR WORKSHOP

Correct the grammar, spelling, punctuation, style, and word choice errors in the following sentences:

1. In america a successful woman could be said to be self assured ambitious and forward looking.
2. Africas position today are to a large extent explaind by it's History.
3. This articles will provide a brief history, and a current report on the status of Women in Contemporary chinese society.
4. Cultural differences effect not only values attitude and management practices; but, also impact the processs of information gathering, and processing.
5. Many articles has been written over the past few years regarding public school Reform.
6. Denmark was the location for the 1997 siec Conference.
7. The university of Mining and metallurgy are located in Krakow polland.
8. Bronx is the only one of New York citys' five boroughs on the mainland of the United States.
9. South Africa has three capitols: Pretoria; Cape town, and Bloemfontein.
10. Africa is the only continent in all four hemispheres Northern Southern eastern and Western.

CHAPTER

3 Communication Technologies and Techniques

Michelle Schroer, Llewellyn Worldwide, Ltd.

LET'S TALK BUSINESS Today's business survives on communication. Finding ways to improve that communication, both internally and externally, gives your company a competitive edge.

E-mail and the World Wide Web are prime examples of communication tools that connect the company to the customer. Through this connection, you are giving your customers another means of contacting you. This electronic contact is as important as all other forms of communication; therefore, normal business communication rules need to be applied. Spelling, punctuation, grammar, and writing style make an impression on the customer. You want to show your current and potential customers you are a professional.

(Continued)

[LEARNING OBJECTIVES]

[1] DISCUSS THE TRENDS AND ISSUES ASSOCIATED WITH THE USE OF COMMUNICATION TECHNOLOGY.

[2] EXPLAIN HOW THE INTERNET AND WORLD WIDE WEB ASSIST BUSINESS COMMUNICATORS IN ACHIEVING THEIR GOALS.

[3] IDENTIFY THE TECHNOLOGICAL TOOLS BUSINESS COMMUNICATORS CAN USE TO IMPROVE WRITTEN, ORAL, AND VISUAL COMMUNICATION.

Remember, with electronic tools and the World Wide Web, your company *and you* are on display to more people than ever before. Incorrect spelling and punctuation, poor grammar, or bad writing style in e-mail or on your Web site can spell disaster for your company.

Make sure you show your customers just how professional you are and gain that competitive edge! •

Today's business professionals operate in a fast-paced, global environment. As Michelle Schroer points out in the Let's Talk Business section, technology can help organizations meet communication challenges and gain a competitive edge. Notebook computers and cell phones have made communication tools portable. The Internet and World Wide Web have opened new markets for products and services and created new avenues through which communication may travel.

The impact of technology has been rapid and dramatic. Information technology manufacturers appear to be engaged in a game of leapfrog—every new product does more than the one that preceded it, and the interval between new products is shrinking. "More, cheaper, faster" has become the norm, and that pattern is unlikely to change. This chapter, therefore, focuses on WHAT the technology does rather than on the specifics of HOW it does it. The goal is to increase your awareness of the ways in which technology can help improve or facilitate business communication.

The chapter begins by looking at some of the trends and issues associated with adopting technology for use in business communication. Next, we look at ways in which the Internet and World Wide Web can help facilitate effective communication. Finally, because much of today's communication is verbal, we end by exploring the tools communicators may use to improve their written and oral communication; visual communication tools are addressed as part of that section.

Trends and Issues

Learning Objective [1]
DISCUSS THE TRENDS AND ISSUES ASSOCIATED WITH THE USE OF COMMUNICATION TECHNOLOGY.

As the use of technology has expanded and assumed a more dominant role in the business communication process, several trends and issues have emerged.

One of the most product-related trends in communication technology is the prevalence of integration. An **integrated program** combines several products (e.g., word processing, spreadsheet, database, and presentation), ensuring compatibility among the different programs. Although integrated software solves the problem of compatibility among programs adopted by one user, incompatibility between software programs used by individual communicators is still possible.

[NOTE 3.1]
Integration helps ensure software compatibility.

The trend toward integration is fueled, in part, by the growth of wireless computer equipment. In the near future, communicators can expect to have Web, e-mail, fax, and phone access through a computer the size of a wristwatch. To learn more about wearable computing, visit **http://www.media.mit.edu/projects/wearables**. These wireless units, like their corded predecessors, will support multitasking. Users

[NOTE 3.2]
Wireless technology will make wearable computing a reality.

will be able to have a phone conversation, surf the Web, analyze data, and view a Webcast, all from a battery-powered computer. In addition, users will download software from the Internet rather than buy it in boxes off the shelf.

[NOTE 3.3] Goods can be bought and sold electronically.

Another trend linked to technology is **electronic commerce** (e-commerce), the buying and selling of goods and services over the Internet. A related concept is **mobile commerce** (M-commerce), which enables users to execute transactions from virtually any location via a cellular phone or other wireless device. M-commerce is used widely in Europe and Asia; rapid adoption and expansion are expected in the United States.

[NOTE 3.4] As e-commerce expands, so will electronic communication.

The idea of Internet-based commerce is appealing to businesses because of the virtually unlimited market expansion it offers. Nearly half of all U.S. households now have computers and, although numbers are smaller in other countries, the growth of the Internet literally makes the world an e-commerce market. In fact, online sales are forecast to be between $100 billion and $600 billion early in the twenty-first century—and that prediction was made before the electronic signature law was signed in the summer of 2000. Success in the international marketplace will depend not only on technology but also on the ability to communicate effectively.

Electronic commerce has already established a firm base. Internet users can order everything from a floral arrangement to an automobile and have it delivered to their home, office, or some other location. How do they pay? By credit card or through a pre-established account. The thought of sending a credit card number across the Internet makes some people reluctant to participate in electronic commerce. Security issues are being addressed by *encrypting* (encoding) the buyer's credit card number, and forecasters now suggest that nearly one quarter of all household expenditures will occur in cyberspace by the year 2005.

As customers become more comfortable with the idea of ordering and paying for goods and services through the Internet, business communicators can expect to process more of their messages electronically. Inquiries and complaints, for example, will arrive and be responded to via e-mail. Many of those messages will be originated by people who do not speak English or for whom English is not their first language. In fact, some Internet watchers believe that people in other countries may learn English not through formal training but rather through their use of the Internet. Translation programs will assist in interpreting and responding to messages in languages other than English, but the need to be aware of and sensitive to cultural differences and the way language translates will be extremely important.

[NOTE 3.5] The Internet can be a data-gathering tool.

Expanded use of the Internet also means that business professionals may find themselves using the Internet not only for secondary research but also for primary research. Many firms already use the Internet for conducting surveys. Having data submitted electronically expedites analysis because the data do not have to be keyed and proofread. Establishing trust will be a key element in the success of electronic surveys.

[NOTE 3.6] Research about Internet users can be controversial.

Internet research is not without controversy. Technology makes it feasible to gather data about computer users without their knowledge or permission, a practice that many consider to be unethical and an invasion of individual privacy. As a result of these concerns, organizations frequently include a privacy statement on their Web sites. The statement explains what data are gathered and how they will be used. The Better Business Bureau assists with this process by sponsoring a privacy program to which businesses may subscribe. To learn more about the program, visit the Bureau's site at **http://www.bbbonline.org/**.

Telecommuting means working from a location other than the office where business is usually conducted. Although anyone who communicates with his or her office from a car, public telephone, hotel, or client's office might be defined as a telecommuter, the term is more widely applied to those who work from their home. Data access and communication with clients, colleagues, and supervisors are accomplished electronically. For organizations doing business across time zones, telecommuting enhances communication by allowing people to talk more conveniently early in the morning or late at night. Increased productivity, reduced employee turnover, and reduced need for costly office space are among the reasons businesses consider permitting employees to telecommute.

[NOTE 3.7]
Communication technology enables workers to telecommute.

Despite its advantages, telecommuting can promote worker isolation. In order to minimize the impact telecommuting can have on worker-worker, worker-supervisor, or worker-organization relationships, some organizations have telecommuters spend one day a week (or some other pattern) in the office. This structure permits organizations to schedule face-to-face meetings and to facilitate development of interpersonal relationships among employees.

Whether its employees work on site or off, organizations must be sure technology is used appropriately. Misuse of e-mail and Internet resources not only threatens productivity and creates legal concerns but also endangers the company's image.

[NOTE 3.8]
Privacy, productivity, legal liability, and image are concerns.

Productivity concerns stem from workers' easy access to e-mail and the Internet. Access to and curiosity about these services, which are provided to facilitate business transactions, create the temptation to waste time. When workers are exchanging e-mail with family and friends, forwarding jokes to coworkers and others, playing games, day trading, or just surfing the Web, they are not engaged in activities that promote the organization or its mission.

Legal concerns about misuse of e-mail and Internet access are related to liability and privacy. Organizations want to trust their employees and respect their privacy, but they fear they may be held liable for the content of e-mail messages. Computer systems can retain messages long after they have been deleted from the user's mailbox. Gossip, derogatory comments, lewd or obscene messages or graphics, harassing messages, or any number of other items could be retrieved from e-mail files and used as evidence in court cases. In addition, having such messages originate or circulate within the workplace negatively impacts the organization's goal of having a harassment-free environment and could ultimately tarnish the organization's good image. Even business-related e-mail can haunt an individual or organization, as demonstrated in the antitrust case against Microsoft in the late 1990s. In this case, e-mail exchanged among Bill Gates and his staff was retrieved and used as evidence.

The fear of litigation and the concern over wasted time have prompted some organizations to monitor workers' use of electronic resources; special network and e-mail software programs exist for just this purpose. Other organizations have chosen to develop clear policies on the use of e-mail and other company resources. Boeing, for example, includes the statement shown in Figure 3.1 in its employee manual.

[NOTE 3.9]
Employers use various methods to alert workers to resource-use policies.

Some companies make employment contingent on a prospective employee's willingness to sign a statement saying that she or he has read, understands, and

Figure 3.1
Resource Use Policy

3. Use of Boeing Resources for Noncompany Purposes

   A. Boeing Communication Systems

   Boeing communication systems and networks are provided for the conduct of company business. However, personal use by employees of Boeing telephones, facsimile machines, and voice mail, E-mail, and Internet systems is permitted within the following guidelines:

   1. The use is of reasonable duration and frequency.
   2. Boeing incurs no added costs, such as long distance telephone charges.
   3. The use is not related to any illegal activity or the conduct of an outside business.
   4. The use would not cause embarrassment to the company.
   5. The use is not in support of any religious, political, or outside organization activity, except for company-requested support to nonprofit organizations as provided in *section 5*.
   6. The use does not interfere with the performance of company business, the employee's assigned duties, or the assigned duties of other employees and does not adversely affect the performance of the employee or the employee's organization.

   Use of Boeing E-mail systems involves additional considerations and requires special care. Employees must bear in mind that E-mail is not private and its source is clearly identifiable. E-mail messages may remain part of Boeing business records long after they have been supposedly deleted. Employees must ensure that personal E-mail does not adversely affect the company or its public image or that of its customers, partners, associates, or suppliers. E-mail may not be used for external broadcast messages or to send or post chain letters, messages of a political or religious nature, or messages that contain obscene, profane, or otherwise offensive language or material that violate company policy or procedure, including Boeing Policy POL-5, "Equal Employment Opportunity."

   Personal use of internal and external networks must also comply with additional requirements in Boeing Procedure IB-ACG-313, "Network Security and Proper Use."

   Issues concerning appropriate personal use of Boeing communication systems within a particular work group are to be resolved by the management of that organization.

   B. Use of Boeing Personal Computers, Copiers, and Similar Office Equipment

   Office equipment, such as personal computers and copiers, is provided for the conduct of company business. The company and its organizations may incur costs based on the rate of use of such equipment. Employees may not use a company mainframe, minicomputer system, or data network for any noncompany purposes except when such use is in accordance with Boeing Procedure IC-ACH-319, "Computer Hardware, Software, and Data Control and Protection." However, occasional personal use of a personal computer, copier, or similar office equipment is permitted within the following guidelines:

   1. The use should be infrequent and minimal.
   2. The use must not be related to any illegal activity or the conduct of an outside business.
   3. The use must not cause embarrassment to the company.
   4. The use should not be in support of any religious, political, or other outside organization activity, except for company-requested support to nonprofit organizations as provided in *section 5*.
   5. The equipment should be used on an off-hour basis, such as during lunch time or before or after work hours.
   6. The use should not interfere with the performance of company business, the employee's assigned duties, or the assigned duties of other employees and should not adversely affect the performance of the employee or the employee's organization.
   7. There should be no incremental cost to the organization or the cost should be insignificant.

   Issues concerning appropriate personal use of Boeing personal computers, copiers, and similar office equipment within a particular work group are to be resolved by the management of that organization.

accepts the organization's computer use policy. Some organizations embed a statement about technology misuse into the system's log-on procedure. Users may not proceed without acknowledging the message and the warning that their computing activities may be monitored.

Other trends and issues will emerge as technology changes the way in which work is accomplished. Being part of that change will be exciting.

The Internet and the World Wide Web

Learning Objective [2]
EXPLAIN HOW THE INTERNET AND WORLD WIDE WEB ASSIST BUSINESS COMMUNICATORS IN ACHIEVING THEIR GOALS.

Advances in technology have enabled people to communicate in ways previously not possible. This section describes several electronic resources.

When two or more computers are linked to facilitate information transfers, they form a **network.** The **Internet** is the world's largest network, but rather than linking individual computers, it links computer networks.

[NOTE 3.10]
The Internet is a worldwide network.

Created in the 1960s as a tool for communication among employees of various government agencies, especially research scientists, the Internet is now an international communication medium used by educators, businesses, nonprofit organizations, and private citizens. One of the factors contributing to the popularity of the Internet was the inception of the **World Wide Web,** commonly referred to as *the Web* and identified by the abbreviation *WWW.*

[NOTE 3.11]
The Web makes Internet access easy.

The Web, which originated at the European Center for Nuclear Research (CERN) in Geneva, Switzerland, has made the Internet more accessible to those who want to tap its resources. Users navigate the system via a *browser* and rely on *hyperlinks* (electronic pointers) to move from one *site* (location) to another. Each site is a hypermedia document that may contain text, sound, and still or video images. Each site has a *URL* (Uniform Resource Locator), an address or reference code the browser uses to contact the site. The standard format for a URL is **transfer protocol://servername.domain/directory/subdirectory/filename.filetype**. URLs typically begin with the letters *http* and often end with the letters *html* or *htm.* The abbreviation **http** stands for *HyperText Transfer Protocol,* the instructions used to transfer documents and data between computers; the abbreviation **html** refers to the *HyperText Markup Language,* a set of commands that describes the file to the browser. As you can see, the Internet has generated its own jargon.

[NOTE 3.12]
As the Internet developed, so did a special vocabulary.

E-mail represents the most common Internet application. The Internet can, however, be used for many other purposes, including research. Information about how to use the Internet as a research tool, how to develop an effective search strategy, how to recognize a credible source, and how to cite Internet resources can be found in Chapter 11. Chapter 16 includes information about how the Internet can be used to research potential employers and be a channel through which people apply for employment.

[NOTE 3.13]
Use the Internet for e-mail, research, and other purposes.

USENET

In the sections that follow, you'll learn about features available through **USENET,** a service that allows Internet users to meet, talk, and exchange ideas about topics in which they have a mutual interest. USENET formats are broadly classified as

[NOTE 3.14]
USENET has several formats.

newsgroups and are often identified by more specific terms such as listservs, bulletin boards, and chat rooms.

The value of each USENET format will vary depending on the purpose for which the user accesses it. In general, each is a good vehicle for idea sharing and for getting leads to credible research sources but less good as a valid source in and of itself. Internet resources such as periodicals, or databases listing periodicals, are typically viewed as being more credible.

[NOTE 3.15]
Users join a listserv.

Listservs A **listserv** is a message-management system that allows participants to exchange e-mail with others who wish to correspond about a topic of mutual interest. When a message is posted to the listserv, it is automatically sent to all those on the list. To participate in a listserv, users must **subscribe,** or sign on. This is accomplished by sending a specific message to a predefined location. Users follow a similar procedure when they wish to **unsubscribe** (leave) the listserv. The format for the address and messages resemble those shown in the following entries.

To: listserv@xxx.edu (*xxx* represents the host computer)
Message: sub *listserv name your name*
Message: signoff *listserv name your name*

Listservs can be a good way to seek and get information about a topic in which you are interested, but be careful. A simple query sent to the listserv can generate hundreds of replies—all directed to your e-mail address. And poorly phrased questions can raise the wrath of irate responders. For a catalog of publicly available listservs, visit **http://www.lsoft.com/catalist.html**.

[NOTE 3.16]
Users visit a bulletin board.

Electronic Bulletin Boards **Electronic bulletin boards** permit users to post or publish messages on the Internet. Unlike listservs, which users must join before they may take part, bulletin boards (and chat rooms) are services that users visit. When users arrive, they view a menu (listing) of options designed to guide them during their stay. Those who post messages are expected to identify themselves and provide information to allow interested readers to contact them via e-mail.

[NOTE 3.17]
Chat room messages are temporary.

Chat Rooms For those who seek a more active experience than that offered by a listserv or bulletin board, chat rooms may prove useful. **Chat rooms** are online discussion groups. When one person keys a comment, others see it within seconds. Unlike items displayed in other formats, chat room comments have a short life; they are not saved indefinitely. When established for and restricted to exchanges about business-related topics, chat rooms can be used to improve customer relations and strengthen communication among employees or other business professionals.

[NOTE 3.18]
Select USENET services carefully.

A Word of Caution USENET attracts a wide variety of users from around the world. Some newsgroups offer intellectually stimulating content, others entertain; some, however, will be perceived by readers to be crude and obscene. The best policy is to visit various USENET sites, screen them carefully, and participate in those you think are appropriate. Also, consider using a screen name alias rather than your own name. When you participate, be sure to follow the "netiquette" guidelines in the Tips and Hints box.

Be a Courteous Network User

TIPS AND HINTS

The following items will help Internet users be good network citizens (netizens) and use appropriate network etiquette (netiquette):

- Read before you write. Familiarize yourself with and write in the style used within the resource.
- Use Frequently Asked Questions (FAQ) listings as a source of information.
- Focus on the topic. Don't introduce irrevelant topics or attempt to terminate a lively debate by introducing a new related topic.
- Think about what you say and how you say it. Don't **spam** (send excessive or unwanted e-mail messages), don't **flame** (send angry messages designed to "burn" other users, especially those who spam).
- Include a signature line even though e-mail information has probably been provided by the system you use. A typical signature line includes a person's postal address, phone number, and fax number; some people include a favorite quote.

INTRANETS

Most of the features discussed in this chapter can be made available on an organization-only basis through an **intranet.** Businesses that develop such systems enable their employees to move information, exchange ideas, and discuss strategy within a company but not to access the external resources available on the Internet. The primary reason for establishing an intranet rather than working through the Internet is the security of having a *firewall* to protect the system from outside intruders, hackers, or others with destructive motives.

[NOTE 3.19]
Intranets operate within an organization.

WEB SITES AND WEB PAGES

A **Web site** is the name given to a group of related Web pages. The opening screen or **home page** of a Web site acts as a table of contents. From this screen, users link to other pages or sites by clicking on icons or phrases designed for that purpose. The convenience and speed of this process relate directly to the way in which the page is organized.

[NOTE 3.20]
A Web site may have one or more pages.

COMMUNICATION QUOTE

Today, one of the most important assets a company holds is information. Customer information. Competitor information. Internal process information. The list goes on and on. One of the most important functions of an organization is disseminating this information and sharing it internally as well as externally in a quick, simple, efficient, and accurate manner. With the surge of Internet-based applications such as corporate information portals, decision support systems, and collaboration tools, it is apparent that the Internet is the perfect vehicle for the upcoming age of information.

Paul Johansen, Rainier.

[NOTE 3.21]
Be sure your Web site is effective.

As Paul Johansen points out in his Communication Quote, information is an organizational asset. Electronic messages written to disseminate that information require the same attention to planning and development as do letters and memos. Building an effective Web site involves five steps:

[1] **Determine the purpose and audience.** Web sites may have one or more purposes. Sites are designed to inform, persuade, and/or entertain. Each site owner also hopes to generate goodwill. If a site has more than one purpose, separate pages should be devoted to each. Once you have determined why your site exists, you are ready to decide to whom it is going to be directed. Although your site may be accessible to the world of Internet users, you should define your target audience. Knowing your audience will help you determine your site's content and design.

[2] **Develop the content.** Site content may consist of original material or material supplemented by links to other sites. Most people who search the Internet are seeking information; a site that contains only links won't meet their primary need and won't be visited frequently. Materials you prepare yourself should adhere to the principles of business communication. If you establish links to other sites, be sure they meet your high standards. Those who view your site will con-

Guidelines for Designing a Web Site

TIPS AND HINTS

Following these guidelines when designing a site can ensure that your receiver will get your message:

[1] **Label your page.** Place the title, purpose, and creation/update date near the top, where it will get strong emphasis.

[2] **Format carefully.** Minimize the number of horizontal and vertical lines; they make the page look busy. Use headlines to summarize topics or to list elements, so your reader can scan your document and locate the desired information quickly. If your site has multiple pages, use the same format on all pages to give your site an identity or image. Keeping navigational information (e.g., "return to home page," "back," "next") in the same place will assist your readers. Encourage feedback and make action easy by providing your e-mail address as a link.

[3] **Use graphics wisely.** A few well-chosen graphics add interest; too many add to the load time. The longer a visitor has to wait before being able to read or use the page, the greater the likelihood he or she will leave and not return to the site. Consider providing a text-only version of your page. If you take images from other sources, do so ethically—respect copyrights and get permission when necessary.

[4] **Select appropriate emphasis techniques.** Bold and italics are generally more effective than blinking text. Colors should complement each other. Background patterns, if used, should be subtle and not detract from the viewability of the page.

struct an image of you based not only on what you prepare but on where you might direct them.

[3] **Design the site.** Organization is the key to site design, and an outline will help you create an easy-to-navigate site. Visiting other sites can help, too. You'll find a list of the Internet's top 500 sites at **http://www.mediamatrix.com/Top500/Top500.html**. The Tips and Hints box on page 68 contains additional items to consider when designing a site.

[4] **Tackle technical issues.** Every Web page is an html document. Users may write their own html, create it using commercial software such as Claris® HomePage[1] or Microsoft® FrontPage®, or hire a commercial service to perform the task. To be accessible to readers, each site must reside on a computer equipped with server software and have a URL.

[5] **Update the site.** Web sites need regular maintenance to retain their value. The site's contents will determine how frequently updates are needed, but quarterly reviews are the outside limit. During an update, verify that all sites to which you link are still active and appropriate; software is available to assist with this task.

Tools for Written Communication

Business communicators have several tools at their disposal when they wish to create written documents. Several of those tools are explained in the sections that follow. As you read the material, note that the features described for one tool may also be part of another and that tools may be linked or integrated to increase their communication value.

Learning Objective [3]
IDENTIFY THE TECHNOLOGICAL TOOLS BUSINESS COMMUNICATORS CAN USE TO IMPROVE WRITTEN, ORAL, AND VISUAL COMMUNICATION.

WORD PROCESSING SOFTWARE

Word processing software is the application package business communicators use most often. The ease with which letters, memos, reports, and other documents can be revised, edited, and formatted draws writers to this tool.

[NOTE 3.22]
Word processing software helps writers draft, edit, and format documents.

Most word processing packages, including Microsoft Word® and Corel® WordPerfect®, contain a thesaurus, spell checker, and style checker. These features help writers to apply the principles of business communication (see Chapter 4).

A **thesaurus** helps you select appropriate words by suggesting a variety of word choices. It also helps you avoid word repetition and bring variety to word choice. A **spell checker** assists with, *but does not replace,* careful proofreading. A spell checker will not detect an error that results in the correct spelling of another word (e.g., *thin* for *than*). Recent versions of word processing software automatically correct certain types of errors. If a writer keys *te* rather than *the,* the software detects and corrects the error. The software also automatically changes the first letter of a sentence from lowercase to uppercase if the writer makes such an oversight. Users may choose to turn off these features. A **style checker** analyzes a document and alerts the writer to potential problems with sentence length, vocabulary level, word choice (e.g., *affect* for *effect*), punctuation, and passive voice. The software does not, however, correct the errors. The writer retains responsibility for ensuring that style

[NOTE 3.23]
Software features don't replace proofreading.

[1] The software programs mentioned in this chapter are only examples of what is available. References to them should not be construed as endorsements.

errors do not create communication barriers. Although they are a good writing aid, style checkers are not perfect; they may question things that are correct or fail to question things that are incorrect. Writers should always revise, edit, and proofread to be sure they have applied the principles of business communication.

The ability to insert, delete, move, and copy text is essential to revising efficiently, and word processing software helps writers accomplish these tasks with ease. The move and copy features can be used across as well as within documents. Duplicating text can bring consistency and continuity to a writer's documents. Unless writers cut and paste carefully and proofread thoroughly, they may find that their messages say something other than what they intended.

Word processing software allows writers to move quickly and easily from one part of a document to another—for example, from the top of the page to the bottom or from page 43 to page 5. Movement also may be linked to words or phrases. Writers can find the next or every occurrence of a character, word, or phrase. When combined with a replace function, the find feature becomes a powerful editing tool, but one that must be used with care. Unless users precisely define what is to be replaced, they may create a problem in addition to solving one. Imagine directing the software to replace all occurrences of *his* with *his and her* only to find that *This idea has merit* becomes *This and her idea has merit.*

[NOTE 3.24]
Enhancement features draw attention to text.

Word processing software can assist writers in giving words and sentences appropriate emphasis. Text may be displayed using **bold,** underscore, *italics,* or other enhancement features. Type fonts (styles) and pitch (size) can be changed. Margins may be widened or narrowed. Tables can be created with ease. Boxes or other borders can be placed around text. Symbols or images may be inserted to draw a reader's attention to important items. Writers who have access to color printers should determine whether using color will enhance the communication, and if so, how much of which color(s) is appropriate. The following Tips and Hints box contains information about colors and their meanings.

TIPS AND HINTS

What Colors Mean

Empirical and scientific evidence points to the belief that color impacts not only our eyes but also our senses and our minds. As you create or design print and electronic documents, consider the following possible meanings your receivers may associate with the colors you choose.

- Blue: patience, guidance, happiness, change
- Brown: earthiness, concentration
- Green: money, growth, prosperity
- Orange: energy
- Pink: romance, friendship
- Purple: power
- Red: strength, passion, courage, health
- Silver: stability
- White: peace, truth-seeking, protection
- Yellow: intelligence, activity, creativity, togetherness

Some colors have significance within a culture. If your message is designed to reach a person or group within a particular culture, include color as part of your audience analysis.

With so many options available, writers must choose wisely. Using too many enhancements in one document could deter rather than facilitate successful communication. Decide what you want to accomplish and then choose the feature that best helps you reach your goal. In other words, analyze your receiver and the communication situation.

[NOTE 3.25]
Choose emphasis techniques wisely.

The features described so far could be used without regard to document type. Some features, though, have a strong relationship to specific writing tasks. Report writers appreciate the automatic page numbering and outline-generating features of word processing software. Those who prepare correspondence will appreciate the letter and memo format templates embedded in the software. (See Appendix A.) The merge feature will appeal to those who wish to personalize a form letter by adding the receiver's name and address. This feature allows writers to fill in the blanks of a form letter with variable information drawn from a mailing list or directory. The information in the following Tips and Hints box will help you write using word processing software.

[NOTE 3.26]
Some features have general appeal, others are task specific.

Writing With Word Processing Software

TIPS AND HINTS

- Don't expect to produce a final copy every time you write. Long or complex messages may require an outline and several revisions. Take full advantage of the editing features the software offers.
- Focus on content before mechanics. Draft your message and, once you verify that it says what you want, check the accuracy of your spelling, grammar, word choice, and punctuation.
- Don't let document format dictate the sequence in which you write. There's no rule that says you must use a top down approach to writing. If you're having trouble with the opening of a message, bypass that part and move on to another section.
- Proofread before **and** after you print.

Although keyboarding remains the primary method by which text is entered, speaking is becoming a viable option. **Voice recognition software** captures spoken sounds, converts them to digital signals, and matches those signals to sounds contained in a database. Matches are then transformed into printed words or action commands.

[NOTE 3.27]
Keyboarding is one text entry method.

Voice recognition software may be a separate application package, such as Dragon Naturally Speaking™ or IBM® ViaVoice™, which works in conjunction with a user's word processing program, or it may be an application within a software program. In either case, the user must "train" the software to recognize his or her distinctive speech patterns. Investing two or more hours in recording time can pay dividends, though, in increased productivity. Depending on the user and the software program, accuracy can reach as high as 98 percent. The software is also an excellent tool for those with disabilities that make it difficult or impossible to use a traditional keyboard. Some programs include foreign language recognition or translation. Some are available in network versions, which allow more users to tap into the software. Newer versions of the software also allow users to customize the program by adding up to 60,000 words.

[NOTE 3.28]
Material may be spoken or scanned into software.

Another popular input device is the **scanner.** When attached to a computer equipped with appropriate software, this device captures characters and other images from a hard copy and converts them to electronic form. Once in electronic form, the scanned document can be manipulated using word processing or other software programs. The time-saving advantages of the scanner are obvious, but there are money-saving benefits as well. For example, scanning items and distributing them electronically eliminates postage costs.

DESKTOP PUBLISHING SOFTWARE

[NOTE 3.29]
Desktop publishing software helps give documents a professional look.

When a computer with **desktop publishing software** is linked to a high-quality printer, writers can produce newsletters, brochures, reports, or other business messages with the quality of a professionally typeset document. Text may be organized into columns of varying length and width. Charts, graphs, diagrams, other illustrations—including photographs—can be made part of the document. Writers may choose to use application software packages such as Adobe® PageMaker® or PrintShop® Deluxe, but full-featured word processing software programs offer many desktop publishing features.

SPREADSHEET SOFTWARE

[NOTE 3.30]
Spreadsheet software is useful for doing calculations.

Writers who need to incorporate financial or other types of numeric data into their documents will find **spreadsheet software** such as Lotus®1-2-3 or Microsoft Excel® helpful. Data are entered into locations called *cells.* Mathematical formulas can then be applied to the cells; some programs also enable users to do basic statistical analyses such as regressions. Tables, graphs, and charts can be created using this type of software. High-end word processing and desktop publishing packages usually allow users to add (import) documents created on spreadsheet software packages.

Spreadsheet software has another advantage in business communication: The data contained in a spreadsheet can often be converted into a visual aid, such as a line graph or pie chart. Displaying information in a format other than text can clarify or reinforce a receiver's understanding of numeric data.

DATABASE SOFTWARE

[NOTE 3.31]
Database software can be used to sort and group data.

Database software such as Corel Paradox® or Microsoft Access® helps writers to organize data. Individual elements (e.g., names, addresses, prices, and quantities) are entered into a computer file. Users may select and group elements having desired features. For example, a user could have the program select from a student database file those whose GPA is greater than or equal to 3.00. The program could then be directed to list those students in alphabetical order by surname. The lists, tables, and other documents created using database software may be incorporated into word processing or desktop publishing documents.

So far, the tools described in this section have focused on the creation of paper documents. In the next sections, we'll consider media that do not rely on paper—electronic mail and fax.

ELECTRONIC MAIL

One of the most common questions business professionals ask today is "What's your e-mail address?" The reason for the query is simple—electronic mail represents a fast, efficient method of exchanging messages. Users may select PC or network versions of commercial packages such as Qualcomm® Eudora Pro® or Cyrusoft

Mulberry™, subscribe to a service such as America Online (AOL), or obtain free e-mail through sites such as **http://www.juno.com** or **http://www.yahoo.com**.

E-mail systems may be internal or external. Internal systems allow users to communicate only *within* an organization. External systems allow users to communicate with others in the same organization or, by using the Internet, to channel messages to users outside the organization. Each user has a unique address that consists of a name and a location. The symbol @, meaning *at,* separates the parts. The name identifies the user; the location identifies the computer on which the e-mail program resides and classifies the organization according to its purpose. The portion of the address that follows the @ is called the **domain.** Figure 3.2 shows a sample e-mail address and lists the possible domains. E-mail addresses for locations outside the United States also carry a country identifier such as *uk* for United Kingdom or *jp* for Japan.

[NOTE 3.32]
E-mail users must have a unique address.

Figure 3.2
E-Mail Addresses and Domains

pharris@d.umn.edu

phariss	Identifies the user by his or her log-in name.
d.umn	Names or identifies the computer on which the message should be directed. In this example, the computer is located at Duluth, at the University of Minnesota.
edu	Identifies the organization as an educational institution.

Domain	Organization Purpose
com	Commercial entity (business)
edu	Educational institution
gov	Nonmilitary U.S. government institution
int	International institution
mil	U.S. military institution
net	Network resource
org	Nonprofit organization

E-mail resembles a memo. The software automatically enters the sender's name and records the date and time of the message. The writer enters the receiver's name and the subject. Salutations, closings, and signatures are not needed, but many users include them to make the message seem more personal. Another technique used to personalize e-mail is a **signature block,** a segment of text appended to the end of a message. Signature blocks typically list alternative contact information and may include other things, such as a quote. Writers should choose carefully when selecting what to include in a signature block. The text will go with *every* message that is sent and, unless deleted by the receiver, stay with the message if it is forwarded.

[NOTE 3.33]
E-mails and memos have a similar format.

E-mail programs vary in the number and sophistication of mail management tools they include. In order to derive the greatest benefit from software, writers should be thoroughly familiar with the programs they use. One common management tool is an **address book.** This feature offers writers the opportunity to store the e-mail addresses of those with whom they frequently exchange messages. To access the address, the writer uses an **alias,** a code or short version of the name. The same concept allows writers to group the mailing addresses of several receivers and enter an identifier to retrieve all of them. For example, rather than entering the full address for each budget committee member every time a message is to be sent, the committee chair might record all information only once and then retrieve it by

[NOTE 3.34]
Aliases save time when sending one message to many receivers.

keying "budgcom" or a similar alias. Your instructor probably uses a feature like this when sending messages to your class.

E-mail programs generally have many of the same features found in word processing software. Users can format messages by adjusting margins and use emphasis techniques such as bold, italics, and underscore. These techniques, however, are generally useful only when senders and receivers use the same software program.

[NOTE 3.35] Emphasis techniques can have special meaning in e-mail.

Certain emphasis techniques have a special connotation in e-mail. Anything displayed entirely in uppercase letters, for example, suggests the sender is shouting at the receiver. Exclamation points, when used often or in a series (!!!), suggest greater volume. To intensify a portion of a message, a sender may *place the text within asterisks.* Other methods of incorporating emotion into informal business messages are illustrated in Figure 3.3 and in the Communication Note below.

Figure 3.3
E-mail Emoticons and Initialisms

Emoticons are the symbols (icons) writers use to reflect emotion in personal or informal business e-mail. Emoticons are built by combining various letters and symbols. To be interpreted correctly, most emoticons must be viewed from the side. **Initialisms** are letter combinations that substitute for words. They are created by using the first letter of each word. The following list includes several frequently used emoticons and initialisms.

Emoticon	Meaning	Initialism	Meaning
:-)	smile	FYI	for your information
%-	confusion	BTW	by the way
:-(	frown	TIA	thanks in advance
:-<	sadness	IMO	in my opinion
:-D	laughter	NRN	no reply necessary
|-|	boredom	PTMM	please tell me more
:-o	surprise	WRT	with respect to
;-)	wink	AAMOF	as a matter of fact
:-#	sealed lips	OTOH	on the other hand

COMMUNICATION NOTE

Help Your Reader "Hear" Your E-mail

By its nature e-mail communication encourages a personal, informal style of writing, a feature most people view as attractive. Writers get into trouble, however, when they assume that readers actually can hear their voices. Although e-mail may be more like oral communication than traditional forms of written communication, it's still writing, not speaking. Your reader cannot hear the inflection of your voice.

To guard against this type of misunderstanding, take this simple precaution: Include a goodwill statement in every message you send. Rather than write "Please come prepared to discuss the report," for example, add another sentence: "As always, I value your experience and insight."

Rather than "Fine," write "Fine. Happy to do it." Rather than "Well, you did it again. Would you mind adapting your presentation for our board?" write "Well, you did it again. Great job! Would you mind adapting . . ."

A goodwill statement is like an insurance policy. It protects you from being misunderstood. Including it reduces the risk of miscommunication when you are writing quickly.

Reprinted with permission of the author, Stephen Wilbers. You can visit his Web page at **http://www.wilbers.com.**

Another similarity between e-mail and word processing is editing. E-mail message software may allow users to check spelling as well as to move and copy passages.

[NOTE 3.36]
Business e-mail deserves the same attention as other written business messages.

If you've used e-mail only to communicate with friends or family, or if you've heard that grammar and spelling aren't important in e-mail, the preceding paragraph might make you wonder why e-mail software has *any* editing features. The reason is simple: The only difference between an e-mail message and a paper message is the channel through which it is transmitted. When e-mail is used in a business setting, the extent to which a writer edits a message depends on his or her analysis of the situation and the receiver. Remember that receivers will judge both you and your organization by the messages you send. You want to create and maintain a professional image. Be sure you apply the same high standards to business-related e-mail and paper messages. To do so, follow the guidelines in the Tips and Hints box on page 76.

Dilbert

Courteous e-mail users check their messages once or twice every day. They are also careful about viewing attachments they receive. Computer viruses are often sent as e-mail attachments; when the attachments are opened, the virus is activated. A good rule is to save the attachment as a file so that virus detection software can be applied.

[NOTE 3.37]
Treat e-mail attachments with care.

The widespread use of e-mail has both positive and negative dimensions. The good news is the speed with which messages are relayed from sender to receiver. Another benefit is that messages can be created and sent at the convenience of the writer and retrieved and read at the convenience of the receiver, often from locations other than the workplace. The downside is that the ease with which messages can be distributed can result in **information overload**—a term that refers to the enormous amounts of data and information that receivers must sort through and interpret. The Communication Note on page 77 describes how e-mail helped a rumor get out of hand and create information overload.

[NOTE 3.38]
Information overload is a problem.

E-mail Guidelines

- **Make the subject line count.** Use the subject line to convey your real message to your receiver. For example, if you are asking the reader for a favor, your subject line might be "Request With Deadline."
- **Keep the subject line short.** Some systems limit display space, and you won't want your subject line to be truncated (cut).
- **Cover only one topic in each message.** Limiting yourself to one topic allows you to use the subject line effectively, helps ensure that each item gets the attention it deserves, and permits the receiver to take action on each message and then delete it.
- **Make your message inviting.** Use short line lengths and short paragraphs. Use traditional format when you key. using all lowercase letters-failing to correct typographical errrs and omitting punctuation may mean you can create messages faster but it makes the message hard to read readers are accustomed to seeing material in a misture of characters and use punctuation to guide them through a message varying from whats normal affects comprehension
- **Use position wisely and keep messages brief.** Deliver the most important information in the opening sentence or paragraph. If the message is longer than one screen, the receiver might not bother reading it. If you need to transmit lengthy documents via e-mail, use the attachment feature.
- **Use attachments carefully.** Not all computer programs are compatible when it comes to attachments. Confirm in advance that your receiver has the software necessary to access what you send. If you're sending a word processed file, for example, tell the receiver what program you used to create it. Opening a Corel WordPerfect file using Microsoft Word can result in a message that resembles hieroglyphics. When you have multiple attachments, consider sending them separately. Some e-mail programs don't support multiple attachments.
- **Hold your temper.** Remember, you're communicating with a person, not a machine. Don't send messages when you're angry or upset.
- **Use emoticons and initialisms wisely.** A good symbol or abbreviation is one your receiver will recognize quickly and interpret correctly. These enhancements are best used only in casual messages and, even then, used sparingly.
- **Know when *not* to use e-mail.** Because it lacks the cues supplied by body language, voice tones, and shared environment, e-mail lacks the communication richness of a face-to-face or telephone communication and the formality or authority of a letter. Consider other communication channels when messages are time sensitive (scheduling or canceling a meeting on short notice), when the topic merits face-to-face discussion (e-mail is really a series of monologues), or when the message contains content that will have significant emotional impact on the receiver (e.g., job termination).
- **Proofread the message before you send it.** Most systems do not allow messages to be canceled or retrieved after a user gives the *send* command. To make matters worse, it takes just a few keystrokes for the receiver to forward the message to one, a few, or literally thousands of additional receivers.
- **Choose "reply" or "reply to all" as appropriate to the situation.** Ensure that your message gets to its target audience and no one else.
- **Set the context for your response.** Edit the subject line *(Request Response–Yes!)*, recap the original message, or include some or all of the original message in your reply. Most e-mail programs distinguish between old and new text by placing a > or other symbol before each line of text retained from the original message.
- **Respect confidentiality.** Never forward confidential information unless you are authorized to do so. If you receive a blind copy (BCC), recognize that the primary receiver doesn't know you also received the message. Do not mention the message to the primary receiver or to anyone else.

TIPS AND HINTS

COMMUNICATION NOTE

E-mail Hoax Causes Overload

Thanks to e-mail, a nonexistent piece of legislation caused headaches on Capitol Hill. The message claimed that congress was considering a bill allowing the U.S. Postal Service to collect 5¢ each time someone sent an e-mail. E-mail users were urged to write their representatives, and they did just that. One representative received thousands of inquiries, most of them by e-mail. He wrote his constituents saying, "It's spinning out of control because the rumor keeps getting circulated over and over by people who keep forwarding the e-mail message to others."

As reported in USA Today, *January 12, 2000, p. 13A.*

The portability of technology compounds the information overload situation by making it more difficult for business and other professionals to leave their work at the office. Programs such as pcANYWHERE© eliminate the need to transport files from one location to another. The software allows use of a remote (home) computer to access and manipulate files on the host (office) computer.

Sally Forth

[NOTE 3.39]
Speed and convenience contribute to e-mail's popularity.

Figures distributed through the popular press or available on the Internet suggest that e-mail use is escalating at an astounding rate. Faced with a large number of e-mail messages, receivers make quick judgments about which to read immediately, which to read later, and which to delete without reading. Some software programs have the capacity to **filter** messages, to sort them based on user-defined criteria. This feature helps receivers screen and assign priority to the messages they receive. Although traditional (paper) messages must also be judged to determine what is read when, the lower volume of paper messages makes the processes quite different. Other programs notify senders when a message has been received or tell them that their receiver will not be available to read their message until a particular day or time.

The need to screen or sort e-mail messages will become more important as the number of e-mail users increases and information overload continues. Conservative estimates indicate that early in the twenty-first century, 8 billion or more e-mails will travel through cyberspace on a *daily* basis. These messages will be generated by over 201 million people who are online throughout the world, over half of them in the United States and Canada (**http://www.nua.ic/surveys/**). According to a research report issued by Pitney Bowes, each U.S. worker receives 201 messages every day (**http://www.pitneybowes.com/whats_new/knowledge_eco.asp**). These messages arrive from internal and external sources through telephone calls and voice mail, e-mail, faxes, and paper messages. The Communication Note below describes how one employer dealt with the large volume of e-mail exchanged among employees.

COMMUNICATION NOTE

Business Takes an E-mail "Time Out"

The chairman of Computer Associates International was pleased to learn that employees were taking advantage of the software company's e-mail system. When he checked further, however, he discovered that managers were getting *hundreds* of messages each day. Rather than speaking with the person in the next cubicle, an employee would send an electronic message. E-mail had evolved from a tool to a nightmare.

To stop the e-mail overload, the chairman created an electronic "time out." He banned e-mail between 9:30 and noon and between 1:30 and 4 p.m. As a result, people once again talked to their coworkers.

Adapted from "Lost in the E-mail," by S. C. Gwynne and John F. Dickerson. Time *149, no. 16, April 21, 1997.*

Some experts in the technology field suggest that instant messaging is the next evolution of e-mail. **Instant messaging** adds a real-time dimension to e-mail. Users are able to determine which of their coworkers are currently online and then send one or more of them a message that is displayed instantly on a pop-up screen on the monitor. Instant messaging is available from Microsoft, AOL, and others.

FAX

[NOTE 3.40] Fax machines send copies.

Fax systems are another popular method by which messages are transmitted electronically. Standalone fax machines digitize printed characters and images and then send them across phone lines. After receiving and interpreting the digitized message, the receiver's machine produces a copy (facsimile) of the original document.

[NOTE 3.41] Fax machines can be standalone or computer based.

Not all fax transmissions rely on paper. Computers can also act as fax machines. Images displayed on the sender's monitor are transmitted and either displayed on the receiver's monitor or printed on her or his fax machine. The process bears a strong similarity to that used in sending and receiving e-mail. Fax, like e-mail, also allows users to group and store receiver information items (phone numbers) so they don't have to be re-entered every time messages are sent.

COLLABORATIVE WRITING SOFTWARE

As organizations have increased their use of cross-functional teams, the need to collaborate on projects such as reports and proposals has also grown. **Collaborative writing software** facilitates group writing. The product allows several users to work on the same document rather than on a printed or electronically transmitted (e-mail attachment) copy of the document.

Collaborative writing may be interactive (synchronous) or independent (asynchronous). When collaboration is interactive, two or more people work with the same document at the same time and see changes as they are made. The document resides on the computer of one of the participants, referred to as the host. Each person who wants to contribute something to the document signals the host, who determines the sequence in which participants will access the document. Interactive collaborative writing sessions resemble meetings in that they must be prearranged. In addition, only the host has access to the document between sessions.

[NOTE 3.42]
Writing teams benefit from collaborative writing software.

In independent collaborative writing, the document resides on a computer that may be accessed at any time by anyone in the writing group. This type of collaboration has the advantage of permitting writers to work on the document at their convenience. The disadvantage is that writers must also check periodically to see what changes their coauthors have made. For this reason, writers tend to rely on strikeout and redline techniques to mark their changes.

Collaborative writing software is one element of a larger software category called **groupware.** Other features available in groupware include shared scheduling and project tracking. When members of a group each have access to other members' schedules, meetings are easier to arrange. Project management has similar advantages. Updates can be entered by one person and quickly seen by all people who are working on the project.

[NOTE 3.43]
Groupware has several features.

Tools for Oral Communication

This section provides an introduction to how technology can improve oral communication.

Learning Objective [3]
IDENTIFY THE TECHNOLOGICAL TOOLS BUSINESS COMMUNICATORS CAN USE TO IMPROVE WRITTEN, ORAL, AND VISUAL COMMUNICATION.

VOICE MAIL

Voice mail is the audio version of e-mail. The service can be obtained through a commercial provider or set up as an independent system within a business. Features include storage and retrieval, message forwarding, group messages, delivery verification, delayed messaging, and password protection. Most systems permit receivers to access mailboxes from remote locations. One recent innovation in voice messaging is voice-activated dialing. Users simply speak the name of someone in the voice mail directory, and the phone will automatically dial the number and send recorded messages.

Whether recording an outgoing message or leaving an incoming message, communicators should analyze their audience and apply the principles of business communication. Messages should be brief, clear, and complete; they should be framed in the you–viewpoint.

[NOTE 3.44]
Analyze your voice mail audience.

WIRELESS MESSAGING SYSTEMS

Pagers and cellular telephones are wireless messaging systems that rely on radio signals to transmit messages. They are used when physical connections, such as telephone lines, are unavailable or inconvenient.

[NOTE 3.45] Pager signals may vary.

Pagers Although pagers do not send or receive oral messages, they can be used to alert the receiver about the need to place a phone call. Basic systems are activated by placing a telephone call to a receiver's pager number. When the connection is made, the caller enters the number the receiver is to call. Advanced systems permit senders to transmit brief written messages. Once the sender completes his or her portion of the process, the message is transmitted to the receiver's pager. The unit beeps or vibrates to catch the receiver's attention. Vibrating pagers have become popular because their signal affects only the receiver.

[NOTE 3.46] Cell phone users should be courteous.

Cellular Telephones **Cellular telephones** are portable devices that permit users to make and receive calls while away from a traditional telephone. Broad area coverage and competitive rates have made cell phones extremely popular not only for business but also for personal use. Cellular service has become so widespread and popular that many people use it exclusively.

The proliferation of cell phone users has created the need for cell phone etiquette. To avoid having a cell phone become a barrier to communication, users should be courteous about when and where they take and make calls. Additional cell phone etiquette practices appear in the following Tips and Hints box.

Cellular Phone Etiquette

TIPS AND HINTS

An estimated 66 million people use cell phones, and the number is said to be growing by 30,000 users a day. The growth has occurred faster than "good use" practices have evolved; the result is phone rage. ("Carded at the Theater, for Using Your Phone" by Csar S. Soriano; *USA Today,* November 15, 1999, p. 4D)

If you use a cell phone, follow these guidelines:

[1] **Answer the phone quickly.** A ringing phone irritates those around you almost as much as the conversation that follows. Set the phone to vibrate or adjust the ring to the lowest possible volume level.

[2] **Speak quietly and end the conversation quickly.** Most cell phone users speak louder than normal to compensate for noises in the surrounding area.

[3] **Avoid taking or making calls when others are present.** Placing or receiving a call during meetings, while at restaurants, or during group events sends the nonverbal message that the person on the phone is more important than those with whom you are interacting face to face. If you must use the phone, excuse yourself and leave the room.

CONFERENCING SYSTEMS

Conferencing enables people to take part in meetings without being at the same location. An **audio conference** occurs whenever two or more people confer by telephone. A **video conference** permits users to see and hear events; a Webcast (audio/video broadcast over the Web) falls into this category. When video conferences become interactive, an **electronic meeting** results. Microsoft NetMeeting® is one example of software used for electronic meetings.

[NOTE 3.47] Electronic meetings are interactive.

In an electronic or *virtual* meeting, some participants may attend face to face while others attend from their office via computer. Interaction among the various participants occurs via video cameras and microphones in the meeting room and on remote attendees' desktop computers. Presentations are broadcast to the desktop units and shown on a large-screen monitor in the meeting room. Remote attendees participate by sending notes via chat and similar instant-messaging technologies. These basic systems may be supplemented to permit participants to make anonymous suggestions during a brainstorming session or cast secret ballots in favor of or in opposition to proposals. Another option is to use an **electronic white board,** a device that enables users to write on the board and have their words, figures, or drawings transmitted to and displayed on local or remote computer monitors.

[NOTE 3.48] Conferencing can save time and money.

Whatever the method, the advantage of using conferencing systems is that employees need not travel to take part in a meeting. The potential for dollar and productivity savings is tremendous. In addition, the quality of the decisions made during a meeting can increase because resource materials are readily available and because the number of people who participate can be expanded.

Technology can help make meetings more effective.

[NOTE 3.49] Conference participation requires planning.

The larger the number of people involved, the greater the need to coordinate the date and time of a conference. Those involved can enhance the quality of the conference by being prepared. The originator should be sure that everyone involved clearly understands the purpose of the meeting. Each participant should review related materials and be sure they are at hand during the call. In addition, participants should make sure that nothing interrupts them during the conference. The best advice for those participating in any type of conference is to behave as though at an in-person meeting.

Tools for Visual Communication

Learning Objective [3]
IDENTIFY THE TECHNOLOGICAL TOOLS BUSINESS COMMUNICATORS CAN USE TO IMPROVE WRITTEN, ORAL, AND VISUAL COMMUNICATION.

The tools discussed in this section differ from those discussed earlier. These tools—graphics and presentation software—contain elements of or can be incorporated into both written and oral messages.

GRAPHICS SOFTWARE

[NOTE 3.50]
Graphics can help receivers interpret a message.

Graphics are images used to represent data or ideas in a format other than text. Writers and speakers use graphics to clarify or reinforce their message. **Graphics software** converts data into a visual aid. Among the most common graphic aids used in business messages are line graphs, bar graphs, and pie charts. Data to create these graphic images may be entered directly into the software program or taken from a spreadsheet or other document.

Depending on the document and audience, writers may also want to incorporate photographs, designs, maps, diagrams, or other visual images into their documents. Software such as Adobe PhotoShop® and Corel Draw® assist with these tasks. For more casual enhancements, writers can buy clip art programs or download clip art files from the Web.

The mere presence of a graphic does not guarantee successful communication. The sender must choose graphic aids carefully, introduce them clearly, and explain them thoroughly. Additional considerations include color and size. Chapter 13 focuses on these and other elements of visual aids.

PRESENTATION SOFTWARE

[NOTE 3.51]
Use presentation software to prepare and deliver a presentation.

Presentation software helps speakers organize, prepare, and deliver clear, effective, interesting presentations. The software allows users to enter new material; to use materials created with word processing, spreadsheet, graphics, or other software; to incorporate sound, video, or animation; and to access resources available through the Internet. Examples of this software include Microsoft PowerPoint®, Corel Presentations®, and Astound.

Materials created with presentation software can remain electronic and be projected onto a screen during a presentation, or they can be made into overhead transparencies or 35mm slides. In addition, the materials can be printed as audience handouts and/or speaker notes.

[NOTE 3.52]
Select features that help your audience.

Presentation software can be a powerful tool. To use it effectively, speakers must select those features that help the audience understand the message. Speakers who choose too many features or who select inappropriate features may find that the audience focuses on the software, not the message. Chapter 15 contains information about how to plan and deliver effective oral presentations.

Summary of Learning Objectives

Learning Objective [1]

Discuss the trends and issues associated with the use of communication technology. Integrated software programs are a positive trend, one that helps eliminate issues associated with software incompatibility. Wireless wearable technology is under development. Telecommuting and electronic commerce are additional trends. Security, privacy, productivity, and legal liability are issues with which business is struggling and will continue to struggle. Other trends and issues will surface as technology changes.

Learning Objective [2]

Explain how the Internet and World Wide Web assist business communicators in achieving their goals. The Internet and World Wide Web help business communicators reach their goal of receiver understanding by expanding the number of resources available to researchers and by making messages easier and faster to send. E-mail is the most widely used, but certainly not the only, resource on the Internet. USENET and related services allow business professionals to ask questions of and exchange ideas with others who have common problems or interests. These services should, however, be used with caution. Web pages help business communicators make information about themselves, their organization, and their organization's products and services available to potential customers worldwide.

Learning Objective [3]

Identify the technological tools business communicators can use to improve written, oral, and visual communication. Word processing, desktop publishing, spreadsheet, and database software programs are the tools available to help communicators improve their written (paper) documents. Word processing features such as the spell checker, thesaurus, and style checker augment the software's powerful editing functions. Some of these features are also available to those who use e-mail as a non-paper method of written communication. Oral communication can be improved by using voice mail, pagers, cellular phones, and conferencing. Graphics and presentation software programs help writers improve the visuals they incorporate into their written and oral communications. Collaborative writing software facilitates group writing. The Internet can also play an important role in improving communication.

DISCUSSION QUESTIONS

1. How will growth in electronic commerce affect business communication? (Objective 1)
2. Explain the relationships among an html document, a Web page, and a Web site. (Objective 1)
3. The Communication Note on page 77 describes an e-mail hoax, but the situation could be real. Would you support a fee or tax on e-mail? Why or why not? (Objective 1)
4. How does the original purpose of the Internet differ from the way in which it is now used? How do you envision the Internet will be used in the future? (Objectives 1 and 2)
5. What is an intranet? Why might a business choose to create one? (Objective 2)
6. How can presentation software assist someone who gives an oral presentation? (Objective 3)

7. Name three technology tools communicators can use to assist with written communication. (Objective 3)
8. Explain why spell checkers and style checkers do not replace proofreading. (Objective 3)
9. Identify one advantage and one disadvantage of voice recognition software. (Objective 3)
10. Describe the features and benefits of voice mail systems. (Objective 3)
11. What is an "alias"? How can it help e-mail users? (Objective 3)
12. List and explain two guidelines to follow when creating an e-mail and one to follow when replying to an e-mail. (Objective 3)
13. Define "electronic information overload." What causes it? Why is it a problem? (Objective 3)
14. Why is audience analysis important when using voice mail? (Objective 3)
15. Explain the difference between a video conference and an electronic meeting. (Objective 3)

APPLICATION EXERCISES

1. Conduct an in-class debate exploring the following question: Should employers monitor worker use of e-mail and Internet resources? (Objective 1)
2. **Teamwork.** Make a list of the reasons you would or would not like to telecommute. Share your list with three or four of your classmates in a small group setting. Note the diversity among members of your group. (Objective 1)
3. **Ethics.** Take the following ethics quiz. Do not put your name on your paper, but submit the results to your instructor. After tallying the results for your class, your instructor will provide information about how the original group of respondents replied. Discuss how results from your class compare to those of the original group. (Objective 1)

The Wall Street Journal *Workplace-Ethics Quiz* (The Wall Street Journal, *Thursday, October 21, 1999, p. B1)*

Office Technology

1. *Is it wrong to use company e-mail for personal reasons?*

   Yes No

2. *Is it wrong to use office equipment to help your children or spouse do schoolwork?*

   Yes No

3. *Is it wrong to play computer games on office equipment during the work day?*

   Yes No

4. *Is it wrong to use office equipment to do Internet shopping?*

   Yes No

5. *Is it unethical to blame an error you made on a technological glitch?*

   Yes No

6. *Is it unethical to visit pornographic Web sites using office equipment?*

   Yes No

4. **Internet.** Use the Internet to find the countries represented by the following Internet domain address codes: (Objective 2)

   a. ar
   b. bo
   c. cl
   d. eg
   e. gr
   f. ie
   g. ly
   h. mx
   i. no
   j. su

5. **Global/Cross-Cultural. Internet.** Access the home page of two companies based in countries other than the United States and two similar companies in the United States (e.g., financial institutions, airlines). In which ways do the home pages for companies based outside the United States differ from those for companies based in the United States? Did any of the companies make their pages available in languages other than English? Present your results in a memo to your instructor. (Objective 2)
6. While attending a social event, you chat with someone who says, "The computer is only good for playing games." What would you say? Outline the points you would use in your response. (Objectives 2 and 3)
7. Interview a business professional engaged in the type of work you plan to do after you graduate. Ask what types of communication technology he or she uses and why each is important. Share your findings with the class. (Objectives 2 and 3)
8. Use the spell check feature of your word processing program to check for errors in the following paragraph. Compare the results with errors you find as you proofread the text. (Objective 3)

Paula were working a loan in the jewelry department. Tree choppers approached the counter while he was rapping an other customers' pack age. Max, the stationary department clerk, offered to provide assistants. Pauline expected. All six customs were served quickly.

9. **Teamwork.** Work with one or two of your classmates to design a "Cell Phone Etiquette" handout that could be used at your school. Produce the handout using word processing, desktop publishing, graphics, or another software program. (Objective 3)
10. Write the text of the voice mail message you would leave on your office phone in the following situation: Tomorrow you leave for a two-week business trip to China. Without returning to your office, you will then take a one-week vacation. You will check your voice mail periodically while you are gone but plan to return only those messages you consider to be urgent. Calls may be directed to your assistant, Marge Blackmarr, at 555-0129. (Objective 3)

11. **Teamwork. E-mail.** Form a group with three or four of your classmates. Each person will read the message he or she wrote in exercise 10. After all the messages have been read, work to incorporate the best components of each into one message. Submit that message to your instructor via e-mail. (Objective 3)

12. **Teamwork.** Form a 4-person group consisting of two 2-person subgroups. Each subgroup will find an appropriate substitute for the words in the following list. One subgroup will use a traditional (book) thesaurus, the other the electronic thesaurus feature of a word processing software program. Both subgroups should record the time it takes to accomplish the task. Compile the findings of the two subgroups into a visual that compares the two methods. (Objective 3)

   a. archaic
   b. monumental
   c. exemplify
   d. preposterous

e. veritable
f. sundry
g. irritable
h. assimilate
i. ubiquitous
j. ameliorate

13. **Internet/E-mail.** Use electronic or print resources to locate an article describing a type of communication technology that has been introduced since this chapter was written. Send an e-mail to your instructor describing the technology and how it can be used to improve business communication.

14. **Teamwork.** Form a four-person group. As a group, select five of the emoticons and five of the initialisms included in Figure 3.3. Format the items as a quiz. Have each group member administer the quiz to five people other than your classmates. Compile the results and submit them as part of a memo to your instructor. (Objective 3)

There are Web exercises at **http://krizan.swcollege.com** to accompany this chapter.

MESSAGE ANALYSIS

J. J. Peak plans to send the following e-mail to his new boss, someone who has been with the company only three weeks. Knowing this is a business message and that J. J. hasn't had much time to develop a casual, working relationship with his new boss, convert the message to one more appropriate to the situation. Send the revised document to your instructor as an attachment to an e-mail, indicating what is attached. If you are unfamiliar with the initialisms and emoticons used in this message, first try to interpret them based on context, then ask your instructor.

THX 4 reviewing the proposal i plan 2 submit 2 Mears, Inc. YOU CERTAINLY MADE LOTS OF SUGGESTIONS!!!! :'(FYI the dew date is 4.1. Then TPTB at Mears will do a prelim screening & invite 3 bidrs to make F2F presentations. I'll let ya know ASAP after I hear from em. FWIW I think r chances are xlnt :-D If u have any ??? pls call. TAFN T2UL8R

GRAMMAR WORKSHOP

Correct the grammar, punctuation, spelling, style, and word choice errors in the following sentences:

1. Thank you for excepting my invitation to speak at next months' meeting of the Assoc. For Electronic Commerce [ACE).
2. 52% of the respondents indicated they plan to lease there next car, 38 percent plan to bye.
3. Mr. Siders said Julia me and Jim did a well job planning the knew member social.
4. While on vacation my office was re-modeled.
5. If I was president of the Company, I'ld make every day "casual day.
6. Each member was asked to eturn their ballots by December 15th.
7. Did Melissa say that "I should bring the package on her desk to the mailroom?".
8. Me and Rob was going to play golf last Saturday, but canceled when we herd about the severe thunderstorm warning.
9. The environmental impact report lead us to quickly decide against purchasing the land.
10. Pamelas younger brother Todd has been offered a job with the fbi in arlington v.a.

PART 2

Developing Communications

CHAPTER:

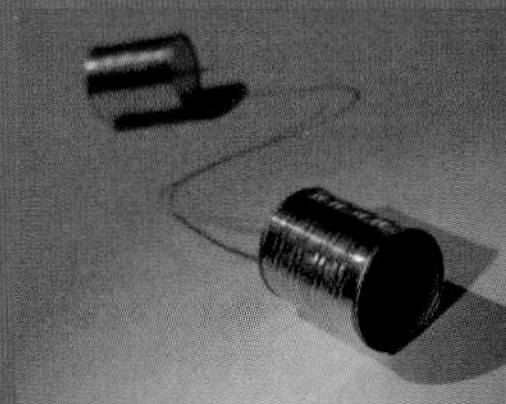

CHAPTER

4 Principles of Business Communication

R. Bruce Ray, President, Ray Products Inc.

LET'S TALK BUSINESS As the president and owner of a plastic thermoforming company in Ontario, California, I am both a customer and a supplier. I firmly believe that a clear and concise writing style is essential to convey our expectations for delivery, quality, and service, and to avoid possible misunderstandings that could cost additional time and money at both ends of the project.

E-mail communication has become a valuable alternative to formal business letters because of the speed with which messages can be sent, received, and processed. Care must still be taken to ensure accuracy and proper business etiquette. Grammar, spelling, and sentence structure should not be compromised

(Continued)

[LEARNING OBJECTIVES]

[1] IDENTIFY WORDS THAT YOUR RECEIVER(S) WILL UNDERSTAND AND THAT WILL ELICIT THE BETTER REACTION YOU NEED.

[2] DISCUSS THE ELEMENTS NEEDED FOR CLEAR, CONCISE, AND EFFECTIVE SENTENCES.

[3] DEVELOP CLEAR, CONCISE, LOGICAL, COHERENT, AND EFFECTIVE PARAGRAPHS.

[4] USE AVAILABLE ALTERNATIVES TO ASSURE UNBIASED LANGUAGE IN BUSINESS MESSAGES.

[5] APPLY YOUR OWN COMPOSING STYLE TO GIVE UNIQUENESS AND LIFE TO YOUR MESSAGES.

because of the perceived informality. We must also keep in mind the fact that messages sent via e-mail are easily forwarded to unknown recipients with whom we have not established a business relationship. Poor communication in any form could jeopardize my company's reputation and our future associations.

The best way to improve your ability to compose effective business messages is to learn and use the principles of business communication. This chapter provides the principles you need for choosing words, developing sentences, and forming paragraphs. The writing proficiency of American students is grim, as reported in the "Grammar 'R' Us" article in the Communication Note box; you can improve your writing ability by learning the principles of business communication.

[NOTE 4.1]
Compose effective messages by using the principles of business communication.

COMMUNICATION NOTE

Grammar 'R' Us

When it comes to the writing proficiency of American students, the news is grim, according to the Nation's Report Card, issued by the Education Department. While students' achievements in science and math jumped between 1984 and 1996, average writing scores of 11th-graders slumped.

As reported in "Washington Insight," Los Angeles Times, *September 3, 1997, p. A5.*

The basic principle of business communication is to keep your message short and simple. Some communicators remember this principle by its initials, KISS, which stands for Keep It Short and Simple. Application of this principle means composing your business messages using short and simple words, sentences, and paragraphs. Your messages, as a result, will be concise, easy to understand, and straightforward.

[NOTE 4.2]
Keep business messages short and simple.

To be an effective, successful business communicator, you will want to adopt the businesslike KISS principle. It may take extra time to compose a shorter, better message; but it will be worth it to you and your receiver.

Most of the 15 principles of business communication that are discussed in the following sections apply to both written and oral messages. A few apply only to written messages.

Choosing Words

Learning Objective [1]
IDENTIFY WORDS THAT YOUR RECEIVER(S) WILL UNDERSTAND AND THAT WILL ELICIT THE REACTION YOU NEED.

Words are the smallest units of messages. You will want to give attention to each word you choose to be sure it is the most effective one. An **effective word** is one that your receiver will understand and that will elicit the response you want. You can improve your ability to choose words by (1) using a dictionary and a thesaurus and (2) following the 15 principles of business communication.

[NOTE 4.3]
Choose effective words.

USE A DICTIONARY AND A THESAURUS

[NOTE 4.4] Use a dictionary to select words.

The two most valuable resources for the business communicator are a dictionary and a thesaurus. A **dictionary** is a word reference book. You can use it to determine a word's meaning(s), acceptable spelling(s), hyphenation, capitalization, pronunciation(s), and synonym(s). Many word processing software packages have a spell checker that can assist you in determining the correct spelling of words.

Successful managers communicate concisely and clearly

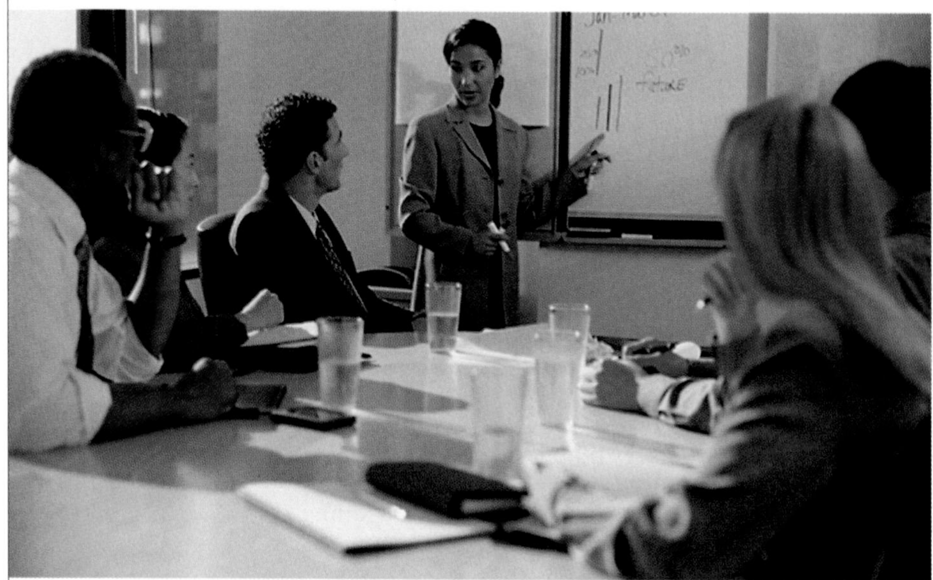

A dictionary is also helpful in choosing correct words. Some words are easily confused and, therefore, at times misused. Examples of such words are *effect* and *affect, capital* and *capitol, principal* and *principle, continuous* and *continual*, and *further* and *farther*. See the Business English Seminar E for an extensive list of easily confused words.

[NOTE 4.5] Use a thesaurus to find synonyms.

A **thesaurus** provides additional synonyms and different shades of meanings. Thesauruses are available in book form or as software; the latter is usually a part of a word processing software package. If you have an idea you want to express, use a thesaurus to check for words that represent the idea and find several alternative words that you can use. Each choice usually has a slightly different connotation. A thesaurus can provide the simplest and most precise words for your message, as well as synonyms to use so that you can avoid repeating a word.

[NOTE 4.6] Use a dictionary and a thesaurus to select appropriate words.

A dictionary and a thesaurus should be at your side when you are attempting to compose effective messages. Your use of them can increase your power to choose the most appropriate words for each of your messages. Reference sites for online dictionaries and/or thesauruses on the Internet include the following:

Merriam-Webster Online Dictionary at **http://m-w.com/**
Yahoo Reference Dictionary at **http://www.yahoo.com/reference/dictionaries**
OneLook Dictionaries at **http://www.onelook.com**

Also, the *Microsoft Encarta '97*, a CD-ROM encyclopedia, includes a dictionary. The *Webster New World Dictionary* by Zane Publishing is also available on CD-ROM. In addition, many libraries have dial-in access to their online unabridged dictionaries and thesauruses; check with your library for local access numbers for this service.

In addition to using a dictionary and a thesaurus, you will want to follow the following 15 principles of business communication when you are choosing words for your messages.

PRINCIPLE 1: CHOOSE UNDERSTANDABLE WORDS

The first principle of word selection is to choose words that your receiver will understand. Prior to composing your messages, you should have analyzed your receiver's knowledge, interests, attitudes, and emotional state. Considering the information you gathered in this analysis and keeping in mind the importance of the you–viewpoint, you will want to choose words that the receiver will understand.

[NOTE 4.7]
Choose words your receiver will understand.

An **understandable word** is one that is in your receiver's vocabulary. Consider your receiver's educational level and experience as they relate to your message when choosing words. The words that will communicate best are those slightly below the receiver's vocabulary level. For most receivers, you should select the more understandable words in the following examples rather than the less understandable ones.

[NOTE 4.8]
Understandable words are words that are in your receiver's vocabulary.

Less Understandable	More Understandable
abdicate	resign
amble	walk
apprehend	arrest
ascent	slope
demonstrate	show
emulate	copy
exonerate	clear
expedite	rush
facilitate	help
finality	end
gelid	icy
incited	provoked
incriminate	blame
initiate	start
oscillate	swing
prerogative	right
perspiration	sweat
utilize	use
verbalize	say
zealot	fanatic

Notice that the more understandable words are the simpler words normally used in everyday conversations. Also, words that are more understandable are usually shorter.

[NOTE 4.9]
Understandable words are generally simpler and shorter.

[NOTE 4.10]
Appropriate technical words can be efficient.

Using appropriate technical words is a special consideration in choosing understandable words. A **technical word**—sometimes referred to as *jargon*—is one with special meaning in a particular field. Technical words can assist in conveying precise, meaningful messages among certain receivers and senders. For example, between two accountants the use of the words *accrued liabilities* will be understandable. Using these technical words enables accountants to be more precise and efficient than using nontechnical language. For most of us, though, *accrued liabilities* is not as understandable as *debts that have not yet been recorded on our books*. Here are some other examples of technical and nontechnical words:

Technical Words	Nontechnical Words
amenities	features of the property
brief	summary of a legal case
cerebellum	lower part of the brain
CRT	terminal
de facto	actual
ferment	sour
gelding	neutered male horse
haute couture	high fashion
juried	judged
symposium	conference

[NOTE 4.11]
Appropriate technical words are those in your receiver's vocabulary.

You will want to use only those technical words that are in your receiver's vocabulary. To do otherwise reduces the receiver's understanding of your message. If you are not sure whether a technical word is in your receiver's vocabulary, do not use it.

In summary, you can best choose understandable words by selecting simple words, short words, and appropriate technical words. The examples that follow assume that the receiver is a typical high school graduate who has no particular technical knowledge.

Less Understandable	More Understandable
She should be on the qui vive.	She should be alert.
Benito formulated the manifesto.	Benito prepared the statement.
Have you ever met a philodox?	Have you ever met a person who loves to hear himself talk?
The altercation between Hilda and Lupe originated following dissension.	The fight between Hilda and Lupe began after a quarrel.
Midori demanded the prerogative to establish her own docket.	Midori demanded the right to set her own schedule.
Mea culpa.	I am at fault.
The boys on the corner were deadbeat after slaving all day.	The boys on the corner were exhausted after working all day.

PRINCIPLE 2: USE CONCRETE WORDS

A **concrete word** is one that is specific and precise. In your business messages use concrete words that are clear so that there will be no question in your receiver's mind as to the meaning you intended.

[NOTE 4.12]
Use concrete words. They are specific and precise.

An **abstract word** is a general word. Abstract words are the opposite of concrete words. Their meanings are less clear than the meanings of concrete words and are more likely to create wrong or confusing connotations in your receiver's mind. Abstract words are appropriate for literary compositions, but you will primarily want to use concrete words in your business messages. Here are examples of abstract words and ways to make them more specific:

[NOTE 4.13]
Abstract words are less clear in meaning.

Abstract	Concrete
automobile	Volkswagen Cabrio
early	5:00 a.m.
hot	100 degrees Fahrenheit
loyal	would give his or her life
most	89.9 percent
office furniture	wooden desk
Olympics	2002 Winter Olympics
others	College of Business Administration students
poor student	Has 1.6 grade point average (4.0 = A)
printer	Hewlett-Packard Laser Jet 4L
soon	7:00 p.m., Tuesday

Notice in the preceding examples that sometimes a few more words are needed to be concrete. These additions to the length of your message are worth the clarity you gain.

PRINCIPLE 3: CHOOSE STRONG WORDS

A **strong word** in the English language will be either a verb or a noun. Verbs are the strongest words, and nouns are next in strength. Adjectives and adverbs, while needed for concreteness at times, are generally weaker, less objective words. (See Business English Seminar A for a review of the parts of speech.)

[NOTE 4.14]
Verbs and nouns are strong words. Adjectives and adverbs are weaker.

You will want to give preference to verbs and nouns in your business messages and avoid the use of subjective adjectives and adverbs. Adjectives and adverbs tend to distract the receiver from the main points of the message. Reducing your use of adjectives and adverbs will help prevent you from overstating a point or position. To have an impact, business messages should convey objectivity by avoiding exaggeration.

A sender who communicates with clarity and forcefulness is often described as "a person of a few words," "the strong, silent type," "straight to the point," and "clear as a bell." A short, powerful message composed of strong words will more likely get the attention of your receiver. Note these examples:

[NOTE 4.15]
Choose strong words for power and objectivity.

Weak	Strong
adventure	war
at this point in time	now

Weak	Strong, *continued*
female parent	mother
initial	first
implement	do
intoxicant	alcohol
passed away	died
room and board with Uncle Sam	imprisonment
situation	problem
suggested	demanded
The Peace Corps sends men and women to third-world countries.	The Peace Corps sends men and women to poor and undeveloped countries.
A careful study of the market is obviously in order.	A study of the market should be made.
I think that perhaps we may want to consider doing something.	We must do something.
Mary told me she has plenty of time to visit since she is waiting for employment.	Mary told me she has plenty of time to visit since she is unemployed.

[NOTE 4.16] Use weak words to soften messages.

Although Principle 3 advocates a preference for strong words, there will be times when you will want to soften a message with weaker words. This is particularly true for a message that is bad news for your receiver. If you have to discuss a problem with a coworker, you will build better human relations and more acceptance of your message if you use the weaker word *situation* instead of the stronger word *problem*. (This use of weak words is fully discussed in Chapter 9.)

PRINCIPLE 4: EMPHASIZE POSITIVE WORDS

[NOTE 4.17] Emphasize positive words and avoid negative words.

A positive, *can-do* attitude is one of the most important attributes you can have in business. Having that attitude is just the first step; you will want to communicate it to your receivers by selecting positive words and avoiding negative words. A **positive word** is one that conveys optimism and confidence. **Negative words** trigger unpleasant emotional feelings in most of your receivers.

[NOTE 4.18] Positive words are more likely to achieve business communication goals.

Positive words in a message help to achieve the business communication goals of securing the needed response, maintaining a favorable relationship, and gaining goodwill. Here are examples of negative words you should avoid using when possible:

Negative Words

contradict	disapprove	deny	thwart
complaint	accuse	stingy	hateful
don't	disgust	discouraging	wrong
problem	obnoxious	blame	improper
impossible	flunked	trouble	disaster
never	unhappy	sorry	regret

Employees who develop a positive, can-do attitude are better communicators.

These examples show that unpleasant and negative words are often strong words. There will be occasions when you will want to use negative words for emphasis. (An example is a claim letter to a vendor to replace china that was broken during shipment; see Chapter 7.)

[NOTE 4.19]
In some situations, negative words can be used for emphasis.

As the next examples show, however, you will more effectively convey a positive attitude and the you–viewpoint if you emphasize what can be done rather than what cannot be done. Both your professional and personal relationships will be served well by selecting positive words and avoiding negative ones.

Negative Phrasings	Positive Phrasings
I cannot attend the meeting today.	I will be available to meet tomorrow.
The item you ordered is not in stock.	We will fill your order on December 5.
You will not regret your decision.	You will be happy with your decision.
We are not open until later.	We open at 10 a.m.
Gloria is never happy before 7 a.m.	Gloria is always happy after 7 a.m.
After my son drove the car to the football game, the tank was half empty.	After my son drove the car to the football game, the tank was half full.
You will not be enrolled at UCSB until after December 2001.	You will be enrolled at UCSB as of January 2002.
I regret to advise that we must decline the refund for your defective lawn mower.	Your lawn mower may be repaired at your convenience by our professional staff.

PRINCIPLE 5: AVOID OVERUSED WORDS

An **overused word** is one used so much in normal conversation or in business messages that it has lost its effectiveness. The continued use of such words makes messages less precise and less understandable. Because we have heard them over and

[NOTE 4.20]
Avoid overused words because they have lost their effectiveness.

over, overused words make messages less interesting. Avoid these and similar overused words:

Overused Words and Phrases

win-win	it goes without saying
awesome	below the belt
really	wannabe
random	interface
strategic planning	very
nice	by leaps and bounds
24/7	mommy track
sure	awful
bottom line	day trader
paradigm	wow

PRINCIPLE 6: AVOID OBSOLETE WORDS

[NOTE 4.21] Avoid obsolete words because they are pompous, dull, or stiff.

An **obsolete word** is one that is out-of-date, pompous, dull, or stiff. Some of these obsolete words were used years ago in business messages and have been adopted by younger managers. Such words are not normally used in everyday conversation and should not be used in business communication.

Sometimes individuals tend to use obsolete words and become formal, stilted, and pompous when writing messages or speaking before groups. They fail to use the desirable conversational language that communicates best with receivers. The following are examples of obsolete words you should avoid:

Obsolete Words and Phrases

above board	grin and bear it	as per
permit us to remind	enclosed herewith	hereby advise
mind your p's and q's	thanking you in advance	in closing
regret to advise	fish out of water	wish to advise
hodgepodge	take the liberty of	tower of strength

As you read through these examples, you quickly realize that most people do not use obsolete words in their everyday conversations. Some do, however, in their writing or public speaking. Such obsolete words should be avoided in all business messages.

COMMUNICATION QUOTE

Good Communication Skills Are Necessary for College Graduates

Communication skills, both oral and written, are essential in every aspect of life. As a recent college graduate now working on my Masters in Business Administration, I have found that communication skills are critical to obtaining a higher educational degree, securing employment, achieving promotions in the workplace, and interacting with members in professional organizations. No matter what you do today or after graduation, communication skills are vital to your success.

Sima Boyajian, Recent College Graduate, California.

Developing Sentences

In the first part of this chapter you learned how to choose effective words. Now you are ready to study the principles that will guide you in combining those words into effective sentences. Businesspeople prefer concise, efficient, effective communication. To be successful, you will want to use clear, short sentences that are in the active voice and that emphasize your most important points. The following are principles of business communication for developing clear sentences.

Learning Objective [2]
DISCUSS THE ELEMENTS NEEDED FOR CLEAR, CONCISE, AND EFFECTIVE SENTENCES.

[NOTE 4.22]
Use short, clear sentences, active voice, and appropriate emphasis.

PRINCIPLE 7: COMPOSE CLEAR SENTENCES

You can compose clear sentences by following the principles for choosing words that were discussed in the preceding sections. A **clear sentence** uses words that are understandable, concrete, strong, and positive. In addition, clear sentences have unity; that is, they normally contain one main idea. Finally, clear sentences are logically composed by keeping related words together.

[NOTE 4.23]
Compose clear sentences with understandable, concrete, strong, and positive words.

Give Sentences Unity **Sentence unity** means that a sentence communicates one main idea—one thought. At times you may also want to include ideas that support the main idea. The general rule, however, is one thought, one sentence. If you have two main thoughts, construct two separate sentences. Examine these contrasting examples of sentences without unity and with unity:

[NOTE 4.24]
Clear sentences have unity.

Lacks Unity	Has Unity
The students at the university were told that the Small Business minor would be changed and the Small Business minor requirements will be listed on the Small Business Web site.	The students at the university were told that the Small Business minor would be changed from last year. The minor's requirements will be listed on the Small Business Web site.

By separating the two subjects—*Small Business minor* and *requirements*—we have made each sentence clearer and have given each subject more emphasis.

Keep Related Words Together **Modifiers** are words, phrases, or clauses that describe or limit other words, phrases, or clauses. Modifiers should be placed close to the words they modify. For the sentence to be clear, the word or words that are being described or limited by the modifier must be obvious. In each of the following examples, a modifier has been placed in italics:

[NOTE 4.25]
Related words are placed close together in clear sentences.

Unclear Relationship	Clear Relationship
When I raise my hand and give you the test, *start taking it.*	When I raise my hand, *start taking* the test I have given you.
For the first time the salesperson filled an order for the new computer.	The salesperson filled an order for the new computer *for the first time.*

Unclear Relationship	Clear Relationship, *continued*
I am *immediately* approving your loan effective so that you can purchase the house.	So that you can purchase the house, I am approving your loan effective *immediately*.
Luke will submit his resume for the *professional trainer position* on Friday.	On Friday, Luke will submit his resume for the *professional trainer position*.

[NOTE 4.26]
Clear sentences are grammatically correct.

Use Correct Grammar Clear sentences are grammatically correct. All parts of a sentence should agree. The subject and verb should agree in tense and number. Pronouns should agree with their antecedents in three ways—number, gender, and clear relationship. Another important form of agreement is parallelism—using the same grammatical form for parts of sentences that serve the same purpose. Correct grammar is discussed in Business English Seminars A and B.

PRINCIPLE 8: USE SHORT SENTENCES

[NOTE 4.27]
Use short sentences. They are more understandable.

A short sentence is more effective than a long sentence. Generally, short sentences are easier to understand.

[NOTE 4.28]
Short sentences should average 15–20 words.

The average length of your sentences will depend on the ability of your receiver to understand. For a middle-level receiver, short sentences should average 15 to 20 words. Generally, you should use sentences of longer average length for receivers with more knowledge about the subject and sentences of shorter average length for receivers with less knowledge about the subject.

[NOTE 4.29]
Vary sentence length for interest.

Vary the length of your sentences to provide interest and to eliminate the dull, choppy effect of too many short sentences. However, you may need a long sentence simply to cover the main idea or the relationship of ideas.

[NOTE 4.30]
Examine sentences with 30 words or more for clarity.

Sentence fragments are used in business messages. Fragments can be as short as one word, for example, *Yes.* A complete sentence will have at least two words—a subject and a predicate; for example, *Paul laughed.* Any sentence that is 30 words or longer is considered a long sentence and should be examined for clarity. The criteria of a **short sentence** for a middle-level receiver is shown in the following Communication Note.

COMMUNICATION NOTE

How Long Is a Short Sentence?

- A sentence fragment can have *1 word.*
- Complete sentences will have at least *2 words* (a subject and a verb).
- Short sentences will average *15 to 20 words.*
- Long sentences are *30 words or longer.*

Short sentences are preferred because of the following advantages: They are less complex, and, therefore, easier to understand. They are efficient and take less time to listen to or read. Short sentences are businesslike—concise, clear, and to the point. Sentences can be shortened by omitting unnecessary words and by limiting sentence content to one major idea.

Omit Unnecessary Words An **unnecessary word** is one that is not essential to the meaning of the sentence. Clear and concise sentences are lean. They have only *essential* words. When composing sentences, try to omit words that are not essential. Compare these examples:

[NOTE 4.31]
Compose short sentences by omitting unnecessary words.

Wordy	Lean
There were five women who attended.	Five women attended.
Automation of the workplace is a critical and necessary activity to make it more effective and efficient in the future.	Automation of the workplace is essential to enhancing productivity.
On the occasion of the company's tenth anniversary, all of its customers were contacted and invited to a gala celebration.	On the company's tenth anniversary, its customers were invited to a celebration.
I met the accountant on only one occasion.	I met the accountant once.
Now seems to be an appropriate time to restructure our own organization to prepare ourselves for the competitive marketplace of tomorrow.	We should restructure the company to be competitive in the future.

Limit Content As you will recall, clear sentences convey one main idea. If you have a sentence that is 30 words or longer, you may want to divide it into two or more sentences. Examine the unity of the sentence to see if it is appropriate to divide it further. Remember, you want just one thought unit for most sentences.

[NOTE 4.32]
Limiting content is another way to achieve short sentences.

Excessive Sentence Content	Limited Sentence Content
On today's visit to IBM, we were happy to have the opportunity to be introduced to Kim Lea; she presented some of the new information on new notebook computers. If you have any questions about these notebook computers, feel free to call her at IBM.	On today's visit to IBM, we were introduced to Kim Lea, who presented information on new notebook computers. If you have questions, call her at IBM.

One technique for changing long sentences to short sentences is to change commas and semicolons to periods when possible. In the preceding illustration you can see that this was done. Often phrases and dependent clauses can be modified so that they can stand alone as short sentences.

PRINCIPLE 9: PREFER ACTIVE VOICE IN SENTENCES

Sentences using the active voice of the verb will communicate more clearly, concisely, and forcefully than those in the passive voice. In the **active voice** the subject does the acting; in the **passive voice** the subject is acted on. For example, *Gloria issued the teaching schedules* (active voice) versus *The teaching schedules were issued by Gloria* (passive voice). The active voice emphasizes Gloria and the action.

[NOTE 4.33]
Prefer active voice. It is clear, concise, and forceful.

The active voice is more direct, stronger, and more vigorous than the passive voice. The active voice usually requires fewer words and results in shorter, more understandable sentences. You will want to make the active voice predominant in your sentences. Look for the advantages of the active voice over the passive voice in these contrasting examples:

Passive	**Active**
The audit was performed by a local company.	A local company performed the audit.
The $1,000 fine was paid by the guilty party.	The guilty party paid the $1,000 fine.
Profits have increased this year at Disney.	Disney reported increased profits this year.
The automobile was purchased from John Coldiron.	John Coldiron sold the automobile.

[NOTE 4.34]
Passive voice can be used for variety and for de-emphasizing ideas.

Although these examples clearly show the power, liveliness, and conciseness of the active voice, there are appropriate uses of the passive voice. Use the passive voice when the doer of the action is unknown or unimportant or when you want to de-emphasize negative or unpleasant ideas. For example, when a customer's order is more important than who shipped it, the passive voice is appropriate:

Active: Nordstrom's delivered the clothing on schedule.
Passive: The clothing was delivered on schedule.

In the passive voice the customer's order is emphasized, thus permitting use of the you–viewpoint. Further, in the passive voice the doer of the action—the vendor—is de-emphasized and appropriately left unnamed.

In the next example you can see how to reduce a negative impression of a doer by using the passive voice. It permits you to leave the doer unnamed.

Active: Nordstrom's delivered your clothing late.
Passive: Your clothing was delivered late.

You will also sometimes want to use the passive voice to provide variety and interest in your messages. Because of its many advantages, however, the active voice should be dominant in your business messages.

PRINCIPLE 10: GIVE SENTENCES APPROPRIATE EMPHASIS

[NOTE 4.35]
Give sentences appropriate emphasis using sentence design.

Giving your sentences **appropriate emphasis** means emphasizing the important ideas and de-emphasizing the unimportant ideas. Every speaker or writer wants a particular message transmitted to the receiver. As you develop each sentence in a message, ask yourself, "Should the main idea of this sentence be emphasized or de-emphasized?" Then design the sentence to give the appropriate emphasis.

There are several ways to emphasize or de-emphasize an idea: Use length of sentence, use location within the sentence, use sentence structure, repeat key words, tell the receiver what is and what is not important, be specific or general, use format, and use mechanical means. Each of these ways is discussed and illustrated in the following sections.

Use Length Short sentences emphasize content and long sentences de-emphasize content. Most of the time you will want to use shorter sentences to give your ideas greater emphasis. Compare these examples:

> The team planned to go to the meeting that will be held on Friday at a little before 7 p.m.
>
> The team planned to attend Friday's meeting just before 7 p.m.

The important content of the message—*Friday's meeting*—receives far more emphasis in the short sentence. The longer version not only changes the main idea to a dependent clause but also surrounds the main idea with excessive, distracting words.

[NOTE 4.36]
Length: Short sentences emphasize; long sentences de-emphasize.

Use Location Beginnings and endings of sentences are the locations of greatest emphasis. What ideas are stressed in these sentences?

> Larry received a raise.
>
> Larry's salary was raised from $30,000 per year to $35,000 per year.
>
> Outstanding performance resulted in a raise for Larry.

[NOTE 4.37]
Location: Beginnings and endings emphasize; middles de-emphasize.

Larry is emphasized in all three sentences. Larry's raise also receives emphasis in the first sentence by its location at the end. The fact that Larry is now earning $35,000 receives emphasis in the second sentence. Finally, in the third sentence Larry's outstanding performance is emphasized.

Sentence beginnings compete for attention with the words that follow them; endings compete for attention with words that precede them. Words in the middle of sentences, however, have to compete with both the preceding and following words and, therefore, are de-emphasized. For example:

> The new position requires a transfer to another facility, but it affords an excellent opportunity for advancement.
>
> Dumsile received her SAT scores; the scores for the ACT test, which was taken earlier, should be sent to her next week.

In the first sentence, *a transfer to another facility* is de-emphasized by its location. In the second sentence, *which was taken earlier* is de-emphasized. Location is an excellent way to give appropriate emphasis.

Use Sentence Structure You give the greatest emphasis to an idea by placing it in a short, simple sentence. If you want to show a relationship between ideas, it is possible to emphasize main ideas by placing them in independent clauses and de-emphasize other ideas by placing them in dependent clauses. The independent clause is similar to the short sentence; it can stand alone. Dependent clauses are not complete thoughts; they do not make sense standing alone. (See Business English Seminar B for a discussion of sentence structure.)

[NOTE 4.38]
Structure: Ideas in independent clauses are emphasized; in dependent clauses, de-emphasized.

The two short sentences that follow give approximately the same emphasis to two main ideas: the *six-figure salary* and *consider opportunities.*

> I prefer to earn a salary in the low six figures. I would consider opportunities at a lower level.

[NOTE 4.39]
Ideas share emphasis in a compound sentence.

If you want the two ideas to share emphasis—each receiving a reduced amount—you can organize them into a compound sentence:

> I prefer to earn a salary in the low six figures and would consider opportunities at a lower level.

By organizing these two ideas into one complex sentence, however, one idea can be emphasized and one de-emphasized. This sentence structure arrangement is called **subordination**. Organizing your sentences using subordination of ideas gives you flexibility in composing your messages. Examine the varying emphases in the following examples:

> Although I prefer to earn a salary in the low six figures, I would consider opportunities at a lower level.
>
> Although I would consider opportunities at a lower level, I prefer a salary in the low six figures.

In the first example, the idea of considering opportunities at a lower level is emphasized by being placed in an independent clause. In the second sentence, the primary idea of a salary in the low six figures gets the attention as an independent clause.

[NOTE 4.40]
Repetition: Emphasize ideas by repeating key words.

Repeat Key Words Main ideas represented by key words can be emphasized by repeating those words within a sentence. Note the emphasis given *defective* and *radio* in this sentence from a customer complaint:

> The radio I purchased from you is defective; please replace this defective radio immediately.

Here is another example of emphasis through repetition of the same root word in different forms:

> Les and Tim flew to Costa Rica on a Boeing 767; the Boeing 767 is a safe plane to fly.

Repetition of key words also provides coherence and movement in a sentence. Coherence and movement are discussed later in this chapter.

[NOTE 4.41]
Explicitness: You can tell the receiver what is important and what is unimportant.

Tell the Receiver What Is Important You can tell your receiver that an idea is important or unimportant by your word choice. For example:

> High grades and high SAT scores are *critical* for gaining acceptance at a top university.
>
> Of *less concern* is that the flight to Krakow, Poland, will be delayed.

Of course, there are many words and constructions you can use to indicate the importance of an idea. You can refer to ideas with such words as *significant, of (no) consequence, (not) a concern, high (or low) priority, (not) critical, fundamental,* and *(non)essential.* Your thesaurus will be helpful in choosing words to tell your receiver that one idea is important and another unimportant.

[NOTE 4.42]
Specification: Specific words emphasize; general words de-emphasize.

Be Specific or General Another way to give appropriate emphasis is to use concrete words (specific words) to emphasize ideas and to use abstract words (general words) to de-emphasize ideas. Here are examples of how this works:

Specific: Craig Jones bought a new *white Porsche Boxter.*
General: Craig Jones bought a new *car.*
Specific: I love to run, swim, and bicycle.
General: I love to exercise.

Use Format The way you arrange and punctuate a sentence can give emphasis to selected ideas. One way to highlight an idea is to separate it from other information in the sentence. Consider this example:

[NOTE 4.43]
Format: Emphasize ideas with punctuation and lists.

One factor is always key at any successful fund-raising event—food!

"Food" stands out because it is set off with a dash and exclamation point. Dashes, colons, and exclamation points are strong punctuation marks and can be used to emphasize ideas. Ideas can be de-emphasized by setting them off with commas or parentheses, which are weaker punctuation marks.

A vertical numbered or lettered list attracts more attention than a list of items simply set off by commas in regular sentence format. This example shows how you can emphasize points by putting them in a numbered list:

The major conclusions of the study are that for a woman to be successful in China she must

[1] Work harder than men,

[2] Be well educated and trained for a specific profession, and

[3] Be able to handle the affairs of the family well and support her husband.

Use Mechanical Means There are several ways you can give emphasis to ideas through mechanical means. You can *italicize* or use **boldface** type. You can use a different color to highlight selected ideas. The previous sentence and the illustrations and marginal notes in this book are examples of the effective use of color. Other mechanical means include type size, typeface, uppercase letters, bullets, arrows, and circles.

[NOTE 4.44]
Mechanics: Emphasize with underlining, type, color, and other means.

Overuse of format or mechanical means to emphasize ideas will reduce their effectiveness and can be distracting. Their use in letters and memos should be very limited and reserved for special situations. The use of mechanical means to emphasize ideas is more common in advertisements, reports, and visual aids.

There are many ways to emphasize and de-emphasize ideas as you develop effective sentences. You will want to practice and use these techniques to strengthen your business communication skills.

Forming Paragraphs

Learning Objective [3]
DEVELOP CLEAR, CONCISE, LOGICAL, COHERENT, AND EFFECTIVE PARAGRAPHS.

Combining sentences into paragraphs is an important part of composing a message. Paragraphs help your receiver organize his or her thoughts and see where your message is going. You can form effective paragraphs by following five basic principles of business communication. These principles will guide you in determining paragraph length, unity, organization, emphasis, and coherence.

[NOTE 4.45]
Paragraphs organize the receiver's thoughts.

PRINCIPLE 11: USE SHORT PARAGRAPHS

[NOTE 4.46] Use short paragraphs. They are easier to understand.

You will want to use short paragraphs in your business messages. A **short paragraph** is easy to understand, helps your receivers organize their thoughts more easily, and appears more inviting to the receiver. Receivers are more likely to read short paragraphs.

Long paragraphs are more complex, appear more difficult to read, and are harder to comprehend. Readers are less likely to read them.

[NOTE 4.47] In letters and memos, paragraphs should average four to five lines. Paragraphs with eight lines or more should be examined.

In business letter and memo writing, short paragraphs average four to five *lines*. If any paragraph in a letter or memo is eight lines or more, it is long and should be examined carefully to see if it can be shortened or divided. Business letters and memos are likely to be read quickly, and short paragraphs aid receiver understanding.

[NOTE 4.48] In reports, paragraphs should average six to seven lines. Paragraphs with twelve lines or more should be examined.

Business reports are more likely to be studied carefully, and the paragraphs can be somewhat longer, but not much longer. In business report writing, short paragraphs should average six to seven lines. Twelve lines or more in any paragraph in a report is a signal that it is long, and its unity (see Principle 12) should be examined carefully. Criteria of a short paragraph for business letters and memos and for business reports are shown in the following Communication Note.

COMMUNICATION NOTE

How Long Is a Short Paragraph?

Business Letters and Memos

- A short paragraph can have *1 line.*
- Short paragraphs will average *4 to 5 lines.*
- Long paragraphs are *8 lines or more.*

Business Reports

- A short paragraph can have *2 lines.*
- Short paragraphs will average *6 to 7 lines.*
- Long paragraphs are *12 lines or more.*

[NOTE 4.49] Paragraph lengths should vary from one line to many.

These guidelines for the lengths of paragraphs in business messages are recommended averages and maximums. The lengths of paragraphs should be varied to accommodate content and to promote reader interest. Paragraphs can and should vary from one line to many lines. They can consist of one sentence or a number of sentences.

[NOTE 4.50] First and last paragraphs are usually shorter for greater emphasis.

In most business letters, memos, and reports, the first and last paragraphs are shorter than the middle paragraphs. Often the first and last paragraphs in letters and memos are one to three lines long and consist of only one or two sentences. In reports the first and last paragraphs may be somewhat longer. Short opening and closing paragraphs are more inviting to the reader. They add emphasis to the message's beginning and ending ideas. In Parts 3 and 5 of this book, there are several examples of letters, memos, and reports in which paragraph size can be examined.

PRINCIPLE 12: GIVE PARAGRAPHS UNITY

[NOTE 4.51] Clear paragraphs have unity.

Paragraphs should have unity. **Paragraph unity** means that all the sentences in a paragraph relate to one topic. The topic should be covered adequately; however, if the paragraph becomes too long, it should be divided into two or more logical parts. Examine the following paragraphs:

> **Lacks Unity:** The baseball game had reached a crucial point. A large crowd had been at the park all afternoon. The weather had been muggy. Vendors were selling hot dogs and soft drinks.

> **Has Unity:** The baseball game had reached a crucial point. It was the bottom of the ninth inning and the score was tied. Two batters were out. The third was at the plate, and the pitcher had already thrown him two strikes and three balls. Yes, this was the most exciting time in the game.

Giving unity to paragraphs is sometimes more difficult than the preceding examples imply. The following example lacks unity. Can you determine why?

> **Lacks Unity:** The College of Business has proposed that all professors submit their professional development plans online in order to save time. The new procedure will require all professional development plans to follow the same format. Using the same format will save time for reviewers of the professional development plans. All College of Business faculty members must publish one refereed article per year and make two presentations at professional conferences.

Did you note that the fourth sentence did not relate directly to the paragraph's main topic? If you did, you are right. The main topic was saving time by submitting professional development plans online. The fourth sentence shifted the topic to publishing a refereed article and making presentations. The fourth sentence is a separate topic that requires its own paragraph or paragraphs.

PRINCIPLE 13: ORGANIZE PARAGRAPHS LOGICALLY

Paragraphs can be organized logically using one of two basic plans: the direct plan (deductive approach) or the indirect plan (inductive approach). In the **direct plan** the main idea is presented in the first sentence of the paragraph, and details follow in succeeding sentences. In the **indirect plan** details are presented first, and the main idea is presented later in the paragraph.

[NOTE 4.52]
Organize paragraphs logically using direct or indirect plans.

The content determines which plan—direct or indirect—you will use. Positive news and neutral news can best be presented using the direct plan. Getting directly to the main point and following it with details helps orient the reader to the content. Negative news or persuasive news can best be presented using the indirect plan. This approach enables you to provide details at the beginning of the message that pave the way for an unpleasant main point, an unfavorable recommendation, or a request for action.

[NOTE 4.53]
Present positive or neutral news using the direct plan.

[NOTE 4.54]
Present negative news or persuasion using the indirect plan.

The sentence that presents the main point of a paragraph is called the **topic sentence**. The topic sentence will either announce the main idea to the reader or it will summarize the content of the main idea. The topic sentence is like the headline on a newspaper story. In using the direct plan, the topic sentence will be the first sentence, as it is in this paragraph. With the indirect plan, the topic sentence will be placed later in the paragraph.

[NOTE 4.55]
The topic sentence presents the main point of the paragraph.

As a general rule, the first sentence in a paragraph should be either the topic sentence or a transitional sentence. How to provide transition (movement) in a first sentence will be explained later, under Principle 15. Unless there is an important

[NOTE 4.56]
The first sentence should be topical or transitional.

reason to locate it elsewhere in the paragraph, the topic sentence should be placed first in business messages. Here are examples of the two basic plans with the topic sentences italicized:

[NOTE 4.57] Neutral news.

Direct Plan (Topic Sentence First): *Most chief business executives rate business communication as the most important skill a manager can possess.* A recent survey of business executives showed that 80 percent of the respondents thought business communication was a manager's most important skill. The remaining 20 percent of the respondents rated business communication second to technical skill. The survey was conducted using a random sample of the presidents of the Fortune 500 companies.

[NOTE 4.58] Persuasion.

Indirect Plan (Topic Sentence Within): Gain the edge in 2001! *Call 1.888.555.2387 and enroll in the International Training Certificate program today.* The International Training Certificate program offers certification in conducting business with people from (1) Asian cultures, (2) European cultures, and (3) Hispanic cultures.

[NOTE 4.59] Persuasion.

Indirect Plan (Topic Sentence Last): Spring is just around the corner. This means that vacation time is almost upon us. When you think about planning your vacation for this year, think of us. *Call the Newport Coast Travel Agency at 949.555.1234, and let us send you the "Summer Vacation Planner's Guide."*

In summary, paragraphs can be organized logically using the direct or the indirect plan. Generally, the direct plan is recommended for good news and neutral news; and the indirect plan is recommended for bad news and persuasion.

PRINCIPLE 14: GIVE PARAGRAPHS APPROPRIATE EMPHASIS

[NOTE 4.60] Give paragraphs appropriate emphasis using paragraph design.

As you will recall from the section on sentences in this chapter, giving *appropriate emphasis* means emphasizing the important ideas and de-emphasizing the unimportant ideas. Many of the same ways for giving appropriate emphasis to sentences apply to giving appropriate emphasis to paragraph content. The applicable ways are summarized here:

[NOTE 4.61] Design paragraph emphasis using length, location, repetition, explicitness, format, and mechanics.

Length	Short paragraphs emphasize content and long paragraphs de-emphasize content.
Location	Beginnings and endings of paragraphs are the locations of greatest emphasis. The middle of a paragraph is the location of least emphasis.
Repetition	Repeating key words throughout the paragraph can emphasize the ideas represented by those words.
Explicitness	You can tell your reader that an idea is important or unimportant.
Format	The way you arrange and punctuate a paragraph—set ideas off with punctuation, listings, wider margins, and so forth—can give emphasis to selected ideas.
Mechanics	You can emphasize ideas using mechanical means: underlining, boldface type, color, type size, typeface, uppercase letters, bullets, arrows, and circles.

PRINCIPLE 15: PROVIDE PARAGRAPH COHERENCE

Providing **coherence** between and within paragraphs means providing for a flow of thought. You want to encourage the logical movement of your receiver's mind from one idea to the next. The primary way to assure coherence is to organize paragraphs logically using the direct or indirect plans discussed in Principle 13.

[NOTE 4.62]
Provide for flow of thought with paragraph coherence.

You can also provide for coherence between and within paragraphs by using transitional words and tie-in sentences. Hints for successfully adopting these latter suggestions follow.

Use Transitional Words A **transitional word** is a helpful bridge from one idea to the next. Transitional words help receivers see where you are leading them, why you are leading them there, and what to expect when they get there. Transitional words provide coherence by holding ideas together logically.

[NOTE 4.63]
Provide coherence with transitional words.

For example, suppose you present an idea in one sentence and you want to expand on that idea in the next sentence. By using transitional words such as *in addition, furthermore,* and *also* at the beginning of the second sentence, you can help receivers see the relationship between ideas. The following example shows this kind of bridging between two sentences:

> **Adding Information:** Monica is a proficient writer. *In addition,* she is an excellent speaker.

There are other transitional words that provide coherence for different situations. Here are some examples:

Contrasts:	but, however, by contrast, nevertheless, on the other hand, on the one hand, from another viewpoint
Examples:	for example, to illustrate, for instance, that is, as follows, like, in illustration
Sequence:	first, second, third; one, two, three; also, in addition, finally; next, then, finally; to sum up; in conclusion
Emphasis:	significant, primarily, most importantly, particularly, especially, in fact, indeed, above all
Conclusions:	therefore, thus, so, consequently, as a result, accordingly, hence
Exclusions:	except, neither . . . nor, except that, all but, except for, all except
Additions:	in addition, furthermore, also, and, similarly, moreover, as well as, too

Use Tie-In Sentences A **tie-in sentence** helps your receiver move from one aspect of the subject to the next. When using the tie-in sentence technique for coherence, repeat the same subject one or more times. To develop tie-in sentences, you can paraphrase the subject, repeat key words that describe the subject, or use pronouns that refer to the subject. Examples of tie-in sentences using these approaches are as follows:

[NOTE 4.64]
Provide coherence with tie-in sentences.

> **Paraphrasing:** The information system in the Sheldon Hotel is *used extensively* for decision making. Because of this *high rate of use,* it is imperative that the data in the information system be up to date.

Repeating Key Words: Ernesto Garcia found that direct mail is a *cost-effective technique* for selling magazine subscriptions. Telemarketing is another proven *cost-effective technique* for promoting subscription sales.

Using Pronoun Reference: *Students* submitting applications to MBA programs must register for the GMAT test by April 1. *They* will receive confirmation of *their* registration by May 1.

USING UNBIASED LANGUAGE

Learning Objective [4]
USE AVAILABLE ALTERNATIVES TO ASSURE UNBIASED LANGUAGE IN BUSINESS MESSAGES.

The use of unbiased language is a final and important consideration in the composition of business messages. Fair and balanced treatment of all individuals regardless of race, gender, culture, age, ability, religion, or socioeconomic status is essential in a democracy. Such treatment is vital to the maintenance of favorable human relationships.

[NOTE 4.65] Message analysis includes assuring unbiased language for fair and balanced treatment of all individuals.

You will want to avoid all words that have unfavorable denotations or connotations in their reflection on any individuals. The use of such language will offend not only those to whom the references are made but also many other persons. Respect for the dignity and worth of all persons is compatible with being a responsible citizen. To increase your effectiveness as a business communicator, analyze your messages to eliminate any biased language.

[NOTE 4.66] Using biased language offends not only those referred to but also many others.

[NOTE 4.67] The English language structure is biased as to gender stereotyping.

Avoid Gender-Biased Language Using unbiased gender language is a special challenge because of the structure of the English language. The English language implies stereotyping of males and females because of (1) the generic use of masculine singular pronouns—pronouns used to represent both men and women; (2) the generic use of the word *man;* (3) the existence of masculine marker words; and (4) the use of certain words, phrases, and constructions that involve stereotyping. Fortunately, the structure of our language does not stereotype individuals on the basis of race, age, religion, and so on.

[NOTE 4.68] Listeners and readers tend to picture a male when *man*, *he*, or *chairman* is used.

Some English language listeners and readers tend to subconsciously picture a male when words such as *man, he,* or *chairman* are used. This is true even though such words are used generically—used to represent both men and women. These images should be avoided in your business messages. The examples that follow suggest that many alternatives to gender stereotyping are available:

[NOTE 4.69] You should avoid these male-only images.

Biased	Unbiased
businessman	businessperson, business executive, manager
chairman	chairperson, moderator, chair, group leader
policeman	police officer
salesman	salesperson, sales agent, sales representative
executives and their wives	executives and their spouses
mankind	humanity, people, human race
manned	staffed
mailman	mail carrier, letter carrier
Each chairman must submit his program to the membership committee.	Each chair must submit a program to the membership committee.

Biased	**Unbiased, *continued***
When an student carries a notebook computer to class, she is able to take notes easily.	When students carry notebook computers to class, they are able to take notes easily.
If an employee is late, give him one warning.	An employee who is late should receive one warning.
the ladies and the men	the women and the men, the ladies and the gentlemen
Gentlemen: Dear Sirs: (letter salutations)	Ladies and Gentlemen: (or avoid salutation by using the Simplified Block Letter style shown in Appendix A)

Avoid Other-Biased Language To be sure that you treat persons of different races and cultures in a bias-free manner, avoid all negative stereotypes of any group. Instead of using a name that may have unfavorable connotations, refer to groups by the name they prefer. For example, African Americans prefer the name *African American* to *Negro, black, colored,* or other terms used years ago. Many Hispanics prefer *Hispanic* to *Chicano* or *Mexican American.*

[NOTE 4.70]
Avoid negative stereotypes.

Avoid emphasizing religion or race when it is not essential to the main point of the message. For example, leave out the terms in italics in the following two sentences: "The *Jewish* investor from New York City funded the construction of the regional mall." "The *white* teacher spoke to the inner-city youth."

[NOTE 4.71]
Terms can be omitted to achieve unbiased language.

To avoid biased language when referring to age, for example, use *older person* or *senior citizen* instead of *elderly person* or *old man, old woman.* When referring to persons with disabilities, use people-first language and focus on the person, not the disability. Use *person with AIDS* instead of *AIDS patient* and *person with mental illness* instead of a *mentally ill woman (or man).*

[NOTE 4.72]
Substitute unbiased language for biased language.

Do not use any language that belittles, offends, embarrasses, or denigrates other persons. Do not imply that a person of a different status (race, gender, religion, culture, age, socioeconomic level, or physical or mental condition) is inferior simply because he or she is of that status. Do not imply by your language that a person of another status is rigid, lazy, stupid, slow, devious, shrewd, dishonest, fanatical, or cold. In addition, do not attribute superior qualities to persons of a certain status.

[NOTE 4.73]
Do not use any language that belittles, offends, embarrasses, or denigrates other persons.

Composing With Style

Learning Objective [5]
APPLY YOUR OWN COMPOSING STYLE TO GIVE UNIQUENESS AND LIFE TO YOUR MESSAGES.

The most effective business communicators use the principles that have been reviewed in this chapter. You, too, should find them effective. There is one other important dimension of your communication—your personality. Your writing and speaking should reflect the interesting, unique person you are.

Be yourself. Use words and combinations of words that not only are understood by your receiver but also reveal who you are—words that give life and distinction to your message. There are many combinations of words that will send the same basic message to your receiver. Use the words that communicate clearly and concisely, and that reflect your personality. Remember writing is easy, as illustrated in the following Communication Note.

[NOTE 4.74]
Compose with style—include your personality.

COMMUNICATION NOTE

Breaking Down Elements of Writing Makes It Easier

Writing is easy. All you need to do is combine letters into words, words into sentences, sentences into paragraphs, and paragraphs into documents or finished pieces.

As reported in "Writing for Business," Orange County Register, *May 10, 1999, p. d21.*

One of America's outstanding orators, Patrick Henry (1736–1799), showed what can be accomplished with style. The first sentence shows how he might have made one of his famous statements; the second sentence is what he actually said:

Not This: If I can't have freedom, then I would rather not live.

But This: Give me liberty, or give me death!

Former President William Jefferson Clinton (1946–) is a highly skilled communicator. What he could have said and what he actually said during his 1997 inaugural address are contrasted in the following example and in the Communication Quote.

COMMUNICATION QUOTE

The preeminent mission of our new government is to give all Americans an opportunity—not a guarantee, but a real opportunity—to build better lives.

President William Jefferson Clinton (1946–), 1997 Inaugural Address.

Not This: The most important thing that we need to do in our government today is to have our foremost mission to be giving all of our countrymen a chance to have a better life and to build better lives.

But This: The preeminent mission of our new government is to give all Americans an opportunity—not a guarantee, but a real opportunity—to build better lives.

One of the leaders in advocating full rights for women, Susan B. Anthony (1820–1906), was extremely effective in awakening the American nation to inequities based on gender. Contrast the way she might have expressed her basic belief in equality for women with the way she actually expressed it:

Not This: There is no reason to give women fewer rights than we give men.

But This: Men, their rights and nothing more; women, their rights and nothing less.

Another powerful communicator who moved Americans, Martin Luther King, Jr. (1929–1968), used the principles of communication coupled with his own unique selection of words. What he could have said and what he did say are sharply contrasted in the following illustration:

Not This: It is hard for others to hold you down if you never give them the chance.

But This: A man can't ride your back unless it's bent.

Finally, from another effective writer and speaker, John F. Kennedy (1917–1963), we have this contrast in what could have been said and what was said:

Not This: Do not inquire about what you can get the government to do for you; instead find out what you can do for the government.

But This: Ask not what your country can do for you; ask what you can do for your country.

Effective communicators give thought and time to what they say and write. You, too, with study and effort, can improve your ability to be an effective communicator in your professional career and your personal life. Remember to use the you–viewpoint, apply the principles of business communication, and be yourself—you will then be a powerful business communicator.

[NOTE 4.75]
Be a powerful business communicator. Use the you–viewpoint and the principles of business communication, and be yourself.

The following checklist will help you use the principles of business communication. When drafting and revising messages, refer to this list to be sure you have used each principle.

Checklist—Principles of Business Communication

When composing the message, did I

- Choose understandable words?
- Use concrete words?
- Choose strong words?
- Emphasize positive words?
- Avoid overused words?
- Avoid obsolete words?
- Compose clear sentences?
- Use short sentences?
- Prefer active voice in sentences?
- Give sentences appropriate emphasis?
- Use short paragraphs?
- Give paragraphs unity?
- Organize paragraphs logically?
- Give paragraphs appropriate emphasis?
- Provide paragraph coherence?

The following Communication Note from "Writing for Business" offers five key elements that may also help you evaluate your writing.

COMMUNICATION NOTE

Evaluate Your Writing: Five Key Elements

You can evaluate the effectiveness of your writing according to five elements of effective communication: approach, development, clarity, style, and correctness.

[1] **Approach:** Tone is appropriate to your purpose, audience, and material.

[2] **Development:** Material is arranged in a logical and coherent sequence.

[3] **Clarity:** Purpose or central idea is stated clearly. Word choice is clear, specific, accurate, unassuming, and cliche- and jargon-free.

[4] **Style:** Action verbs are used instead of weak verbs. Active voice is used instead of passive voice. A variety of sentence structure and sentence length is used.

[5] **Correctness:** Rules and conventions of spelling, grammar, usage, idiom, and punctuation are followed. Copy is free of mechanical errors.

As reported in "Writing for Business," Orange County Register, *February 15, 1999, p. d21.*

Summary of Learning Objectives

Learning Objective [1]

Identify words that your receiver(s) will understand and that will elicit the reaction you need. Words are the smallest units of messages, and you will want to be sure to choose the most effective words for your messages. The six principles of choosing words are (1) choose understandable words; (2) use concrete words; (3) choose strong words; (4) emphasize positive words; (5) avoid overused words; and (6) avoid obsolete words. The two most valuable resources for the business communicator are the dictionary and the thesaurus. Remember to have both a hard copy and an electronic copy of each.

Learning Objective [2]

Discuss the elements needed for clear, concise, and effective sentences. Businesspeople prefer concise, efficient, effective communication; therefore, you will want to use clear, short sentences that are in the active voice and that have appropriate emphasis. The four principles of developing sentences are (1) compose clear sentences with understandable, concrete, strong, and positive words; (2) use short sentences since they are more understandable; (3) use the active voice in sentences where the subject does the acting; and (4) give your sentences appropriate emphasis using sentence design.

Learning Objective [3]

Develop clear, concise, logical, coherent, and effective paragraphs. Combining sentences into paragraphs is an important part of composing a message. Paragraphs organize the receiver's thoughts. The five principles of forming paragraphs are (1) use short paragraphs since they are easier to understand; (2) give paragraphs unity, which means that all the sentences in a paragraph relate to one topic; (3) organize paragraphs logically using the direct or indirect plan; (4) give paragraphs appropriate emphasis by stressing the important ideas and de-emphasizing the unimportant ideas; (5) provide for flow of thought with paragraph coherence.

Use available alternatives to assure unbiased language in business messages. Message analysis includes assuring unbiased language for fair and balanced treatment of all individuals regardless of race, gender, culture, age, ability, religion, or socioeconomic status. You will want to avoid all words that have unfavorable denotations or connotations in their reflection on any individuals.

Learning Objective [4]

Apply your own composing style to give uniqueness and life to your messages. The most effective business communicators use the principles that have been reviewed in this chapter. There is one other important dimension of your communication—your personality. Use words and combinations of words that not only are understood by your receiver but also reveal who you are—words that give life and distinction to your message.

Learning Objective [5]

DISCUSSION QUESTIONS

1. Define the KISS principle of business communication and address the advantages of its use. (Objective 1)
2. Explain how a word processing software package can help you be a more effective communicator. (Objective 1)
3. Discuss the differences between concrete and abstract words. Which should you use in your business messages? (Objective 1)
4. Explain how the use of appropriate technical words can assist communicators. Give an example. (Objective 1)
5. Explain what must be done to assure that sentences are grammatically correct. (Objective 2)
6. Why are short sentences preferred in business communication? How can sentences be shortened? (Objective 2)
7. Discuss the advantages of using the active voice and of using the passive voice in sentences. Write a sentence in active voice then change the sentence to passive voice. (Objective 2)
8. Explain why a sender should use short paragraphs in business messages. Tell what the average length of short paragraphs should be for (a) letters and memos and (b) reports. (Objective 3)
9. Explain how you can use alternative wording to assure unbiased language in business messages. Give an example. (Objective 4)
10. How can you follow the principles of business communication in your composing efforts and still reflect your own personality in your messages? (Objective 5)

APPLICATION EXERCISES

Instructions. For each principle of business communication listed, follow the directions given for its exercises. Keep the basic meaning contained in each of the exercises, and use examples that are different from those in this chapter. Use a dictionary and a thesaurus to assist you in these exercises. Assume that your receiver is a high school graduate with a tenth- to eleventh-grade vocabulary level and no particular technical expertise.

Principle 1: Choose Understandable Words (Objective 1)

1. **Select simple words.** Select simpler words to replace these difficult words: (a) mesmerize, (b) exemplary, (c) garner, (d) protocol, (e) decorum, (f) illicit, (g) adversary, (h) jeopardy, (i) segregate, (j) advocate, (k) beguile, (l) impeccable, (m) propriety, (n) proponent, (o) sequester.
2. **Use short words.** Select short words to replace these long words: (a) whimsical, (b) facsimile, (c) consolidate, (d) reproduction, (e) reasonable, (f) confederate, (g) vacillation, (h) prerogative, (i) clandestine, (j) amalgamate, (k) representation, (l) incorporate, (m) surreptitious, (n) lackadaisical, (o) capacitate.
3. **Use appropriate nontechnical words.** Select nontechnical words to replace each of these technical words: (a) dividend, (b) prosthesis, (c) equity, (d) hypothesis, (e) asset, (f) invoice, (g) accounts payable, (h) tabloid, (i) exempt employee, (j) debug, (k) carcinoma, (l) accounts receivable, (m) generate, (n) chronicle, (o) matriculate.

Principle 2: Use Concrete Words (Objective 1)

Select concrete words to replace these abstract words: (a) book, (b) industry, (c) building, (d) equipment, (e) nice, (f) flower, (g) soon, (h) early, (i) transportation, (j) periodically, (k) car, (l) tree, (m) airline, (n) slow, (o) country.

Principle 3: Prefer Strong Words (Objective 1)

Select strong words to replace these weak words: (a) let go, (b) remiss, (c) inexpensive, (d) request, (e) comply, (f) overlooked, (g) ask, (h) refrain, (i) purchase, (j) resist, (k) decline, (l) comply, (m) withstand, (n) overdue, (o) suggest.

Principle 4: Emphasize Positive Words (Objective 1)

List five positive words that would be good to use in business messages and five negative words a sender should avoid using.

Principle 5: Avoid Overused Words (Objective 1)

List five overused words or phrases a sender should avoid using.

Principle 6: Avoid Obsolete Words (Objective 1)

Develop ten sentences using obsolete words or phrases. Rewrite these sentences avoiding the use of the obsolete words or phrases.

Principle 7: Compose Clear Sentences (Objective 2)

1. **Give sentences unity.** Rewrite the following long sentences. Divide them into a number of sentences each of which possesses unity.

The new product was online to be produced by October 1, but the necessary parts inventory was not available in time to start production as scheduled; to solve this problem, the purchasing agent and the expediters located alternative vendors.

The planning was to be carried out by the end of January, but the information needed to complete the planning was not available in time; to solve this problem, the vice president of operations decided to extend the planning calendar through February so that production could continue using the current procedures.

2. **Keep related words together.** Revise the following sentences so that there is a clear relationship between the modifiers and the words they modify:
   - **a.** E-mail work journals are due by 5 p.m. each Wednesday promptly.
   - **b.** To all employees the cards must be given before Monday.
   - **c.** The fax machine needed repair which was purchased last year.
   - **d.** The employee was too ill to come to work because he sent his report by fax.
   - **e.** The information was not available needed to complete the project.
   - **f.** The computer needed repair which was purchased recently.
   - **g.** A copy was mailed of the policy to each manager on September 15.

Principle 8: Use Short Sentences (Objective 2)

Shorten the following sentences by omitting unnecessary words and limiting content:

- **a.** We received your letter on company letterhead that was dated January 1, 2001.
- **b.** As head of the human resources department, Dr. Srinivas was happy to have the opportunity to conduct a search for new professors.
- **c.** Our services include a logistic audit to evaluate your transportation department, warehouse operation, and the ability to get your products to market.
- **d.** Our goal is to affect your bottom line directly in a positive manner.
- **e.** I will call you within the next several days to see when we might schedule an exploratory meeting.
- **f.** The prices which are for the nonfat variety of milk are going up in price.
- **g.** The time of the next cross country meet will be determined, set, and announced on October 1 at the first cross-country meet.

Principle 9: Prefer Active Voice in Sentences (Objective 2)

Change the following sentences from the passive voice to the active voice:

- **a.** A lecture must be prepared by the professor.
- **b.** The deed of trust must be signed by the owner of the property.
- **c.** Proposals are to be prepared in triplicate.
- **d.** The information was faxed to Brunswick Company on Thursday by Cindy Greene.
- **e.** Graduation check forms must be prepared in triplicate.
- **f.** The cross-country race was won by Liz Morse.
- **g.** The money was stolen by the girl with the black skirt.

Principle 10: Give Sentences Appropriate Emphasis (Objective 2)

Following the guideline instructions for emphasis, create one to three sentences for each situation:

1. **Use length.** You want to help students at a local high school understand the importance of performing well on their upcoming ACT test for college admission. Emphasize this point by the length of your sentence(s).
2. **Use location.** You want to stress to students the importance of attending every class session. Emphasize this point at the beginning of your sentence(s).
3. **Use sentence structure.** You have to tell a group of jazz band students that they have not been accepted to perform at Disneyland. Use sentence structure to de-emphasize the *no* in your sentence(s).

4. **Repeat key words.** Repeat key words in your sentence(s) to emphasize that we conduct business in a global society.
5. **Be specific or general.** Be general in your sentence(s) to de-emphasize the grade that you received on your chemistry final.
6. **Use format.** Use format in your sentence(s) to emphasize the number of students in your graduating class that will be continuing their education at graduate schools.
7. **Use mechanical means.** Use mechanical means in your sentence(s) to emphasize the importance of attending the business education seminar at the Marriott Hotel.

Principle 11: Use Short Paragraphs (Objective 3)

Indicate the recommended average number of lines for short paragraphs in (a) letters and memos and (b) reports. Also indicate the number of lines for paragraphs that are considered long for (c) letters and memos and (d) reports. Finally, indicate (e) the number of lines in the shortest possible paragraph.

Principle 12: Give Paragraphs Unity (Objective 3)

Indicate the sentence that does not belong in each of the following paragraphs:

- **a.** Business communication instruction offers students an important opportunity. That opportunity is a chance to strengthen the most critical skill they can possess—the ability to communicate. Most managers, when asked, say that strong communication skills are essential to success. Specifically, this success depends on several subskills. Included in these subskills is knowing how to develop a business message. Also, understanding how to delegate and how to provide constructive criticism are crucial to managerial success. Basic to managerial achievement, however, is understanding how to analyze the receiver for the you–viewpoint.
- **b.** Colleges are preparing for the increased number of students applying for admission. Over the next ten years, the number of applicants is expected to increase 25 percent. This influx of students is called Tidal Wave 2. Students like college. The colleges are building more classrooms and hiring more professors to accommodate more students.
- **c.** Only recently have women had the opportunity to hold positions of leadership in unions. In fact, by 1993 there were only three women presidents of national unions affiliated with the American Federation of Labor–Congress of Industrial Organizations (AFL-CIO). Important progress during the 1980s and early 1990s was made by women who penetrated the middle levels of management. One of the first women involved in union leadership was Delores Huerta who cofounded the United Farm Workers (UFW) union with Cesar Chavez.

Principle 13: Organize Paragraphs Logically (Objective 3)

Using the direct plan, indicate the most logical order of these two groups of sentences by listing their letters in that order:

- **a.** This new marketing plan should increase sales significantly.
- **b.** The increased sales will justify the intensive planning effort.
- **c.** The vice president for sales approved the new marketing plan.
- **d.** I think you will agree that the planning effort was worthwhile.

- **a.** The facts in your request clearly supported your position.
- **b.** Your request to attend the conference is approved.

c. Report these expenses to me when you return.

d. Please keep a careful record of your travel expenses.

Principle 14: Give Paragraphs Appropriate Emphasis (Objective 3)

1. Create a paragraph that emphasizes the importance of getting a college education and de-emphasizes the time commitment that is required.
2. Create a paragraph that emphasizes the importance of having a computer connected to the Internet for use in your homework, and de-emphasizes the cost of making the arrangements for Internet service and purchasing the equipment.

Principle 15: Provide Paragraph Coherence (Objective 3)

Using the indirect plan, indicate the most coherent order for these sentences by listing their letters in that order:

a. Why should you join the National Business Education Association?

b. Don't wait. Join NBEA today!

c. You will receive valuable publications.

d. In addition, you can exchange ideas with other teachers.

a. The University of Michigan has offered Jean Almarez a teaching contract.

b. She received her bachelor of science degree from the University of Loyola and her Ph.D. from the University of Illinois.

c. Dr. Almarez is excited about her new position as associate professor.

d. She loves to sing and dance.

e. Dr. Almarez has taught management for more than 10 years.

Comprehensive Exercise 1—Principles 1–15

Teamwork. Ethics. Form a group of two to three students and use your creativity to rewrite the following sentences. While retaining the basic meaning of the original version, be sure to draw on your own unique personalities in determining the wording of the revised versions. Present your rewritten sentences to your instructor. (Objective 5)

1. Communication skills are important for success in business.
2. Using the Internet is important for students today.
3. Teamwork is important in business.
4. Last year was the best ever for the Corona del Mar girls' cross-country team.
5. The dress cannot be returned to the department store; the tags have been torn off and the dress has been worn.
6. Being ethical is important for many reasons.
7. Preparing for retirement is important to all individuals.
8. Achieving financial stability is important for each and every person.
9. Learning a foreign language is essential for conducting business abroad.
10. The key variables of performance are ability, motivation, clarity of expectations, and opportunity.

Comprehensive Exercise 2—Principles 1–15

Diversity. Change the language in the following sentences so that it is unbiased as to race, gender, culture, age, or disability, as appropriate: (Objective 4)

1. Jack is confined to a wheelchair. (*Hint*: Avoid emphasizing the limitation of the disability.)
2. That the company merged with a small company that was owned by an older, white female was the headline of the news release. (*Hint*: Avoid emphasizing age, race, and gender when it is not essential to the main point of the message.)
3. The exercise program was developed for handicapped people. (*Hint*: Avoid emphasizing the limitations of the disability.)
4. As you know, Mexicans take siestas because they are lazy. (*Hint*: Avoid implying that persons have limitations because of their nationality.)
5. This is obviously man's work. (*Hint*: Avoid language that is demeaning, patronizing, or limiting.)
6. The student should determine which type of math problem gives him the most difficulty and then ask the instructor for help. (*Hint*: Avoid language that is limiting.)
7. Dear Sirs: Please accept my application for the position as human resource manager. (*Hint*: Avoid language that is limiting.)

Comprehensive Exercise 3—Principles 1–15

Teamwork. Using unbiased gender language is a special challenge because of the structure of the English language. Form a group of four or five students and develop a list of ten biased words and the unbiased alternatives. Develop a sentence for each of the words and their alternatives.

TECHNOLOGY EXERCISES

1. **E-mail.** Send an e-mail message to your instructor explaining why you took the class. Apply the principles of business communication you have studied in this chapter.

There are Web exercises at **http://krizan.swcollege.com** to accompany this chapter.

MESSAGE ANALYSIS

Rewrite the well-intended but poorly written memo that follows. Apply the principles of business communication you have studied in this chapter. Include in your memo only the information you think is important for potential customers to know about your consulting services.

Are you faced with questions like, "Are distribution cost to high?" "How well are we servicing our customer's needs? Or "How can we improve getting our goods to market?"

If these questions are concerns then we can help you get some answers. Top Electronics, ABC Systems, and Nomo Technology are a few of the clients we have consulted with, providing favorable results by improving their logistic functions.

Our services include a logistic audit to evaluate your transportation department, warehouse operation and the ability to get your products to market. The enclosed brochure further details our services. With 10 years experience we can readily identify potential savings and formulate a set of recommendations designed to reduce your expenses and improve performance.

All we need to get started is a short initial visit to gather information. Please call us within the next few days so that we might be able to schedule a meeting.

GRAMMAR WORKSHOP

Correct the grammar, spelling, punctuation, style, and word choice errors in the following sentences:

1. Large amounts of our Colleagues are retiring, his positions either remain vacant; or, are filled by inadequate trained teachers.
2. Before going Sally packed her back pack laid out her clothes and read one chapter in Phyllis A. Whitneys book Start Flight.
3. Shiori Sakamoto PhD has been researching the fatal voyage of the Titantic which occurred in April 1912.
4. The guitar players strolled between the diners in the spanish restaurant.
5. Jose interrupted a private discussion among Patty and me.
6. All of the students had his resumes already to hand in at the beginning of english 101.
7. Mr. Ringi Nisimura a Financial Advisor gives people advise on money matters.
8. What is the amount of students' that will graduate in June?
9. Todays computer technology, and presentation software increases flexibility, capability and editing power.
10. Woman in technical education includes women who work in non traditional jobs.

CHAPTER

5 Developing Effective and Ethical Business Messages

Andrea Anast Tunks, vice president of a major international bank, with over 21 years of credit risk management experience

LET'S TALK BUSINESS The competition in today's business environment, and the expectation of constantly improving performance of public companies in a "hot" market, has resulted in a focus on current results. Decisions are often made based on the immediate impact on earnings and stock price rather than the implications for the long-term viability of the business. This myopic view can result in behavior contrary to the continuing health of our companies and the success of individual employees. The irony is that if we focus on the long-term health of our businesses, short-term benefits typically will accrue, albeit sometimes at a slower pace.

To be consistently successful in business, you must be able to communicate clearly, interact ethically, and operate honestly.

Communicate Clearly As you write, remember that the goal of business communications is to convey and support your point of view, not to impress the recipient with your vocabulary or prose. The real message can be lost in

(Continued)

[LEARNING OBJECTIVES]

[1] USE A THREE-STEP PROCESS FOR PLANNING AND COMPOSING EFFECTIVE BUSINESS MESSAGES.

[2] DESCRIBE HOW THE VOCABULARY LEVEL OF BUSINESS MESSAGES CAN BE DETERMINED.

[3] DESCRIBE HOW TO CHOOSE ETHICAL CONTENT FOR BUSINESS MESSAGES.

[4] EXPLAIN HOW TO ASSURE THE LEGALITY OF BUSINESS MESSAGES.

seemingly unending paragraphs of grandiloquent vocabulary, in a pedantic style that obscures the point with sheer bombast. In other words . . . keep it simple so your point doesn't get lost. Save your fancy vocabulary for fiction, and keep business communications at a high school level.

Interact Ethically Always say and do "the right thing" . . . if you don't, it *will* come back to haunt you when you least expect it. The "golden rule" can, and should, apply in the business world. In my experience with hundreds of businesses, those individuals that treat their customers, suppliers, bankers, and employees with respect, honesty, and consideration are consistently the most successful over time. They are perceived as having integrity and being trustworthy. They get the benefit of the doubt in close calls, and over time, people prefer to do business with them . . . even if it costs them more.

The implications of an ethical approach to printed communications are obvious. But remember, e-mails can be forwarded . . . they can also be saved to a disk, printed, and taken home as evidence. (I've seen e-mails that would make a litigator jump for joy.) Voice mails can also be forwarded, recorded, and transcribed. If in doubt, leave it out . . . or consult your attorney.

Operate Honestly Always assume that your written communications *will* get into the wrong hands. After you have finished a written communication, take a break and then reread it as an impartial third party.

The legality of your messages should be assured if you follow the above rules. Also remember that there are many types of business communication, and the rules should be applied consistently to each.

Best Formula I believe the best formula for business success is a combination of behaviors consistent with the long-term viability of the organization . . . in other words, the application of a sound set of business ethics or values.

The planning and composing process for developing all types of written and oral business messages is the same. The process consists of the following three tasks:

- Determine the message's purpose(s).
- Analyze the receiver(s) for the you–viewpoint.
- Compose the content of the message.

[NOTE 5.1]
Use the same planning and composing process for all messages.

Carrying out this process may take from a few seconds for a simple oral message to several days for a long written report. Following the process is essential for developing effective business messages.

[NOTE 5.2]
Analyze your messages.

Message analysis is a related aspect of developing effective business messages. Control the vocabulary level of your messages so that it fits your receivers. In addition, be sure that your messages are ethical and meet legal requirements.

This chapter discusses how to develop effective business messages. The how-to of planning, composing, and analyzing business messages is presented. Remember to keep in mind the importance of planning and sending the appropriate business message, as suggested in the following Communication Note.

COMMUNICATION NOTE

Letters, Memos, and E-Mail Can Send a Message About You

Beside obvious no-nos such as poor spelling and grammar, experts cite a number of things to bear in mind when writing. Here are a few of them:

[1] **Goal.** Before starting out, make sure you understand what your goal is and the message you want to deliver.
[2] **Clarity.** Make sure your points are clear and obvious. Avoid ambiguous language that might confuse readers.
[3] **Tone.** Carefully consider the feeling or impression you want to leave in your message.

As reported by David R. Olmos in "Letters, Memos, and E-Mail Can Send a Message About You," Los Angeles Times, *June 8, 1998, p. 13.*

Learning Objective [1]
USE A THREE-STEP PROCESS FOR PLANNING AND COMPOSING EFFECTIVE BUSINESS MESSAGES.

Planning and Composing Business Messages

[NOTE 5.3]
The process: Determine purpose, analyze receiver, and compose content.

The three-step process for planning and composing business messages is simple but critical to your success in communicating. The process incorporates and applies topics covered in Chapter 1, "Business Communication Foundations," and Chapter 4, "Principles of Business Communication."

[NOTE 5.4]
Message purpose will vary.

STEP 1: DETERMINE THE MESSAGE'S PURPOSE(S)

[NOTE 5.5]
First: Analyze the situation.

The primary and secondary purposes for a specific business message will vary depending on the communication situation.

[NOTE 5.6]
Who is the receiver? Does the message contain positive, neutral, negative, or persuasive information? What is the main content?

Analyze the Communication Situation Your first task in determining the purpose or purposes of a message is to decide what is involved in a specific communication situation. When analyzing the communication situation, you will want to ask yourself the following questions:

[1] Who will receive the message?

[2] Will the message be positive, neutral, negative, or persuasive for my receiver(s)?

[3] What will be the main content of the message—the main idea and the supporting ideas?

Figure 5.1 shows the parts of the communication situation analysis.

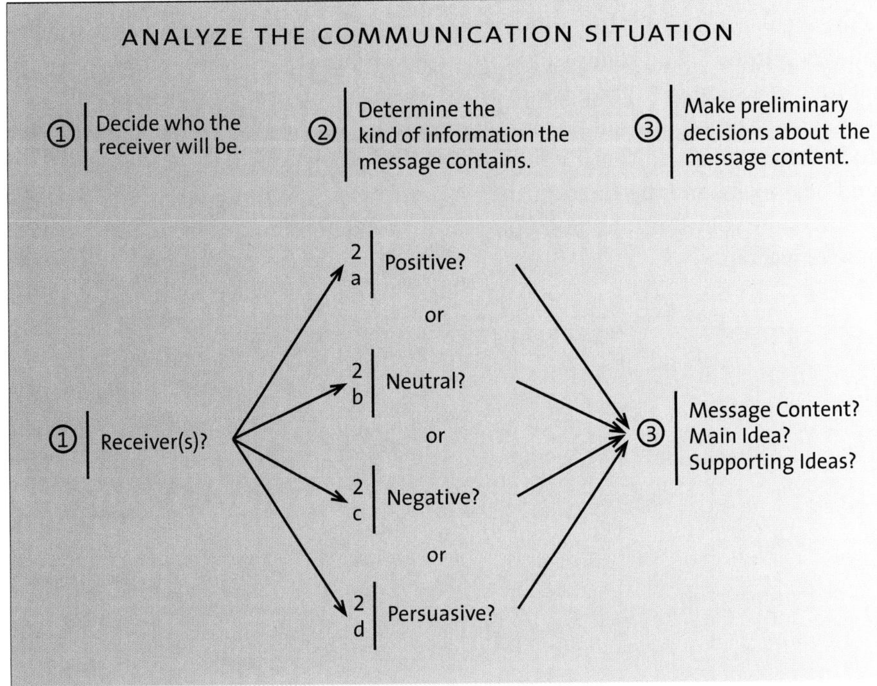
ANALYZE THE COMMUNICATION SITUATION
① Decide who the receiver will be.
② Determine the kind of information the message contains.
③ Make preliminary decisions about the message content.
① Receiver(s)?
2a Positive?
or
2b Neutral?
or
2c Negative?
or
2d Persuasive?
③ Message Content? Main Idea? Supporting Ideas?

Figure 5.1
Analyzing the Communication Situation

More specific questions you might ask yourself when analyzing the communication situation include the following:

[1] Can I say *yes* to an employee's request for a vacation during the first two weeks in August?

[2] How can I initiate a communication to my customers to promote a summer clearance sale?

[3] How do I say *no* to a customer who wants to return a computer for a full refund of its purchase price?

The analysis of the communication situation may be done mentally in a few seconds before you write a memo or place a telephone call. On the other hand, the communication situation analysis may involve collecting extensive information and may be written. This would be the case for an involved business report to be submitted to a board of directors.

[NOTE 5.7]
Analysis may take a few seconds or several days.

Establish Primary and Secondary Purposes Following the analysis of the communication situation, your second task is to establish the primary and secondary

[NOTE 5.8]
Second: Establish purpose within the framework of goals.

purposes of your message. This will be done within the framework of the four business communication goals:

[1] Receiver understanding

[2] Necessary receiver response

[3] Favorable relationship

[4] Organizational goodwill

[NOTE 5.9] Message purpose: Main and supporting ideas.

[NOTE 5.10] The purpose can be simple.

The message's main idea is the primary purpose, and its supporting ideas are the secondary purposes. For example, assume that you can say yes to an employee's request to take a vacation during the first two weeks of August. This message can be oral, will be positive, and will be sent to a receiver you know well. The message will include the yes, plus additional information about work priorities—work that should be done before the vacation and work that can wait until afterwards. Figure 5.2 shows how your purposes might appear for this communication situation if they were written.

Figure 5.2
Simple Message Purposes

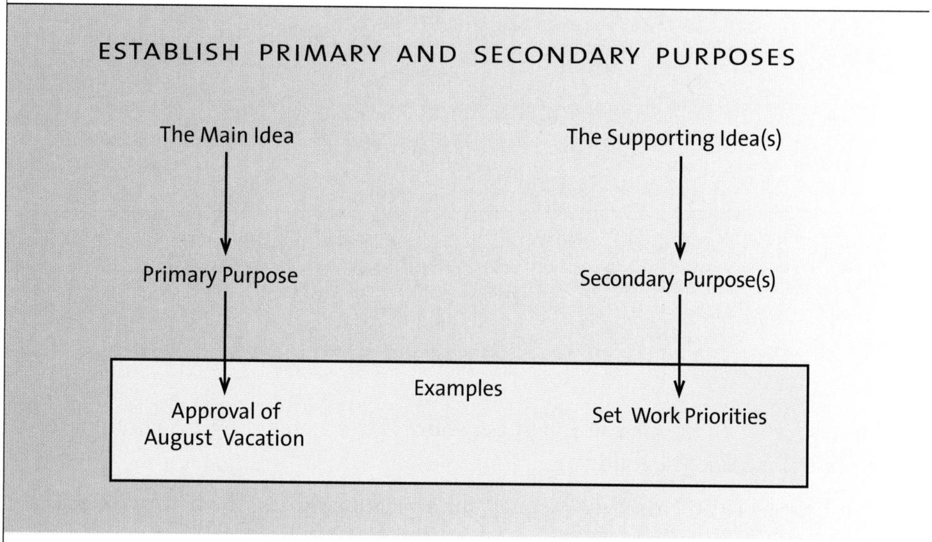

ESTABLISH PRIMARY AND SECONDARY PURPOSES

The Main Idea → Primary Purpose → Approval of August Vacation

The Supporting Idea(s) → Secondary Purpose(s) → Set Work Priorities

Examples

[NOTE 5.11] The purpose can be involved.

Another example shows how establishing primary and secondary purposes for a specific message can be more involved. Assume that the message you are developing is a written annual departmental report. The message category will likely be mixed. There may be some positive information, some neutral information, some negative information, and some persuasive information in the report. The receivers of the report could include employees who report to you, managers at your level in other departments, and upper management of the organization. The primary and secondary purposes for your departmental report might be as shown in Figure 5.3.

When you have analyzed the communication situation and have determined the primary and secondary purposes of the message, you are ready to analyze your receivers to enable you to use the you–viewpoint.

Involved Message Purposes

Primary Purposes

1. To document clearly the department's accomplishments for 200–.
2. To persuade upper management to meet the department's future needs.

Secondary Purposes

1. To instill pride of accomplishment in the department's employees.
2. To inform managers at your own level of the department's activities and needs.
3. To inform upper management of the contributions your department and its employees have made.
4. To convince upper management to finance the department's continuing operation and proposed projects.
5. To maintain favorable relationships with others.
6. To build organizational goodwill for the department.

Figure 5.3
Involved Message Purposes for Department Report

STEP 2: ANALYZE THE RECEIVER(S) FOR THE YOU–VIEWPOINT

The second step in planning and composing an effective written or oral business message is to analyze the receiver or receivers for the you–viewpoint. Because this step is discussed fully in Chapter 1, only a brief summary of it is given here.

Analyze the Receiver For some communication situations, you will know the receiver of your message quite well. Little or no analysis of the receiver may be necessary. By contrast, it may be necessary for you to do a careful, detailed analysis of the receiver in other communication situations. Whether your analysis of the receiver requires a limited or an extensive amount of research, the approach is the same. You analyze your receiver in four areas—knowledge, interests, attitudes, and emotional state—as shown in Figure 5.4.

[NOTE 5.12]
Analyze receiver's knowledge, interests, opinions, and emotional state.

If you have multiple receivers of your message, you need to analyze each receiver in the group. For example, if you are giving a speech to a Rotary Club, you should visualize the various members of the audience. If you are writing a memo to five other people in your office, analyze each receiver. To achieve the goals and purposes of your message with all your receivers, the message must be understandable to the receiver in the group with the least amount of knowledge about the subject, the lowest vocabulary level, and the most emotional opposition to the message.

[NOTE 5.13]
If you have multiple receivers, analyze each one.

[NOTE 5.14]
A message must be composed so all receivers can understand it.

Your analysis of the receiver will give you better information about the receiver's vocabulary, interests, possible biases, and emotional state. From your analysis you can determine the ideas, words, and approach that will communicate best in each situation. This kind of information is essential if you are to use the you–viewpoint.

Use the You–Viewpoint Based on the analysis of your receiver, you will be able to use the powerful you–viewpoint in developing your message. When using the you–viewpoint, give highest priority to what you think will be your receiver's perception of the message. You are trying to achieve receiver understanding and to obtain appropriate receiver reaction. The receiver's perception of your message is your message.

[NOTE 5.15]
Use the you–viewpoint for receiver understanding and reaction.

Figure 5.4
Analysis of the Receiver

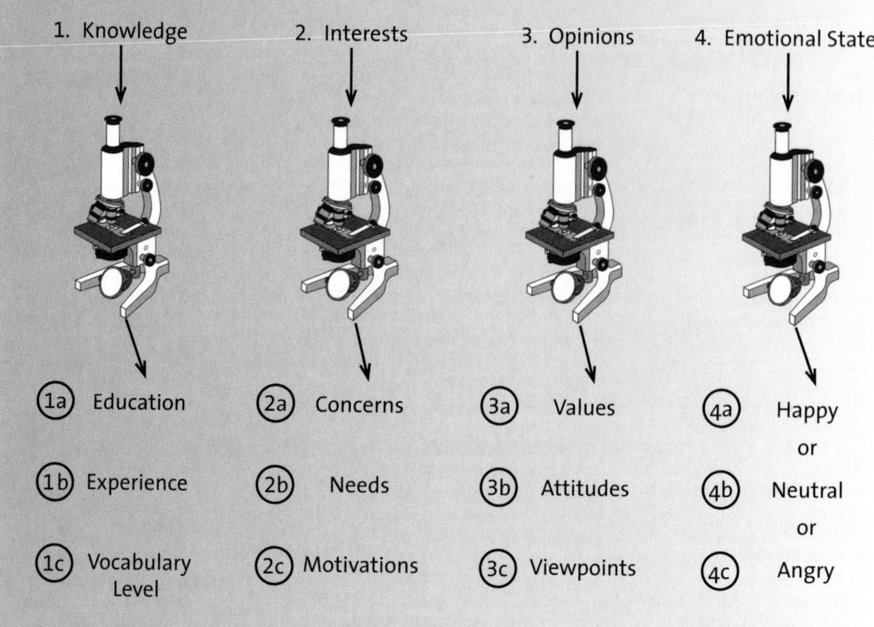

[NOTE 5.16] The receiver's perception is the message.

[NOTE 5.17] Using the you–viewpoint is critical to success.

Using the you–viewpoint means choosing words that are understandable and acceptable to your receiver. It also means considering the receiver's knowledge, interests, opinions, and emotional state. Using the you–viewpoint in composing the content of your message is critical to the success of your message.

STEP 3: COMPOSE THE CONTENT OF THE MESSAGE

[NOTE 5.18] Six tasks are involved in composing message content.

The third step in developing an effective business message is to compose the content of the message. Composing the message content involves the following six tasks: (1) selecting the type of message, (2) selecting the organizational plan, (3) outlining the content, (4) drafting the message, (5) editing and revising the message, and (6) proofreading the final product. See Figure 5.5 for the six tasks involved in composing message content.

[NOTE 5.19] Composing tasks can be done mentally or on paper.

Many of the composing tasks may be done mentally for simple, short messages. Which tasks you do on paper will depend on the complexity and the length of the message.

[NOTE 5.20] First: Select the type of message.

Select the Type of Message Your initial task is to decide whether to use a written message or an oral message. Once you make this choice, you have many variations of either type of message to consider. For example, written messages can be handwritten, typed, or printed. They can take the form of e-mail, diskette, letter, memo, written report, fax, or many other forms. Oral messages include telephone calls, voice mail, face-to-face meetings, small group presentations, and

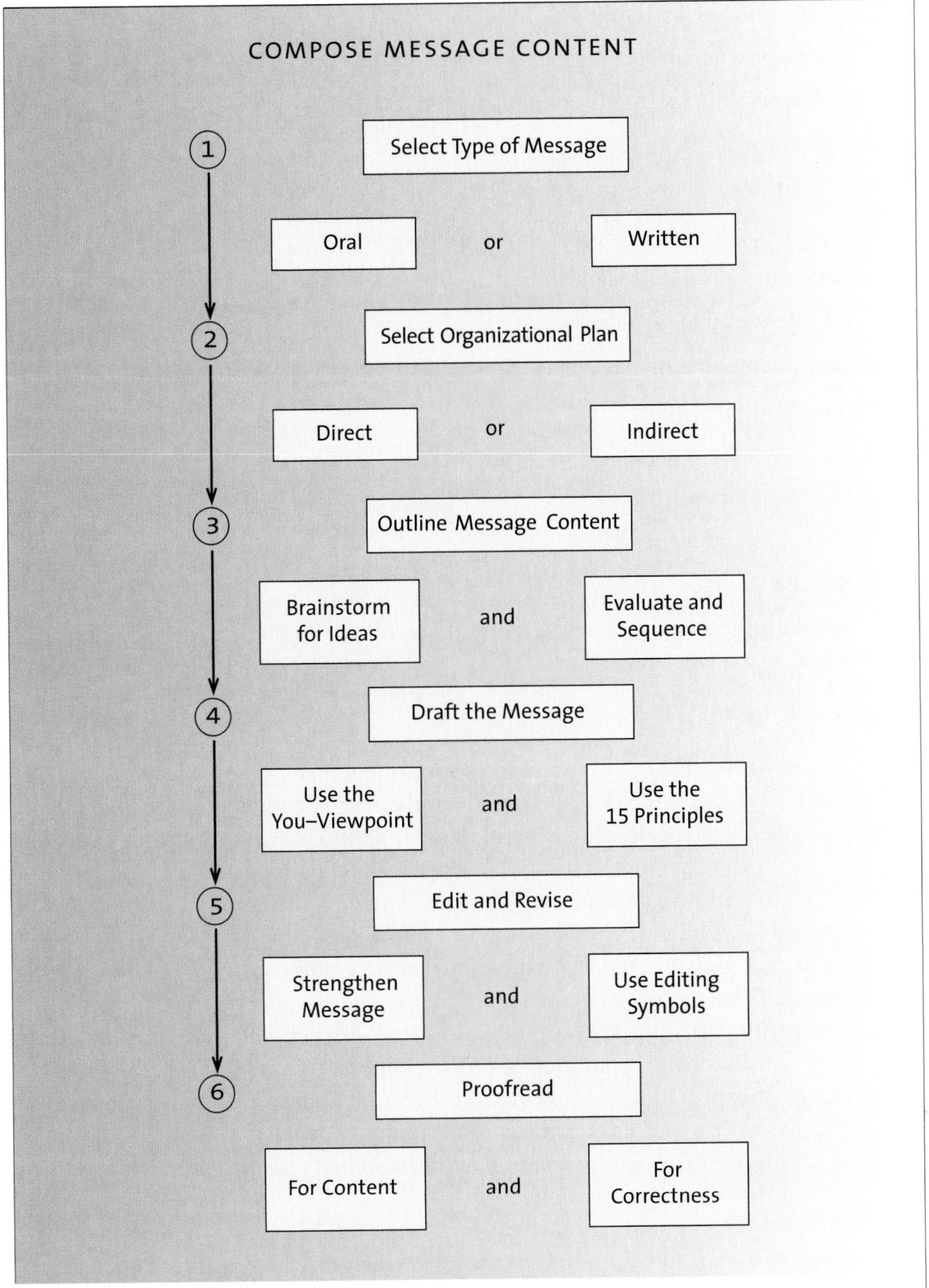

COMPOSE MESSAGE CONTENT

1. Select Type of Message
   - Oral or Written
2. Select Organizational Plan
   - Direct or Indirect
3. Outline Message Content
   - Brainstorm for Ideas and Evaluate and Sequence
4. Draft the Message
   - Use the You–Viewpoint and Use the 15 Principles
5. Edit and Revise
   - Strengthen Message and Use Editing Symbols
6. Proofread
   - For Content and For Correctness

Figure 5.5
Composing the Message Content

public speeches. Each of these messages varies in the way it can be composed and transmitted.

The advantages of oral messages are that they

[1] Can be quickly transmitted

[2] Are more personal

[3] Allow immediate feedback

[NOTE 5.21]
Each type of message has advantages and disadvantages.

The disadvantages are that they

[1] Lack a permanent record

[2] Are unsuitable for highly complex material

[3] Permit only limited reflection by the receiver

The advantages of written messages are that they

[1] Provide a permanent record

[2] Accommodate lengthy and complex content

[3] Can be reread and studied

[4] Can be edited and revised

The disadvantages are that they

[1] Are generally transmitted slowly

[2] Are more formal

[3] Delay and reduce feedback

[4] Require storage

[NOTE 5.22] Select the best type of message for the situation.

Based on the advantages and disadvantages of oral and written messages, you can select the type of message that will best achieve your purposes and best communicate with your receiver.

[NOTE 5.23] Second: Select an organizational plan.

[NOTE 5.24] Use the direct plan or the indirect plan.

Select an Organizational Plan Two organizational plans are used for both oral and written messages: the direct (deductive) plan and the indirect (inductive) plan. There are many variations of these two plans. In Part 3 and Part 5 of this text, alternative ways to use the direct and indirect approaches are discussed. These alternatives apply to both written and oral messages. The direct and indirect plans for messages are shown in Figure 5.6.

[NOTE 5.25] The direct plan is best for positive or neutral information; the indirect plan is best for negative information or persuasion.

The **direct plan** attempts to achieve the primary purpose (main idea) of the message immediately by placing the main idea in the opening. The details supporting or explaining the primary purpose follow the opening. The **indirect plan** opens on neutral ground or on a point of agreement. The opening is followed by supporting reasons or explanations and moves to the primary purpose later in the message. Research has shown that in most situations the direct plan is more effective for positive information or neutral information, and the indirect plan is more effective for negative information or persuasion.

When developing international business messages, keep in mind that many cultures around the world communicate almost exclusively using the indirect plan. Included in the cultures that respond more positively to the indirect plan are Asian, Spanish-speaking, Middle Eastern, Southern European, and cultures located near the equator. Northern American and Northern European cultures respond more positively to the direct plan.

After selecting the type of message you will use—written or oral—and the organizational plan for your message—direct or indirect—you are ready to outline message content.

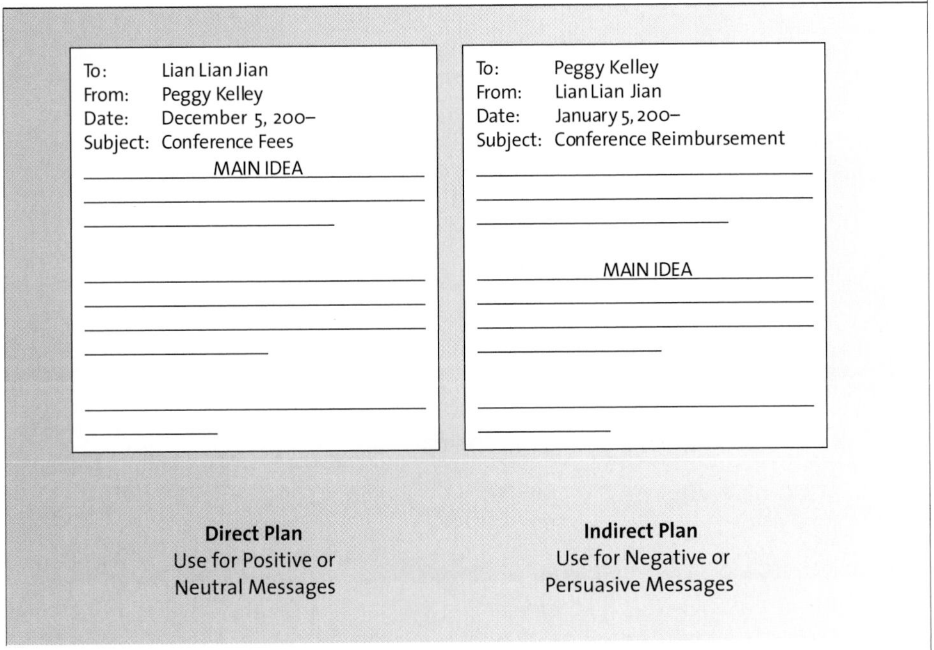

To: Lian Lian Jian
From: Peggy Kelley
Date: December 5, 200–
Subject: Conference Fees
MAIN IDEA

Direct Plan
Use for Positive or
Neutral Messages

To: Peggy Kelley
From: Lian Lian Jian
Date: January 5, 200–
Subject: Conference Reimbursement

MAIN IDEA

Indirect Plan
Use for Negative or
Persuasive Messages

Figure 5.6
Organizational Plans for Messages

Outline the Message Content In outlining message content, you are simply organizing your ideas for the message in your mind or on paper, diskette, or other medium.

[NOTE 5.26]
Third: Outline the message content.

Start the outlining process by brainstorming for ideas. **Brainstorming** involves (1) concentrating on both the purpose(s) of your message and your receiver(s), and (2) listing all the ideas that you think should be included in the message. Let this activity take place randomly. Do not evaluate the ideas in detail; just record them. As you do this, you may find it necessary to gather helpful information from files, other employees, or other sources.

[NOTE 5.27]
Keeping purpose(s) and receiver(s) in mind, brainstorm content.

Assume, for example, that you have received a claim letter from a customer asking for a refund for a piano that she bought on sale. Although the customer's letter is not very well written, the message is clear—she wants her money back. You will have to tell her no—send her a negative message—because you do not give refunds for items bought on sale. You brainstorm ideas for the content of your response. Your notes, written on the claim letter you received, might appear as in Figure 5.7 on page 131.

The second part of the outlining task is to evaluate and sequence the ideas you developed during your brainstorming session. Arrange the ideas you want to use in a logical order following the organizational plan you chose. In your response to the claim letter, you will want to use the indirect plan because you must give the customer negative information. The order in which you would sequence ideas for the positive message is shown in Figure 5.7 by the number in parentheses following each idea. After completing the sequencing of ideas, you are ready to draft the message.

[NOTE 5.28]
Evaluate and sequence ideas.

Draft the Message Using your mental or recorded notes from the outlining process, you next draft the message. You may draft the message by dictating,

[NOTE 5.29]
Fourth: Draft the message.

Employees brainstorm for ideas for a message.

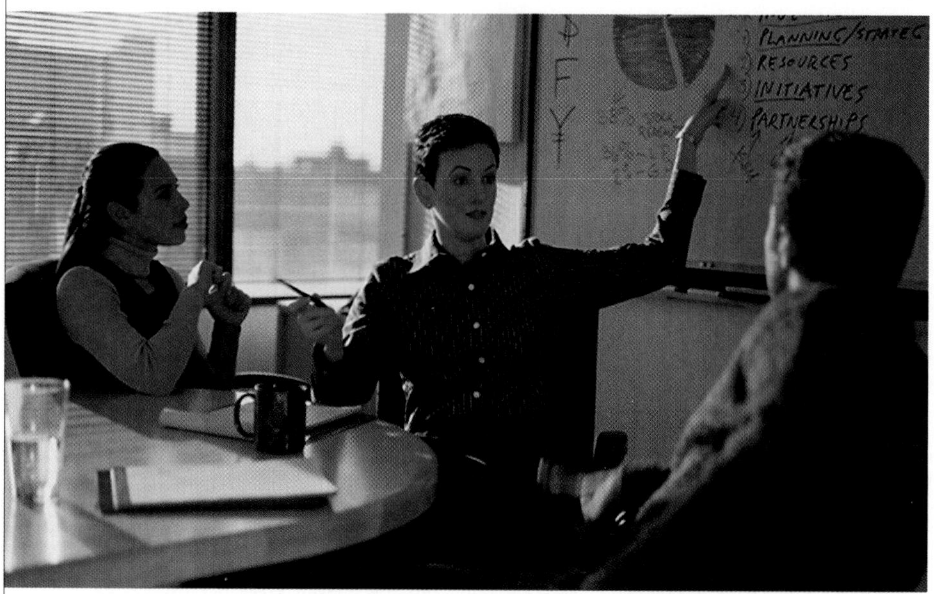

keyboarding, or handwriting it. It is important to use the 15 principles of business communication given in Chapter 4 when drafting messages. Also, be sure to use the you–viewpoint. Put yourself in the place of your receiver.

[NOTE 5.30] You may have one or more drafts.

For simple situations your first draft may be the final version of the message. For difficult messages you may have a rough first draft and then one or more improved draft versions of the message. With the development of word processing software, it is much easier to have multiple drafts of messages because only the changes need to be keyed. Word processing software and its features are more fully explained in Chapter 3.

[NOTE 5.31] Word processing software makes second and succeeding drafts easier to do.

You may or may not prepare a complete draft for an oral message. You may transmit oral messages from mental notes or written notes. If you prepare a complete draft of a speech, you should use notes for the actual presentation of the speech. Reading an oral message from a complete, written draft is not recommended except in circumstances where you must be extremely cautious in what you say. An example of this would be reading a prepared statement during a press conference.

[NOTE 5.32] If you know you will edit and revise, just get something in writing at the start.

If you are drafting a message that you know you will edit and revise, it is more important to get something down in writing than it is to get the initial copy perfect. Experienced writers know that the clearest, most effective communication results from editing and revising drafts of messages.

[NOTE 5.33] The clearest messages come from editing and revising drafts.

You will, of course, prepare complete drafts of your written messages. For example, the first rough draft of the negative message to Ronalee Reid about the piano is shown in Figure 5.8 on page 132. After reviewing the first draft of a message, you can either decide that it will be your final version or that you will edit and revise it.

[NOTE 5.34] Fifth: Edit and revise the message.

Edit and Revise the Message When editing and revising, keep the primary and secondary purposes of the message in mind. Edit the message from your receiver's point of view using the principles of business communication to guide your improvements.

Purpose of message:
Reject request for refund on piano.
Maintain customer's business.
Increase organizational goodwill.

3623 Happy Valley Lane
Lafayette, CA 94549
April 24, 200–

Ideas for Content: Express appreciation for purchase. (1)
Neutral spending – "do all we can." (2)
Recommend purchase of $125.95 for foam baffles. (7)
Thank for making Yamaha part of their life. (8)
Amount of savings – $4,000. (4)

Mr. Richard Spear
Store Manager
Pacific Fields Piano
1800 Mount Diablo Blvd.
Lafayette, CA 94549

Dear Mr. Spear:

I want my money back on the G2F PE Yamaha acoustic piano I bought from you during your "Winter Sale." After I had the piano delivered, my neighbors complained that my son's piano practicing made too much noise. This piano will not work in this house! Please send me the refund check for $13,899.75, and I will have Orange Coast Piano Movers return it to your Lafayette store.

Sincerely,

Ronalee Reid

Ronalee Reid

Volume purchases/ cut overhead. (5)

Reinforce purchase decision. (3)
No–All sales final. (6)

Figure 5.7
Brainstorming the Message Content on Claim Letter

Editing and revising are the best ways to strengthen the quality of your messages so that they achieve their purpose in the most effective manner. The results of editing and revising can be seen in Figure 5.9 on page 133. Note the clarity, power, and you–viewpoint that have been added in this second draft of the letter.

[NOTE 5.35]
Keep purpose(s) and receiver(s) in mind while editing and revising.

Standard symbols for editing and revising, used in Figure 5.9, are shown in Figure 5.10 on page 134. Editing symbols are helpful devices for communication between the originator and the preparer of messages. It is suggested that you learn to use these symbols in your editing, revising, and proofreading efforts.

[NOTE 5.36]
To aid communication between message preparer and originator, use editing symbols.

Give the editing and revising tasks the highest priority for important or lengthy, complex messages. This is your opportunity to strengthen your word choice, sentence development, and paragraph formation. You can check that you have used the chosen organizational plan effectively. In addition, revising gives you another chance to add distinctiveness—a part of your personality—to the message.

[NOTE 5.37]
Give the editing and revising tasks highest priority.

You may edit and revise some messages many times. Long business reports often are revised three, four, or more times. Continue editing and revising until you have a version of the message in the you–viewpoint that is clear, concise, and businesslike.

1800 Mount Diablo Blvd.
Lafayette, CA 94549
(714) 283-5000

May 1, 200–

Mrs. Ronalee Reid
3623 Happy Valley Lane
Lafayette, CA 94549

Dear Mrs. Reid:

We appreciate your recent purchase of a G2F PE Yamaha acoustic piano. You certainly have chosen an extremely high-quality parlor grand piano that will give you many years of joy and satisfaction. A Yamaha piano is the instrument of choice by many of the world's top artists. We want to ensure that enjoyment is possible.

You made a good decision when you bought a G2F PE Yamaha acoustic piano during the Pacific Fields Piano "Winter Sale." The tremendous savings you got on this sale totaling almost $4,000 were made possible in two ways: We (1) buy merchandise in large volumes whenever we can, and (2) cut overhead and pass the savings on to our customers.

One of the ways we cut overhead is to make all sales final on items purchased during the "Winter Sale." We make every effort to be sure all our customers are aware of this policy by noting it in all advertisements and posting signs throughout the store.

You will be very glad to learn that you can easily make the piano quieter by purchasing a set of foam baffles. These foam baffles are installed under the piano between the ribs in order to quiet the sound. For $125.95 you can purchase the foam baffles that have complete directions and guides for installation. You can either "do-it yourself" or have one of our technicians take care of it for you at cost. Please call us collect at (714) 555-9011 and tell us your preference.

Once again, thank you for making Yamaha part of your life.

Sincerely yours,

Richard Spear

Richard Spear, Manager
Keyboard Division

Figure 5.8
First Rough Draft of a Negative Message

[NOTE 5.38]
Sixth: Proofread the message.

[NOTE 5.39]
Proofread to catch all spelling, punctuation, and grammar errors and to check format.

[NOTE 5.40]
Follow these steps when proofreading a document.

Proofread the Message The proofreading task is different from the editing and revising task. Proofreading is checking each word to be sure that it is spelled correctly. It is assuring yourself that proper punctuation and grammar have been used, that your sentences are complete and properly constructed, and that your format meets appropriate standards.

Careful proofreading involves (1) reading the message for content and (2) reading it again for correct grammar, spelling, and punctuation. Some proofreaders can find more spelling errors by reading the copy backwards. If you are using word

1800 Mount Diablo Blvd.
Lafayette, CA 94549
(714) 283-5000

May 1, 200–

Mrs. Ronalee Reid
3623 Happy Valley Lane
Lafayette, CA 94549

Dear Mrs. Reid:

~~We appreciate~~ Your recent purchase of a G2F PE Yamaha acoustic piano *is appreciated*. You ~~certainly~~ have chosen a~~n extremely~~ high-quality parlor grand piano that *can* ~~will~~ give you many years of joy and satisfaction. A Yamaha piano is the instrument of choice by many of the world's top artists. We want to ensure that enjoyment is possible *for you with your new piano.*

You made a *wise* ~~good~~ decision when you bought a G2F PE Yamaha acoustic piano during the ~~Pacific Fields Piano~~ "Winter Sale." The tremendous savings *of* almost *$4,000 that* you *realized* ~~got~~ on this *purchase* ~~sale totaling~~ ~~$4,000~~ were made possible in two ways: (1) We buy merchandise in large volumes ~~whenever we can~~, and (2) *we* cut overhead and pass the savings on to ~~our~~ *the* customers.

One of the ways we cut overhead is to make all sales final on items purchased during the "Winter Sale." We make every effort to be sure all our customers are aware of this policy by noting it in all advertisements and posting signs throughout the store.

You will be ~~very~~ glad to *know* ~~learn~~ that you can easily make the piano quieter by purchasing a set of foam baffles. These foam baffles are installed under the piano between the ribs in order to quiet the sound. For *only* $125.95 you can purchase the foam baffles that have complete directions ~~and guides~~ for *their* installation. You can either "do-it yourself" or have one of our technicians take care of it for you at cost. Please call us collect at (714) 555-9011 and tell us your preference.

Once again, thank you for making Yamaha part of your life.

Sincerely yours,

Richard Spear

Richard Spear, Manager
Keyboard Division

Figure 5.9
Edited and Revised Negative Letter

processing software, you may have a spell-check feature to assist you in finding errors. You may also have document analysis software (style checker) to help you detect possible errors. Spell checkers and style checkers do not eliminate the need for proofreading; they just make the task easier.

[NOTE 5.41]
Spell checkers and style checkers assist with proofreading.

Errors detract from the clarity of the message and reduce your credibility in the mind of the receiver. Therefore, you or some other competent person should proofread each message carefully. As the one who submits the report or signs the letter or memo, you have the ultimate responsibility for both the

Figure 5.10
Editing Symbols

EDITING SYMBOLS

Defined		Examples
Paragraph	¶	¶ Begin a new paragraph at this point.
Insert a character	∧	Insrt a letter here.
Delete	ℓ	Delete these words. Disregard.
Do not change	stet or ------	the previous correction.
Transpose	tr	To transpose is to around turn.
Move to the left	[	Move this copy to the left.
Move to the right	]	Move this copy to the right.
No paragraph	no ¶	no ¶ Do not begin a new paragraph here.
Delete and close up.		Delete the hyphen from pre-empt and close the space.
Set in caps	Caps or ≡	a sentence begins with a capital letter.
Set in lower case	lc	This Word should not be capitalized.
Insert a period	⊙	Insert a period ⊙
Quotation marks		Quotation marks and
Comma		a comma should be placed here he said.
Insert space	#	Space between thesewords.
Apostrophe		An apostrophe is whats needed here.
Hyphen	=	Add a hyphen to African American
Close up		Close the extra spa ce.
Use superior figure		Footnote this sentence.
Set in italic	italic or ______	Set the words, sine qua non, in italics.
Move up		This word is too low.
Move down		This word is too high.

content and the accuracy. Proofreading procedures include the following steps:

[1] If you are using a word processing program, use your spell checker and grammar checker to check for errors. Next, proofread the copy on screen and print a copy of the document in double-spaced format.

[2] Proofread the copy by reading the document aloud from beginning to end, focusing on the content. Reread the document looking for spelling errors, grammatical errors, punctuation errors, and style errors. Pay special attention to personal names, numbers, addresses, information in brackets, words that are capitalized, and unusual words.

[3] After you have completed proofreading the document, ask a colleague or associate to proofread the document. It is better to have another person proofread the document because you will be tired of looking at it. If you have columns of numbers, consider reading the document aloud with a partner.

[4] Make the corrections as required and then reprint the document for an additional reading.

Several proven procedures and techniques for effective proofreading can be found in books at the library. You may also check the Online Writing Lab (OWL) at the Purdue University Web site at **http://owl.english.purdue.edu/** or the Resources for Writers Web site by Jack Lynch at **http://andromeda.rutgers.edu/~jlynch/** for additional guidelines on proven methods of proofreading.

After completing the tasks involved in composing the content of your message, you arrive at its final version. This version should be understood clearly by your receiver, stimulate the action you want, build a favorable relationship between you and the receiver, and increase organizational goodwill. In addition, your message should achieve its specific purposes for the communication situation.

[NOTE 5.42]
Following the planning and composing process will achieve the goals and purposes of your message.

Determining Vocabulary Level

As you know, one of your primary concerns in composing effective business messages is using a vocabulary level that your receiver will understand. **Vocabulary level**, as used in this book, refers to the level of difficulty of the words and combinations of words in messages.

[NOTE 5.43]
Message analysis includes determining vocabulary level to assure receiver understanding.

READABILITY FORMULAS

There are several readability formulas you can use to calculate vocabulary levels for your messages. These formulas—such as the Gunning, Flesch, Dale-Chall, and Fry—are described in materials available in most libraries or on the Web. They generally measure the average length of sentences and the percentage of "difficult" words. Although the counting necessary to use the formulas can be done manually, several of the formulas have been computerized and can be easily used with electronic media. Many grammar-checker software programs are able to calculate the vocabulary level of your message.

Learning Objective [2]
DESCRIBE HOW THE VOCABULARY LEVEL OF BUSINESS MESSAGES CAN BE DETERMINED.

[NOTE 5.44]
Readability formulas can be used to check vocabulary levels.

READABILITY RATINGS

[NOTE 5.45] Readability ratings show approximate grade level.

The vocabulary level ratings obtained from readability formulas generally reflect the approximate grade level a person would need to understand the written material. For example, a rating of 12 would mean that a person would have to be able to read at the twelfth-grade level to comprehend the material fully.

[NOTE 5.46] Common sense must be used with readability ratings.

Readability analysis does not check the actual words you use or the manner in which you combine those words into sentences. An analysis will not show whether the writing is accurate or inaccurate, interesting or dull, valuable or not valuable to a receiver. Use readability ratings as guides, and use common sense in applying them.

A message may have a low readability rating because it uses short words and short sentences even though it uses difficult technical words. By contrast, a message may have a high readability rating because it uses long words and long sentences, even though the sentences are easy to understand and the words are familiar. In addition, an appropriate grade level for a message does not necessarily guarantee that the message will communicate effectively. An inappropriate grade-level rating for a message, however, does mean that the message should be examined for word choice and sentence length.

VOCABULARY LEVELS

[NOTE 5.47] A message at too high a level will not be understood; too low is insulting.

As you compose a message for a given communication situation, keep in mind the estimated vocabulary level of your receiver. A message at too high a vocabulary level will not be understood clearly by your receiver. A message at too low a vocabulary level will insult your receiver, or not hold his or her attention and interest.

[NOTE 5.48] The middle-level receiver is between grades 8 and 12. Most high school graduates read at grade levels 10 to 12.

The middle-level receiver's vocabulary level will fall between grades 8 and 12 for a typical business person. Most high school graduates have vocabulary levels between grades 10 and 12. Business messages written at the eighth- to twelfth-grade levels will communicate clearly with most receivers.

Readability formulas are important tools for analyzing your messages. Use these tools regularly to analyze the vocabulary levels of form letters or memos, newsletters, speeches, magazines, books, and similar materials that will be read (or heard) by many receivers. Use these tools periodically to check the vocabulary levels of your messages to only one receiver.

Being Ethical

[NOTE 5.49] Being ethical is essential for success.

Being ethical in your communication is essential to a successful personal life and business career. Effective interpersonal relationships are built on trust, honesty, and fairness. Promises made are kept. Fair disclosure of information is provided.

[NOTE 5.50] Unethical messages are costly.

Being ethical is enlightened self-interest. You will pay far more in time, money, and effort to repair the damage caused by false messages than truthful, forthcoming messages would cost in the first place. In addition, it is not always possible to repair the damage caused by an unethical message. Your credibility is lost, your interpersonal relationships are destroyed, and your career is impaired.

HOW YOU CAN BE ETHICAL

How can you be sure you are an ethical communicator? First, you determine exactly what ethical communication is. Second, you adopt principles or develop systems that work best for you in choosing ethical content for your messages.

Defining Ethical Communication The word **ethics** is derived from the Greek word *ethos,* meaning character. Being ethical means doing what is right to achieve what is good. In business communication what is right refers to the responsibility to include information in your messages that ought to be there. What is good refers to the end result of the communication. The ethical end result is to strive for the highest good attainable for all of those involved in the communication. Therefore, **ethical communication** strives for the highest good for all involved and provides information that is fully adequate for the circumstance, truthful in every sense, and not deceptive in any way.

[NOTE 5.51]
Being ethical means
- Doing what is right
- Achieving the highest good

Choosing Ethical Content for Your Messages Choosing ethical content for messages requires the same analytical and practical skills as does sound business leadership. Being ethical in your communication requires that you determine—from among all the alternatives—the right and good information in given situations. Figures 5.11 and 5.12 show contrasting choices for message content.

Learning Objective [3]
DESCRIBE HOW TO CHOOSE ETHICAL CONTENT FOR BUSINESS MESSAGES.

[NOTE 5.52]
Choosing ethical content requires analytical skills.

ETHICS IN BUSINESS

Today we frequently learn about unethical behavior in business and government through the news media. Insider trading, bribery, misleading advertising, misrepresentation of facts, cover-ups, and stonewalling are seemingly common.

[NOTE 5.53]
Unethical behavior receives much publicity.

In fact, only a small percentage of business and professional people behave in unethical ways. Those who are unethical do not succeed in the long run, and most of them are not successful even in the short run. Millions of business transactions based on trust and honesty are successfully completed each day. Merchandise is fairly advertised, orders are received, and quality products are shipped and payment is made on time. If businesses and their customers did not relate this way, businesses could not exist.

[NOTE 5.54]
Most people are ethical.

In our modern global economy, managers are facing new issues on how to operate ethically in foreign lands. To conduct business ethically in another culture, managers must be aware of that culture's values and ethics. A Web site for business ethics in different countries can be found at **http://www.pitt.edu/~ethics/**. Companies must help managers distinguish between practices that are merely different from those that are wrong. "Values in Tension: Ethics Away From Home" in the following Communication Note outlines the guiding principles that shape the ethical behavior of companies.

COMMUNICATION NOTE

Values in Tension: Ethics Away From Home

When it comes to shaping ethical behavior, companies must be guided by three principles: (1) respect for core human values, which determine the absolute moral threshold for all business activities; (2) respect for local traditions; and (3) the belief that context matters when deciding what is right and what is wrong.

As reported by Thomas Donaldson in "Values in Tension: Ethics Away From Home," Harvard Business Review, *September–October 1996, p. 52.*

BIKES, INC.

INTEROFFICE MEMO

To: All Employees
From: Bill McKeiver, President
Date: February 1, 200–
Subject: New Shift

Beginning on February 3, 200–, and for an indeterminate time, there will be a newly established third shift running from 12 midnight to 8 a.m. One third of the employees in each department on the 8 a.m. to 4 p.m. shift and one third on the 4 p.m. to 12 midnight shift will be assigned to the new midnight shift. The employees who will have their shifts changed will be notified via a paycheck insert tomorrow.

Lead time is unreasonably short.

No explanation for the action is given.

Lacks consid... of what is g... the employe...

Figure 5.11
An Unethical Message

[NOTE 5.55]
Today, about 90 percent of large U.S. companies have codes of ethics.

The most successful businesses are managed and operated by ethical employees. Research shows that today about 90 percent of all Fortune 500 companies have codes of ethics to help guide their employees' behavior. Codes of conduct must provide clear direction about ethical behavior when the temptation to behave unethically is strongest. The pronouncement in a code of conduct that bribery is unacceptable is useless unless accompanied by guidelines for gift giving and suggested employee responses to unethical situations such as offers of bribes. Executives must practice the ethical standards outlined in the codes of ethics if the company is to have a successful ethics program. The Science Applications International Corporation (SAIC) is an example of an organization with a well-established and defined code of ethics that communicates the conduct that is expected of all employees. The SAIC *credo* is shown in Figure 5.13.

[NOTE 5.56]
After years of inattention, businesses are now stressing ethical behavior.

Many companies have training sessions in which the codes are discussed and procedures for assuring compliance throughout the company are explained. Lockheed Martin, an aerospace company, has gone a step further by creating an innova-

BIKES, INC.

INTEROFFICE MEMO

To: All Employees
From: Bill McKeiver, President
Date: February 1, 200–
Subject: New Shift

As you are aware, we are experiencing sharply increasing customer demand for our bikes. Such demand improves the company's outlook and strengthens employee security in these trying economic times. Meeting the increase in demand, however, is overloading our equipment and causing machine failures and unacceptable downtime.

To meet the demand and to solve the equipment problems, Employee/Management Group C recommends that, for a three-month trial period, a third shift running from 12 midnight to 8 a.m. be added. I am approving this recommendation.

We will implement the third shift on March 1. The employees on the third shift will be paid a 10 percent bonus. Because we will need one-third of the employees from each department from the 8 a.m. and 4 p.m. shifts to move to the third shift, we are seeking volunteers who are willing to change their shifts. Volunteers will be accepted on a first-come, first-served basis. If there are not enough volunteers to reach the one-third departmental goals, employees will be drawn by lot to serve on the new shift on a weekly rotating basis.

Your support of this new approach to meeting current customer demand will be greatly appreciated. If the higher level of demand continues throughout the three-month trial period of the new shift, a reassessment of how we will meet the demand will be made. Alternatives to be considered at that time will be either to continue the third shift or to increase investment in production equipment.

If you are interested in volunteering for the third shift for the three-month trial, call the Human Resources Department at extension 3636.

ound infor- is given.

entation air.

Employees were involved in the decision.

Full information is provided on the plan.

Action required is clear and easy to take.

Figure 5.12
An Ethical Message

tive site on the World Wide Web that gives employees, customers, and suppliers access to the company's ethical code and a chance to voice complaints and concerns.

The use of toll-free hot lines has been on the rise in corporate America as a way for employees to obtain advice on ethical matters. For example, the Sears Assistance Line[1] provides Sears associates, contractors, and vendors with advice on ethical concerns. The Assistance Line has six full-time employees trained to answer questions and receives about 15,000 calls annually.

Most businesses now realize the importance of a strong sense of individual and corporate values. The following examples of ethical and unethical communication can serve to illustrate the importance of ethics in business.

[NOTE 5.57]
Examples of ethical communication situations: Human resources cases.

HUMAN RESOURCES CASES

Texaco Incorporated On January 6, 1999, Texaco Incorporated, an oil giant based in White Plains, New York, agreed to pay $3.1 million, without admitting any

[1] Daryl Koehn, "Extolling the Virtues of Hot Lines," *Workforce,* June 1998, v77, n6, pp. 125–127.

Figure 5.13
The Science Applications International Corporation (SAIC) Credo
http://www.saic.com/company/mission.html

SAIC Credo

We, as Science Applications International Corporation Employees, are dedicated to the delivery of quality scientific and technical products and services contributing to the security and well-being of our communities throughout the world. We believe high ethical standards are essential to the achievement of our individual and corporate goals. As such, we fully subscribe to the following commitments:

To Our Customers:

- We shall place the highest priority on the quality, timeliness, and competitiveness of our products and services.
- We shall pursue our objectives with a commitment to personal integrity and high professional standards.

To Our Fellow Employees, Present and Prospective:

- We shall promote an environment that encourages new ideas, high-quality work, and professional achievement.
- We shall treat our fellow employees honestly and fairly; and we shall ensure equal opportunity for employment and advancement.
- We shall share the rewards of success with those whose honest efforts contribute to that success.

To Our Vendors, Suppliers, and Subcontractors:

- We shall be fair and professional in all our business dealings and shall honor our commitments to our business partners.
- We shall endeavor to select vendors, suppliers, and subcontractors who will adhere to our ethical standards and commitment to quality products and services.

To Our Neighbors:

- We shall be responsible citizens, respecting the laws and customs of each community in which we live and conduct business.

To Our Shareholders and Employee Owners:

- We shall conduct ourselves so as to enhance and preserve the reputation of the company.
- Consistent with the commitments expressed above, we shall strive to provide our shareholders a fair return on investment.

violations, to 186 female employees who were underpaid for work done between 1993 and 1996.[2] This seems small in comparison to the $176 million settlement the company paid in the 1996 racial discrimination case over tape recordings by senior executives casting disparaging comments about black employees. Part of the settlement for the 1996 case was the development of a diversity program and the creation of an "equality and tolerance task force" empowered to shape personnel decisions affecting women and minorities. Texaco confirmed that it has made significant progress toward the goals of its diversity program, which allows all employees and business partners to contribute equally and be compensated fairly.[3]

[2] "Texaco Will Pay $3.1 Million to 186 Female Managers," *Los Angeles Times,* January 7, 1999, p. C1.
[3] "Texaco Claims Diversity Moves," *The Oil Daily,* February 4, 1998, v48, n23, p. 7.

Advantica's Denny's Inc. In 1999, Denny's launched a $2 million advertising campaign in an effort to address the problems the company has endured ever since settling a $45.7 million discrimination suit filed by black customers in 1994.[4] David Margullis, a Dallas-based crisis communication consultant, has designed the antiracism television ads that address the issue. Denny's diversity initiatives are an example of ethical communication that follows from sound, ethical decision making.

Mitsubishi Motor Manufacturing of America Black employees of Mitsubishi Motors filed a class-action lawsuit in federal court in January 2000. They claimed they had been denied promotions, raises, and job training because of their race.[5] This came just two years after Mitsubishi paid a record $34 million to settle federal charges that it had done nothing to stop sexual harassment at its assembly plant. Mitsubishi Motors has spent $200 million on programs for minority groups as a result of claims of racial discrimination and sexual harassment.[6] The Mitsubishi case demonstrates the need to reinforce sexual harassment policy and diversity programs with efforts such as regularly held workshops and seminars.

GLOBAL CASES

[NOTE 5.58]
Example of ethical communication situations: Global cases.

Levi Strauss Levi Strauss, located in San Francisco, California, had a supplier that posed an ethical problem. The Tan family, a large supplier for Levi Strauss, allegedly forced 1,200 Chinese and Filipino women to work 74 hours per week in guarded compounds in the Mariana Islands. Levi Strauss, after repeated warnings—good examples of ethical messages—to the Tans, broke off the business arrangement. Levi Strauss relied on the company's Global Sourcing and Operating Guidelines when figuring out how to deal with the Tan family. These ethical guidelines state that Levi Strauss will "seek to identify and utilize business partners who aspire as individuals and in the conduct of all their businesses to a set of ethical standards not incompatible with our own."

Merck & Co. Merck & Co. is one of the largest producers of prescription drugs in the world. Merck was voted one of *Fortune* magazine's top 10 "Best Companies to Work For" in 1998. Embedded in the culture of Merck is founder George W. Merck's philosophy that medicine is for people, not for profits. Merck, an innovative company, has contributed millions of dollars to the development and distribution of Mectizan, a drug used to treat river blindness, in third-world countries.[7] At Merck, management believes that three principles are important for global success: (1) product innovation, (2) consensus on core values that guide actions and decisions, and (3) an adherence to the highest standards of ethical behavior.[8] Merck's management has found that ethical decisions affect not only the employees who work for them but also those individuals who rely on their medicines and services worldwide.

[4] Bruce Smith, "Denny's Is Televising Anti-Racism Ads That Address Past Problems," *Orange County Register,* January 13, 1999, p. C5.

[5] "Mitsubishi Workers File Lawsuit Alleging Racial Discrimination," *The Wall Street Journal,* January 20, 2000, p. B21.

[6] Tracy Corrigan, "Barriers Begin to Crack," *The Financial Times,* February 3, 1997, p. 13.

[7] Gareth R. Jones, Jennifer M. George, and Charles W. L. Hill, *Contemporary Management,* Boston: McGraw-Hill, 2000, pp. 81–82.

[8] Raymond V. Gilmartin, "Innovation, Ethics, and Core Values: Keys to Global Success," *Vital Speeches,* January 15, 1999, v165, i7, p. 209.

The Communication Note that follows presents information regarding ethics in today's global economy.

COMMUNICATION NOTE

Global Ethics Codes

A Conference Board survey of 124 companies in 22 countries found that 78 percent of boards of directors are setting ethics standards, up from 41 percent in 1992 and 21 percent in 1987. Business leaders see the self-regulation as a way to avoid legislative or judicial intrusions into their operations. Ethics codes also help promote tolerance of diverse practices and customs while doing business abroad.

As reported by Helene Cooper in "Global Ethics Codes," The Wall Street Journal, *August 19, 1999, p. A1.*

[NOTE 5.59] Example of ethical communication situations: Environment cases.

ENVIRONMENTAL CASES

Tom's of Maine Tom's of Maine is a socially responsible company that has achieved rapid growth and profitability by focusing on respect for the environment. Founded by Tom and Kate Chappell, the company produces personal care products, such as toothpaste, that will not pollute the environment. The ethical standard that the company lives by is reflected in the last phrase of its mission statement: "To be a profitable and successful company while acting in a socially and environmentally responsible manner."[9] Tom's of Maine behaves ethically in its communications as well as its actions.

Patagonia, Inc. Patagonia, an outdoor clothing and gear company, was founded in the early 1970s with the goal to "do the right thing." At first that meant making useful and durable products, then progressed to manufacturing clothing with an eye to minimizing waste and damage to the environment. The environmentally responsible company donates 1 percent of sales revenue to environmental groups. One recipient was the campaign against dams that block rivers used by spawning salmon.[10] Yvon Chouinard, the founder, states that "profit is what happens when you do everything right." Patagonia communicates ethical practices by being socially responsible.

[NOTE 5.60] Example of ethical communication situations: Product cases.

PRODUCT CASES

Prudential Insurance Company Prudential Insurance Company has had an excellent reputation for selling insurance products to lower-income families since 1875. Its slogan "Get a piece of the rock" symbolizes not only the financial strength of the company but also the integrity of the products it sells. Prudential faced an ethical crisis in 1996 when it was fined $35 million for misleading sales practices. The agency had failed to communicate to its customers that the new policies they were buying would be more expensive than the ones that they had previously held.

The new products, which could be purchased from the built-up cash value of older policies, were interest-rate sensitive. If the interest rate stayed the same or rose, the customer would pay the premium that had been quoted; however, if the interest rates dropped, which they did, the customer would have to pay Prudential more

[9] Tom Chappell, *Managing Upside Down: The Seven Intentions of Values-Centered Leadership*, New York: William Morrow and Company, Inc., September 1999, pp. 75–77, 211.

[10] Roger Rosenblatt, "Reaching the Top by Doing the Right Thing," *Time,* October 15, 1999, pp. 87–91.

money. Prudential Insurance Company engaged in misconduct in that it failed to communicate honestly with its customers. Since then Prudential has taken positive steps toward improving corporate communication both internally and externally. Communicating legally as well as ethically is essential for a company's reputation and its bottom line.

[NOTE 5.61]
Johnson & Johnson provides a classic example of an ethical communication.

Johnson & Johnson A review of the ideal way Johnson & Johnson and its managers faced an ethical situation may illustrate how most businesses try to operate today. In 1982 an unknown criminal poisoned Tylenol capsules, which led to the deaths of seven people. Unaware of the cause of the deaths, Johnson & Johnson managers based their ethical and decisive reactions to this crisis on the company's 45-year-old credo, which can be accessed on its Web site at **http://www.jnj.com**. This credo is based on the belief that business is a moral undertaking for the benefit of society, with responsibilities that go far beyond sales and profits.

[NOTE 5.62]
A company credo guides ethical behavior.

[NOTE 5.63]
Johnson & Johnson believes it exists to benefit society.

COMMUNICATION QUOTE

As a leader in health care, we believe we have a special responsibility to enhance the quality of life for our customers, employees, and the community at large. This responsibility goes beyond producing high-quality products. It also involves conducting our business in accordance with the highest ethical standards, treating our employees sensitively and fairly, and helping to meet critical community needs.

Ralph S. Larsen, Chairman and Chief Executive Officer of Johnson & Johnson, stresses the importance of the company credo.

Johnson & Johnson developed communications to alert the public and medical community, removed all Tylenol capsules from stores, halted production, and completely cooperated with the media and public health officials. Society was well served by this private company. Its managers' ethical behavior was the foundation for the comeback of Tylenol in new tamper-proof containers. Less than six months after the tragedy, Johnson & Johnson had regained 70 percent of its previous market and Tylenol was again available to the public. The Johnson & Johnson story is a model of ethical managerial decisions and communications.

[NOTE 5.64]
The Tylenol crisis was handled ethically.

In many communication situations, you will be faced with gray areas. Very few situations in the real world are entirely right or entirely wrong. There may be competing interests among your superiors, subordinates, customers, suppliers, stockholders, and others. Principles and systems that can help you make decisions on ethical content for your messages are presented in the following sections.

[NOTE 5.65]
You will be faced with gray areas and competing interests.

AN EXAMPLE OF AN ETHICAL SITUATION—COMMUNICATING ABOUT COCA-COLA'S DOWNSIZING PROGRAM

As you study the principles and systems for making ethical decisions, think about the following example. The Coca-Cola Company's significant restructuring of its operations in January 2000 involved the largest downsizing of employees in its 113-year history.[11] Assume that you are Douglas Daft, the company's president and

[NOTE 5.66]
Reflect on this communication situation as you review the ethical principles and systems.

[11] Betsey McKay and Joann S. Lublin, "Coke Planning Sweeping Job Reductions," *The Wall Street Journal,* January 26, 2000, p. A3.

chief operating officer, responsible for developing and transmitting messages that will announce to various receivers that the company has a suffered a loss for the fourth quarter and plans a layoff of 6,000 employees. The job cuts include about 2,500 in Atlanta and affect nearly 21 percent of the company's 29,000 employees in the global workforce.[12] The receivers of your messages will include the company's current employees, businesspeople in the communities where the company is located and where the employees live, suppliers to the company, local and state government officials, managers and supervisors within the company, the company's stockholders, the company's customers, and the general public.

Reflect on the receivers' needs in this communication situation. The employees need to know about the company downsizing several months in advance so they can search for other jobs. The local community and government officials need to know so they can seek other industries to replace the lost jobs and tax income. The suppliers need to know so they can seek replacement customers. The company managers and stockholders want a smooth transition and need the restructuring program to boost Coca-Cola's reputation and market leadership. The company needs to maintain a positive image with its customers and the general public.

How do you decide what is the *right information* that ought to be in your messages to these receivers? How do you resolve what is the *highest good* attainable for all those involved? After the following ethical principles and systems have been presented, the company downsizing communication situation will be analyzed.

ETHICAL PRINCIPLES AND SYSTEMS

Some of the ethical principles and systems that have worked well for others are provided in the following sections. These principles and systems can be helpful to you in being an ethical communicator. Choose among these suggestions to find the one or the combination that works best for you. Use the principles and systems you choose on a daily basis to ensure that your business messages are ethical.

[NOTE 5.67] Do unto others as you would have them do unto you.

The Golden Rule The Golden Rule is "Do unto others as you would have them do unto you." This simply stated, fundamental moral imperative is a helpful ethical principle for many business communicators. They analyze the communication problems facing them. Then they analyze the alternative content they could select for their messages. They choose content that will provide the full disclosure, truth, and straightforwardness that they would want to have if they were the receiver(s).

[NOTE 5.68] Choose content that produces the most good and least harm.

The Social-Utility Concept The concept of social utility provides a higher-level system than does the Golden Rule principle. To determine ethical content for a message using this approach, you first list all the alternative content from which you could choose. You then consider the positive and negative impacts of each of the alternatives on all those affected by your message. Those content alternatives that produce the greatest good and the least harm for all affected are chosen for inclusion in the message. Using this approach, self-interest is overridden by the requirement that everyone's good be counted equally.

[12] Henry Unger, "Coke CEO Says Growth Targets Are Out of Reach," *The Atlanta Journal and Constitution,* January 26, 2000. Distributed by *Knight-Ridder Business News,* January 26, 2000.

The Universal-Law Concept Using the universal-law approach, the actions and the alternatives that could be chosen for message content are categorized as good or evil for society as a whole. The question the business communicator asks is, "Would I be willing to require all others in the same circumstances to send the same kind of message I am sending?" The answer has to be yes. You would have to be willing, for the welfare and betterment of society, to establish a universal law requiring all others to behave as you are behaving.

[NOTE 5.69]
Be willing to require everyone to send the same kind of message.

The Four-Way Test Rotary International, a service club with members throughout the world, has a unique set of questions for promoting ethical decisions, behavior, and communication. The test, referred to as The Four-Way Test of Things We Think, Say, or Do, is outlined in the Communication Note that follows.

[NOTE 5.70]
Be sure your content is truthful, fair, friendly, and beneficial to all.

COMMUNICATION NOTE

The Four-Way Test

[1] Is it the TRUTH?
[2] Is it FAIR to all concerned?
[3] Will it build GOODWILL and BETTER FRIENDSHIPS?
[4] Will it be BENEFICIAL to all concerned?

Source: Rotary International, One Rotary Circle, Evanston, IL, 60201.

This test stresses truth, fairness, goodwill, good interpersonal relationships, and benefits to all concerned. It is a helpful, practical way for many to implement the social utility and universal law concepts.

Other Practical Approaches Another decision-making form that may be helpful to you is advocated by Frank Navran, director of training, at the Ethics Resource Center. The *ethics filter* helps the decision maker determine the right thing to do in any situation.

The Generic Form of the Ethics Filter Is **PLUS.**

P = POLICIES AND PROCEDURES
What organizationally imposed requirements are applicable?
L = LAWS AND REGULATIONS
What externally imposed requirements are applicable?
U = UNIVERSAL ORGANIZATIONAL VALUES
What universal organizational values must I take into consideration?
S = SELF
What personal values must I consider?

Once you have used the PLUS filter and considered all the options, your decision should be clear. Anything less would be wrong, and, as we have all been told, "There is no right way to do the wrong thing."[13]

[NOTE 5.71] Test your content against community standards, the law, your conscience, and a higher power.

In determining whether a situation is ethical, you should first make sure your message content meets applicable community and society standards of behavior. Second, you should make sure your message is legal. Third, you should apply your own personal values to the content. Fourth, you should seek guidance from a higher power. This system emphasizes using acceptable standards of conduct in ethical decision making.

An excellent source of information on business ethics and ethical communication is the following nonprofit organization:

Ethics Resource Center
1747 Pennsylvania Avenue, NW
Suite 400
Washington, DC 20006
Phone: 202.737.2258
Fax: 202.737.2227
E-mail Address: ethics@ethics.org

The Web site of the Institute for Business and Professional Ethics, **http://www.depaul.edu/ethics**, is ranked among the top 5 percent of Web sites by the Internet-by-Point Survey and has been awarded three stars by Magellan. This Web site is one of the first ethics-related resources to create a hypertext-linked network on the Internet. This Web site provides ethics resources for businesspeople as well as teachers.

[NOTE 5.72] Web sites are excellent sources for information on ethics.

Another organization that provides information on ethics is The International Business Ethics Institute (Washington, D. C.), at **http://www.business-ethics.org**, which is dedicated to disseminating business-ethics information. The Business Research in Information and Technology (BRINT) site provides access to full-text articles and papers for business information on ethics at **http://www.brint.com**. Business Ethics Resources on WWW at **http://www.ethics.ubc.ca/resources/business/** lists many companies' codes of ethics.

AN ANALYSIS OF THE EXAMPLE ETHICAL SITUATION—COMMUNICATING ABOUT COCA-COLA'S DOWNSIZING PROGRAM

Let's apply the ethical principles and systems given in the preceding section to the Coca-Cola Company's downsizing situation described earlier. As you will recall, you are the manager responsible for announcing Coca-Cola's downsizing to various receivers.

[NOTE 5.73] The Coca-Cola downsizing communication situation involves competing interests.

The ethical issues in this communication situation involve competing interests. The company's managers and stockholders want a cost-effective downsizing that does not involve employee turmoil. The company's employees will need to find other jobs. Government officials will be concerned about lost tax revenue and community development. Suppliers will be concerned about replacing lost business. The company's customers will need a new source of supply. Finally, the public at large will have a general interest.

[13] Frank Navran, "Hypothetically Speaking: The Experts Give Their Read of the Situation," *Ethics Today*, spring 1997, pp. 8–10.

When do you send the messages? What information do you include in different messages for different receivers? How do you best achieve the highest good for all those involved in the communication?

The principles and systems can guide you to develop ethical messages that contain full information and provide the greatest good to all receivers. With some assumptions about detailed facts in this communication situation, here are logical, ethical decisions regarding your messages:

[NOTE 5.74]
Seek the greatest good for all receivers.

[1] The messages will go out at the same time. They will be sent several months in advance of the downsizing to give the large number of people who will be affected time to take corrective actions.

[2] A truthful, open explanation of how the downsizing and restructuring is intended to streamline the company will be given. Information will be shared on how the changes in the company's organization will enable Coca-Cola's line managers around the world more autonomy to better serve their markets.[14]

[3] Information will be provided to the company's employees and managers to assist them in the transition. Departing Coca-Cola employees will leave with one of the more generous severance packages in recent history. The $800 million in severance benefits will also provide affected employees with resume, job search, and other outplacement services.[15]

[4] The company's stockholders and managers will be reminded of how the timing and content of your messages—to employees, customers, the general public, and others—best serves the company's long-term interests. The move is aimed at cutting costs and boosting earnings. Coca-Cola said the restructuring will yield about $300 million in annual cost savings once it is completed.

FINAL COMMENTS ON BEING ETHICAL

Being ethical in your communication is not only essential and the right thing to do, it is also contagious. Others will follow your lead when they observe the success you experience in interpersonal relationships and in your career. All will benefit from being ethical.

[NOTE 5.75]
Being ethical is contagious.

Assuring Legality

Learning Objective [4]
EXPLAIN HOW TO ASSURE THE LEGALITY OF BUSINESS MESSAGES.

You and your organization could be sued or prosecuted if you violate the law in your business messages. Thousands or even millions of dollars could be lost. Prison terms might have to be served. To assure the legality of your written or oral messages, you must be aware of the laws, court decisions, and administrative regulations that apply to those messages. Ignorance of the law and related information does not excuse violators.

[NOTE 5.76]
Learn the legal requirements that relate to your work.

If you are considering content for a message and are not sure about its legality, you should consult with an attorney or other authority. Many companies have

[14] James F. Peltz, "Coke Will Slash 21% of Worldwide Work Force," *Los Angeles Times*, January 27, 2000, pp. C1, C8.

[15] Tammy Joyner, "Coke Tries to Soften Blow of Layoffs With Generous Severance Package," *Knight-Ridder Business News*, January 26, 2000.

attorneys who are available to employees. In addition, some company officials—personnel officers, purchasing agents, and others—have specialized knowledge of legal requirements in their areas of responsibility.

A review of some of the most important legal considerations will assist you in assuring the legality of your messages. The Communication Note that follows shows that laws are required to maintain social order but that we should strive for a higher moral code of conduct.

COMMUNICATION NOTE

I Did Nothing Illegal!

- *Legal standards* are the minimal standards. They provide the outer boundaries of conduct. They tell you what you *can't* do, but provide no positive guidance about what you *should* do.
- *Ethical standards* are the next step up in the hierarchy. Ethical conduct is the set of behavior standards established for a group of people working together in the same place, same group, or same profession.
- *Moral conduct* implies the highest standards of conduct guided by personal principles, values, and virtues.

In short, the law tells you what you should not do, ethics tell you what you should do, and morals tell you what you should aspire to do.

Source: Nan DeMars, You Want Me To Do WHAT? *New York: Fireside, 1997, p. 104.*

CONTRACT COMMUNICATION

The oral and written communications with the customers of your company must meet the requirements of several laws. Among the most important forms of communication is the contract.

[NOTE 5.77] "Plain English" laws are common.

"Plain English" Laws Several states have "plain English" laws requiring that contracts be written so consumers can understand them. Some states specify readability levels, average number of syllables per word, layout, size of print, and many other content details. These laws require careful analysis of a contract's content. Other states have more general guidelines, such as requiring contracts to contain understandable words, short sentences, and short paragraphs. If the principles of business communication given in Chapter 4 are followed, the requirements of "plain English" laws would be met.

[NOTE 5.78] Warranties can be express or implied.

Warranties and Guarantees The Uniform Commercial Code, the Consumer Product Warranty Act, the Federal Trade Commission Improvement Act, and similar legislation cover express warranties (promises made willingly by the seller) and implied warranties (promises created by law). An example of an express warranty is a manufacturer's written promise to replace a product during the first year if it proves defective due to quality of construction or materials. An example of an implied warranty provided by law is that the product must be satisfactory for the purpose intended. Promises to consumers and others can be made orally or in writing, so be sure you warrant only to the extent you intend.

CREDIT AND COLLECTION COMMUNICATION

Many state and federal laws specify the responsibilities of businesses in issuing credit and collecting debts. Here are some of the more important federal laws.

[NOTE 5.79]
Credit must be equally available.

Businesspeople must be sure they use plain English in their contracts.

Equal Credit Opportunity Act This law requires that credit be equally available to all credit-worthy customers. It also covers how credit worthiness is determined. The content of credit applications and any oral questioning of credit applicants must not include references to race, color, religion, or national origin. Credit decisions cannot be based on age, marital status, or future personal plans. Credit refusals must be in writing.

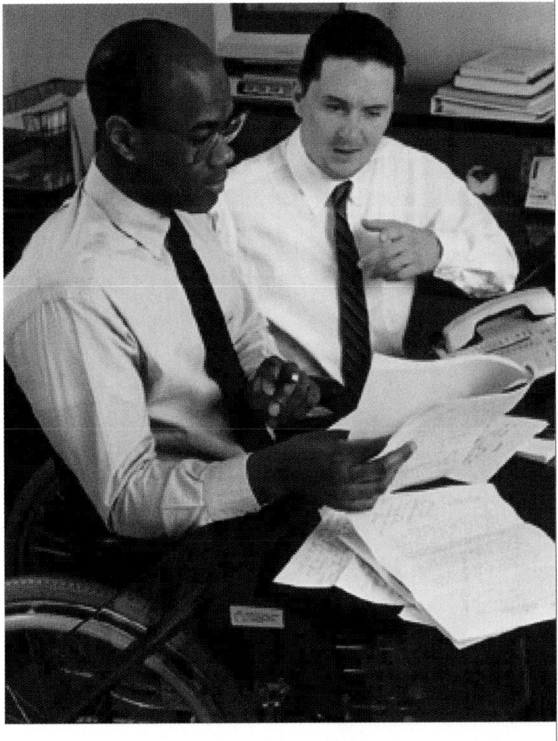

Fair Credit Billing Act This law protects credit card users against false charges made to their accounts. The act specifies in detail those procedures that consumers and creditors must follow to resolve problems.

Fair Debt Collection Act This law specifies in detail what bill collectors can and cannot do. What you can and cannot say, how many times you may call the debtor, and to whom you may write (not relatives or employers) are among the requirements included.

[NOTE 5.80]
Billing and collection procedures must be specific.

Federal Truth-in-Lending Act Requirements for full disclosure of credit terms to consumers are stated in this law. Lenders and creditors must clearly disclose service charges, finance charges, and the effective annual interest rate. How the terms and conditions of loans must be specified—such as number of payments and due dates of payments—is covered in this law. It also provides that the borrower has the right to cancel within three business days after signing the contract.

[NOTE 5.81]
Credit terms must be clear.

EMPLOYMENT COMMUNICATION

Managers, supervisors, and employees need to know the legal requirements affecting employment communication. Much of what can and cannot be said or written about employees is specified in the following laws.

The Civil Rights Act This law and its amendments prohibit discrimination in employment. Hiring, firing, compensation, and other conditions of employment cannot be based on race, color, religion, gender, or national origin. This act, first passed

[NOTE 5.82]
Discrimination in employment communication is illegal.

in 1964 and since amended, is landmark legislation. Every business communicator should be aware of its requirements. Affirmative action programs have evolved from the Civil Rights Act, the Equal Employment Opportunity Act, and other extensive federal, state, and local employment regulations.

[NOTE 5.83] ADEA deals with the changing demographics of the American workforce.

The Age Discrimination in Employment Act The ADEA has been designed to deal with a shift in the demographics of the American workforce. The ADEA was enacted to prohibit discrimination in workers over 40 years of age. This act requires much greater due diligence, record keeping, and documentation on the part of employers in firing or letting go of employees.

[NOTE 5.84] Communications between labor and management must meet legal requirements.

Labor-Management Relations Act Communications between managers and workers, particularly concerning unions, are guided by this law. Details regarding the implementation of this law are provided by the National Labor Relations Board.

[NOTE 5.85] Information about employees must be kept private.

The Privacy Act This law gives employees access to information about themselves. It also limits the use of personnel information to the purpose for which it was collected. For example, it is important when serving as a reference that you respond only to specific requests that have been approved by the employee. Further, your comments should relate only to documented job performance. Any reference should be objective, given in good faith, and without malice.

[NOTE 5.86] Persons with disabilities must be treated fairly.

Americans With Disabilities Act This 1990 act, covering some 43 million Americans with disabilities, is referred to as the most important employment legislation since Title VII of the Civil Rights Act. This act makes it unlawful to discriminate against people with disabilities in regard to hiring, firing, compensation, training, and advancement. Communicators must be aware of language that the courts might rule discriminatory, such as job descriptions and advertisements calling for *high energy level, able bodied,* and so forth. Both physical and mental disabilities are covered by the law. Persons with disabilities are qualified applicants and employees if they "can perform the essential functions of the job." If so, employers must reasonably accommodate their disabilities.

[NOTE 5.87] FMLA helps nontraditional and dual-income families.

Family and Medical Leave Act The FMLA was passed in 1993. This act recognizes the responsibilities of mothers, fathers, and other caregivers in nontraditional situations and dual-income households to take care of children and their families.[16] The act has been extremely burdensome to administer because of additional administrative and time-keeping requirements.[17]

[NOTE 5.88] Copyright laws prohibit copying most materials without the originator's permission.

COPYRIGHT AND FAIR-USE COMMUNICATION

Copyright laws vary throughout the world, and managers must be aware of the laws within the country where they are communicating. Copyright laws in the United

[16] Gillian Flynn, "Looking Back on 100 Years of Employment Law," *Workforce,* November 1999, v78, i11, p. 74.

[17] Gillian Flynn, "Prediction About the Future of Employment Law," *Workforce,* January 2000, v49, i1, pp. 78–80.

States, with limited exceptions, prohibit copying material without the owner's permission. The related fair-use doctrine permits the making of single copies for noncommercial purposes. Material does not have to be registered with the U.S. Copyright Office to be copyrighted.

[NOTE 5.89]
The fair-use doctrine permits limited copying.

Protection of intellectual property is an ongoing concern, and copyright laws have been enacted to protect the originators' interests in their ideas, writings, and other creations. You may have to obtain permission to use the information, and you will be required to give credit to the originator as the source. In addition, the originator may require you to pay a fee for its use. Even if the information is excluded from the coverage of the copyright laws, ethical standards require that you give credit to the originator as the source. (The format for source credits is shown in Appendix B.)

[NOTE 5.90]
Secure permission for sources; give them credit.

You do not have to cite a source for information that is general knowledge, such as "communicators should be sure their messages are ethical and legal." You can say that on your own even though you might have read it in this book or in some other publication. Copyright laws and the fair-use doctrine are complex. Most libraries have the material published by the copyright office on these topics. Business communicators must make themselves aware of the laws and guidelines that apply to their messages. Please refer to the Appendix B for information on citation formats.

Using others' materials without giving credit is called *plagiarism* or *paraphrasing,* depending on the manner in which the material is used. These two terms are defined as follows:

- **Plagiarism** means stealing and using someone else's ideas or words as your own without giving the other person(s) credit as the source.
- **Paraphrasing** means restating (in your own words) and using the ideas belonging to another without giving the other person(s) credit as the source.

[NOTE 5.91]
Plagiarism is stealing and using another's ideas.

[NOTE 5.92]
Paraphrasing is restating another's words.

Plagiarism and paraphrasing can cause communicators serious legal and ethical problems. You can avoid these problems by (1) understanding and obeying the copyright laws, (2) giving credit to others when using their ideas or words, or (3) not using others' ideas and words.

DEFAMATION AND FRAUD

Common law and other legislation cover such important legal considerations as defamation and fraud.

Defamation The law does not permit you to make statements that injure the reputation or character of another person. Such statements, called **defamation**, are libelous (written) or slanderous (oral). To be considered defamation, the statements must be false, made for or read by a third person, and must cause some injury. True statements can be considered defamation if they are made with the intent of harming the other person.

[NOTE 5.93]
Libel and slander are statements that injure a reputation.

Fraud Lying that causes another person monetary damage is called **fraud.** Fraud exists when these conditions are proven: (1) a communicator misrepresents or conceals a material fact, (2) the misrepresentation was made knowingly or with a reckless disregard for the truth, (3) the misrepresentation was made with the intent to deceive,

[NOTE 5.94]
Fraud is lying that causes another person monetary damage.

(4) the deceived person relied on the false statement, and (5) monetary damage was incurred by the deceived person. Fraud can be committed by words or conduct and includes false advertising and false endorsement of products or services.

[NOTE 5.95]
You can develop effective business messages by using the planning and composing process, controlling vocabulary level, being ethical, and assuring legality.

You can develop effective business messages by following the process and guidelines outlined in this chapter. The process for planning and composing business messages—determining the purposes, analyzing the receiver, and compose the content—is a proven approach. The recommendations for determining vocabulary level, being ethical, and assuring legality can assist you further in developing business messages that communicate effectively with your receiver.

Summary of Learning Objectives

Learning Objective [1]

Use a three-step process for planning and composing effective business messages. The three-step process for planning and composing business messages is simple but critical to your success in communicating. The three steps are as follows:

Step 1: Determine purposes. The primary and secondary purposes for a specific business message will vary depending on the communication situation.

Step 2: Analyze the receiver for the you–viewpoint. The second step in planning and composing an effective written or oral business message is to analyze the receiver or receivers for the you–viewpoint.

Step 3: Compose message content. The third step in developing an effective business message is to compose the content of the message. Composing the message content includes the following tasks: selecting the type of message, selecting the organizational plan, outlining the content, drafting the message, editing and revising the message, and proofreading the final product.

Learning Objective [2]

Describe how the vocabulary level of business messages can be determined. Using a vocabulary level that your receiver will understand is a primary concern in composing effective business messages. Vocabulary level, as used in this book, refers to the level of difficulty of the words and combinations of words in messages.

There are several readability formulas that can be used to calculate vocabulary levels for your messages. Many grammar-checker programs are able to calculate the vocabulary level of your message. Business messages written at the eighth- to twelfth-grade levels will communicate clearly with most receivers.

Learning Objective [3]

Describe how to choose ethical content for business messages. Being ethical in your communication is essential to a successful personal life and business career. Effective interpersonal relationships are built on trust, honesty, and fairness. The ethical end result is to strive for the highest good attainable for all those involved in the communication. Therefore, ethical communication strives for the highest good for all involved and provides information that is fully adequate for the circumstance, truthful in every sense, and not deceptive in any way.

Choosing ethical content for messages requires the same analytical and practical skills as does sound business leadership. Being ethical in your communication requires that you determine—from among all the alternatives—the right and good information in given situations.

Explain how to assure the legality of business messages. You and your organization could be sued or prosecuted if you violate the law in your business messages. To assure the legality of your written or oral messages, you must be aware of the laws, court decisions, and administrative regulations that apply to those messages. Ignorance of the law and related information does not excuse violators.

Learning Objective [4]

If you are considering content for a message and are not sure about its legality, you should consult with an attorney or other competent authority. A review of some of the most important legal considerations will assist you in assuring the legality of your messages.

DISCUSSION QUESTIONS

1. Describe how to analyze a communication situation. (Objective 1)
2. Explain the two tasks involved in determining purposes of business messages. (Objective 1)
3. Explain how to analyze the receiver for the you–viewpoint. (Objective 1)
4. Explain how you can select the correct type of message. (Objective 1)
5. Discuss how word processing software programs affect the drafting of messages. (Objective 1)
6. Explain the importance of vocabulary level in composing effective business messages. (Objective 2)
7. What are readability formulas? Why should one use these tools? (Objective 2)
8. Define ethics. Explain what ethical communication is. (Objective 3)
9. What is The Four-Way Test? What does the test stress? (Objective 3)
10. Define fraud. List the conditions that are necessary to prove fraud exists. (Objective 4)

APPLICATION EXERCISES

1. **E-mail.** Briefly describe (a) two situations in which you would use oral messages and (b) two situations in which you would use written messages. Send an e-mail message to another student and your instructor describing the situations. (Objective 1)
2. Briefly describe (a) five situations in which you would use the direct plan for messages and (b) five situations in which you would use the indirect plan for messages. Give a typed copy of these situations to your instructor. (Objective 1)

3. **Global/Cross-Cultural.** Interview a person of another culture. Describe for the interviewee the direct and indirect plans for organizing messages as they are explained in this chapter. Ask the interviewee the following questions: (Objective 1)
   a. Which organizational plan is used for most messages in your culture?
   b. What types of messages in your culture use the direct plan?
   c. What types of messages in your culture use the indirect plan?

   Report your findings to the class.
4. Assume that you are writing a memo to your instructor to recommend that student oral reports be videotaped. List four ideas for content for this memo in a logical sequence for an indirect plan. (Objective 1)
5. Edit and revise the following message so that it communicates more clearly and concisely to a middle-level American receiver: (Objective 2)

It is excruciatingly clear that in order to ascend to the new heights of sales to achieve the new sales quotas the salesmen and saleswomen must dramatically and definitely increase their efforts.

Here are the things they must do whenever: (a) Get out in the field more of the time (b) practice, practice, practice and improve their presentations that they make. This will ultimately result in more—more commissions for them and more income over expenses, or profit, for the company organization.

6. **Ethics. /Teamwork.** In a group of three to five students, brainstorm the challenges that one faces being ethical in business. Present your ideas in a memo to your instructor. (Objective 3)

7. **Ethics. /Teamwork.** Form teams of three to five students and locate in the newspaper an example of an ethical situation that a company is facing or has faced. Within your group, discuss how you would handle the situation and present your findings to the class. (Objective 3)

8. **Ethics.** Over a 48-hour period, record all reports of illegal business communication that you hear or see on television or radio. Report your findings to the class. (Objective 4)

9. **Ethics. /Teamwork.** Form a group of three to five students, and develop a code of ethics for a company that you may want to start once you graduate from college. Remember to include the following: responsibility to customers; responsibility to employees; responsibility to communities; and responsibility to stockholders. Present your code of ethics to the class for discussion.
10. Using the principles of business communication, edit and revise the following message:

Title 7 of the Civel Right's act prohibits discrimination on the bases or ace, religion, gender or national origen. The Age Discrimination in Employement act (adEa) prohibits employer discrimination agin any one over fourty years of age.

Unlike the Civel Right's act, AdEA, provide for a trail by Jury and can lead to possible ciminal penalty. Trail by Jury is important because Jury's do not typically act favorably to discrimination agin older workers.

The American's with Disabilities act is a comprehensive anti discrimination statute designed to fairly provide equal assess to "qualified individuals with disabilityes". Title 1 of the AdA act which becomes effective 7/26/92 prohibit discrimination in employeement.

11. **E-mail. /Ethics.** Send an e-mail message to your instructor describing an ethical situation that you had to handle at your job or in the classroom. Apply the principles of business communication you have studied.

12. **Ethics. /Teamwork.** *Ethics in Business: A Study of the Bank of Alma.* The Bank of Alma is a community bank with seven branches in Alma, Michigan, and surrounding communities. Alma is a small rural community, and the Bank of Alma emphasizes customer service including individual attention, and speedy loans.

    Ethics and ethical communication in the banking industry are very important, especially in small community banks that rely heavily on word-of-mouth endorsements from satisfied customers.

    After viewing the video *Ethics in Business: A Study of the Bank of Alma,* complete the following and submit a memo to your instructor outlining your answers and recommendations.

a. List the four ethical issues for the Bank of Alma.
b. Explain why each of the ethical issues are important in any bank institution.
c. Form a group and discuss ethical issues you encounter in your job and how you handle them.

There are Web exercises at **http://krizan.swcollege.com** to accompany this chapter.

MESSAGE ANALYSIS

Using what you have learned in this chapter and previous chapters, edit and revise the following letter to assure that it is accurate, ethical, legal, and unbiased. Also be sure that the vocabulary is appropriate for a person who is a high school graduate.

Dear Sirs: It is with a great deel of pleasure and personnel enthusiasm that I communicate to you the introduction of a new insurance policy written and designed exclusively for the small businesses run by businessmen in our iner city area. Our Chairmen will be holding a special conference to explane the covrage on February 30, 2001.

This knew policy is written for small businesses only so if you have sales over $250K per year and purchase this policy we might have to report you're attempt to the authorities. This policy not only offers the small businessmen the coverage they need and have been asking for, but it also is offered at a very low price.

You're business is greatley appreciated! We are glad you choose Protection Mutual for your Insurance needs. For your convient in replying to let us know if you may attend the session conducted by our Chairman in February, we have enclose is a postage-payed, addressed form.

Very Sinerly Yours

GRAMMAR WORKSHOP

Correct the grammar, spelling, punctuation, style, and word choice errors in the following sentences:

1. A System of morale principals is a definition for the word Ethics.
2. The DARE police have spoken to the stanford High school students on many occasions.
3. The *ABC Journal* publish articles on Business Communication.
4. Listening speaking writing and reading is not discrete subjects.
5. Effective teachers teaches the listener the speaker, and the writer.
6. Students acquire oral communication skill through both formal, and informal speaking activities.
7. Basic communication skills is fundamental for successful, work in the business-field.
8. To be an effective writing one must be give attention to the composing process.
9. Please be sure to provide time for the students to discuss the tylenol Case.
10. Before opening a Exit Door on a Air Plane look thru a window too check for smoke and fire.

CHAPTER

6 Interpersonal Communication and Teamwork

Brian Delegan, Morningstar, Inc.

LET'S TALK BUSINESS In the business world, dynamic environments create unique challenges requiring unique solutions. Alongside change resides confusion.

Pablo Picasso claimed, "Every act of creation is first an act of destruction." As I participated in data department re-engineering at Morningstar, I found this to be very true.

In the initial stages of change, there was chaos. Several coworkers fled, fearing or rejecting the new vision. Facilitating change requires communication; there needs to be understanding. Everyone involved in the change needs to be aware why and how the change will occur.

As catalysts for change, leaders need to communicate the information clearly, completely, and in a timely manner. They need to convey the strategy

(Continued)

[LEARNING OBJECTIVES]

[1] IDENTIFY THE COMPONENTS OF INTERPERSONAL COMMUNICATION.

[2] ENHANCE YOUR ABILITY TO BUILD POSITIVE RELATIONSHIPS.

[3] GIVE CRITICISM EFFECTIVELY AND RECEIVE IT APPROPRIATELY.

[4] DESCRIBE TECHNIQUES FOR RESOLVING CONFLICTS.

[5] DEVELOP THE SKILLS ASSOCIATED WITH LEADING AND PARTICIPATING IN TEAMS.

[6] DESCRIBE THE FEATURES OF AND PROCESS USED BY A WRITING TEAM.

so subordinates can share and feel ownership in the vision. Holding back information leads to speculation within the workforce. Speculation that is built on incomplete or inaccurate information leads to disruption and inefficient operations.

Leaders aren't the only ones who must communicate during times of change. Colleagues must also communicate with and support each other. Suppressed information or feelings inevitably trigger greater confusion, which leads to discontent. At Morningstar, even some who embraced the wave of change were close to giving up on the vision. Support from their colleagues helped to get them through the process and to flourish in the new environment.

Tight-knit teams are always important, but during periods of change, they are vital. •

Brian Delegan's experience during his first year at Morningstar underscores the importance of communication at both corporate and individual levels. His example illustrates how formal communication from executives to employees sets the tone for change and how interpersonal communication among workers provides the support they need to accept and survive change. Interpersonal communication—what it is and how it is used in business settings—is one of the topics we explore in this chapter.

The Elements of Interpersonal Communication

Learning Objective [1]
IDENTIFY THE COMPONENTS OF INTERPERSONAL COMMUNICATION.

Interpersonal communication is the term applied to the verbal and nonverbal interactions in one-on-one or small-group settings. "People skills" and "soft skills" are terms often used to describe someone's interpersonal abilities.

[NOTE 6.1]
Interpersonal communication skills are used in one-on-one and small-group interactions.

Interpersonal communication is a cornerstone in what social scientists refer to as the **communication climate**—the quality of the personal relationships that exist within an organization. The communication climate reflects the workers' perceptions of whether the organization trusts, respects, and values them—factors related to job satisfaction and commitment. Interpersonal communication is linked to leadership potential, a quality employers seek in those they hire. Therefore, one key to success in business is learning to create a positive communication climate.

[NOTE 6.2]
Organizations that demonstrate trust, respect, and value of workers have a good communication climate.

Interpersonal skills have always played a role in business, but that role grew in importance as the United States moved from being an industrial to a service-oriented economy. Service thrives on positive working relationships between coworkers, departments, and organizations. Recall that developing and maintaining these relationships is a goal of business communication.

Workplace diversity, globalization, organizational restructuring, worker specialization, and technology contribute to the current emphasis on interpersonal skills. Workplace diversity and globalization call upon workers to be aware of and sensi-

[NOTE 6.3]
Various factors contribute to the current workplace focus on interpersonal skills.

tive to the ways in which an individual's culture affects his or her attitudes and actions in the office. Organizational restructuring, often resulting in downsizing, has redistributed the workload and placed pressure on those who remain. Worker specialization increases the likelihood that senders and receivers won't speak the same technical language. Technology has increased the speed at which work is processed and reduced the number of face-to-face encounters. Failure to recognize and adapt to these factors can create communication barriers.

Interpersonal communication skills exhibit themselves in the style with which people write and speak. Techniques for enhancing your written communication skills are covered in the correspondence section of this book. Here, we focus on how listening, speaking, and nonverbal communication are used to build positive relationships, to give and receive criticism comfortably, to manage conflict effectively, and to negotiate productively.

Learning Objective [2]
ENHANCE YOUR ABILITY TO BUILD POSITIVE RELATIONSHIPS.

Positive Relationships

[NOTE 6.4] Positive relationships don't happen by chance.

Positive relationships don't just happen. They are built over time, and they require ongoing maintenance. This section focuses on three topics related to building and maintaining positive relationships—conversations, office politics, and relationship repair.

CONVERSATIONS

[NOTE 6.5] Relationships begin with cautious conversation.

Relationships generally begin with conversations. At first, the interaction will probably be cautious. Then, as trust and comfort grow, participants begin to reveal more of their personalities and to share information about their lives. People begin to connect on intellectual, personal, and emotional levels. At the office, this may mean speaking about family or friends, hopes and fears, and problems and solutions. The nature and extent of the topics discussed will vary with each relationship. A worker might share less with a superior or subordinate than with a colleague, and more with one colleague than another. The key elements are trust and comfort.

[NOTE 6.6] Workplace relationship patterns parallel personal relationship patterns.

This pattern of trust and sharing in the workplace parallels that used in other parts of life. Consider your best friend. How did you meet? What were your early conversations about? What do you discuss now? Do you share things with one friend that you do not talk about with another? The patterns you observe in your school and social life will be evident in your work life as well.

As Brad Fujii notes in his Communication Quote on page 159, one-to-one oral communication, including conversation, is a valuable business tool. In fact, it is probably the most important form of interaction used in business. It occurs in both structured and social business settings, it is essential to good customer service, and it forms the foundation for workplace interactions among employees. More critical business decisions are made during conversations between two people than in any other forum.

Whether conversations occur in person, via the telephone, or during a computer-based video conference, they are constantly changing situations. Sometimes you will be a message sender; sometimes you will be a receiver. Therefore, you must listen carefully (Chapter 14), continually analyze your receiver (Chapter 1), and adjust your delivery based on feedback (Chapter 1). In addition, you must apply the principles of business communication (Chapter 4). The success of a conversation also

COMMUNICATION QUOTE

One of the most effective business tools I use from day to day is talking with people. Although technology offers efficient alternatives to the spoken word, there is no substitute for a phone call or face-to-face conversation.

Brad Fujii, Purchasing Manager, Council for Jewish Elderly.

depends on using care in developing and sending the message (Chapter 5) and on eliminating communication barriers that threaten the conversation (Chapter 1).

Before we identify factors associated exclusively with successful face-to-face and successful telephone conversations, we must understand the conversation process.

The Conversation Process Conversations generally take place in five stages:

[NOTE 6.7] Conversations occur in stages.

[1] Greeting

[2] Introduction

[3] Exchange

[4] Summary

[5] Closing

Greeting The greeting opens the channel for a conversation. "Hello," "Good morning," and "Jose, this is Marla" are verbal greetings; a wave and a smile are nonverbal greetings.

[NOTE 6.8] Greetings consist of words and actions.

Through gestures, tone, and words, you provide information about your relationship with the receiver. Smiling warmly, extending your hand, and saying "Hi, Bob. It's good to see you again" portrays a very different relationship than does a stern face and a curtly uttered "Hello." Similarly, you might greet a coworker or personal friend by saying "Yo, Mary" but choose "Good afternoon, Mrs. Baumann" for a prospective client or the president of your firm. Whatever your relationship with the receiver, be sure that the tone of your greeting matches the tone of your message. A positive, upbeat, carefree greeting would not be a good match for a message conveying bad news. Once the greeting has occurred, the conversation moves to the introduction stage.

Introduction During this stage, the person initiating the conversation previews what will follow. Introductions should be brief and informative. "Tony, you've had experience with just-in-time inventory systems. What do you see as their strengths?" alerts the receiver to the topic of the conversation and helps frame the context for his or her role in it.

[NOTE 6.9] Introductory remarks should be brief yet informative.

An introduction may be direct or indirect. For example, if you believe you deserve an above-average increase in salary and your analysis of your boss tells you she or he prefers the direct approach, introduce your conversation topic by saying "Considering my performance this past year, I think that I deserve an above-average raise. Can we discuss this?" Your introduction makes your position on the topic clear. On the other hand, when a manager needs to discuss a budget cut with a supervisor, he or she might say "We need to discuss your department's budget request." This introduction defines the topic, provides a buffer to the negative news, and serves as a smooth transition between the greeting and the exchange, the third stage of the process.

[NOTE 6.10] Business is transacted during the exchange.

Exchange As the word *exchange* implies, the business of a conversation is conducted in a give-and-take format. During this stage of the process, the purpose of the conversation comes to the forefront. For example:

Elaine: Jack, are you free to meet with Ced and me at 2 tomorrow afternoon? We need to discuss plans for this year's division retreat.

Jack: Possibly. How much time will we need? I know I have a staff meeting at 3.

Elaine: Thirty or forty minutes should do it.

Jack: OK. I'll put it on my calendar. Will you confirm with Ced?

Elaine: Sure.

In this example, the exchange is brief and direct. In another situation, the exchange might be longer and use the indirect approach. Specific techniques for a productive exchange are offered in the Keys for Successful Face-to-Face Conversations section below.

[NOTE 6.11] The summary recaps the exchange or leads to the close.

Summary The fourth stage in the conversation process, the summary, allows the parties to reflect on the exchange, to recap the items discussed during a long or complex exchange, and to signal that a conversation is ending. This stage of the process does for the end of a conversation what the introduction does for the beginning: It serves as a bridge.

Either the sender or the receiver may summarize a conversation. By saying "Please have the revised budget on my desk by Friday morning" or "Call me if you have questions," a supervisor signals to a worker that their budget conversation is about to end. By saying, "I'll make the changes we've agreed to and have the revised budget on your desk by Friday morning," the employee indicates readiness to end the exchange and move to the final stage, the closing.

[NOTE 6.12] The closing should be cordial.

Closing The closing is the cordial conclusion to the conversation. Depending on the situation, the closing may be verbal, nonverbal, or a combination of the two. After finalizing a sale with a new customer, for example, a sales representative might say, "It's been a pleasure doing business with you, Mr. Maestas. I'll process the order today and phone you about a week after the printer has been installed to be sure you're satisfied with it. Good-bye." The wording makes it clear the conversation has ended; the process has been completed.

Whether spontaneous or planned, successful conversations are honest, objective, sincere, and reasonable. Effective interpersonal relations and communications depend on these attributes. The process and techniques described in this section apply to all conversations; those described in the next two sections relate to special forms of conversation—face-to-face and telephone.

[NOTE 6.13] Work to make conversations productive.

Keys for Successful Face-to-Face Conversations Face-to-face conversations have an advantage over written and telephone communication because both the sender and receiver can use nonverbal cues to help them interpret a message. The following techniques will help make a face-to-face exchange productive:

- Carefully choose the location.
- Minimize interruptions.
- Speak effectively.
- Send clear, appropriate nonverbal cues.

- Ask questions.
- Accommodate diversity.
- Listen with your ears and eyes.

Carefully Choose the Location Conversations may take place in your office, in someone else's office, or at a neutral site. The purpose of the meeting should dictate the site and seating arrangement. Furniture can be a barrier to open communication. In a small office, a chair placed beside the desk creates a more welcoming atmosphere than does a chair placed opposite the desk. When you are uncomfortable with the seating arrangement in an office other than your own, ask politely to change it; do not move chairs without permission.

[NOTE 6.14]
Place furniture carefully.

Restaurants are neutral sites that provide the opportunity for both social and business interaction. When meeting a business associate at a restaurant, select a table away from major traffic flows and wait for your guest there. Seat yourself across the table from your guest; be sure the guest has the seat with the fewest distractions.

Minimize Interruptions Interruptions affect your ability to hold a meaningful conversation. Ask staff to intercept telephone calls, have your calls transferred directly to voice mail, or simply let your phone ring. Keep your office door partially or fully closed to discourage in-person interruptions. When off-site, turn off your pager or set it to signal messages by vibrating rather than ringing. Make similar adjustments to your cellular phone.

[NOTE 6.15]
Give the conversation your full attention.

Speak Effectively Strong, effective messages are short and simple. Always think before you speak, and structure your sentences so that the receiver will understand them. Most receivers want to hear only those details they need to understand the message. They react favorably to the ideas of a sender who is concise and to the point without being abrupt. People also appreciate having others call them by name. The following Tips and Hints box provides helpful suggestions on this topic.

[NOTE 6.16]
Apply the principles of business communication.

TIPS AND HINTS

The Importance of a Name

A person's name is his or her most important possession. Until asked to do otherwise, use the courtesy title and surname of customers, clients, or people who hold positions above yours within your organization. Address peers or others in the organization by their given name.

When you forget someone's name, be open and honest; admit your memory lapse. The specific approach you take will depend on the situation. When someone who phones you fails to give her or his name and you are unable to identify the caller by voice or from context, apologize and ask the caller's name. If the individual approaches you and addresses you by name, say, "It's good to see you again. I remember meeting you (indicate event or time) but don't recall your name." To initiate a conversation, begin by introducing yourself and reminding the person about where and when you met. Use the same strategy if you begin conversing with someone and sense he or she doesn't remember your name. Comfort, not embarrassment, is your goal.

Vary your pitch, speed, and volume to hold your listener's interest and to emphasize important points. Enunciate words clearly and pronounce them correctly. Eliminate vocal distractions such as *um* and *ah*. Avoid vocal gestures that show impatience (humming, speaking abnormally fast) or do not support your message (sighing).

Your purpose, analysis of the situation, and analysis of the receiver will guide you in determining how assertive you should be. Remember, though, that assertiveness does not mean aggressiveness; assertiveness does not alienate others. Be assertive by stating your views in a clear, straightforward manner appropriate to the circumstance.

[NOTE 6.17] Control your emotions.

In business relationships people are expected to be calm, cool, and controlled, so keep your emotions in check. It is possible to disagree without being disagreeable. Successful businesspeople do not argue, they discuss. They avoid sarcasm, vulgarity, and inappropriate tears or laughter. They don't embarrass themselves or others.

[NOTE 6.18] Use nonverbal cues that match the situation.

Send Clear, Appropriate Nonverbal Cues If appropriate to the situation, smile. When you offer someone a genuine smile, you show acceptance and build trust. People speak more freely when they feel safe, and a smile conveys safety.

Generally, the gestures and other movements used during conversations are smaller and more subtle than those used when speaking before a group. The proximity of the person or group with whom you are conversing makes your facial expressions more noticeable. Be sure any touch is appropriate to the situation and the person. Touch can be perceived to signal playfulness, control, support, gratitude, affection, intimidation, harassment, aggression, or other motives. Respect the personal space of those with whom you speak.

Limited eye contact may be thought to signify dishonesty, fear, or lack of interest—all barriers to effective communication. Recall that the appropriate level of eye contact varies among cultures. Let your receiver and the circumstances govern your behavior.

[NOTE 6.19] Use questions to obtain facts and learn about feelings.

Ask Questions One of the best ways to encourage another person to communicate is to ask questions. Carefully structured questions can help you gather facts, determine your receiver's needs, and encourage dialogue. Good communicators understand and use both closed- and open-ended questions.

[NOTE 6.20] Use closed- and open-ended questions.

A **closed-ended question** is designed to produce a one- or two-word answer; this type of question works best for fact finding. An **open-ended question** requires a longer answer and promotes a dialogue. Use this type of question when you want expanded answers or background information. Open-ended questions also work well when your receiver or the situation is emotional.

If, for example, you are trying to help a subordinate improve the quality of his or her work, you will have a more meaningful exchange if you ask "What can I do to help you do a better job?" than by asking "Do you need help to do your job?" The open-ended question invites the employee to suggest things that each of you can do to improve the work. In this situation, the closed-ended question invites a one-word response—and resentment or anger. Conversely, if you need to know when a contract was signed, you will get the data you want faster by asking "What is the signature date on the contract with Recore?" than by asking "What's the history of the Recore contract?"

Once you've asked a question, give the receiver time to respond. Fast-paced questioning could be perceived as interrogation, which will stifle rather than stimulate discussion. Refer to the following Tips and Hints box for information on the part questions play in social conversation.

TIPS AND HINTS

Social Conversations

Questions play a role in conversations during business-related social functions. A good host or hostess will introduce guests to one another and, as part of the introduction, will offer information on which discussion can commence. For example, a host might say "Selina, this is Yuri, who just returned from a business trip to London." Turning to Yuri, the host might then say "Selina enjoys theater and has seen productions in New York and in London."

Savvy conversationalists ask receiver-centered questions that respect an individual's privacy. They might ask people where they work but not what they paid for their house or what they earn. People interested in developing positive relationships avoid hot-button topics—those that will evoke emotional responses or provoke confrontation. Religion and politics are classic examples. When the person with whom you are speaking introduces a topic you don't wish to discuss, simply listen, make a noncommittal response such as "That's interesting," and then change the subject to something noncontroversial.

Accommodate Diversity Recognize and accommodate cultural or other differences during your conversations. Consider language differences; nonverbal communication differences; and factors such as values, attitudes, religion, political systems, and social orders. Be alert to and sensitive about physical and other disabilities that affect communication. Chapter 2 provides information about various cultures. The Tips and Hints box on page 164 provides helpful information about communicating with people who have various disabilities.

Listen With Your Ears and Eyes When people are conversing, they often think about what they are going to say next instead of listening to what the other person has to say. By giving the speaker your full attention, you can participate effectively in the conversation and make the other person believe she or he is important and interesting.

[NOTE 6.21]
Attentive listening shows your interest in the speaker.

Giving the speaker your full attention will allow you to "hear" both verbal and nonverbal cues. Any deviation from the person's normal speech pattern and nonverbal behavior must be considered in the context of the situation. Negative words or an angry tone may signal disagreement or fear; a fast pace may signal enthusiasm, excitement, or anxiety. Darting eye movements, frequent shifts of body weight, and changes in posture must also be interpreted. You may tell an employee that you have decided to give a desirable assignment to a coworker. If the employee's shoulders slump or if he or she becomes teary-eyed while saying "Fine. Good." you know that

Tips for Communicating With People Who Have Disabilities

TIPS AND HINTS

When a person has a . . .	You should . . .
Visual impairment	• Speak directly to the person, not through an interpreter or other person unless requested to do so. Ask how he or she communicates best and honor the preference. • Introduce yourself and others. Give names, titles, and locations (e.g., "To my right is Greg Peters, project director"). Tell the person when someone joins, leaves, or changes location within the group. • Accept that "I'll see you later" and other colloquial expressions containing sight terms will not be viewed as offensive.
Hearing impairment	• Use a light touch on the shoulder, a wave, or other signal to gain attention. • Minimize visual distractions, including bright sunlight. • Look directly at the person. Keep your hands away from your face. • Speak clearly and rephrase if necessary. Write your message if further clarification is needed. • Accept that "Did you hear?" and other colloquial expressions containing sound terms will not be viewed as offensive.
Mobility impairment or other physical disability	• Ask whether assistance is needed, and wait for a response before taking action. Carefully follow all instructions. • Create a comfortable viewing angle for someone who uses a wheelchair. Eye level is best but, if you must stand, move back enough to minimize the angle without having to raise your voice to be heard. • Offer to shake hands. People who have limited use of their right arm or hand or who use an artificial limb often use their left hand in greetings.
Speech impairment	• Try to speak in a quiet location. • Be patient. Allow the speaker to finish sentences; don't complete them for him or her. • Paraphrase and ask if you have understood what's been said. Ask to have statements repeated when you don't understand what has been said.

the employee does not view your decision as either fine or good. Feelings must be addressed before you can move forward with business discussions.

[NOTE 6.22]
Paraphrasing helps you clarify and retain what you hear.

To verify or acknowledge what you hear, paraphrase the message or ask relevant questions. Repeating what was said will help you retain what you have heard. When the speaker pauses, count to three before you speak. Interruptions can destroy the comfortable atmosphere you want to create, but a carefully placed "You seem frustrated," or "So, what you said is . . ." can keep the line of communication open.

Empathy means understanding how a person feels; it does not mean you agree with how the person feels. Listening with empathy is especially important when someone comes to you with a problem. After the problem has been described, ask how you can help. Offer advice only when encouraged to do so. Sometimes just listening is all the help the person needs.

[NOTE 6.23]
Listen with empathy.

Keys for Successful Telephone Conversations The telephone is important for sending and receiving business messages and can be valuable in building interpersonal relationships. For some message receivers, the entire image of a company rests solely on the quality of their telephone interactions with representatives of the organization. The following will help you improve the quality of your telephone conversations:

[NOTE 6.24]
Telephone conversations are important business tools.

- Use the telephone equipment and system properly.
- Be businesslike.
- Be considerate.

Use the Telephone Equipment and System Properly Hold the telephone mouthpiece one to two inches from your mouth and talk directly into it. Speech faults, accents, and other sounds are magnified during telephone conversations. Never chew gum, eat, or drink while on the phone; remove earrings, bracelets, and similar jewelry before placing or receiving a call. Know how to transfer calls, arrange conference calls, use a speaker phone, set up callbacks, and use other special features of your system. Employees who are not able to use the company telephone system properly will be perceived as inefficient, as will the organization.

[NOTE 6.25]
The telephone amplifies sounds.

Be Businesslike When answering the telephone, identify yourself immediately. Some phone systems produce a different ringing sound or have a screen display code to indicate whether a call originated inside or outside the organization. You may wish to include your organization and department name only for calls from outside the organization.

As you speak, create and hold a mental image of the person you call. This technique will help you to maintain a businesslike manner. The method will also help keep the conversation receiver-centered and your voice conversational. Because you cannot be seen, your voice has to carry the whole message and convey its tone. Use cordial terms such as *please, thank you,* and *I appreciate.* Remember to smile; the tone of your voice is more pleasant when you smile.

After the conversation has ended, let the caller hang up first. This simple gesture reinforces the impression that the caller is important and has your undivided attention. It also minimizes the need for a second call because the sender thought of something else to say but was cut off before he or she could do so.

When you place a call, the telephone may be answered by a support staff member or channeled to a *voice mail* system. Be prepared to leave a clear, complete message that includes at least your name, your phone number, and the purpose of your call. Be sure to pronounce and spell your name clearly; slow down when giving your phone number.

[NOTE 6.26]
Create meaningful voice mail messages.

Whether at home or at the office, be sure your outgoing message is current and complete. Resist the temptation to record a generic "I'm unavailable to take your call" message; provide your callers with real information about when you will be available to take or return calls. Invite your caller to leave a message. Be sure, too, that your message is businesslike. Friends or family members may enjoy a humorous greeting, but a client or prospective employer could view the greeting—and you—as unprofessional. Also, international callers may be confused by messages using colloquial English or by messages recorded at a faster than normal speaking rate. Read the following Tips and Hints box to learn about telephone communication with those who speak with foreign accents.

Tips for Handling Telephone Conversations With People Who Have Foreign Accents

TIPS AND HINTS

Call it simple kindness or call it common sense, but learning to deal with accents that are foreign to you can definitely be good for business. More than one million legal immigrants enter the United States each year, and most of them have one thing in common: English is their second language. This population represents a sizable market for any corporation selling products or services in the United States.

The phone calls you answer may be from people whose accents are unfamiliar to you. Here are six easy points to remember when dealing with a foreign accent:

[1] Don't pretend to understand. If you don't understand the caller, it's perfectly okay to say gently that you're having a little difficulty understanding him or her. Ask the caller to slow down so you can get all the information correct.

[2] Don't rush. Rushing threatens callers. Listen to the caller's pattern of speech. You'll be able to pick up key words. Repeat the key words to them; they'll appreciate the fact that you're really listening.

[3] Don't shout. The difficulty is with language, not volume.

[4] Don't repeat unnecessarily. People with an accent usually speak two or more languages, so it will take them a little longer to go through the thought process: their native language for thinking, English for communicating with you. Repeating the same word over and over to be sure they understand is unnecessary.

[5] Don't be rude. If you've ever told a caller, "I can't understand you," or "Huh?" or even "What did you say?" you've been a little rude, whether you intended that or not. It's much better to stop, take full responsibility, and explain you're having difficulty understanding. Say, "If you'll repeat it for me again, I'll be able to help you." It's a subtle difference, but a key one.

[6] Do keep a job aid available. If most of the calls you receive are predominantly from one particular ethnic group, keep a list with a few commonly used phrases near your phone. For example, in Spanish "Uno momento, por favor" means "one moment, please." Even if you pronounce it poorly, this phrase would be appreciated by a Latino whom you are having difficulty understanding. You can then pause and bring someone to the phone who can help.

Adapted from materials produced by American Media Incorporated, 4900 University Avenue, West Des Moines, IA 50266-6769; used with permission.

Be Considerate Place your own calls. Having an assistant place your calls and then keeping the called party waiting while you get on the line makes it appear that you believe your time is more valuable than the receiver's. Such a procedure is inconsiderate and gets the conversation off to a bad start.

[NOTE 6.27]
Placing and taking your own calls is efficient and courteous.

When taking calls, answer on the first ring, if possible, but certainly no later than the third. When you must ask a caller to wait while you gather information, return at 15- to 30-second intervals to report your progress and assure him or her that you will be back to the conversation as soon as possible. If it becomes obvious that your off-phone efforts will take longer than a minute or two, offer to return the call at a specified time. Be sure to keep a pencil and notepad close to the telephone. Before using a speaker phone, ask whether the other person objects; honor the person's preference for privacy.

[NOTE 6.28]
Keep callers informed about delays.

OFFICE POLITICS

Office politics is the name given to the competitive environment created whenever three or more people work in an organization. The competition may be for tangibles such as equipment, pay raises, promotions, or office space; it may also be for intangibles such as status or influence. Any workplace action that represents an informal attempt to protect self-interest, meet personal needs, and advance personal goals could be termed office politics. The way in which office politics affects a relationship depends on the situation and the people involved—sometimes it can be benign; other times, incendiary.

[NOTE 6.29]
The office is a competitive environment with its own politics.

Each of us may want to believe that the workplace is fair and that gains come solely through hard work. We may want to believe that we can trust everyone, that comments can be made without fear of retaliation, and that statements made in confidence will remain confidential. We want to believe that rules exist and that everyone will follow them. In reality, that is not the case. Written rules seldom address competitive strategies and, even when they do, bending and breaking occur. These comments may sound cynical, but they are not meant to be. Their purpose is to introduce a topic that can best be described as a gray area in communication, an area dependent as much on perception as on fact. Consider the following example.

[NOTE 6.30]
Office politics have no written rules.

B. J. and Shawn worked in different units of a large organization. B. J. had been with the company for about two years and worked in an entry-level position; positive performance reviews resulted in pay raises and increased levels of responsibility but no promotion. Shawn had been with the company for over ten years and managed a growing division. The two, both of whom were interested in physical fitness, had no real interaction until they joined a new health club near their homes. Over the next several months, their common interest outside the office led to conversations at work. People began to notice and, when B. J. applied for and was hired for a supervisory position in Shawn's division, people began to talk. "It's office politics," they said, "B. J. didn't earn that promotion. At least six people in Shawn's division are more qualified. B. J. was hired just because of their friendship. Shawn didn't even know who B. J. was until they met at that health club. I heard that B. J. joined that health club because several managers belonged."

Was the meeting between B. J. and Shawn coincidence or strategy? Was their friendship genuine or contrived? Did Shawn hire B. J. because of qualifications or friendship? Was the promotion a function of networking? office politics? neither? both? The answers are anything but clear.

[NOTE 6.31] Assess the political environment in your organization.

One thing is clear: Because people are human and have emotions, politics exist in every organization. Once you acknowledge the reality, you can assess the political landscape—who's who and how things get done—and decide at what level to participate. The choices run along a continuum anchored by "light" and "heavy," but there are no standard definitions of the type of behavior associated with each. Light participation in one organization may consist of participating in the grapevine only when the information is not destructive to someone. In another organization, light participation may involve identifying one or two strengths of an influential manager and supporting and playing to those strengths.

Ronna Lichtenberg, author of *Work Would Be Great if It Weren't for People,* contends that skill alone is insufficient for survival in today's organizations; people must be good at office politics, too.[1] This view is shared by others, among them Rebecca Luhn Wolfe, author of *Office Politics: Positive Results From Fair Practices,* who advocates practical, ethical choices based on five rules:[2]

[1] Understand your corporate culture. Follow policy unless you are in a position to change it.

[2] Know when to hold and when to fold. Each is appropriate depending on the situation; be flexible.

[3] Believe in win-win situations. Being able to negotiate a solution can help you survive.

[4] Play fair. Respect yourself and others.

[5] Think first, act later. Results will be better if based on reason rather than emotion.

You probably won't be able to assess the political environment in an organization until you begin working there. If you find yourself working in an organization where the politics don't match your beliefs or ability to play, you may benefit by changing employers.

RELATIONSHIP REPAIR

[NOTE 6.32] With effort, damaged relationships can be repaired.

Sometimes, despite the good intentions of those involved, relationships are damaged. Rather than let pride or indifference cause them to walk away from a damaged relationship, effective communicators take steps to rebuild it.

The obvious thing to do, of course, is apologize. Sometimes a simple "I'm sorry" is all that's needed. When this simple statement doesn't accomplish its goal, however, the speaker must make an additional effort. Acknowledging that he or she played a part in the failure is an option, but the speaker must do so sincerely and without expectation that the receiver will also claim responsibility. Relinquishing dual responsibility is a sacrifice that demonstrates the speaker's commitment to rebuilding the relationship.

[1] "Office Politics," *Executive Excellence,* October 1998, pp. 14.

[2] Rebecca Luhn Wolfe, *Office Politics: Positive Results From Fair Practices,* Menlo Park, Calif.: Crisp Publications, Inc., 1997.

Depending on what caused the relationship to weaken, actions may be the glue that's needed to mend it. This is especially true when the relationship has a history of broken promises. Actions can replace or complement an apology or acknowledgment.

Finally, both parties must let go of the problem that caused the relationship failure. Until they do, the relationship cannot regain its strength or grow stronger.

Criticism

Learning Objective [3]
GIVE CRITICISM EFFECTIVELY AND RECEIVE IT APPROPRIATELY.

Praise is easy to give and nice to receive. For most people, the opposite is true of criticism. Despite our dislike for it, criticism is a fact of workplace life. Therefore, it is important that we learn to deliver it effectively and accept it without becoming defensive.

[NOTE 6.33]
Criticism contributes to improved performance.

GIVING CRITICISM

The following list contains suggestions to help you maximize the chances of having your receiver understand and accept criticism:

[NOTE 6.34]
Receiver understanding and acceptance are the goals.

[1] Be sure you have the authority to critique the receiver. If you don't, he or she will most likely reject the criticism and resent you for delivering it.

[2] Criticize one relevant concern at a time. People become overwhelmed, confused, or dejected when faced with a long list of complaints. Be assertive but consistent. Repeat and clarify the issues, but do not argue about them.

[3] Check your facts. If your receiver identifies even one small element of your concern as being false, he or she could focus on it, argue about it, and move the conversation away from the issue at hand. Once a sender's credibility on an issue is tainted, the goal cannot be accomplished.

[4] Criticize privately, preferably face-to-face. Criticism is difficult enough to receive without being embarrassed in the process. Give the receiver an opportunity to retain his or her dignity and to use every available verbal and nonverbal cue. Be sure no one interrupts your meeting with a phone call or office visit.

[5] Offer only constructive criticism. Comments that are clear, specific, and show receiver benefit will be most effective. Rather than say "Your proposal is disorganized, contains computational errors, and is a writing disaster" say "All the elements of a good proposal are here, they just need to be reordered. By placing the strongest element first, we can capture and hold the reader's attention. Double check your figures and be sure grammar and punctuation are correct."

[6] Use the you–viewpoint; criticize the action or item, not the person. "Being abrupt with a customer portrays the company as uncaring" or "You'll make a more positive personal and corporate impression if you are courteous with customers" works better than "You are abrupt with customers."

[NOTE 6.35]
Focus on the receiver; use the you–viewpoint.

[7] Be sure the receiver knows your criticism in one area won't cloud your overall judgment of him or her. Show respect and appreciation for what the person has done in other areas. Criticize personal items (e.g., hygiene, dress) only when they relate to work performance.

[8] If appropriate, accept partial responsibility for the problem. An introduction such as "Perhaps my directions weren't clear" can temper the impact of the criticism that follows.

[9] Be aware of the verbal and nonverbal cues that accompany your message. Use a conversational pace and tone. Use "blameless" gestures. Pointing with a pen or your finger, for example, creates an aura of accusation.

[NOTE 6.36] Allow the receiver to absorb and respond.

[10] Allow the receiver time to process and respond. Even when the receiver knows the purpose of the meeting is to discuss behavior or work performance, hearing the message may have an emotional impact. Accept silence and emotional displays. Listen actively and empathetically. When people believe they have been heard and understood, they are less defensive.

RECEIVING CRITICISM

[NOTE 6.37] Accept criticism without becoming defensive.

Perhaps the only thing more difficult than giving criticism is receiving it. When faced with criticism, people generally respond with "fight or flight" behavior. Fighting manifests itself as defensive, argumentative, or counterattack remarks. Fleeing can be physical (e.g., avoiding face-to-face or telephone contact) or mental (e.g., tuning out). In the long run, neither method solves the problem as effectively as (1) agreeing with the criticism or (2) seeking more information.

[NOTE 6.38] Agree with the facts; influence the perception they create.

Agreeing Criticism can be based on facts, perceptions, or both. If, for example, your supervisor identifies computational errors in your work, he or she may perceive these facts as being related to inability or carelessness. Arguing about the facts (computational errors) is futile, but you can redirect the perception by pointing out that these errors are the exception, not the rule, in your work performance. You can, however, acknowledge that you understand why he or she might feel you let him or her down. Acknowledging the other person's feelings doesn't mean you agree with them. Say what you will do to minimize the likelihood the problem will be repeated.

[NOTE 6.39] Clarify the concern by seeking more information.

Seeking More Information Showing interest in what prompts the criticism can help you decide how to fix whatever prompted it. To that end, consider doing the following:

- Ask for specific examples. "Can you show me where the errors are?"
- Describe a situation and ask whether it illustrates the problem. "Does the formula error in the spreadsheet I prepared on the Miller account illustrate your concern?"
- Paraphrase the criticism to focus on an outcome. "Are you saying that when my work contains errors it creates problems for the people who must use it?"
- Ask how you can improve. "Other than proofreading more carefully, do you have specific suggestions that might help me?"

Learning Objective [4]
DESCRIBE TECHNIQUES FOR RESOLVING CONFLICTS.

Conflict

[NOTE 6.40] Conflict can arise from various sources.

Conflict is inevitable. To deny it is to prove it. Conflict can occur in your personal life or at work. In the workplace, conflict may arise between you and a coworker, between two employees you supervise, between your department and another, or between your organization and a customer or client. Its source can be differences in personalities (e.g., extrovert and introvert), goals or expectations, values or beliefs, circumstances (e.g., money and time), or facts (e.g., different sources). Conflicts associated with values and beliefs tend to be the most difficult to resolve because they are so deeply rooted. When faced with conflict, you have four options:

- **Yield.** This approach should be used when the issue is less important to one person than to the other or when maintaining the relationship is more important than the issue. It is also the logical approach when one person knows he or she can't win or wants to bank a favor.
- **Compromise.** This approach works best when the parties have some areas of agreement on which a mutually agreeable solution can be built or, as in yielding, when the relationship is more important than the issue.
- **Overpower.** This approach should be used only in an emergency or when the issue is more important than the relationship.
- **Collaborate.** This approach requires people to work things out. It fits best in situations that may repeat themselves or when the relationship has been long term.

[NOTE 6.41]
Responses to conflict vary by person and situation.

As you can see by these descriptions, the option that could work best will vary with the situation and the people involved. This is true within as well as across cultures. When Tinsley[3] analyzed responses that Japanese, German, and American managers gave to a hypothetical conflict scenario, she learned that (1) Japanese managers preferred deferring to status power more than German and American managers; (2) German managers rated applying regulations and integrating interests equally; (3) Germans' preference for applying regulations was greater than that of American and Japanese managers; and (4) American managers preferred integrating interests more than did German and Japanese managers. Research by Morris, et al[4] found that U.S. managers, because of their relatively high value on individual achievement, rely on a competing style of conflict resolution. Chinese managers, on the other hand, rely on an avoiding style because of their relatively high value on conformity and tradition.

[NOTE 6.42]
Conflict may be good or bad.

Conflict may be healthy or destructive. At its best, conflict fosters creative thinking and the opportunity to improve. Healthy conflict is marked by the ability to disagree on one issue while working collaboratively on others. At its worst, conflict sabotages relationships, destroys morale, and polarizes people. Unhealthy conflict is not issue specific; it transcends both time and situations. Fortunately, destructive conflicts can be resolved. The techniques that follow can be used either when you are directly involved in the conflict or when you are an outside party with a vested interest in seeing it resolved.

GENERAL TECHNIQUES

[NOTE 6.43]
Conflict resolution requires good interpersonal skills.

Several conflict resolution techniques apply to situations in which you are a participant and to those in which you are facilitator:

- **Act promptly.** The longer a problem goes unattended, the greater the chance it will escalate into a major issue. If the conflict involves emotions, the parties will need time to cool off; 24 to 48 hours should be sufficient.

[3] C. Tinsley, "Models of Conflict Resolution in Japanese, German, and American Cultures," *Journal of Applied Psychology,* 83, 1998, pp. 316–323.

[4] M. W. Morris, et al, "Conflict Management Style: Accounting for Cross-National Differences," *Journal of International Business Studies,* 29, 4, 1998, pp. 729–747.

- **Schedule a meeting.** Whenever possible, meet face to face so that the participants can take advantage of nonverbal cues. Choose a neutral location so neither party has a territorial advantage.
- **Use active listening.** Every conflict has two sides, and each person fervently believes his or hers is the accurate or "right" side. Both people want to be heard and understood. Before a conflict can be resolved, both parties must be able to separate what happened from how they feel about it. Paraphrasing can be valuable in this effort.
- **Focus on the problem, not the person.** Laying blame delays resolution. The parties must respect themselves and each other.
- **Brainstorm solutions.** Look for win-win opportunities; negotiate if necessary.
- **Formalize the solution.** Putting the solution on paper allows both parties the opportunity to see as well as hear it and minimizes the likelihood that they will later disagree on the solution.
- **Implement the solution and set a date for follow-up.** The follow-up creates an air of accountability.

WHEN YOU ARE INVOLVED

[NOTE 6.44] Take the first step.

One person in a conflict must initiate resolution. Although some perceive the person who takes the first step as the weaker party, others believe he or she is the stronger. In the workplace, the latter is more likely to be true.

Before you approach the other person, critically analyze the situation and your role in it. If you don't know the basis for your position, you won't be able to explain it. Bring your emotions under control; place organizational goals above personal goals.

When you approach the other person, do so with sincerity. Issue an invitation rather than a directive. Telling the other person that you must meet will create more tension.

[NOTE 6.45] Listen before speaking.

[NOTE 6.46] Collaborate on a solution.

During the meeting, let the other person tell his or her story first. Paraphrase to verify that you understand both facts and feelings. Ask for specific examples and facts, but choose your words and tone carefully. Getting angry, arguing, telling the person how he or she should feel, making statements that ridicule or criticize the other person, or telling him or her to be quiet and listen will make the situation worse. As you listen, look for areas of agreement. When you tell your story, begin by citing areas on which you agree. Then move to those on which resolution will be necessary. If the list is short or simple, begin immediately to look for solutions. If the list is long or complex, schedule a second meeting with the understanding that you'll each come to it with possible solutions.

WHEN YOU ARE A FACILITATOR

[NOTE 6.47] Left unattended, conflict will escalate.

As a supervisor or manager, you will have responsibility for building a team, a group that will work with each other and with you to achieve goals. Productivity declines, lowered morale, absenteeism, accidents, and emotional outbursts are all signs that conflict may exist. When conflict emerges within your group, you have an obligation to see that it is resolved.

You may learn about a conflict by (1) observing it, (2) being told of it by one or both parties involved in it, or (3) being informed by a third party. Sometimes intensity can be mistaken for conflict; simply hearing raised voices isn't sufficient to presume conflict exists. If you believe you observe conflict or are told of it by a third party, document it.

If one party to a conflict tells you about it, the situation is more tenuous. You must acknowledge what you are told without giving the impression that you agree with the person. Taking sides or giving the impression that you are taking sides creates animosity and enemies. Similarly, you must refrain from placing blame or forcing the parties to apologize. Trying to identify who is at fault is unproductive; it causes you to look backward rather than forward. Being forced to apologize humiliates the parties and can increase the animosity between them.

[NOTE 6.48]
Be objective.

Regardless of how you learn about a conflict, deal with it in private. Invite the parties to meet with you separately and then together. Use the individual meetings to ascertain the real source of the conflict and its severity. Sometimes people argue about secondary concerns. Unless the key issue is identified and resolved, it will resurface. Use the group meeting to encourage teamwork and problem solving. During the joint meeting, the facilitator acts as an emcee; he or she introduces topics, clarifies, refocuses, and summarizes. Remember that your goal is to help the parties resolve their disagreement. If you approach the situation with the goal of saving or rescuing, you could cause resentment.

Learning Objective [5]
DEVELOP THE SKILLS ASSOCIATED WITH LEADING AND PARTICIPATING IN TEAMS.

Teamwork

Teamwork has permeated the corporate and nonprofit sectors of American organizations. The concept is simple—by working together, people can accomplish more than any individual can achieve by working alone—but the execution can be complex. A successful team requires persistence, energy, and focus on the part of the team leader and the team participants. Because teams are so common, it is to your advantage to know about the various types of teams, to know how teamwork benefits you and the organization, to be aware of the conditions that must exist for effective teamwork, and to learn how to be a good team leader and a good team member. As illustrated in the Communication Note on page 174, teams are so important that organizations are looking for nontraditional ways in which to develop teamwork skills. In the process, participants learn more about themselves and others, about how to maximize strengths and compensate for weaknesses.

[NOTE 6.49]
Together **E**veryone **A**chieves **M**ore.

Sally Forth

COMMUNICATION NOTE

Cooking Classes Become Teamwork Training Tools

What does cooking have to do with teamwork? A great deal if one is to believe the latest trend in management teamwork training. Participants work together to produce a meal; in some programs, they also take a personality test. What do the tests show? According to Rick Phillips, a senior trainer at the Culinary Institute of America's team-building program, the relationship between kitchen behavior and workplace traits is strong:

A person who . . .	**is . . .**
Doesn't read the recipe through	A micro-manager, not a strategic planner
Prepares all of the ingredients	More practical than visionary
Balks at holding an onion	Reluctant to tackle new things
Arranges a dish artfully	Customer-oriented; thinks about how a product is going to be received by people who are buying it
Produces *al dente* risotto	A good time manager and planner; this is a multitasker
Whips his or her own cream or makes his or her own salad dressing	Independent; likes to work on his or her own and control the environment
Washes the dishes	A team player—follows through, is responsible, compassionate.

Drawn from "Memo to the Team: This Needs Salt!" by Eileen Daspin. Printed in The Wall Street Journal, *April 4, 2000, pp. B1, 14.*

TYPES OF TEAMS

[NOTE 6.50] Teams may be categorized by type.

Teams can generally be categorized as being self-managed, process-improvement, or cross-functional.

Self-Managed Teams Teams that have a great deal of autonomy are considered to be self-directed or self-managed. Self-managed teams are ongoing groups with decision-making authority for virtually every aspect of product production or service delivery. Their responsibilities generally include planning daily work as well as hiring, firing, and training. This structure exists in organizations that have adopted teamwork as an operational model.

Process-Improvement Teams As the name implies, process-improvement teams are charged with making changes to a process. Their focus may be increasing quality, reducing costs, providing speedier service, or eliminating redundancy. Once changes have been proposed and/or implemented, the team is disbanded.

Cross-Functional Teams Members of these teams are drawn from various functional areas and charged with accomplishing a particular task, completing a particular process, or providing ongoing input about various issues. This type of team draws its strength from the perspectives and diverse viewpoints its members can present.

Regardless of the purpose for which the team was created, you will want its members to have complementary traits such as those described in the following Communication Note.

[NOTE 6.51]
Team members need complementary skills.

COMMUNICATION NOTE

The Dream Team

According to David G. Rohlander, one key to creating a perfect team is attaining behavioral diversity. The perfect team would demonstrate the characteristics shown in the following chart:

Direct
- Directive behavior
- Impatient
- Action-oriented

Focuses on getting meetings underway; pushes for closure and results. Must be balanced with needs of other members.

Steady
- Dependable
- Agreeable
- Calm

Holds the group together. Will perform tasks consistently and dependably. Excellent at following up once decisions are made.

Influencer
- Talkative
- Optimistic
- Persuasive

Most concerned with how people are interacting. Wants the process to be enjoyable for those involved. Good at presenting ideas to management and others outside the team in a persuasive, convincing way.

Cautious
- Task-oriented
- Perfectionistic
- Sensitive

Completely analyzes each decision. Leans toward perfection, so information will probably reach a higher standard because of his or her input.

Adapted from "Effective Team Building," IIE Solutions, *31, 9, September 1999, pp. 22–23.*

BENEFITS AND DRAWBACKS OF TEAMWORK

Teams have both advantages and disadvantages.

[NOTE 6.52]
Teams have personal and organizational impact.

[NOTE 6.53]
Effective participation can advance your career.

On a personal level, participating on a team can help you increase your knowledge of the organization, broaden your perspective of areas within the business, develop a sense of camaraderie with coworkers, be more visible within the organization, learn about the various management styles used by team leaders, and improve your own project management skills.

At the organizational level, teams help corporations gain a competitive advantage. In addition, they can help increase productivity, improve communication, encourage creativity, facilitate problem solving, and increase the quality of decisions. As Julie Tapp notes in her Communication Quote, good communication helps team members achieve organizational goals.

COMMUNICATION QUOTE

Interpersonal communication skills are critical in my role as an analyst. As a member of a project team working to develop an automated system, the analyst is responsible for identifying and bridging gaps between business expectations and requirements. Effective listening, as well as good oral and nonverbal communication skills, are essential; they help the project team define the business requirements and manage business expectations. Ultimately, this will aid in the design and development of a system that meets the company's needs.

Julie Tapp, Analyst, Federated Insurance.

The negatives of working in a group include loss of control, pressure to conform, and uneven distribution of workload, a phenomenon also known as "free riding" or "social loafing." With effective team leadership and participation, these disadvantages can be neutralized or eliminated.

CONDITIONS FOR EFFECTIVE TEAMWORK

[NOTE 6.54] Communication, cohesiveness, and potential for growth foster team success.

For teams to function effectively, the following conditions must exist:

- **Communication must be open and honest.** Members must trust and respect one another. Ideas should be offered freely and listened to with patience and courtesy. Decisions should be based on an idea's merits, not on the popularity or power of the person who offers it. Personal attacks reduce the comfort level within the team and can promote retaliation or reduced participation.
- **The team must be cohesive.** Members must share and be committed to the team's goals and vision. When some members are excluded, the spirit of cooperation is threatened. Members must be free to interact with each other and with the leader.
- **Growth should be fostered.** The needs of the individual, the team, and the organization must be considered. At the individual level, participation should offer the opportunity for personal and professional growth. Keeping the group to a workable size helps make this happen. When teams exceed ten members, communication and coordination pose challenges. Balanced contributions are more difficult to achieve in a large team; some members may even try to be anonymous.

The following Communication Note describes the stages of the team development life cycle.

COMMUNICATION NOTE

Five Stages in the Project-Team Development Life Cycle

[1] *Forming.* Team members come together with a sense of anticipation and commitment. Motivation is high, but effectiveness is moderate since members are still unsure of each other.
[2] *Storming.* Members challenge the view of others and express their own. Finding areas of disagreement causes both motivation and effectiveness to drop.
[3] *Norming.* Although there may be some preconceived opinions, members agree on the principles of cooperation. Ideas are exchanged openly; motivation and effectiveness begin to increase.
[4] *Performing.* Members have built strong relationships and trust each other; motivation and effectiveness are high.
[5] *Mourning.* The team reaches the end of its work. Effectiveness can either increase as members make one concerted effort to complete the task or fall as they regret the end of the project and breaking up of the relationships they have formed.

A. A. Bubshait and G. Farooq, "Team Building and Project Success," Cost Engineering, *41, 7, July 1999, pp. 34–38.*

MEETING LEADERSHIP AND PARTICIPATION

Meetings are the common vehicle through which teams develop plans, report on progress, and coordinate efforts toward reaching their goals. Depending on their jobs and the industries in which they work, managers report spending anywhere from 30 to 60 percent of their time in meetings. Unfortunately, many businesspeople view meetings as boring, intrusive time wasters. Knowing how to lead and participate in meetings is, therefore, essential to helping you make them worthwhile, productive experiences. The suggestions offered in the following Communication Note may also be useful.

[NOTE 6.55]
Meetings are vehicles for sharing information and solving problems.

COMMUNICATION NOTE

Ways to Add Life to Your Meetings

A. Have a Team Tug of War
Author Stephen S. Kaagan (*Leadership Games: Experiential Learning for Organizational Development*) recommends holding a "tug of war" when teams are divided on an issue. The two opposing viewpoints are clearly stated and sides of the room designated for each opinion. After members have moved to the side matching their view, each group attempts to pull members of the other group to its side using reasoning and persuasion.

Reported by Melissa Master in "Lessons From the Playground," Across the Board, *36, 4, April 1999, p. 62.*

B. Get a Rise Out of Meetings
Management researchers at the University of Missouri ran a series of tests and found that when meeting participants were asked to stand during the session, meetings were 34 percent shorter and the quality of the decision making was not impaired. Those who stood reported greater satisfaction with the meeting.

Reported in "Golden Business Ideas," Journal of Accountancy, *188, 6, December 1999, p. 128.*

Keys for Effective Small-Group Meeting Leadership Sometimes effective teams arise naturally; more often, they need guidance and leadership. The person primarily responsible for the success of a team is the leader. The keys for successful small-group leadership are presented in the following paragraphs.

[NOTE 6.56]
The way a group operates is influenced by its purpose.

Determine the Purpose of the Group The scope of the group's responsibility and authority must be defined. Will it make recommendations, or does it have the power to act? Is the group an ongoing one, designed to share information and solve problems as they arise, or is it a special team formed to brainstorm solutions to a specific dilemma? The purpose of a group will influence the way in which it accomplishes its work. Therefore, the leader must ensure that the group's purpose is clear, communicated to, and understood by all members.

Determine the Purpose of Each Meeting Planning, brainstorming, sharing information, solving problems, and training are among the reasons for which meetings may be held. Groups that meet regularly (e.g., weekly meeting of department managers) may have more than one purpose for each meeting. Members might share information about human resource needs and, at the same meeting, brainstorm about ways in which space may be reallocated.

[NOTE 6.57]
Hold meetings only when necessary.

Before scheduling a face-to-face meeting, be sure it needs to be held. Meetings, even regularly scheduled weekly or monthly meetings, should be canceled if no issues need to be discussed or no decisions need to be made. Consider, too, whether another format might better serve the group. A two- or three-person conversation, an e-mail, or a telephone conference might be more efficient. Although face-to-face meetings have a social dimension, socializing should not be the only reason for meeting.

[NOTE 6.58]
Keep groups to a manageable size.

All too often, people are invited to meetings because the leader doesn't want them to feel left out. Although appropriate in many settings, courtesy is insufficient reason for including someone at a meeting. The larger the group, the less productive the session will be. Limit attendance to those who are instrumental in achieving the group's goals.

[NOTE 6.59]
Prepare and distribute agenda and related materials in advance.

Plan the Meeting Agenda The group leader must prepare the meeting agenda carefully. The topics to be discussed should be listed in some logical order, in a sequence that serves the purpose of the group. For a formal meeting, copies of the agenda and all related materials should be distributed a few days in advance of the meeting so that the members can prepare. When the volume of attachments is small, e-mail is a suitable distribution method. Outlines for two styles of agenda are presented in Figure 6.1. Either could be modified to include the name of the person responsible for each item and to indicate the approximate time to be devoted to each item. For informal meetings with very limited scope, a telephone message describing the date, time, place, and topic may be sufficient.

[NOTE 6.60]
Weigh the effects of start time, end time, and duration.

The time at which a meeting is held can have an effect on its success. Scheduling a meeting for early morning (e.g., 8:15 a.m.) suggests importance; starting at an off-hour time (e.g., 10:45 a.m.) encourages punctuality; selecting an odd starting time (e.g., 1:17 p.m.) captures interest; and scheduling meetings for times just before lunch or at the end of the day encourages timely adjournment. Finally, keep meetings brief. Attention and interest wane after about 45 minutes. If meetings must be longer than an hour, schedule a short break, then reconvene.

Traditional Agenda	Functional Agenda
Group Name Time, Day, and Date of Meeting Location	Group Name Time, Day, and Date of Meeting Location
Participants and Guests Call to Order Minutes of Previous Meeting Reports of Standing Committees Reports of Special (ad hoc) Committees Old Business New Business Announcements Adjournment	Participants and Guests Action Items Discussion Items Information Items

Figure 6.1
Sample Agenda Outlines

The first time a group gathers, list the names of participants on the agenda. Be sure to list the names of guests any time they attend. Knowing who will attend a meeting helps participants plan for the event.

Select and Prepare the Meeting Facility Most routine business meetings are held on-site. Off-site meetings encourage efficiency by minimizing interruptions such as telephone calls; the rental, transportation, and time costs may, however, make them desirable primarily for sessions devoted to strategic planning or similar purposes.

[NOTE 6.61]
Consider site options.

The group leader or a support staff member should arrange for the meeting room and be sure that it is properly prepared. Items to be considered include adequate seating; writing surfaces and supplies; extra copies of the agenda and related materials; room temperature and ventilation; audiovisual equipment, cords, and power sources; lighting and location of light switches; and refreshments. Preparations should be completed well in advance of the meeting and checked about an hour before the meeting starts. The leader should arrive a few minutes early to make a final check of the facility.

Lead the Group Discussion During the meeting, the primary role of the leader is to assist the group in achieving its purpose. This means keeping the group focused on its tasks and not allowing the discussion to stray to unrelated topics. It also means moving from one item on the agenda to the next in a timely manner without stifling adequate discussion. The leader must discourage private discussions among members. Asking members to share their comments with the entire group could bring new insights to the topic or discourage future side conversations. Another strategy is to stop the meeting until the side discussions cease.

[NOTE 6.62]
Lead the discussion to achieve the group's purpose.

A good group leader actually talks very little during a meeting. Rather, he or she serves as a facilitator, a catalyst—someone who motivates participants to work together effectively and who secures group decisions after adequate discussion. Unless the leader anticipates having to exercise authority during a meeting, she or he should sit among the members rather than at the head of the conference table.

Encourage Appropriate Participation The group leader is responsible for eliciting the best contributions possible from each participant. The Tips and Hints box on page 180 lists ways to encourage members to participate in discussions. She or he should

[NOTE 6.63]
Encourage meaningful contributions.

create an environment in which ideas are offered freely and responded to constructively. Whenever anyone presents an idea, ask the others to indicate its strengths as well as its weaknesses and to suggest specific ways to eliminate the weaknesses. If the group is a committee formed of employees from different levels in an organization, some higher-level people might intimidate some of the lower-level people. Avoid creating this situation. While formed into a group with a specific purpose, all employees should be considered equal in order to obtain effective contributions from all participants.

Tips for Encouraging Appropriate Participation in Discussions

TIPS AND HINTS

When members speak too much

[1] Thank the speaker, summarize his or her views (this shows you've listened), and invite another member to speak.
[2] Stress to the whole group that it is important for everyone to have an equal chance to comment.
[3] Suggest that the group is beginning to cover the same territory again and that it needs to move on.
[4] Remind the whole group at the start of the meeting that participation should be uniform.
[5] Sit next to the perpetually dominant person to make it more difficult for him or her to get the leader's attention.
[6] Ask the talkative person to serve as recorder so he or she has less time to participate.
[7] Speak with the member individually after the meeting.

When members speak too little

[1] Ask direct questions; draw on the individual's particular expertise relative to the topic.
[2] Have one member summarize the ideas presented by another speaker.
[3] Ask members for their viewpoints on several safe topics before seeking input on controversial items.
[4] Speak to members individually outside the meeting setting. Tell them that their contributions have value and ask what could be done to make them more active participants.

[NOTE 6.64] Be aware of time without discouraging discussion.

Be Time Conscious The group leader should start and adjourn the meeting on time. Periodically, the leader may need to remind the group of its time constraints. Comments on time must be made judiciously, however, or they will restrict discussion.

Be sure to stick to the agenda. Allowing a member to introduce topics not on the agenda usually results in hasty, uninformed decision making. The group is disadvantaged because only the person who introduces the new topic has had adequate time to prepare to discuss it. Manipulative group members may try to use this tactic to advance a personal or hidden agenda. Such behavior destroys team unity.

Just before the meeting ends, summarize what has been accomplished and clearly state who is to do what by when. If appropriate, set the date of the next meeting.

[NOTE 6.65] Resolve conflicts before they damage teamwork.

Resolve Group Conflicts Often participants in group meetings take opposing positions. This is natural and healthy. When disagreements intensify, however, they can lead to animosity or hostility and destroy a group's ability to work as a team. The leader must resolve conflicts before they reach a destructive level. When conflicts arise within your group, follow the suggestions in the following Tips and Hints box.

Tips for Resolving Group Conflicts

TIPS AND HINTS

The first task in conflict resolution is to be sure the basic issue in the disagreement is clear. If the conflict continues after the issue is clarified, the leader has several options including the following:

[1] Take a vote, leaving the decision to majority rule.
[2] Postpone discussion, giving time for reflection.
[3] Submit the conflict to an arbitrator, such as a superior officer in the company.
[4] Create subgroups and ask each to work independently for 10 to 15 minutes. When the time ends, ask each group to report its proposed solution or compromise.
[5] Move to the next agenda item after deciding the conflict is not worthy of the group's time.

Maintain Appropriate Records The leader should ensure that a record of the group's activities is maintained. Some groups conduct highly structured meetings. These groups closely follow the rules of parliamentary procedure and keep detailed records. Most business meetings, however, are far less structured. Decisions are reached by consensus rather than by vote. If motions are made, they typically follow discussion rather than precede it.

Depending on the formality of the group, photocopying notes made on the agenda may be a sufficient record. If a more formal written record must be maintained, delegate the recording task to someone who isn't part of the group. Having a support staff member or other individual take notes gives members the opportunity for full participation without distraction. If staff support isn't available, the leader should keep the record or ask a member to do so. The member may volunteer, be elected, or agree to serve when asked. In groups that meet regularly, the task of recording and distributing minutes is often rotated among members. Another option is to have major points or actions listed on newsprint or flip charts during the meeting so that all members can see and agree on what is to be recorded. Minutes are then prepared from these notes. Suggestions for preparing traditional minutes for group meetings are given in Chapter 13.

[NOTE 6.66]
Appropriate records must be maintained and shared in a timely manner.

Minutes or notes should be distributed promptly following each meeting. This procedure will enable members to note any corrections while the meeting is still fresh in mind. Minutes of one meeting also serve as a platform from which the agenda for a subsequent meeting can be developed. E-mail can be an effective tool for distributing and receiving feedback about meeting records.

The fluid nature of business suggests that someone may be the leader of one group and a participant in another. To be effective, the business professional must recognize and accept his or her role in each situation.

Keys for Successful Small-Group Meeting Participation The following keys for successful small-group participation will increase your effectiveness in team meetings.

[NOTE 6.67]
Participation requires preparation.

Prepare to Participate Every member of a team should learn as much as possible about the group's purpose. If an agenda is provided in advance, information can be gathered on each topic to ensure intelligent participation. All available background information should be studied.

[NOTE 6.68]
Leave personal and work-related problems behind.

Participate Appropriately Members should arrive on time and be ready to devote their full attention to the meeting. Other work-related problems should be set aside temporarily. Members should participate by making clear, concise comments; asking relevant questions; and voting on issues. Participants must maintain objectivity in their comments and control their emotions. Lively debate is healthy; arguments are destructive. Honesty must permeate all discussions. Withholding information is unethical.

[NOTE 6.69]
Concentrate on what speakers say.

Listen Effectively Meetings can challenge listening skills. Group members will spend most of their time listening to other participants' comments and must strive to keep their concentration. Members should not have side conversations, gaze into space, or exhibit other behavior that detracts from effective listening. Participants can be surprised when, without warning, a speaker asks them what they think. Listeners must be ready to become speakers at any time.

Take Thorough Notes Bring paper and a pen to every meeting. Use them to record key words, ideas, dates, and activities. Using an outline format will help you take notes while still being an active participant in discussions.

[NOTE 6.70]
Be courteous and fair to speakers.

Be Courteous Participants must respect the rights and opinions of others. Opinions should be expressed tactfully, avoiding any indication of self-righteousness. By accepting different viewpoints and by being willing to discuss them, participants can help encourage open discussion. Members should not interrupt, even when the speaker pauses midthought. Avoid sarcasm; use humor carefully.

OTHER MEETING FORMATS

[NOTE 6.71]
Alternative formats can be effective.

Now and in the future, we can expect more work to be accomplished by **virtual teams**—people who are connected via e-mail, groupware, and conferencing software.

One advantage of virtual teams is that groups can transcend the boundaries of time and location. A company with offices in North America and Europe can establish teams with members on the two continents and effectively lengthen the work day by having the project handed from one team to another across time zones.

Virtual teams also level status differences that can occur when people representing various levels within an organization meet in person. As a result, ideas are more likely to be evaluated on merit; team members contribute more often and more freely because they feel a certain level of anonymity when communicating electronically. In addition, the convenience of these meetings often means that more people can contribute; better decisions may result from broader input as well as from ready access to files and other materials.

Although some managers perceive that motivation and morale building are more difficult in virtual teams, computer technology has been so well integrated into our personal and professional lives that concerns about the ability to create team spirit without face-to-face meetings is waning. People now initiate and maintain relationships via the Internet.

The following paragraphs describe four common ways in which technology can be used in virtual teams.

E-mail and Groupware E-mail (electronic correspondence) and groupware (calendaring/scheduling, real-time meetings, bulletin boards, group document handling, and project tracking) support the work of virtual teams by allowing team members to exchange messages and share documents. These items are discussed more fully in Chapter 3 and referenced elsewhere throughout this text.

[NOTE 6.72]
Technology supports virtual teams.

Audio Conferencing Audio conferences use telephone technology to link participants. The typical audio conference begins with a roll call to determine whether all participants are online and whether the connection is clear. Next, the leader verifies that all participants have received the agenda and appropriate supplementary materials. If not, accommodations must be made (fax or e-mail the materials; summarize materials as items are presented). Once these tasks have been accomplished, the group works through the agenda.

[NOTE 6.73]
Audio conferences use modified meeting procedures.

Because members cannot see one another and may not recognize a speaker's voice, participants should introduce themselves every time they speak. Speaker identification also helps the recorder keep accurate notes. If a member must leave the call for any reason, he or she should announce the departure.

Although audio conferences do not permit use of visual cues, the absence of eye contact sometimes makes people more willing to speak. For some people, meetings are more free and less intimidating in this mode.

Video Conferencing Video conferencing is the electronic version of a long-distance, face-to-face meeting. It is preferred over audio conferencing when the meeting involves bargaining, persuasion, images, or complex topics. The ability to see participants' faces and observe their body language enhances the communication.

[NOTE 6.74]
Video conferences permit long-distance, face-to-face communication.

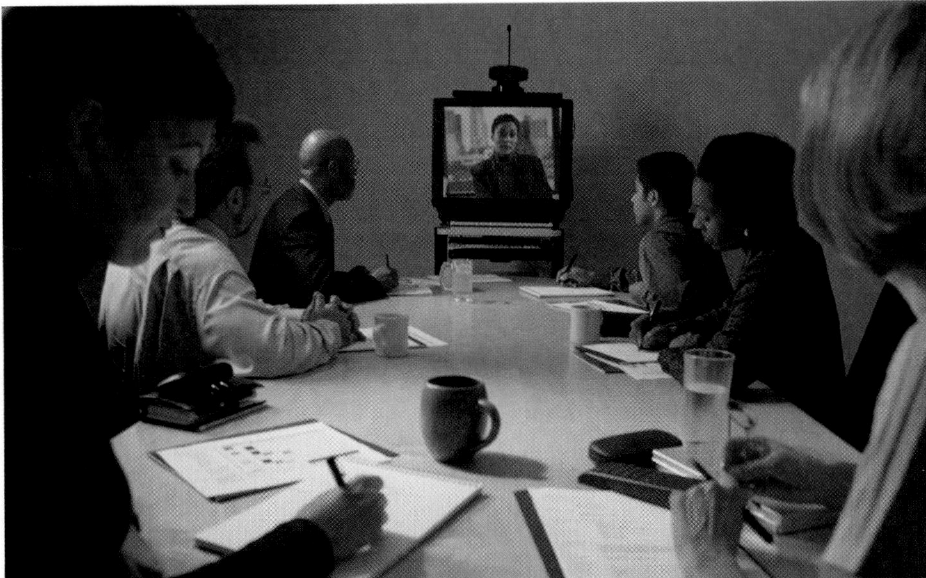

Video conferencing allows participants to take advantage of nonverbal cues.

In order to take part in a video conference, each meeting participant must be at a site equipped with a camera, microphone, and viewing screen. Depending on the organization, the site may be an individual's office, a conference room, or a commercial facility. The equipment the individual uses may be a simple, relatively inexpensive PC-based system or a costly, highly sophisticated system requiring special operating equipment and technical support personnel. The quality of the picture and the number of sites that can be displayed simultaneously vary with the nature of the equipment.

[NOTE 6.75] Whether basic or sophisticated, equipment should be tested in advance.

Regardless of the site or the nature of the equipment, the procedures for conducting a video conference parallel those used to conduct an audio conference. The meeting begins with a roll call to ensure that all group members are connected and that the equipment works properly. If participants are not familiar with one another, each displays a large-print name card at his or her station. The meeting then proceeds according to the agenda and within the framework of the technology used to link the sites.

Electronic Meetings Group decision support system (GDSS) software combines the power of networked personal computers with specialized software to enable teams to work together better and faster whether at the same site or at different locations. The number of participants is limited only by the number of stations on the network.

[NOTE 6.76] Electronic meetings allow anonymous input.

GDSS meetings begin with members signing in and, if the group is meeting for the first time, entering a brief biographical sketch describing the skills and experiences they bring to the meeting. This process parallels the oral introductions common in face-to-face meetings. Unlike oral introductions, which may be forgotten soon after they are made, the biographical sketches are stored and made available to members throughout the meeting. The constant availability of information doesn't end with personal sketches. Participants may also use their computers to retrieve data from any other source normally accessible through the network used to link group members.

As the meeting progresses and issues arise, participants offer facts or opinions by keying them at their PCs. When a member is satisfied with the message, he or she submits it. All submissions are anonymous, so members are less reluctant to participate. Contributions are evaluated and responded to solely on their merit.

[NOTE 6.77] Electronic meetings can be fast paced.

A facilitator receives all comments and, unless directed to screen them, makes them available to all group members. The method used to view the shared comments varies with the situation in which the group operates. If members are gathered in a room designed specifically for GDSS meetings, items are projected on a large screen for all to see. If members are working from remote PCs, comments are displayed on their computer screens. Contributions may be made (keyed) simultaneously, not sequentially as in oral communication. This means that the pace of the meeting is more rapid than in other formats. In her Communication Quote, Blanca Arellano describes how a GDSS system facilitated collaboration between public and private entities in Southern California.

Voting, too, can be accomplished quickly and easily. In fact, the ease with which votes can be taken encourages groups to use methods other than the traditional yes or no vote. Allocation, multiple choice, and ranking votes can be tallied and analyzed almost effortlessly.

COMMUNICATION QUOTE

Collaboration between public and private entities is critical to accomplishing PED Corp.'s mission. Since economic development is driven by private investment and facilitated by the public sector, the Pomona Economic Summit focused on bringing the two stakeholders together to improve the quality of life in the city. The Summit was facilitated by the technology utilized at the Group Decision Support Systems (GDSS) room at Cal Poly. It allowed the "best minds" in each of the issue forums (Image/Marketing, Public Safety, Economic Development, Infrastructure/Transportation, Workforce Development) to anonymously evaluate Pomona's strengths and weaknesses, to suggest improvements and identify opportunities for ongoing collaboration.

Blanca Arellano, CEO, Pomona Economic Development (PED) Corp.

When the meeting ends, all input is automatically stored on the computer, replacing minutes as the permanent record of the meeting. The record can be printed or saved to diskette for future reference.

Whether the meetings you attend are conducted face-to-face or by another method, be sure to follow the techniques associated with good meeting leadership and participation.

Learning Objective [6]
DESCRIBE THE FEATURES OF AND PROCESS USED BY A WRITING TEAM.

Writing Teams

So far, information in this chapter has focused on skills other than writing. Sometimes, though, the product or outcome of teamwork is a written document such as a long report or a complex proposal. Therefore, it seems appropriate to comment on writing teams in this chapter rather than in one devoted to writing.

[NOTE 6.78]
Teamwork can involve writing.

THE WRITING TEAM

The composition of a writing team varies with the task to be accomplished. For one message, the team might be you and your boss; for another message, the team might consist of persons from various departments, computer and research specialists, and an editor.

Regardless of its size and membership, a writing team will face the same challenges and use the same communication skills as those of teams formed for other purposes. Members must communicate well verbally and nonverbally. They must be effective listeners. Effective group dynamics have to prevail during team meetings. Team members must respect each other and have complementary skills. In a shared writing effort, team members must be open to constructive criticism and be able to disagree with each other without being disagreeable. A group loyalty must develop. Team members must understand the writing process and be able to implement it. They have to agree on a schedule and adhere to it.

[NOTE 6.79]
Writing teams have the same characteristics and challenges as other teams.

Productive collaborative writing depends on an effective team effort that competently implements the planning and composing process. In the appropriate communication situation, collaborative writing can result in a message that is comprehensive, accurate, and concrete—a message that is more powerful than an individual could develop.

THE TEAM WRITING PROCESS

[NOTE 6.80] Adapt the three-step writing process to the team format.

In team writing, the planning and composing process described in Chapter 5 is usually carried out in the following manner:

Step 1: Determine the Purposes. Step 1 is a group effort. Team members analyze the communication situation and agree on the primary and secondary purposes.

Step 2: Analyze the Receiver for the You–Viewpoint. Step 2 is also a cooperative effort. Team members discuss and agree about which reader benefits will be used.

Step 3: Compose Message Content. Although message planning can be accomplished in a group setting, the physical act of writing is more efficient when done by an individual. Therefore, part of Step 3 is performed by the group and part by individuals as follows:

- Selecting the type of message and organizational plan is usually done in team meetings.
- Outlining the message content is usually divided. Broad concepts developed during a team brainstorming session are refined by the individual to whom the drafting task is assigned.
- Drafting is accomplished by one person, who makes individual contacts with others to obtain data necessary to make the document clear and complete. When two or more people meet to draft a document, the process becomes inefficient. Different thinking and writing styles prolong the process and actually reduce the quality of the product.
- Revising, editing, and proofreading responsibilities are split. The person who drafts the document shares it (electronically or in paper form) with members of the team. Each member suggests changes to content and organization and notes typographical, grammar, punctuation, and style errors. When documents are shared electronically, members see all suggestions offered by other team members; when paper is the medium, changes are generally referred to the draft's author. The document may go through several iterations of revising and editing before the group meets to review the final product.

Summary of Learning Objectives

Learning Objective [1]

Identify the components of interpersonal communication. Interpersonal communication refers to the verbal and nonverbal interactions in one-to-one or small-group settings. Listening, speaking, and nonverbal communication are the primary elements of a person's "people skills," but writing can also reflect them. Interpersonal communication has a major influence on the communication climate of an organization.

Enhance your ability to build positive relationships. Conversations, the core of positive relationships, follow a five-step process: greeting, introduction, exchange, summary, and closing. The effectiveness of a conversation can be enhanced when participants pay attention to the location, minimize interruptions, speak skillfully, send appropriate nonverbal cues, ask questions, listen for words and emotions, and accommodate diversity. Efficient and effective equipment operation, consideration, and a businesslike manner will help make telephone conversations and voice mail messages successful. Conversations are part of office politics, a competitive environment that affects an interpersonal relationship. Once damaged, a relationship can be repaired by words and/or actions only if both parties are willing to let go of the problem that caused the damage.

Learning Objective [2]

Give criticism effectively and receive it appropriately. Criticism that is given constructively and received without being defensive can help an individual grow. Criticism should be given in private and be limited to documented, relevant, work-related concerns. Focus attention on the behavior, not the person; don't let criticism in one area cloud your judgment in another. Accept partial responsibility if appropriate. Use and read nonverbal cues carefully; allow the receiver time to consider and respond to the message. Agreeing and seeking more information are strategies to use when receiving criticism.

Learning Objective [3]

Describe techniques for resolving conflicts. When faced with conflict, people have four options: yield, compromise, overpower, or collaborate. The option chosen will vary with the people and situation; culture is a factor. Techniques that apply both to participants and to facilitators are acting promptly, scheduling the meeting, using active listening, focusing on the problem, brainstorming solutions, formalizing the solution, and implementing and following up on the solution. When a participant initiates resolution, he or she should first do a self-assessment, then sincerely approach the other person. Active listening combined with paraphrasing should reveal areas of agreement as well as areas to be resolved. Both parties should be involved in developing a solution. Techniques used to facilitate conflict resolution will vary depending on how the facilitator learned of the conflict but generally include arranging a meeting; introducing topics; and clarifying, refocusing, and summarizing discussions and agreements.

Learning Objective [4]

Develop the skills associated with leading and participating in teams. Teams—whether self-managed, process-improvement, or cross-functional—have personal and organizational advantages and disadvantages. To be effective, a team must engage in open, honest communication, be cohesive, and foster growth. Meetings are the vehicle through which teams plan, report on, and coordinate efforts to achieve goals. Both the leader and the participants have responsibilities in ensuring that meetings are productive. Although most business meetings are face-to-face gatherings, other formats are possible.

Learning Objective [5]

Describe the features of and process used by a writing team. Successful collaborative writing depends on the ability of the writing team members, the dynamics of the writing team, group loyalty, and the ability of the members to agree on a schedule and adhere to it. The tasks associated with the three-step writing process are completed either individually or as a group.

Learning Objective [6]

DISCUSSION QUESTIONS

1. What is "communication climate"? Why is it important ? (Objective 1)
2. Why do employers seek employees with good interpersonal communication skills? (Objective 1)
3. Name the five stages in the conversation process and indicate the role each plays in a successful conversation. (Objective 2)
4. Distinguish between being assertive and being aggressive during a conversation. (Objective 2)
5. Name the two types of questions and give an example of each. (Objective 2)
6. Explain how to "hear" verbal and nonverbal cues. (Objective 2)
7. How can relationships be repaired? (Objective 2)
8. Identify four factors to consider when giving criticism. (Objective 3)
9. How can a receiver seek more information about criticism he or she receives? (Objective 3)
10. What four options do people have when faced with conflict? Explain. (Objective 4)
11. What steps should you take to resolve a conflict in which you are a participant? (Objective 4)
12. How is someone who facilitates a conflict like an emcee? (Objective 4)
13. How do individuals benefit by team participation? (Objective 5)
14. Briefly describe what a meeting leader and participant should do before, during, and after a meeting. (Objective 5)
15. Define team writing and explain how teams approach the three-step writing process. (Objective 6)

APPLICATION EXERCISES

1. Interview five people. Ask each to describe the features he or she most appreciates in a best friend and a good boss. During a class discussion, combine your findings with those of other class members, paying special attention to those you would consider interpersonal skills. (Objective 1)
2. Convert the list prepared in Exercise 1 into a self-assessment. For each item, rate yourself on a 5-point scale, where 1 = poor and 5 = excellent. Identify two items on which you wish to improve and make a personal commitment to do so. (Objective 2)
3. Observe a clerk and a customer as they interact with one another. Write notes of how each uses (a) facial expressions, (b) eye contact, (c) gestures, (d) posture, and (e) other body actions. Be prepared to discuss your findings in class. (Objective 2)

4. **Teamwork.** As best as possible, create and complete this scenario within your classroom or another room at your school: You are attending the social that precedes the business meeting of the local chapter of the Society for the Betterment of Management. Your instructor will give you a card indicating the role you are to take (e.g., officer, membership committee member or chair, speaker, speaker's spouse/guest, prospective member, new member, other member, founding member). Take on this role as you mingle within the group and engage in conversation with individuals or small groups. Remember to introduce yourself or others as appropriate. Spend 15 to 20 minutes in this activity, then discuss the exercise as a class. (Objective 2)

5. **Ethics.** Picture yourself as the author of the "Ask Andy" column in your company newsletter. This month, you receive a letter from Edna, who writes "I'm tired of all the

office politics here. I think that those who participate in office politics are unethical. Do you agree?" Respond to "Edna the Ethical Engineer." (Objective 2)

6. **Teamwork.** Recall a recent face-to-face conversation you have had. Plan a three- to four-minute presentation that (1) describes the conversation and how it paralleled the five-step process described in this chapter, (2) identifies the strengths and weaknesses of your role in the conversation, and (3) suggests improvements to be made in your next conversation with this person. Working in small groups assigned by your instructor, give your presentation. (Objective 2)

7. **Teamwork.** As your instructor directs, role play one or more of the following situations in which you are required to give constructive criticism: (Objective 3)
   - **a.** One of the workers in your office has complained to you that another worker has offensive foot odor. You have checked the facts and must now discuss the problem with the second worker and agree on a way to solve it.
   - **b.** Clerks in the retail store you manage were encouraged to participate in the mall's Halloween festivities by wearing costumes to work. One person has chosen to wear something you believe is inappropriate to the image of your store. Handle the situation.
   - **c.** During the past month, several customers have hinted that one of your customer service representatives treated them rudely. Convey the message to the representative.

8. **Teamwork.** Conduct a classroom "tug of war" on one of the following items or a controversial issue at your school: (Objective 4)
   - **a.** Dress code for business students at your university
   - **b.** Employer's right to monitor workers' e-mail
9. Another "Ask Andy" writer (see Exercise 5) says, "Lately, I'm uncertain about what's expected of me. I think the major cause is the incomplete notes I take at meetings." Prepare the response you'll include in your column. Address your response to "Clueless in Payroll." (Objective 5)

10. **Teamwork.** In a group of three to five students, brainstorm the challenges that one faces when collaborating on the writing of a student project. Present your ideas to the class. (Objective 6)

11. **Teamwork. E-mail.** Work with one other student in your class. Identify and arrange to attend a regularly scheduled meeting of some group (e.g., student organization, faculty/staff committee, professional society) at your school or in your community. (Objective 5 and 6)
    - **a.** Prepare a written report that describes the extent to which the leader and participants followed the guidelines presented in this chapter.
    - **b.** E-mail to your instructor a message in which you describe how you and your teammate divided the work on this project.

There are Web exercises at **http://krizan.swcollege.com** to accompany this chapter.

MESSAGE ANALYSIS

Arrange the following items into the agenda for a meeting. Use the functional format. Correct typographical errors.

Bob Harman (chair)
January 1/16
Approve minute of last Week's meating
Hillary Patberg (guest; staff representative to benefits task force; guest)
Sybil Hutchinson—need to decide on property insurance cararier
2–3 a.m.
Chad Donald—update on computer upgrades
Art Westberg wants us to review the equipment acquisition procedure
Wilma Marvin—will have recommmendations from benifits task force
next Tuesday
Conference Room B
Budget Committee
Distribute budget planning forms for next fiscal year; fist draft due March 22

GRAMMAR WORKSHOP

Correct the grammar, spelling, punctuation, style, and word choice errors in the following sentences:

1. Mr. Maki enquired if the crowd had disbursed.
2. The polls show people thing the irs has made process toward improving it's level fo consumer service
3. A mix of stocks bonds and short term reserves will help you achieve a secure financial future.
4. Built in 1997 fore approximately $15.9 million dollars the River Road development contains 224 one, two, and three-bedroom apartments in seven three-story bldgs..
5. Everybody whom attended the demonstration were able to get their questions answered during the ten minute question:answer section that followed the 20 minute presentation.
6. For your convienence I have inclosed a coupon good for a ten % discount which means you'll pay only 13.95 for a full-year of "The Money Manager's Guide".
7. Knowing how much you enjoy sweats, the desert bar will include a assortment of cakes, cookys, pies, bars, and tarts: all of em calorie free.
8. 4,400 companies—about 1/3 of those operating within the State has less then 5 hundred employees.
9. The manger will of course consider both personal and financial resource implications before deciding how to procede with the expandsion.
10. When you visit any of the sights discribed on the enclosed brochure the the history of our Country will come alive.

PART 3

Correspondence Applications

CHAPTER

7 Positive and Neutral Messages

Dick Anderson, BellSouth Corporation

LET'S TALK BUSINESS In my role as President—Customer Markets for BellSouth Corporation, I use verbal and nonverbal communication skills daily to deliver a positive or neutral message. As an example, I might speak to the industry press regarding the introduction of a new BellSouth product or service or discuss the advantages of BellSouth as a communications provider with a major client, both of which rely on the ability to emphasize the positive.

My responsibilities include leadership of all domestic sales and marketing operations with $18 billion in annual revenue. With customers, it is essential to be able to concisely and with confidence present information, offer an explanation, personalize the appeal, and then close with conviction. It is

(Continued)

[LEARNING OBJECTIVES]

[1] DESCRIBE POSITIVE AND NEUTRAL MESSAGES.

[2] DESCRIBE THE FOUR SPECIFIC GUIDELINES FOR USING THE DIRECT PLAN.

[3] DISTINGUISH BETWEEN POOR AND GOOD POSITIVE AND NEUTRAL MESSAGES.

[4] PREPARE COMPETENTLY A VARIETY OF POSITIVE AND NEUTRAL MESSAGES USING THE DIRECT PLAN.

essential because your competitor may have used the same approach to position its offer earlier in the day.

Equally, BellSouth's sales associates use the direct approach to describe BellSouth's position in the market and the prospects for our future.

In a world increasingly dependent on e-business, concise e-mail messages are essential to success. E-mail has the power to shorten decision cycles by conveying needed information without the normal protocols around hierarchy. It is most effective for decisions when it conveys only the most critical facts and advocates a decision or point of view. •

Learning Objective [1]
DESCRIBE POSITIVE AND NEUTRAL MESSAGES.

A **positive** or **neutral message** conveys pleasant, favorable, or neutral information to the receiver. Such a message may (1) inquire about a service, a product, or a person; (2) approve a request that has been made of you or your organization; (3) announce an upcoming sale or a new product; or (4) be used in internal communication to announce promotions, expansions, salary increases, or improvements in fringe benefits. The receiver will be getting information that is favorable or neutral and will accept easily the contents of the message. The message should be constructed using the direct plan so the receiver can readily see the benefits. As illustrated in the following Communication Note, communicating information in a positive manner can be beneficial.

[NOTE 7.1]
Positive and neutral messages give favorable or neutral information.

COMMUNICATION NOTE

Keeping Track of Guests

Marriott International uses special customer management software to send positive messages in an effort to keep customers happy and hopefully keep them coming back. In 1998, this approach helped generate an additional $55 million for the large hotel chain.

Marriott's software allows hotel representatives to pull together information from a number of internal departments and various resorts on any particular returning guest. Representatives then can use this information to send positive messages regarding that guest's unique needs. Imagine how a customer feels when they contact the Marriott and the agent already knows what type of room they require, whether they need a rental car, which special events or activities to offer to book for them, and more. This kind of information frees the customer from hours of planning, and can leave the guest with a wonderful feeling.

Hotel agents are also beginning to use this customer information to market Marriott properties around the world to guests. Individual customers aren't the only ones benefiting from Marriott's new technology. Businesses are also finding it easier to use the Marriott. With their needs on file, an activity planner can leave it to the Marriott to do all the legwork.

Adapted from Amy Borrus's "How Marriott Never Forgets a Guest," Business Week Online, *February 21, 2000.*

Claim messages are also discussed in this chapter because they follow a plan similar to that used for positive information. Even though claim messages may be communicating bad news—the sender is indicating that he or she has been wronged—receivers should welcome them because they assist in improving products or services. Claim messages are strengthened when written in the direct plan format.

Use the Direct Plan for Positive and Neutral Messages

[NOTE 7.2]
The direct plan immediately gives the receiver positive or neutral information.

[NOTE 7.3]
The direct plan increases the likelihood that the receiver will read the entire message.

[NOTE 7.4]
The direct plan gets the receiver in a positive frame of mind.

The **direct plan** should be used in transmitting all positive and neutral messages, written and oral. The direct plan will immediately give the good or neutral information to the receiver, who will then respond favorably to the remainder of the message. An advantage of this plan is that the receiver will know at once that the message is conveying information that is going to be beneficial (or at least not harmful). If the positive or neutral information—the purpose of the message—is not at the beginning, the receiver may lose interest and may not finish the message.

Another advantage of giving the positive or neutral information at the beginning of the message is to put the receiver in an agreeable frame of mind before presenting an explanation of the conditions related to the positive or neutral information. The explanation will have a much better chance of acceptance if the receiver is in a good mood rather than in an apprehensive state.

Learning Objective [2]
DESCRIBE THE FOUR SPECIFIC GUIDELINES FOR USING THE DIRECT PLAN.

How to Use the Direct Plan

[NOTE 7.5]
The direct plan has specific steps.

You should incorporate into your positive and neutral messages the business communication fundamentals that were presented in Chapters 1, 4, and 5. In particular, analyze your receiver and use the you–viewpoint, as discussed in Chapter 1. The four stages in the direct plan for presenting positive or neutral information are detailed in Figure 7.1.

[NOTE 7.6]
The direct plan should be used for messages presenting positive information, neutral information, and claims.

The direct plan is used for a variety of positive messages—approved adjustments, requests, credit applications, and employment applications; favorable decisions; or any other favorable information. The direct plan is also used for neutral information and claim messages. The content of the message must be decided before the direct plan can be implemented.

[NOTE 7.7]
The content of the message is developed after the situation is analyzed and its purposes are determined.

The situation must be analyzed and the primary and secondary purposes of the communication determined before any message can be composed. If the primary purpose is transmitting positive or neutral information, the direct plan should be used in organizing the message. Before composing a positive or neutral message, you must answer the following questions:

[1] What is the most favorable information?

[2] How will this information benefit the receiver?

[3] What additional information should be given to the receiver?

[4] Would a convincing sales appeal be appropriate in this message?

[5] What friendly message can be transmitted in the close to build goodwill?

Once you have determined the purposes and content, you are ready to implement the direct plan. The parts of the direct plan outline are discussed in the following sections, and the most important considerations are reviewed.

Direct Plan for Positive and Neutral Messages

I. The **Opening**
   A. Give the positive or neutral information.
   B. Be optimistic.
   C. Provide coherence.
   D. Use emphasis techniques.
   E. Stress receiver interests and benefits.

II. The **Explanation**
   A. Present related information.
   B. Be objective.
   C. Be concise.
   D. Be positive.

III. **Sales Appeal** (if appropriate)
   A. Personalize appeal.
   B. Suggest alternatives if appropriate.
   C. Aim for quick action.

IV. The **Friendly Close**
   A. Build goodwill.
   B. Be concise.
   C. Be positive.
   D. Express appreciation.

Figure 7.1
Direct Plan Outline

OPENING

In the direct plan, the memo or letter should give the positive or neutral information in the **opening**—the first paragraph of the message. Give the positive information immediately, be optimistic, provide coherence, use emphasis techniques, and stress receiver interests or benefits.

[NOTE 7.8]
In the direct plan, messages begin with positive or neutral information.

The first sentence of the first paragraph should contain the information that will be most beneficial to the receiver. Only positive words should be used in describing the information. The paragraph should be short for emphasis. The receiver's interest will be aroused if the benefits of the good information are stressed in the opening. For coherence, information should be provided so that the receiver will know which request, order, contract, or previous transaction is being discussed. This identification may be placed in a reference line.

EXPLANATION

The second part of a message using the direct plan should contain the explanation. The **explanation** presents any additional information that relates to the positive or neutral information presented in the first paragraph. The explanation is factual and, therefore, needs to be presented in an objective manner. It should be concise

[NOTE 7.9]
The supporting explanation should follow the positive or neutral opening.

but still contain all the details the receiver needs. The explanation should be written optimistically.

SALES APPEAL

[NOTE 7.10]
The sales appeal should be used when appropriate.

The **sales appeal** is the portion of a message in which the writer attempts to persuade the reader to take a specific action. It can be effective in many positive and neutral messages, but is not appropriate in all of them. Situations in which a sales appeal should be used include letters approving charge accounts, letters informing students that they have been accepted into a program, and messages approving claims. Situations in which a sales appeal would not be appropriate include claim letters and messages agreeing to speak at a meeting.

[NOTE 7.11]
The sales appeal should follow the explanation.

The sales appeal, if used, should come after the explanation. Depending on its length and nature, the sales appeal may be placed in a paragraph by itself or combined with the closing paragraph. Adapt the appeal to the situation; if possible and desirable, provide alternatives for the receiver. The sales appeal may tell about an upcoming sale or a new product. Personalize the appeal to convince the receiver that it is in his or her best interest to take immediate action.

FRIENDLY CLOSE

[NOTE 7.12]
A properly written close builds goodwill.

The friendly close is the final paragraph of a message. Its primary purpose is to build goodwill. Goodwill is built by being personal and optimistic. The close may express appreciation for an employee's past service or for a customer's business. The close may move to a related subject, or it may unify the message by referring to the good information given in the first paragraph. The close in a positive or neutral message is normally short and avoids clichés.

Learning Objective [3]
DISTINGUISH BETWEEN POOR AND GOOD POSITIVE AND NEUTRAL MESSAGES.

Implementing the Direct Plan

[NOTE 7.13]
A communication case will help illustrate how to compose positive information messages.

The direct plan is illustrated in the following case, which shows the development of a positive information letter to a customer. You could follow this same plan when organizing your thoughts prior to telephoning a customer. Here are the details of the communication situation.

THE JAMES THOMAS CASE:

James Thomas recently retired from Hard Rock Gas Company. He was employed by Hard Rock for more than 30 years. During these years he held various administrative positions and the company has decided to establish an endowed scholarship in Mr. Thomas' name that each year would award $5,000 to a student. You are Director of Human Resources for Hard Rock. You will write a letter to Mr. Thomas informing him of this scholarship and asking him to develop the guidelines for the scholarship. The Human Resources Department will need details such as the type of major to receive the scholarship, the GPA and ACT score that would be required, the student's need for financial aid, and whether the student should be an incoming freshman or an upperclassman. In addition, you will need to ask Mr. Thomas if he or one of his family members wishes to serve on the selection committee.

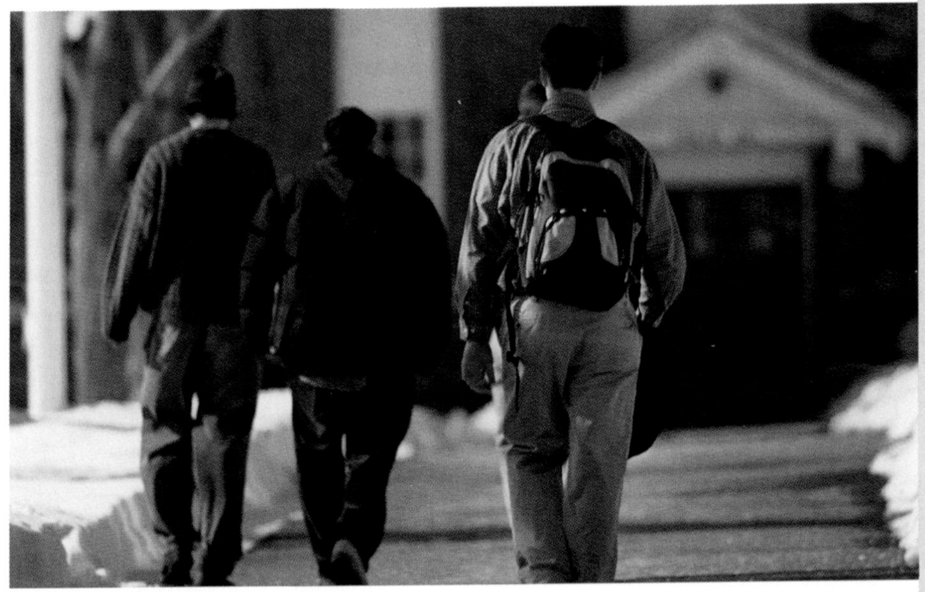

Students will be awarded the James N. Thomas Endowed Scholarship.

The first step in writing is to analyze the situation and determine the purposes and content that will most effectively accomplish the objective of the communication. In the James Thomas letter, the objective is to transmit positive information—the establishment of a scholarship. For this situation the ideas should be developed and organized using the direct plan. The following sections illustrate how the content of the positive information letter could be developed. Each section discusses a stage of the direct plan and presents an example of *poor writing* and an example of *good writing*.

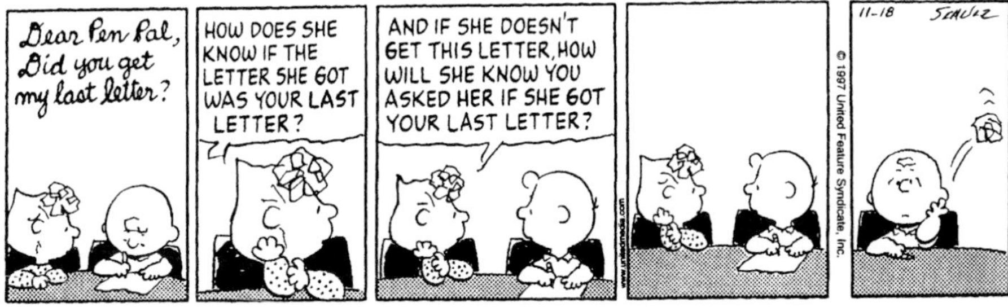

Open With the Positive Information

A **poor** opening presenting the positive information follows:

- The Hard Rock Board of Directors had its quarterly meeting yesterday. Its members have directed me to inform you that a scholarship will be established in your name.

[NOTE 7.14]
The example of a poor opening lacks the you–viewpoint.

This poorly written opening stresses the writer's interest instead of the receiver's interest and benefits. Note that the positive information, the establishment of a scholarship, is not given until the second sentence and the scholarship is not clearly described. The paragraph is also written in a stiff, impersonal manner rather than in a positive, friendly style. After reading the opening, James will be neither excited nor eager to read about the scholarship.

The following would be a **good** opening for this case problem:

[NOTE 7.15] The good opening meets all requirements for presenting positive news.

- To honor you for your many years of dedicated service, a James N. Thomas Endowed Scholarship awarding $5,000 a year will be established. This scholarship was created by the Hard Rock Board of Directors at its quarterly meeting yesterday.

In contrast to the poorly written opening, this paragraph meets all the requirements of properly presenting positive information in a message. It opens with positive information and the you–viewpoint is emphasized. The establishment of a scholarship is specifically identified in two sentences, thus providing coherence. Because this first paragraph has a positive, personal tone, James will be excited about reading the rest of the message.

Provide an Explanation

The next step in composing a message using the direct plan is to present an explanation of the conditions under which the positive information—the establishment of a scholarship—will be carried out.

A **poor** way to present an explanation to James follows:

[NOTE 7.16] The poor explanation lacks the you–viewpoint and is negative.

- I need to know what you want to include in the guidelines for the $5,000 scholarship. I need to know who should receive the scholarship each year. We have never established a scholarship fund before, so I don't know what all you need to include in the guidelines. I do need these guidelines by the end of the month.

The style of this poor explanation is similar to the style of the poor opening; it stresses the writer's interests rather than the receiver's benefits. Lack of a you–viewpoint and the tone of the message make the explanation negative. The explanation should contain all relevant facts so that the receiver will not have any questions. In this example, no assistance is given concerning the types of information to include in the guidelines. The explanation could be made more concise by stating that you would be willing to meet with James to develop the guidelines.

In contrast, a **good** explanation follows:

[NOTE 7.17] The good example meets all requirements for a positive explanation.

- This $5,000 endowed scholarship bearing your name will be awarded each year to a student from the university or college of your choice who meets the guidelines that you establish. The following information should be included in the guidelines: specific major of the recipient, required minimum GPA, required minimum ACT score, and classification of the recipient (incoming freshman or upperclassman).

This explanation presents the facts in an objective way and answers the receiver's questions. The paragraph is written positively. It contains enough information so that the receiver understands the conditions of the positive information. After presenting the explanation, the writer should consider using a sales appeal.

Consider a Sales Appeal

A sales appeal should be used whenever a writer attempts to obtain additional business from the receiver. The sales appeal, depending on its length and nature, may be written as a separate paragraph(s) or as part of the final paragraph of the letter. Topics for sales appeal may include information about additional services that the business may provide, an upcoming sale, or a new product.

In this case the following is an example of a **poor** appeal for James to serve on the selection committee:

- We will use a selection committee to pick someone for the scholarship. Since you are retired and have plenty of free time, why don't you serve on the committee?

[NOTE 7.18]
The poor example of a sales appeal is cold and impersonal.

Note the impersonal tone of the message. There is no you–viewpoint in the sales appeal and the second sentence is more likely to discourage than encourage James to serve on the committee.

- Each year a selection committee will be established to select an outstanding student to be awarded the James N. Thomas Endowed Scholarship. The selection committee will evaluate the student applications and select the student who best meets the guidelines that you establish. Jim, would you or one of your family members wish to serve on the selection committee?

[NOTE 7.19]
The good example of a sales appeal is positive and personalized.

This example of a sales appeal is written in a personalized way; it encourages James to serve on the selection committee. It briefly explains the purpose of the committee, and it politely asks James whether he or a member of his family would be willing to serve on the committee.

End Your Letter With a Friendly Close

A positive or neutral message should conclude with a friendly close that builds goodwill. A **poor** close, such as the one that follows, would guarantee ill will:

- Don't forget that I need the guidelines by the end of the month. I cannot establish the scholarship until you let me know how you want the guidelines written.

[NOTE 7.20]
The example of a poor close is negative and does not build goodwill.

An example of a **good** friendly close that will do much to establish goodwill follows:

- Jim, future students will be grateful to have part of their education paid for because you were such an outstanding employee of Hard Rock Gas. Please have the guidelines to me by the end of the month so that students can begin reaping the benefits.

[NOTE 7.21]
The example of a good close is friendly and builds goodwill.

This friendly close is written in a positive, personalized, and concise way. Appreciation is shown for James's long service.

Summary—Poor and Good Messages to James Thomas

Poor and good messages are used to demonstrate how effective positive messages are written. The *poor* paragraphs are combined as a letter in Figure 7.2. This **poor** message fails to use the direct plan for positive information and fails to incorporate the communication fundamentals that are presented in Chapters 1, 4, and 5.

[NOTE 7.22]
Contrasting poor and good letters to James Thomas are presented in Figures 7.2 and 7.3.

Employee goodwill is promoted in the positive letter shown in Figure 7.3. This letter combines the *good* paragraphs. It integrates communication fundamentals into the direct plan message to produce an effective business communication.

An unsolicited positive message has been used to illustrate how the direct plan is used to communicate a positive message. To demonstrate further how the direct approach is used in actual business correspondence situations, several other examples of good and poor positive and neutral messages are presented in the following pages.

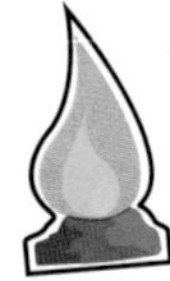

Hard Rock Gas Company
3478 Lamar Avenue
Houston,TX 77025-1135
(713) 555-6391 Fax (713) 555-2833

November 14, 200–

Mr. James N. Thomas
690 Bishop Drive
San Angelo, TX 76901

Dear Jim:

The Hard Rock Board of Directors had its quarterly meeting yesterday. Its members have directed me to inform you that a scholarship will be established in your name.

I need to know what you want to include in the guidelines for the $5,000 scholarship. I need to know who should receive the scholarship each year. We have never established a scholarship fund before, so I don't know what all you need to include in the guidelines. I do need these guidelines by the end of the month.

We will use a selection committee to pick someone for the scholarship. Since you are retired and have plenty of free time, why don't you serve on the committee?

Don't forget that I need the guidelines by the end of the month. I cannot establish the scholarship until you let me know how you want the guidelines written.

Sincerely,

Charles Giese

Charles Giese
Vice President

Weak positive news.

Explanation is impersonal and negative.

Sales appe presented harsh tone

Impersonal close.

Figure 7.2
Example of a Poor *Positive Message*

Learning Objective [4]
PREPARE COMPETENTLY A VARIETY OF POSITIVE AND NEUTRAL MESSAGES USING THE DIRECT PLAN.

Inquiries

[NOTE 7.23]
Use the direct plan with inquiries because persuasion is not needed.

Businesspeople periodically make routine requests for information. Routine **inquiries** are neutral messages that require no persuasion and, therefore, should be written using the direct plan. These inquiries may be about a product, a service, or a person.

[NOTE 7.24]
Inquiries should ask specific questions.

A message of inquiry must be written so that the writer will obtain all the information necessary to make a decision about a product, service, or person. Consider what you or your company needs to know and ask specific questions. Your letter of inquiry should be written so that the receiver can reply easily, quickly, and completely.

[NOTE 7.25]
The message receiver should be glad to receive an inquiry about products or services.

An inquiry about products or services should make the receiver of the message glad to respond. The inquiry may include only one sentence requesting a pamphlet or catalog, or it may have several paragraphs in which questions are asked. If several questions are asked, listing and numbering them will aid the receiver in responding. Use the direct plan outline by presenting your request and stating the reason for it

Hard Rock Gas Company
3478 Lamar Avenue
Houston, TX 77025-1135
(713) 555-6391 Fax (713) 555-2833

November 14, 200–

Mr. James N. Thomas
690 Bishop Drive
San Angelo, TX 76901

Dear Jim:

To honor you for your many years of dedicated service, a James N. Thomas Endowed Scholarship awarding $5,000 a year will be established. This scholarship was created by the Hard Rock Board of Directors at its quarterly meeting yesterday.

This $5,000 endowed scholarship bearing your name will be awarded each year to a student from the university or college of your choice who meets the guidelines that you establish. The following information should be included in the guidelines: specific major of the recipient, required minimum GPA, required minimum ACT score, and classification of the recipient (incoming freshman or upperclassman).

Each year a selection committee will be established to select an outstanding student to be awarded the James N. Thomas Endowed Scholarship. The selection committee will evaluate the student applications and select the student who best meets the guidelines that you establish. Jim, would you or one of your family members wish to serve on the selection committee?

Jim, future students will be grateful to have part of their education paid for because you were such an outstanding employee of Hard Rock Gas. Please have the guidelines to me by the end of the month so that students can begin reaping the benefits.

Sincerely,

Charles Giese

Charles Giese
Vice President

ve good
ing.

Facts are presented in a positive manner.

Sales appeal is presented in a polite invitation.

Friendly close expresses appreciation.

Figure 7.3
Example of a Good *Positive Message*

(if necessary) in the opening paragraph. In the second part of your message, give enough information so that the receiver can respond intelligently. Close your message by requesting action. Inquiries usually do not have a sales appeal section.

Figure 7.4 is an example of a **poor** inquiry in the form of an e-mail requesting the status of a purchase order. The inquiry is not specific enough to enable the sales department to respond with the information Tim Miller needs to make a decision. It would be difficult for the sales department to determine when the order was placed, what items were ordered, why they have not been sent, or when Tim Miller may expect to receive the order.

The letter in Figure 7.5 is an example of a **good** inquiry in the form of an e-mail requesting the status of a purchase order. The letter starts by stating the date that the original order was placed. Sufficient information is provided to the sales department so that it can provide the necessary details in its reply. The listed and numbered items make it easier for the sales department to respond. The close is positive and encourages a prompt reply.

Subject: Inquiry About My Order
Date: Tue, 15 Feb 200- 17:04:19 -0600
From: Tim Miller<tim.miller@aol.com>
To: Sales@compsales.com

I have not received my order of computer equipment and supplies. When can I expect to get these items?

I have been buying items from your organization for five years and normally I get my supplies much quicker. Let me know if and when you are going to send this order to me. If you are not going to send it to me soon, I will order from someone else.

I am looking forward for your reply.

Impersonal, negative, and demanding opening.

Explanation does not provide the receiver with necessary information.

Weak close.

Figure 7.4
Example of a Poor E-mail Inquiry

[NOTE 7.26]
Inquiries about persons should include only relevant questions and should promise confidentiality.

An inquiry about a person must be made carefully to protect the rights of the individual. You should ask only questions that are relevant to the situation. Information obtained should be kept confidential. State whether the person about whom you are inquiring authorized your request. Begin your inquiry by clearly identifying the person and stating your need for the information. The explanation should contain relevant facts—pertinent information that the individual shared with you, requirements that must be met (job, loan, award, etc.), or questions that you need answered. Close by stating that you would appreciate the receiver's sharing the information and by promising to keep the information confidential.

Request Approvals

[NOTE 7.27]
Businesses receive many requests.

[NOTE 7.28]
Most requests are approved.

A **request** is a message expressing the writer's needs or desires; it usually asks for a response. Managers of business organizations receive requests from their customers, their employees, and others. These requests may include, for example, a request from an employee for six months' parenting leave or a request from a civic organization for the manager to speak at a conference. Requests should be carefully considered and approved whenever feasible.

[NOTE 7.29]
Goodwill can be improved with proper handling of requests.

The proper handling of a request can build goodwill for an organization. For instance, approval of a parenting leave will gain goodwill for the organization. The employee taking the leave will have a sense of obligation to the company and will

Subject: Computer Equipment and Supplies Order
Date: Tue, 15 Feb 200- 17:04:19 -0600
From: Tim Miller<tim.miller@aol.com>
To: Sales@compsales.com

The following six items were ordered from your company on February 1:

1. 1-HP Color Laserjet 4500 Series Printer
2. 1-500 Sheet Feeder
3. 2-HP CLJ 4500 Toner Cartridge-Black
4. 1-HP CLJ 4500 Toner Cartridge-Cyan
5. 1-HP CLJ 4500 Toner Cartridge-Magenta
6. 1-HP CLJ 4500 Toner Cartridge-Yellow

Along with the order, I sent you my credit card number so that you would not have to wait for a check to clear the bank. My company really needs these items, so please let me know the status of this order.

Your prompt reply would be appreciated so that I will know when to expect the printer and the supplies.

Direct opening that gives the date of the order.

Facts are given to assist the reader in locating the order.

tails are presented
positive manner.

loses with a
equest for
rompt reply.

Figure 7.5
Example of a Good *E-mail Inquiry*

return refreshed and enthusiastic about the job. Goodwill, no doubt, will spread throughout employee groups and the worker's friends and neighbors when they observe the company's humanistic philosophy. Accepting an invitation to speak at a meeting of a civic organization can build goodwill for the company among those attending the meeting. The acceptance letter should convey enthusiasm about the prospect of appearing before the group; it should in no way indicate a duty to perform a community service. The acceptance letter should emphasize the positive aspects of accepting the invitation to speak.

[NOTE 7.30]
Request approvals should stress the positive news.

To illustrate how the direct plan can be used in a positive message communicating approval of a request, assume that you are the human resources manager of Kwik Start Batteries. Rachel Coker, an assembly line worker, has requested a change from the day shift to the night shift. This change will allow Rachel to eliminate babysitting services and enable her husband to take care of their children while she is at work. Because you want to build goodwill and because there is a shortage of workers on the night shift, you would write a memo to her approving this change and providing details about it.

A **poor** approval memo for this request is shown in Figure 7.6. It does little to build employee morale and goodwill for the company. Note the absence of the you–viewpoint. Also, notice that the positive information is not given until the second paragraph.

The **good** memo in Figure 7.7 uses the direct plan and should influence positively Rachel's attitude toward the company. It gives Rachel the positive

INTEROFFICE COMMUNICATION

TO: Rachel Coker

FROM: Angel Keller

DATE: September 22, 200-

SUBJECT: Request for Shift Change

I have received your request dated September 15 to change from the day shift to the night shift.

I have approved the request effective October 1. I will have everyone notified by then, so you can start the late shift on that day.

I hope this allows you to work out all your problems.

Approval is not given in the first paragraph.

Explanation is not clear.

Negative close.

Figure 7.6
Example of a Poor *Request Approval Memo*

information in the first sentence. The second paragraph presents an explanation that is factual, positive, and concise. A friendly close is given in the final paragraph. A sales appeal—the optional third step in the direct plan—is not appropriate for this situation.

Claims

[NOTE 7.31] Claims take many forms.

Claims include requests for merchandise exchange, for refunds on defective or damaged merchandise, for refunds for unsatisfactory service, and for correction of work. Your complaint receives greatest emphasis when the complaint is the first item in the message. Generally, the receiver wants the claim information so that he or she can make necessary corrections as soon as possible. For this reason, and to give strength to your claim, use the direct plan.

[NOTE 7.32] Claims are presented using the direct plan.

The plan for claim messages can easily be adapted from the direct plan used for positive and neutral information shown in Figure 7.1. The claim should be presented in an objective way, without a display of anger and without placing blame on the receiver. The *opening* should present immediately the claim and its impact. The impact could include the inconveniences suffered and identification of specific damages. The *explanation* should provide all necessary additional background that

INTEROFFICE COMMUNICATION

TO: Rachel Coker

FROM: Angel Keller

DATE: September 22, 200-

SUBJECT: Request for Shift Change

Your transfer to the night shift has been approved. I am sure you will enjoy working with Matt Douglas, your new shift leader.

You begin working the night shift (midnight to 8 a.m.) on Monday, October 1. Please continue working the day shift through Friday, September 28.

Rachel, you are an asset to our company, and we are pleased to approve this change to assist you in improving your child-care arrangements.

Positive information is given immediately.

Clear explanation stresses the receiver's interests.

Friendly close builds goodwill by being personalized and positive.

Figure 7.7
Example of a Good *Request Approval Memo*

relates to the claim. In this section provide facts supporting the claim, describe actions that have been taken, and enclose relevant documents (invoices, etc.). In addition, you should specify actions that you want the receiver to take and set a deadline by which corrective action should be taken. There would be no *sales appeal* in a claim letter. Finally, the *friendly close* should be optimistic.

Figure 7.8 is an example of a **poor** claim letter from a jewelry store that received some broken china in a shipment from a wholesaler. Note that the main objective of the letter—notification that the china was received in unsatisfactory condition—did not appear until the second paragraph. Also note that the letter implies blame; the claimant should avoid accusing the receiver because the receiver will only be angered by this approach. The claim was not clearly identified—how many and which pieces of china were broken? The receiver needs this information but is not interested in sender-related details such as the claimant's order number. Lastly, this letter is not written in a considerate tone.

A preferred letter for the same situation is shown in Figure 7.9, an example of the **good** use of the direct plan for a claim. This letter is objective and courteous. The problem and its impact are specified in the opening. A copy of the invoice is enclosed, and the damaged items are clearly identified. A concise explanation of the circumstances is given in the second paragraph. A deadline as to when replacement china is needed is given politely in the third paragraph. The close is friendly and optimistic.

Exquisite Diamonds and Glass
3258 Lake Travis Drive • Austin, TX 78744-2134
(512) 555-7594 • Fax (512) 555-6363

May 11, 200–

Diane Faske
Hampton Fine Jewelry
4231 Main Street
Sealy, TX 77474-2137

Dear Diane:

As your records will show, on April 18 I ordered three complete sets of Corigan China (my order 2538X). The units were shipped to me by Southwest Van Lines (your invoice 4274) and arrived at my store May 10.

At the time of delivery the receiving clerk noticed that two of the boxes were smashed in on the side. Further inspection showed that your organization used cheap cartons to ship expensive china. As a result of the inferior cartons and the rough handling of the china, over half of it is broken.

It is hard for me to understand how a wholesaler who handles china could permit such inadequate treatment of its products. I do not accept this shipment of china. Further, I want this broken china taken off my hands and replaced with new pieces. Because I will be holding my annual Memorial Day sale May 28, I insist that the replacement Corigan China reach me by May 20.

Sincerely,

Nicole Thorpe

Nicole Thorpe
Owner

mc

Although providing transition, poor opening does not clearly identify the damages.

Explanation is not written in a considerate tone.

Negative and demanding close.

Figure 7.8
Example of a Poor *Claim Letter*

Adjustments

[NOTE 7.33] Legitimate claims should be approved quickly.

Business firms that receive claim messages should respond to them quickly in order to maintain the goodwill of the customer. A positive response to a claim is known as an **adjustment**. If there is any doubt about the legitimacy of a claim, the customer usually receives the benefit of the doubt.

[NOTE 7.34] Use the direct plan for adjustment letters.

A letter approving a claim is positive information and should use the direct plan. The letter should begin with the positive information—the adjustment. This immediate positive information will aid in eliminating any negative feelings the customer has toward the company. The explanation should be convincing to regain the customer's confidence. An effective, personalized sales appeal gives the company an opportunity to emphasize to the customer the quality of the product or service. To avoid ending on a negative note, an adjustment letter should never close with an apology.

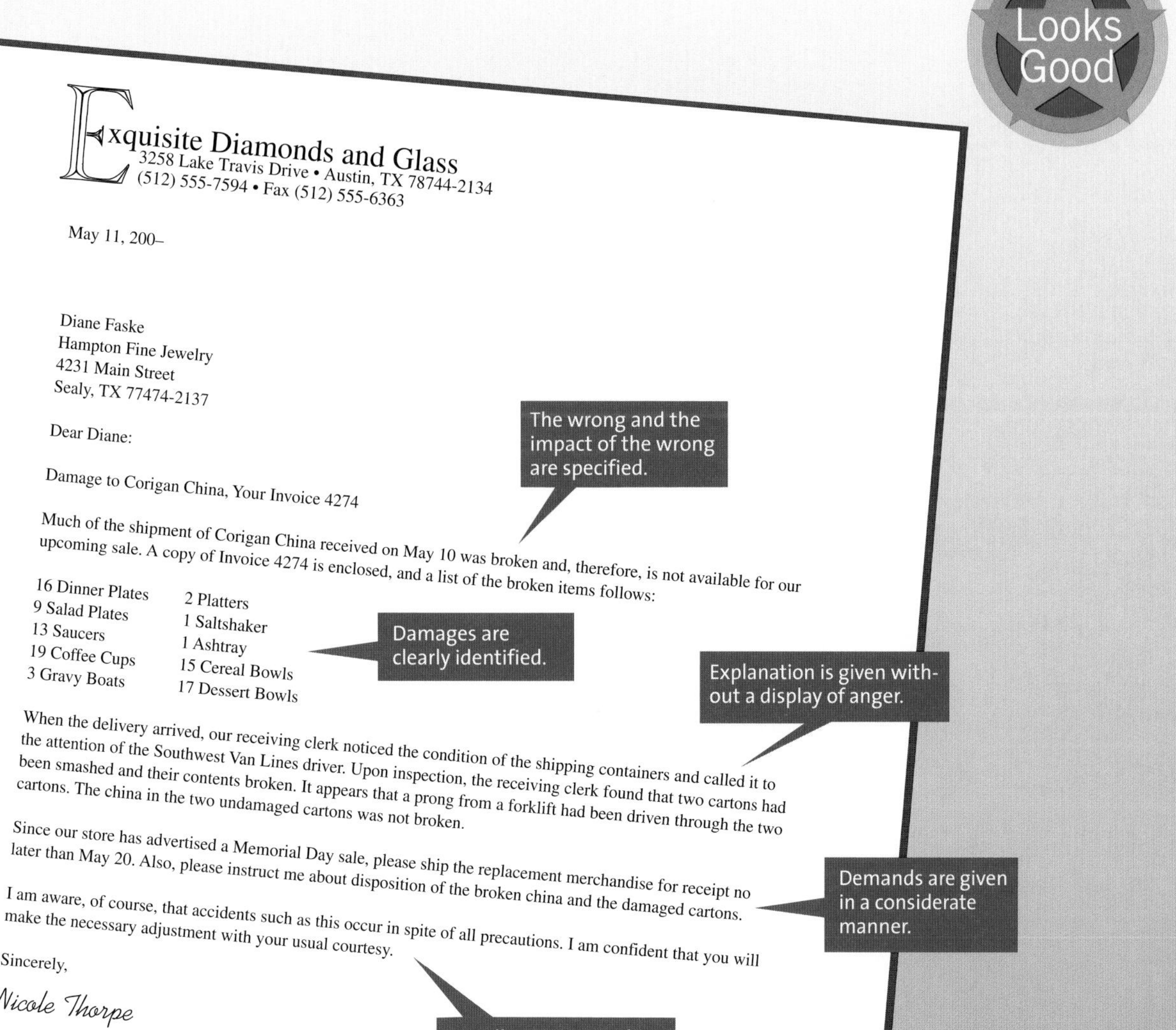

Looks Good
Exquisite Diamonds and Glass
3258 Lake Travis Drive • Austin, TX 78744-2134
(512) 555-7594 • Fax (512) 555-6363
May 11, 200–
Diane Faske
Hampton Fine Jewelry
4231 Main Street
Sealy, TX 77474-2137
Dear Diane:
Damage to Corigan China, Your Invoice 4274
Much of the shipment of Corigan China received on May 10 was broken and, therefore, is not available for our upcoming sale. A copy of Invoice 4274 is enclosed, and a list of the broken items follows:
16 Dinner Plates
9 Salad Plates
13 Saucers
19 Coffee Cups
3 Gravy Boats
2 Platters
1 Saltshaker
1 Ashtray
15 Cereal Bowls
17 Dessert Bowls
When the delivery arrived, our receiving clerk noticed the condition of the shipping containers and called it to the attention of the Southwest Van Lines driver. Upon inspection, the receiving clerk found that two cartons had been smashed and their contents broken. It appears that a prong from a forklift had been driven through the two cartons. The china in the two undamaged cartons was not broken.
Since our store has advertised a Memorial Day sale, please ship the replacement merchandise for receipt no later than May 20. Also, please instruct me about disposition of the broken china and the damaged cartons.
I am aware, of course, that accidents such as this occur in spite of all precautions. I am confident that you will make the necessary adjustment with your usual courtesy.
Sincerely,
Nicole Thorpe
Nicole Thorpe
Owner
mc
The wrong and the impact of the wrong are specified.
Damages are clearly identified.
Explanation is given without a display of anger.
Demands are given in a considerate manner.
Friendly, optimistic close.

Figure 7.9
Example of a Good Claim Letter

An example of a **poor** adjustment response to the claim letter about the broken china is shown in Figure 7.10. This letter does not get to the positive information until the third paragraph. The explanation places the blame on the delivery company and is not convincing. The repeated references to the trouble and inconvenience continually remind the receiver of the negative aspects of the situation. Details as to when the replacement items are to arrive are omitted. The hollow apology in the close does not build the goodwill of the customer. The you–viewpoint is absent from the letter.

An example of a **good** letter approving an adjustment is shown in Figure 7.11. Note that this letter begins immediately with the positive information. The explanation emphasizes not the wrong itself but what was done to correct the wrong. This explanation should help regain the customer's confidence. In the third paragraph, the writer uses a personal approach when describing an item that Ms. Thorpe may be

Hampton Fine Jewelry

4231 Main Street, Sealy, TX 77474-2137 (409) 555-2859

May 12, 200–

Ms. Nicole Thorpe
Exquisite Diamonds and Glass
3258 Lake Travis Drive
Austin, TX 78744-2134

Dear Ms. Thorpe:

We have received your May 7 claim reporting that our shipment of china was damaged. We regret the inconvenience this caused you and understand your unhappiness.

Following our standard practice, we investigated the situation thoroughly. We found that a forklift operator had driven a fork through the cartons when loading the cartons into the delivery truck. We can assure you that Southwest Van Lines will not be used to deliver any more of our merchandise.

I am pleased to report that we are shipping replacement items. The shipment will be made using Van Horn Truck Lines.

Again, we regret the trouble that the damaged china has caused you.

Sincerely,

Diane Faske

Diane Faske
Shipping Manager

pd

Negative opening does not give positive information.

Impersonal, unconvincing explanation.

Positive information should be in first paragraph and should use the you–viewpoint.

Negative final apology.

Figure 7.10
Example of a Poor *Adjustment Letter*

An unscheduled pay increase is an example of an unsolicited positive message.

interested in selling. The close ends the letter on a happy, positive note.

Unsolicited Positive and Neutral Messages

An **unsolicited positive** or **neutral** message is a communication initiated by an organization. Examples of unsolicited positive or neutral messages to customers may include an announcement of new products or services, notification of new

Hampton Fine Jewelry

4231 Main Street, Sealy, TX 77474-2137 (409) 555-2859

May 12, 200–

Ms. Nicole Thorpe
Exquisite Diamonds and Glass
3258 Lake Travis Drive
Austin, TX 78744-2134

Dear Ms. Thorpe:

Your replacement china will reach you by May 18, in time for your Memorial Day sale. Fast delivery of the replacement china is our way of proving to you that we value your business. Do not return the broken china; please dispose of it.

Because your continued business is important to us, we have carefully examined the handling of your order. It was determined that a forklift operator for Southwest Van Lines accidentally drove a fork through two of the cartons. The manager of the van lines assures me that the forklift operator has been given additional training and will be more careful in the future.

Ms. Thorpe, jewelry stores throughout the United States are having excellent sales with our new add-a-pearl necklace. The necklace chain is made of 14-karat gold and comes in 16-, 18-, 24-, or 30-inch lengths. The pearls are white and of the highest quality. A sample necklace containing six pearls is enclosed. Also enclosed is a convenient order form listing prices for your use. Why not order now so you will have this new profit-making item in your store for your sale.

Best wishes for a successful Memorial Day sale.

Sincerely,

Diane Faske

Diane Faske
Shipping Manager

pd
Enclosures

Positive information is given immediately.

Convincing information.

Announces a new item for sales appeal.

Positive close.

Figure 7.11
Example of a Good Adjustment Letter

hours of operation, reductions in prices of merchandise, relocation to a new building, or employment of new customer representatives. Unsolicited positive messages to employees may announce new fringe benefits, an unscheduled pay increase, or a promotion.

Unsolicited positive or neutral messages should employ the direct approach. In the example in Figure 7.12, Alyson misses an opportunity to build on the goodwill that was gained when Goff Enterprises gave everyone a bonus. The letter is written from the viewpoint of the business rather than from employees.

In the example of a **good** unsolicited positive information letter shown in Figure 7.13, Alyson increases the morale of the employees. Note how the you–viewpoint is used to enhance the positive information.

Skillfully used, the direct plan is appropriate for messages that request information, convey favorable information, convey neutral information, or make or settle

[NOTE 7.35]
Businesses send both internal and external unsolicited positive or neutral messages.

[NOTE 7.36]
Use of the direct plan in positive and neutral messages increases their effectiveness.

Subject: Profit at Goff Enterprises
Date: Fri, 12 Mar 200– 11:23:00 EST
From: Alyson Mendez<alyson.mendez@goffent.com>
To: AllEmployees@goffent.com

Goff Enterprises has made numerous administrative changes in the past year. We have been investigating all opportunities that would increase our profit. These changes have resulted in Goff Enterprises making more money.

I am extremely pleased to inform you that we will give a bonus on April 1. The management of Goff Enterprises has worked hard to earn this profit so that we can give you extra money.

We hope that everyone continues working hard so that Goff Enterprises can continue increasing its profits.

Opening does not use the you–viewpoint.

Positive information needs to be in the first paragraph and should stress receiver interest.

Benefits to the company should be de-emphasized.

Figure 7.12
Example of a Poor *Unsolicited Positive E-mail Message*

claims. With the direct plan, effective messages can increase employee morale, promote customer goodwill, and positively affect those who receive them.

Summary of Learning Objectives

Learning Objective [1]

Describe positive and neutral messages. A positive or neutral message conveys to the receiver information that is pleasant, favorable, or neutral. The receiver will be getting information that is favorable or neutral and will accept the contents of the message easily; therefore, the message should be constructed using the direct plan.

Learning Objective [2]

Describe the four specific guidelines for using the direct plan. Open the letter or memo with the positive or neutral information. In the opening paragraph be optimistic, provide coherence, use emphasis techniques, and stress receiver interests or benefits. In the second part of the message, the explanation, present additional information that relates to the positive or neutral information that was presented in the first paragraph. Present the explanation in a concise and objective manner but still include all details that the receiver needs. In the third section, the sales appeal, attempt to persuade the reader to take a specific, desired action. Not all messages

Looks
Good

Subject: Employee Bonus
Date: Fri, 12 Mar 200– 11:23:00 EST
From: Alyson Mendez<alyson.mendez@goffent.com>
To: AllEmployees@goffent.com

You will receive a bonus check on April 1, 200–.

Your bonus will be 3 percent of your current salary. The bonus will be a one-time payment, and taxes will be deducted from the calculated amount.

The effort that each of you has given to the success of Goff Enterprises has led to an extremely productive year. You are a major participant in this success and, therefore, the Board of Directors is happy to reward each of you.

Thank you for your efforts!

Positive, you-oriented, strong beginning.
The positive benefits are clearly explained.
Complimentary remarks will build goodwill.
Positive close.

Figure 7.13
Example of a Good Unsolicited Positive E-mail Message

need a sales appeal. Complete the message with a friendly close. Build goodwill by being personal and optimistic.

Learning Objective [3]

Distinguish between poor and good positive and neutral messages. A good positive and neutral message stresses the reader's interest, the you–viewpoint; a poor message stresses the writer's interest, the I–viewpoint. A good message is written in a positive and friendly style instead of an impersonal manner. The explanation in a good message is concise but gives necessary details whereas the explanation in a poor message does not contain all relevant facts. A good message uses the you–viewpoint to appeal for additional business whereas a poor message will be more impersonal. A good message concludes with a friendly close that builds goodwill.

Learning Objective [4]

Prepare competently a variety of positive and neutral messages using the direct plan. Incorporate the communication fundamentals in a direct plan when preparing inquiries; request approvals, claims, adjustments, and unsolicited positive and neutral messages. Present the information optimistically using the you–viewpoint. Use the direct plan: (1) Opening—start with the main idea of the message. (2) Explanation—present additional information concisely but completely. (3) Sales Appeal—persuade reader to take specific action that is on a related item. (4) Close—build goodwill by being personal and optimistic.

DISCUSSION QUESTIONS

1. Discuss factors that should be considered in selecting the medium to use for transmitting positive or neutral information? (Objective 1)
2. List four characteristics of the opening section of the direct plan. (Objective 2)
3. Identify and discuss three characteristics of the explanation section of the direct plan. (Objective 2)

4. **Ethics.** Describe the process of gathering information about a person that should be followed to ensure that the individual's rights are protected. (Objective 2)
5. Explain why a positive message should use the direct plan. (Objective 2)
6. Which of the following paragraphs would be more appropriate for a sales appeal of a request approval? Explain why. (Objective 3)

Mr. Williams, I want to invite you to our annual sale. We have many new appliances that would look nice in your home. We are giving our customers a 25 percent discount during this sale.

Mr. Williams, you may be interested in browsing through our store and selecting from the many washers, dryers, freezers, dishwashers, etc. that would complement the refrigerator that you recently purchased. These appliances are now being featured during our annual 25 percent off sale. You may be especially interested in the new 45" flat-screen television that is being offered at a 35 percent discount during this sale.

7. Explain why the following paragraph would be weak in opening a request approval letter: (Objective 3)

Your interest in obtaining a membership in the Calloway Country Club is appreciated. You have been a valuable asset to our community the five years that you have lived here.

8. Compare a request approval written to an external audience with one written to an internal audience. (Objective 4)
9. Identify three types of positive messages that could be referred to as unsolicited. Use examples other than those in the text. (Objective 4)
10. Discuss five characteristics of an inquiry. (Objective 4)

APPLICATION EXERCISES

1. **E-mail.** Develop a message that could be sent via e-mail to business students at your school inviting them to attend a meeting of a student professional organization. You may include details such as a guest speaker, free pizza, or any other activity that would be attractive to the students. E-mail a copy of this message to your instructor. (Objective 3)
2. Visit two retail stores in your community and ask how they handle adjustment messages. Get copies of their letters, if possible, and share this information with the class. (Objective 4)
3. Inquire at several organizations about the various situations in which they use a neutral message. Determine the frequency of its use. What organizational plan is followed for presenting the neutral message?

4. **Teamwork.** Form a team of three or four students and develop a questionnaire to determine why students selected their majors and why they chose to attend your

school. Have each member of the team survey at least ten students and combine the results for the team. Write one memo from the team to the instructor reporting the results of the survey.

5. **E-mail.** You are the regional manager of 11 video stores. Assume your instructor is the manager of one of the stores in your region. The employees of your instructor's store have had the lowest absentee record in the region for the past two quarters. Send an e-mail to your instructor acknowledging this accomplishment. Consider the four parts of a direct plan when preparing this message.

There are Web exercises at **http://krizan.swcollege.com** to accompany this chapter.

CASE PROBLEMS

Inquiries

1. You have recently been elected vice president for programs of Young Business Professionals of America. This organization has approximately 1,500 members and holds a national conference in a major U.S. city each year. The major responsibility for the vice president for programs is to plan and coordinate the national conference in four years.

   Develop a form letter that could be sent to the vice presidents who coordinated the last five conferences. Ask these individuals for advice in beginning your preparations. Some of the questions you may want to include are pitfalls in the preparations, types of committees that you should form to assist you in planning the conference, tips on negotiating with hotels, advice on whom to ask and whom to avoid in keynote speakers, and travel arrangements.

2. **Teamwork.** National Cinema wants to build a movie theater in a neighboring state. Form a committee of four students and develop a plan to find the best town for the new theater. Remember that information will be needed about town populations, community interests, and cost of land. Write a memo to your instructor detailing the results of the project. Attach letters that could be sent to agencies requesting information needed to narrow the list of possible sites for building the movie theater.

3. **Global/Cross-Cultural.** Mandy McKinney would like to take her husband, Paul, on a vacation to Germany for their tenth wedding anniversary. She is doing all the planning for this event so she can surprise him with the trip. She will need to contact the Tourist Information Office, Schumannstrasse 27, 50201, Salzburg, Germany, for information and land costs. Write a letter that Mandy McKinney could use to obtain pertinent information. Be sure to include necessary details to make this a complete inquiry.
4. You and a friend are considering a safari to Africa. You have heard that True Adventures of New Orleans, Louisiana, provides excellent safaris. You need to know the cost, including airfare, equipment required, length of the safari, success rate of the safari, immunization requirements, and visa information. Write a letter to True Adventures obtaining this and other pertinent information.

5. **E-mail.** You are interested in buying a basset hound. Develop a message that could be sent via e-mail to a dog breeder obtaining information on any basset hounds that he or she may have for sale. Information you wish to obtain includes the age of the dog, the gender of the dog, its color pattern, its pedigree, and the price. After adding details to make the message complete, send it via e-mail to your instructor.

Request Approvals

6. This past spring your organization constructed a Wellness Center for use by all employees. After the Center was in operation for several weeks, the employees requested that their lunch hour be extended to 1½ hours to allow more time to exercise, to shower, and to eat a quick lunch. You, as director of human resources, realize the benefits that the employees are gaining from the Center. After conferring with top management, you write a memo to all employees informing them that they can take a 1½ hour lunch break to use the Wellness Center but will have to make up the extra half-hour by starting at 7:30 a.m. or by working until 5 p.m. Give the memo to your instructor.
7. You are the credit manager for Kevin's, a family clothing store, in Paducah, Kentucky. Amanda Hyde has applied for a Kevin's charge card. Write Amanda a letter approving her request. Assign her a $5,000 credit limit and explain the details of the charge card. Add necessary facts to make the letter complete.

8. **E-mail.** You are the office manager for Family Care Clinic. Today you received an e-mail from Charley Hess who explains that he was billed $60 for a physician's office visit on May 11. He did not see Dr. Charles Clark, a physician at the clinic, on May 11 because he was out of town on vacation the first 15 days of May. He requests that his account be credited for the $60 office visit. After checking your records, you determine that Mr. Hess is correct. Prepare an e-mail confirming the error and telling Mr. Hess that his account will be credited. Send the message to your instructor via e-mail.
9. ElectroCon, an electrical contracting company, has been in operation for one year. It has requested a line of credit of $100,000 from Mesquite Supply. You have a leaflet describing payment for line-of-credit accounts. As finance manager of Mesquite Supply, write ElectroCon approving its request and including this leaflet. Be sure to include necessary details to make this letter complete.
10. As director of customer service for Harvey's, a regional department store, you receive the following letter from Salley Standfast:

I opened an account with your store on September 28 and charged merchandise in the amount of $74. On December 4 I called your billing office to find out why I had not received a statement. I learned that you had been sending the statement to the wrong address. I was told that my account balance is now $114 due to interest and late fees.

Since you were sending the statement to the wrong address, I do not feel obligated to pay interest and late fees. I am enclosing a check for $74, which was the original charge. Please adjust my account so that my balance is $0.

Write a letter to Salley approving her request. Supply details to make this a complete request approval.

Claims

11. Wilson Chemicals sent $1,188 to Executive Seminars for six employees to attend a two-day hazardous waste handling seminar. After the registration forms and fees for this seminar were submitted, Wilson Chemicals received an unexpected large order. The company will be unable to release the six employees for the seminar. Write a letter to Executive Seminars requesting a refund for $1,188. Be sure to supply details.
12. You are the store manager of Tabitha's Apparel. Last week you received a shipment of 48 dresses. You inspected the dresses on their arrival, and all of them seemed to be in

excellent condition. Yesterday, as one of your valued customers was trying on a size 12 dress, it was apparent that the dress was no larger than a size 8. On closer inspection of the remaining 47 dresses, you found five others that appeared to have been sized incorrectly. You would like six replacement dresses as quickly as possible. Write a letter to Connie's Collections requesting these replacements within two weeks. Make the claim message complete by adding necessary facts.

13. This past summer you purchased by mail order from MicroCompu an Executive 900 microcomputer for home use. The microcomputer is a Pentium 200 with 64 MB of RAM. You purchased this microcomputer primarily for its speed. While using a statistical package on the computer, you found that it did not make the calculations faster than the 486 microcomputer you replaced. Write a letter to MicroCompu explaining that you want to return the microcomputer and be refunded the $1,575 that you paid for it. Supply details that are necessary to make a complete claim letter.

14. You, as manager of Thurman Furniture in Lincoln, Nebraska, ordered ten sets of brocade pinched-pleated drapes to use in displays. When the drapes arrived from Lillie's Window Fashions, you thought they appeared to be a lighter weight fabric than advertised. The sample swatch given you by Lillie's sales representative is also a higher quality material. Write a claim letter requesting a full refund and asking for instructions on how to return the merchandise. Supply details to make this a complete claim letter.

15. Approximately three months ago you purchased a MovieWatcher VCR that came with a one-year warranty. After watching a movie, you cannot get the VCR to eject the tape. When you took the VCR to an authorized repair shop, you overheard another customer complaining about a similar problem. Not wanting to "get stuck" with a faulty machine when the warranty expires, you decide not to have the machine repaired but return the VCR for a full refund. Write a letter to MovieWatcher requesting this refund. Be sure to include details to make this letter complete.

Adjustments

16. Clean Air Appliances manufactures freestanding gas ranges. Ted's Appliances purchased three of the ranges and has sold one. This range was converted to propane upon installation. Ted's customer is unhappy with the oven's performance. The customer states that the oven is very erratic. Sometimes the food is burned and other times the food is underdone. Ted's service representative has tried unsuccessfully to adjust the oven's thermostat. Due to this poor performance, Ted's would like to return all three ranges. You feel the problem is with the conversion to propane but are willing to accept the return. Write a complete letter containing a sales appeal section to Ted's Appliances giving your decision.

17. Dixie Lee Collins purchased a recliner that was manufactured by Comfy Seats. After using it for four months, she noticed a tear in a seam on the armrest. Dixie Lee has written requesting either new upholstery or a full refund for the purchase price of the recliner. As a customer relations specialist for Comfy Seats, write a letter to Dixie Lee asking her to take the recliner to any upholstery shop and get it recovered. Explain in the letter that the upholstery shop should send you the bill for its services. In addition, you should ask Dixie Lee if she is interested in purchasing a love seat that would complement the recliner and mention that she would receive 40 percent off the regular price.

18. You are owner of Mountain Crafts in Asheville, North Carolina. Deanna Roberts lives in Broken Arrow, Oklahoma, and purchased an expensive handmade quilt at your

store when she was vacationing in Asheville. Ms. Roberts has returned the quilt because she noticed some stains on it when she got home. She has requested that you replace her quilt with a similar one that does not contain any stains.

Write a letter to Ms. Roberts approving her request and informing her that you have received some beautiful handmade baskets that she might be interested in purchasing. Supply necessary details to make a complete adjustment.

19. Oscar's Sportswear creates designer shirts. Recently, Marty's Sporting Goods purchased a dozen shirts from Oscar's. Marty's has returned one of the shirts for tests because one of its customers reported that his shirt shrunk. Marty's would like to return the other 11 shirts for full credit. The test failed to find proof of shrinkage, but you will be willing to accept the return of the shirts to maintain your good relationship with Marty's. Write a letter to Marty's explaining your decision.

20. Roscoe's Personalized Printing specializes in customized printing of items used for business advertisements. Jennifer Fairbanks designed an unusual calendar to be given to her customers during the holiday season. In October Ms. Fairbanks phoned in an order for 11,000 calendars. You shipped these calendars to her in early December. On January 9, you receive a letter from Ms. Fairbanks stating that she only ordered 7,000 calendars. She is willing to pay $3,500 for the calendars but not the $5,500 you charged her. You believe that she ordered more calendars than she needed; however, you are willing to adjust her bill to continue getting her business. Write a letter to Ms. Fairbanks explaining your decision to adjust the charge in her account to $3,500, and add details to make the letter complete.

Unsolicited Positive and Neutral Messages

21. You are chief of information systems at the Bank of Newberry. Due to increased demands on information processing, you have decided to divide the Division of Administrative Services into two units: Administrative Services and Telecommunications. Send a memo to Margaret Collins appointing her as head of the telecommunications division.

22. Harry Ferguson has served the city of Paris in various capacities during the past 25 years. The Allegro Foundation Board of Directors has decided to honor Mr. Ferguson by creating a scholarship in his name. Assume that this scholarship will be given at your school. Write a letter informing Mr. Ferguson of Allegro's decision. Add necessary information.

23. Last month a severe thunderstorm in the area interrupted cable reception for three days. As director of public relations for Trinity Cablecomm, you need to prepare a message that could be inserted in the monthly statement for all Trinity subscribers. This message should restore subscriber confidence in Trinity. The cable company is giving credit for three days' service; the credit will appear on next month's statement. Provide details to make this message complete.

24. American Quality Paper has sales representatives throughout the United States. It has set a goal of increasing its sales 25 percent during the next 12 months. As an incentive to the sales representatives, the company is offering to send the three representatives who increase their sales the most during the 12-month period on an all-expense-paid trip to Hawaii for five days. Each representative would be permitted one guest. Write a letter to the sales representatives informing them of the incentive program. Add necessary details.

25. Clarksville Progressive Business Leaders (CPBL) has been actively involved with Clarksville's educational system. To show its support for higher education, CPBL has decided to award $1,000 scholarships to five Clarksville High School graduates. As the CPBL president, write a letter to the principal, Ms. Louise Hendricks, informing her of the five scholarships and explaining to her the procedure that will be used to select the winners. Add information to make the letter complete.

MESSAGE ANALYSIS

Correct the following message that has been written to Amber Henderson, who has been approved for a credit card with Cisco Financial Institution:

The Cisco Financial Institution's credit card may be used in most business establishments throughout the state. We have been in existence for more than 20 years.

Our credit committee approved your application for a credit card today. We are certainly glad that we can serve someone like you. The Cisco credit card has a 9 percent interest rate for the first year. This rate will change at the end of the first year and may be higher. The payment for your credit card is due by the 10th of each month. When you don't make the minimum payment by the 10th, you will be assessed a 1 percent penalty.

I want to invite you to use your credit card whenever you can. We will consider changing your credit limit of $1,000 as soon as you have shown that you can make payments on time.

We are glad that you are doing business with us. If there is anything else I can do, please call.

GRAMMAR WORKSHOP

Correct the grammar, spelling, punctuation, style, and word choice errors in the following sentences:

1. Last week one of the forty band members reports that his instrument was stole during the Marching Contest.
2. Although Monday is Labor Day, the United Nations Security Council is meeting to discuss the deployment of troops.
3. The interior decorater select drapes that complimented the pattern of the sofa.
4. Becky used her capitol for collateral in purchasing the apartment building after she was ensured that the property would appreciate in value.
5. A armored truck carrying $40,000,000.00 of the super bowl receipts turned over on the Interstate.
6. Once your cleaning shores have been completed you can go to the movies or the golf course.
7. Despite being Chief Executive of a $50 million-a-year business Marty drove a 1967 pick up truck.
8. Both the internet and the Fax is a tool that business graduates must understand to be successful.
9. Either Joe or Mike will resign from their positions after their council inform him of the charges.
10. Can I leave if it starts snowing so that I can get home safe.

CHAPTER

8 Goodwill Messages

Andrea Holle,
Edward Jones

LET'S TALK BUSINESS As an Edward Jones investment representative, I use goodwill messages to extend birthday wishes, get well wishes, condolences, and often notes of congratulations.

Goodwill messages help build relationships in which selling investments is enjoyable. I strengthen current relationships with my clients and build future business prospects by sending Thanksgiving notes telling my clients I appreciate their business or birthday cards telling them I remember their special day.

It is essential to build a strong relationship with all business contacts since the financial business is very competitive. Contacting business

(Continued)

[LEARNING OBJECTIVES]

[1] DESCRIBE GOODWILL MESSAGES.

[2] COMPOSE THE SIX COMMON TYPES OF GOODWILL MESSAGES.

[3] DESCRIBE THE CRITERIA FOR SELECTING THE STYLE FOR A GOODWILL MESSAGE.

associates or clients in their time of need or at a time of celebration will strengthen your business relationships and set you apart from your competitors.

Learning Objective [1]
DESCRIBE GOODWILL MESSAGES.

In previous chapters it has been suggested that one maintains good relationships with receivers by personalizing positive, neutral, negative, and persuasive messages. Andrea Holle uses goodwill messages to maintain and build good relationships with her clients. The use of goodwill messages provides Ms. Holle with a competitive edge over her competitors.

[NOTE 8.1]
The purpose of some messages is to promote goodwill.

A **goodwill message** is written to communicate your concern and interest. Sending a goodwill message shows that you care about the receiver. Avoid canceling the positive effects by inserting statements that will cause the receiver to think you are simply trying to further a business relationship. Your goodwill messages should cause your receiver to form a positive opinion of you—the sender of the message. Timeliness is of utmost importance; goodwill can be lost if a message is received several weeks after an event occurs.

[NOTE 8.2]
Positive opinions are formed by goodwill messages.

Learning Objective [2]
COMPOSE THE SIX COMMON TYPES OF GOODWILL MESSAGES.

Types of Goodwill Messages

The types of goodwill messages are congratulations, condolence, appreciation, invitation, holiday greetings, and welcome.

[NOTE 8.3]
Certain occasions call for goodwill messages.

CONGRATULATIONS

Everyone enjoys receiving praise. A message that praises the receiver for an accomplishment or an achievement is referred to as a message of **congratulations**. One of the reasons that congratulatory messages are so effective in building goodwill is that organizations and businesspeople do not use them very often. Congratulatory messages may be as formal as a typewritten letter about a promotion or as informal as a handwritten note attached to a newspaper clipping of a birth announcement.

[NOTE 8.4]
Congratulatory messages build goodwill.

A letter of congratulations may be presented along with a plaque or a pin.

[NOTE 8.5] Congratulatory messages are sent for accomplishments or special occasions.

Congratulatory messages are sent both to individuals and organizations. Occasions that warrant such messages may be either personal or business in nature. A congratulatory message may be sent to an individual on the occasion of a business-related accomplishment, such as attaining the highest sales for the month, retiring after 30 years of service, or receiving a promotion. You also may send a congratulatory message to an individual for a personal event, such as a birthday, an engagement, a marriage, a birth, or an election to office in a social or civic organization. A business firm could receive a message of congratulations for expansion of its company, relocation to a new building, announcement of a new product, or celebration of an anniversary.

[NOTE 8.6] A direct approach should be used in composing a congratulatory message.

Congratulatory business messages should be written in a personal, sincere manner. A direct approach should be used by immediately mentioning the honor or accomplishment. The message should focus on the receiver from start to finish. A closing that refers to the writer's assistance to the receiver in his or her achievement diminishes goodwill. A congratulatory letter to an individual who is being nominated for a board position is shown in Figure 8.1.

Figure 8.1
Congratulatory Letter

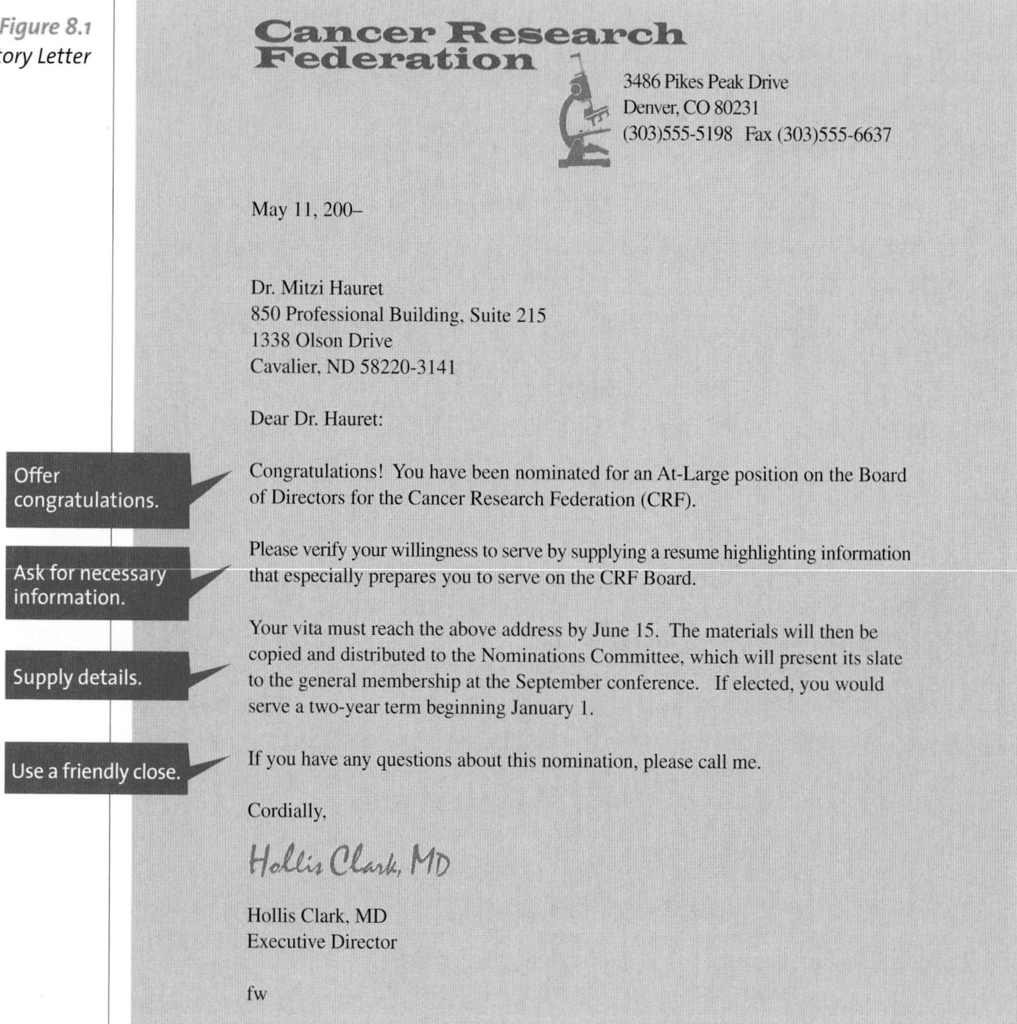

Cancer Research Federation

3486 Pikes Peak Drive
Denver, CO 80231
(303)555-5198 Fax (303)555-6637

May 11, 200–

Dr. Mitzi Hauret
850 Professional Building, Suite 215
1338 Olson Drive
Cavalier, ND 58220-3141

Dear Dr. Hauret:

Congratulations! You have been nominated for an At-Large position on the Board of Directors for the Cancer Research Federation (CRF).

Please verify your willingness to serve by supplying a resume highlighting information that especially prepares you to serve on the CRF Board.

Your vita must reach the above address by June 15. The materials will then be copied and distributed to the Nominations Committee, which will present its slate to the general membership at the September conference. If elected, you would serve a two-year term beginning January 1.

If you have any questions about this nomination, please call me.

Cordially,

Hollis Clark, MD

Hollis Clark, MD
Executive Director

fw

CONDOLENCE

A letter of **condolence** or sympathy is difficult to write because it deals with misfortune. When written properly, however, it should leave no doubt about your empathy. More importantly, your message should help ease the pain felt by the receiver.

[NOTE 8.7]
Messages of condolence must be sincere.

Messages of sympathy may be sent for an illness, death, natural disaster, or other misfortune. They may be typewritten or handwritten, or they may be in the form of a printed card. Handwritten messages are by far the most personal and will be the most appreciated.

[NOTE 8.8]
Make a sympathy letter short and positive.

The direct approach should be used for condolence letters. Begin with the purpose of the message—conveying sympathy. Only the necessary details need to be mentioned, and these should be treated positively and sincerely. For example, it is better to assure the survivor that she or he was appreciated and loved by the deceased person, in a letter of sympathy prompted by the death of a loved one, rather than eulogizing the deceased person. It is also appropriate to mention a personal detail of the deceased if such details are known to the writer; for example, "I remember your mention of the wonderful summer vacations you spent with your grandmother. I know that these memories will be even more precious to you now and in the future."

If appropriate, a letter of condolence can offer assistance; however, avoid a cliché ending. Make sure your offer is specific and genuine. Your message may be concluded by referring to the future in a positive way. Figure 8.2 shows an e-mail sent to a friend in another state whose mother has been hospitalized with a life-threatening illness.

Figure 8.2
Condolence Message

Subject: Mary Ann's Illness
Date: Fri, 10 Apr 200– 16:30:09 –0500
From: Dave Eldredge <dave.eldredge@dwbp.com>
To: Donald.Boecker@jiffy.com

I was shocked to learn that your mother is in the hospital with a serious illness. This must be a difficult time for you.

Convey sympathy.

Since your mother lives with you and your family, her absence has made a big change in your daily life. I hope that she will be returning to your home in the near future. Your children must really miss their grandmother reading to them at night.

Give words of encouragement.

Donald, the doctors at Trinity General have excellent credentials. Under their guidance your mother is receiving the best care possible.

Use a positive close.

APPRECIATION

Most people do not expect rewards for acts of kindness or thoughtfulness; however, we all enjoy knowing that our efforts are appreciated.

[NOTE 8.9]
Messages of appreciation show your gratitude.

A letter of **appreciation** may be sent for long-time thoughtfulness or for a one-time favor. Some examples of individuals who have shown sustained thoughtfulness include a long-standing, loyal customer, a faithful employee, a friend who has consistently recommended a company and brought it many customers, and a volunteer who has generously contributed time and effort to charitable causes.

Letters expressing thanks to such persons are always appropriate. Examples of letters of gratitude for one-time favors include a complimentary letter from a customer to a service department, a letter to a guest speaker who has given an excellent presentation, a letter to a new customer, a letter to a new member of an organization, and a letter to someone who has found a lost article and returned it to the owner.

[NOTE 8.10] Thank the receiver in the first paragraph.

Letters of appreciation should follow the direct approach. The good news—the expression of gratitude—should be given in the first paragraph and be followed by supporting evidence in a second or succeeding paragraphs. The letter should conclude with a comment of appreciation in the final paragraph; however, different words should be used in the opening and closing paragraphs. The thought of the letter, not the length of the letter, is the important consideration. A letter thanking a volunteer for participating in a fund-raising phonathon is shown in Figure 8.3.

Figure 8.3
Letter of Appreciation

MAIN STREET YOUTH, INC.
480 Main Street
Terra Ceia, FL 34250-1240
(813) 555-6635
Fax (813) 555-4389

March 6, 200–

William Taylor
4284 Starfish Drive
Terra Ceia, FL 34250-1221

Dear Bill:

Say thank-you.

Thank you for participating in the Main Street Youth Phonathon, which culminated on March 3. This four-week event provided more than $150,000 in pledges to Main Street Youth, Inc. This figure represents a 41 percent increase over last year's total.

Give supporting comments.

A level of success such as this could not have been achieved without your support and that of other volunteers. Please accept my deepest appreciation for your participation in the 200– MSY Phonathon. Main Street Youth, Inc. is fortunate to have volunteers who are dedicated to providing a productive environment for the youngsters of this community.

Express appreciation.

Thanks again for your contribution to the success of the 200– MSY Phonathon. We could not have done it without you.

Sincerely,

Emily Lacewell

Emily Lacewell
Phonathon Director

ts

INVITATION

A business **invitation** is a request for an individual's presence and is used in various situations. Inviting employees to a small social gathering, asking prominent community members to attend a fund-raising event, inviting civic leaders and selected customers to a company open house are all examples of invitations that are currently used in the business community. A form letter inviting selected local citizens to a $15-a-plate dinner recognizing honor students is shown in Figure 8.4.

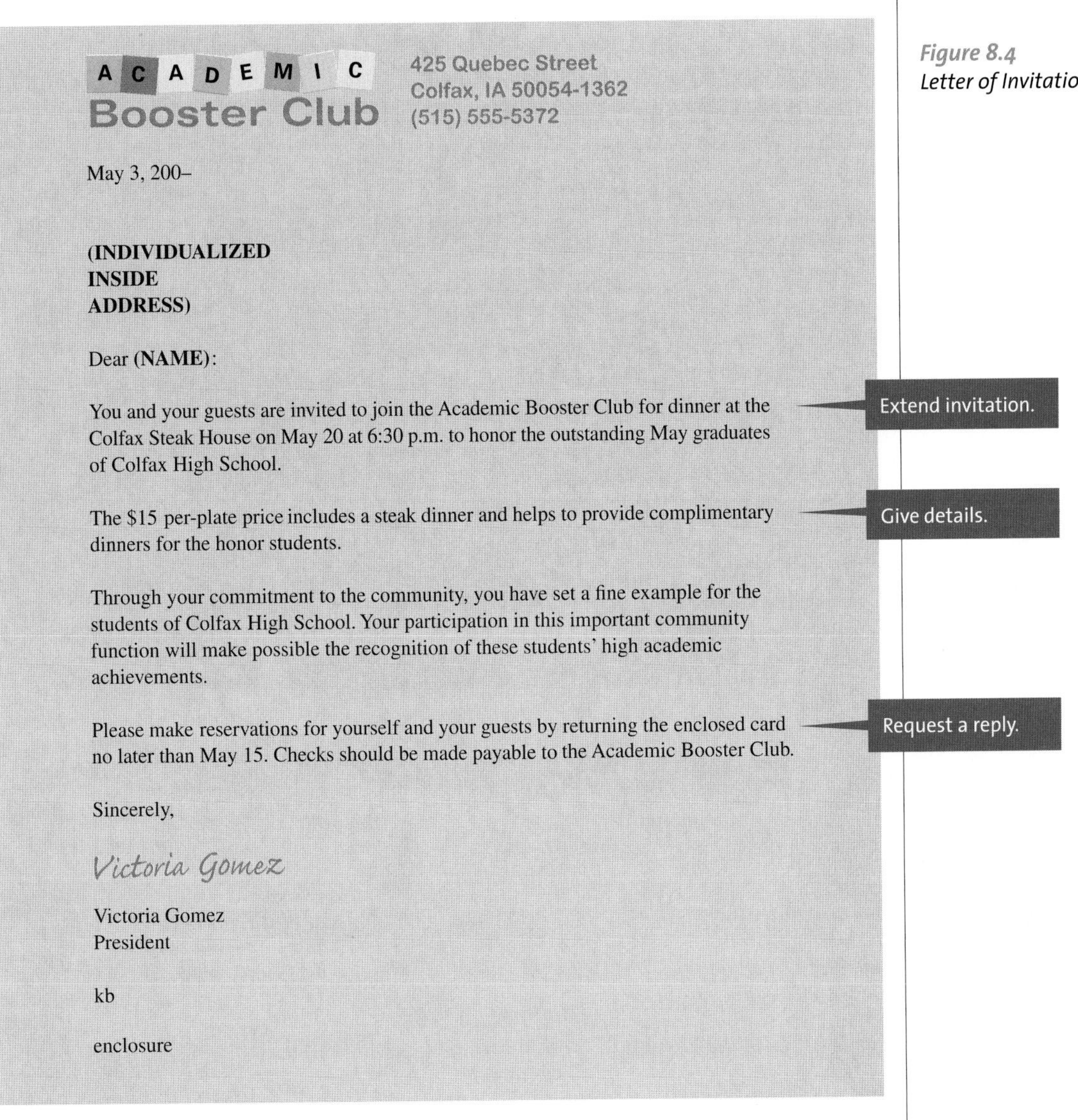

ACADEMIC Booster Club

425 Quebec Street
Colfax, IA 50054-1362
(515) 555-5372

May 3, 200–

(INDIVIDUALIZED
INSIDE
ADDRESS)

Dear **(NAME)**:

You and your guests are invited to join the Academic Booster Club for dinner at the Colfax Steak House on May 20 at 6:30 p.m. to honor the outstanding May graduates of Colfax High School.

The $15 per-plate price includes a steak dinner and helps to provide complimentary dinners for the honor students.

Through your commitment to the community, you have set a fine example for the students of Colfax High School. Your participation in this important community function will make possible the recognition of these students' high academic achievements.

Please make reservations for yourself and your guests by returning the enclosed card no later than May 15. Checks should be made payable to the Academic Booster Club.

Sincerely,

Victoria Gomez

Victoria Gomez
President

kb

enclosure

Extend invitation.
Give details.
Request a reply.

Figure 8.4
Letter of Invitation

An invitation may be handwritten, typed on company stationery, or printed as a formal invitation. It should include all the necessary details such as the date, time, place, suggested dress, and whether the receiver may bring a guest. Be sensitive to diverse living arrangements (guest versus spouse). In order to plan efficiently, an invitation should include an *RSVP;* that is, a request for a reply to the invitation.

[NOTE 8.11]
An invitation may be formal or informal.

The *RSVP* should specify the method by which to respond and the date by which the response is requested:

RSVP 555-7803 by October 31	or	Regrets only 555-6249

HOLIDAY GREETING

[NOTE 8.12]
Holiday greetings may be sent to celebrate festive seasons.

A **holiday greeting** may be sent before or during any festive season. New Year's Day, Easter, Labor Day, Thanksgiving, Hanukkah, and Christmas are holidays generally celebrated in the United States. Businesses participating in international trade should be aware of and acknowledge appropriate holidays in the countries where they have employees, customers, or suppliers.

[NOTE 8.13]
A greeting card is used often.

Many companies send season's greetings cards to customers or suppliers. The majority of letters and cards sent during December now say "Holiday Greetings" rather than "Merry Christmas," because of diversity in the workplace. These greetings usually have the company name printed on the card. Executives and sales representatives may use a different kind of company card on which they can write personalized greetings to business friends and colleagues. Some companies send distinctively designed cards that bear the company name and logo. This type of card is impressive because it is unique to the organization sending it. Individualized holiday greeting letters are sent by some business firms.

Figure 8.5 shows the Thanksgiving message to clients that Andrea Holle refers to in the Let's Talk Business section at the beginning of the chapter. Along with extending wishes for a happy holiday season, the letter anticipates prosperity.

Figure 8.5
Holiday Greeting

Gain attention.

Extend greetings.

Thanksgiving

Turkey and dressing, mashed potatoes and gravy, pumpkin pie and whipped cream—the Thanksgiving holiday is so much more than the feast we enjoy on this special day.

The true meaning of this holiday lies in giving thanks for all that we have. This year, look around and count your blessings—the special people who share the holiday with you (and those who would like to, but can't), the delicious food you enjoy, the roof over your head.

This Thanksgiving, we are grateful for many things, including a loving family, good friends, and good health. We're also grateful for the faith you've placed in us and Edward Jones. We are humbled by your trust, and we remain dedicated to providing exceptional service while helping you reach your financial goals.

Happy Thanksgiving. May you enjoy a bountiful harvest of friends, good health, and prosperity.

Your Friends at Edward Jones

Jo Yount Andrea Holle Joy Jenkins Donna Garcia

WELCOME

A **welcome** message is used to greet new employees, new customers, and newcomers to a community. Many cities have organizations, such as the Welcome Wagon, that send welcome letters to persons moving into the community. A new employee welcome is aimed at familiarizing new employees with the company and at building goodwill. Figure 8.6 is an example of such a letter.

Welcome letters are frequently sent to new customers, particularly to those who are establishing credit with the business. These messages are used to congratulate the customer on opening a charge account with the business and to offer an incentive to the new customer to use the business's facilities in the near future.

[NOTE 8.14]
Welcome letters are appropriate for new employees, new customers, or new community members.

HARRIS, LOCKE, & WILLIAMS, Inc.
1638 Pebble Valley Lane
Evansville, IN 47701-1426
(477) 555-5218 Fax (477) 555-6831

August 3, 200–

Ms. Carolyn Fields
538 Hillcrest Drive
Evansville, IN 47712

Dear Carolyn:

Welcome! You have selected an excellent company with which to begin your professional career.

Harris, Locke, & Williams, Inc., is a well-established company with an outstanding reputation. The company places trust in its employees, and they are encouraged to use innovative ideas in meeting their daily challenges. Our employees are so satisfied with their jobs that we have one of the lowest employee turnover rates in the industry.

As you were informed during your employment interview, Harris, Locke, & Williams, Inc., provides its employees with excellent fringe benefits. Please contact Jennifer Wolfe at extension 3279 to set up an appointment to learn how these benefits can be of value to you.

Carolyn, our company is very pleased that you have selected us. We hope that you have many successful and rewarding years with us. If I can be of any assistance, please let me know.

Sincerely,

Harry Standfast

Harry Standfast
Human Resource Manager

Welcome employee.

Provide information.

Show appreciation.

Figure 8.6
Welcome Letter

Style in Goodwill Messages

Learning Objective [3]
DESCRIBE THE CRITERIA FOR SELECTING THE STYLE FOR A GOODWILL MESSAGE.

A goodwill message is an effective way to build a positive relationship with a customer, an employee, or a supplier. Style is important in accomplishing the purpose of the communication. Goodwill messages come in many forms. The following Communication Note describes a goodwill message sent in an unusual style.

COMMUNICATION NOTE

Campaign for Signatures on Good-Luck Banner

As the Indian cricket team prepared to compete in the 1999 World Cup, a banner was circulated for signatures in 72 cities in India. The campaign, "Sign Lagao—India Jitao" (Sign your name—make India win), aimed to present a goodwill message on the world's largest banner. The banner stretched for 10.45 kilometers. The giant banner was presented to the Indian team on the eve of its departure for the World Cup.

Adapted from "Signature Campaign to Wish Indian Team," The Hindu, http://www.usa.cricket.org, *April 8, 1999.*

HANDWRITTEN VERSUS TYPEWRITTEN VERSUS PRINTED MESSAGES

[NOTE 8.15] A goodwill message may be handwritten, typed, or printed.

You must decide whether a goodwill message should be handwritten, typewritten, or printed. A handwritten note is appropriate in times of sorrow, but a printed invitation to a social function is preferred, whether it is for a small wedding or a dinner and dance for several hundred people. A typewritten message is normally used to welcome a customer or employee to a business. The form that is most effective for conveying your message should be the basis of your decision.

CARD VERSUS LETTER VERSUS E-MAIL

[NOTE 8.16] Whether to send a card or a letter depends on the occasion.

Using a commercially produced card is less time consuming and frequently is more suitable than a typed letter. A short, handwritten note on a holiday greeting card or a card of sympathy may mean more to the receiver than a long, formal letter. However, a typewritten welcome letter to a new credit customer is the preferred business style. Messages sent via e-mail are rapidly gaining popularity as a means of delivering goodwill to employees, customers, and friends. E-mail is inexpensive and timely.

FAMILIARITY VERSUS FORMALITY

[NOTE 8.17] How well you know the receiver dictates the formality of the message.

The formality of a goodwill message depends on the purpose of the message you are sending and on how well you know the receiver. Put yourself in the place of the receiver and write a letter that you would like to receive—whether the message must, of necessity, be phrased in formal language or whether the nature of the message permits you to be relaxed and informal.

Summary of Learning Objectives

Describe goodwill messages. A goodwill message is written to show that you care about the receiver. Goodwill messages should not be used as sales messages. Goodwill messages must be sent promptly. *Learning Objective* [1]

Compose the six common types of goodwill messages. The types of goodwill messages are congratulations, condolence, appreciation, invitation, holiday greetings, and welcome. A message of congratulations praises the receiver for an accomplishment or an achievement. Messages of condolence or sympathy may be sent for an illness, death, natural disaster, or other misfortune and are prepared using the direct approach. Letters of appreciation are sent to acknowledge thoughtfulness and are also prepared using the direct approach. A business invitation is a request for an individual's presence. An invitation may be handwritten, typed, or printed. Holiday greeting messages may be sent during any festive season. A welcome message is used to greet new employees, new customers, and newcomers to a community or an organization and is prepared using the direct approach. *Learning Objective* [2]

Describe the criteria for selecting the style for a goodwill message. Style is important in accomplishing the purpose of the communication. A goodwill message may be handwritten, typewritten, or printed. A handwritten note is appropriate in times of sorrow, but a printed invitation is preferred for a social function. A typewritten message is normally used to welcome a customer or employee to a business. Commercially produced cards generally are used for brief personal messages, whereas typewritten letters are used more often for less personal goodwill messages. The purpose of the goodwill message and your familiarity with the receiver determine the formality of the message. *Learning Objective* [3]

DISCUSSION QUESTIONS

1. Describe similarities and differences between goodwill messages and positive messages. (Objective 1 and Chapter 7)
2. Indicate two situations for which it would be appropriate to send congratulatory messages to an individual and two situations for which it would be appropriate to send congratulatory messages to a business. (Objective 1)
3. Discuss the three major elements that should be included in an appreciation message. (Objective 2)
4. Describe the content that should be included in an invitation. (Objective 2)
5. Discuss the criteria that should be considered when deciding whether to use a handwritten note, a typewritten message, or a printed message for goodwill. (Objective 3)
6. Should goodwill messages be written using formal or informal language? Explain. (Objective 3)

APPLICATION EXERCISES

1. Select a business in your community and interview a supervisor to learn how he or she handles condolences with employees, with customers and clients (both long-term

and new), and with community leaders who are not customers or clients. Obtain copies of the messages, if possible, and report your findings to the class. (Objective 1)

2. Describe to the class any unique holiday greetings that you have received from businesspersons. Determine how they handle sympathy or condolences with their clients, customers, and/or employees. Compare your findings with the suggestions described in the text. (Objective 2)
3. Design an invitation to participate in a charity golf tournament that your school is sponsoring. The proceeds from the tournament will go toward scholarships. (Objective 2)

4. **Teamwork.** Divide into teams of three or four students and design a message that could be placed in your school paper welcoming new students to campus on behalf of a student organization. This message also needs to inform the students of the student organization. (Objective 2)

5. **E-mail.** Your instructor has been hospitalized for emergency surgery and is now recovering at home. He or she can access e-mail. Compose an appropriate condolence message and send it to your instructor using e-mail. (Objective 3)

There are Web exercises at **http://krizan.swcollege.com** to accompany this chapter.

CASE PROBLEMS

Congratulations

1. James Ferguson, your information systems manager, was recently named by the Information Systems Association (ISA) the Outstanding Information Systems Manager of the year in the United States. As the human resources manager in your company, write a letter to James congratulating him on his accomplishment. Add details to make this a complete letter.
2. You are the human resources manager in your company, and you belong to several professional organizations. Yesterday, you read in *Professional Managers,* a newsletter from one of the organizations, that Theresa Goodman has been promoted to president of her company. Write a letter to Theresa, a long-time friend, congratulating her on the promotion. Add details to make this a complete letter.
3. David Mikulcik, owner of The Green House, has developed a new variety of rose. Its blossoms are turquoise and it has an unusually sweet smell. David has been working on this project since graduating from college 15 years ago. Write a letter to David congratulating him on his accomplishment. Add details to make this a complete letter.
4. Hudson Filters is moving into a new 50,000-square-foot manufacturing plant. The modern design is attractive and a welcome addition to your community. The plant will contain the latest technology. Write a letter to Hudson Filters congratulating it on the new building. Add details to make this a complete letter.

Condolence

5. You are the executive director for the chamber of commerce in your town. Last week a group of tourists ate contaminated turkey in a local restaurant and 14 of them were hospitalized. It has been determined that this contaminated turkey was the fault of the food supplier and not of the restaurant. However, the news has attracted much negative media attention and has resulted in greatly reduced business. The

restaurant, Ethel's, is owned by one of your chamber members. Write a letter to Ethel Thompson, expressing your condolences and asking her how you can be of assistance. Add details to make this a complete letter.

6. Todd Ledbetter was a sales representative for your company for eight years. Yesterday, he died of AIDS. Write a letter to his family expressing your sympathy.
7. Sure Tuff Tires has operated a plant in your community for 27 years. Yesterday, it was announced in the local paper that the plant will close at the end of the year. This unexpected shutdown will affect the company's 600 employees, many of whom are not eligible for retirement. Write a letter to the editor of the local paper expressing your company's concern for Sure Tuff's employees. Add details to make this a complete letter.
8. Heavy rains have caused the Ohio River to flow over its banks in many areas. Addyston, Ohio, is no exception; much damage has occurred because of flooding. Your company, Industrial Plastics, has a plant in Addyston. Many of your company's Addyston employees have had excessive damage to their homes. As president of Industrial Plastics, write a form letter that can be sent to the Addyston employees expressing your condolences.

Appreciation

9. Margie Boldt, an accounting professor, has been of great assistance in getting you a job after your graduation from college with a degree in accounting. She wrote several letters of recommendation and gave you names of several contacts. One of these contacts resulted in your present job. Write a letter of appreciation to Margie, and send a copy of the letter to the dean of your school. Add details to make this a complete letter.
10. You are program coordinator for Young Urban Professionals. Chris Madden spoke on "Professionalism" to your organization. Supply supporting details and write a letter thanking him for his presentation.

11. **Global/Cross-Cultural.** Hans Gerhardt, a German high school soccer star, spent three weeks visiting relatives in your town. While he was in town, he held a one-week soccer camp for the recreational league. Your business sponsors one of the teams in the league. Hans has returned to Germany. Write a letter thanking him for conducting the soccer camp.

12. **E-mail.** A Relay for Life celebration was held this past weekend in your town. The celebration was extremely successful and raised more than $200,000 to fight cancer. Five of your employees have been involved with organizing this project for the past four months. Develop a message that could be sent via e-mail to the employees; be sure to supply details. Send this message to your instructor.

Invitation

13. Dr. Eva Schultz, a noted botanist, is scheduled to present a program at City Hall on October 12, 200–, and the admission will be $5 per person. Dr. Schultz has recently returned from South America and will present a program on the plight of the rain forest. Compose an invitation that could be placed in the local newspaper advertising this program. Supply details to make this a complete letter.
14. Bluebonnet Electric is having an open house to celebrate moving into a new facility. Write a form letter that can be personalized and sent to all customers inviting them to the open house.

15. The art club at your school is displaying its art projects from the past year. Write a memo that the school can send to invite the families of the art students to the fair.

16. The president of your organization, Kern Alexander, is retiring after 32 years of service. A dinner honoring him for his long service to the company, community, and region will be held on September 24. One of his closest friends, Kristi Urquhart, lives in a community 200 miles away. Write a letter inviting her to the dinner and asking her to present a brief tribute to Kern. Remind her that many others will be giving similar presentations so she must keep her remarks brief.

Holiday Greeting

17. **E-mail.** Your company is holding a Sweetheart Dinner and Dance for its employees and their sweethearts on February 14. The dinner and dance will be held from 6 p.m. to midnight at Brian's Steak House and Lounge. Prepare a message that could be sent via e-mail to your employees.

18. Guardian Savings and Loan Association closes to honor the memory of Martin Luther King, Jr. Design a notice that could be placed in a local newspaper informing its readers that Guardian Savings will be closed for the entire day.

19. Red Rose Ice Cream is holding a one-mile fun run followed by an ice cream social on Labor Day. All individuals participating in the fun run at 10 a.m. will receive a free T-shirt. Everyone in town is invited to the ice cream social from noon to 2 p.m. at Jackson Park. Design a notice that could be placed in a local newspaper to advertise the festivities. Include a registration form for the fun run.

20. As part of the city's Memorial Day festivities, L&H Petroleum is sponsoring a concert by Leaping Lizards. The band will perform at the football stadium at 7 p.m. There will be no charge for the concert. Create a notice that could be placed in the local newspaper promoting this concert.

Welcome

21. Randi Sawyer has been approved for a credit card from your company. Her card has a credit limit of $2,000. Write a letter that could be used to welcome Randi. Include a brochure that was prepared earlier describing the details of the credit card.

22. The Health Academy opened last month and is rapidly expanding its membership. Prepare a form letter that could be used to welcome all of its new members. Be creative and add details.

23. Businesses in your area are interested in building better relations with students from your college. As executive director of the chamber of commerce in your town, you need to prepare a flyer announcing a free ice cream social for all students. This flyer will be given to students at registration. Be creative and add details to make this a complete flyer.

24. Panorama Cablevision has recently purchased another cable company. The president of Panorama would like you to write a memo to the employees of the newly acquired company welcoming them to Panorama. This memo needs to make the new employees feel they are equal to the original Panorama employees.

Message Analysis

Correct and strengthen the following message that has been written to congratulate an employee for completing her bachelor's degree:

Pearl, I know that you are glad that you finally got your degree. The 11 years that it took you to complete this degree must have seemed like an eternity.

I am glad that you are finally through. This will bring our percentage of college graduates to 92%. Our branch will now earn a plaque for having more than 90 percent college graduates.

Hopefully your degree will help you do a better job with our company. Once again, I am glad that you are now finished with your studies.

GRAMMAR WORKSHOP

Correct the grammar, spelling, punctuation, style, and word choice errors in the following sentences:

1. The tornado blew a tree on Douglas car; twisted the television antenna on Joys' house; and flattened Bob's and Reba's home.
2. Prior to locating the Starlite theatre he drove South on 18th street, turned west on Main street, and finally drove North on Poplar Avenue.
3. The instructor asked the computor students why they had doubled spaced they're reports.
4. Sara Redden the company President met with the board of directors in the morning, and played golf with Amy in the afternoon prior to leaving for Tulsa.
5. Erosion occured as rainwater run out of the gutter, however; the rain was needed bad due to the draught.
6. Monday at the annual stock holders meeting the company comptroler stated, all common share stock holders will receive a 5% dividend.
7. Get these legal documents to Mr. McDaniels' whose in the office next door.
8. In order to meet more frequently the world war II Aviators changed it's meetings from monthly to bi-monthly.
9. This is the briefest letter that I have ever send to the Sales Representatives.
10. Wow. The St. Louis zoo has numerous exotic monkies, colorful peasants, and sleek tigers.

CHAPTER

9 Negative Messages

Tim Farmer, Co-owner, ComputerLand of Paducah, Kentucky

LET'S TALK BUSINESS As a business owner, I am faced with a difficult customer from time to time. The old saying in the retail industry is "the customer is always right." Sometimes, however, it seems impossible to satisfy customers. No matter what action or method the business takes, it is never enough to please some customers. At other times, a customer will disappoint the business by failing in financial obligations. No matter what the circumstances, when the business or the customer is unhappy, the business stands at a crossroads with a difficult decision. Do you continue to do all that you can to try to accommodate a customer at any cost? Or, do you decide to end the relationship?

Let me share an example of a situation in which I believe it would be in the best interest of a business to sever the relationship with the customer and de-

(Continued)

[LEARNING OBJECTIVES]

[1] DESCRIBE THE NATURE OF NEGATIVE MESSAGES.

[2] LIST THE ADVANTAGES OF USING THE INDIRECT PLAN FOR EFFECTIVE COMMUNICATION OF NEGATIVE INFORMATION.

[3] DESCRIBE THE FIVE SPECIFIC GUIDELINES FOR USING THE INDIRECT PLAN.

[4] PREPARE COMPETENTLY A VARIETY OF NEGATIVE MESSAGES USING THE INDIRECT PLAN.

[5] PREPARE NEGATIVE MESSAGES USING THE DIRECT PLAN WHEN IT IS APPROPRIATE.

scribe the communication I would use in handling this situation. In some instances, customers routinely do not pay their bills in a timely manner even after they are sent several past-due statements. At this time, it becomes necessary to begin sending the customers several letters stating that their account is past due. The first letter I use begins and ends with a positive paragraph thanking the customer for his or her business. However, the second and third letters I send are more direct and usually state my negative message in the opening paragraph. After these conventional attempts have been made to rectify the problem, more drastic measures may be required, such as writing a letter indicating my company's desire to end the relationship.

Letters of this nature are the hardest ones to write considering the company may have had a long-standing relationship with the customer or if he or she happens to be a personal friend. Nevertheless, a final letter to sever the partnership between the business and customer is sometimes inevitable. In this final letter, I begin by thanking the customer for his or her business and conclude by stating my desire to end the business relationship. Furthermore, I describe with detail the reasons or circumstances that led to this difficult decision.

Negative messages are always the most difficult correspondence to write. If written properly, however, your image and your company's image will remain a positive one. •

Learning Objective [1]
DESCRIBE THE NATURE OF NEGATIVE MESSAGES.

A **negative message** is one that is likely to be viewed as unpleasant, disappointing, or unfavorable by the receiver. A negative message, for example, may be written to refuse a request that has been made of you or your organization. The message may provide information about a change in policy that employees do not particularly favor or a price increase that customers prefer to avoid.

[NOTE 9.1]
Negative messages give unfavorable information.

As Tim Farmer states in the opening quotation of this chapter, a negative message is a challenge to compose. At the same time, it is an opportunity for you as a writer or speaker to resolve a common business problem successfully. You can even win a friend for yourself or a customer for your organization with an effectively conveyed negative message.

Use the Indirect Plan for Negative Messages

The general strategy for conveying all types of negative messages is to use the indirect plan. With the indirect plan, the sentence or the section of the message that conveys the disappointing idea follows reasons that explain why you must refuse a request or why you must provide unfavorable information. The indirect plan prepares your receivers for the negative information. Research has shown that receivers are more accepting of negative information when they have been prepared to receive it.

[NOTE 9.2]
The indirect plan prepares the receiver for negative news.

[NOTE 9.3]
Research supports the effectiveness of the indirect plan.

Learning Objective [2]
LIST THE ADVANTAGES OF USING THE INDIRECT PLAN FOR EFFECTIVE COMMUNICATION OF NEGATIVE INFORMATION.

Important advantages of the indirect plan are that it enables receivers (1) to accept the negative information you must give them and (2) to maintain a satisfactory relationship with you.

[NOTE 9.4]
The indirect plan enables receivers to accept negative information and to maintain their relationship with you.

The indirect plan has these advantages because it maintains calm through its gradual approach. It gives time for the receiver's anxiety to subside. The indirect plan affords the opportunity for reason to prevail and for understanding to develop. If the negative information is given first, the receiver may ignore the rest of the message; even a fair, reasonable explanation following the bad news may never be accepted.

[NOTE 9.5]
The indirect plan
- Maintains calm
- Permits reason to prevail
- Changes a negative situation to a positive one

If your message is written or spoken thoughtfully and carefully in the you–viewpoint, the receiver may even agree that the negative information is appropriate and acceptable. An effective presentation of the message may clearly show that the negative information is, in fact, in the best interest of the receiver. It may represent a decision that benefits the receiver. The achievement of a positive receiver reaction is your goal in preparing negative messages.

Learning Objective [3]
DESCRIBE THE FIVE SPECIFIC GUIDELINES FOR USING THE INDIRECT PLAN.

How to Use the Indirect Plan

[NOTE 9.6]
There are specific steps in the indirect plan.

In this section specific guides for using the indirect plan for writing negative messages are given. In addition, you will want to use the fundamentals of effective business communication that are presented in Chapters 1, 4, and 5. Figure 9.1 outlines the steps and specific guides for using the indirect plan to present negative information.

The indirect plan can be used effectively for a variety of written and oral negative messages—refused claims, refused requests, unfavorable decisions, or any unpleasant information. Written messages are shown in this chapter to illustrate clearly the use of the indirect plan for negative messages.

DETERMINATION OF CONTENT

[NOTE 9.7]
The situation must be analyzed before the indirect plan is implemented.

Each communication situation must first be analyzed to determine (1) primary and secondary purposes and (2) the basic content of the message. The following questions must be answered for negative messages: What ideas can I use in the opening to establish coherence and build goodwill in this particular situation? Why is it in the receiver's interest for me to refuse the request or present the unfavorable information? Is there an alternative course of action that I can recommend to this receiver? What friendly message can I convey in the off-the-subject close?

Once you have determined the purposes and content of the negative message, you are ready to implement the indirect plan. In the following sections, the indirect plan outline is discussed; and the most important considerations are reviewed.

OPENING BUFFER

[NOTE 9.8]
Use the opening buffer to
- Provide coherence
- Build goodwill
- Be positive
- Maintain neutrality
- Introduce the explanation

In the indirect plan, the opening buffer should meet the following requirements: provide coherence, build goodwill, be positive, maintain neutrality, and introduce the explanation. The opening buffer usually will consist of one to three sentences. It will serve as the first paragraph in a memo or a letter.

To provide coherence, the opening buffer puts you and your receiver on the same wavelength. The negative message is tied to a previous conversation, a point of agreement, a memo or letter received earlier, a prior transaction, or some other common ground.

Figure 9.1
Indirect Plan Outline

Indirect Plan for Negative Messages

I. The **Opening Buffer**
   A. Provide coherence.
   B. Build goodwill.
   C. Be positive.
   D. Maintain neutrality.
   E. Introduce the explanation.

II. The **Logical Explanation**
   A. Relate to the opening buffer.
   B. Present convincing reasoning.
   C. Stress receiver interests and benefits.
   D. Use de-emphasis techniques.
   E. Be positive.

III. The **Negative Information**
   A. Relate to the logical explanation.
   B. Imply or give negative information explicitly.
   C. Use de-emphasis techniques.
   D. Give negative information quickly.
   E. Be positive.
   F. Say what can be done (not what cannot).
   G. Avoid an apology.

IV. The **Constructive Follow-up**
   A. Provide an alternative solution.
   B. Give additional reasoning.

V. The **Friendly Close**
   A. Build goodwill.
   B. Personalize the close.
   C. Stay off the negative subject.
   D. Be warm.
   E. Be optimistic.

You will want to build goodwill by using courteous, polite words such as *thank you, please,* and *I appreciate,* and by keeping the receiver's interests central to your opening buffer. Use positive words; avoid negative words. Using positive words helps set a favorable tone and makes your message more acceptable to the receiver. It is possible, in fact desirable, to compose negative messages without using a single negative word.

The two final requirements for a good opening buffer—maintaining neutrality and introducing the explanation—are closely related. You will want your receiver to read through the opening buffer into the logical explanation that follows. You do not want to suggest the negative information in the opening. Therefore, the opening buffer should not imply either a yes or a no. It should not lead the receiver in either direction; it should be neutral.

The final requirement of the opening buffer is to set the stage for the explanation, that is, introduce the explanation. In the last sentence of the buffer, give your receiver some indication of the thrust of the explanation. In effect, give the receiver the "headline" for the explanation that follows in the next paragraph(s). This sets up the strategy for the logical explanation, which is the next part of your message, and it assists in providing coherence.

LOGICAL EXPLANATION

[NOTE 9.9]
Logical explanation follows the opening buffer and precedes the negative information.

The second part of the indirect plan is the logical explanation. In a memo or letter, the logical explanation usually begins after the opening buffer and often can be handled in one paragraph. If the explanation is short, the negative information may be included in the same paragraph. In some situations the constructive follow-up can immediately follow the negative information in the same paragraph. This buries the negative news in the middle of a paragraph. In other written message situations, the logical explanation may be so long that it requires two or more paragraphs.

[NOTE 9.10]
The logical explanation

- Justifies the negative information
- Provides coherence
- Presents convincing reasoning
- Uses rules of emphasis
- Accents positiveness

One of the most important aspects of the indirect plan is that the reasoning that justifies the negative information is presented *before* the negative information. After the opening buffer, you present the reasons explaining why you must convey the negative information. If at all possible, these reasons should show how the negative information will be in the best interest of your receiver. This reasoning, in order to be effective, must be presented in a calm, convincing, and pleasant manner using the you–viewpoint. The following Communication Note indicates that company policy, without explanation, should not be used as justification for bad news.

COMMUNICATION NOTE

Company Policy Is NOT Justification

Company policy, in and of itself, is not sufficient justification for negative news. Readers could argue that the policy should be changed or that their situation deserves an exception. Writers should explain the reason behind the policy.

The specific requirements for the logical explanation are that it relates coherently to the opening buffer, presents convincing reasoning, stresses receiver interests and benefits, uses emphasis techniques, and is positive.

The opening buffer will have introduced the explanation. The beginning of the logical explanation should use coherence techniques to relate it to the opening and to facilitate the flow of thought. You may use repetition of key words, a tie-in sentence, or some other coherence technique to ensure that the logical explanation follows the opening.

The convincing reasoning, which supports the unfavorable information, should be composed with the receiver's interests or benefits as the focal points. The receiver's favorable reactions to the words you choose will be your goal. In fact, if at the end of the reasoning the receiver agrees that the negative information represents the best alternative in this situation, you will have composed the ideal negative message.

Although the ideal logical explanation presents the reasoning in terms of receiver benefit, circumstances will not always permit you to compose the ideal message. You may have to base your reasoning on what is fair for all concerned. Also, there may be occasions when confidentiality precludes giving any specific reasons. In these situations, you will want to communicate convincingly and persuasively that the matter was carefully considered in the interest of the receiver before the decision was reached.

You will want to use rules of emphasis in the logical explanation. Start with the points that are most favorable to your receiver, and, as you move deeper into the paragraph, deal with the least favorable aspects of your reasoning.

Finally, the logical explanation should be positive. Avoid all negative words. For example, use *situation* instead of *problem* and *needed change* instead of *correction.* In referring to the negative information, avoid such words as *failure, cannot, trouble, inadequate,* and *defective.*

NEGATIVE INFORMATION

After the opening buffer and the logical explanation, you are ready to present the negative information. This step in the indirect plan consists of the request refusal, unfavorable decision, or other disappointing information. If the opening buffer and the logical explanation have been effective, receivers will be expecting the negative information. In fact, in most circumstances, it is possible for you to prepare your receivers so well that they will easily accept the information, refusal, or decision.

[NOTE 9.11]
The negative information follows the logical explanation.

The primary goal in presenting negative information is to be sure that the receiver clearly understands this part of your message. In communicating with Americans, Europeans, Australians, and others with similar cultures, you will want to imply or state explicitly your decision. Wording such as "... therefore, it would seem better for you to follow the company policy" may leave a question in the mind of your receiver. With this lack of clarity, the receiver may think that the decision is still up for discussion or that he or she could decide what to do. However, in many parts of the world—Asia and Latin America, for example—people prefer a lack of clarity because it makes the moment more pleasant. In some cultures the words *yes* and *no* do not always have the same meaning, as noted in the following Communication Note.

[NOTE 9.12]
Be sure negative information is clear.

COMMUNICATION NOTE

They Don't Say "No" in Asia

In Thailand, there is no word for *no.* In Japan, there are over 20 ways to avoid saying *no* directly. The Koreans try to avoid giving bad news. Asians answer practically all questions either with *yes* or *maybe.* If you ask, "Do you want to buy this product?" you may get a *yes* that means "I heard your question." *Yes* does not always mean *yes* in Asia.

Even with cultures that prefer more directness and clarity, it is desirable in most situations to imply the negative information. It softens the bad news and permits you to present negative information in a positive manner. For example, "Smoking is permitted in the hallways only" is much more acceptable to most people than "Smoking is prohibited in the classrooms and offices." These statements both say basically the same thing; the first just says it positively. For effective communication of negative information, it is better to say what can be done rather than what cannot be done.

[NOTE 9.13]
It is best to imply the negative information.

[NOTE 9.14]
Stress what can be done (not what cannot be done).

There are situations when the negative information should be given in explicit terms. These are the times when you believe that an implied refusal would not be strong enough or might be misunderstood by your receiver. In the case of rejecting admission to a college, for example, it may not be possible to imply the refusal. In this type of situation, it is better to present the logical explanation and then explicitly state the refusal in clear terms, such as ". . . therefore, the committee has not approved your application for admission." This wording can leave no doubt in the receiver's mind. In most cases, though, you will want to imply the negative information to reduce its emphasis.

[NOTE 9.15] De-emphasize the negative information by placing it in the middle of a paragraph.

The recommended placement of the negative information section of the message is immediately following the logical explanation. In a written message, never place the negative information in a separate paragraph. In order to de-emphasize the negative information, place it in the middle of a paragraph. The negative news may be followed by an additional reason or suggested alternative(s). This placement would tuck the negative information inside the paragraph and de-emphasize it.

[NOTE 9.16] State the negative information quickly.

[NOTE 9.17] Be positive.

The negative information should be given in as few words as possible. Ideally, you can further de-emphasize the unfavorable news by placing it in a dependent clause. As in all sections of a negative message, you will want to use positive words and avoid negative words—say what can be done and not what cannot be done. Also, in most cases you will want to avoid apologies throughout the message because they only call further attention to the negativeness of the situation. Do not use apologies such as, "I am sorry I must refuse your request."

[NOTE 9.18] Avoid an apology.

In summary, negative information is implied or stated explicitly, follows the logical explanation, uses techniques to de-emphasize it, is given quickly, is positive, says what can be done, and avoids apologies. After giving the negative information, your next step in the indirect plan is to provide constructive follow-up.

CONSTRUCTIVE FOLLOW-UP

[NOTE 9.19] Constructive follow-up consists of other solutions or additional justification.

In the constructive follow-up section of a negative message, you provide other solutions to the problem or, if that is not possible, you give an additional reason justifying the unfavorable news.

For example, one good way to strengthen your communication and to build improved human relations is to do more than is expected by offering an alternative solution to the receiver. If you were asked to return to your high school on October 24 to speak to seniors about attending college and your schedule would not permit you to do so, you could suggest an alternative speaker or an alternative date. Even though you have to refuse the request, your suggested alternative may solve the problem and maintain effective human relations. In the case of adjustment refusals, you can make a special offer or resell the customer on the product or service.

If you cannot suggest an alternative or offer a solution to the problem, it will be important for you to save part of the logical explanation and place it following the negative information. This helps the receiver accept the bad news by de-emphasizing its importance and giving him or her additional justification for it.

FRIENDLY CLOSE

[NOTE 9.20] The friendly close

- Builds goodwill
- Is off the subject

The friendly close moves the receiver's mind away from the problem—the negative information—and provides an opportunity to build goodwill. If you must refuse a customer credit, you will want him or her to continue to buy with cash. If you have to refuse an employee's request, you will want to maintain good human relations and not reduce the employee's productivity.

You can build goodwill in the friendly close by ensuring that it is personalized, off the subject, warm, and optimistic. The wording of the friendly close should fit the receiver and the particular situation. The close should relate to the topic while avoiding the bad news. It could make further reference to the constructive follow-up, or it could express appreciation to a customer for his or her business.

The friendly close should not include anything that reminds the receiver of the negative information you have given. It should be off the subject of the negative information. The friendly close should not include an apology such as, "Again, let me say how sorry I am that we cannot honor your claim." This only reminds the receiver of the problem. The close can include any friendly remark appropriate to your receiver. The prime requirement for the friendly close is to regain the goodwill that may have been lost due to the negative information.

Implementing the Indirect Plan

The step-by-step development of a memo to employees who must be given negative information shows clearly how the indirect plan works. Although negative messages often are best presented orally, a written message will be developed for this case to illustrate the content. Here are the details of the communication situation.

[NOTE 9.21]
A communication situation will help illustrate how to compose negative messages.

THE KREBS FURNITURE CASE

Krebs Furniture has manufacturing plants in six locations within the United States. Its Georgetown, Texas, plant manufactures collectible reproductions and has been operating for 35 years. It currently has 150 employees who have excellent fringe benefits and earn above-average salaries for the Georgetown area. Krebs began its operation in Georgetown with 12 employees and steadily grew to more than 250 employees. About five years ago competition in producing collectible reproductions, especially from international companies, increased tremendously. This competition forced Krebs to downsize its workforce to its present size of 150 employees. Now Krebs' management, realizing that it cannot compete with the lower production costs due to the low wages that international companies pay, has decided to close its Georgetown plant at the end of the year. Your task is to write a memo conveying the negative information to the employees and, at the same time, to make that information acceptable and maybe even desirable for them.

Determine Appropriate Content

The first step in writing a message is to determine its purposes and content. The primary purpose of your memo to Krebs' employees will be to convey clearly the negative information, and the secondary purpose is to make that information acceptable and maybe even desirable for them. The content of the memo must be developed and organized for each step in the indirect plan. Examples of *poor* and *good* content you could decide to use are illustrated in the following sections.

Write an Effective Opening Buffer

The five qualities of a good opening buffer described previously can best be illustrated for this communication situation through contrasting examples. An example of a **poor** opening buffer for a memo to Krebs' employees follows:

[NOTE 9.22]
The poor opening starts with negative information and lacks the you–viewpoint.

- It is my unfortunate duty to inform you that Krebs Furniture is closing its plant in Georgetown, Texas, on December 31, 200–.

In analyzing this poor opening buffer, note the lack of you–viewpoint and absence of goodwill. Also, the receivers' interests are ignored. Finally, this opening buffer reveals the negative information, the closing of the plant, immediately. There is no motivation for the employees to read the logical explanation that is to follow the opening.

An example of a **good** opening buffer for this situation follows:

[NOTE 9.23]
The good opening meets all requirements for an effective buffer.

- Krebs Furniture has been operating a plant in Georgetown for 35 years. During these years you have produced quality furniture that our customers have been proud to place in their homes. Your dedication to our company has made it possible for us to offer excellent benefits and above-average salaries.

In contrast to the poor opening buffer, this paragraph effectively meets all the requirements of a good buffer for a negative message. Coherence and goodwill are built by reminding the employees that they have received excellent salaries and fringe benefits.

Goodwill is further built through commending the employees for the quality product they have produced. This good opening buffer is neutral—it does not disclose the plant closing. It introduces in a positive manner the logical explanation by mentioning salaries and fringe benefits which result in high production costs.

Provide a Convincing Logical Explanation

The next step in the indirect plan is to build on the opening buffer with a logical explanation justifying the negative information.

A **poor** logical explanation to Krebs' employees might read as follows:

[NOTE 9.24]
The poor logical explanation fails to justify the negative information.

- I know that this plant closing comes at a bad time. However, there is no good time for employees to lose their jobs. Krebs cannot continue losing money at this plant because of the high wages and excellent fringe benefits that you receive. This continuous loss is not fair to the employees at the other five plants that are making a profit. The closing of this plant will give us the opportunity to pay higher dividends to our stockholders.

This logical explanation shows—as did the poor opening buffer—a lack of positiveness and you–viewpoint. This poorly worded explanation is negative and ignores receivers' interests. The statement "However, there is no good time for employees to lose their jobs" will sound unsympathetic to individuals losing their jobs. Inability to pay "higher dividends" is not convincing reasoning to use in this explanation.

Conversely, a **good** logical explanation for this communication situation could read as follows:

[NOTE 9.25]
This example meets all requirements for a good logical explanation.

- You have been rewarded with excellent salaries and benefits for producing quality furniture. Our company is facing the challenge of maintaining our quality products at a competitive price while providing excellent salaries and security for employees. International companies can produce collectible reproductions at a much lower cost due to the availability of cheaper labor in their locations.

This logical explanation coherently follows the good opening buffer by picking up on the ideas "excellent salaries and benefits" and "producing quality furniture." The most-positive ideas are presented early in the paragraph with a gradual movement to less positive ideas. This is an effective use of the rules of emphasis.

After reading this logical explanation, the employees may not understand how the low wages paid by international companies have caused them to lose their jobs, but at least they will believe you have presented them with a fair, logical explanation. They will be prepared for the negative information that will be presented to them later in the paragraph.

Give Negative Information Positively

A **poor** way to tell the employees that the plant is closing follows:

- It is my unfortunate duty to inform you that Krebs Furniture is closing its plant in Georgetown, Texas, on December 31, 200–.
  I know that this plant closing comes at a bad time.

[NOTE 9.26]
This poor presentation states the negative information immediately.

The letter begins with the negative, harsh words "... unfortunate duty to inform you...." The second paragraph begins in the I–viewpoint rather than the you–viewpoint. The letter overemphasizes the problem by using negative words *(unfortunate, closing,* and *bad)* in both paragraphs.

A **good** way to inform the employees of the plant closing follows:

- After analyzing production costs at all plants, management has decided to close its Georgetown plant on December 31. The other five Krebs' plants will continue producing furniture.

[NOTE 9.27]
This good presentation de-emphasizes the negative information.

This negative information is presented at the end of the logical explanation paragraph. The plant closing is de-emphasized by being placed within the explanation. Instead of an apology, which would emphasize the negativeness of the situation, the explanation paragraph ends with a statement using positive words that should give hope to the employees for employment at another Krebs' plant.

Because you prepared the employees to receive negative information, this plant closing will likely be acceptable to them. In fact, as suggested earlier, they may prefer the alternative solution that you will give them in the next paragraph—the constructive follow-up. They will also know you respect them because you took the time to explain the decision to close the plant.

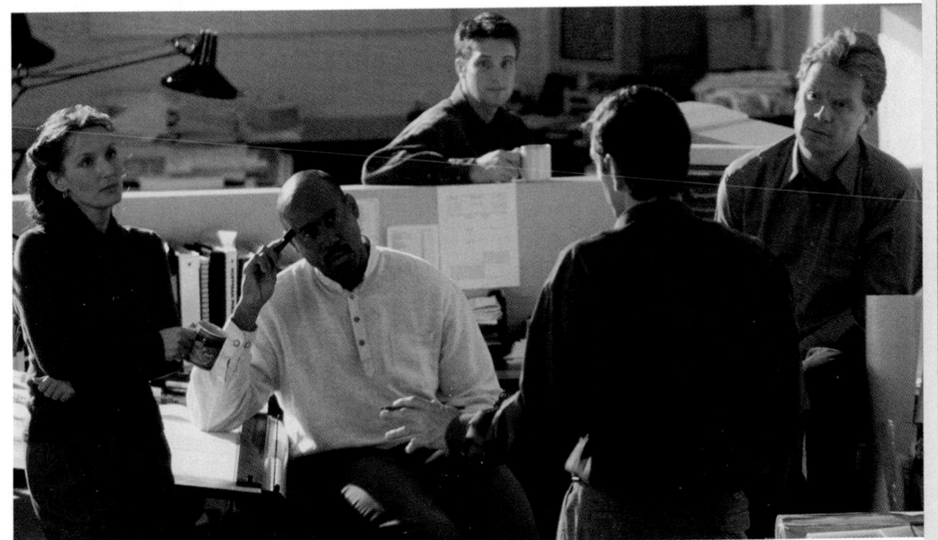

A manager's justification can make negative information acceptable and the decision preferable.

Assist the Receiver With Constructive Follow-Up

Is there an alternative solution you can suggest to the Krebs' employees in this communication situation? The following is an example of a **poor** constructive follow-up section of your memo to the employees:

[NOTE 9.28] The poor constructive follow-up example does not really help, whereas the good example does more than is expected.

- I hope you find another job soon.

A **good** constructive follow-up section would be:

- Krebs has five manufacturing plants that are in need of good employees. Employees at the Georgetown plant will be given priority for filling vacancies at the other plants. Human resources personnel from the five plants will be here next week to discuss opportunities and interview interested employees for these positions. Attached is a flyer describing activities at each of these plants and times for interviews with human resources personnel.

This constructive follow-up suggests a possible solution for the Krebs' employees. If it is not the solution the employees want, it is at least one employment opportunity for them. Note that the good suggested alternative is longer than the poor suggested alternative. This is often true of you–viewpoint writing or speaking. In effective business communication, the additional effort and additional words are worthwhile.

Build Goodwill in a Friendly Close

The last part of the indirect plan is the friendly close. A **poor** friendly close for the employees' memo might read this way:

[NOTE 9.29] The poor friendly close contains an apology.

- Again, let me say I am sorry that the Georgetown plant has to close. If I can be of any further help, please let me know.

Obviously, the apology serves no purpose other than to remind the employees of the negative information they have received. In fact, the negative information is re-emphasized. Also, the last sentence in the poor example sounds condescending and seems hollow.

A **good** friendly close for the employees' memo is as follows:

[NOTE 9.30] The good friendly close is in the you–viewpoint and builds goodwill.

- Please contact my secretary, Pam, if you would like to schedule an interview with a representative from one of the plants. It appears to be a good alternative for many of you. Your excellent work is appreciated, and I hope you stay with Krebs Furniture for many years to come!

This friendly close meets all the requirements. It builds goodwill. It is personalized, warm, and optimistic. It also meets the important requirement of being off the subject—it does not refer to the negative information.

Summary—Poor and Good Memos to the Krebs' Employees

[NOTE 9.31] Contrasting memos to employees of Krebs Furniture are presented in Figures 9.2 and 9.3.

In reviewing how to write effective negative messages, two example memos—one poor and one good—have been presented. Both of these memos carry the negative information about the plant closing. The **poor** memo (see Figure 9.2) shows a failure to use proven communication guides that enhance understanding and acceptance of negative messages. The poor memo also fails to use the indirect plan to present the message.

The **good** memo to the employees shown in Figure 9.3 incorporates the recommended guidelines for effective business communication. The good memo shows how the indirect plan, properly implemented, builds goodwill and improves human relations.

To illustrate further how the guides apply to actual business situations, several other examples of poor and good negative messages are examined in the following pages.

Learning Objective [4]
PREPARE COMPETENTLY A VARIETY OF NEGATIVE MESSAGES USING THE INDIRECT PLAN.

Request Refusals

[NOTE 9.32]
Businesses receive many requests.

Business firms frequently receive requests—for example, a request from a senior citizens' organization for a contribution to its greenhouse project or a request from a local Boy Scout troop to use a bank's community meeting room on the first Wednesday night of each month. Many of these requests are reasonable, and companies will want to respond positively.

Sometimes, however, a **request refusal**—a denial of something asked for—must be sent. For example, the company receiving the senior citizens' request may budget all charitable contributions once a year; therefore, no allocation is available at the time of the request. The company must then refuse this worthy request—at least at this time. The constructive follow-up in this negative message might be that the company will be glad to consider the request when the next budget is planned.

[NOTE 9.33]
Some requests must be refused.

In the case of the local Boy Scout troop's request to use the bank's meeting room, this kind of use may be exactly the type the bank intended for the meeting room. However, if the room is scheduled for use by the League of Women Voters on the first Wednesday night of each month, the bank must refuse the request. The bank, if possible, will suggest an alternative night for the Boy Scouts.

In any request refusal situation, it will be important to a business to maintain goodwill. At the same time, the business has to send a message that the receiver does not want to receive. Effective use of the indirect plan will make the refusal more acceptable.

[NOTE 9.34]
Use the indirect plan for refusals.

Here is another situation that illustrates the use of the indirect plan for a request refusal: Assume that you are the owner of six Good Neighbor Pharmacies in the area. You receive an e-mail from Sheri Jackson, department manager, who is requesting a vacation for the period from February 6 to 19. Each year your pharmacies do their annual inventories during the first two weeks of February. No one is permitted to take a vacation during this period. You must send an e-mail to Sheri denying her request for vacation during the inventory period. Figure 9.4 shows a **poor** e-mail message for this situation.

The **good** e-mail message for this request refusal, shown in Figure 9.5, builds goodwill by explaining the situation and suggesting an alternative for Sheri.

Adjustment Refusals

Handling customer claims is a common task for most business firms. These claims include requests to exchange merchandise, requests for refunds, requests that work be corrected, and other requests for adjustments. Most of these claims are approved because they are legitimate. However, some requests for adjustment must be denied, and an **adjustment refusal** message must be sent. Adjustment refusals are negative messages for the customer. They are necessary when the customer is at fault or when the vendor has done all that can reasonably or legally be expected.

TO: Employees of Krebs Furniture

FROM: Nancy Eudy

DATE: June 22, 200–

SUBJECT: Closing of Krebs' Georgetown Plant

It is my unfortunate duty to inform you that Krebs Furniture is closing its plant in Georgetown, Texas, on December 31, 200–.

I know that this plant closing comes at a bad time. However, there is no good time for employees to lose their jobs. Krebs cannot continue losing money at this plant because of the high wages and excellent fringe benefits that you receive. This continuous loss is not fair to the employees at the other five plants that are making a profit. The closing of this plant will give us the opportunity to pay higher dividends to our stockholders.

I hope you find another job soon.

Again, let me say I am sorry that the Georgetown plant has to close. If I can be of any further help, please let me know.

Negative reference.

Poor Buffer.

Explanation lacks receiver benefit; negative refusal.

Trite expression.

Negative apology

Figure 9.2
Example of a Poor *Negative Message*

[NOTE 9.35]
Businesses try to retain customers when making refusals.

An adjustment refusal message requires your best communication skills because it is bad news to the receiver. You have to refuse the claim and at the same time retain the customer. You may refuse the request for adjustment and even try to sell the customer more merchandise or service. All this is happening when the customer is probably angry, disappointed, or inconvenienced.

You will want to use the indirect plan effectively for the presentation of this negative information. As a case in point, consider a customer who wants to return 24 dresses that do not meet her expectations. Figure 9.6 shows a **poor** letter in which the dress manufacturer fails to implement the indirect plan and probably makes an enemy.

On the other hand, the same basic message can be written using the indirect plan and result in keeping a good customer. Figure 9.7 is a **good** example of how this letter refusing the return of the dresses could be written.

TO: Employees of Krebs Furniture
FROM: Nancy Eudy
DATE: June 22, 200–
SUBJECT: Krebs' Georgetown Plant

Positive reference.

Krebs Furniture has been operating a plant in Georgetown for 35 years. During these years you have produced quality furniture that our customers have been proud to place in their homes. Your dedication to our company has made it possible for us to offer excellent benefits and above-average salaries.

Good opening buffer.

You have been rewarded with excellent salaries and benefits for producing quality furniture. Our company is facing the challenge of maintaining our quality products at a competitive price while providing excellent salaries and security for employees. International companies can produce collectible reproductions at a much lower cost due to the availability of cheaper labor in their locations. After analyzing production costs at all plants, management has decided to close its Georgetown plant on December 31. The other five Krebs' plants will continue producing furniture.

You–viewpoint is reassuring; negative information is de-emphasized.

Krebs has five manufacturing plants that are in need of good employees. Employees at the Georgetown plant will be given priority for filling vacancies at the other plants. Human resources personnel from the five plants will be here next week to discuss opportunities and interview interested employees for these positions. Attached is a flyer describing activities at each of these plants and times for interviews with human resources personnel.

Alternative is suggested.

Please contact my secretary, Pam, if you would like to schedule an interview with one of the plants. It appears to be a good alternative for many of you. Your excellent work is appreciated, and I hope you stay with Krebs Furniture for many years to come!

Attachment

Goodwill and off-the-subject close.

Figure 9.3
Example of a Good *Negative Message*

Credit Refusals

Buying on credit using in-store credit cards as well as national and international credit cards is common today. Most businesses permit and even encourage qualified customers to buy on credit. It is a strategy that increases sales. The discussion in this section is more relevant to in-store credit cards.

[NOTE 9.36]
Buying on credit is common.

Customers who have good credit ratings or who have sufficient assets for collateral will be granted credit. Customers who have problems paying their bills or who own nothing of sufficient value to use as collateral may be refused credit. A message rejecting a request for credit is called a **credit refusal**.

[NOTE 9.37]
Some customers must be refused credit.

Business firms attempt to communicate credit refusals in a manner that makes the answer acceptable to the customer. Businesses want to do this out of common decency and also because they want to continue to serve the customer on a cash basis if possible.

[NOTE 9.38]
Credit refusals usually are in the customer's interest.

Negative reference.

Subject: Denial of Request for Vacation
Date: Thu, 18 Jan 200– 10:15:25 –0500
From: Sheri Jackson <Sjackson@gnp.com>
To: Cody.Cook@gnp.com

Lacks buffer; lacks you–viewpoint.

I must deny your request for a two-week vacation from February 6 to 19. I cannot let you go during that period.

Lectures receiver.

This is a busy period for all six locations of Good Neighbor Pharmacies and you must be here. Plan your vacation at a different time.

Figure 9.4
Example of a Poor *Request Refusal*

Looks Good

e reference.

Subject: Request for Vacation
Date: Thu, 18 Jan 200– 10:15:25 –0500
From: Sheri Jackson <Sjackson@gnp.com>
To: Cody.Cook@gnp.com

Sheri, thank you for your e-mail requesting vacation time from February 6 to 19. You have been doing an excellent job as department manager and certainly deserve your two-week vacation.

Good Neighbor Pharmacies is conducting its annual inventory during the first two weeks of February. It is important for all employees to perform their normal duties during this period. Your supervision of your department has made it one of our most successful areas, and your assistance during the inventory will be of great value.

The inventory will be completed by February 14. You can begin your two-week vacation anytime after February 15. Please e-mail me the dates for the two-week period that you choose for your vacation.

Your excellent work is appreciated, and I hope that you will be associated with Good Neighbor Pharmacies for many years.

Buffer has a neutral opening.

Logical explanation stresses reader's responsibility.

The negative information is implied.

A helpful alternative is suggested.

Off-the-subject, friendly close.

Figure 9.5
Example of a Good *Request Refusal*

Credit refusals are communicated in the following four basic ways: (1) personalized letters, (2) form letters, (3) telephone calls, or (4) face-to-face conversations. In all these cases the indirect plan is used for communicating the credit refusal.

Figure 9.8 is a **poor** example of a personalized letter in which a bank denies a customer's application. The indirect plan is not used in this letter.

An improved letter for this circumstance is shown in Figure 9.9, a **good** example of the use of the indirect plan for a credit refusal. A mutually satisfactory business relationship could develop from this credit refusal.

Unsolicited Negative Messages

Not all negative messages are in response to a request or an inquiry. An **unsolicited negative message** is a bad news message initiated by the sender. Examples of such unsolicited negative messages include communications about price increases for products or services, budget reductions, and staff reductions (layoffs). These messages are especially difficult to compose because they initiate the bad news.

[NOTE 9.39]
Sometimes businesses must initiate negative messages.

In Figure 9.10, you can feel the negative impact of the **poor** interoffice memo informing sales representatives of a product recall. The indirect plan and the guides for its implementation were not used.

2640 Poidres Lane • Dallas, TX 75236-2721
(214) 555-3265 • Fax (214) 555-7381

March 18, 200–

Ms. Renee Black
Susie's Fashions
1438 Commerce Street
Marion, IL 62959-4143

Dear Ms. Black:

We are sorry we cannot honor your request to return the 24 dresses that you recently purchased from us. You can see that these dresses are made of a high-quality material.

We feel sure that with a little effort, you can sell these dresses. We have been making dresses for a long time, and all of our customers are always satisfied. We have sold you dresses before, and you were able to sell them. Our profit would be reduced if we allowed our customers to return dresses without their trying to sell them. I am sure you can understand why we can't let you return these dresses.

Again, let us say we are sorry that you will not be allowed to return these dresses. Don't forget to place your order for fall dresses no later than July 1.

Sincerely yours,

Michelle Miller

Michelle Miller
Marketing Manager

tp

Gives negative information first; is negative; talks down to the receiver.

Explanation is not in the you–viewpoint; is not logical.

Negative final apology; constructive follow-up is poorly written and out of sequence.

Figure 9.6
Example of a Poor *Adjustment Refusal Letter*

Figure 9.11, a **good** example of an unsolicited negative message, shows how the same information can be conveyed in a more acceptable manner. Sale representatives are not going to be happy about having to inform their customers that a toy is being recalled, but at least the situation is more acceptable when the indirect plan is used. There is no need for a communicator to anger, disturb, or hurt receivers—intentionally or inadvertently—through poorly conveyed messages.

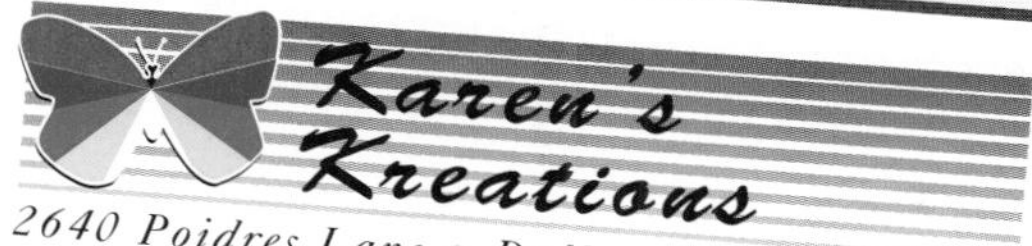

2640 Poidres Lane • Dallas, TX 75236-2721
(214) 555-3265 • Fax (214) 555-7381

March 18, 200–

Ms. Renee Black
Susie's Fashions
1438 Commerce Street
Marion, IL 62959-4143

Dear Ms. Black:

Thank you for your recent purchase of 24 dresses. You selected stylish, high-quality dresses that will be extremely easy to sell. These elegant dresses are luxurious to the touch while simple and versatile.

Neutral opening introduces explanation.

The dresses that you purchased are of the highest quality. As you know there is a 10 percent variation in the weight of material for dresses of this kind. The standard industry practice of permitting a variation of 10 percent is necessary due to the number of sources from which material is purchased. Few customers would be aware of a 10 percent variation in the weight of material for these dresses. These dresses should sell easily. With a 50 percent markup on these dresses, you will earn more than $1,500 when all 24 dresses are sold.

Convincing reasoning is positively presented; receiver benefits are stressed; negative information is implied and de-emphasized.

Many of our customers inform us that these dresses are among the leading sellers in their stores for this season. Their customers are extremely pleased with the workmanship and the split-shawl collar. Many of the stores have already placed a second order for these dresses. We feel sure that your customers will be equally pleased with the dresses.

Additional reasoning is given.

Best wishes for a successful summer season.

Goodwill, off-the-subject close.

Sincerely yours,

Michelle Miller

Michelle Miller
Marketing Manager

tp

Figure 9.7
Example of a Good *Adjustment Refusal Letter*

Use the Direct Plan for Negative Messages When Appropriate

Learning Objective [5]
PREPARE NEGATIVE MESSAGES USING THE DIRECT PLAN WHEN IT IS APPROPRIATE.

You are already familiar with the direct plan for message preparation; that is, the main idea of the message is conveyed in the first sentences. There are occasions when the direct plan is used for negative messages—when the negative information

[NOTE 9.40]
The direct plan gives negative information first.

Livingston Bank and Trust
2148 Market Street, Navasota, TX 77868-3217
(979) 555-5363

January 29, 200–

Mr. Wendell Tucker
1475 River Road
Navasota, TX 77868-7213

Dear Mr. Tucker:

I am sorry to inform you that the Livingston Bank and Trust cannot approve a $75,000 loan for you at this time. We would like to give you a loan, but our bank's policy does not permit us to make business loans to customers with no experience.

Navasota is a small town with seven florists. Managing a floral shop with no experience can be disastrous. You may not realize that many small businesses go bankrupt each year due to inexperience of the owner. We cannot take a chance by loaning money to someone who has no experience in a business area in which they are wanting to enter. We know that you have good intentions, but experience is what counts.

Again, let me say that I am sorry that we cannot give you a loan at this time. If you are interested in any other banking service, please let Livingston Bank and Trust help you.

Sincerely,

Sabrina White

Sabrina White
Loan Officer

kw

Negative opening gives bad information; is not in the you–viewpoint.

Not personalized; is not in the you–viewpoint; negative.

No constructive follow-up to the negative information; negative final apology; poor reselling.

Figure 9.8
Example of a Poor *Credit Refusal Letter*

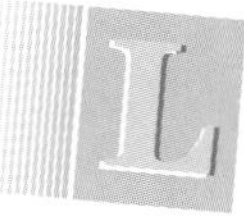

Livingston Bank and Trust
2148 Market Street, Navasota, TX 77868-3217
(979) 555-5363

January 29, 200–

Mr. Wendell Tucker
1475 River Road
Navasota, TX 77868-7213

Dear Mr. Tucker:

Thank you for your loan application. Providing support and assistance to new business owners is one of Livingston Bank and Trust's most important goals. If you are successful, your bank will be successful.

Information from several sources is examined by Livingston Bank and Trust before approving a loan to support a business venture. This analysis is always done with the applicant's success in mind. You have expressed a desire to locate a floral shop, Basket of Joy, in the city of Navasota. The city of Navasota, with a population of approximately 10,000, currently has seven established florists. Your college degree in agriculture did not include courses that would give you experience in managing a floral shop. Due to this lack of experience, you would need $18,750 (25 percent) cash for investment in the shop before Livingston Bank and Trust would consider approving a $75,000 loan.

We recommend that you gain some floral shop management experience before making such a huge investment in the business. When you attain a couple of years' experience, please resubmit a loan application and we will reevaluate it based on local economic conditions at that time.

Livingston Bank and Trust provides many banking services to businesses and individuals. Currently customers earn 6.5 percent on a six-month $5,000 certificate of deposit. Please stop in and speak with Desi, our investment consultant.

Best wishes, Mr. Tucker, in entering the florist profession. Your business is important to us, and we hope to be of service to you in the future.

Sincerely,

Sabrina White

Sabrina White
Loan Officer

kw

Good opening buffer builds goodwill; is neutral.

Explanation is logical; stresses receiver interests.

Negative information is implied.

Alternative solution.

Resells.

Friendly, off-the-subject close; warm and personalized.

Figure 9.9
Example of a Good Credit Refusal Letter

DATE: November 15, 200–
TO: Sales Representatives
FROM: Mei-ling Sheng, Production Manager
SUBJECT: Recall of Defective Doll

I hate to tell you that you will have to contact all of the stores in your area and inform them that they must return Longneck the Giraffe.

I know that this recall comes at a bad time. Most of the stores will have these dolls on their shelves and will be mad at you for having to rearrange their displays. We must get these dolls back since we have determined that children may easily remove the heads and possibly swallow them. This problem can result in many lawsuits and many dollars in damages.

Again, let me say that I am sorry that you will have to spend your valuable time informing the stores about this recall. If there is anything that I can do, please contact me.

kt

Opening gives unfavorable information explicitly and negatively.

Lacks you–viewpoint (receiver's interest is ignored); negative.

Close is not off the subject; limited offer to help.

Figure 9.10
Example of a
Poor *Unsolicited Negative Memo*

is given first. Your analysis of the situation and the receiver will help you determine when you can use the direct plan.

[NOTE 9.41]
The direct plan may be used
- For some receivers
- For routine information
- To emphasize sorrow
- For situations involving ethics
- To emphasize negative information

You may use the direct plan when you know your receiver prefers to learn the bad news first and the reasons or rationale for it later. For example, if your receiver's personality is the type that prefers directness, use the direct approach.

Likewise, in online customer relations situations, the responder should use the same style as the person making the request—if the request is direct, the response should be, too, even if it's negative news.

INTEROFFICE MEMO

DATE: November 15, 200–
TO: Sales Representatives
FROM: Mei-ling Sheng, Production Manager
SUBJECT: Longneck the Giraffe Doll

You have done an outstanding job in selling our products for the upcoming holiday season. Your efforts have contributed to Gizmos & Doodads' having its most profitable year ever. Our toys attract children's interest and make your job of selling much easier.

As you know, Gizmos & Doodads does extensive research and throughly tests all of its products before releasing them to the public. One phase of the testing involves putting the toy in the hands of hundreds of children. After the children keep the toy for a month, the toy is sent back to the lab for additional testing. In spite of this extensive testing, sometimes problems with these toys will not appear until after they have been distributed nationwide. This is the case with Longneck the Giraffe. All of these dolls must be returned to our warehouse because under extreme conditions the heads may become loose.

Gizmos & Doodads has decided to release Patty the Panda to replace Longneck. Notify us of the stores wanting this replacement doll, and we will ship the dolls via overnight express with no shipping cost to the stores. The return shipping costs for Longneck will also be paid by Gizmos & Doodads.

This holiday season will be an appropriate ending to a banner year. By working together we can all look forward to good years ahead.

kt

Good opening buffer builds coherence; is positive, neutral, and sets the stage for the explanation.

Convincing logical reasoning precedes the negative information.

Negative information is de-emphasized by its position in the paragraph.

Receiver's interests are stressed in the helpful alternative solution.

Friendly close is warm and optimistic.

Figure 9.11
Example of a Good *Unsolicited Negative Memo*

You may also use the direct plan when the negative information is routine and will not be upsetting to your receiver. For example, a receiver will not be upset to learn that a nonessential meeting has been canceled.

Another instance in which the direct plan may be used is when you want to emphasize how sorry you are about the negative situation. An example of this is a sympathy note sent regarding a death or tragedy.

In another situation, ethical behavior may be the issue and directness would strengthen a negative message and regain the trust of the customer. An example is an automobile service center billing for work that is covered by warranty. A message

Automotive Warranty Services, Inc.
1710 Magnum Drive, Los Angeles, CA 90078-9712 (714) 555-3333

June 20, 200–

Ms. Shannon L. Fuentes
3033 Velazquez Place
Rolling Hills, CA 90274-2274

Dear Ms. Fuentes:

The Rolling Hills Service Center has been having a lot of problems and we are trying to straighten them out. They should have repaired your automobile's transmission and not have sent you a bill for the total charges.

I hope you will return to the Rolling Hills Service Center for all your future automotive repairs as we intend to do a better job for you in the future. Thanks for your past business.

Sincerely,

Jeffrey W. Innis

Jeffrey W. Innis
President

pjr

Enclosure: Refund check

Opening lacks an apology and is not in the you–viewpoint.

Explanation lacks clarity and openness.

Customer trust is not regained.

Figure 9.12
Poor *Negative Message Using the Direct Plan*

dealing with this ethical problem should use the direct approach and include an apology. Figure 9.12 is an example of a **poor** negative message using the direct plan that likely will not resolve the ethical problem or regain customer trust. Figure 9.13 provides an example of a **good** negative message using the direct plan that should regain trust and correct the problem.

Automotive Warranty
Services, Inc.
1710 Magnum Drive, Los Angeles, CA 90078-9712 (714) 555-3333

June 20, 200–

Ms. Shannon L. Fuentes
3033 Velazquez Place
Rolling Hills, CA 90274-2274

Dear Ms. Fuentes:

Please accept our apology for the inconvenience you experienced when our branch service center in Rolling Hills billed you for the replacement of your transmission. Charging for warranty work is not good business practice, and steps have been taken to assure that this does not happen in the future. New management is now in place at this center—a management team committed to high-quality, ethical, economical service.

Opening apologizes and deals directly with the ethical issue.

A refund check for $1,378.34, the cost of parts and labor incurred in the replacement of the transmission on your automobile, is enclosed. Your 10-year limited service warranty will be fully honored in the future.

Appropriate correction of the problem.

Your business is greatly appreciated. Automotive Warranty Services assures you that any future needs you have for repair will be met promptly and fairly by the Rolling Hills Service Center.

Customer trust should be regained.

Sincerely,

Jeffrey W. Innis

Jeffrey W. Innis
President

pjr

Enclosure

Figure 9.13
Good *Negative Message Using the Direct Plan*

Another instance in which the direct plan may be used for negative messages is when the negative information needs to be emphasized. In the chapter opening, Tim Farmer says that he uses the direct plan in the second and third letters he sends to customers who do not pay their past-due bills. The direct plan emphasizes the negative message that Tim must send in these situations.

In most negative message situations, however, you will want to use the indirect order of presentation because of its many advantages.

Summary of Learning Objectives

Learning Objective [1]

Describe the nature of negative messages. A negative message is one that is likely to be viewed as unpleasant, disappointing, or unfavorable by the receiver. A negative message is a challenge to compose. At the same time, it is an opportunity for you as a writer or speaker to resolve a common business problem successfully.

Learning Objective [2]

List the advantages of using the indirect plan for effective communication of negative information. Important advantages of the indirect plan are that it enables receivers (1) to accept the negative information you must give them and (2) to maintain a satisfactory relationship with you. The indirect plan has these advantages because it maintains calm through its gradual approach. The indirect plan affords the opportunity for reason to prevail and for understanding to develop. If the negative information is given first, the receiver may ignore the rest of the message; even a fair, reasonable explanation following the bad news may never be accepted.

Learning Objective [3]

Describe the five specific guidelines for using the indirect plan. Messages using the indirect plan consist of an opening buffer, logical explanation, negative information, constructive follow-up, and friendly close. The opening buffer should meet the following requirements: provide coherence, build goodwill, be positive, maintain neutrality, and introduce the explanation. The logical explanation usually begins after the opening buffer and often can be handled in one paragraph. The negative information follows the logical explanation and is short—normally one sentence. It may be implied or given in explicit terms and should be de-emphasized. Solutions are provided or additional justification of the unfavorable information is given in the constructive follow-up section. The friendly close should be personalized, off the subject, warm, and optimistic. The friendly close should move the receiver's mind away from the negative news.

Learning Objective [4]

Prepare competently a variety of negative messages using the indirect plan. Incorporate the communication fundamentals in an indirect plan when preparing request refusals, adjustment refusals, credit refusals, and unsolicited negative messages. You should present the information positively using the you–viewpoint. Organize the message in the following order: opening buffer, logical explanation, negative information, constructive follow-up, and friendly close.

Learning Objective [5]

Prepare negative messages using the direct plan when it is appropriate. Analyze the situation and the receiver to determine when the direct plan should be used with a negative message. Use the direct plan when you know your receiver prefers to learn the bad news before the reason(s) for it. It may also be used when the negative information is routine and will not be upsetting to your receiver. When using the direct plan with negative messages, start the message with the negative information and follow with the explanation.

DISCUSSION QUESTIONS

1. What benefits may a writer gain by effectively composing a negative message? (Objective 1)
2. List and discuss the advantages of the indirect plan for negative messages. (Objective 2)
3. How can a writer use a friendly close to build goodwill? (Objective 3)
4. Describe how to ensure that the logical explanation coherently follows the opening. (Objective 3)
5. Describe how to present convincing reasoning and use emphasis techniques in the logical explanation. (Objective 3)
6. Define (a) a request refusal, (b) an adjustment refusal, (c) a credit refusal, and (d) an unsolicited negative message. (Objective 4)
7. If a person is a bad credit risk, why shouldn't a writer simply begin the negative message by telling the receiver that he or she doesn't meet the minimum credit standards of the company? (Objective 4)
8. Why do businesses attempt to communicate credit refusals in a way that makes the message acceptable and helpful to customers? (Objective 4)
9. Describe a circumstance where a businessperson would have to transmit an unsolicited negative message. (Objective 4)
10. Are there any circumstances under which a writer would present the negative information before giving a buffer of explanation? Explain. (Objective 5)

APPLICATION EXERCISES

1. Analyze the following sentences for their effectiveness in opening a negative message: (Objective 3)
   a. Your credit history prevents us from issuing you a credit card.
   b. Thank you for your interest in the show, "Patsy Cline Returns to the Ryman."
   c. Your check for four Super Bowl tickets is enclosed.
   d. When you were hired, you were told that you could not take vacation the first two weeks in April.
   e. Your registration for the computer application workshop has been received.

2. **Global/Cross-Cultural.** Interview a person from a culture other than your own and determine how negative information is transmitted effectively in the interviewee's culture. Report your findings to the class. (Objective 1)
3. Analyze your personal experiences in receiving negative information. Record the strengths and weaknesses of the quality of these messages. Share your findings with the class. (Objective 2)
4. Change the following statements to reflect what can be done instead of what cannot be done: (Objective 3)
   a. No smoking in this building.
   b. Don't touch any of the artwork.
   c. No refunds will be made without the sales slip.
   d. This telephone cannot be used for personal calls.
   e. The computer lab is closed on Saturdays and Sundays.

5. Contact the loan officer at a local bank and ask him or her what is the most effective way to convey negative information to a customer. Be prepared to share your findings with the class. (Objective 2)
6. Select one of the five parts of an indirect plan for negative messages, and prepare yourself for a class debate. Attempt to convince the class that the part you selected is the most important in effectively delivering negative messages. (Objective 2)
7. Ask a businessperson or an instructor at your school in what situations he or she uses the direct approach in conveying negative information. Share your findings with the class. (Objective 5)

8. **E-mail.** Your instructor has asked you to speak to the faculty club at your school. Your speech is to be about the benefits of belonging to a student organization. You are unable to make the presentation. Send an e-mail message to your instructor declining the invitation. Add any necessary details. Remember that you will need this instructor to write a recommendation letter for you. (Objective 4)

There are Web exercises at **http://krizan.swcollege.com** to accompany this chapter.

CASE PROBLEMS

Request Refusals

1. You are the owner of Brian's Gourmet Diner, a low-cost, high-quality restaurant. Last week Angie Laird, a representative from Single Parents Association (SPA), visited your establishment and spoke to you about being affiliated with SPA. Businesses that are associated with SPA pay a small monthly fee and give members belonging to SPA a 20 percent discount on purchases. Supposedly, belonging to SPA would increase your customer base. Today you receive a letter from Angie asking you once again to become a SPA affiliate. You have thought about affiliating with SPA and have decided against it. Your diner is doing quite well, and giving the 20 percent discount to members would definitely cut into your profit margins. Write a letter to Angie declining the offer without offending her. Add any necessary details.

2. **E-mail.** The Colonial Apartment complex in your town is one year old and has a heated swimming pool, a fully furnished exercise room, and a party room. It caters to adult tenants. Its pet policy allows only cats. Jennifer Wolf is interested in renting one of the units. She has e-mailed you, the apartment manager, requesting an exception to the policy that would allow her to move into the unit with her two birds. Compose an e-mail reply that would deny the exception to the pet policy; send your message to your instructor.

3. **Global/Cross-Cultural.** You are the international marketing manager for Global Sales, Inc., in New York City. One of your responsibilities is contracting with agencies to sell Global products in countries throughout the world. The standard agreement is that the foreign sales agency receives a 20 percent commission. You have negotiations underway with the Mohr Agency in Bamberg, Germany. Mohr has requested that a special dispensation be made and that its agency receive a 25 percent commission on sales. Say no to Mohr, but try to retain it as Global's sales agency in northern Bavaria. Add any necessary details to make your letter complete.
4. You have accepted a volunteer job as editor of your professional journal. One of the undesirable parts of the job is to send rejection letters to persons who have submitted articles for publication. Many of these articles are well written but do not contain appropriate content for the journal. The letter must be written so that it won't offend

the writer, who is a member of your professional organization. Write a form letter that would deny publication in your journal.

5. **Teamwork. Ethical/Legal.** You have just learned that one salesperson at Replacement Windows, Inc., has been promising customers installation dates that could not possibly be met. His unethical mode of operating, to get the sale, involves letting the customer request any date he or she wants.

    You, the sales manager, and four ethical salespersons on your staff meet to write a form letter suitable for sending to the customers involved. Your writing team's challenge is to compose an effective message that will convey the negative information that you cannot install the windows on the dates promised. In addition, you will try to keep their business. Your installation schedule will permit you to install the windows approximately three months after the promised date. Add details to make this a complete request refusal letter.

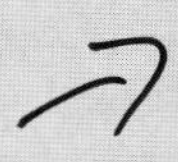

6. You are the manager of a franchise for Pizza Stores, Inc. An executive of a manufacturing plant near your restaurant has asked you whether he may have his employees attend a pizza party at your restaurant at 9 p.m. on Thursday. You would have to close your restaurant two hours early to accommodate the large number of his employees. Because you do not feel it is possible for you to close your restaurant to the public two hours early, you will have to turn down the request. You would be glad, however, to cater a pizza party at some other location. You can do this in the manufacturer's plant, at the community center, or at some other location of the executive's choosing. Write a letter to the executive that will turn down his request and keep the business. Add any necessary details.

Adjustment Refusals

7. Angela and Richard Little have been remodeling their house for more than a year. About six months ago they special ordered a prefabricated countertop with a 3-inch lip that goes against the back wall. While visiting with some friends, they learned that a Formica countertop would be better. They contacted your company, Woodson Supply, and stated that they wanted to exchange the original countertop for a Formica countertop. As general manager you have to deny their request. The prefabricated countertop was cut specifically to their measurements and would be next to impossible to sell to someone else. As an alternative, you may offer the Formica countertop at your cost. Write a letter to Angela and Richard giving them your decision. You do not want to lose their business in the future.

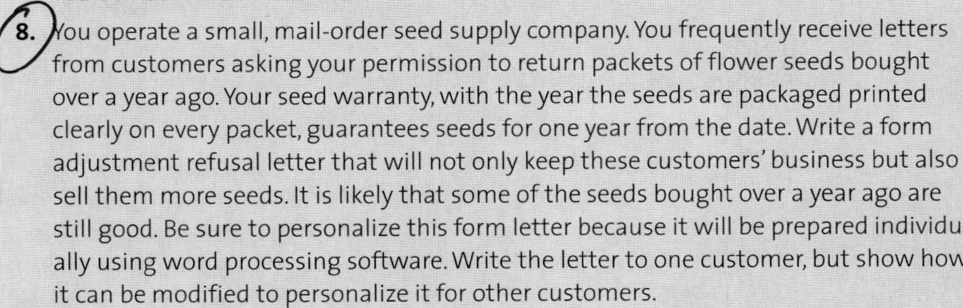

8. You operate a small, mail-order seed supply company. You frequently receive letters from customers asking your permission to return packets of flower seeds bought over a year ago. Your seed warranty, with the year the seeds are packaged printed clearly on every packet, guarantees seeds for one year from the date. Write a form adjustment refusal letter that will not only keep these customers' business but also sell them more seeds. It is likely that some of the seeds bought over a year ago are still good. Be sure to personalize this form letter because it will be prepared individually using word processing software. Write the letter to one customer, but show how it can be modified to personalize it for other customers.

9. **Global/Cross-Cultural.** Baseballs Limited is an American-owned company that manufactures its products in Mexico and sells them all over the world. As marketing manager at Baseballs Limited, you have just received a letter from Rinji Nitobe, purchasing agent for Tokuda, Inc., Kushiro, Japan. In the letter he asks for a 50 percent refund on the purchase price for 10,000 baseballs Tokuda bought for resale to little league

teams throughout northern Japan. His justification for this request is the complaint by some team managers that the balls are livelier this year than last. He says that, as a matter of goodwill, Tokuda would like to make 50 percent refunds to all its customers who bought from this shipment. Write a positive, courteous adjustment refusal letter. The team managers' complaints are without foundation. Newly manufactured balls are regularly subjected to random tests to assure the same degree of resiliency year-to-year. These tests are conducted by the International Baseball Association, a highly reliable organization.

10. You are the owner of Tuff Built Implements, a firm that sells farm machinery to equipment dealers. Tieman Tractors purchased one of your medium-size tractors and sold it to Ken Robertson. After using the tractor for one season, Ken has returned the tractor to Tieman Tractors and demanded a full refund. While investigating the transaction, you learn that Ken purchased a new 22-foot field cultivator and was unable to pull it with the Tuff Built tractor that he had purchased a year earlier. The tractor was not designed to pull implements as large as the 22-foot cultivator. Write a positive, courteous adjustment refusal letter to Tieman Tractors. Suggest to them that Mr. Robertson use a smaller cultivator or trade his medium-size tractor for a larger model. You are willing to sell Tieman Tractors one of your larger tractors at a greatly reduced price.

11. Frank Electronics sells televisions, radios, CD players, cell phones, and other electronics equipment. In addition to operating his retail store, Frank publishes a catalog each month. Part of the catalog is devoted to clearance merchandise. Frank has received many returns of catalog clearance sale merchandise even though it clearly states in the catalog that it is not possible to return merchandise that has been purchased from the clearance sale section of the catalog. Prepare a form letter that Frank could use to deny the claims for clearance sale merchandise.

12. Billy Ray's Ready Mix delivers a variety of concrete, sand, rock, gravel, fill dirt, and so forth. Its 60-truck fleet makes deliveries in six counties. As manager of Billy Ray's, you received from Jack Drum a huge order for fill dirt. He was planning to build a shopping mall on 40 acres of undeveloped land. For two months you delivered fill dirt to the location and leveled the land. One week after billing Mr. Drum for your work, you receive a letter from him stating that he will not pay the charges because he was expecting top soil and not fill dirt. He had changed his mind about building a shopping mall and had decided instead to construct a par 3 golf course. A golf course needs grass, and it will not grow on fill dirt. Write a letter to Mr. Drum informing him that he is responsible for the work done since fill dirt was requested in the original order. You may suggest that he replace the top 12 inches of fill dirt with top soil.

Credit Refusals

13. You are the owner of Dale's Clothiers for Men, a business designed to serve white-collar professionals. The policy of your store is to provide credit cards for individuals who have good jobs and excellent credit. One day you receive an application from Jason Williams, a full-time graduate student at your local university. Jason went from high school to college to graduate school without ever working full time. He has few assets but not many liabilities since his parents paid for all of his expenses until he started graduate school. He is scheduled to graduate with an MBA in a year. You have decided to refuse his application but do not want to alienate him because he may become a good customer after graduation. Write him a refusal letter adding necessary details.

14. Raymond Parker has just placed a $7,000 order for home building supplies with Contractor Supplies, Inc. Unfortunately, Mr. Parker's credit record with Contractor Supplies is so poor that management has decided that he must be refused further credit until he pays his current account balance of $14,200, which is now 60 days overdue. As the manager of accounting services for Contractor Supplies, write a credit refusal letter to Mr. Parker using the direct approach. In your letter, try to keep Mr. Parker as a customer. Of course, business with him will have to be on a cash basis until he pays his past-due account.

15. **E-mail.** You are the loan officer for LuckyOnes Bank. Shane and Karen Fletcher have sent an e-mail asking about LuckyOnes approving a $200,000 loan application to build a weekend home in the country. They purchased a $300,000 home in town three years ago with a loan from your bank. Shane is an account executive and Karen is a systems analyst. Both jobs pay well; however, the Fletchers are spending beyond their means. Periodically they are late in making payments on their home and two sports cars. You would like to keep them as customers, but at this time you must send them an e-mail denying the loan for the weekend home. Prepare the message, adding details, and send the message via e-mail to your instructor.
16. A young married couple, Manuel and Bella Silva, are in the process of furnishing their first apartment. Because they are young, neither has established a credit record. They have come to your furniture store, HomeQuarters, to look at living room and bedroom furniture and kitchen appliances. Your advertised policy is to sell furniture and appliances for no money down, interest free for the first year, with no payments due for 90 days to customers with good credit records. Bella and Manuel have asked you whether they qualify for this type of financing, but you must tell them no. Your objective is to ensure a sale to Manuel and Bella. However, because they lack a credit rating, they must pay one-third down on the purchase and start making payments within 30 days. What are you going to say to them? Use the indirect plan for this message.
17. Lynn Cooper has moved into your town and is interested in becoming a painting contractor. She has requested a line of credit with your home decorating store. The problem with her application for the line of credit is that her information is sketchy. You have been unable to contact her references, and she has refused to furnish you her employment history. You would like to do business with Lynn on a cash basis but cannot approve a line of credit until you obtain more creditable information. Write a letter to Lynn denying her line of credit but encouraging her to buy on a cash basis. Add necessary details.
18. You are the owner of Oliver's Food Market, a small grocery store. Oliver's success has been largely due to its personable and friendly service. Over the past 20 years you have not accepted credit cards but have allowed your faithful customers to charge their groceries until the end of the month. Recently, two large chain groceries have moved into town forcing you to lower your prices to remain competitive. Reducing the price of your groceries has greatly cut into your profit margin. As you analyze your entire operation, you determine that permitting customers to charge for 30 days is becoming too costly; therefore, you decide to terminate your credit plan at the end of next month. Write your customers informing them that as of the end of the month, you will no longer permit customers to charge their purchases. Add details.

Unsolicited Negative Messages

19. Place yourself in the position of the plant manager of Mighty Pressure Compressors, Inc. Your sales representative in Texas, Victoria Morales, sold one of your largest and

most powerful air compressors to Mesquite Drilling Company. Victoria promised the purchasing manager of Mesquite Drilling, Charles Harrell, that the air compressor would be delivered in two weeks; however, due to the increased drilling of oil and gas wells, you have a backlog of deliveries and will not be able to deliver the compressor for at least 90 days. You do not want to lose this order or jeopardize any future business with Mesquite Drilling. Write Mr. Harrell a letter explaining the delay in delivery of his compressor. Add information to make the letter realistic.

20. The Good Sam Camper's Club prints a journal describing desirable camp sites, interesting places to visit, health tips, and other items of interest to campers. Write a form letter to the members of the Good Sam Campers' Club telling them that their dues will be increased by $5 next year. Costs to print the journal, operate national headquarters, and provide member hotline services have increased significantly over the past ten years, but there has been no increase in dues.

21. You are the administrative manager of Sunnyvale Medical Center. The center has 28 doctors with various specialties. A popular family physician, Dr. Linda Seabolt, is moving to an out-of-state hospital at the end of June. The center has another family physician, Dr. Ali Raj, and is searching for an additional family physician. Write a form letter that could be sent to all of Dr. Seabolt's patients informing them of her departure and encouraging them to see Dr. Raj or the new doctor when he or she arrives. Add information to make the letter realistic.

22. Teamwork. Global/Cross-Cultural. You have over 2,000 wholesale dealers in Canada who regularly buy high school graduation rings from your American company. Price levels for these rings have not been changed in four years. Because of the increase in the world price of gold over the past 24 months, your company is going to have to increase the price level of your ring line by 12 percent. Appoint a writing team from management to write the form letter that will maintain the goodwill of your customers, keep their business, and help them accept your bad news. Add details to make the letter complete.

23. For the past ten years Boone, Texas, has held a Freedom Fest celebration during the Fourth of July week. One of the highlights of Freedom Fest has been a performance by a country and western entertainer followed by a fireworks display. Fans attending the performance paid a small fee, and the rest of the expenses were paid by a local company. This company has informed you, the Boone city manager, that it will no longer sponsor the event. As city manager you need to write a negative message that could be put in the local newspaper stating that this year's Freedom Fest will not feature an entertainer.

24. You are manager of Gerald's Home Improvement Center. Your 20,000-square-foot building is one of the largest in the area. To escape the weather, many individuals use your facility for their daily walking exercise. The number of people using your facility has increased to a point that it is interfering with your business. Write a notice that could be placed in the local newspaper explaining that walkers will no longer be able to use your facility for exercise. Word the notice so you do not offend anyone.

MESSAGE ANALYSIS

Steve Armstrong has been a marketing representative with your company for eight years. He has written you requesting a promotion to sales director. Steve has been a marginal employee for the entire time he has been with your company; however, as he gains experience and maturity, he has potential for being an excellent employee. Edit and revise the following memo that could be sent to Steve denying his promotion request:

I cannot believe that you think you are ready to be promoted to sales director. This position requires interpersonal skills, initiative, and complete honesty. You have a difficult time in communicating with others and must be given detailed instructions in order for you to complete a job. In the past three months you have had your travel expense voucher returned twice because it had been padded. I am sure you will work on these problems so the next time a position opens, you will be better prepared.

GRAMMAR WORKSHOP

Correct the grammar, spelling, punctuation, and word choice errors in the following sentences:

1. Transportation and a car is provided for you, when you spend three or more days at our luxurious resort.
2. Our policy is to reject them accounts who are not financial secure.
3. Saras' graph compliments the text in her report.
4. Although drinking stations for walkers and joggers was added to the trails it remain an ecologically-sound facility.
5. Nearly three-fourths of the fruit crop were lost due to the extreme cold temperatures.
6. Andy wrote the book "Getting Along With Your Mother in Law."
7. Pat and Bonnie were the first to excuse theirselves from the meeting, so that they could go golfing.
8. The shipment included apples oranges and bananas, but did not include tomatoes or onions.
9. After completing a three day inventory of the stock Darcy finds a 10% shortage.
10. Judy appeared relaxed at the musical as she looked contented at her class.

CHAPTER

10 Persuasive Messages

David E. Alexander,
Vice Chairman—
Area Practices and Management Committee Member
Ernst & Young LLP

LET'S TALK BUSINESS From my early years at Ernst & Young as a staff accountant to my current role as vice chair, the power and importance of effective communication have been constantly reinforced. Persuasive messages are a part of everyone's daily business because we are all in "sales." We may not be directly involved in selling products or services to external customers, but success requires that each of us be able to "sell" ideas to our internal customers—those we report to, our peers, and those who report to us. The objective may be to gain support, develop alliances, advance a career, or create opportunities. In fact, I have found that I often have to "sell" my internal customers and gain their acceptance before I can work on taking new ideas, products, and services to our client market.

(Continued)

[LEARNING OBJECTIVES]

[1] DESCRIBE A PERSUASIVE MESSAGE.

[2] LIST THE PURPOSES OF A PERSUASIVE MESSAGE.

[3] DESCRIBE THE FOUR SPECIFIC GUIDELINES FOR USING THE INDIRECT PLAN FOR PERSUASION.

[4] WRITE DIFFERENT KINDS OF PERSUASIVE MESSAGES USING THE INDIRECT PLAN.

[5] WRITE MESSAGES THAT ARE USED FOR THE VARIOUS STAGES OF COLLECTION.

For me, the starting point in developing a persuasive message is a thorough understanding of my audience and what they value. If I am making a presentation to a potential client, I always take the time to research the company and its decision makers to understand what business opportunities and challenges they are facing. My goal is not to communicate just what I want them to know, nor what they want to hear, but to construct and communicate a message that will lead to a positive impact on their business. I clearly communicate the value of my message in terms they can relate to—cost savings, increased profits, better efficiency, and improved market strength.

Once I've developed the framework of a message, I find it extremely helpful to get the input of others who can build on and enhance the communication. I test the message to be sure it is clear and compelling. An objective third party may be used to identify potential points of confusion or gaps in information that I have overlooked.

Finally, make your persuasive message concise. Over-communicating can be just as ineffective as under-communicating. Present your message in the fewest words possible. Your brevity will be appreciated by your busy audience and hopefully rewarded with the response you seek.

Learning Objective [1]
DESCRIBE A PERSUASIVE MESSAGE.

A **persuasive message** is (1) a request for action when you believe the receiver may be unknowing, disinterested, or unwilling, or (2) a communication to try to change the opinion of a receiver. These messages will be viewed as neither positive nor negative by the receiver.

[NOTE 10.1]
Persuasive messages are used to convince receivers to take action or change an opinion.

Persuasive messages are used in both internal and external communication. Examples of persuasive messages in internal communication include a speech asking employees to volunteer to work on upcoming weekends, an employee's memo to a manager requesting that the organization initiate a flextime policy, an employee's recommendation or proposal to establish a day care center, and a letter to employees requesting donations for a charity that has just been endorsed by the company.

[NOTE 10.2]
Persuasive messages are used for a variety of purposes in internal and external communication.

A **sales message** is a communication that includes a description of a product, its benefits, available options and models, price, and related services. It is the most common persuasive message in external communication. Other examples of persuasive messages used in external communication include a telephone call to ask the manager of another company to be the keynote speaker at an annual banquet or a letter to persuade readers to respond to a questionnaire. Persuasive messages also include letters requesting employment with an organization.

In the Let's Talk Business section, David Alexander supports the idea that persuasive messages must be designed to convince receivers that taking the requested action is in their best interest. The supporting facts in the message must be presented as useful or profitable to the receiver. Persuasive messages should usually be presented using an indirect approach.

[NOTE 10.3]
Receivers will have to be convinced that it is in their best interest to take action.

Use the Indirect Plan for Persuasive Messages

[NOTE 10.4]
The indirect plan assists in convincing a receiver to take action.

[NOTE 10.5]
The indirect plan conditions a receiver to accept the message.

The *indirect plan* should be used for messages that attempt to convince the receiver to take an action. The advantage of using the indirect plan for persuasive messages is that it enables the sender to present first the benefits that the receiver may gain from fulfilling the request. This puts the receiver in the proper frame of mind to consider the request. If the request were given prior to the explanation, the receiver might form objections that would be difficult to overcome. The receiver also might not read the part of the letter that contains the benefits. The indirect plan does require the use of more words than the direct plan, but the result is worth the additional words.

[NOTE 10.6]
The you–viewpoint should be used.

If the message is positively constructed in the you–viewpoint, the receiver will more likely be in a positive mood to consider the value of the entire message and will more likely agree with its contents. An effective presentation will associate the message with the motivating factors in the receiver's mind.

[NOTE 10.7]
Carefully analyze receiver to determine motivational factors.

How to Use the Indirect Plan

Learning Objective [2]
LIST THE PURPOSES OF A PERSUASIVE MESSAGE.

Analyzing your receiver is especially important when planning a persuasive message. You will have to anticipate what motivates the receiver—his or her goals, values, and needs. You must then build your persuasive message around these factors using the you–viewpoint. Do this by stressing the receiver's interests and benefits.

[NOTE 10.8]
Purposes of a persuasive message are to have receiver consider entire message and then to take requested action.

The two primary purposes of a persuasive message are (1) to get the receiver to read or listen to the entire message, and then (2) to have the receiver react positively to the request. These purposes are more easily achieved when the indirect plan is used in constructing the message. The specific guides for using the indirect plan to construct persuasive messages are shown in Figure 10.1.

Figure 10.1
Indirect Plan Outline for Persuasion

Indirect Plan for Persuasion

I. Attention
- A. Attract receiver's attention in opening sentence.
- B. Cause receiver to read or to listen to rest of message.
- C. Be positive and brief.

II. Interest
- A. Build on attention gained in the opening.
- B. Show benefits to receiver.
- C. Motivate receiver to continue reading.

III. Desire
- A. Build on receiver's attention and interest by providing proof of benefits.
- B. Re-emphasize benefits to the receiver.
- C. Downplay any negative points or obstacles.

IV. Action
- A. Motivate receiver to take immediate action.
- B. Be positive.
- C. Make action easy.

The indirect plan can be used for a variety of persuasive messages—requests, recommendations, special claims, sales, collection, and employment. The organization and development of the first five types of persuasive messages are discussed in this chapter, and employment messages are covered in Chapter 17. An analysis of the indirect plan for persuasion will be helpful prior to discussing the construction of five sample persuasive messages.

[NOTE 10.9]
Persuasive messages include requests, recommendations, special claims, sales, collection, and employment.

Learning Objective [3]
DESCRIBE THE FOUR SPECIFIC GUIDELINES FOR USING THE INDIRECT PLAN FOR PERSUASION.

ATTENTION

The opening in any persuasive message must attract the receiver's attention. A persuasive message is successful only when the receiver takes the desired action. The desired action is not likely to be taken unless the receiver is motivated to read or listen to the entire message. An attention-getting opening increases the chances that the receiver will read or listen to the entire message and then take the desired action.

[NOTE 10.10]
A receiver's attention must be gained to ensure message is read or heard.

The receiver's attention must be captured in the opening sentence. It is important that the opening be concise and positive. In a well-planned persuasive message, the receiver's curiosity is aroused when a message opens with an interesting point. When a positive emotion is aroused, the receiver will continue reading.

[NOTE 10.11]
Get the receiver's attention immediately.

Many different methods have been used successfully by communicators to capture the receiver's attention. These methods include using mechanical devices (such as color or drawings), the receiver's name in the sentence, rhetorical questions, and interjections. The you–viewpoint must be considered when organizing the content of the message. Any method that gets the receiver's attention may be used if it is relevant to the topic of the message and is not trite or high-pressure. Gimmicks may be used but should not give the receiver the impression that an attempt is being made to mislead him or her. For example, beginning a letter with, "Your investment of $10 may grow to a million dollars by the end of the year," will probably cause the receiver to read no further because the message is unrealistic.

[NOTE 10.12]
Senders use different techniques to gain receiver's attention.

INTEREST

The receiver's interest must be held after his or her attention is gained. The topic of the first paragraph is expanded while maintaining the interest of the receiver. Interest will be maintained when the receiver sees benefits for himself or herself. When taking the requested action will result in several benefits to the receiver, the benefits may be emphasized by listing them. The receiver may hesitate to take the desired action unless he or she clearly sees the value of taking such action. Using the proper mechanical device for presenting the message can affect receivers' interest. The Communication Note on page 268 demonstrates how the improper selection of a mechanical device to deliver a message can negatively affect the receiver's interest.

[NOTE 10.13]
To hold interest, make the receiver aware of the benefits of taking the action.

DESIRE

Once you have the receiver's attention and interest, offer proof of the benefits the receiver can gain. Doing so will motivate the receiver to take the requested action. Remember, the purpose of the persuasive message is to move the receiver to take the desired action. Details of the message are used to intensify the interest of and create desire in the receiver. Anticipate the receiver's negative reactions to taking the desired action; attempt to overcome these feelings by showing proof of the benefits. Facts and figures can be valuable but should not be overused. Too many numbers or testimonials will confuse or bore the receiver.

[NOTE 10.14]
Providing proof of the benefits and values increases a receiver's desire to take action.

COMMUNICATION NOTE

Importance of Proper Packaging of a Message

The Wisconsin legislature passed a $1 billion tax relief package that included $700 million in sales tax rebates to 2.5 million taxpayers. The rebate checks were mailed as postcard-sized items that were mistaken for junk mail by many recipients. Many of the recipients improperly disposed of the rebate checks.

When this problem was brought to the attention of the Wisconsin Revenue Department, it redesigned the checks for easier identification. The replacement checks were sent in a blue, business-sized envelope, which was easier for recipients to identify.

Adapted from "Replacement Rebate Checks Being Sent," Duluth News-Tribune, *January 21, 2000.*

The *interest* and the *desire* sections of a persuasive message may be combined by listing a benefit and then immediately providing proof of that benefit. This arrangement would be used until all the benefits have been discussed.

ACTION

[NOTE 10.15] The receiver should feel that taking the action is a logical conclusion.

You are ready to ask the receiver to take immediate action once you have built his or her interest and desire. The action you request the receiver to take should be a logical next step. This action should be requested in a direct and positive manner.

[NOTE 10.16] Make it easy to take the action.

The message sender must ensure that minimal effort is required for the receiver to take the necessary action. Ask for a simple action such as checking a choice and returning an enclosed card rather than for a time-consuming action such as writing an entire letter.

[NOTE 10.17] If a deadline is necessary, give it.

When the desired action is required by a certain date, be sure that this date is clearly stated. If no time limit is involved, encourage the receiver to act quickly.

[NOTE 10.18] Various methods of getting the receiver to take action exist.

Many techniques can be used to influence the receiver to take the desired action immediately. A sales letter can offer coupons to be redeemed, specify a date that the offer ends, or suggest that supplies are limited. Collection letters can offer assurance that the receiver's credit will not be damaged if payment is received by a certain date. Including the receiver's name in a drawing for a free prize if he or she returns a questionnaire can be used with requests. All these techniques are effective if the receiver feels no undue pressure and what is offered has value to the receiver.

Implementing the Indirect Plan

[NOTE 10.19] A communication case will help illustrate ways to compose persuasive messages.

The use of the indirect plan for persuasion will be illustrated through the development of a manager's request to an employee asking her to transfer to a new facility. Here are details of the communication case problem.

THE JERI MATTHEWS CASE

Jeri Matthews has been a computer specialist for Samson Foods Distribution in Jackson, Tennessee, for seven years. Samson Foods is opening a new distribution center in Little Rock, Arkansas, this fall. The vice president for operations recently spoke to Jeri about the new facility. At that time, he did not tell Jeri about the possibility of her transferring to Little Rock. Now, he would like Jeri to make a lateral transfer to Little Rock and assume the duties of computer analyst. It would not be a promotion for Jeri nor would there be an increase in pay; however, the company will pay moving expenses and a relocation allowance. Jeri would have to move to a new city and get a system operating for the new distribution center. Write a memo to Jeri convincing her that she should accept the new position.

As is the case in developing all business messages, you must first analyze the situation to determine the content that will best accomplish the purpose of the communication. The following sections show how the content of the Jeri Matthews memo may be developed. Each section discusses a stage of the indirect plan for persuasive messages and presents an example of poor writing and then an example of good writing.

Capture the Receiver's Attention

The first step in writing a persuasive message is to capture the receiver's attention. A **poor** way of gaining Jeri's attention is shown here:

- The new distribution center for Samson Foods in Little Rock, Arkansas, needs a computer analyst. You have been working with computers for a long time and should take this job.

[NOTE 10.20]
The poor opening is negative and impersonal.

This poorly written opening paragraph begins by immediately telling Jeri that she should transfer to a new location and take a different job. It may get her attention but not in a positive way. The paragraph is impersonal and shows a lack of appreciation for Jeri's service with the company. She may be reluctant to continue reading the memo if she immediately senses that the company may be taking advantage of her.

In contrast, a **good** opening to gain Jeri's attention follows:

- Your work as a computer specialist has been outstanding for the past seven years. You really learned how computer systems operate while you were at the University of Memphis, and you have done an excellent job in applying this knowledge to your position at Samson Foods.

[NOTE 10.21]
The good opening is positive and personal.

This good opening gains Jeri's attention by recognizing her longtime dedication to the organization. This paragraph uses both a positive approach and the you–viewpoint. It should interest her because it praises her for her previous service. Everyone likes to receive recognition, and this acknowledgment of her efforts should motivate Jeri to read the remaining portion of the memo with an open mind.

Build the Receiver's Interest

After you have captured the receiver's attention, concentrate on building his or her interest in accepting the request. A **poor** way of building Jeri's interest follows:

[NOTE 10.22]
The poor message lacks a you–viewpoint.

- This job is not a promotion. You would continue earning the same salary that you presently make. Samson Foods has been looking for a competent computer analyst, and your record shows that you could become one.

This poor attempt to build the receiver's interest is similar to that of the poor opening in that it focuses on the negative and trivializes her transfer. The paragraph is cold and lacks a you–viewpoint; it is of no help in building Jeri's interest in accepting the transfer.

A **good** paragraph, which should build Jeri's interest, follows:

[NOTE 10.23]
The good message aids in building receiver's interest.

- As I mentioned to you last week during our discussion, Samson Foods is opening a distribution center in Little Rock, Arkansas. This distribution center will be fully operational by November 1, 200–. The center needs a computer analyst who has experience in the foods distribution industry. The possibility of promotion is great at our new facility, even though your transfer would not mean an immediate promotion. On a personal note, Little Rock is the capital of Arkansas, and you will find museums, theaters, and other cultural activities unique to metropolitan areas.

This good paragraph describes the opening of the new center and a benefit of the transfer in a positive manner. Jeri's interest, now stimulated, will peak in the next paragraph.

Funky Winkerbean

Promote Desire in the Receiver

This section should emphasize the benefits that Jeri would receive by taking the requested action and attempt to overcome any negative thoughts that Jeri may have. A **poor** attempt to create desire is illustrated here:

[NOTE 10.24]
The arguments in this poor example are presented from a selfish point of view.

- I know that this job would present many challenges, but you could learn from them. It is always interesting and educational when starting an operation in a new location. I know that you would have to leave many friends and relatives in Jackson; however, you can make new friends in Little Rock.

This approach will do little to motivate the reader to accept the transfer. The paragraph is written from the sender's point of view—not from the receiver's. Jeri will look at the transfer as nothing more than having to move and having to learn a new job.

A **good** attempt to stimulate Jeri's desire to accept the transfer follows:

- The facility in Little Rock will have state-of-the-art equipment. You would be involved in planning and implementing the distribution operations for the southwest region of Samson Foods. Your moving expenses will be paid by Samson Foods, and you will receive a moving allowance of $1,000.

[NOTE 10.25]
This good example points out or proves the benefits to the receiver.

The benefits that Jeri can gain from the transfer are clearly explained in the good example. The negative aspect of the transfer—that she will have to move to a new city—is handled in a positive way. Jeri should now be looking forward to accepting the transfer.

Request Action From the Receiver

Once Jeri has been motivated to accept the transfer, request that she do so immediately. Jeri's action of accepting the transfer should be made as easy as possible for her.

A **poor** example of requesting action is shown here:

- Jeri, if you decide to accept this job as computer analyst in Little Rock, please send me a letter of acceptance. Make sure that you let me know if you don't want the new position so I can get someone else.

[NOTE 10.26]
This poor request for action is presented in a negative manner.

This paragraph does little to motivate Jeri to accept the transfer. The you–viewpoint is absent. The paragraph is negative; it emphasizes the alternative that she does not have to accept the transfer.

A **good** example of requesting action may be written as follows:

- Jeri, please accept the computer analyst position in our Little Rock distribution center. Please e-mail your response to me no later than August 25 at dmartin@samsonfoods.com.

[NOTE 10.27]
The sender of this good example makes it easy for receiver to take action.

Notice the direct, positive approach used in this paragraph. Accepting the transfer is made easy for Jeri; she can simply e-mail her acceptance.

Summary—Poor and Good Messages to Jeri Matthews

Good and poor persuasive messages have been illustrated. The poor paragraphs are combined as a memo in Figure 10.2. This persuasive request does not follow the indirect plan outline as shown in Figure 10.1.

The chances of Jeri's accepting the transfer are improved in the good message shown in Figure 10.3. This effective persuasive message follows the guidelines described earlier in this chapter.

This case problem shows how the indirect plan can be effective in communicating persuasive messages. To help you better understand the use of the indirect plan in organizing persuasive messages, several examples of both good and bad messages are illustrated in the following pages.

Learning Objective [4]
WRITE DIFFERENT KINDS OF PERSUASIVE MESSAGES USING THE INDIRECT PLAN.

Persuasive Requests

[NOTE 10.28]
Organizational plans for requests may be
- Simple—direct
- Complex—indirect

Organizations use both simple requests and complex requests. The simple request was discussed in Chapter 7 and should be constructed with the direct plan. The **complex request** is a persuasive message because in it you will have to

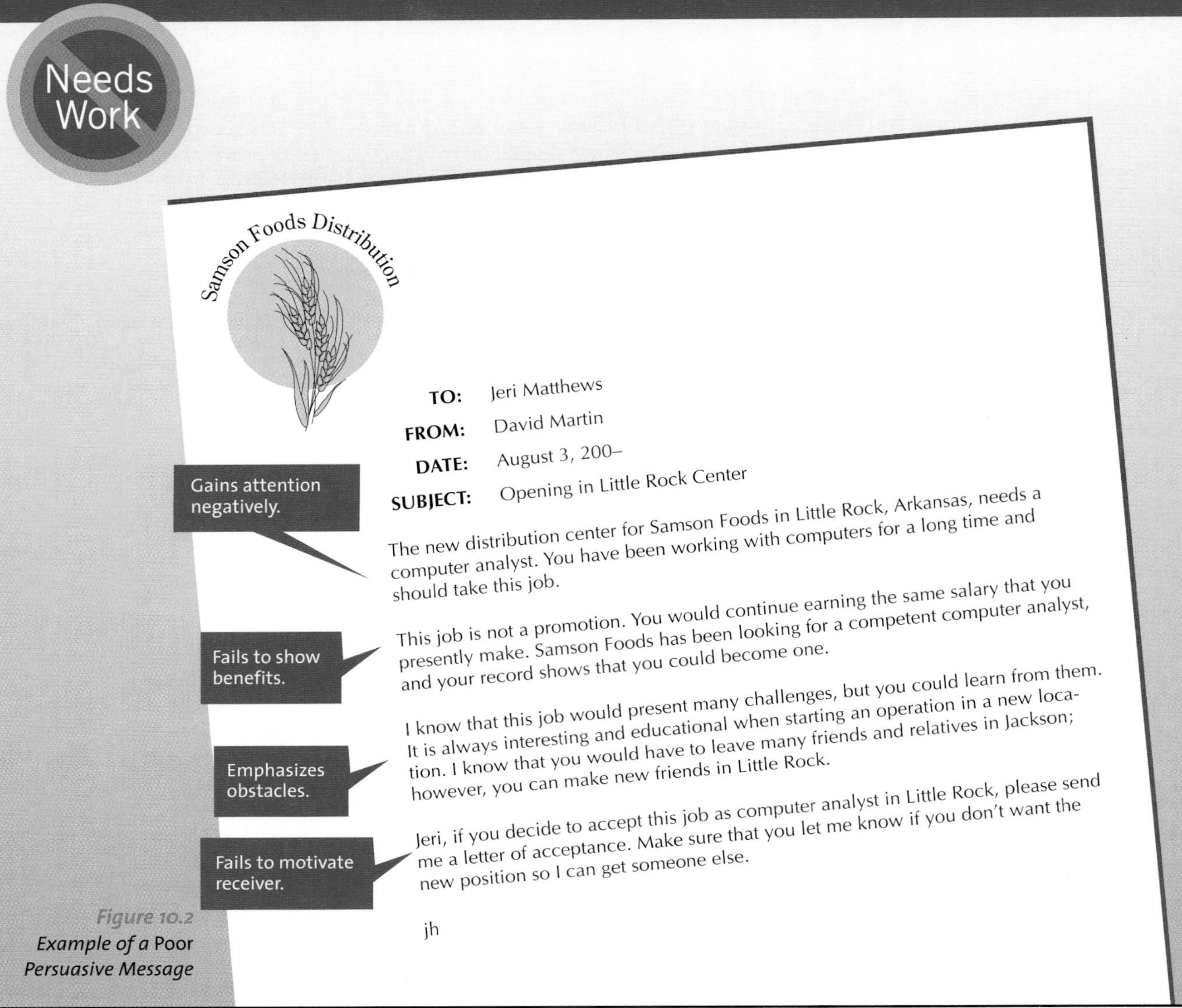

Samson Foods Distribution

TO: Jeri Matthews

FROM: David Martin

DATE: August 3, 200–

SUBJECT: Opening in Little Rock Center

The new distribution center for Samson Foods in Little Rock, Arkansas, needs a computer analyst. You have been working with computers for a long time and should take this job.

This job is not a promotion. You would continue earning the same salary that you presently make. Samson Foods has been looking for a competent computer analyst, and your record shows that you could become one.

I know that this job would present many challenges, but you could learn from them. It is always interesting and educational when starting an operation in a new location. I know that you would have to leave many friends and relatives in Jackson; however, you can make new friends in Little Rock.

Jeri, if you decide to accept this job as computer analyst in Little Rock, please send me a letter of acceptance. Make sure that you let me know if you don't want the new position so I can get someone else.

jh

Gains attention negatively.

Fails to show benefits.

Emphasizes obstacles.

Fails to motivate receiver.

Figure 10.2
Example of a Poor *Persuasive Message*

convince the receiver to take action. The complex request should use the indirect plan.

In this section we will be concerned only with complex (persuasive) requests. Examples of persuasive requests are those that (1) seek an increase in a department's budget, (2) ask for a donation to a community organization, (3) look for participants for a research project, (4) desire a change in a work schedule, and (5) recruit volunteers.

Figure 10.4 shows a **poor** persuasive request for employees to donate to a company-sponsored charity. This example does not create any receiver interest. The memo is written in the I–viewpoint rather than in the you–viewpoint. The employees will have little motivation to support this year's fund drive.

Figure 10.5 shows a **good** interoffice memo written in the you–viewpoint. The message creates receiver motivation for the same situation. The memo gains attention, builds interest, creates desire, and makes taking action easy.

Looks Good

Samson Foods Distribution

TO: Jeri Matthews
FROM: David Martin
DATE: August 3, 200–
SUBJECT: Opening in Little Rock Center

Your work as a computer specialist has been outstanding for the past seven years. You really learned how computer systems operate while you were at the University of Memphis, and you have done an excellent job in applying this knowledge to your position at Samson Foods.

As I mentioned to you last week during our discussion, Samson Foods is opening a distribution center in Little Rock, Arkansas. This distribution center will be fully operational by November 1, 200–. The center needs a computer analyst who has experience in the foods distribution industry. The possibility of promotion is great at our new facility, even though your transfer would not mean an immediate promotion. On a personal note, Little Rock is the capital of Arkansas, and you will find museums, theaters, and other cultural activities unique to metropolitan areas.

The facility in Little Rock will have state-of-the-art equipment. You would be involved in planning and implementing the distribution operations for the southwest region of Samson Foods. Your moving expenses will be paid by Samson Foods, and you will receive a moving allowance of $1,000.

Jeri, please accept the computer analyst position in our Little Rock distribution center. Please e-mail your response to me no later than August 25 at dmartin@samsonfoods.com.

jh

Focuses attention on receiver.

Continues interest and keeps attention that was gained in first paragraph.

Emphasizes proof of benefits to receiver.

Motivates receiver and makes taking action easy.

Figure 10.3
Example of a Good Persuasive Message

The following table summarizes the approach used for the two types of requests:

Request	Approach
simple or routine	direct
persuasive or complex	indirect

Recommendations

A **recommendation** is a message that attempts to persuade the receiver to take an action proposed by the sender. Individuals in business, government, and civic organizations periodically submit recommendations to receivers who are above, below, and at their organizational level. Recommendations are most effective when the indirect persuasive plan is employed. Examples that should use the indirect plan include

[NOTE 10.29]
Recommendations are submitted at all organizational levels.

[NOTE 10.30]
Recommendations are best when organized in the indirect persuasive plan.

comfy furniture
interoffice memorandum

TO: All Employees
FROM: Felicia Downs, Human Resources Director FD
DATE: November 3, 200-
SUBJECT: Mountaintop Children's Home

The committee for selecting a charity for Comfy Furniture to sponsor has chosen Mountaintop Children's Home this year. We need you to send your donation no later than November 20.

We need to beat the $8,700 that we gave to Needline last year. We think that Mountaintop is in more need than was Needline. This year's goal is $10,000.

If you need more information, read the enclosed brochure that gives all the details.

tm

Enclosure

Impersonal—does not gain attention.

Selfish—does little to build interest.

Vague—difficult for receiver to take action.

Figure 10.4
Example of a Poor *Persuasive Request*

recommendations to a company officer to advise the firm to replace obsolete equipment, to a manager to change a company policy, and to a civic leader to use a tract of land for a city park rather than a housing project.

Figure 10.6 shows a **poor** recommendation from Derrick Martin, a vice president, to Kern Allen, the president. Derrick is responding to a memo from Mr. Allen concerning renovation. Derrick probably will not be successful in his recommendation if the poor memo is submitted. This memo is not written with the you–viewpoint. It also displays bitterness, which hinders communication. In addition, the memo is not written using the indirect plan—the key to successful persuasive messages.

The **good** memo in Figure 10.7 should increase the chances that Mr. Allen will proceed with the proposed renovation. Note how the indirect persuasive plan presents the *benefits*—improved production and increased employee morale—before the *recommendation*. This memo gains the president's attention in the

comfy furniture

interoffice memorandum

TO: All Employees
FROM: Felicia Downs, Human Resources Director FD
DATE: November 3, 200-
SUBJECT: Mountaintop Children's Home

Gains attention.

Imagine Thanksgiving without turkey or summer without a vacation.

The Mountaintop Children's Home makes sure that the 45 children who live there have those things. Mountaintop is a nonprofit organization that provides care for children who have lost their parents. A brochure describing the facilities and services provided at the home is enclosed.

Builds interest.

Each year a committee consisting of one member from each department selects a charity for the Comfy Furniture employees to sponsor. This year they are asking us to pledge our support to Mountaintop. Last year the employees of Comfy generously gave $8,700 to Needline, and we know that you will help meet this year's $10,000 goal for the Mountaintop Children's Home.

Provides details that stimulate desire.

Please return the enclosed pledge card by November 20. The amount you select will be deducted from your paycheck. Your contribution is tax deductible. The Mountaintop children will greatly appreciate and benefit from your generosity.

tm

Enclosures

Makes taking action easy.

Figure 10.5
Example of a Good Persuasive Request

opening, uses the you–viewpoint in presenting the reasons supporting the recommendation, and presents the recommendation in a positive, professional manner.

Special Claims

Special claims are unique and should use the indirect persuasive plan. Routine claims use the direct plan and are discussed in Chapter 7. **Special** or **nonroutine claims** are those in which the fault is disputable. The sender may need to convince the receiver that the adjustment or refund is appropriate.

[NOTE 10.31]
Special claims should use the indirect plan.

Examples of special claims that should be organized as persuasive messages include the following: You want a roofing contractor, who has guaranteed his work, to replace the shingles on your office building because they are not aligned properly.

ALLENIndustries, Inc.

TO: Kern Allen, President

FROM: Derrick Martin, Vice President

DATE: October 11, 200–

SUBJECT: Renovation of Facilities

You should not even consider renovating our present facilities. It will cost so much money and you will still have an old, outdated building.

Renovation of this building is ridiculous. We could have a new building that would be modern and attractive; however, if you want to renovate the present building, we can do it. We will have to move to a temporary site during the construction.

If you decide to go ahead with this renovation, I will begin planning the move to a temporary location.

gw

Negatively influences receiver.

Displays negative attitude; does not show benefits.

Begrudgingly accepts responsibility.

Figure 10.6
Example of a Poor *Recommendation Memo*

A transportation company has purchased a fleet of 25 trucks, 20 of which have had their transmissions replaced in the first six months. The company wants the manufacturer to absorb the cost of the new transmissions. A work of art, which was purchased for $50,000, was found to be a forgery; the buyer demands reimbursement from the gallery that sold it.

Figure 10.8 is a **poor** special claim letter from Terry McNichols, owner of Terry's Antiques. Terry purchased an antique doll that was of lesser quality than advertised. The writer of this letter is upset. The receiver's attention may be gained in the opening paragraph, but not in a way that will get the desired reaction. The writer clearly does not give the necessary details. The entire letter is negative, which will irritate the receiver and hinder getting the desired action—a refund.

ALLEN Industries, Inc.

TO: Kern Allen, President
FROM: Derrick Martin, Vice President
DATE: October 11, 200–
SUBJECT: Renovation of Facilities

Allen Industries has become one of the most successful businesses in the state. It has more than doubled its sales and profit in the past three years. This success is expected to continue in the future.

I agree with you that the increased volume of business has resulted in Allen Industries' facilities being inadequate. Renovation of our facilities would greatly benefit our company. Enlarging the facility would aid production and contribute to increased sales. Attractive, modern offices will boost the morale of our employees.

Relocation of our operation during renovation can be accomplished easily if we follow the proposed relocation plan that I have attached to this memo. Interruption of production should be minimal during the renovation process. Employees will readily accept this relocation plan because they look forward to the increased efficiency of the renovated facilities.

I recommend that you proceed with the renovation plan that you proposed.

gw

Enclosure

Gains the manager's attention.

Builds interest.

Stimulates desire.

Gives a recommendation.

Figure 10.7
Example of a Good *Recommendation Memo*

The letter in Figure 10.9 covers the same situation but is a **good** message. Notice how the writer shows the receiver the benefits to be gained by adjusting the purchase price of the doll. The writer of this letter remains calm and explains the necessary details for the receiver. The positive tone of the letter will encourage cooperation from the receiver. The writer is courteous throughout the complaint but emphasizes that the doll is of lesser quality than advertised. Notice that the receiver may fax her response.

The following table summarizes the approach used for the two types of claims:

Claim	**Approach**
simple or routine	direct
special or nonroutine	indirect

TERRY'S
ANTIQUES
1230 MAGNOLIA DRIVE, GREENSBORO, GA 30642-1252
(404) 555-6891 FAX (404) 555-7733

February 23, 200–

Ms. Marie Coltharp
Wholesale Antiques & Collectibles
3245 Bayou Circle
Houston, TX 77040-2132

Dear Ms. Coltharp:

I want the $2,700 back for the doll that I ordered because it is not of the quality that you promised.

You promised that the doll was of museum quality. It is NOT! Someone painted over several of the bad spots trying to hide the chips that the doll had. Your sorry antique may make me lose a good customer.

I want you to either send me back my $2,700 and I will return the doll, or I will keep the doll and you refund me $300 because it is not of the quality that you promised. I need you to let me know quickly so that I can tell my customer.

Sincerely,

Terry McNichols

Terry McNichols
Owner

Is negative.

Shows anger.

Demands action rather than making a request.

Figure 10.8
Example of a Poor *Special Claim Letter*

[NOTE 10.32]
Most sales messages are prepared by advertising professionals.

[NOTE 10.33]
A careful analysis of the product or service should be completed before composing the sales material.

Sales Messages

Sales messages come in many different forms, such as letters, brochures, leaflets, catalogs, radio and television commercials, and billboards. Most of these messages are prepared by advertising professionals; however, you may one day be asked to compose one.

Before you compose a sales message, know the product or service you are going to sell. Know its strengths, its weaknesses, its competitors, and its market. As you

TERRY'S
ANTIQUES
1230 MAGNOLIA DRIVE. GREENSBORO. GA 30642-1252
(404) 555-6891 FAX (404) 555-7733

February 23, 200–

Ms. Marie Coltharp
Wholesale Antiques & Collectibles
3245 Bayou Circle
Houston, TX 77040-2132

Dear Ms. Coltharp:

Your dealership has provided my shop with many beautiful, authentic antique pieces during the past 15 years. On January 25, I ordered from you a Fortune Teller doll for $2,700. One of my clients wanted this doll as a Valentine gift for his wife.

The mid-1800s doll is extremely rare. You advertised it as museum quality with original painted wooden features. Upon close inspection it is obvious that the doll's paint has been touched up. This painting alteration lowers the doll's antique value.

My client is willing to keep the doll but is not willing to pay the original price. He thinks that the touch-up painting has lowered the doll's value by $300; therefore, I am requesting a refund of that amount. If a partial refund is not possible, I will return the doll and expect a total refund of $2,700. Please call me or fax your decision so that my client may be promptly informed.

Sincerely,

Terry McNichols

Terry McNichols
Owner

Attracts attention with praise.

Gains interest by giving detail.

Adds detail.

Makes polite request.

Figure 10.9
Example of a Good Special Claim Letter

compose the message, emphasize the strengths and omit any mention of weaknesses. Your market should be researched carefully to determine how to appeal to your customers and to get their business.

Various techniques are used in sales messages to gain the receiver's attention: color, sentence fragments, catchy slogans, famous quotations, testimonials from celebrities, and descriptions of benefits. A salutation is frequently omitted from the message.

[NOTE 10.34]
Receiver's attention is gained through different techniques.

[NOTE 10.35]
An interested receiver will hear or read all of the message.

Once you gain the receiver's attention, you must maintain his or her interest to ensure that the entire message is read or heard. A careful analysis of the receiver is critical in preparing the message from the receiver's point of view. Extra care must be taken in the analysis of the receiver because sales messages are usually prepared for multiple receivers.

A **poor** sales message to the Russells about a golfing vacation is shown in Figure 10.10. This message is not written from the you–viewpoint. The letter fails to point out the benefits of the vacation resort. The resort's features are given, but the writer does it in a negative manner. The request for action is weak. How should the customer "let us know"?

A **good** sales letter is shown in Figure 10.11. Note how this letter stresses the benefits that the Russells will gain from the "Spring Fling." The subject line is effective in gaining the reader's attention. Mentioning golf and relaxation will build interest. Notice how the letter integrates the golf course and the other facilities of the vacation resort. Ms. Burgess makes it easy for the Russells to take action—to reserve their room.

Learning Objective [5]
WRITE MESSAGES THAT ARE USED FOR THE VARIOUS STAGES OF COLLECTION.

Collection Messages

[NOTE 10.36]
Collection messages are designed to collect money and retain goodwill.

A collection message is used by business firms to collect overdue accounts. The two purposes of collection messages are (1) to collect the money due and (2) to retain goodwill with the customer.

[NOTE 10.37]
Collection messages are written in three stages.

Collection messages, generally, are written in three stages—reminder, appeal, and warning. Each stage is progressively more persuasive, and each stage has several steps. The number of steps in each stage will vary according to the type of business involved and the credit rating of the customer.

[NOTE 10.38]
The reminder stage is for customers who forgot to pay.

REMINDER STAGE

The reminder stage is for customers who intend to pay but just need a reminder. The **reminder** is a simple and sometimes comical message intended to get a receiver to pay a bill. Collection messages in this category are direct and friendly; they must never offend the receiver. These messages are normally only short notes or a sticker on a bill.

Examples of collection messages in the reminder stage include the following:

Past Due
Reminder
Please Remit

Messages in the reminder stage are very courteous because failure to make a payment is often only an oversight. A harsh reminder may well alienate a customer who had intended to pay on time. If the reminder fails, the collection process will proceed to the appeal stage.

APPEAL STAGE

An **appeal** is stronger than a first-stage message because the customer has failed to heed the reminder notice. You need to analyze the customer carefully before writing a letter of appeal. You will have to select the type of appeal that will persuade the customer to pay. You may appeal to the customer's pride, credit rating, morality, or reputation. Once you have selected the type of appeal to use, construct the message using the indirect persuasive outline.

[NOTE 10.39]
The appeal stage must effectively persuade the receiver.

A **poor** collection letter in the appeal stage is shown in Figure 10.12. This letter is too harsh. It is written from the writer's point of view and will cause anger, which will reduce rather than increase the chances of collection. Necessary details such as the amount due are not furnished.

The **good** collection letter in Figure 10.13 is recommended for the appeal stage. It is written in a positive, courteous tone. The opening paragraph will get the customer's attention by appealing to his pride. The customer should believe that the store is trying to help him maintain his excellent credit reputation. The store's chances of collecting are greatly increased with this letter.

WARNING STAGE

Reminders and appeals may not succeed in collecting all past-due bills. When these efforts fail, you must move into the final stage—warning. Until now, you were interested in maintaining the customer's goodwill while trying to collect. When the warning stage is reached, you are interested only in collecting the past-due amount.

A **warning** is the last opportunity for a customer to pay an account before it is transferred to a collection agency, a credit bureau, or an attorney. Use the direct plan to develop your message for this stage. Sending the warning letter by registered mail—so a signature is required—stresses the importance of the message and creates a sense of urgency.

[NOTE 10.40]
The warning stage is used only when the other stages have failed.

A **poor** warning stage collection message is shown in Figure 10.14 on page 286. In this poor example, the customer will be inclined to resist because the writer does not get directly to the warning in a firm manner without displaying anger. Notice that the amount due is never given. The use of threats is illegal and will not increase the writer's chances of collection.

Figure 10.15 on page 287 shows how a **good** collection letter in the warning stage should be written. This letter gets directly to the main idea—the customer's account is past due, and no attempt is being made to correct the problem. Facts are

PARADISE TRAVEL
428 SEASIDE LANE, HILTON HEAD, SC 29928-3175
(803) 555-4279 FAX (803) 555-5831

March 18, 200–

Marc and Janet Russell
2841 Mountain View Road
Asheville, NC 28800

Dear Marc and Janet:

Paradise Travel is offering a three-day, two-night vacation at Sanddollar Golf Course and Hotel for only $750 a couple.

Sanddollar has spent a lot of money remodeling its hotel and reworking its golf courses. It has even hired a golf pro to manage the course. The greens on the 18-hole course are in good shape even for this time of the year. March temperatures are better in Hilton Head than they are in Asheville.

If you don't like to golf, you can always swim or play tennis. Sanddollar has 3 pools and 12 tennis courts. If you don't like to swim or play tennis, you can soak in the hot tubs or lift weights in the exercise room. If you work up an appetite, you can eat at one of our three restaurants. They serve a variety of food.

Let us know if you want to vacation at the Sanddollar facility. Reserve a room in March and we will give you four coupons for dinner.

Sincerely,

Kay Burgess

Kay Burgess
President

Opening is not from the you–viewpoint.

Receiver's benefits are not pointed out.

Receiver's benefits are not re-emphasized.

Request for action is not positive.

Figure 10.10
Example of a Poor *Sales Message*

PARADISE TRAVEL
428 SEASIDE LANE, HILTON HEAD, SC 29928-3175
(803) 555-4279 FAX (803) 555-5831

March 18, 200–

Marc and Janet Russell
2841 Mountain View Road
Asheville, NC 28800

Dear Marc and Janet:

SPRING FLING WITH GOLF!

Spring is a time for new beginnings! Come enjoy the championship Sanddollar Golf Course on Hilton Head. A three-day spring fling of golf, tennis, and relaxation will renew your outlook on life. Enjoy three days of golf and tennis and two nights of relaxation in the luxurious Sanddollar Hotel for only $750 a couple.

Mention of golf and relaxation gains attention.

The 18-hole Sanddollar Golf Course provides great challenges with inclined and narrow fairways demanding greater accuracy. The course contains many water hazards along the fairways, and natural flora adds to its beauty. The beautifully landscaped course and the comfortable March temperatures make each day a golfer's paradise.

The features of the golf course are given.

In addition to enjoying the luxurious golf course, you may play on the 12 tennis courts, swim in the 3 pools, relax in the 3 hot tubs, exercise in the fitness room, or dance in the romantic lounge. You may enjoy a variety of fresh fish, steaks, Italian pasta specials, and tempting salads in our three specialty restaurants.

Describing additional facilities builds desire.

Please reserve your room for this exciting, relaxing spring fling by calling our toll-free number, 1-800-555-GOLF. If you take advantage of this spring fling in March, you will receive coupons for four free dinners at any of our three specialty restaurants!

Action can be taken easily.

Sincerely,

Kay Burgess

Kay Burgess
President

Figure 10.11
Example of a Good Sales Message

WAGGONER'S
CLOTHING
1728 FULLER STREET
ATLANTA, GA 30351-72283
(404) 555-3279

February 17, 200-

Mr. Alvah Tucker
1753 Johnson Boulevard
Athens, GA 30611-4812

Dear Mr. Tucker:

I am totally disappointed with you for not making a payment on your overdue account. We must have our money now.

We were generous when we extended credit to you, but then you let us down. I will have to inform the Credit Bureau if I don't receive a payment in ten days.

Once again I appeal to you to make an immediate payment so I don't have to destroy your credit reputation. I am expecting payment by return mail.

Sincerely,

Maria Ortiz

Maria Ortiz
Credit Manager

dw

Attacks the receiver too severely.

Uses I–viewpoint.

Makes a demand.

Figure 10.12
Example of a Poor *Collection Message—Appeal Stage*

presented in a positive tone with no sign of anger. In the last paragraph, the customer is told exactly what must be done to avoid legal action.

Finally, let us summarize the approach that is used in each stage of collection messages:

Stage	**Approach**
reminder	direct
appeal	indirect
warning	direct

WAGGONER'S CLOTHING
1728 FULLER STREET
ATLANTA, GA 30351-72283
(404) 555-3279

April 5, 200-

Mr. Alvah Tucker
1753 Johnson Boulevard
Athens, GA 30611-4812

Dear Mr. Tucker:

You take pride in your appearance because you selected our suits for your wardrobe. I know this pride extends to other aspects of your life.

You have been a valued credit customer of ours for many years, and we would like this relationship to continue. For some reason you have not responded to the reminders that were sent on December 20, January 20, and February 2. Your account is three months overdue.

Please send a check for $725.90 in the enclosed envelope by March 1 so that your credit reputation can remain in good standing.

Sincerely,

Maria Ortiz

Maria Ortiz
Credit Manager

dw

Enclosure

Uses pride appeal.

Reviews past actions courteously.

Motivates receiver to take action.

Figure 10.13
Example of a Good Collection Message—Appeal Stage

Your use of the indirect plan outline will enable you to compose most effective persuasive messages. The ability to do so will serve you well throughout your career.

Summary of Learning Objectives

Learning Objective [1]

Describe a persuasive message. A persuasive message is (1) a request for action when you believe the receiver may be unknowing, disinterested, or unwilling, or (2) a communication to try to change the opinion of a receiver. These messages will be viewed

WAGGONER'S CLOTHING
1728 FULLER STREET
ATLANTA, GA 30351-72283
(404) 555-3279

April 5, 200-

Mr. Alvah Tucker
1753 Johnson Boulevard
Athens, GA 30611-4812

Dear Mr. Tucker:

We have been trying for five months to get you to pay the balance due on your account. We can no longer tolerate your getting by without paying when all the rest of our customers pay promptly.

We are going to turn your account over to our attorney if we do not get the money by April 12. You will be sorry when this happens because we are giving the attorney full authority to do anything to collect the money.

Sincerely,

Maria Ortiz

Maria Ortiz
Credit Manager

dw

Neglects the you–viewpoint.

Threatens receiver.

Figure 10.14
Example of a Poor *Collection Message—Warning Stage*

as neither positive nor negative by the receiver and may be used in both internal and external communication. The supporting facts of persuasive messages must convince receivers that taking the requested action is in their best interest. Persuasive messages should almost always be presented using an indirect approach.

Learning Objective [2]

List the purposes of a persuasive message. The two primary purposes of a persuasive message are (1) to get the receiver to read or listen to the entire message, and then (2) to have the receiver react positively to the request.

Looks Good

WAGGONER'S CLOTHING
1728 FULLER STREET
ATLANTA, GA 30351-72283
(404) 555-3279

April 5, 200-

Mr. Alvah Tucker
1753 Johnson Boulevard
Athens, GA 30611-4812

Dear Mr. Tucker:

Your account balance of $725.90 is five months past due, and you have ignored all our collection attempts. Your failure to respond leaves us no choice but to turn the account over to our attorney.

Legal action is not pleasant for either of us, but it is necessary because of your failure to respond to our previous notices. A lawsuit will be expensive and embarrassing to you.

Our attorney assures us that if your account balance is paid by April 12, no legal action will be taken; your credit reputation will be maintained. Please send the check in the enclosed envelope prior to April 12 to avoid this action.

Sincerely,

Maria Ortiz

Maria Ortiz
Credit Manager

dw

Enclosure

Gains reader's attention.

Reminds reader of past actions.

Motivates receiver to take immediate action.

Figure 10.15
Example of a Good Collection Message—Warning Stage

Learning Objective [3]

Describe the four specific guidelines for using the indirect plan for persuasion. The four parts of an indirect plan for a persuasive message are the following: (1) Attention—the receiver's attention must be gained in the opening to ensure the message is read or heard. (2) Interest—benefits must be shown to hold the receiver's interest. (3) Desire—providing proof of the benefits will motivate the receiver to take action. (4) Action—make it easy for the receiver to take action and motivate him or her to take the action quickly.

Learning Objective [4]

Write different kinds of persuasive messages using the indirect plan. Use the indirect plan when preparing complex (persuasive) requests; recommendations; special claims; and sales, some collection, and employment messages. The indirect plan for persuasion includes attention, interest, desire, and action.

Learning Objective [5]

Write messages that are used for the various stages of collection. The three stages normally used in collection messages are reminder, appeal, and warning. The reminder stage is a short, direct, polite message to a customer who simply forgot to pay. In the appeal stage, use the indirect plan for persuasion. When the other stages fail to collect, move into the warning stage. Messages in the warning stage are constructed using the direct plan and are not concerned about maintaining the receiver's goodwill.

DISCUSSION QUESTIONS

1. What is a persuasive message? How does anticipated receiver reaction influence the organizational plan used to write a persuasive message? (Objective 1)
2. Why is analyzing your receiver important when planning a persuasive message? (Objective 2)
3. Describe three characteristics of the interest section of the indirect plan for persuasion. (Objective 3)
4. Briefly describe the plan that should be used in organizing most persuasive messages. (Objective 3)
5. Identify the organizational plan that should be used by a grocery owner who wants the store's entire parking area resurfaced because asphalt is cracking after only three months' use. Explain why the organizational plan was selected. (Objective 4)
6. Explain why the following paragraph would be ineffective as the final paragraph of a letter to Becky trying to convince her to assume the duties of newsletter editor. Rewrite the paragraph to be more effective. (Objective 4)

Becky, if you feel that you can spare the time to be newsletter editor, I would appreciate your writing a letter stating so. Make sure that you let me know because if you don't accept, I will have to find someone else.

7. Should you respond to all requests the same way? Explain. (Objective 4)
8. Explain why the following paragraph would be ineffective in opening a sales message. Rewrite the paragraph to be more effective. (Objective 4)

We need to sell many briefcases. Our warehouse is full, and bills need to be paid.

9. Why is it especially important that a writer carefully analyze a customer before writing a collection letter in the appeal stage? (Objective 5)
10. Are the objectives the same for all three stages of collection messages? Explain your answer. (Objective 5)

APPLICATION EXERCISES

1. Analyze a sales letter that has been received in your household. Identify the parts of the message that correspond to the parts of the organizational plan for persuasive messages. (Objective 3)
2. Outline the ideas to be included in the interest and desire sections of a message to send to your school's administration recommending that final examinations be eliminated. (Objective 3)
3. Discuss several situations in which someone tried to persuade you to do something. Analyze the strengths and weaknesses of these oral or written messages. (Objective 3)
4. Write a memo to your instructor recommending that students be permitted to work in teams to prepare class projects. (Objective 4)
5. Write an article that could be used in your school newspaper for recruiting new members to your communication club. (Objective 4)

6. **E-mail.** All of your grades in your business communication class except one have been good. The poor grade came at a time during which you were extremely busy with extracurricular activities. This one poor grade may lower your average for the class by one letter. Send a persuasive e-mail to your instructor asking that he or she permit you to do an additional assignment for extra credit. Use facts to support your persuasive message. (Objective 4)

There are Web exercises at **http://krizan.swcollege.com** to accompany this chapter.

CASE PROBLEMS

Persuasive Requests

1. Your company has selected FreeMed Insurance to provide your employees a plan that takes advantage of tax laws. Individuals enrolling in the plan can pay their share of certain insurance premiums tax-free. The plan also permits employees to set aside money tax-free to help pay for expenses not covered by medical insurance. As director of human services, write a memo that would persuade employees to attend a meeting in which FreeMed personnel would be available to explain this tax-saving plan.
2. You are the business manager of Missouri Ostrich, Inc. The company's primary income comes from selling ostriches. The ostrich market, however, is not well established. A $25,000 payment on a loan is due on April 15, and you are unable to make the payment. Write a letter to Ruben Hurwitz, Loan Officer, Houston County Bank, Mountain Grove, Missouri 65711-1402, requesting that payment be postponed for three months. You have some good birds that will be ready for sale in three months. Ruben will need to be persuaded because ostrich farming is new and risky.
3. Star Electric has provided electricity to the area for many years. Recently Star upgraded all of its wiring to fiber optics and is now expanding into digital cable services. As marketing manager for Star Electric, write a letter that could be sent to residents in the area persuading them to take advantage of these services. These letters may be sent to current as well as potential electrical customers. Add details to make it a complete letter.

4. **Global/Cross-Cultural.** You are program director for the student economics organization on your campus. You have done such an outstanding job that you have been

asked to obtain the keynote speaker for this year's state conference. You would like to get an economist from Germany. Write a letter to the head of the economics department at the University of Heidelberg in Germany requesting that he or she furnish a speaker at no cost, except travel-related expenses, for the state conference. Add details needed to make this a complete request.

5. You are the director of a wellness clinic at a local hospital. Doctors in the clinic wish to conduct a research project to help people lower their blood pressure and cholesterol levels through diet and exercise rather than medication. Volunteers are needed to participate in the program. Write a personalized form letter to be sent to patients to persuade them to volunteer for the project. Note that no monetary compensation will be given but that the weekly checkups are provided without cost.

Recommendations

6. Alyssa Johnston has been working for you as a communication specialist for seven years. She is interested in advancing to a more challenging job, but your organization currently has no room for advancement. She has applied for the director of public relations position at Freeman International and has requested that you write a letter of recommendation for her. She has been an excellent employee for you, and you do not want to lose her; however, you feel obligated to write her a letter that would influence Freeman International to hire her. Write a complete letter of recommendation for her.
7. You are the president of the Student Government Association for your school. Numerous students have complained of difficulty in finding parking spaces on campus. You have noticed an empty parking lot behind a vacant building one block from campus. Write a letter to the owner recommending that students be permitted to park on the lot during the week.
8. Becky Wolf is an excellent clarinetist. She received many honors in high school. She is now working in Memphis, Tennessee, and has been identified as a potential member of the city's symphonic orchestra. She needs a personal letter of recommendation. Write a letter to the Memphis Symphony Orchestra Board of Directors telling them what an asset Becky would be.
9. The city in which you go to school needs a new administration building. One location being considered for the building site is a public park in the downtown area. If this park area is used, many beautiful old trees would be destroyed. An alternative location would be property owned by the city at the edge of town. Write a recommendation letter to the city officials persuading them to select the alternative site. Add details.
10. Bellville Savings and Loan has a policy that customers may borrow money only for a home in which they will reside. Many customers would like to purchase other property, such as rental property or weekend homes. Bellville Savings and Loan cannot lend the money for these purchases but will recommend applicants to another financial institution. Write a personalized form letter that could be used to recommend these individuals. Supply details.

Special Claims

11. You and a friend have saved for a year to take a cruise during spring break. You contacted a reputable travel agency and purchased a five-day luxury cruise for $1,950.

The cruise was a disaster. The rooms were too small, the food tasted as if it were cooked in the college cafeteria, the ship was too crowded, and the service was awful. Write a special claims letter to your travel agency requesting a full refund for the cruise. Add details.

12. You were recently involved in an automobile accident. As you were going to work early one morning, a deer jumped in your path. You were traveling at such a high rate of speed that you could not avoid hitting the animal. Damages to your car are estimated at $1,495. An accident report was filed, and you did not receive a ticket. Your insurance company will pay only $800; it feels you were partially responsible because you were traveling too fast. Write a letter to your insurance company asking it to pay the full amount less the $100 deductible.

13. You purchased a microcomputer on line and discovered when you unpacked it that it did not work. You called the company's technical support division and spoke to Rebecca Manning. On hearing the symptoms, Rebecca stated that the power supply was faulty and recommended that you return the CPU. When the replacement unit arrived, the monitor did not work. Experiencing these problems, you decide to return the entire computer for a full refund. Write a letter to CompuCo requesting a refund for the microcomputer, including shipping costs. Add details to make the letter complete.

14. Mayes's Leadership analyzes a company and then provides personnel training seminars to improve the organization's operating efficiency. As human resources director, you hired Mayes's Leadership to improve the morale and reduce absenteeism. Mayes's conducted many seminars for all levels of employees and managers over a three-month period. Nine months later you have noticed no significant improvement. In fact, absenteeism has increased and morale is at an all-time low. Write a letter to Mayes's Leadership requesting a refund of $95,000 for its consultant work. Add details.

15. Holiday Tours is an agency that arranges package tours for clients. Often clients return from a tour and complain that accommodations did not meet the standards described in the brochures. Prepare a personalized form letter that could be sent to hotels and motels asking for a refund for a dissatisfied customer.

Sales Messages

16. You are treasurer of your student business organization and have made arrangements with a local nursery for your organization to receive $2 for each mum corsage sold for homecoming. Write a form letter that could be sent to students promoting the sale of these corsages. Add details to make the letter complete.

17. **Teamwork. Global/Cross-Cultural.** You are a member of your school's Humanities Student Association, which has decided to organize a retired-persons' tour to the Black Forest of Germany for its service project. Several tasks must be accomplished for this project. Your tasks include the following:

a. Contact a travel agency or airline to obtain airfare information.

b. Write a letter to a tourist information office in one of the towns in the Black Forest area to obtain necessary information for developing a sales letter about the tour.

c. Find the exchange rate for German deutsche marks to U.S. dollars.

d. Write a form letter that could be sent to the retired people in the area advertising this tour. The letter should include the cost of the tour (airline tickets, lodging, food, and ground transportation). Have interested individuals send a deposit for the tour.

18. Arnold's Fitness Center provides a complete program for a healthy body. It offers aerobic classes, seminars on nutrition and stress management, weight training, and a variety of exercise equipment. Arnold's has hired you to create a flyer announcing a program for students interested in building and maintaining a healthy body. This flyer will be placed on various bulletin boards on your campus encouraging students to enroll in the program. Create this flyer adding details.

19. Claudia's, a clothing boutique, has contacted your student business organization for help in promoting a Valentine's Day sale. Claudia's would like your organization to sell coupons for $5 each. The boutique would be closed one evening, and the only way a person could enter the store would be with this coupon. In addition to admitting the person, the coupon would entitle the customer to free refreshments and a 25 percent discount on all purchases. Claudia's would donate all of the coupon monies to your organization. Design an advertisement that could be used in the local or school paper to help your organization with this fundraiser.

20. Andy Gatts is starting Andy's Web Creations, a small business that will build Web pages for organizations. Andy's can customize Web pages to meet the needs of a client's organization—as complex or as simple as desired. Fees to create Web pages are based on an hourly rate. Write a letter that Andy can send to organizations in the area inviting them to investigate his services. Add details.

Collection Messages

21. Patsy Simmons owns a large condominium complex. Approximately two years ago she hired Jimmy Gee, a local plumber, to renovate the plumbing in the complex. Jimmy completed the renovation and sent her an invoice for $32,500. Patsy has not paid any of the charges and has not responded to any of the numerous appeals that Jimmy sent her. Jimmy would like you to write a letter to Patsy asking for the money and informing her that if the money is not received within three weeks, he is going to contact his attorney. Add details to make this a complete warning letter.

22. Kent Fulsom has been a credit customer of Thurman Furniture Store for eight years. He is a good customer but periodically fails to make payments on his account. He is currently four months past due ($235.81); several reminders have produced no response. As credit manager of Thurman's, write an appeal collection letter to Kent requesting payment.

23. Mary Lou's Family Cooking has been operating for 25 years. Several chain restaurants have moved into the area resulting in a highly competitive market. Mary Lou's currently owes an $18,750 balance to Hillman's Wholesale for grocery products that is eight months past due. Because the bill has not been paid, you changed the policy for this restaurant to pay for all groceries on delivery. This policy has worked well, but Mary Lou's has made no payment toward the $18,750 past-due balance. Write a letter that will encourage the restaurant to begin paying on the past-due amount. You realize that it may take a year to reduce the balance to zero.

24. Hal Montgomery purchased a ring from your jewelry store when he became engaged to Kimberly Fairbanks, the daughter of a prominent family in the community. The financial agreement that Hal signed when he purchased the ring stated that Hal would pay $550 down and $150 a month until the account was paid in full. The balance on the account is $1,450 and Hal has made no payment during the last eight months. Your appeal letters to him have produced no response, and he has not done any other business with your store. Write a letter to Hal informing him that he must pay the entire balance on the account or the debt will be turned over to a collection agency.

25. Acme Finance Company's primary business is lending money to individuals who are purchasing used cars. Often individuals make several payments and then suddenly stop. Sometimes a reminder will get them to continue their payments; sometimes it will not. Write a form letter that could be individualized for each customer requesting payment to update the account. Add details.

MESSAGE ANALYSIS

Correct the errors in the following letter that has been written to Bill and Emily Chadwick, who have not made a payment for the past five months on their home bought through Habitat for Humanity:

When are you going to begin making your monthly house payment? Since you moved into the house we at Habitat for Humanity remodeled for you, you have made only two payments on it.

We at Habitat want our money. We made it clear to you that you were geting a good deal by paying the low 2% interest rate. We were able to provide this low rate because our Habitat members worked on the house for free and many of the materials were donated. We know that you were happy to get the lovely home for such low cost that we would hate to take it away from you. However, you must start making payments immediately or else we will have to give the house to someone else.

We will be expecting to get your $260 check to cover this month's $210 payment and $50 to be applied to the past-due balance by March 15 or we will have to take other action.

GRAMMAR WORKSHOP

Correct the grammar, spelling, punctuation, and word choice errors in the following sentences:

1. Employers expects employees to have writing skills that clearly communicates information.
2. The members of the union has not voted but when they do they will not pass the agreement as a matter of principal.
3. Young investors that want a good retirement should invest in Stocks Bonds and Mutual Funds.
4. Last month Ricardo speak at Universities in Oxford, Mississippi, Dallas, Texas, Grand Forks, North Dakota, and Duluth, Minnesota.
5. Susan's parents could not hardly wait to congratulate her for graduating with Honors.

6. Charlie submitted a article for publication in the January 15, addition of "Readers' Digest".
7. Harold set at the desk and begun his paper that was dew tommorrow.
8. Jose' learned to talk english in a class that he took at midwest college.
9. Troy ran the marathon and 100 meter dash threw the javelin and discus and participated in the mile relay during the Spring Meet.
10. Last week the system analysts surveyed the employees; studied workflow in the plant; and are writing their report.

PART 4

Written Report Applications

CHAPTER:

CHAPTER

11 Business Research and Report Writing

Connie Cushing, CPA, Manager, O'Sullivan Hicks Patton, LLP

LET'S TALK BUSINESS As a tax manager in a CPA firm, I conduct research as an integral part of my day-to-day responsibilities. Tax laws and cases related to them sometimes change on a daily basis, so we must do research before we can give a client advice about a certain tax position. In addition, we have to stay on top of all changes in the tax law in order to make sure our clients are not paying excess taxes.

In this fast-moving, high technology society, it is imperative that CPA firms have online Internet access to a tax service that is updated daily. Knowing how to do effective, thorough research both online and by using printed

(Continued)

[LEARNING OBJECTIVES]

[1] IDENTIFY AND USE THE FIVE STEPS FOR CONDUCTING RESEARCH.

[2] DISTINGUISH BETWEEN FORMAL AND INFORMAL REPORTS.

[3] IDENTIFY THE TYPES OF INFORMAL REPORTS.

[4] DESCRIBE THE COMPONENTS OF A FORMAL REPORT.

[5] LIST THE ADVANTAGES OF CORRECT REPORT FORMATTING.

[6] WRITE FORMAL AND INFORMAL REPORTS.

tax service materials, law books, and tax books is very high in our criteria for job promotion. •

Research and report writing are activities common in business. As Connie Cushing indicates in Let's Talk Business, research helps her advise clients about tax issues. Research can have other purposes, too. It can be used to develop procedures, to test products, to explore markets, to gather opinions, or for numerous other purposes. The results of research may be reported orally or in writing, informally or formally.

[NOTE 11.1]
Research has many uses in business.

Regardless of their purpose or destination, reports must be based on thorough, accurate research. Because the information gathered through business research becomes the basis for decisions by managers, research reports must be written and formatted to ensure readability and understanding. This chapter, which builds on the communication basics introduced in earlier chapters, is devoted to discussing research techniques and report writing, including formatting. Techniques for making effective oral presentations are discussed in Chapters 14 and 15. Because visual aids may be used in both oral and written communication, that topic is covered separately, in Chapter 13.

Research Techniques

Learning Objective [1]
IDENTIFY AND USE THE FIVE STEPS FOR CONDUCTING RESEARCH.

The systematic procedures used to conduct a business study are called **research methods**. Those who expect to pursue careers in any business field should know how to plan and conduct a research project.

[NOTE 11.2]
There is a common, overall approach for conducting business research.

THE STEPS IN CONDUCTING RESEARCH

The five steps in conducting research are

[1] Plan the research.

[2] Gather information.

[3] Analyze the information.

[4] Determine solution(s).

[5] Write the report.

PLAN THE RESEARCH

Planning the research includes stating the problem, setting the boundaries, identifying and analyzing the audience, and deciding on the procedures to be followed.

Stating the Problem The **statement of the problem** is a clear, accurate, description of what is to be studied. Prior to finalizing the problem statement, managers or other key people might discuss what the research should accomplish or agree to conduct a preliminary investigation. Examining files, talking with employees, reading similar reports, speaking with vendors, or making inquiries are activities that could help the researcher(s) clarify what needs to be done. Here are examples of problem statements for studies:

[NOTE 11.3]
Start by stating the problem.

Discussions held before research begins help clarify project goals.

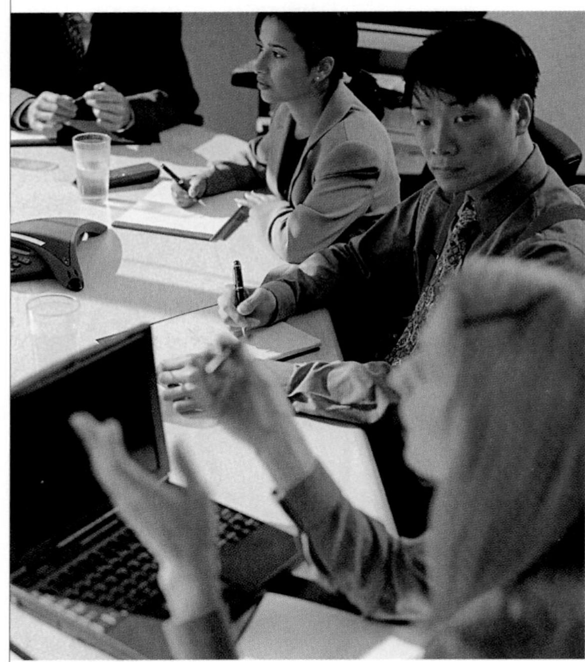

[1] To determine ways to improve the morale of ABC Company employees.

[2] To design a new procedure for processing online orders.

[3] What is the best location for cash registers?

[4] Should we replace paper towel dispensers with air dryers in all public restrooms?

[NOTE 11.4] Problem statements can use either the infinitive or the question form.

Notice that the first two examples are infinitive statements whereas the last two examples are pre-sented as questions. Either form is appropriate.

[NOTE 11.5] Set the research boundaries.

Setting the Boundaries of the Research Research needs to have boundaries. These boundaries are affected by the scope, time schedule, and budget for the project.

[NOTE 11.6] What factors will you research?

Scope The **scope** of the research is determined by the factors that will be studied. It is best to limit the amount of information you will gather to the most needed and most important factors. The factors for one of the problem statements given previously might look like this:

> **Statement of Problem:** To determine ways to improve the morale of ABC Company employees.
>
> Factors:
>
> [1] Salaries
> [2] Fringe benefits
> [3] Work assignments
> [4] Work hours
> [5] Evaluation procedures
> [6] Recognition programs

You could research many other factors relative to improving employee morale, and you might want to consider some of them later. For any one research project, however, a reasonable scope must be clearly defined.

Time Schedule The person who assigns the project and the person who conducts the research should agree on a completion date. The schedule is set by working back from the report deadline. The **time schedule** should show the major steps in the research and report writing process and when each is to be completed. Figure 11.1 illustrates a time schedule known as a **Gantt chart**.

[NOTE 11.7]
What time schedule will you follow?

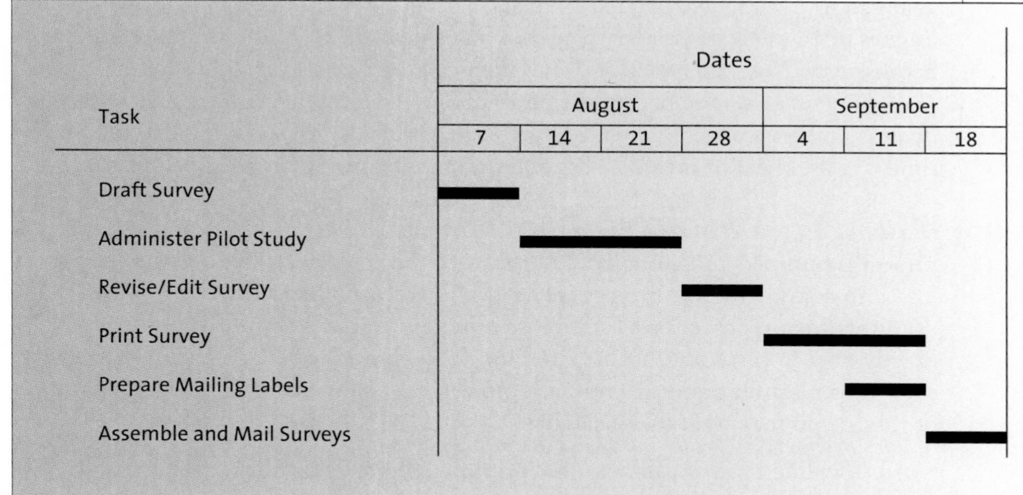

Figure 11.1
Gantt Chart

As you view the chart, notice that several tasks can be worked on at the same time. For example, you can prepare mailing labels while the survey document is being printed. Time schedules should include enough detail for everyone associated with the project to understand exactly what is to be done and when.

Budget All studies cost money. Even studies that are conducted within an organization will have some costs above normal operating expenses.

[NOTE 11.8]
How much will the research cost?

Dilbert

A large organization may use a charge-back system to bill one department for having work done by another. For example, if you are conducting a survey for the human resources department, the graphic arts department might charge your unit for printing the questionnaire and the final report. In addition, the information systems department might charge for processing the survey results. Other research costs could be incurred for items such as personnel time, supplies, and postage. All costs should be estimated and a budget approved before work begins.

[NOTE 11.9]
Analyze the receivers of the report.

Determining the Audience Effective communication depends on using the you–viewpoint in all written and oral messages. This is certainly true for written reports. The way in which you write the results of your research should be determined by your readers' knowledge, interests, opinions, and emotional reactions—the key factors in analyzing readers.

When there will be primary and secondary readers of a report, both should be analyzed. If, for example, you are a financial manager writing a report for which colleagues in the field are primary readers, you can use the technical language of finance because it will be understood by other financial managers. If members of the general management staff, members of the production management staff, general employees, or stockholders are secondary readers, you may want to define your terms the first time you use them or include a list of terms and definitions as an appendix.

[NOTE 11.10]
Decide on procedures.

Deciding on the Research Procedures Comprehensive research will result if the project is outlined and completed in a step-by-step sequence. The steps to be followed in completing the project are known as **research procedures**.

Deciding on procedures for each step in your research simply means deciding exactly how to carry out that step. Although the procedures you actually select will vary from research project to research project, the following can serve as an example of things you may wish to consider:

- Am I willing to invest the money and time required to gather current data?
- Will I use information that is already printed about the topic?
- Will I survey employees?
- Will I seek information from outside the company?
- Will I use a computer to gather or analyze the information?
- Will the report be printed internally or externally?

[NOTE 11.11]
Surveys must have validity and reliability.

When conducting research, you may want to seek the advice of one or more specialists. If, for example, you are going to use statistical procedures to analyze survey data, you could seek the help of a statistician. He or she can assist with sample selection and help ensure that your survey has validity and reliability. **Validity** means the survey measures what it intended to measure; **reliability** means the survey is likely to produce consistent results.

GATHER INFORMATION

[NOTE 11.12]
Information sources can be primary or secondary.

You may gather information for your research from one or more sources. There are two types of information sources: secondary and primary. **Secondary sources** of information are the published materials on the topic. **Primary sources** include individuals, company files, observations, and experiments.

If your research requires gathering information from both primary and secondary sources, gather secondary source information first. The published information may contain good ideas on what primary information you should gather and how to gather it.

[NOTE 11.13]
Secondary sources contain the published information about the topic.

Secondary Sources of Information Published materials on most topics are readily available in company, public, and college libraries. Experienced reference librarians can provide valuable assistance in finding published information that will be helpful in your research. They can direct you to print or electronic indexes, catalogs, reference books, government documents, computer databases, and other helpful secondary sources of information.

When gathering secondary information be sure to do a careful evaluation of the sources. Not all information found in print or available through the Internet is accurate. When examining a print source, consider the following items:

[NOTE 11.14]
Carefully evaluate all sources.

- *Timeliness.* Is the information current?
- *Relevance.* Is the information related to the specific topic I am researching?
- *Approach.* Is the work an opinion piece or a research report? Are opinions supported by facts or research? Is the research complete and thorough? Was appropriate methodology used to conduct the study? Is the research unbiased?
- *Outlet.* Is the publication reputable? Was a review process used to screen the work for publication? Who are the reviewers? What are their qualifications?
- *Author.* Is the author an authority in this particular area of research? What are his or her credentials and reputation in the field?

Since no one controls who posts what to the Internet, you'll want to consider the following if your secondary information source is a Web site:

- *Type/Purpose.* Is the site a personal page or one geared toward advocacy, marketing, information, or news? For help in distinguishing among the categories, consult the Harvard University Widener Library site at **http://www2.widener.edu/Wolfgram-Memorial-Library/webeval.htm.**
- *Sponsor.* Is the page owner a group, organization, institution, corporation, or government agency?
- *Perspective.* Do either the author or the sponsor bring a bias to what is posted at the site?
- *Author/Contact Information.* Who wrote or gathered the materials? What credentials does the person or group possess? Can the credentials be verified?
- *Completeness.* Does the site include up-to-date links to other relevant sites? Are links purely internal (same site), exclusively external (outside site), or mixed?
- *Attribution.* Is the information contained at the site original? If not, have the authors appropriately cited their sources?
- *Timeliness.* How current is the information? When was the site last updated?

Many university libraries offer advice to students about how to evaluate Web sites. In addition to the Widener Library site mentioned previously, you may find these sites useful:

http://thorplus.lib.purdue.edu/%7Etechman/eval.html
http://www.library.ucla.edu/libraries/college/instruct/web/critical.htm

Traditional Searches An assortment of reference materials can be used in conducting library research: handbooks, almanacs, yearbooks, encyclopedias, dictionaries, books, periodicals, reports, directories, government publications, and audiovisual materials. Figure 11.2 briefly explains each source.

[NOTE 11.15]
Reference librarians can assist you in locating print and electronic sources.

Computerized Searches Of particular value to businesspeople today are computerized searches of published information on a given topic. Most reference librarians

Figure 11.2
Traditional Reference Sources

Reference Sources Used in Conducting Research

Traditional Sources

Handbooks and Almanacs	When approaching a new subject, these sources can assist you in developing a brief topic overview. Topics covered by handbooks and almanacs include accounting, economics, finance, management, marketing, human resources, and so forth. Examples include the following: *AMA Management Handbook, Handbook for Business Writing, Handbook of Accounting and Auditing, The Real Estate Handbook, The World Almanac and Book of Facts,* and *Insurance Almanac.*
Yearbooks and Encyclopedias	Like handbooks and almanacs these reference materials cover a full range of business topics. Most yearbooks are published annually and include statistical information and important events during the year. Encyclopedias include histories of important events and people, definitions of terms, and a comprehensive coverage of various subjects. Examples include the following: *Business Statistics, Statistical Yearbook, Collier's Encyclopedia, Encyclopedia Americana, The Encyclopedia of Associations, Encyclopedia Britannica,* and *Encyclopedia of Business Information Sources.*
Dictionaries	Dictionaries provide brief definitions of key terms in fields such as accounting, economics, finance, management, marketing, human resources, and so forth. New buzzwords and jargon make dictionaries obsolete overnight. Examples include the following: *New Webster's Dictionary of the English Language, Webster's Unabridged Dictionary, Dictionary of Business and Management,* and *The Business Dictionary.*
Books	Hundreds of business books are published annually. Books range from etiquette to resume writing to telecommuting. Consult a book review publication for recommendations. Books used to locate books include the following: *Bibliographic Guide to Business and Economics, Subject Guide to Books in Print, Business Periodicals Index,* and *Publisher's Weekly.*
Periodical Literature	Thousands of periodicals are published annually worldwide. When searching for periodical literature, it is important to begin with a subject index. A subject index will provide you with lists of articles arranged by both broad and narrow subject headings. Periodicals are an important source of current information. Examples include the following: *Business Week, Forbes, Fortune, The Economist, Financial Times,* and *Wall Street Journal.*
Reports	Business reports are published for private, limited circulation and may be obtained directly from the company. Examples include the following: corporate annual reports, market research reports, and various census reports.
Directories	Business directories provide entries for companies, products, and individuals. Directories are considered essential for marketers and others who are prospecting. Examples include the following: *Directory of Directories, AT&T Toll Free 800 Directory, Mail Order Business Directory, Standard & Poor's 500 Directory,* and *Official Airline Guide.*

continued

Government Publications	The United States Government is one of the largest publishers of business information and should be a prime source in business research. The subject areas are varied. Examples of directories of government publications include the following: *Guide to Popular U.S. Government Publications, Directory of Government Document Collections & Librarians,* and *Free Publications From U.S. Government Agencies.*
Audiovisual Materials	Audiovisual materials include motion pictures, videocassettes, videodiscs, slides, filmstrips, transparencies, computer programs, and audiocassettes. Audiovisual materials are effective for making presentations. Examples of sources include the following: *Ambrose Video Publishing, Inc., AV Market Place, Books on Cassette,* and *Dartnell.*

Adapted from Ernest L. Maier, Anthony J. Faria, Peter Kaatyrude, Elizabeth Wood, *The Business Library and How to Use It,* Detroit, Mich.: Omnigraphics, Inc., 1996.

Figure 11.2 *Traditional Reference Sources Cont.*

can assist you in searches that quickly give you an up-to-date bibliography of reference materials on your topic. Some online sources also provide the full text of the articles they index.

Computerized sources can be categorized as either commercial or open access. As the name implies, **commercial sources** require users to pay for materials, which may be provided as a CD-ROM or online. Some of the more popular commercial sources of business information are listed in Figure 11.3. Many business periodicals, newspapers, and journals offer subscriptions to online versions of their publications. In addition, professional associations may make databases or other resources available to members either free or for a modest fee. Professional organizations may also sponsor newsgroups, listservs, or chat rooms where members can pose questions. Although these online forums can provide leads to reputable sources, they are seldom viewed as credible in and of themselves.

[NOTE 11.16]
Some computerized sources are free; others are fee-based.

Secondary research encompasses both traditional and electronic sources.

Figure 11.3
Commercial Sources of Computerized Business Information

ABI Inform
First Search (includes AcxiomBiz, Article First, Consumers Index, Wilson Business Abstracts, and WorldscopeS)
Business Reference Suite (includes *Business and Industry, Business and Management Practices,* and *TableBase*)
FEDSTATS
Global Access (formerly called Disclosure)
InfoTrac (includes General Business File ASAP)
LEXIS-NEXIS
Research Insight
RIA Checkpoint
Stat-USA
Statistical Universe

[NOTE 11.17]
Subject directories are similar to indexes in a book.

Open-access sources are available free to anyone who has access to the Web. Because anyone can publish anything and post it on the Web, finding good material related to your topic can be challenging unless you have a search strategy. Begin by using a **subject directory**, a hierarchically organized index of subject categories similar to those found in books. These indexes will help direct you to the Web site with information on your research topic.

[NOTE 11.18]
Search engines are often referred to as *spiders* or *crawlers*.

Once the appropriate subject is identified, an in-depth search can be completed using a search engine. **Search engines**, also referred to as *spiders* or *crawlers,* require the use of keywords pertinent to your area of research. Although all search engines perform the same task, it is unlikely that any two will produce identical results. If you do not obtain the results you want from one search engine, try others.

[NOTE 11.19]
Multithreaded or "meta" search engines search multiple databases simultaneously.

Because of the growth in search engines, **multithreaded**, or "**meta**," search engines have been developed. Users enter their query only once, and the engine searches multiple databases concurrently.

Figure 11.4 lists some of the search engines, metasearch engines, and directories available on the Internet. More information about these and similar sources may be found at sites such as Search Engine Watch, **http://www.searchenginewatch.com**, or Search Engine Showdown, **http://www.searchengineshowdown.com**. As Tracy Marks notes in the following Communication Quote, to search these or other sources effec-

COMMUNICATION QUOTE

Hints for Searching the Internet

In order to search effectively, we have to be able to define what we are seeking and to develop the discipline to not be distracted by the hundreds of fascinating but irrelevant URLs we find along the way. But because the Net is so vast and the satisfactions of passive surfing are so tempting, it is easy for us as trainers and for our students to lose our own center of gravity and to become lost in the waves rather than sail our own ships through them.

Tracy Marks, Windweaver Web Resources at http://www.windweaver.com/index.htm.

tively and efficiently, you must clearly define the research topic. Doing so will help you select the keywords you will use during your search. Most computer searches follow the principles of Boolean logic, which relies on three operators: *OR, AND,* and *NOT.* Search engine sites typically offer suggestions on how to use these operators effectively. In addition, the site at **http://www.albany.edu/library/internet/boolean/html** offers an easy-to-understand explanation of Boolean logic and Internet searches.

Figure 11.4
Search Engines, Metasearch Engines, and Directories

Search Engines

Alta Vista	**http://www.altavista.com/**
Anzwers.com	**http://www.anzwers.com/**
Ask Jeeves	**http://www.aj.com/**
Direct Hit	**http://www.directhit.com/**
DisInformation	**http://www.disinfo.com/**
*Excite	**http://www.excite.com/**
Fast Search	**http://www.ussc.alltheweb.com/**
Google	**http://www.google.com/**
GovBot	**http://ciir2.cs.umass.edu/Govbot/**
HotBot	**http://hotbot.lycos.com/**
*Infoseek	**http://infoseek.go.com/**
*Look Smart	**http://www.looksmart.com/**
*Lycos	**http://www.lycos.com/**
*Magellan	**http://magellan.excite.com/**
MSN Search	**http://search.msn.com/**
Northern Light	**http://www.northernlight.com/**
*Snap	**http://www.snap.com/**
WebCrawler	**http://www.webcrawler.com/**
*Yahoo!	**http://www.yahoo.com/**

Metasearch Engines

Debriefing	**http://www.debriefing.com/**
Direct Search	**http://gwis2.circ.gwu.edu/~gprice/direct.htm**
DogPile	**http://www.dogpile.com/**
Galaxy	**http://galaxy.einet.net/search.html**
Highway 61	**http://www.highway61.com/**
Inference Find	**http://www.infind.com/**
Internet Sleuth	**http://www.thebighub.com/**
Mamma	**http://www.mamma.com/**
MatchSite	**http://www.matchsite.com/**
MetaCrawler	**http://www.go2net.com/index.html**
MetaFind	**http://www.metacrawler.com/index_metafind.html**
ProFusion	**http://www.profusion.com/**
SavvySearch	**http://savvy.search.com/**

Directories

About.Com	**http://www.about.com/**
Argus Clearinghouse	**http://www.clearinghouse.net/index.html**
OneKey	**http://www.onekey.com/**
Open Directory	**http://dmoz.org/**
WWW Virtual Library	**http://vlib.org/**

*Search engines that also have directories.

When you find a good source, either record the Universal Resource Locator (URL) or save it as a bookmark on your browser. Keep all of your bookmarks in a booklist that acts just like your own personal menu.

[NOTE 11.20] Accurately cite all sources.

Be sure that you get complete bibliographic information on published materials while you work with them so that it will be available for footnotes and the bibliography. Most published materials are copyrighted. You may have to obtain permission to use such information, and you will be required to give credit to the originator as the source. **Plagiarism** is using someone else's ideas or words without giving him or her credit. To avoid plagiarism you must correctly document information found in all data sources including the Web. Information on documenting sources is given in Appendix B. Plagiarism and paraphrasing are also discussed in the Copyright and Fair-Use Communication section of Chapter 5.

[NOTE 11.21] Primary sources provide unpublished information on the topic.

[NOTE 11.22] Surveying people is a way to get primary information.

Primary Sources of Information Your research may require gathering original information—information about your topic that has not been previously published. This primary information may come from an examination of original company records, a survey of knowledgeable individuals, a focus group, an observation of an activity, or an experiment.

Original records and files are obvious sources of historical information that may be helpful to you. Other sources of primary information—surveys, focus groups, observations, and experiments—may not be as obvious.

[NOTE 11.23] Each survey method has advantages and disadvantages.

Surveys To gather opinions and facts from individuals, you can survey them. Surveys can be conducted in person, by telephone, by mail, or electronically. Each method has advantages and disadvantages.

Compared with other survey methods, in-person interviews are expensive. Personnel must be trained, scheduling and conducting the interviews is time-consuming, and transportation can be costly. The process does, however, produce the most in-depth responses.

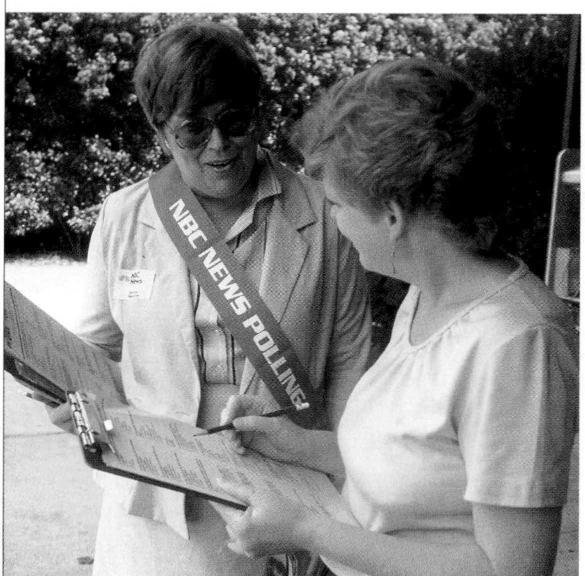

Trained personnel conduct in-person surveys.

Telephone surveys can be conducted fairly quickly and can be relatively inexpensive if done within a local calling range. Those who conduct the interviews generally read from a script and are cautioned not to deviate from it, so training costs are minimized. Response rates for telephone surveys will generally be higher than for those conducted by mail, but establishing credibility can be challenging in an era when telemarketing has become commonplace.

Because they require fewer people to conduct them, mail surveys are generally less expensive than telephone or face-to-face surveys. The process is quite slow; it can take months to get an acceptable number of responses, even with follow-up mailings to those who don't respond to the initial mailing.

Electronic surveys may be conducted online through a Web site or via e-mail. In a Web-based survey, e-mail is sent to potential respondents inviting them to complete the survey located at a particular URL. This method enables the researcher to incorporate color, graphics, and audio features into the survey. In addition, the software used to create the survey can be programmed to collect data automatically and to generate ongoing data summaries. The disadvantage of this method is that potential respondents who have e-mail without access to the Web could not respond. See Figure 11.5 for an example of an online questionnaire used by AmericanWest Bank to get feedback from its customers.

[NOTE 11.24]
E-mail and Web-based surveys are becoming popular.

The simplest way to conduct an e-mail survey is to embed the questions into a message that is sent to potential respondents. Receivers are told to use the reply function and answer the questions as they scroll through the message. The simplicity of this method is offset by the limits placed on the researcher's ability to incorporate emphasis techniques such as the type of font and size variations, color, and graphics into the document. Pretesting the survey is essential to ensure alignment is maintained through transmission and to verify that entering a response will not adversely affect the format of subsequent items.

One way to overcome concerns about format is to send the survey as an e-mail attachment. The respondent can download the attachment and use a word processing program to respond. The completed survey can then be sent as an e-mail attachment to a "reply" message. The number and complexity of steps in this process may deter people from responding. Another, perhaps stronger, deterrent is the respondent's fear of infecting his or her computer with a virus passed through an e-mail attachment.

Regardless of whether e-mail surveys are embedded or attached, their response rate could be negatively affected by the lack of anonymity associated with e-mail transmissions. In addition, e-mail is very easy to ignore or delete, especially if it spans multiple screens.

When designing a questionnaire, be sure to follow the principles of business communication. The following guidelines may also be useful:

[NOTE 11.25]
Questionnaires used in surveys should be developed carefully.

[1] *Develop the survey questions from the factors being studied.* In a survey to assess employee morale, you might develop questions to seek opinions or facts about employee salaries, fringe benefits, work hours, and so forth.

[2] *Sequence questions appropriately.* Start your questionnaire with easy questions that will encourage respondents to continue. Group similar topics. For example, put all questions on salaries in the same section. Arrange questions in logical order—the way people commonly think of the topics.

Figure 11.5
Online Questionnaire

AmericanWest Bank

AMERICANWEST ON-LINE CUSTOMER SURVEY

We want our service to be the best it can be.

At AmericanWest Bank we are continually looking for ways to improve our service. We would like to hear from you. If you have an idea for a new or improved service or a suggestion on how we can serve you better, please let us know.

Thank you for for taking a minute to fill out our On-Line Survey. Your answers and opinions will help us to further improve the quality of service you expect and deserve. Please know the results of this survey are for our information and will be kept confidential.

Thanks again.

1. Please tell us how satisfied you are with the service you receive from AmericanWest Bank:
   Not at all / Occasionally / Fair / Good / Very Good

2. Do you use an ATM? Yes / No
3. Do you know that you can ask for cash back at the grocery store when using our VISA Debit Card? Yes / No
4. Do you have a VISA Debit Card? Yes / No
5. If not, would you like one? Yes / No
6. Is *AmericanWest Bank* your Primary Financial Institution? Yes / No
7. Are our tellers courteous and friendly? Yes / No
8. Did our new accounts people offer you more services than you asked for? Yes / No
9. Do you know that we have an investment counselor available? Yes / No
10. If we offered Home Banking by computer, would you use it? Yes / No
11. If we offered a Bill Paying Service, would you use it? Yes / No
12. Do you know that you can access your account information by our Telebank phone number 24 hours a day? Yes / No
13. Were you aware that *AmericanWest Bank* offers all types of Commercial, Agricultural, Consumer, and Real Estate loans? Yes / No
14. Do you feel that our service is worth recommending to others? Yes / No

I would like to recognize ______
for the following example of his/her First Class Service:

The Branch where I bank is:

Main Street, WW **Eastgate, WW** **Waitsburg** **Dayton**

Name		Daytime Phone	
Email Address		Address	
City, State, Zip			

Thank you again for taking a moment to fill out our On-line Survey. When you are satisfied with the answers you've provided, click the "send survey" button. If you wish to start again, just use the reset button.

Send Survey | Reset Form

Equal Housing Lender / Member **FDIC** and of the communities we serve.

Site designed and maintained by Dennis Jones for Madison Avenue West.
Direct questions or comments about this site to webmaster@wallawallawa.com

Reprinted with permission of American West Bank, Walla Walla, WA.

[3] *Use clear questions.* Phrase each item so that it will be interpreted uniformly by all respondents. A question such as, "What kind of car do you own?" is vague. Based on the respondents' interpretations, the answers could be *convertible, Chevrolet, sports, foreign,* and so on. An example of a clearer way to obtain specific information is, "Please indicate the name of the manufacturer of the car you drive most often."

[4] *Ask only for relevant demographic data.* If factors such as age, gender, marital status, income, and so on won't be used in your analysis, don't ask respondents to provide the data.

[5] *Avoid leading questions.* Leading questions influence readers to give a biased answer. Questions such as, "Would it be a good idea to improve the arrangement of our work hours?" will likely be biased toward a yes answer. A better method would be to ask the respondent to rate his or her satisfaction with current work hours. The rating could be along a numeric (e.g., 5 high, 1 low) or verbal (e.g., very satisfactory, satisfactory, unsatisfactory, or very unsatisfactory) indicator known as a **Likert scale**.

[NOTE 11.26]
Leading questions produce biased responses.

[6] *Provide for all possible responses in the answer options.* When it is not possible to be all inclusive, include an "other" option and encourage respondents to write an explanation.

[7] *Avoid skip-and-jump directions.* For example, "If your answer to Question 9 is no, skip Questions 10, 11, and 12 and go directly to Question 13. If your answer is yes, also answer Question 10, but skip 11 and 12 if you do not have children."

[8] *Choose the appropriate type of question.* Forced-answer questions will outnumber open-ended questions in mail, telephone, and electronic surveys; the opposite is true in face-to-face interviews. Open-ended questions let respondents answer in their own words. These kinds of questions must be worded carefully in order to obtain the desired information. Data obtained through open-ended questions can be difficult to interpret and analyze, which is why forced-answer questions are used wherever possible. In the forced-answer question style, the researcher provides possible answers to the questions, and the respondents choose among the alternatives. The possible answers should be discrete; that is, use 25–29, 30–34, 35–39 instead of 25–30, 30–35, 35–40. Provide lines or boxes for easy check-mark answers. The lines or boxes for the responses should precede the possible answers.

[NOTE 11.27]
The two basic types of questions are open-ended and forced-answer.

Once the survey has been drafted, field test or "pilot" it. The feedback you get from this process will assist you in revising the document prior to distribution.

Brief, attractively designed documents accompanied by a message that explains the purpose of the survey help to convey a professional image and encourage receivers to respond. One sheet of paper (8½ × 11, 11 × 14, or 17 × 11) printed on both sides and folded to resemble four "book" pages is more inviting than four single-sided, stapled pages. Including a confidentiality statement similar to that shown in Figure 11.6 also encourages receivers to reply and enables the researcher to code the questionnaires so that reminders or follow-up requests can be sent to those who do not respond.

[NOTE 11.28]
Questionnaires should encourage response.

To save time and money, researchers usually send surveys to a few people who are representative of a larger group. This type of survey is called a **sample survey**. A

[NOTE 11.29]
Surveys are usually conducted using samples.

Figure 11.6
Confidentiality Statement

No. *56*

Your individual responses will be kept confidential; data will be reported only in the aggregate. The number on this form will be used only to follow up with nonrespondents. Once an acceptable number of responses has been received, all documents linking surveys to respondents will be destroyed.

statistician can help determine how to select the sample, how many surveys to distribute, and the minimum number of responses necessary to draw conclusions about the entire group from responses provided by the sample.

[NOTE 11.30]
Focus groups solicit qualitative data.

Focus Groups When you are seeking ideas or feedback in qualitative rather than quantitative format, focus groups are an appropriate research method. These groups, frequently used in market research, involve 6 to 12 participants and a moderator. Clearly defined research objectives; unbiased, randomly selected participants; and a trained moderator are critical success factors. A comfortable site that creates a relaxed atmosphere also contributes to success.

Under the guidance of the moderator, the group discusses a series of ideas or issues—the focus. The moderator must ensure that everyone's thoughts are heard and that no one is influenced by others in the group. The task of keeping records also falls to the moderator. Note-taking is kept to a minimum during the session so that the moderator can concentrate on what is being said and keep the discussion flowing in an appropriate direction. Immediately after the session, he or she will summarize the positive and negative points that arose during the discussion. This information will be used when the moderator prepares his or her report.

Although most focus groups are in-person events, online focus groups are possible. The technique is fairly new, however; and, as detailed in the Communication Note on page 311, several questions about it are yet to be answered.

[NOTE 11.31]
Observations may be used to gather primary information.

Observations Observation is another way to gather primary information for a research project. This technique involves one or more observers watching and recording facts about an activity. Although the observation technique can incur high personnel costs, it is a way to obtain precise information.

A common use of the observation technique is to gather information on how a worker operates a machine in a factory. The worker's repetitive movements might be timed, production records maintained, and conclusions drawn about the efficiency of the procedures. Similarly, observers might be posted in selected areas of cities to count out-of-state cars in order to get a measure of tourist traffic. Many managers and employers use informal observation to obtain information that is helpful to them in performing their jobs. This kind of information, although not scientifically obtained, can be of value in a limited way.

[NOTE 11.32]
The observation technique must be carefully controlled.

The observation technique requires careful control. All observers must look for the same thing and record their observations in the same way for the information to be of comparative value. Proper control requires that observers and subjects do not interact.

[NOTE 11.33]
Experiments may be conducted to gather primary information.

Experiments The last way to gather primary information for a research project is the experiment. Experiments in business are usually used to compare two ways of

COMMUNICATION NOTE

Online Focus Groups

Judith Langer is president of Langer Associates, Inc., a qualitative research firm that has conducted some online research and plans to investigate the medium more. While recognizing that online focus groups have advantages, Langer acknowledges that questions need to be answered through further research. Among the questions she raises are these:

- Are respondents who they really say they are? Is the information they provide when signing up on the database or at the time of screening for a particular focus group true? How can we be sure that someone else hasn't substituted for them?
- How often should online respondents participate? Some may be signing up regularly because they enjoy the experience and/or the incentives.
- Are online focus groups less likely to be free of group dynamics bias than in-person ones, or do they just have different dynamics?
- Does the anonymity of a screen name make online respondents more honest, saying what's really on their minds rather than being polite? Are they more open about sensitive subjects? And is the bluntness and so-called *flaming* in chat rooms true candor or just rudeness?
- Are focus groups in this interactive medium truly interactive? How much moderator-respondent and respondent-respondent interaction really takes place if respondents are busy typing?
- Can researchers and observers gain a clear sense of individual respondents the way they can in physical observation?
- What ways can be found to encourage respondents to give longer answers rather than one- and two-sentence replies?
- How much is lost by the absence of body language and vocal inflection?

Taken from Judith Langer, "'On' and 'Offline' Focus Groups: Claims, Questions," Marketing News *34 (12), June 5, 2000, p. H38.*

doing something so that the better way can be identified. For example, employees in one plant might be placed on a four-day work week, while employees in another plant would be kept on a five-day work week. The employees in the two plants would then be observed and surveyed periodically to determine their productivity and their satisfaction with work hours.

Another approach would be to conduct a presurvey and a postsurvey of a group of employees that you plan to change from a five-day work week to a four-day work week. In this approach, employees who are on a five-day work week could be asked a series of questions about the effect their work schedule has on their productivity and job satisfaction. Then their five-day work week would be changed to a four-day work week. After three months pass, the employees would be asked the same set of questions they were asked before their work schedule was changed. Then the two sets of answers would be compared.

Experiments are not as common in business as they are in scientific laboratories, but experiments do have their uses. In an experiment, you can easily compare the old way with the new way, compare Method A with Method B, or test-market a new product. Experiments can be expensive. Carefully designed and controlled experiments, however, have provided businesspersons with much valuable information.

[NOTE 11.34]
Experiments are a good way to make comparisons.

ANALYZE THE INFORMATION

[NOTE 11.35] Analysis may be a short and clear or a long and complex process.

Once you have planned your research and gathered information, you are ready to begin your analysis. The information you gathered may speak for itself. It may clearly say yes to adopting a new procedure or product. The information you gathered may clearly say that employees overwhelmingly prefer the four-day to the five-day work week. Under these circumstances, the analysis may take only a few minutes. On the other hand, you may have gathered a great amount of complex information. It may take you days, weeks, or months to complete the analysis.

[NOTE 11.36] Analysis should be objective.

The word **analysis** means to look at the parts of things separately or in relationship to the whole. The various parts of your information are compared and contrasted in an effort to try to develop new or better ideas. Separate facts and figures are interpreted by explaining what they mean—what significance they have. You will not want personal bias of any kind to enter into the analysis. Use your brain power—objectively and unemotionally.

For example, if you were doing research to determine which computer to buy for your office, you would collect information on the type of work you are currently doing and the kinds of work you want to do. Next you would gather information on computers, including cost, software compatibility, speed of operation, machine capacity, machine dependability, maintenance availability, potential for upgrading, and other factors. Then you would compare the machines to determine how well they can do what you want done, what their potential is, how dependable they are, and so on. Once you have completed the analysis, you would be ready to determine solutions.

DETERMINE SOLUTION(S)

Based on your analysis, you will be ready to offer a solution or solutions to the problem you have been researching. Your solution will be framed as conclusions and recommendations.

[NOTE 11.37] Solutions may consist of conclusions and recommendations.

A **conclusion** is an inference drawn from the facts; it is a reasoned judgment that you make from your analysis. If you were to select the most important ideas suggested by your analysis, these ideas would be your conclusions. Based on your conclusions, you could state the research answer or **recommendation**—the research solution. In formal studies and reports, you can draw conclusions from your analysis and state them separately from the recommendation(s).

The conclusions and recommendations must be based on the findings and your objective analysis, not your personal opinion of what a good solution would be. Your conclusions and recommendations for a report might look like this:

Conclusions:

[1] Procedure B appears significantly more cost-effective than Procedure A in the two installations studied.

[2] Dependable equipment for implementing Procedure B on a wide-scale basis is not currently available.

[3] The XYZ Manufacturing Company currently has in stock 20 Model 3CA machines that can be used to implement Procedure B.

[4] The XYZ Manufacturing Company projects that it will have 500 Model 3CAs available within six months.

Recommendations:

[1] Immediately lease the 20 Model 3CAs from XYZ and continue to compare Procedure A with Procedure B for three more months.

[2] Enter an option to purchase 500 Model 3CAs from the XYZ Manufacturing Company.

[3] If the additional research continues to show that Procedure B is significantly more cost-effective than Procedure A, exercise the option with XYZ to purchase the 500 Model 3CAs.

WRITE THE REPORT

The final step in a research project is to write the report. This is an important step because you will want to present your results effectively. The writing process for reports parallels that for other messages. You will draft, revise, and edit your report before submitting it.

[NOTE 11.38]
Reports must be written to be readable and understandable.

The time and effort spent in researching and writing a report are wasted unless the report is read and understood. The probability that a report will be read and understood is increased when certain principles of formatting are followed. The remainder of this chapter discusses the various report types and the formatting principles to follow for effective report preparation.

Learning Objective [2]
DISTINGUISH BETWEEN FORMAL AND INFORMAL REPORTS.

Learning Objective [6]
WRITE FORMAL AND INFORMAL REPORTS.

Report Types and Characteristics

Written reports vary from short, informal reports to long, formal reports. The language can vary from conversational, first-person language to highly structured, third-person language. This section provides a brief introduction to informal and formal reports; each type is then discussed individually.

[NOTE 11.39]
Written reports may be formal or informal.

Informal reports are generally brief. They can consist of a body and a title page or of a body only; informal reports are often formatted as memos or letters. **Memo reports** communicate information to individuals within an organization. This style is used primarily for reporting routine information concerning day-to-day operations or to provide a written record. **Letter reports** use a letter format to present information and make recommendations to individuals outside an organization; a subject line may be used to identify the topic of the report. A report in letter format is shown in Figure 11.7. When formatted as correspondence, informal reports use side headings to guide the reader from topic to topic. This type of report will not contain graphic aids or draw on material from secondary sources. Informal reports are usually written in the first person (I recommend that . . .).

[NOTE 11.40]
Informal reports are shorter and less structured than formal reports.

A **formal report** may consist of all or some of the following parts: title page, authorization message, transmittal message, table of contents, list of illustrations, abstract, body, glossary, appendix, and bibliography. The body of the report will span several pages and include multiple levels of headings. Content could be drawn from primary and/or secondary sources. Visual aids assist readers to interpret information presented as text. Formal reports are usually written in the third person (It is recommended that . . .). Recent trends, however, suggest that informality is acceptable in formal reports. The degree of formality is determined after the report originator has analyzed the receiver.

Figure 11.7
Letter Report

JULIA'S
1428 Riverside Road
Waco, TX 76708-2142
Telephone (817) 555-4281
Fax (817) 555-8364

To Our Shareholders:

JULIA'S achieved record sales during fiscal 1999. The company's sales increased 7.8% to a record $108 million. Our earnings per share were $.57 in fiscal 1999 compared to $.45 in fiscal 1998. Our earnings increase can be attributed to increased sales, decreased expenses in many stores, and improved marketing. Fiscal 1999 includes a charge of $.07 per share for the write-off of deferred financing and other costs associated with a previous banking agreement.

Growth and Expansion

We continued our program of expansion and renovation to position us to gain greater market share. During the year, we opened 18 new stores and renovated 11 of our older stores. Our expenditures on stores accounted for most of our $3.9 million of capital expenditures. As a result of these activities, we ended the year with 212 stores.

For fiscal 2000, we plan to spend $6.9 million on capital improvements, of which over 60% will be spent on our store base. We expect to open 30 new stores and renovate 15 of our older stores. We have already signed leases for 12 new stores. We expect these new and renovated stores to significantly increase our income in the future.

Operational Developments

During fiscal 1999, we reevaluated store staffing to reflect the level of business activity and to simplify operating procedures. In the benefits area, we reduced

continued

Informal Written Reports

Learning Objective [3]
IDENTIFY THE TYPES OF INFORMAL REPORTS.

Learning Objective [6]
WRITE FORMAL AND INFORMAL REPORTS.

In business, the informal report is used much more frequently than the formal report. There are many different types of informal reports; three of the most common—progress, periodic, and technical—are discussed in the following sections.

PROGRESS REPORTS

[NOTE 11.41]
Significant events and changes in a project are reported in a progress report.

A **progress report** (also called a *status report*) is used to inform readers about the status of a particular project. The report assists managers in monitoring and making decisions about the project. The report should inform the reader about the work that has been accomplished, the work that is being done currently, and the work that is scheduled to be done in the next reporting period. Any significant progress or problems should be discussed in the report. The frequency of the reports will depend on the type or nature of the project being discussed. An example of a progress report is shown in Figure 11.8 on page 316.

workers' compensation costs by implementing a new self-insurance program. As we move into fiscal 2000, we have reincorporated the Company from Delaware to Texas, which will reduce our state tax burden.

Marketing Developments

We are planning to source more of our private label abroad to enhance our markup while offering our customers more value. We are also investigating the latest computer-aided design technology to increase the effectiveness and productivity of our company.

During 1999, we implemented our style locator program, which allows our stores to better serve our customers. Using our point-of-sale terminals, our associates can locate out-of-stock merchandise for our customer in another store and send the item directly to the customer.

Outlook

We expect 2000 to be another year of intense competition. Consumers will remain focused on value, seeking the best quality and price they can find. We will continue our aggressive efforts to win market share from our competitors and to reduce our cost structure.

Sincerely,

Julia Swanson

Julia Swanson

President and CEO

Figure 11.7
Letter Report Cont.

PERIODIC REPORTS

A **periodic report** provides managers with statistical information at regularly scheduled intervals. These intervals may be daily, weekly, monthly, quarterly, or annually. Periodic reports follow no set format; many organizations use preprinted forms. A form used to indicate the security status of facilities is shown in Figure 11.9 on page 317.

TECHNICAL REPORTS

A **technical report** conveys specialized or scientific information. There are no standard formats or organizational plans for technical reports. However, organizations will often specify particular formats and plans to be used for internal reports. Standardized formats make it easy for readers to scan reports for information of particular interest to them. An example of a technical report in memo format is shown in Figure 11.10 on page 318.

Technical terms need not be defined when a technical report is prepared for someone familiar with the terminology. If the reader does not have the appropriate technical expertise, however, words used in the report must be clarified. A good rule to follow is to remember the principles of business communication discussed in Chapter 4.

[NOTE 11.42]
Technical terms must be defined if they are likely to be misunderstood by the reader.

Figure 11.8
Progress Report

Subject: Project Status
Date: August 9, 2000
To: John Thompson
Nursing Home Administrator
From: Roger Outland RO
Facilities Manager

The following is the status of work items you requested:

1. **Askin Laundry**
   New washing machines have been installed. New dryers are scheduled to arrive August 15 and will be installed the following week. Interior walls have been painted. New flooring will be laid before dryers are installed.

2. **Blackburn Wing Renovation**
   Jones Construction Company of Bellville is the contractor. The project will span nine months, due to the coordination required to minimize disruption. Work on Phase I began June 3, 2000. Work is progressing with few problems.

3. **Miller Recreation Center**
   Exterior painting has been delayed due to weather conditions. Interior painting is complete. The trees (Leland Cypress) have been planted on the north and west sides. Carpeting of the floor is complete.

4. **Winslow Dining**
   Windows have been replaced, and window a/c units have been reinstalled. This project is complete.

Learning Objective [4]
DESCRIBE THE COMPONENTS OF A FORMAL REPORT.

Formal Written Reports

[NOTE 11.43] A formal report normally is written for upper management.

A formal report is prepared for and read by individuals in top levels of management and possibly individuals outside the writer's organization. It may take from several weeks to several months to research and write the report. These activities can be completed by one person or by a team.

[NOTE 11.44] Formal reports generally have preliminary, body, and supplementary sections.

A formal report generally contains three major divisions: the preliminary section, the body, and the supplementary section. A formal report may contain all or some of the following parts:

Parts of Formal Reports

[1] Preliminary Section

a. Title Page
b. Letter or Memo of Transmittal
c. Table of Contents

DAILY SECURITY CHECK OF FACILITIES		
FAIRCHILD, INC.		
FACILITY	**TIME**	**RESULTS**
Conference Room		
Dining Area		
Human Resources		
Accounting		
Purchasing		
Advertising		
Laboratory		
Assembly Room		
Warehouse #1		
Warehouse #2		
Warehouse #3		
Parking Lot		
OFFICER'S NAME		
OFFICER'S ID NO.		
DATE		
OTHER INFO.		

Figure 11.9
Periodic Report

Parts of Formal Reports (*continued*)

d. List of Illustrations
e. Executive Summary

[2] Body

a. Introduction
b. Procedures
c. Findings
d. Analysis
e. Conclusions
f. Recommendations

[3] Supplementary Section

a. Glossary
b. Appendix
c. Bibliography

Figure 11.10
Technical Report

ELECTRICAL CONTRACTING
1556 B EAST EMMA AVE., SPRINGDALE, ARKANSAS 72784
Telephone (501) 555-9393 Fax (501) 555-2718

TO: Ralph Mustain
FROM: Robert Hess RH
DATE: November 18, 200–
SUBJECT: Status of the Seabolt Farms Project

The Seabolt Farms Project, which began on July 1, is nearing completion. The December 15 deadline should be met if the supplies arrive within a week.

Pickens Supply has assured me that the following supplies will be delivered by November 21:

1 100A 30 4wire Main Circuit Breaker 42 slot Nema
1 120/208Volt Panel
2 3Pole 50AMP Bolt In Breakers
2 60AMP 3Pole 3Fuse 250Volt Nema 1 Heavy Duty Disconnect
6 40AMP FRN Fuses
2 1" Offset Nipples

Marc Schecter at Paris Supply informed me that the following materials were shipped on November 17 and should arrive today or tomorrow:

200' 3/4" EMT Conduit

200' 3/4" EMT Conduit
500' #8 THHN Copper Wire
20 3/4 1-hole Straps
1 #10 x 1" Plastic Anchor Kit
4 3/4 EMT Compression Connectors
20 3/4 EMT Compression Couplings
2 3/4 LB Condulets

I will need to pull one worker from David Waldrop's crew and one worker from Ray Rumfelt's crew next week. I will inform Ramona of the crew changes so that she can transfer the charges to the Seabolt project.

ev

c: Ramona Newberry
Ray Rumfelt
David Waldrop

Figure 11.13 (see pages 328–329) contains an actual business report that features many of the parts described in the following sections. Although the report's authors adopted a format different from the one described in this chapter, the document is visually appealing and easy to follow; the style is consistent throughout. Appendix C contains a report that illustrates the content and format guidelines described in this chapter. This report is also visually appealing and formatted for readability. Although different in style, the reports have one thing in common—both were written to meet the needs of their audience.

PRELIMINARY SECTION

The **preliminary section** contains all the parts of a report that precede the body. The specific preliminary pages included in the report will vary with the formality of the report. A discussion of the individual parts follows.

Title Page A **title page** typically contains the title of the report; the writer's name, title, and department; and the date of submission. The name of the person or company receiving the report is used when reports are prepared for clients or others outside the organization. The title should indicate the purpose and content of the report.

[NOTE 11.45]
All formal reports should contain a title page.

Some organizations have specific guidelines for the preparation of title pages; others permit artistic freedom. If specific guidelines do not exist, the traditional format may be the best choice. In traditional format, each line on the title page is centered horizontally with equal vertical spacing between items. Titles containing more than one line are single spaced. The title should be all capitals; other lines may be either all capitals or initial capitals.

Letter or Memo of Transmittal The **letter** or **memo of transmittal**, if used, is written by the report writer and is used to introduce the report to the reader. A report to readers outside the organization would contain a letter, whereas reports for internal use would contain a memo. In more formal reports, a preface or foreword may be used.

[NOTE 11.46]
A letter or memo of transmittal contains items you would tell the reader if you were to deliver the report personally.

The letter or memo of transmittal should be concise and may be subjective—that is, the writer may offer a suggestion or opinion not supported by data. It may contain personal comments. The letter or memo may also refer readers to parts of the report of special interest or suggest special uses of the information. In general, any item worthy of discussion may be included in the letter or memo of transmittal. The message typically ends with a statement expressing appreciation for the opportunity to participate in the project.

Table of Contents A **table of contents** lists all major sections that follow it and the page on which each begins. Its purpose is to aid the reader in quickly locating specific information in the report. A table of contents normally is not used in reports of fewer than five pages. Section heads should be listed exactly as they appear in the body and should be connected to the page number by dot leaders (horizontally spaced periods). Page numbers are optional for subheadings. The table of contents normally is prepared after the report is typed or printed in its final form.

[NOTE 11.47]
Use a table of contents only when a report exceeds four pages.

[NOTE 11.48] A list of illustrations summarizes the visual aids used in the report.

List of Illustrations Visual aids are identified in a **list of illustrations**. The list may be on the same page as the table of contents, or it may begin on the page following the table of contents if the report contains more than four illustrations. The list of illustrations uses the same format as the table of contents, with illustration captions instead of section heads. A report may group all visual aids into one list of illustrations, or it may group each type (table, chart, graph, etc.) separately. This section is normally prepared after the report is typed or printed in its final form.

[NOTE 11.49] An executive summary is a capsule form of the report.

Executive Summary An **executive summary** is a brief version of the report; it restates each section of the report in abbreviated form with an emphasis on findings, conclusions, and recommendations. Other common names for an executive summary are *summary, abstract, overview,* and *synopsis.*

The summary, which is approximately 10 percent of the length of the report up to a limit of two single-spaced pages, saves readers time by providing an overview of its contents. Reports that include a synopsis in the letter of transmittal generally do not contain an executive summary. Figure 11.11 illustrates an executive summary.

BODY

[NOTE 11.50] The body of a report may use the direct or the indirect approach.

Most formal reports will contain all the information presented in the sections discussed in this part of the chapter; however, some of the sections may be combined. The material in the body may be presented using the direct or the indirect approach. The conclusions, recommendations, or both come at the beginning of the body when the direct approach is used; they come at the end of the body in the indirect approach.

[NOTE 11.51] The introduction assists the reader in understanding the rest of the report.

Introduction The **introduction** provides adequate background concerning the study so that the reader can understand the scope and sequence of the report.

[NOTE 11.52] The background sets the context for the report.

Background The introduction often begins with the **background**, a general description of the problem that was studied and the main issues involved in it. The background leads to the statement of the problem.

[NOTE 11.53] The specific topic of the study is given in the statement of the problem.

Statement of the Problem The **statement of the problem** clearly identifies the specific problem that was researched. The statement of the problem should be brief but informative.

[NOTE 11.54] The purpose provides the reason for the study.

Purpose of the Study The **purpose of the study** indicates why the study was conducted. The purpose should help convince the reader of the worthiness of the report. The purpose may be stated as a question ("Which insurance company will best serve our needs?") or as a statement ("The purpose of this study is to provide information so that the insurance company with the most effective plan will be selected.").

[NOTE 11.55] The scope lets the reader know the extent of the research.

Scope The **scope** of the research is defined by the main factors that were studied and generally appears next in the introductory section. It lets the reader know the extent of the research. Boundaries set by the researcher as well as factors over

Introduction and Executive Summary

South Shore Investment Consulting, Inc. has been retained by the Bell University Foundation, Inc. (the Foundation) to conduct an Asset Allocation Modeling Study for the Foundation's endowed and other assets with a long-term investment horizon. The Investment Committee is seeking to determine the most efficient and effective portfolio construction to enable the foundation to meet its long-term growth and spending objectives.

Returns for all asset classes during the recent 10 to 15 years have been high relative to historic norms. South Shore believes that the returns realized in the traditional domestic stock and bond markets over the last decade are unlikely to be repeated into the next decade. The Investment Committee has expressed a desire to evaluate the alternative allocation strategies that might be appropriate for assets that will be invested in the Foundation's Long-Term Investment Pool and explore the benefits of continuing to utilize diversifying asset classes such as international equities and small cap domestic equities.

Following a brief review of the asset modeling process (Section II), South Shore presents an analysis of the Foundation's current asset allocation and four alternative asset allocations for consideration. It is generally accepted that the asset allocation maintained by an investor is by far the most important determinant of the returns and volatility of returns (risk) experienced over time. Although other investment policy–related issues and the selection of quality investment managers are also important, South Shore considers the selection of an appropriate long-term strategic asset allocation to be the most important issue under consideration.

The following observations summarize the analysis:

- The results of the analysis support maintaining significant equity exposure and increasing diversification among equity subsectors. With the exception of the most aggressively postured alternative allocation strategy, each of the allocations exhibits a higher return per unit of risk compared to the Current Portfolio due to the benefit of increased diversification.
- The use of a reasonable exposure to asset classes which are not closely correlated with domestic stocks and bonds can increase expected portfolio return while decreasing downside risk.
- The study supports the expectation that increasing total equity exposure increases the probability of achieving higher returns in exchange for greater volatility. The results of the study indicate that, even with as much as 80 percent of total assets dedicated to the equity sector, there is a high probability of achieving a positive rate of return over periods of five years or longer.
- Two primary long-term investment objectives for the Foundation's endowed assets are 1) growth net of inflation and 2) growth in spending. By diversifying and maintaining a significant equity exposure, the foundation has a high probability of achieving a level of investment returns over long investment horizons, which would support the attainment of these objectives.

South Shore Investment Consulting, Inc. Bell University Foundation, Inc.

Figure 11.11
Executive Summary

which the researcher had no control are listed in this section of the introduction. These limitations can include lack of resources, lack of time, or geographic boundaries.

Related Literature **Related literature** is material collected while doing research on a topic being studied. A review of related literature may be included in the introduction if only a limited amount of literature is available about the topic. A separate section should be used when extensive amounts of related literature are reviewed.

Unfamiliar Terms Definitions of terms unfamiliar to the reader can be included in the introductory section. When many terms need to be defined, however, a glossary should be included in the supplementary section.

[NOTE 11.56]
The steps used in conducting the study are described in the procedures section.

Procedures The **procedures**, or methodology, section describes the steps taken in conducting the study. One purpose of this section is to allow readers to determine whether all aspects of the problem were adequately investigated. This section can also be used by another researcher to conduct a similar study that could validate or disprove the results of the original study.

[NOTE 11.57]
The results of the study are presented in the findings section.

Findings **Findings** are results discovered during the research. This section should be presented in a factual and objective manner without personal opinions or interpretations. Present all findings—positive and negative. Visual aids such as those presented in Chapter 13 can be used to assist the writer in communicating the findings of the study.

[NOTE 11.58]
Significant outcomes and relationships are discussed in the analysis section.

Analysis The **analysis** section contains the writer's interpretation of the qualitative or quantitative assessment of the findings. If prior research on the topic exists, the writer compares its results with the findings of the current study. Information in the analysis section assists the reader in determining which relationships are important.

[NOTE 11.59]
Conclusions are drawn from the findings of the study.

Conclusions A **conclusion** is a statement of reasoning made by a researcher after a thorough investigation. All conclusions should be made using the findings of the study and should be based on the analysis section of the report. In many studies, conclusions are summary statements of the content of the analysis section. No new data should be presented in this section. A study may have one or several conclusions. Because these statements become the basis for the writer's recommendations, the two sections may be combined.

[NOTE 11.60]
Recommendations are based on conclusions.

Recommendations A **recommendation** is the writer's suggestion to the reader as to the action(s) that should be taken to solve the problem that was studied. Recommendations should develop logically from the findings, analysis, and conclusions of the study. A study can result in one or more recommendations. If three or more recommendations are presented, they can be listed and numbered. This section may contain only the recommendations, or it may contain both the recommendations and the supportive reasoning for their development.

SUPPLEMENTARY SECTION

The final section of a written report contains material that relates indirectly to the main topic of the study. This section may consist of one or more subsections, such as a glossary, an appendix, and a bibliography.

Glossary A **glossary** is an alphabetic list of terms used in the report, terms with which the reader might be unfamiliar. It is used only when numerous unfamiliar terms are included in the text. When the report contains only a few specialized terms, the writer should define them in the introduction or when they first occur in the text.

[NOTE 11.61]
Unfamiliar terms are defined in the glossary.

Appendix An **appendix** contains related information excluded from the body to improve its readability. When appending two or more items, label each separately and identify it with a capital letter:

Appendix A: Computer Printout of Daily Sales
Appendix B: Sample Follow-Up Letter

[NOTE 11.62]
Indirectly related material is placed in an appendix.

All appendixes should be referred to in the body of the report. If the material is not referred to in the body, it is not relevant enough to be included as an appendix. Some items commonly included as appendixes include questionnaires, computer printouts, follow-up letters, reports of similar studies, working papers, intricate tables, and supporting material.

Bibliography A **bibliography,** also known as a reference list, is an alphabetical list of all references used as sources of information in the study, including those that do not appear in footnotes. Consult Appendix B or a reference manual for information on how to display entries for various sources.

[NOTE 11.63]
All references are listed in a bibliography.

Learning Objective [5]
LIST THE ADVANTAGES OF CORRECT REPORT FORMATTING.

Learning Objective [6]
WRITE FORMAL AND INFORMAL REPORTS.

Mechanics of Formal Reports

The mechanics of a written report—format, spacing, footnotes, and so forth—are as important as the mechanics of a letter or memo in that they make the first impression on the reader. The reader's first impression of the report will be based on its appearance. A negative first impression may increase the time it takes for a reader to gain confidence in the report writer's credibility.

[NOTE 11.64]
The outward appearance of a report influences the reader of the report.

When preparing the document, the writer must consider general guidelines of report mechanics as well as the guidelines and policies of the organization. The primary consideration in the physical presentation of a written report is that the mechanics improve the readability of the report. Readability is one of the report characteristics cited by Howard Kruse in the Communication Quote on page 324. Paragraphs averaging six to seven lines make it easy for the reader to concentrate on the written material. Proper spacing between paragraphs and correct margins make it easy for the reader to follow the material. Headings lead the reader from one section to the next by announcing the next topic.

COMMUNICATION QUOTE

Report preparation—most important for making good decisions. Decision makers need clear, concise, accurate, and readable reports. Good reports make for good decisions.

Howard W. Kruse, President, Blue Bell Creameries, Inc.

COVER

[NOTE 11.65] The cover provides information and protects the report.

The **cover** protects the contents of the report; therefore, it is often constructed of light-weight card stock. Information can be printed on the cover or displayed through a cutout section (window). The cover should be attractive and may contain an appropriate picture or drawing that will add to the impact of the report. Many organizations use preprinted covers on which the author can place the variable information. The four items generally displayed on a report cover are the title, the name of the receiver, the name of the author, and the date the report was submitted. Normally, the title is in uppercase letters, and the author's name has initial capital letters. Covers usually are used only on long, formal reports.

MARGINS

[NOTE 11.66] Margins add to the attractiveness of the report.

Proper **margins** in a report are important because they create the white space that makes the report visually appealing to the reader. As a general rule, report margins should be 1 inch on all sides. However, reports that are bound at the left should have a 1½-inch left margin, and reports that are bound at the top should have a 2-inch top margin. Preliminary parts, supplementary parts, and the opening page of major sections typically have larger (2-inch) top margins.

SPACING

[NOTE 11.67] Most reports are single-spaced, but double spacing is acceptable.

Reports may be **single-spaced** or **double-spaced**. The trend in business organizations is toward single spacing to reduce the number of sheets of paper that have to be handled. In reports using double spacing, paragraph indentations should be ½ inch from the left margin; no space is added between paragraphs. Single-spaced reports should be double-spaced between paragraphs; indenting the first line of the paragraph is optional.

HEADINGS

[NOTE 11.68] Structural or informative headings may be used.

Appropriate headings help the reader follow the report organization and enable him or her to refer quickly to specific sections within the report. Sections that are of little interest can be skipped or scanned quickly.

Headings may be either informative or structural. An **informative heading** indicates the content of a section and orients readers so that they can more easily understand the material. A **structural heading** emphasizes the functional sections within the report. Once the type of heading is selected, it should be used consistently throughout the report. An example of each follows:

Informative Heading:

CUSTOMERS' ATTITUDES TOWARD TELEVISION AS AN ADVERTISING MEDIUM

Structural Heading:

FINDINGS

The ways headings are presented vary according to the style manual used by the organization. Regardless of the method selected, consistency of presentation is vital. An explanation of one widely accepted method follows.

First-level headings (main headings) are centered on the page in uppercase letters. Main headings may be printed in boldface uppercase letters but preferably not in uppercase letters and underscored. **Second-level headings** (side headings) begin at the left margin, and the first letter of each main word is capitalized. Side headings are often underlined or boldfaced for emphasis. The **third-level heading** (paragraph heading) begins one-half inch from the left margin, is underlined or boldfaced, and has the first letter capitalized. An example of this method is shown in Figure 11.12.

The headings at each level must be constructed so that they are grammatically parallel. For example, all first-level headings must be parallel; however, first-level headings do not have to be parallel with second-level headings. In the following example, the second-level headings are parallel, but the first-level headings are not:

[NOTE 11.69]
Headings within a level must be parallel.

INCOME FOR FIRST QUARTER

Rent

Dividends

WAYS THAT FIRST QUARTER INCOME IS SPENT

Wages

Insurance

Travel

This example could be corrected by changing "WAYS THAT FIRST QUARTER INCOME IS SPENT" to "EXPENSES FOR FIRST QUARTER."

The rules of outlining should be followed when preparing headings in a written report. That is, when second- or third-level headings are used, each level must have at least two headings.

All first- and second-level headings within a report should be set off from preceding and following text by a double space. Text for sections with third-level headings begins two word spaces after the period in the heading. This method of organizing headings is shown in Figure 11.12.

FOOTNOTES

Footnotes must be used to give credit to the source of quoted or paraphrased material. Reports in the business community do not contain as many footnotes as reports in

[NOTE 11.70]
Information obtained from secondary sources must be footnoted.

Figure 11.12
Levels of Headings

FIRST-LEVEL HEADING

xxxxxxxxxxxxxxxxxxxxxxxxxxxxxxxxxxxxxxxxxxxxxxxxxxxxxxxxxxxxxxxxxxx
xxxxxxxxxxxxxxxxxxxxxxxxxxxxxxxxxxxxxxxxxxxxxxxxxxxxxxxxxxxxxxxxxxxxxxxx
xxxxxxxxxxxxxxxxxxxxxxxxxxxxxxxxxxxxxxxxxxxxxxxxxxxxxxxxxxxxxxxxxxxxxxxx
xxxxxxxxxxxxxxxxxxxxxxxxxxxxxxxxxxxxxxxxxxxxxxxxxxxxxxxxxxxxxxxxxxxxxxxx

Second-Level Heading

xxxxxxxxxxxxxxxxxxxxxxxxxxxxxxxxxxxxxxxxxxxxxxxxxxxxxxxxxxxxxxxxxxx
xxxxxxxxxxxxxxxxxxxxxxxxxxxxxxxxxxxxxxxxxxxxxxxxxxxxxxxxxxxxxxxxxxxxxxxx
xxxxxxxxxxxxxxxxxxxxxxxxxxxxxxxxxxxxxxxxxxxxxxxxxxxxxxxxxxxxxxxxxxxxxxxx

Third-level heading. xxxxxxxxxxxxxxxxxxxxxxxxxxxxxxxxxxxxxxxxxxxxxxx
xxxxxxxxxxxxxxxxxxxxxxxxxxxxxxxxxxxxxxxxxxxxxxxxxxxxxxxxxxxxxxxxxxxxxxxx
xxxxxxxxxxxxxxxxxxxxxxxxxxxxxxxxxxxxxxxxxxxxxxxxxxxxxxxxxxxxxxxxxxxxxxxx

Third-level heading. xxxxxxxxxxxxxxxxxxxxxxxxxxxxxxxxxxxxxxxxxxxxxxx
xxxxxxxxxxxxxxxxxxxxxxxxxxxxxxxxxxxxxxxxxxxxxxxxxxxxxxxxxxxxxxxxxxxxxxxx
xxxxxxxxxxx

Third-level heading. xxxxxxxxxxxxxxxxxxxxxxxxxxxxxxxxxxxxxxxxxxxxxxx
xxxxxxxxxxxxxxxxxxxxxxxxxxxxxxxxxxxxxxxxxxxxxxxxxxxxxxxxxxxxxxxxxxxxxxxx
xxxxxxxxxxxxxxxxxxxxxxxx

Third-level heading. xxxxxxxxxxxxxxxxxxxxxxxxxxxxxxxxxxxxxxxxxxxxxxx
xxxxxxxxxxxxxxxxxxxxxxxxxxxxxxxxxxxxxxxxxxxxxxxxxxxxxxxxxxxxxxxxxxxxxxxx
xxxxxxxxxxxxxxxxxxxxxxxx

Second-Level Heading

xxxxxxxxxxxxxxxxxxxxxxxxxxxxxxxxxxxxxxxxxxxxxxxxxxxxxxxxxxxxxxxxxxx
xxxxxxxxxxxxxxxxxxxxxxxxxxxxxxxxxxxxxxxxxxxxxxxxxxxxxxxxxxxxxxxxxxxxxxxx

FIRST-LEVEL HEADING

xxxxxxxxxxxxxxxxxxxxxxxxxxxxxxxxxxxxxxxxxxxxxxxxxxxxxxxxxxxxxxxxxxx
xxxxxxxxxxxxxxxxxxxxxxxxxxxxxxxxxxxxxxxxxxxxxxxxxxxxxxxxxxxxxxxxxxxxxxxx
xxxxxxxxxxxxxxxxxxxxxx

other fields because business reports usually contain only information that is based on data gathered through primary research. Two commonly used methods for citing sources follow.

[NOTE 11.71]
Commonly used footnoting methods are
- Traditional
- Contemporary

The traditional method of footnoting is convenient for the reader when a report contains information gathered from a number of sources. Material to be footnoted is marked by an Arabic numeral that is placed at the end of the quoted material and raised ½ line (superscript). The footnote numbers begin with 1 and are consecutive throughout the report. The footnote is separated from the text by a 1-inch or 2-inch horizontal rule beginning at the left margin 1 line below the last line of the text material. The footnote is typed or printed on the second line under the rule; it is single-spaced, with the first line indented ½ inch from the left margin. The superscript number identification precedes the citation.

The footnoting feature of word processing software makes enumeration and placement easy, but the report writer must still ensure that the citation is complete and correct. Information contained in traditional footnotes varies depending on the source—book, periodical, encyclopedia, government publication, newspaper, or unpublished material. An example of a traditional footnote for information taken from a periodical follows. Footnotes for material from other sources vary slightly.

> The number of new oil wells being drilled has decreased by 10 percent from the number drilled last year.[1] There will be a shortage of oil products if the trend of drilling fewer wells continues for the rest of this decade.
>
> ---
>
> [1]A. W. Hodde, "Oil Production in 1997," *Petroleum Quarterly* 9, (1998) p. 8.

A contemporary method of footnoting information is more appropriate for reports that contain information from only a few sources. These sources can be documented easily by placing the information (name of author, date of publication, and page number) in parentheses at the end of the sentence relating to the citation. For information about the source, a reader would refer to the bibliography. An example of this method follows:

> The number of new oil wells being drilled has decreased by 10 percent from the number drilled last year (Hodde, 1998, p. 8). There will be a shortage of oil products if the trend of drilling fewer wells continues for the rest of this decade.

See Appendix B for a more detailed description of procedures to follow when constructing footnotes and other citations.

PAGE NUMBERS

Pages in reports of only one or two pages do not have to be numbered. Pages in long reports should be numbered consecutively. Preliminary pages (pages prior to the body of a report) should be numbered by placing small Roman numerals (ii, iii, iv, etc.) at the center of the page, one inch from the bottom, beginning with the second page. The title page is considered page i, even though no page number is displayed.

[NOTE 11.72]
Reports containing more than two pages should be numbered.

The body of the report should begin as page one, identified with Arabic numerals (1, 2, 3, 4, etc.). For each section or chapter that is started on a separate page, the page number should be centered one inch from the bottom. On the remaining pages of unbound or left-bound reports, the number should be placed on the fourth line from the top of the page in the right margin; on top-bound reports the page number should be centered and one inch from the bottom edge of the page. The page numbering feature of word processing software simplifies the placement process. An example of a formal report appears in Figure 11.13.

Figure 11.13
Formal Report

IMPACT STUDY:

Duluth Botanical Gardens/Conservatory

Date:

August 30, 1999

Richard Lichty
with Jean Jacobson
and Arnela Smajlovic

Bureau of Business and
Economic Research
University of Minnesota Duluth

-1-

Figure 11.13
Formal Report Cont.

IMPACT STUDY

Duluth Botanical Gardens/Conservatory

August 30, 1999

In this study:

-2-

Figure 11.13
Formal Report Cont.

INTRODUCTION

This study was requested by the Bayfront Visions citizen s group to muster impact data for presentation to the Duluth City Council and planning committee in support of a proposal to build a conservatory and botanical garden for Duluth in the area known as the Bayfront. Assumptions for new visitors and other tourism-related impacts are discussed below, but represent preliminary notions about possible numbers. Data are supplied and analysis is accomplished by the IMPLAN software model and data.

BACKGROUND

THE IMPACT MODEL AND DATA

IMPLAN Professional is an economic impact assessment modeling system. IMPLAN allows the user to build economic models to estimate the impacts of economic changes in their states, counties, or communities. The IMPLAN system is comprised of two pieces purchased separately. The first is the IMPLAN Professional software. The second piece is the IMPLAN database. You need both software and data to create an economic impact model. Software IMPLAN Professional¤ is an economic impact assessment software system. IMPLANPro¤, combined with MIG databases, allows the user to develop local level input-output models that can estimate the economic impact of new firms moving into an area, professional sports teams, recreation and tourism, and many more activities.

DATABASE COMPONENTS

IMPLAN databases consist of the following components: Employment; Industry Output; Value Added; Employee Compensation; Proprietary Income; Other Property Type Income; Indirect Business Taxes; and more.

DATABASE SOURCES

U.S. Bureau of Economic Analysis Benchmark I/O Accounts of the U.S.
U.S. Bureau of Economic Analysis Output Estimates
U.S. Bureau of Economic Analysis REIS Program
U.S. Bureau of Labor Statistics ES202 Program
U.S. Bureau of Labor Statistics Consumer Expenditure Survey
U.S. Census Bureau County Business Patterns
U.S. Census Bureau Deciennial Census and Population Surveys
U.S. Census Bureau Economic Censuses and Surveys
U.S. Department of Agriculture
U.S. Geological Survey

-3-

Figure 11.13
Formal Report Cont.

THE NATURE OF IMPACTS

Assumptions:

Several assumptions are necessary in any impact analysis. This was especially true in the case of the tourism impact analysis of the proposed Duluth Botanical Gardens/ Conservatory since time and money did not allow for surveys or other methods aimed at fine-tuning the analysis.

The following assumptions apply to the impacts here reported:

¥ **Production, Not Sales**

The impacts reported here are based on production, not sales. This is a common approach using the models and tools used for this analysis.

What does this mean? The primary implications from these assumptions are for retail and wholesale trade. An example might help: If I buy a car from a local car dealer for $20,000, how much was produced in Duluth? Well, the car dealer did not manufacture the car. So we can deduct $15,000 or so that went to Detroit or Japan. Perhaps the owners do not reside in Duluth. We can deduct their earnings from profit that goes to wherever they reside. That leaves local sales people, maintenance people, for a local impact.

We call that proportion of total sales by the car dealership in our example *margins*. Margins represent the contribution to local production by the local dealership. This means that the output impacts will be much less than the total sales impact. However, the output impact is a true production impact upon which decisions can be made. Since tourism deals mostly with retail establishments, to use sales as an estimator is misleading relative to the true impact.

¥ **Employment Assumptions**

Employment figures are based on Department of Commerce definitions. This means that a part-time employee is counted as one employee. There are no adjustments toward full-time equivalent measures.

Once again, this assumption has its greatest effect on sectors such as retail trade. Retail trade hires a significant number of part-time employees. This means that any impact measure in this sector will be inflated when compared to full time equivalent definitions.

Another required assumption for employment impacts is that there is no excess capacity in the community. New levels of sales require new employees, and we are assuming these new employees are available. Any other assumption would require more time and budget than is available for this analysis.

-4-

Figure 11.13
Formal Report
Cont.

- ¥ **The Source of Margins**

For this analysis, the margins were initially taken from the default values contained in IMPLAN. Each was then reviewed based on other data, such as the Census of Retail Trade, Department of Commerce and a few adjustments were made.

- ¥ **Prices in 1996 Dollars**

The most recent IMPLAN model contains a database based on 1996 information. This is taken as the base year for this analysis. An inflation rate of 2 percent is then factored into the model for each year of the analysis. All figures provided were deflated by this factor. Of course, if there is a desire to have the impacts stated in current dollars, the factor can be added back in.

- ¥ **High and Low Assumptions for New Visitor Days**

Probably the most heroic assumption regards tourists. It is difficult to understand what motivates a tourist to come into our region without surveys of our major markets. These markets pretty much follow Interstate 35, with the Twin Cities being our biggest customers, Iowa coming second, Missouri third, and so on. There is some evidence that Chicago residents are increasing in number for our tourist base.

Our assumption is that one major motivator for tourism in the region is to see the Lake and related environment offered by Duluth. The landscape proposal being analyzed here maximizes this exposure.

Why is this important? Because only new tourist expenditures should be included in any tourism project impact statement. If a new operation only results in a tourist spending money in one Duluth store instead of another, the net impact is zero.

For this initial impact study, we present high and low assumptions: a high of 70,000 new visitor days for Duluth because of this operation, or a low of 35,000 new visitor days for Duluth because of this operation. For occupancy we assume that an average stay in a hotel/motel is one night.

- ¥ **Personal Tax Assumptions**

It is important to note that tax impacts extend beyond those directly paid by employees of the operation. Impacts include the indirect and induced (see below) effects from an initial change in activity. Even if an assumed operation resulted in no direct tax impacts from its own operations, the indirect and induced effects could be quite large.

The tax impact model assumptions for this study come from the IMPLAN tax impact structure, as built into the IMPLAN Pro 2.0 model and data.

-5-

Figure 11.13
Formal Report Cont.

¥ **Other Assumptions**

There are several other assumptions associated with the IMPLAN model used in this analysis. The reader is referred to the *IMPLAN User's Guide* for a list of these assumptions.

TYPES OF MULTIPLIERS

There are several types of multipliers used in this analysis, speci cally, the Direct, the Indirect, and the Induced. The total of these three make up the Total Impact. In the impact data to be presented, all of these impacts will be listed.

The following de nitions apply:

¥ **Direct**

The direct impact comes from the operation itself. Remember that, in the case of retail or service operations, margins constitute the basis for direct impact estimates.

¥ **Indirect**

The indirect impacts stem from the interaction between the facility and other local businesses. The interaction comes from the facilities purchases of locally produced producers. Only purchases and sales from *local* businesses count in this calculation.

It is important to note that the purchases by the facility under consideration are the direct impacts. The indirect impacts come from these second-round businesses purchasing needed local goods and services in order to provide for the increased production in the region as a result of the initial, direct expenditures. Then third round increases in activity occur, fourth round, and so on until the multiplier has played itself out.

¥ **Induced**

Induced impacts stem from the earnings of employees in each round of impact activity. Employees spend a portion of their personal income in the region, creating rounds of induced activity.

¥ **Total**

The total impact is simply the direct, plus the indirect, plus the induced impacts.

TYPES OF MEASURES

Our impact estimates include the following measures: output, employment, personal income, and personal taxes. Each will be described in a sentence:

-6-

Figure 11.13
Formal Report
Cont.

¥ **Output**

Output impacts represent the new direct, indirect, and induced *production* from local industries as a result of the new facility. Output is generally not the same as sales, as discussed above.

¥ **Employment**

Employment impacts are the direct, indirect, and induced impacts from industry activity in the region as a result of the new operation. Remember, an employee is an employee, whether full- or part-time.

¥ **Personal Income**

Personal income impacts are the direct, indirect, and induced impacts from industry activity in the region as a result of the new operation. Personal income includes employee compensation plus proprietor s income if the proprietor is a local individual.

¥ **Taxes**

Tax impacts are based on household factors and on indirect taxes. Household taxes include personal taxes and property taxes, as well as estimates of various other income based taxes. Indirect taxes include sales taxes and excise taxes. All tax estimates are for state and local taxes. Federal taxes are not included.

IMPACTS FROM CONSTRUCTION

The construction associated with this project is assumed to take place in the year 2000. All construction expenditure estimates were provided by the supporters of this development plan. We then discounted these estimates to 1996 dollars based on the 2 percent per annum inflation rate assumed for this project. The initial assumptions for this impact were a total construction cost of $7,250,000. Of course, the construction impacts are for one year only and do not extend into the future.

Table 1 presents the direct, indirect, and induced impacts from the assumed construction activity.

Table 1: Construction

	*Direct**	*Indirect**	*Induced**	*Total**
Labor Income	$2,040,403	$815,031	$776,467	$3,631,900
Output Impact	$6,643,396	$2,086,144	$1,900,508	$10,630,04
Employment	74.6	34.6	36.1	145.3
*1996 dollars				

-7-

Figure 11.13
Formal Report Cont.

IMPACTS FROM OPERATIONS

The operations associated with this project are assumed to begin in the year 2001. The impacts listed here are for that one year. The assumption is that the operations impact would continue indefinitely into the future. The initial assumptions for this impact were a total operations cost of $1,514,400.

Table 2 presents the direct, indirect, and induced impacts from the operations assumptions.

Table 2: Operations

	*Direct**	*Indirect**	*Induced**	*Total**
Labor Income	$417,876	$143,425	$152,633	$713,934
Output Impact	$1,057,774	$392,216	$373,589	$1,823,579
Employment	19.5	6.2	7.1	32.7
*1996 dollars				

IMPACTS (HIGH, MEDIUM, AND LOW ASSUMPTIONS) FROM NEW VISITOR DAYS

Table 3 reflects high (70,000), medium (35,000), and low (10,000) assumptions of additional visitor days for the region to take advantage of this new park. This number would begin with the operations in the year 2001. The expenditures of these tourists are assumed to concentrate in a few local industries. Impacted industry sectors included are retail, eating & drinking, lodging, advertising, theater, sports, motion pictures, transportation, food stores, banking, and Rental.

Remember that the direct impact on retail trade is based on margins, not on sales.
Table 3 presents the direct, indirect, and induced impacts from the new tourism in the region.

Table 3: Tourism

	*Direct**	*Indirect**	*Induced**	*Total**
HIGH:				
Labor Income	$2,106,985	$702,055	$763,852	$3,572,892
Output Impact	$6,314,169	$2,010,325	$1,869,630	$10,194,124
Employment	144.3	30.8	35.5	210.6
MEDIUM:				
Labor Income	$394,613	$138,324	$144,920	$677,857
Output Income	$1,240,351	$398,739	$354,710	$1,993,800
Employment	29.9	6.1	6.7	42.7
LOW				
Labor Income	$925,417	$300,759	$333,429	$1,559,605
Output	$2,758,642	$861,954	$816,114	$4,436,709
Employment	62.2	13.1	15.5	90.8
*1996 dollars				

-8-

Figure 11.13
Formal Report
Cont.

IMPACT FROM TAXES

Table 4 presents the household-based tax impact and indirect business-tax impact in the region.

Table 4: Tax Impact

	Household-Based Taxes	*Indirect Business Tax*
Construction	$133,307	$329,611
Operations	$25,812	$46,352
Tourism (High)	$128,849	$534,370
Tourism (Medium)	$24,454	$110,601
Tourism (Low)	$6,987	$31,600
High TOTAL	$287,968	$910,333
Medium TOTAL	$183,573	$486,564
Low TOTAL	$166,106	$407,563

-9-

Figure 11.13
Formal Report Cont.

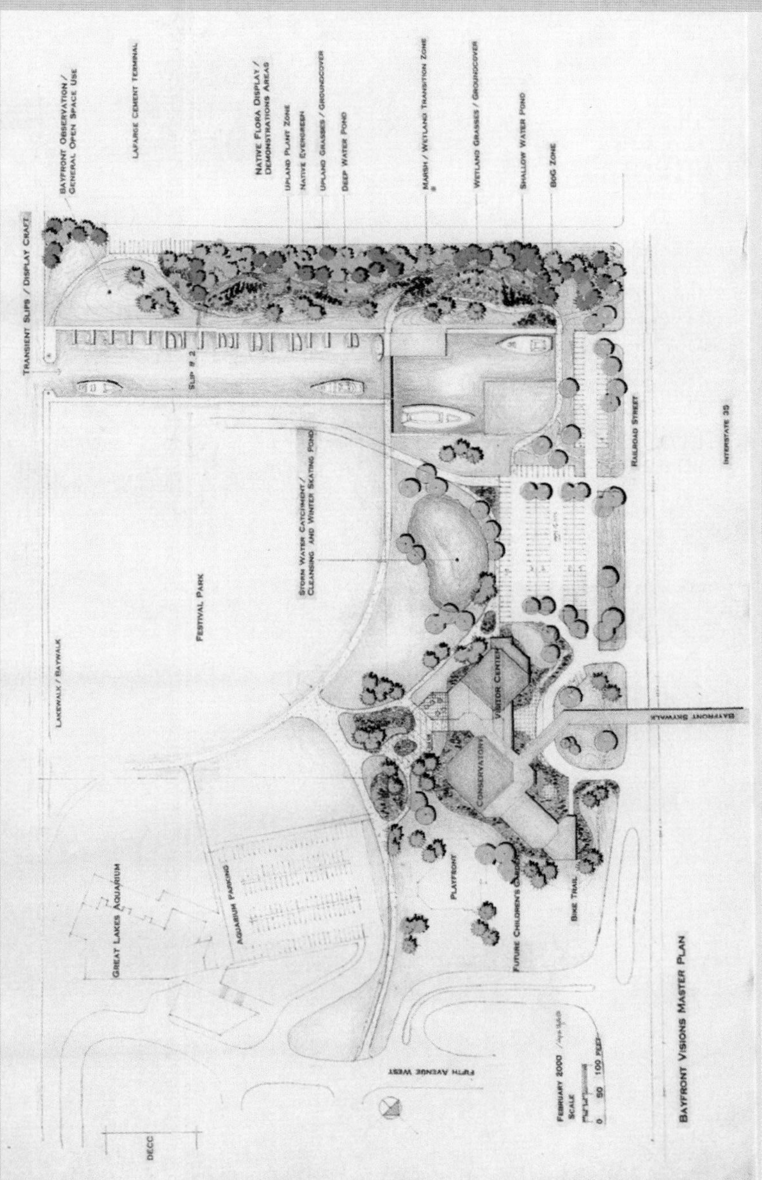

Figure 1 Bayfront Visions Master Plan, prepared by Bayfront Visions Group, April 1999

-10-

Figure 11.13
Formal Report
Cont.

REFERENCES

Data and Software:

Minnesota IMPLAN Group, Inc., IMPLAN System (1996 data and software), 1940 South Greeley Street, Suite 101, Stillwater, MN 55082, http://www.implan.com, 1997.

Written Guide:

Olson, Doug and Scott Lindall, "IMPLAN Professional Software, Analysis, and Data Guide," Minnesota IMPLAN Group, Inc., 1940 South Greeley Street, Suite 101, Stillwater, MN 55082, http://www.implan.com, 1996.

Figure 11.13
Formal Report Cont.

APPENDIXES AND SUPPORTING IMPLAN DATA

For Appendixes and Supporting IMPLAN Data Tables please see the UMD Bureau of Business and Economic Research, including:

Tourism (High, Medium, and Low Assumptions)
Labor Income Impact, Output Impact, Employment Impact, Tax Impact
Construction
Labor Income Impact, Output Impact, Employment Impact, Tax Impact
Operations
Labor Income Impact, Output Impact, Employment Impact, Tax Impact

-12-

Summary of Learning Objectives

Learning Objective [1]

Identify and use the five steps for conducting research. The five steps in conducting research are: (1) *Plan the research.* Planning the research includes stating the problem, setting the boundaries, determining the readership, and deciding on the procedures to be followed. (2) *Gather information.* You may gather information for your research from one or more sources. There are two basic types of information sources: secondary and primary. The Web has become an essential tool for conducting research. (3) *Analyze the information.* The purpose of the analysis is to make sense, objectively, of the information you have gathered. You will not want personal bias of any kind to enter into the analysis. (4) *Determine the solution(s).* Based on your analysis, you will be ready to offer a solution or solutions to the problem you have been researching. For formal studies and reports, you may draw conclusions from your analysis and state them separately from the recommendation(s). (5) *Write the report.* The final step in a research project is to write the report. It is an important step; you will want to present your results effectively.

Learning Objective [2]

Distinguish between formal and informal reports. A formal report may consist of all or some of the following parts: title page, letter or memo of authorization, table of contents, list of illustrations, abstract, body, glossary, appendix, and bibliography. An informal report may consist of a body and a title page or of a body only; it may also be formatted as correspondence. Formal reports are usually written in the third person, but informality is becoming more acceptable; informal reports are usually written in the first person. Both formal and informal reports use headings to guide the reader through the document.

Learning Objective [3]

Identify the types of informal reports. The three most common informal reports are progress, periodic, and technical. A progress report informs readers about the status of a particular project. A periodic report provides managers with statistical information at regularly scheduled intervals. A technical report conveys specialized or scientific information.

Learning Objective [4]

Describe the components of a formal report. The report cover, which contains the report title and author's name, protects the contents of the report. Report margins are generally 1 inch on all sides. Reports may be single- or double-spaced. Single-spaced reports should be double-spaced between paragraphs. Headings may be informative or structural. Informative headings indicate the content of a forthcoming section; structural headings emphasize the functional sections within the report. Footnotes give credit to the source of quoted or paraphrased material. Pages of short reports may not be numbered; pages of long reports should be numbered. Preliminary pages are normally numbered with Roman numerals whereas pages containing the body and supplementary parts of the report are numbered with Arabic numerals.

Learning Objective [5]

List the advantages of correct report formatting. Correct report formatting will cause the reader to have a good first impression of the report. It decreases the time necessary for a reader to gain confidence in the report writer's credibility. Formatting a written report properly will improve its readability. Properly formatted reports help the reader follow the organization of the material by using appropriate headings.

Write formal and informal reports. Informal reports are normally written in the first person. They usually do not contain visual aids or material from secondary sources and may be formatted as letters or memos.

Learning Objective [6]

DISCUSSION QUESTIONS

1. List the five steps in conducting research and explain each step. (Objective 1)
2. Name and explain what must be done to plan a research project. (Objective 1)
3. What factors should a researcher consider when assessing the value of traditional and computerized secondary sources? (Objective 1)
4. Name the four major sources of primary information and briefly describe each one. (Objective 1)
5. List and explain three of the guidelines to follow when designing a questionnaire. (Objective 1)
6. How do formal and informal reports differ? (Objective 2)
7. What format options exist for informal reports? (Objective 2)
8. What information should be included in a progress report? (Objective 3)
9. How does an organization benefit from establishing a standard format for its technical reports? (Objective 3)
10. List and briefly describe the three major divisions of a formal report. (Objective 4)
11. What is an executive summary? Why is it used? (Objective 4)
12. How does a writer determine whether to include material within the body of a report or as an appendix to the report? (Objective 4)
13. Explain when to use Roman numerals and when to use Arabic numbers in a formal report. (Objective 5)
14. Distinguish between a structural heading and an informative heading. Given an example of each. (Objective 5)
15. Explain why correctly formatting a report improves its readability. (Objective 5)

APPLICATION EXERCISES

1. **Teamwork.** Form teams to do research to determine students' attitudes toward an important current student issue on your campus. Implement all the major steps in conducting business research except writing the report. In a group meeting of all teams, fairly assign a portion of the research to each team. Prepare a memo to your instructor outlining what each team will do and the time schedule for the project. (Objective 1)
2. Indicate what would be (a) an appropriate statement of the problem and (b) an appropriate list of factors for comparative research of the relative cost-effectiveness of two procedures for processing employment application forms in a human resource office. (Objective 1)
3. You plan to determine whether students prefer debit cards or credit cards. State the problem, list the research factors, and indicate the way you would gather data. (Objective 1)

4. **Teamwork.** Form teams to develop a questionnaire that could be used to survey student opinions on the quality of student advisement in your school. (Objective 1)

5. **Teamwork.** Pilot-test, revise, and then administer the questionnaire developed in Application Exercise 4 to the students in three business classes. Tabulate the students' responses and analyze the data. As your instructor directs, report your findings in a memo or an oral report. (Objectives 1, 3, and 6)

6. **Teamwork.** Repeat Exercise 4 using the focus group technique. As your instructor directs, report your findings in a memo or an oral report. (Objectives 1, 3, and 6)
7. Contact a local grocery store manager and obtain permission to observe customers as they pass through the checkout line during set times over a three-day period. Your goal is to obtain data to determine whether plastic or paper bags are preferred. Incorporate other relevant factors into your observation. Report your results in a memo report to your instructor and in a letter report to the store manager. (Objectives 1, 3, and 6)

8. **Teamwork.** Design an experiment to compare the speed and output of two search engines. After getting feedback on your design from members of another team, conduct your experiment. Submit an informal report to your instructor. (Objectives 1, 3, and 6)

9. **Teamwork.** Form a group and develop a questionnaire that could be uploaded on the Web to evaluate the favorite videos, movies, and music of college students. Present a copy of your questionnaire to the class for discussion and present a copy to your instructor. You may consider distributing the questionnaire to students in your class. (Objective 1)

10. **Internet.** The increased use of computers within your organization has prompted your supervisor, R. J. Tibbs, to become concerned about repetitive strain injury (RSI). R. J. has asked you to research the topic; specifically, she is interested in information on prevention, symptoms, and treatment. Use traditional and/or computerized search techniques to gather your information, then prepare an informal report. (Objectives 1, 3, and 6)

11. **E-mail.** Send an e-mail note to a student in your class with a copy to your instructor. In the e-mail explain why you think your favorite search engine is the best one. (Objective 3)

There are Web exercises at **http://krizan.swcollege.com** to accompany this chapter.

CASE PROBLEMS

1. The employees of Hazel Savings have asked about the possibility of classes being offered on-site. Upon inquiring at State College, you learn that up to two classes could be taught if enough students enroll to make the classes cost-effective. A survey was taken; 131 of Hazel Savings' 162 employees responded. The results follow. Write a memo report to the human resources director, Teresa Trevino, giving the results of the investigation and your recommendations.

1. *What courses would you be interested in taking? (Give your top 3 choices as 1, 2, and 3.)*

	1	2	3
Business Communication	*14*	*14*	*17*
Human Relations	*28*	*9*	*16*
Computer Applications	*32*	*17*	*14*

	1	2	3
Financial Accounting	*9*	*23*	*18*
Marketing	*7*	*22*	*8*

2. *What would be the best day for the class?*

Monday	*15*
Tuesday	*52*
Wednesday	*32*
Thursday	*32*
Friday	*0*

3. *What would be the most convenient time for the class?*

7 a.m.	*12*
5 p.m.	*41*
6 p.m.	*52*
7 p.m.	*26*

2. Northeastern Savings and Loan's contract with an insurance company lapses in four months. It is trying to determine its employees' attitudes toward medical coverage. Following are the results of a survey to which 89 of the 105 employees responded. The responses have been organized into three groups—single persons, individuals with one dependent, and individuals with two or more dependents. Use the data to prepare a report that could be sent to the company's president.

	Single	1 Dependent	2+Dependents
1. *Which type of coverage is best?*			
a. Employee only	*25*	*5*	*1*
b. Family plan	*5*	*16*	*37*
2. *What coverage(s) should be available? (Check all that apply.)*			
a. Basic medical	*30*	*21*	*38*
b. Major medical	*30*	*21*	*38*
c. Hospitalization	*30*	*21*	*38*
d. Dental	*16*	*12*	*32*
e. Optical	*9*	*7*	*32*
f. Prescriptions	*20*	*15*	*25*
3. *What limit should a policy place on out-of-pocket expenses?*			
a. $ 500	*21*	*13*	*31*
b. $1,000	*6*	*5*	*6*
c. $2,500	*1*	*1*	*1*
d. $5,000	*2*	*2*	*0*
4. *Should the company offer a menu insurance program in which an employee can choose the type of coverage desired?*			
a. Yes	*28*	*19*	*37*
b. No	*2*	*1*	*2*
5. *Which would you prefer?*			
a. Minimum coverage—company pays premium	*22*	*12*	*25*

		Single	1 Dependent	2+Dependents
b.	*Increased coverage—employee shares in paying premium*	*8*	*9*	*13*

6. *What should be the maximum premium that the employee must pay each month?*

		Single	1 Dependent	2+Dependents
a.	*$ 0*	*23*	*13*	*30*
b.	*$ 25*	*5*	*2*	*4*
c.	*$ 50*	*1*	*4*	*2*
d.	*$100*	*1*	*2*	*2*

3. As program planner for the local entertainment league, you surveyed your 396 season ticket holders to determine what plays they are interested in seeing during the following season. You listed the play possibilities and asked respondents to indicate their interest level in each (1 = low; 4 = high). Although patrons prefer musicals, past experience dictates that a schedule that excludes comedy and drama results in lower-than-average attendance. This year, you also wanted to gather information about when ticket holders prefer to have performances. Data from 302 respondents is summarized below. Analyze the data and prepare a memo report to the entertainment league's president, Mildred Babcock, who will use the information when she negotiates with agents. (Numbers may not total 302 due to incomplete responses on some survey returns.)

Plays	**1**	**2**	**3**	**4**
1776	*57*	*55*	*101*	*86*
A Chorus Line	*17*	*77*	*73*	*135*
A Flea in Her Ear	*209*	*53*	*25*	*13*
A Streetcar Named Desire	*12*	*73*	*183*	*31*
Ah, Wilderness!	*113*	*45*	*74*	*70*
Barefoot in the Park	*93*	*72*	*81*	*55*
Cabaret	*4*	*60*	*124*	*110*
Cats	*2*	*35*	*83*	*181*
Charley's Aunt	*161*	*52*	*71*	*18*
Chicago	*71*	*49*	*79*	*103*
City of Angels	*77*	*84*	*58*	*78*
Conversations With My Father	*44*	*134*	*67*	*48*
Dancing at Lughnasa	*44*	*81*	*148*	*29*
Death of a Salesman	*76*	*72*	*80*	*74*
Eleemosynary	*55*	*207*	*27*	*10*
Fiddler on the Roof	*114*	*59*	*103*	*26*
Grease	*1*	*39*	*258*	*4*
Hamlet	*70*	*79*	*77*	*75*
How to Succeed in Business Without Really Trying	*93*	*144*	*56*	*3*
Inherit the Wind	*31*	*127*	*126*	*18*
Jeckyll & Hyde	*102*	*87*	*76*	*35*
Jelly's Last Jam	*40*	*94*	*86*	*78*
Les Miserables	*103*	*157*	*30*	*2*
Little Shop of Horrors	*183*	*11*	*56*	*52*
Lost in Yonkers	*149*	*51*	*91*	*11*

Plays	**1**	**2**	**3**	**4**
Man of LaMancha	79	86	77	60
Peter Pan	21	96	133	52
Rent	3	34	111	153
Show Boat	16	237	25	24
Six Degrees of Separation	98	78	82	41
South Pacific	64	170	46	16
Stomp	121	32	126	23
The Fantasticks	80	200	16	4
The Secret Garden	68	64	96	74
The Sound of Music	94	163	23	17
The Sunshine Boys	108	104	79	11
The Glass Menagerie	111	103	80	1
The Last Night of Ballyhoo	90	46	43	116
The Lion King	36	6	92	168
The Phantom of the Opera	14	63	173	52
The King and I	53	115	63	64
The Homecoming	134	122	27	19
Victor/Victoria	22	89	146	44

Scheduling Preferences: Days	**1**	**2**	**3**	**4**
Monday	273	26	3	1
Tuesday	132	8	129	33
Wednesday	45	10	68	177
Thursday	6	92	63	109
Friday	206	74	16	4
Saturday (matinee)	244	51	8	0
Saturday (evening)	20	9	253	19
Sunday (matinee)	237	20	32	13
Sunday (evening)	84	6	157	55

Scheduling Preferences: Months	**1**	**2**	**3**	**4**
September	37	102	114	49
October	22	70	144	64
November	55	110	103	34
December	193	19	85	5
January	88	100	112	2
February	16	130	133	22
March	82	64	76	79
April	71	80	85	64
May	55	83	70	93
June	122	86	58	36

4. While working in the human resources department, you have become concerned about the effects that computers may be having on your company's employees. The tabulations of the 147 survey responses that you received from the company's 163 employees follow. Write a memo report to the company's general manager explaining the results of your survey and making any recommendations that you deem necessary.

1. *Average number of hours you spend in front of your computer each work day:*

	Number of Respondents
More than 6	*14*
5 or 6	*42*
3 or 4	*68*
1 or 2	*18*
Fewer than 1	*5*

2. *The computer*

	Strongly Agree	Agree	Disagree	Strongly Disagree
Increases my productivity	*78*	*43*	*18*	*8*
Forces me to work alone	*31*	*66*	*39*	*11*
Gives me job security	*40*	*48*	*42*	*17*
Makes my job frustrating	*14*	*52*	*43*	*38*
Helps me solve problems	*32*	*74*	*29*	*12*
Requires me to get training	*61*	*27*	*31*	*28*
Requires me to think	*18*	*81*	*35*	*13*

3. *What impact has the computer had on you?*

	Strongly Agree	Agree	Disagree	Strongly Disagree
Helps me get pay raises	*43*	*68*	*22*	*14*
Makes my job more challenging	*15*	*92*	*30*	*10*
Gives me more career options	*37*	*88*	*17*	*5*
Weakens my job security	*16*	*43*	*46*	*42*
Makes me wish I had selected another field	*11*	*16*	*92*	*28*

5. Barnard's Industrial Supply is attempting to improve its image. It is conducting a workshop on ethical business practices. A questionnaire sent to employees asking them to rate selected aspects of their behavior as *Never, Rarely, Sometimes,* and *Often* was returned by 243 of Barnard's 287 employees. Use the following results to write a memo report that could be distributed to the employees at the workshop.

In the past five years I have

	Never	Rarely	Sometimes	Often
1. *Taken money illegally from the company*	*225*	*16*	*1*	*1*
2. *Withheld truth to cover my mistakes*	*76*	*87*	*59*	*21*
3. *Withheld truth to cover others' mistakes*	*54*	*63*	*103*	*23*
4. *Reported hours that weren't worked*	*198*	*12*	*24*	*9*
5. *Made personal long-distance calls on business phones*	*17*	*53*	*97*	*76*

	Never	Rarely	Sometimes	Often
6. *Taken supplies for personal use*	*51*	*17*	*42*	*133*
7. *Given false reasons for missing work*	*36*	*69*	*107*	*31*
8. *Used unethical behavior to make a sale*	*202*	*21*	*9*	*11*
9. *Submitted false expenses for travel*	*164*	*33*	*28*	*18*
10. *Stayed past break or lunch periods*	*8*	*14*	*168*	*53*
11. *Used equipment for personal projects*	*21*	*37*	*149*	*36*
12. *Made illegal copies of software*	*104*	*52*	*71*	*16*

6. Peoples Bank is exploring the possibility of building a wellness center for its employees. Harold Shen, bank president, has asked the human resources department to survey the bank's employees to learn what facilities they would most likely use. Eighty-one of Peoples' 97 employees responded. The results of the survey follow. Write a memo report to Mr. Shen explaining the results of the survey and offering your recommendations.

	Male	Female
1. *How often would you use the facility?*		
Once a week	*2*	*4*
2–3 times a week	*9*	*14*
Daily	*14*	*16*
Once or twice a month	*2*	*2*
Never	*6*	*12*
2. *When would you use the center? (Check all that apply.)*		
Before work	*10*	*3*
Lunch hour	*11*	*23*
After work	*4*	*6*
Evening	*2*	*4*
3. *Would you like the center to open on weekends?*		
Yes	*26*	*12*
No	*1*	*24*
4. *Check all the activities in which you would participate:*		
Weights	*21*	*18*
Jogging/walking	*6*	*26*
Basketball	*16*	*5*
Racquetball	*18*	*17*
Stairmaster	*12*	*16*
Other	*9*	*11*
5. *How often would you like to meet with medical staff for consultation?*		
Weekly	*0*	*1*
Monthly	*0*	*3*
Quarterly	*2*	*4*
Semi-annually	*8*	*24*
Annually	*11*	*3*
Never	*6*	*1*

7. The human resources department surveyed the company's 74 employees to determine how best to structure the work week. The results of the survey follow. Write a memo report to the company president, Connie Trevathan, giving the results of the survey and your recommendations.

	Number of Respondents
1. Preference for 4-day or 5-day week:	
Four 10-hour days	*53*
Five 8-hour days	*18*
No preference	*3*
2. Work hours preferred if 8-hour days with 1-hour lunch break:	
7 a.m. to 4 p.m.	*4*
8 a.m. to 5 p.m.	*15*
9 a.m. to 6 p.m.	*4*
All work 10 a.m. to 3 p.m., flexible hours for other 4	*48*
No preference	*3*
3. Work hours preferred if 10-hour days with 1-hour lunch break:	
6 a.m. to 5 p.m.	*3*
7 a.m. to 6 p.m.	*14*
8 a.m. to 7 p.m.	*4*
All work 9 a.m. to 4 p.m., flexible hours for other 4	*50*
No preference	*3*

8. As a field associate for a national marketing research firm, you surveyed 50 women to learn whether they perceived the scent of several hand and body lotions were (1) appropriately named and (2) attractively packaged. Summarize the results of your research in an informal report that will be sent to the national office with your raw data. The question and coding scheme used in the interviews are as follows:

Age: 1 = under 25 2 = 26–34 3 = 35–44 4 = 45–54 5 = 55 or over

Educational level: 1 = high school 2 = some post-secondary 3 = associate degree or certificate 4 = bachelor's degree 5 = graduate degree

Fragrance rating: 1 = low 5 = high

Attractive packaging: 1 = yes 2 = no

Respondent Number	Age	Educ. Level	Almond Blush	Rose Garden	Mountain Spring	Rainwater Fresh	Autumn Day	Package Rating
1	*1*	*4*	*5*	*3*	*1*	*1*	*2*	*1*
2	*4*	*2*	*3*	*3*	*5*	*2*	*2*	*2*
3	*3*	*3*	*4*	*5*	*5*	*1*	*3*	*1*
4	*4*	*4*	*5*	*3*	*2*	*1*	*4*	*1*
5	*4*	*5*	*3*	*1*	*4*	*5*	*2*	*2*
6	*2*	*3*	*5*	*1*	*1*	*4*	*5*	*1*
7	*3*	*3*	*4*	*4*	*4*	*3*	*3*	*2*
8	*2*	*1*	*5*	*5*	*4*	*4*	*1*	*2*
9	*5*	*3*	*3*	*4*	*2*	*2*	*5*	*1*

Respondent Number	Age	Educ. Level	Almond Blush	Rose Garden	Mountain Spring	Rainwater Fresh	Autumn Day	Package Rating
10	4	4	2	4	5	3	3	1
11	1	1	3	3	3	3	3	2
12	3	1	2	3	4	4	2	2
13	3	2	4	5	5	1	2	2
14	2	4	2	4	2	4	1	2
15	3	1	4	5	5	5	4	1
16	5	1	3	3	2	4	5	1
17	4	4	4	3	2	3	1	1
18	1	2	2	3	4	4	4	1
19	4	2	2	4	3	5	5	2
20	2	4	2	2	3	4	5	1
21	2	4	3	3	4	5	2	1
22	1	2	1	1	3	4	2	2
23	1	3	4	3	5	5	4	1
24	2	3	4	4	1	1	2	2
25	4	5	3	3	1	2	5	2
26	1	1	2	2	4	3	5	1
27	1	2	3	4	5	5	3	2
28	1	3	2	2	4	3	5	1
29	3	1	5	5	5	5	5	1
30	2	4	2	3	2	1	2	2
31	5	4	3	3	3	3	3	2
32	1	3	2	4	5	5	1	1
33	3	3	3	3	4	1	2	1
34	4	3	5	4	5	3	4	1
35	1	2	2	2	3	3	2	2
36	5	3	5	5	3	3	5	1
37	2	1	3	3	3	3	3	2
38	1	4	2	2	2	4	5	1
39	3	1	5	4	3	5	4	1
40	2	2	5	4	1	1	1	2
41	5	5	5	3	2	2	1	1
42	3	2	4	5	4	3	2	2
43	1	1	1	2	3	2	1	1
44	2	3	5	5	3	4	2	1
45	5	2	3	4	3	4	4	1
46	4	2	1	3	5	3	2	2
47	4	1	2	2	4	4	5	1
48	5	4	2	4	3	3	4	2
49	2	5	3	2	4	3	4	2
50	1	2	3	3	4	2	3	2

MESSAGE ANALYSIS

Format the following text as a short, informal report. Give the report a descriptive title, organize the text logically, develop transitions, write a summary, and insert headings where appropriate. Correct grammar, punctuation, and spelling errors.

Business travel is becoming increasingly complex. Deadlines, delayed or canceled flights, crowded airports and airplanes, and hotel stays are just a few of the challenges travelers face. The suggestions presented in this report may help weary travelers to cope with the stress and meet those challenges. If your flight is canceled, call your travel agent or the airline to get a new reservation. By doing this, you will avoide the crowds at the airport ticket counters. If you have carry-on bags, ask to be seated near the rear of the aircraft; You board first and have easier time stowing your bags. Become familiar with the local laws and customs of the countries to which you are traveling. Making telephone calls through a hotels' in-room telephone service is very expensive. For cheaper rates, use a long distance calling card. When staying in a hotel, try to stay between the second and seventh floor. This can help to avoid break-ins while remaining in reach of emergency ladders. Always be sure to request automatic locks when renting a car. These are a valuable safety measure when driving and parking in unfamiliar areas. If you regularly travel to the same destination investigate corporate housing for stays of more then a week. You can go home for the weekends and still keep the lower rates. To minimize the expensive refueling charges when renting a car, note the location of a gas station as you leave the airport. When you returning the car, you will know where to refuel. Keep clothing wrinkle free by rolling articles in dry-cleaning bags when packing. Learn the carry-on bag size restrictions of the airlines you use before you get to the gate and have to forfeit your bag. If you loose your passport while traveling internationally, immediately contact the Embassy or Consulate for assistance right away. Make photocopies of your prescriptions for medicines and eye-glasses, as well as credit cards. This will speed the process of obtaining new ones while on the road. Always be sure to keep a copy of your ID and/or passport in your luggage and at home in case of theft or loss. Place any breakable items, like perfume or cologne, in bubble warp and sealed plastic bags prior to packing to protect them and avoid a mess in the event that they should break. Avoid isolated phones payphones or ones in dimly-lit areas. Face outward while calling to stay alert to possible intruders, and hang onto your belongings. When boarding your fight or checking into your hotel room, always note the location of emergency exist.

GRAMMAR WORKSHOP

Correct the grammar, spelling, punctuation, style, and word choice errors in the following sentences:

1. Miss Beth Hustad and here husband Mark well attend the Opening Ceremonies at the 2004 summer olympics.
2. Can I take you the check and paperwork to your house?
3. Carpal tunnel syndrome is an repetitious, stress injury that effects the nerves in the hands.
4. Tiger Woods oneof Today's best golfers is winning manhy tournamints with his short game.
5. Sherri will of coarse reimbursed you fore yore business related expanses.

6. The rules, and how you should behave regulations, is designed for you're comfort and safety.
7. A senior citizen will receive a free nights lodging when they join our travel club.
8. The news paper re-porter will phone again latter if she has anymore quotations about the emerger.
9. No topic is mere passionately contested then how to raise children correct, and many parents' find that the government and themedia undermine parental authority.
10. Many analyzers believe the Stock MARKET will continue to grow; due to a strong economy, low inflation, and low un-employment.

CHAPTER

12 Proposals, Business Plans, and Special Reports

Bruce Ray, President, Ray Products

LET'S TALK BUSINESS As president of a plastics thermoforming company in Ontario, California, I can attest to the importance of the proposal/quotation/bid process. A clear and concise proposal is essential in order to meet the expectations of the customer. When bidding on a job, we are careful to include the following: scope of the project, detailing what will be supplied by us and by the customer (i.e., design, engineered prints, tooling, material, assembly), a lead time, pricing, quantity, method and schedule of payment, delivery dates and locations, and the period of time for which the quote is valid. It is also important to specify whether the material and/or final product must meet federal (UL) standards, to establish who obtains the clearance, and

(Continued)

[LEARNING OBJECTIVES]

[1] IDENTIFY THE DIFFERENT TYPES OF PROPOSALS.

[2] WRITE FORMAL AND INFORMAL PROPOSALS.

[3] DRAFT A BUSINESS PLAN.

[4] REPORT THE PROCEEDINGS OF A MEETING EFFECTIVELY THROUGH THE USE OF MINUTES.

[5] DEVELOP CLEAR POLICY STATEMENTS.

[6] WRITE AN EFFECTIVE NEWS RELEASE.

[7] PREPARE A CONSTRUCTIVE PERFORMANCE APPRAISAL.

to set the time for first inspection and approval. A bid that includes all of these components helps us avoid misunderstandings and ultimately leads to repeat business and referrals. •

Formal reports are not the only structured documents used within organizations. Proposals and business plans fall into this category, as do a variety of special reports. Each of these document types is discussed in this chapter.

Learning Objective [1]
IDENTIFY THE DIFFERENT TYPES OF PROPOSALS.

Proposals

A **proposal** is a persuasive message in which a writer analyzes a problem and recommends a solution. The problem may be a need for equipment, services, research, a plan of action, or other things. The recommended solution may be products, personnel, a business study, a description of work to be performed, or any of several other outcomes. Proposals are common in business and, as Bruce Ray notes in Let's Talk Business, it is important that they be clear, be concise, and meet reader expectations.

[NOTE 12.1]
Proposals analyze problems and provide solutions.

Businesspeople look for initiative. They welcome suggestions about how to change things for the better. Customers and suppliers want to receive proposals that will benefit them and you. Successful organizations depend on the creation of ideas that will improve productivity and profitability.

[NOTE 12.2]
Proposals present ideas for improving productivity and profitability.

Proposals are gambles. They take time to develop and they often are rejected. Some proposal developers believe that they are doing well if they win acceptance of one of every ten proposals. Effective proposal writers are risk takers; they assess the probability of success and then decide whether to proceed.

[NOTE 12.3]
A proposal is a gamble.

TYPES OF PROPOSALS

Proposals can be external or internal, solicited or unsolicited, formal or informal.

[NOTE 12.4]
Proposals may be
- External or internal
- Solicited or unsolicited
- Formal or informal

External proposals go outside an organization to current or prospective customers, to government agencies, or to private agencies and foundations. These messages include proposals to supply products at given prices, to build roads, or to perform audits. This category also encompasses requests for grants of money or goods to support the work of not-for-profit agencies or other groups hoping to meet some societal or humanitarian need. Such requests are submitted to foundations established solely for the purpose of funding projects in areas such as the arts, education, the environment, or human services. They are also submitted to corporations, whose missions often include returning a portion of their profits to the communities or regions in which they do business.

Receiving approval of external proposals is essential to the success of many for-profit and not-for-profit organizations. The Tips and Hints on page 354 offer several sugges-tions about writing a grant proposal. Libraries and the Web are other sources of information and sample proposals. The sites at **http://www.fdncenter.org** and **http://www.npguides.org** are good online sources of information about proposal writing. The site at **http://www.foundations.org/grantmakers.html** contains a directory of corporate and private foundations.

Always Be Certain

TIPS AND HINTS

Whenever you prepare a proposal to submit to a foundation, always be certain you

- Know the reason why you are writing the grant. If it doesn't make sense to you, it won't make sense to the reader. You must be able to explain in clear, easily understood language how the grant will significantly advance the mission of your organization.
- Do your homework. Carefully research the foundation and pay attention to its criteria.
- Read the entire grant application. Take time to read every sentence of the application; then write your grant request in response to the information asked of you.
- Check your spelling. A spell checker does not catch words spelled correctly but used inappropriately. Present a neatly typed proposal, on clean paper, in a font size that a person with normal eyesight can read.
- Send your proposal to a person. Never use "Dear Sir or Madam" or "To Whom It May Concern."
- Adhere to their deadline. If you have doubts about it, phone them. And, if you receive a grant where a response is requested to indicate your acceptance of the terms, respond immediately.
- Keep your proposal people-centered. Foundations aren't interested in things, they are interested in what the things can do to benefit people.
- Have measurable outcomes. It is not sufficient to say you served more people than ever before. Say how many and what happened to them over what time period.
- Demonstrate the sustainability of your project. What will happen when the funding expires?
- Secure external validation. Letters others write in support of your request validate that others know and value your organization.
- Indicate your intent to collaborate with others. Very few ideas are truly unique; provide documentation that shows how you will work with other organizations also interested in the problem.
- Thank the foundation for its support. Do this not once but every time you report on your project. Keeping the foundation informed about your progress and the support you receive from others helps them know that their investment was a wise one.

From Norma K. Murphy, "The ABCs of Grant Writing or 'Always Be Certain,'" *Fund Raising Management* 30 (6), August 1999, pp. 30–31.

Proposals sent to others within an organization are **internal proposals**. These can be proposals to solve problems or to meet needs by improving procedures, changing products, adding personnel, reorganizing departments, expanding facilities, reducing budgets, or making other changes. Ideas for internal improvement, creatively developed and effectively presented, are the lifeblood of organizations.

A **solicited proposal** is prepared in response to a request for proposal (RFP). The solicitation may be made face-to-face, by telephone, or in writing. Solicited proposals are generally submitted externally. When responding to solicitations for proposals, writers must provide all the requested information and use the specified format. Failure to do so may eliminate the proposal from consideration.

Proposals prepared at the writer's initiative rather than in response to an RFP are called **unsolicited proposals**. These proposals represent an independent analysis of another's problems or needs and the creation of possible solutions. Unsolicited proposals may be internal or external. When submitting proposals to foundations or government agencies, writers must match the goals of the writer's organization to those of the foundation or agency.

Informal proposals generally take the form of letters (external) or memos (internal). Some foundations, corporations, and government agencies encourage or require proposal writers to submit preproposals or letters of inquiry. These documents, which are submitted without attachments, provide a succinct description of the project. After review, the funding agency either rejects the proposal or directs the writer to submit a full proposal.

Learning Objective [2]
WRITE FORMAL AND INFORMAL PROPOSALS.

QUALITIES OF A SUCCESSFUL PROPOSAL

[NOTE 12.5]
Successful proposals have excellent content that is presented clearly.

Successful proposals have qualities that separate them from unsuccessful proposals. Although success sometimes depends on factors such as luck, politics, timing, and reputation, most proposals must have excellent content and be clearly presented to be accepted. The following qualities usually are required for a successful proposal:

- The purpose of the proposal is stated clearly.
- The problem or need is understood and defined clearly.
- The solution is innovative and presented convincingly.
- The benefits outweigh the costs.
- The personnel implementing the solution are qualified.
- The solution can be achieved on a timely basis.
- The proposal is honest, factual, realistic, and objective.
- The presentation is professional and attractive.

To convey these qualities in the proposal, the writer must carefully analyze the situation and the receivers, use the you–viewpoint, and apply the principles of business communication.

[NOTE 12.6]
Proposals should be powerful, persuasive messages.

The proposal should be a powerful, persuasive message. The receivers are going to be looking for the benefits to them, their department, the company, the community, the society, or some other group to which they belong. The proposal should get the receivers' attention, show clearly the benefits of accepting the proposal, give proof of those benefits, and motivate favorable action.

THE ELEMENTS OF A FORMAL PROPOSAL

Items contained in a proposal vary with the situation and the reader. As you'll learn by reading the Communication Notes on pages 356–358, an audit proposal, a sales proposal, and a grant proposal are similar but not identical.

[NOTE 12.7]
Successful proposals contain specific elements.

A successful proposal contains essential elements or parts. In solicited proposals, the elements are specified in the RFP. Careful and complete responses should be made to all the elements requested in the RFP. If you think elements necessary to the acceptance of your proposal are missing from the RFP, then you should try to work those parts into the specified format. In unsolicited proposals, you must

COMMUNICATION NOTE

The Audit Proposal

Accounting firms are often asked to submit written proposals and make oral presentations to substantiate their expertise and demonstrate their ability to serve a client. The proposal-writing process generally has four elements: fact-finding and research, strategy development, content, and design.

The content of the proposal will vary with the scope and nature of the proposal and the requirements of the RFP. Some of the more important items that usually become part of every proposal are

- *Background.* Discuss the key management and industry issues facing the reader's organization.
- *Team information.* Provide information on the experience and background of those who will work on the engagement team; include a graphic representation of the organization chart.
- *Experience.* Demonstrate the firm's depth of knowledge by listing similar work done for other clients in the reader's industry.
- *Audit plan/consulting approach.* Respond to the specifics of the RFP. Include some detail on how you plan to audit the transactions or compliance issues that are unique to an industry or a specific company. In consulting proposals, demonstrate your experience and understanding of the project by providing details about your objectives, steps and procedures, and deliverables.

Excerpted from Bob Stewart, "First Impressions," CA Magazine *133 (2), March 2000, pp. 39–40.*

decide which elements to include. What follows is a list of possible proposal elements:

- Cover letter or memo
- Title page or cover
- Reference to authorization
- Table of contents
- List of illustrations
- Proposal summary
- Purpose
- Problem or need
- Background
- Benefits of the proposal
- Description of the solution
- Evaluation plan
- Qualifications of personnel
- Time schedule
- Cost
- Glossary
- Appendixes
- Reference list

COMMUNICATION NOTE

The Sales Proposal

To be successful, a sales representative needs to be able to write effective proposals to customers. They can be 1-page letters or 100-page tomes that include charts and graphs. They can be delivered in hard copy or online, but every proposal must clearly offer a customer the reasons why a product or service should be purchased. Writing proposals has never been easy, but today it's even more complex as salespeople need to appeal to a broader and more time-sensitive customer base that is often looking for multiple solutions. The writing process is simplified, though, by breaking a proposal into the following five distinct elements:

[1] *Executive summary.* Succinctly and clearly offer the customer one point—your understanding of his or her needs. Spell out the customer's problems, the proposed solutions, their benefits, and any customer concerns. This may be the only part of the proposal that some key receivers ever read; therefore, it should be 2 pages or less for proposals with 50 or fewer pages.

[2] *Need/solution/benefit analysis.* Expand on the summary. Include pertinent design material, explain the sales organization's understanding of the customer's needs and problems, provide the solutions to those problems/needs, and explain the financial and resource benefits of the solutions. The focus of this entire section is not on the product or service but on the receiver.

[3] *Company description.* Demonstrate why your company is the best vendor. Include case histories of customers who solved similar problems with similar solutions. Large firms will stress strength; small firms will emphasize flexibility and personal attention.

[4] *Pricing and sales agreement.* Describe the product, list the price, and identify the delivery schedule. This section typically represents the easiest part of the proposal.

[5] *Sales agreement.* Ask for the business. Base the agreement on what the customer must buy to achieve the benefits described in the proposal. When appropriate, note or guarantee any return on investment analysis that was part of the proposal.

From Joseph Conlin, "The Write Stuff," Sales and Marketing Management *150 (1), January 1998, pp. 71–75.*

Although all these elements are important for many large proposals, the key elements are the purpose, problem or need, benefits of implementing the solution, description of the solution, qualifications of personnel, time schedule, and cost. All the proposal elements are described in the following sections.

Cover Letter or Memo The **cover letter** or **memo**, also referred to as a *transmittal message,* introduces the proposal to the reader. A letter is used for an external proposal and a memo for an internal proposal. The cover letter or memo should include content that provides coherence for the reader, reviews the highlights of the proposal, and encourages action.

[NOTE 12.8]
The cover letter or memo highlights the contents and encourages action.

Title Page or Cover The information contained on the **title page** or **cover** of a proposal can include the title of the proposal, name and location of the receiver, name and location of the submitter, date of submission, principal investigator,

[NOTE 12.9]
The title page or cover includes essential information.

COMMUNICATION NOTE

The Grant Proposal

A grant proposal must convince the prospective donor of two things: (1) that a problem or need of significant magnitude exists and (2) that the applicant agency has the means and the imagination to solve the problem or meet the need.

When no specific format or guidelines are provided by the funding source, assume the proposal should be no more than 15 single-spaced pages and that it should include the following:

- Summary (½ page)
- Qualifications of the organization (1–2 pages)
- Problem statement or needs assessment (3–4 pages)
- Program goals and objectives (1–2 pages)
- Methodology (4+ pages)
- Evaluation (1–2 pages)
- Future funding (½ page)
- Budget
- Appendixes

The proposal is submitted with a one- to two-page cover letter addressed to the person responsible for the funding program. The letter provides a brief overview of the organization and its purpose, includes the reason for the request and the amount (if required by the funder), and provides the name and phone number of a contact at the requesting organization. The letter should be signed by someone who can speak with authority on behalf of the organization.

Excerpted from "Elements of a Grant Proposal," at **http://www.silcom.com/~paladin/promaster.html**.

proposed cost, and proposed duration of the project. The title should be concise, preferably under ten words. Consider which of the six "W and H" questions—what? when? where? who? why? how?—must be answered by the title. The title of the proposal should attract the reader's attention and, because it will be used to identify the proposal, it should be easy to remember. Eliminate meaningless words such as "A Study of" or "An Examination of"; use descriptive adjective–noun combinations.

[NOTE 12.10] If the proposal is solicited, its authorization should be noted.

Reference to Authorization If the proposal is solicited, the request should be noted in a **reference to authorization**—the permission or request for the proposal. The information contained in the reference to authorization depends on the RFP. For an informal or short RFP, the reference could be as simple as listing the RFP number on the cover or including a line in the cover letter or memo that says "This proposal is in response to your telephone call of May 5, 200–." For a formal RFP, the reference to authorization could be one or more pages following the title page or cover. A lengthy RFP may require an abstract as a reference to authorization.

[NOTE 12.11] The table of contents orients the reader and serves as a reference.

Table of Contents The **table of contents** lists the titles and page numbers of all the major sections of the proposal. It will assist in orienting readers and will serve as an aid to locating specific information. The names and page numbers of the appendixes are also included in the table of contents.

List of Illustrations The titles and page numbers of any tables, figures, graphs, or other illustrations are placed in a **list of illustrations** immediately following the table of contents.

[NOTE 12.12]
The list of illustrations contains the titles and locations of visual aids.

Proposal Summary The **proposal summary** is the proposal in capsule form. This section, which contains the most vital information from each of the major sections of the proposal, is prepared after the proposal has been written. It should be short. The summary is designed to give busy people a quick but complete overview of the proposal. For short proposals the summary may be just a paragraph. For a long proposal of 100 to 500 pages, the summary might be 1 to 10 pages. If the RFP specifies a length, be sure to make the summary that length and no longer.

[NOTE 12.13]
The summary provides an overview of the proposal.

Purpose Following the summary, the actual proposal begins. The purpose should be stated first. The **purpose statement** helps the reader understand clearly (1) the reason you are making the proposal and (2) the nature of the proposal—how it will accomplish the purpose. Example purpose statements follow:

[NOTE 12.14]
The purpose statement clearly describes the reason for and nature of the proposal.

> This is a proposal to reduce manufacturing costs 10 percent by replacing the Assembly Line A conveyor system.
>
> The purpose of this proposal is to increase sales by adding commission sales personnel.
>
> The purpose of this proposal is to improve the quality of life of Middleton's senior citizens by securing funding and constructing a senior center adjacent to the community library.

These purpose statements may stand alone or they may be followed by brief explanations. The amount of explanation given depends on the reader's knowledge and his or her need for information.

Problem or Need The next section should describe the problem being solved or the need being met. This section should use coherence techniques to link it to the section in which the purpose was stated. For example, the first purpose statement given in the previous section might be followed by a problem statement such as the following:

[NOTE 12.15]
State the problem being solved or the need being met.

> Manufacturing costs for the second quarter are up 5 percent over the first quarter. Most of this cost increase can be attributed to the new labor agreement that became effective March 1. To meet competition, we must find new ways to reduce manufacturing costs.

Background If necessary for your reader's complete understanding, you should provide background data on the problem. The background section may be combined with the problem/need section or, if both sections are long, it can be presented separately. In the **background** section, you may explain the problem—how it developed, its magnitude, and the consequences if nothing is done.

[NOTE 12.16]
Limit background information to what the reader needs.

[NOTE 12.17] Benefits, the outcomes of implementing the solution, must outweigh costs.

Benefits of the Proposal The benefits of the proposal are important. **Benefits of the proposal** represent the outcomes of the implementation of the proposed solution. The benefits must be stated in the you–viewpoint; they must clearly serve the interests of the reader and/or his or her organization. The benefits must outweigh their cost. (The cost data will be given later in the proposal.) If your proposal is competing with other proposals, the benefits you cite must be more cost-effective than your competitors' benefits for your proposal to be the winning one.

[NOTE 12.18] Emphasize the benefits.

When presenting the benefits of the proposal, use the emphasis techniques discussed in Chapter 4, but be careful not to overstate the benefits. Make them concrete, realistic, and honest.

[NOTE 12.19] The description of the solution is the most important proposal section.

Description of the Solution The description of the solution is the most important section in the proposal. It will likely be the largest section. It contains the solution to the problem or the way you recommend meeting the need.

The description of the solution section must tie coherently to the information given previously in the proposal. References must be made in this section to the purpose, the problem or need, and the benefits of the proposal. Your readers must clearly understand your solution and be convinced that it achieves the purpose, solves the problem, and provides the benefits cited earlier.

The description of the solution should include specifically what you are proposing be done, who will do it, when it will be done, where it is to be done, how it will be done, and why it should be done. As mentioned earlier, proposals submitted in response to an RFP must carefully provide all the information called for in the request.

[NOTE 12.20] Be sure the description is realistic and persuasive.

You will want to stress the innovative aspects of your proposal, the special nature of the resources you are recommending, and the strength of your solution's rationale. Show how these features of your proposal fit your reader's needs or mission. A good way to do this is to relate your solutions directly to each of the benefits given earlier. Those benefits might be listed individually, with each followed by an appropriate part of the description of the solution. The intent is to show clearly that (1) you have carefully thought through all aspects of the proposed solution; (2) it represents a realistic, feasible, and desirable way of solving the problem or meeting the need; and (3) you, your department, or your organization are capable of implementing the solution.

[NOTE 12.21] An evaluation plan provides a way to judge the success of proposal implementation.

Evaluation Plan If appropriate for your proposal, you will want to include an evaluation plan. The **evaluation plan** is a way to measure the degree of success achieved if your proposal were implemented. The evaluation plan could consist of a record-keeping system; a review by a panel of experts; statistical analysis procedures; a reporting system; or any number of control, analysis, measurement, or judgment techniques.

An evaluation plan is a major element in proposals for research studies. In other proposals, such as increased staffing proposals, the evaluation system might be an employee performance review procedure already in place. In this case, only a brief reference to the existing plan would be needed.

[NOTE 12.22] The personnel qualifications section shows ability of participants to provide proposed services.

Qualifications of Personnel In the qualifications of personnel section, you provide biographical information about each key participant involved in implementing the proposal. You show his or her qualifications to provide the services proposed.

The information should include the education, experience, accomplishments, successes, and evidences of achievement that directly relate to each participant's involvement in the proposed solution. In this section, you are justifying to the reader that these persons are fully qualified to serve in their assigned roles. The appropriate types of data are discussed in detail in Chapter 16.

Depending on the nature of the proposal, the amount of data presented for each individual will vary from a few lines to several pages. In some proposals, brief summaries are presented in the qualifications of personnel section and full resumes are provided in an appendix. If you are responding to an RFP, provide exactly the amount and type of personnel information specified.

Time Schedule The time schedule shows when activity is to start and when it is to be completed. For simple proposals, the time schedule may consist of a listing of activities and their beginning and ending dates. For elaborate proposals, it may be necessary to use more complex task-time analysis charts such as Gantt, PERT (Program Evaluation Review Technique), or Milestone.

[NOTE 12.23]
The time schedule shows when activities begin and end.

If you need assistance in selecting a time-schedule format, most libraries have good reference materials you can use. Your responsibility in this section is to show the reader a realistic time schedule.

Cost The cost or the price of the proposed solution is shown next. This section may be labeled *Cost, Prices, Budget,* or given another appropriate title. The cost may be presented in logical parts, such as personnel, supplies, equipment, and facilities; or it may be organized by benefits, parts of the description of the solution, time phases, or other appropriate categories.

[NOTE 12.24]
The cost section shows the cost of the proposed solution.

The cost of the proposed solution must cover your expenses and, if appropriate, a profit. It also must be reasonable in relation to the benefits and the products or services to be provided. If you are following the guidelines in an RFP, the format for the cost section will likely be specified and should be used.

Glossary Based on a careful analysis of your readers, you may decide to include a glossary in your proposal. A **glossary** lists alphabetically the unfamiliar terms used in the proposal and gives their definitions. Include a glossary only when many unfamiliar, specialized, or technical terms have to be used. When there are only a few such terms, define them the first time they are used.

[NOTE 12.25]
The glossary defines unfamiliar terms.

Appendixes To keep the body of the proposal as short and readable as possible, it is sometimes appropriate to place complex supporting information in an appendix. An **appendix** contains items that are indirectly related to the proposal but are excluded from the body to improve readability.

[NOTE 12.26]
Complex supporting information is shown in the appendixes.

It was suggested earlier that resumes of key personnel might appropriately be placed in an appendix. Other information that might be placed in appendixes includes your organization's history, product specifications, records of past successes with similar projects, letters of support, details that support information in the description section, a questionnaire to be used for the proposed research, or other supporting and reference materials.

An RFP may specify what appendixes are to be included. Be sure to include only those appendixes essential to the reader's understanding and decision making.

[NOTE 12.27]
Limit appendixes to information that is essential to the reader's needs.

If the proposal becomes too bulky, it will be less acceptable to a potential approver, funder, or purchaser.

[NOTE 12.28] The reference list contains information about the sources used in the proposal.

Reference List If you think it strengthens your case, include a reference list in the proposal. A **reference list** is an alphabetical listing of all sources of information in the proposal, including those items presented as footnotes.

WRITING A PROPOSAL

[NOTE 12.29] A proposal may be written by a team or by an individual.

For a long, complex proposal, a writing team may be formed. Sections of the proposal may be assigned to different individuals for writing. In this case, it is important to have one chief writer to assure consistency throughout the proposal and to tie all the parts together coherently.

For short proposals one person is responsible for the writing. It may or may not be appropriate for that writer to ask others to read the proposal before it is finalized and submitted.

Whether written by one person or a team, proposals—like correspondence and reports—require planning. The principles of business communication must be applied as the document is drafted, revised, and edited.

[NOTE 12.30] Use format to enhance readability.

Format, too, plays a part in readability and can help to generate interest in the proposal. Headings, margin notes, bullet points, outlines, charts, and diagrams can serve as road signs to guide the reader. White space can help to highlight important items.

Figure 12.1 is an example of a **poor** internal proposal in which the rideshare coordinator is recommending a proposed change in Metrolink reimbursements. This chapter's suggestions for writing successful proposals are not implemented in this memo. An improved proposal for the same situation is shown in Figure 12.2. This example of a **good** informal proposal follows the guidelines for developing and writing successful proposals.

Figure 12.3a is an example of a **good** external proposal submitted by Goodwill Industries, a not-for-profit agency, to secure funding to hire a consultant to guide it through a strategic planning activity. Figure 12.3b is the final report submitted to the funding agency, and Figure 12.3c is a follow-up letter of appreciation. Note that Figures 12.3b and 12.3c include items described in the "Always Be Certain" Tips and Hints on page 354.

[NOTE 12.31] Well-written proposals can help you advance your career.

Proposals are the way that new ideas are conveyed to decision makers. Most of the recommendations in this section on proposals apply to both written and oral proposals. Successful businesspeople develop and submit many proposals in their careers. They are not deterred by rejections. They keep developing and submitting proposals and realize professional and personal gains when their proposals are accepted.

Learning Objective [3] DRAFT A BUSINESS PLAN.

Business Plans

[NOTE 12.32] Business plans are special-purpose proposals.

A **business plan** is a special type of proposal, one designed to persuade a financial institution or a private party to invest money to support a particular venture. The investment may be in a start-up company or in a business that wishes to expand.

The plan provides all the information necessary for the project to be evaluated by the funding source.

This section contains a brief description of what a business plan contains and offers several presentation suggestions. When faced with the task of developing a business plan, most people consult with an accountant or a business development specialist. Numerous print and electronic resources are also available to provide background information beyond what is available here. In addition, there are numerous free or low-cost services provided through agencies such as the Small Business Administration. The SBA's Web site at **http://www.sba.gov** is one of many online that provide sample business plans.

[NOTE 12.33]
Seek help from specialists when preparing a business plan.

Although the actual format and organization may vary, a business plan will contain the following elements:

[NOTE 12.34]
Financial institutions expect business plans to contain certain information.

[1] *Executive summary.* The executive summary describes the highlights of the plan. To help capture the interest of the reader, provide a brief, crisp introduction that discusses the nature of the business and its proposed location; how much funding you need and why; and the time period in which money is needed.

[2] *Ownership/management/staffing.* This section describes the proposed ownership and legal structure; it gives information about the experience, skills, training, and qualifications of key personnel.

[3] *Product/service/market identification.* When describing the products or services, identify the size, location, demographics, and other relevant information about your market. Explain your pricing strategy and how you plan to advertise and market the product or service.

[4] *Administration/production factors.* Next, provide information about equipment and facilities, production techniques, quality control mechanisms, management structure, accounting systems and controls, and any other factors specific to your product or service.

[5] *Growth and development potential and plans.* Present a one- or two-year projection linked to improving or expanding products, services, or markets; changes in required staffing; and additional investment that might be required.

[6] *Financial information.* Provide detailed, realistic information about how much the project will cost, money that will be provided through other sources, and what financial security you can offer lenders. Develop a one-year monthly operating budget and cash flow projection. Forecast a first-year return on investment. Identify the break-even point. Supply projected income statements and balance sheets for two years.

[7] *Appendixes.* Documents that relate to or further explain or support the plan are included in an appendix or appendixes. Resumes of key personnel, letters of intent, and copies of contracts or leases are among the items that may be included.

As you can tell from the item descriptions, the business plan is a complex document—one that poses a writing challenge. As Steve Schneberger notes in the

LEVCO

Interoffice Memo

To: David M. Pedersen, Director
Environmental Health and Safety

From: Michelle Howe
Rideshare Coordinator

Date: April 25, 2000

Subject: Shuttle Service

We are now incurring unnecessary expenses on our Metrolink rider reimbursement program. We have been reimbursing riders $60 of their monthly ticket expense plus we have been giving them free transportation from campus to the Metrolink station. This transportation is not cost-effective in that two shuttles are in service, but ridership is below capacity. Foothill Transit now offers the same shuttle service free to Metrolink ticket holders. We are, therefore, spending money on a shuttle service that is underutilized and for which an acceptable alternative is available at no expense. We need to curtail our shuttle service or reduce the monthly ticket reimbursement to save money and will poll the users to get their opinion.

I hope you will consider this situation when you prepare the Rideshare budget for the next year. We can save a significant amount of money—between $10,500 and $12,000 annually—by taking one of these steps. We can offer each rider either a $60 ticket reimbursement with no shuttle service or a $10 ticket reimbursement with shuttle service. Either way we will save over $10,000. Clearly, there are economic advantages to making these changes.

Subject line is not specific.

Purpose is not stated clearly.

Problem clear, cor or concre

Background information is not organized logically; not all the information is helpful.

Benefits are not emphasized or presented clearly.

Proposed action is not clear.

Figure 12.1
Example of a Poor *Internal Proposal*

Communication Quote on page 377, success depends in part on your ability to present (sell) your ideas clearly and covincingly.

Like other forms of business writing, the business plan should reflect the principles of business communication and show evidence of thorough planning. As a persuasive message crafted to sell your idea, the plan should contain the attention,

LEVCO

Interoffice Memo

To: David M. Pedersen, Director
Environmental Health and Safety

From: Michelle Howe
Rideshare Coordinator

Date: April 25, 2000

Subject: Proposed Change in Metrolink Reimbursements

Subject is clear.

The Purpose

Headings orient reader.

The purpose of this proposal is to seek to reduce the costs of funding the Metrolink shuttle service by implementing a two-tier method of reimbursement.

Purpose is given first.

The Metrolink Shuttle Problem

The cost for providing a shuttle service is $50 per day or approximately $1,000 per month (based on a 20-day month). If we are to provide two shuttles, the cost is $70 per day or approximately $1,400 per month. Each shuttle can hold 15 passengers; and, at this point, the ridership does not justify the use of two shuttles.

Problem is stated concretely.

When we started the shuttle service in 1993, there was no public transportation available to take our employees from the train station to campus. Within the last few months, Foothill Transit has established a new bus route, which conveniently serves the Claremont and North Pomona Metrolink station. Buses are running approximately every 30 minutes throughout the day. There is no cost to ride these buses for Metrolink riders. They only have to show their Metrolink pass and the bus ride is free.

Helpful background information is provided.

Metrolink riders are reimbursed up to $60 per month for the purchase of a train ticket. During the last three months, we have averaged 23 riders per month with a monthly reimbursement cost of $1,105.

The Benefits of Implementing the Proposal

At this point, we are spending $12,000 a year to provide what is, in essence, a parallel transportation service. We are also reimbursing employees up to $60 a month to ride the train. If we estimate the average monthly reimbursement for 23 employees to be $1,105, then we are

Figure 12.2
Example of a Good *Internal Proposal*
Page 1

interest, desire, and action elements described in Chapter 10 and be designed to reflect a professional image. The Tips and Hints on page 377 offer suggestions related to these topics.

Many universities, economic development agencies, and other organizations conduct business plan competitions and award cash prizes to those who write what

David M. Pedersen, Director
Page 2
April 25, 200–

spending $13,260 per year for reimbursements. The estimated total costs for both the shuttle service and Metrolink ticket reimbursements are $25,260.

1. If we were to discontinue the shuttle service and continue paying the $60 per month reimbursement, the annual expense would be approximately $13,260. Compared to our current costs, this is a $12,000 saving.

2. If we drop the reimbursement to $10 per month for those who use the Metrolink shuttle (23 passengers), then our monthly costs would be $230 for the reimbursement and $1,000 for the shuttle. The estimated annual costs would be $14,760. Compared to our current costs, this is a $10,500 savings.

The price difference between proposals 1 and 2 is $1,500.

Recommended Action

I propose we let the Metrolink riders choose which option they want for the 00/01 budget year. Those who want to continue riding the shuttle will receive a $10 monthly reimbursement. Those who want to continue receiving the $60 monthly reimbursement would take the bus or arrange their own transportation to campus. We could easily implement the two-tier system because we receive a daily sheet from the shuttle service listing all the riders by name and department.

A questionnaire listing Options 1 and 2 will be sent to the Metrolink riders. We will also ask for their comments regarding this situation. Based on the information they send us, we can decide what option or options would be best.

Benefits are stated clearly and emphatically.

Proposed action is presented clearly and concretely.

Figure 12.2
Example of a Good *Internal Proposal Page 2*

judges deem to be outstanding business plans. The title page, table of contents, and statement of purpose displayed in Figures 12.4a, 12.4b, and 12.4c are taken from an award-winning plan from a competition held in Superior, Wisconsin. The complete plan is available at the Web site for this book, **http://krizan.swcollege.com**. Business owner Eric Goerdt, who authored the plan, offers his thoughts in the Communication Quote on page 381.

Figure 12.3a
Example of a Good *External Proposal*

700 Garfield Avenue Duluth, Minnesota 55802
Tel: (218) 555-6351 Fax: (218) 555-8108 E-mail: goodwillduluth@servegroup.com

May 3, 1999

Ms. Sharon K. Sederstrom
Program Officer
Duluth-Superior Area Community Foundation
618 Missabe Building
227 West First Street
Duluth, MN 55802

Dear Ms. Sederstrom:

Enclosed is Goodwill's request for a grant of $3,100 to enable a professional facilitator to lead our agency in the development of a strategic plan. The funds will be used to cover the cost of phase three of a three-part strategic planning process as follows:

Phase 1: Background, research, and material review phase.
Phase 2: Solicitation of feedback via surveys, interviews, and focus groups phase.
Phase 3: Development of written strategic plan phase with staff and board participation.

With the recent change in executive leadership at Goodwill Industries, the timing is perfect to reexamine the agency's role in the community and to plan for the future. We estimate the strategic planning process would take between six and nine months to complete and produce a final document. Using a facilitator with an in-depth knowledge of the community would be the most efficient and timely way to accomplish this.

The Board of Directors and staff at Goodwill are enthusiastic to begin the process. With the support of the Duluth-Superior Area Community Foundation and other community resources, we hope to begin this spring and conclude sometime in the late fall.

The outcome of the strategic planning process will be an organization with an enhanced leadership and managerial capacity to meet the human services needs of the community over the next three to five years.

Thank you for considering this request for funding. If you have questions or need additional information, please give me a call at 555-6351.

Sincerely,

Douglas M. Werber
Executive Director

DW/bb
Enclosure: Funding Application

"Our Business Works. So People Can."
Equal Opportunity Employer/Contractor

ccirf
Accredited by the Commission on Accreditation of Rehabilitation Facilities

Figure 12.3a
Example of a Good *External Proposal Cont.*

Minnesota Common Grant Application Form

Date of Application: May 3, 1999

COVER SHEET

(You may reproduce this form on your computer)

ORGANIZATION INFORMATION

Goodwill Industries Vocational Enterprises, Inc.
Legal Name of Organization

700 Garfield Avenue
Address

Duluth, MN 55802	(218) 555-6351	(218) 555-8108
City, State, Zip	*Telephone*	*FAX*

Individuals Responsible:

Douglas M. Werber	Executive Director	555-6351 Ext. 120
Name of top paid staff	*Title*	*Direct dial phone #*
Same		
Contact person (if different from top paid staff)	*Title*	*Direct dial phone #*

Organization Description: *(2–3 sentences)*
The Duluth Goodwill Industries has been providing job training and employment services to people with disabilities since 1919. Goodwill's purpose is to help people overcome barriers to employment and become self-sufficient through employment.

Is your organization an IRS 501(c)(3) not-for-profit? __X__ YES ____ NO

If no, is your organization a public agency/unit of government or religious institution? ____ YES ____ NO

If no, name of fiscal agent (fiscal sponsor) ________

AMOUNT AND TYPE OF SUPPORT REQUESTED

The dollar amount being requested: $3,100.00

Funds are being requested for (make sure the funder provides the type of support you are requesting, then check the appropriate line)

____ general operating support	____ capital	____ Other: ________
__X__ project support	____ endowment	
____ start-up costs	____ technical assistance	

If a project, give project duration __May__ Month __1999__ Year to __Dec.__ Month __1999__ Year

If operating support, fiscal year: ____ Month ____ Year to ____ Month ____ Year

BUDGET

Total annual organization budget: $4,001,010.00

Total project budget (for support other than general operating): $ 9,300.00

PROPOSAL SUMMARY

(If operating or start-up support, relate to the organization. If project and other support, relate to the project.)

Project name (if applying for project support): Strategic Planning Facilitator

____ Please give a 2–3 sentence summary of the request: Goodwill Industries is seeking funds to engage a professional facilitator to lead the organization in the development of a strategic plan. The plan will enhance Goodwill's capability to help people with disabilities or disadvantaged backgrounds become self-sufficient through job training and employment.

Geographic area served:
Northern Minnesota and Northwest Wisconsin

Population Served:
Goodwill Industries serves people with physical or mental disabilities as well as people with disadvantaged backgrounds lacking employment skills.

AUTHORIZATION

Name of top paid staff and/or Board Chair (type): Douglas M. Werber Executive Director

Signature *Douglas M. Werber*

80th ANNIVERSARY 1919–1999

700 Garfield Avenue Duluth, Minnesota 55802
Tel: (218) 555-6351 Fax: (218) 555-8108 E-mail: goodwillduluth@servegroup.com

A Funding Request to the Duluth-Superior Area Community Foundation for a facilitator to guide Goodwill Industries through the development of a strategic plan

1. **GENERAL INFORMATION**
1999 marks the 80th anniversary of Goodwill Industries in Duluth, Minnesota. In North America there are 187 chapters of Goodwill Industries, all of which are members of Goodwill Industries International (GII), headquartered in Bethesda, Maryland. Minnesota has two chapters of Goodwill Industries: Duluth and St. Paul.

Goodwill Industries in Duluth has a territory assigned by GII consisting of 25 counties in Minnesota, or approximately the northern half of the state, and the top four northwest counties in Wisconsin. The agency's annual operating budget is approximately $4,000,000 with 50 percent of its operating revenue coming from the sale of recycled household items in eight thrift stores located throughout its territory.

Goodwill's mission is to provide vocational evaluation, training, extended employment, job placement, and related vocational rehabilitation services to persons with disabilities and others with barriers to employment. The agency serves approximately 300 people annually with the majority of clients being served in the Extended Employment Program. The primary disability served is mental retardation, followed by mental illness. Other disabilities typically include cerebral palsy, epilepsy, learning disability, and traumatic brain injury. A variety of training and employment opportunities is available to clients within the facility, including industrial sewing, wood working, assembly and packaging, and the manufacture of rubber stamps. Community-based training and employment opportunities are found in janitorial and lawn maintenance work, food growing, and frozen food processing.

2. **PROJECT INFORMATION**

A. NEED FOR THE PROGRAM
Goodwill Industries does not have a strategic plan in place guiding the agency. With the recent change in executive directors in September 1998, the time is ideal for the development of one. The process would take between six and nine months. A facilitator with a broad knowledge of the community would enhance Goodwill's ability to identify the unmet employment and training needs of people with disabilities and/or disadvantaged backgrounds in northern Minnesota and northwest Wisconsin. The process will analyze the agency's internal strengths and weaknesses in addition to external opportunities and threats. Goodwill Industries needs to develop a long-range programmatic vision to provide a framework for its programs of service to people experiencing barriers to employment. The result of the strategic planning process will be an agency with a renewed commitment to serve the community and an enhanced capability to help people with special needs become self-sufficient through employment.

B. TARGET POPULATION AND INTENDED BENEFICIARIES
For the 1997–1998 program year, Goodwill provided vocational services to 184 unduplicated people with disabilities or special needs. Mental retardation comprised the largest disability group at 39 percent, and mental illness was second at 24 percent. The remaining 37 percent of clients served included those with learning disabilities, seizures, cerebral palsy, chemical dependency, hearing impairments, visual impairments, cardiac conditions, arthritis, diabetes, physical disabilities, and traumatic brain injury. A community needs assessment will most likely broaden the types and numbers of people served. One of the keys to Goodwill's longevity and success has been its ability to be flexible and to develop programming to meet changing community needs.

C. ANTICIPATED RESULTS
The outcome of a strategic planning process would be an organization with an enhanced management capability and an improved communication system. The organization would have a refocused mission, most likely encompassing a broader range of community needs. In turn, the long-range stability and strength of the organization would be enhanced through the establishment of goals leading to steady growth and diversification. Overall agency morale would increase as the natural creativity of staff members is given full expression. In addition, the strategic planning process will produce an agency road map for the future and a means to measure progress toward mutually agreed upon goals and objectives.

D. PLAN OF ACTION
A strategic planning committee has been formed composed of board members, staff, and volunteers. The strategic planning process would take between six and nine months. The facilitator would guide the organization through the eight steps in the strategic planning process as follows:

Figure 12.3a *Example of a* Good *External Proposal Cont.*

Figure 12.3a
Example of a Good External Proposal Cont.

1. **Situation Audit**
   Assist the agency in interpreting its operating environment by examining agency history, territory demographics, and current financial position. Assist in the clarification of agency core values and the development of a long-range programmatic vision, using observations, trend analysis, and feedback from stakeholders.
2. **Community Needs Assessment**
   Assist the agency in determining the employment and training needs of people with disabilities or disadvantaged backgrounds in the community. Guide the development and implementation of surveys and other vehicles to reach stakeholders for their opinions and observations of Goodwill Industries. Conduct research on existing community needs studies of people with disabilities or disadvantaged backgrounds.
3. **Risk Analysis**
   Lead the organization in an analysis of its internal strengths and weaknesses and external opportunities and threats.
4. **Mission Statement**
   Guide the organization through a reexamination of its mission statement. Help define the mission narrowly enough to encompass existing programming and funding sources yet broad enough to allow for growth and diversification.
5. **Determination of Organizational Objectives**
   Assist in the development of programmatic and operational goals and objectives in line with the overall mission of the organization.
6. **Development of Action Steps**
   Provide guidance in the development of action steps and strategies required to achieve objectives.
7. **Implementation**
   Give guidance and direction to the organization on how to gain cooperation and acceptance of the strategic plan among staff, clients, and board members. Provide a framework for linking annual planning and short-term activities with the achievement of long-term strategic goals.
8. **Evaluation of Plan**
   Assist in the development of a process for ongoing evaluation and revision of the strategic plan.

3. **PLAN FOR EVALUATING THE PROJECT**
   A review of the strategic plan would be part of the annual agency planning and budgeting process. Progress or difficulties in achieving stated goals and objectives would be discussed at the Board of Directors meetings on an annual basis. The plan would be updated on an as-needed basis following periodic reviews by the Board of Directors.

Figure 12.3a
Example of a Good External Proposal Cont.

700 Garfield Avenue Duluth, Minnesota 55802
Tel: (218) 555-6351 Fax: (218) 555-8108 E-mail: goodwillduluth@servegroup.com

STRATEGIC PLANNING PROJECT BUDGET

I. INCOME	
Foundation Grants	
Duluth-Superior Area Community Foundation	$3,100.00
Northland Foundation	3,100.00
Ordean Foundation	3,100.00
TOTAL INCOME	$9,300.00
II. EXPENSE	
Facilitator Fee	$8,500.00
Board/Staff Planning Retreats (2)	500.00
Facilitator/Staff Travel Expense	150.00
Mail Survey/Postage Expense	150.00
TOTAL EXPENSE	$9,300.00

GOODWILL INDUSTRIES VOCATIONAL ENTERPRISES, INC.
Agency Budget/Year-to-Date Actual
Fiscal Year 1998–1999

	1997–98 Actual	1998–99 Budget	1998–99 Actual 7/98–3/99
REVENUE			
Program Srv. Fees—DRS	130,247	128,000	94,558
Job Coach Fees—DRS	17,116	18,750	16,803
DRS Wage Equity	13,503	0	3,716
TBI Project Support	65,953	63,530	42,670
DRS Extended Employment	308,915	280,000	210,128
Program Serv Fees—Other	6,996	7,000	5,235
St. Louis County	109,721	98,000	73,317
Area County Support	16,157	15,000	17,433
United Way–Dul/NE Carlton Co.	102,261	102,900	79,402
Sales to the Public			
Contracts & Chore Services	896,064	937,000	620,861
Retail Sales	1,776,710	1,838,700	1,331,800
Textiles	343,230	249,900	66,401
CBE Wage Reimbursement	79,959	70,000	69,531
Interest Income	29,372	27,000	21,402
Contributions	33,347	5,000	7,050
Contributions—Goods Value	290,449	299,300	259,360
Rental/Miscellaneous	8,022	5,000	14,231
TOTAL REVENUE	4,228,022	4,145,080	2,933,898
DIRECT COST OF SALES			
Production Supplies/Inventory	306,123	351,970	231,112
Client Labor	884,334	900,000	707,231
Client Benefits	11,256	12,250	7,574
Client Payroll Taxes	84,271	94,700	66,035
TOTAL DIRECT COST OF SALES	1,285,984	1,358,920	1,011,952
STAFF SALARY & OTHER EXPENSE			
Staff Salary	1,505,600	1,647,690	1,199,559
Staff Benefits	177,211	211,500	168,429
Staff Payroll Taxes	136,698	161,000	108,462
TOTAL STAFF SALARY & OTHER EXPENSE	1,819,509	2,020,190	1,476,450
OTHER EXPENSE			
Occupancy	280,845	292,000	219,038
Maintenance/Repair—Bldg	42,257	20,000	20,833
Telephone	13,373	13,760	9,830
Insurance	37,419	40,000	22,250
Freight & Shipping	27,729	27,460	15,603
Maintenance/Repair/Rental—Equip.	60,697	51,600	29,248
Travel	25,977	23,450	16,202
Professional Fees	20,190	23,700	14,939
Office Supplies	13,044	12,820	10,238
Postage	6,587	7,000	4,928
Advertising & Printing	30,065	26,500	11,326
Interest	33	100	440
Membership Dues	52,555	45,300	33,866
Miscellaneous	54,632	41,900	46,969
TOTAL OTHER EXPENSE	665,403	625,590	455,710
TOTAL EXPENSE	3,770,896	4,004,700	2,944,112
INCOME IN EXCESS OF EXPENSE	457,126**	140,380	(10,214)

** *Note:* Expense does not include depreciation ($175,092 for 1997–98); revenue does not include any Plant & Equipment Fund revenue ($7,950 for 1997–98).

Figure 12.3a
Example of a Good *External Proposal Cont.*

Figure 12.3b
Follow-Up message

700 Garfield Avenue Duluth, Minnesota 55802
Tel: (218) 555-6351 Fax: (218) 555-8108 E-mail: goodwillduluth@servegroup.com

June 29, 1999

Ms. Beverly Bryant
President
Duluth-Superior Area Community Foundation
618 Missabe Building
227 West First Street
Duluth, MN 55802

Dear Beverly:

Thank you very much for the $3,100 grant from the Corporate Leaders Fund for our Strategic Planning project. Enclosed is the signed Grant Agreement for your files.

Thank you again for helping Goodwill Industries plan new ways of serving people with disabilities in the Duluth-Superior area.

Sincerely,

Douglas M. Werber
Douglas M. Werber
Executive Director

Enclosure: Signed Grant Agreement

"Our Business Works. So People Can."
Equal Opportunity Employer/Contractor

Special Reports

Learning Objective [4]
REPORT THE PROCEEDINGS OF A MEETING EFFECTIVELY THROUGH THE USE OF MINUTES.

Some business reports require special content or format considerations. Four common special reports are minutes, policies, news releases, and performance appraisals.

MINUTES

[NOTE 12.35]
Minutes serve as the official report of a meeting.

Minutes are an official report of the proceedings of a meeting. They should be concise, accurate, and well organized. Minutes serve as an official record, assist in refreshing memories of participants, provide information to individuals who were not present, and help prepare members for upcoming meetings.

[NOTE 12.36]
Only pertinent information should be included in minutes.

Minutes should be brief and should include only pertinent information that accurately summarizes the meeting. All motions and resolutions should be recorded word-for-word as presented. Individuals presenting motions and resolutions should

700 Garfield Avenue Duluth, Minnesota 55802
Tel: (218) 555-6351 Fax: (218) 555-8108 E-mail: goodwillduluth@servegroup.com

March 13, 2000

Ms. Sharon K. Sederstrom
Program Officer
Duluth-Superior Area Community Foundation
618 Missabe Building
227 West First Street
Duluth, MN 55802

Dear Sharon:

I apologize for the delay in sending you the final project report for our Strategic Planning project.

Enclosed is the final project report, although we are not completely finished with the project. All the research, community interviews, and focus group meetings in phase one and phase two have been completed, leaving only the last part of the project, the development of a Work Plan with action steps and timelines, to be done. I expect the project will be finished by the end of March.

Ellie Thompson, our facilitator, has completed her work. She was very helpful in steering Goodwill through the planning process over the past eight months.

Thank you very much for the $3,100 grant that allowed Goodwill Industries to develop a strategic plan. A copy of the plan will be sent to you when it is completed.

Sincerely,

Douglas M. Werber

Douglas M. Werber
Executive Director

DW/bb

cc: Jeffrey Packard, President

A United Way Agency

"Our Business Works. So People Can."
Equal Opportunity Employer/Contractor

Accredited by the Commission on Accreditation of Rehabilitation Facilities

Figure 12.3c
Final Report

be identified by name in the minutes. It is important to indicate that a motion was seconded, but the name of the individual who seconds a motion need not be recorded. The outcome—approval or defeat—should be included also.

The parts that normally are included in minutes are the following: name of the committee or organization conducting the meeting; date, time, and location of the meeting; listing of those who attended; approval of the minutes of the previous meeting; record of the meeting in chronological order; time of adjournment; and

[NOTE 12.37]
Not all minutes will contain the same parts.

Figure 12.3c
Final Report Cont.

DULUTH-SUPERIOR AREA COMMUNITY FOUNDATION
FINAL PROJECT REPORT

The Community Foundation needs to gather evaluative information on the projects it has funded. We, therefore, respectfully request that you prepare a Final Project Report by completing this cover sheet and answering the questions on the following page. Please focus your comments on project outcomes. Return your completed report to the Community Foundation by the date specified in your grant notification letter. Thank you, in advance, for your compliance with this grant requirement.

GRANTEE: Goodwill Industries Vocational Enterprises, Inc.

PROJECT TITLE: Strategic Planning

CONTACT PERSON: Douglas M. Werber

PROJECT GOALS & OBJECTIVES: Development of an Agency Strategic Plan with the assistance of a professional facilitator.

GRANT AMOUNT: $3,100

TIME PERIOD COVERED BY GRANT: June-December 1999

COMMUNITY FOUNDATION BOARD APPROVAL DATE: June 23, 1999

GRANT CONDITIONS: Fund phase three of three-part planning process.

NAME OF PERSON PREPARING REPORT: Douglas M. Werber

TITLE: Executive Director

TELEPHONE: 555-6351

DATE: March 13, 2000

Figure 12.3c
Final Report
Cont.

GOODWILL INDUSTRIES Vocational Enterprises, Inc.

700 Garfield Avenue Duluth, Minnesota 55802
Tel: (218) 555-6351 Fax: (218) 555-8108 E-mail: goodwillduluth@servegroup.com

FINAL PROJECT REPORT
ON THE
GOODWILL INDUSTRIES
STRATEGIC PLANNING PROJECT

I. Program Information

Under the guidance of the project facilitator, Ellie Thompson, the first two phases of the Strategic Planning project have been completed. The last portion of phase three, developing a Work Plan, is in the final stages of completion. The Work Plan accompanies the more general strategic plan (already completed) and sets forth specific objectives and timelines for completion.

Our first estimate of six to nine months to complete the project seems to be more realistic than the revised six-month timeline. Once the Work Plan is finished, the project will be completed. That should occur by the end of March.

II. Financial Information

The $3,100 grant from the Duluth-Superior Area Community Foundation was coupled with identical grants from the Ordean Foundation and the Northland Foundation to fund the entire project budget of $9,300.

From the attached Expenditure Summary, you can see how the funds were applied. Any expenses greater than the available grants were funded by Goodwill Industries. If any additional expenses are incurred in the completion of the Work Plan, they too will be covered by Goodwill.

III. Related Publicity Materials

Because the project did not involve services to clients, no photos were taken that can be shared with funding sources or the community. The project will, however, enhance our ability to serve the employment needs of people with disabilities or disadvantaged backgrounds in northern Minnesota and northwestern Wisconsin.

3-13-00
DW/bb

A United Way Agency

"Our Business Works. So People Can."
Equal Opportunity Employer/Contractor

carf
Accredited by the Commission on Accreditation of Rehabilitation Facilities

Figure 12.3c
Final Report
Cont.

STRATEGIC PLANNING EXPENDITURE SUMMARY
January 31, 2000

Phase I

Professional fees		
May:	initial meeting, tour, and a review of materials	$675.00
June:	timeline revision, research & review of available data, county survey	1,225.00
July:	research community data	500.00
Aug.:	review data & summarize for retreat	600.00
		$3,000.00
Administrative staff cost (1 meeting)		144.00
TOTAL cost of Phase I		$3,144.00

Phase II

Professional fees		
July:	develop focus group questions, conduct multiple focus groups, summarize results	$2,000.00
Aug.:	plan retreat, planning committee meeting	350.00
		$2,350.00
Administrative staff cost (2 meetings)		434.00
Mailings: surveys, focus group notices		111.21
Meeting refreshments & lunches		208.34
TOTAL cost of Phase II		$3,103.55

Phase III

Professional fees		
Sept.:	board focus group, facilitate retreat	$1,700.00
Oct.:	planning meeting, revision of plan	500.00
Nov.:	work plan development	400.00
		$2,600.00
Administrative staff cost (5 meetings)		1,081.00
Retreat accommodations		262.14
Meeting refreshments & lunches		146.56
TOTAL cost of Phase III		$4,089.70

TOTAL PROJECT COST	$10,337.25

Figures 12.3a, b, and c are reprinted with permission. Some names and contact information have been omitted or changed.

signatures of the secretary and/or chairperson. These parts will vary depending on the purpose and formality of the meeting. Style will also vary based on the parliamentary authority used by the group. Figure 12.5 shows an example of minutes for a meeting of a committee of a national organization.

Learning Objective [5]
DEVELOP CLEAR POLICY STATEMENTS.

POLICIES

[NOTE 12.38]
Policy statements serve as guidelines for operation of a business.

A **policy statement** in a business organization serves as a guideline that employees must follow. Policy statements normally will be assembled into a manual. This manual can be used to orient new employees and can serve as a reference for long-time employees.

COMMUNICATION QUOTE

It is difficult to overstate the value of a well-thought-out and well-written business plan. Perhaps the most common use of the written business plan is in the procurement of the financing needed to start or expand a business. In many cases, the loan applicant meets with and presents the loan request to a single loan officer, but loan approvals may be issued only after a higher lending authority such as a senior lender, a loan committee, or a board of directors (and sometimes all three) has reviewed and approved the loan request. In some instances, the specific loan request may be eligible for assistance under one of a number of entrepreneurial loan programs or perhaps the request will be approved only if it qualifies under one of the loan guaranty programs.

Circumstances such as these are not uncommon, and when they arise, the availability of a thoroughly conceived and well-written business plan will increase the likelihood that the entrepreneur's story will be accurately communicated to all parties involved, with minimal loss of critical content.

The following advice is offered to business plan writers:

[1] Be thorough. Seek and use all available resources as you research and write your plan. The perspective gained from sharing ideas with individuals whose profession regularly involves them in this type of activity will produce a better business plan, one that is viewed by the reader as realistic, easy to comprehend, and devoid of mistakes and redundancies.

[2] Include all key assumptions used in preparing financial projections. Support for the assumptions should also be included whenever the reason for their selection is not obvious.

[3] Strive for accuracy. If the reader discovers inaccuracies or unfounded statements, he or she may question the writer/entrepreneur's competence. In some cases, inaccuracy could be interpreted as an intentional attempt to mislead the reader. Obviously, neither of these conclusions is desirable from the writer's perspective.

[4] Be enthusiastic. While your plan must come across as reasonable and realistic, your commitment and enthusiasm for your project must also be conveyed to the reader.

Steve Schneberger, Vice President, Commercial Loans, National Bank of Commerce.

Business Plan Do's

- Keep your plan concise—20 to 40 single-spaced pages plus appendixes.
- Make sure the plan is easy to read and to understand—use headings or tabbed dividers.
- Eliminate typographical and grammatical errors.
- Accurately describe the market opportunities for the business.
- Acknowledge and address the risks involved.
- Convey the strength and depth of your management team.
- Explain your assumptions; make certain they are realistic.
- Limit your use of jargon and technical details. Define any terms you must use.
- Refrain from providing highly confidential or proprietary information.
- Use professional packaging (cover sheet, binding) that reflects the type of business you are proposing; gimmicks detract from content.

Figure 12.4a
Business Plan Title Page

Business Plan

May 2000

TABLE OF CONTENTS

Figure 12.4b
Business Plan Table of Contents

Figure 12.4c
Business Plan Statement of Purpose

NAME AND STATEMENT OF PURPOSE

Northern Waters Smokehaus
Eric and Lynn Goerdt, Sole Proprietors
Superior, Wisconsin 54880

Statement of Purpose

Northern Waters Smokehaus is committed to providing premium smoked salmon and other quality handmade products to the communities of Superior and Duluth. We are committed to providing a quality of life for the owners and employees and being an asset to the business community in Superior.

Reprinted with permission; some names and contact information have been modified. The remainder of the business plan is available at http://krizan.swcollege.com

COMMUNICATION QUOTE

The business plan is very important because it encompasses in written form all the emotions, hard work, dedication, and financial risk that one puts into a small business. If the business plan accurately depicts the excitement that an owner has for a business, the plan will very likely pique the interest of funding sources or investors. The plan is the bridge between the entrepreneur and those who can make the dream a reality, so it must be well written.

Eric Goerdt, Owner, Northern Waters Smokehaus.

Dilbert

www.dilbert.com scottadams@aol.com

Policy statements should be written in the third person and should be clear, concise, and complete. Policies written for managerial personnel are broad guides that allow flexibility, whereas policies for nonmanagerial personnel are narrower and more restrictive. An example of a policy memo is shown in Figure 12.6.

[NOTE 12.39] Policies should be broad for managerial personnel and specific for nonmanagerial personnel.

NEWS RELEASES

Learning Objective [6] WRITE AN EFFECTIVE NEWS RELEASE.

A **news release** is a special business report containing information that will be of interest to the public. News releases need to be newsworthy, accurate, timely, concise, and positive. Common subjects for news releases include promotions, business expansion, employee layoffs, and introduction of new products.

[NOTE 12.40] News releases build good public relations.

The **inverted pyramid format** should be used for news releases. The inverted pyramid format begins with a summary lead that tells who, what, where, when, and sometimes why or how. The body of the release should be developed by giving details in descending order of importance—most important facts first and least important facts last. A news release should not contain a conclusion.

[NOTE 12.41] News releases should be written in the inverted pyramid format.

Figure 12.5
Minutes of a Meeting

Membership Affairs Committee (MAC)
Minutes
August 5–6, 2000
Chicago, Illinois

The following were present for all or part of the meeting:

Members: Phil Brigham (Chair), Sylvia Cotting, Adam Dougherty, Seth Finch, Tonya Hawkins, Julia Lloyd, Walter Murphy. **Staff:** Mike Castro, Elsa Craig, Don Patberg. **Guests:** Jim Elwood, Jeremy Vieth, Vince Vincent.

Meeting Details
The Committee met in executive session from 9 a.m .until noon on Saturday, August 5, and from 8:30 a.m. until 11:30 a.m. on Sunday, August 6. The Subcommittees on Member Services (MS), Member Recruitment/Retention (MRR), and Membership Categories/Dues (MCD) met separately from 1:30 p.m. until 4:30 p.m. on Saturday, August 5.

1. **Approval of Minutes of the May 14–15, 2000, Meeting**
   The minutes were approved with one correction: page 3, ". . . The conference will be held in Arlington, Texas, . . ." [Cotting/Finch/unanimous]

2. **Chair's Report**
   Brigham reviewed what MS/MRR Joint Task Force has done on insurance benefits. Dougherty suggested the group investigate long-term care insurance.

   Brigham referred to a letter from the Committee on Professional Affairs (CPA), which plans to survey members under age 40. MAC was invited to suggest topics. The matter was referred to the MRR, which will be asked to report at the next meeting.

3. **Membership Certificate Presentation**
   Jeremy Vieth of the Board of Directors made a presentation about membership certificates. During discussion, a question arose about whether years as a student affiliate were counted when a member applied for emeritus status. The matter was referred to the MCD for discussion.

4. **Committee Web Site**
   Patberg reviewed the Committee Web site. He encouraged members to look at the Web site (www.membership.acu.org/mac). A counter and "mail to" links have been added; surveys can be conducted through the site. The Committee asked staff to consider the following questions and report at the next meeting:
   1. Should Committee and Subcommittee minutes go on the Web page?
   2. How should page traffic be tracked?
   3. Will inserting meta tags improve searchability?
   4. Who reviews content? How often?

5. **Subcommittee Reports**
   <u>Membership Services—Tonya Hawkins, Chair</u>
   ACTION: Support the Subcommittee recommendations for expanding the nontechnical members' benefits in 2001 and 2002 to include worldwide Internet access. [Hawkins/Vieth/unanimous]

   <u>Member Recruitment/Retention—Julia Lloyd, Chair</u>
   ACTION: Accept the Subcommittee recommendation that a notebook be awarded to 10-year members and a pen to 25-year members and that both bear the association logo and year milestone. [Lloyd/Murphy/passed]

   <u>Membership Categories/Dues—Sylvia Cotting, Chair</u>
   No recommendations were forwarded for Committee action.

Mike Craig

Mike Craig

Figure 12.6
Policy Statement

POLICY NUMBER: 23
SUBJECT: Working Hours
APPLIES TO: Staff
EFFECTIVE DATE: July 1, 200–
REVISED FROM: January 1, 2000

WORKING HOURS

1. **Work Week**
   a. The normal work week for full-time employees is either 37½ or 40 hours measured from Friday midnight until midnight of the following Friday. (Saturday through Friday)
   b. Employees of several departments of the resort regularly work 40 hours per week. Schedules for these hours are established by each department.

2. **Shifts**
   a. The normal office hours of the resort are 7½ working hours per day, 8:00 a.m. to 4:30 p.m. (1-hour lunch)
   b. Employees may be required to work shifts different from normal, such as afternoons, evenings, and/or weekends. The supervisor shall base assignment of an employee to a shift on the needs of the department, work performance, and seniority.

3. **Days**
   a. The normal work week is five (5) days.
   b. Several departments require a seven-day-per-week operation. Employees working in these departments will be required to revise schedules to meet the needs of these departments. The supervisor shall base the assignment of an employee to a schedule on the needs of the department, work performance, and seniority.

The news release should be double-spaced with the company's name and address typed or printed at the top. The contact person's name and telephone number also should be on the news release. Special instructions ("FOR IMMEDIATE RELEASE," "FOR RELEASE ON MAY 2") should be typed in all capital letters at the top. The release text is immediately preceded by city, state, and date. A news release should end with "-30-" or "###" beneath the last line to inform the news agency that the release is complete; for releases longer than one page, "more" should be printed on the bottom of each page that is to be continued. Figure 12.7 shows a sample news release.

[NOTE 12.42]
News releases should end with "-30-" or "###."

Figure 12.7
News Release

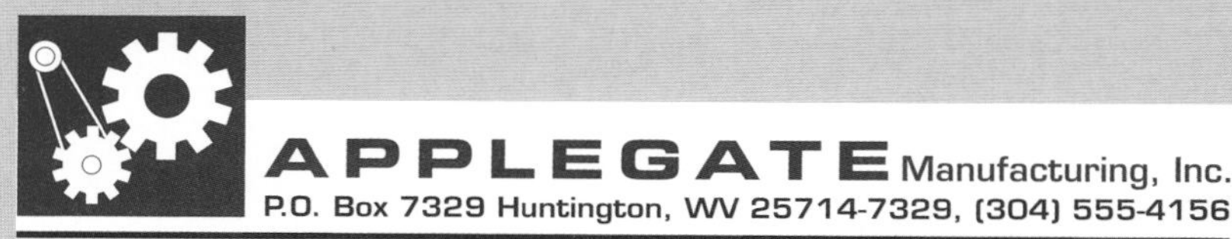

NEWS RELEASE

FOR IMMEDIATE RELEASE

Applegate Manufacturing Declares Dividends

Huntington, WV (April 13, 200–) Applegate Manufacturing, Inc. announced today that its Board of Directors declared a quarterly dividend of $0.175 a share on the company's Common Stock and $0.875 a share on its Preferred Stock, both payable April 15, 200–, to stockholders of record on March 16, 200–.

Applegate Manufacturing is a leading North American plastics manufacturer specializing in products used in food packaging. Based in Huntington, West Virginia, the company also has facilities in El Paso, Texas, and Salem, Oregon.

CONTACT:

Walter Henry
304.555.4082
W.Henry@applegate.paper.net

###

Learning Objective [7]
PREPARE A CONSTRUCTIVE PERFORMANCE APPRAISAL.

PERFORMANCE APPRAISALS

[NOTE 12.43]
Performance appraisals help the employee and the organization.

A **performance appraisal** reports a supervisor's evaluation of his or her employees' job performance. The appraisal is a tool for helping to improve subpar performance and for identifying leadership potential. Written appraisals are prepared, then discussed with the worker before becoming part of his or her employment record. Often the employee is asked to sign the appraisal to acknowledge that the supervisor has discussed it with him or her. Employees who disagree with the supervisor's appraisal may have an opportunity to write a response and have it included in the file, too. Information contained in Chapter 6 will be useful in preparing for and conducting the performance appraisal meeting.

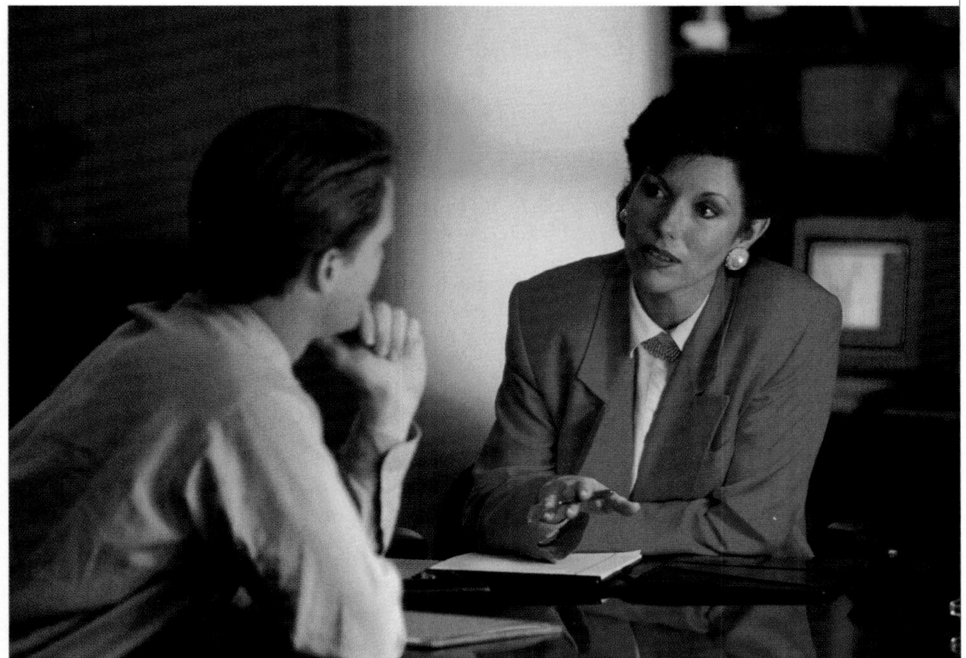

A supervisor and worker discuss the worker's performance appraisal.

No employee should be surprised by information contained in a written performance appraisal. Good management practice dictates that duties and expectations be conveyed to employees in advance and that informal feedback—praise, criticism, and suggestions for improvement—become a routine part of supervision. Nevertheless, supervisors must approach the writing of a performance appraisal as they would any other business document. They must identify the purpose, analyze the receiver, and select the appropriate approach.

[NOTE 12.44]
Performance appraisals formalize elements of the supervision process.

An evaluation that will be received positively or neutrally should follow the direct pattern; evaluations that contain negative news should be presented indirectly. Because the appraisal will become the basis for human resource decisions such as pay raises, promotions, discipline, and terminations, assessments must be supported by factual evidence. Saying "Paul has submitted 4 of his last 6 monthly reports 3 to 10 days after they were due" is more descriptive than "Paul does not submit reports in a timely manner."

Brevity is also a factor in preparing performance appraisals. Many organizations have developed forms that supervisors must use, and space is usually limited. If necessary, the writer should continue his or her comments on another sheet and attach it to the form. The organization may ask that the worker sign both the form and the supplement. Figure 12.8 represents one section of a performance appraisal. An honest appraisal, devoid of humor and sarcasm, is most effective. Omit comments such as "He sets low standards and consistently fails to achieve them." The Tips and Hints on page 386 offer more suggestions related to the performance appraisal process.

Figure 12.8
Performance Appraisal

Performance Appraisal

Employee: Barbara Wriggly **Department:** Administration

Duty: Employee is responsible for greeting visitors, issuing visitor badges, and notifying employees that their guests have arrived.

Standard: Visitors should be greeted within 30 seconds after entering the lobby. No guests should pass beyond the lobby without a visitor badge. No guests should pass beyond the lobby without an employee escort.

Evaluation: Barb performs her duties efficiently. Guests are greeted in a timely manner and served in the sequence in which they arrive. Her smile and the warm, friendly tone of her voice create a positive impression on our guests. Barb needs to ensure that she exhibits these positive traits in her interactions with employees as well as guests. During the past three months, I have received calls from four employees expressing concern that Barb has become sharp with them if she must phone them more than once. They fear that guests may hear her and react negatively.

Action/ Follow-up: Barb and I will develop several strategies for handling delays and review their effectiveness after two weeks and again after six weeks.

Employee's Signature: *Barbara Wriggly* Supervisor's Signature: M. P. Arb
Date Reviewed: June 16, 200–

The Performance Appraisal Process

TIPS AND HINTS

- Effective reviews cannot be written the night before. The process should begin days or even weeks in advance.
- Keep "performance flashes" about each worker. These notes, which reflect positive and negative work occurrences and detail what happened when, will help reinforce the appraisal by providing specific examples.
- Focus your requests for improvement. A long list of needed changes can be overwhelming to the employee. Stress your top priorities and plan to monitor them.
- The ability to deliver powerful, motivating performance reviews is something that happens only with practice. Openness, honesty, and trust are keys to excellent appraisals and leadership.

Adapted from John Farr, "Beat the Performance Appraisal Blues," *Restaurant Hospitality* 82 (9), September 1998, p. 38.

Summary of Learning Objectives

Learning Objective [1]

Identify the different types of proposals. A proposal is an analysis of a problem and a recommendation for a solution. The recommended solution may be products or personnel, a business study, work to be performed, or any of several other ways of solving a problem. Proposals may be external or internal, solicited or unsolicited, formal or informal. External proposals can be directed to prospective clients, government agencies, or private agencies/foundations.

Learning Objective [2]

Write formal and informal proposals. Proposals are common in business and must be written as persuasive messages designed to win the reader's approval of the writer's recommendation. Successful proposals must have excellent content and be clearly presented.

Learning Objective [3]

Draft a business plan. A business plan is a proposal for funding to start or expand a business. The proposal will provide information about the people, products, potential, and financing of the business. A realistic, well-thought-out, well-written business plan has the greatest opportunity for success.

Learning Objective [4]

Report the proceedings of a meeting effectively through the use of minutes. Minutes of a meeting should be brief and contain only relevant information. Motions and resolutions should be recorded exactly as presented. The name of the individual presenting a motion or resolution should be included in the minutes along with the outcome of the motion.

Learning Objective [5]

Develop clear policy statements. Policy statements serve as guidelines for the operation of a business. They should be clear, concise, and complete.

Learning Objective [6]

Write an effective news release. News releases should be written in the inverted pyramid format. The body should contain the important facts first and least important facts last. It should not contain a conclusion.

Learning Objective [7]

Prepare a constructive performance appraisal. Performance appraisals provide feedback to workers and help them improve their performance. They typically become the basis for human resource decisions such as pay raises, promotions, discipline, and termination. Statements should be concise, clear, and concrete. Comments should be organized directly for positive, neutral evaluations and indirectly for negative evaluations. A written evaluation should be discussed with and signed by the worker to show he or she has reviewed it.

DISCUSSION QUESTIONS

1. Define and explain the various types of proposals. (Objective 1)
2. Discuss the qualities of successful proposals. (Objective 2)
3. Why is it necessary for a proposal to include information about the qualifications of personnel? (Objective 2)

4. What is a glossary? When should it be included in a proposal? (Objective 2)
5. What is a business plan? For whom is it prepared? (Objective 3)
6. Briefly describe the nature of the materials included within a business plan. (Objective 3)
7. List the purposes of meeting minutes. (Objective 4)
8. How do policy statements written for managerial personnel differ from those written for nonmanagerial personnel? (Objective 5)
9. Describe the inverted pyramid format for composing news releases. (Objective 6)
10. What is a performance appraisal? What purpose does it serve? (Objective 7)

APPLICATION EXERCISES

1. **Internet. Teamwork.** Individually or as a group, develop a proposal on one of the following topics. If possible, use the Web to research the topic. The proposal is to be sent to the dean or president of your college, as appropriate for the topic. (Objectives 1 and 2)
   a. Requiring all students to have laptop computers
   b. Establishing a "Club Member of the Term" award
   c. Instituting a career shadowing program in local businesses
   d. Requiring all business students to complete an internship
   e. Operating on a four-day school week
   f. Installing baby diaper changing stations in all (male and female) restrooms
   g. Requiring all business students to complete 200 hours of volunteer work
   h. Increasing summer school offerings
   i. Sponsoring a blood drive
   j. Sponsoring a "Business Jeopardy" competition among student organizations

2. **Internet. Teamwork.** Write an informal proposal to your instructor in which you recommend that your business communication course be offered on the Internet. Think carefully about the purpose, the problem, and the benefits of this proposal. Use a Web search engine to locate other schools that offer courses on the Internet. Consider working with a team to brainstorm the recommended action. (Objective 2)
3. Interview the development officer at your school, the director of a not-for-profit group within your community, or the director of a local foundation to learn about the proposals they write or fund. Report your findings to the class. (Objectives 2 and 3)
4. Write a complete proposal using all 18 proposal elements discussed in this chapter. The subject of your proposal can be (1) combatting fatigue by allowing workers to take short naps during the work day or (2) instituting self-appraisal or peer review as part of the performance evaluation process within the organization. (Objectives 2 and 7)

5. **Teamwork.** Work with two or three students who are pursuing the same degree as you and design an Internet-based business. As your instructor directs, prepare all or selected parts of a business plan designed to obtain the funding necessary to start your business. (Objective 3)

6. **E-mail/Internet.** Use the Internet to identify three foundations that fund tech-nol-ogy related proposals from post-secondary schools. Compare their application requirements and funding guidelines; report your findings to your instructor via e-mail.
7. A copy of the minutes of the Butler Insurance Company Fringe Benefits Committee meeting follows. List the items that have been omitted from the minutes. (Objective 4)

MINUTES

FRINGE BENEFITS COMMITTEE

The meeting was called to order at 10:30 a.m. on April 18, 200–.

Copies of the last meeting's minutes were distributed.

Ms. Carson presented a proposal on the new procedures for vacations. Mr. Wilson moved that the proposal be approved.

The committee unanimously approved the motion.

The proposal for adding dental insurance to the family policy was defeated by a 5 to 2 vote.

The president appointed Mr. Thomas to gather information on eye care insurance. He was directed to report his findings at the next committee meeting.

The meeting was adjourned at 11:15 a.m.

8. **Internet/E-mail.** Many organizations and local government bodies now post minutes of their meetings on the Web. Check to see whether organizations to which you belong or the city in which you reside has adopted this policy. Report your findings to your instructor in an e-mail and, if one or more of these groups have not adopted this policy, prepare an informal proposal suggesting that one of them do so. Submit your proposal not only to your instructor but also to the organization or government body. (Objectives 1, 2, and 4)
9. You are a member of the student government association at your school. The association has passed a resolution that prohibits smoking in classroom buildings. Develop a policy statement concerning this issue that could be submitted to the administration for consideration. (Objective 5)
10. **E-mail.** Write (or e-mail) three businesses and request copies of their policy on reimbursing employees for business-related travel. Summarize your findings in a memo to your instructor. Include information about the format of the policies, including whether they are numbered, dated, and so on. (Objective 5)
11. A student organization to which you belong is holding a regional conference on your campus. Assume a well-respected, nationally known business leader has accepted your invitation to be the keynote speaker at the event. Prepare an appropriate news release; add details to make the release interesting. (Objective 6)

There are Web exercises at **http://krizan.swcollege.com** to accompany this chapter.

MESSAGE ANALYSIS

Rewrite and improve the quality of the following policy statement. Implement the guidelines given in this chapter.

Due to the increasing litter problem on the head quarters building, the following poster policy is in effect. This affects all posters, flyers, handbills, and other publicity materials posted on the walls. ANY POSTER, NOT APPROVED OR LACKING INFORMATION WILL BE TAKEN DOWN. See the Public Relations Office manager for detales; the Hr director can give special approval of items that do not fit these criterion.

1. *All posters must contain the following information:*
   - *Sponsoring Organization (internal grapes take priority)*
   - *Time of the event*
   - *Place of the event*
   - *Cost to attend the event*
   - *Who the event is open to*
2. *Posters must not exceet a size of 22 x 14.*
3. *Each poster must be individually stamped and initialed by the Pr receptionist.*

Posting

1. *Posters can only be only posted in one of the approved posting locations. See Approved Posting Areas.*
2. *Posters CAN NOT be put on department bulletin boards, painted surfaces, wood surfaces, wall-papered surfaces, metal surface, glass surfaces, directional signs*
3. *Masking tape is the only adhesive you can use. Other tapes or poster mounts are not permeated.*
4. *Please remove posters after the even has occured. This will help keep advertising activities effective and keep the accumulation of posters to a minimum.*

GRAMMAR WORKSHOP

Correct the grammar, spelling, punctuation, style, and word choice errors in the following sentences:

1. This mourning I got in touch with the 800 number and telephoned the magazine to change the addres.
2. In todays' male a postcard from Allen's in New Zealand arrived?
3. Your card and note is hear on my desk sitting an reply.
4. You we're choosed to participate in the program and should have received the letter of acceptance soon.

5. Edw. he learned that Abby got promoted so he sended here a congratulate card.
6. A passport and visa is required for intry in to China: a visa is not require for Hong Kong unless you are on an immigrant visa of SouthEast Asia.
7. After you pass the class we will reimburse your tuition and fees; the from you must complete fill out is availabe at the HR websight.
8. One of the first woman involved in leadership of unions is Dolores Huerta who co-founded the United farm workers Union with Cesar Chavez.
9. All of her children is activists witch make Dolores especially proud of.
10. Cicily chose verticle blinds for her office, they will be instilled early next month?

CHAPTER

13 Visual Aids

Lawana Duncan Sleadd, Information Systems Manager, Dana Corporation, Plumley Division

LET'S TALK BUSINESS Visual aids are a powerful means for communicating valuable information. Our business uses a variety of visual aids to keep associates informed.

The financial well-being of our company is regularly communicated to all employees through the use of visuals. We are given a clear picture of how actual numbers relate to the planned or budgeted numbers. We can see how we are measuring up to our corporate goals. We can see at a glance how the current year compares to prior years. Graphs can serve as a benchmarking tool

(Continued)

[LEARNING OBJECTIVES]

[1] DESCRIBE THE PURPOSES OF VISUAL AIDS IN WRITTEN AND ORAL COMMUNICATION.

[2] EXPLAIN WHERE TO PLACE A VISUAL AID WITHIN A REPORT.

[3] LABEL VISUAL AIDS PROPERLY.

[4] CONSTRUCT TABLES THAT PRESENT STATISTICAL INFORMATION.

(Continued)

for comparisons to other divisions within the corporation, to other companies of like size, and to competitors.

Graphs are also valuable tools for tracking projects or programs. Timelines are effective for showing the progress of a project. Timelines from completed projects are a resource for estimating other projects. "Red/Yellow/Green" charts are used to follow a project's status. At a quick glance we can see by the "red" status what projects are having problems.

Flowcharts are used throughout the company. Organizational charts give a clear picture of employee reporting lines, and the proper placement of solid versus broken lines is critical for understanding the authority structure. Flowcharts are particularly useful in the Information Systems Department.

Visual aids have become important tools for businesses to use in communicating with employees, customers, and suppliers. Using accurate and well-defined visual aids enables you to provide important information quickly and effectively. •

[5] CONSTRUCT THE THREE TYPES OF CHARTS THAT COMMONLY APPEAR IN BUSINESS REPORTS.

[6] CONSTRUCT THE VARIOUS TYPES OF BAR GRAPHS AND LINE GRAPHS.

[7] DESCRIBE HOW MISCELLANEOUS VISUAL AIDS ARE USED.

[8] SELECT THE APPROPRIATE TYPE OF VISUAL AID TO COMPLEMENT AN ORAL PRESENTATION.

[9] EXPLAIN HOW RECEIVERS CAN AVOID BEING DECEIVED BY VISUAL AIDS.

[NOTE 13.1]
Visual aids make a report more understandable.

A **visual aid** is an illustration used to clarify points and improve comprehension of material in a written report or business presentation. Visual aids may be in the form of tables, graphs, charts, drawings, photographs, diagrams, or maps. These illustrations are used to complement the communication. Visual aids for written reports may reduce the volume of text, but they do not eliminate the written material completely. Visual aids can clarify complex data in an oral presentation without lengthy explanation.

Use of Visual Aids

[NOTE 13.2]
Appropriate visual aids will improve communication.

When used properly, visual aids can be helpful in effectively communicating ideas. Indiscriminate use of visual aids may impede rather than promote communication. The selection of effective visuals requires a basic knowledge of the purposes of visual aids and the design elements of these visuals, as well as careful consideration of how they will be used to complement the written or spoken word.

Effective use of color in a graphic aid can help receivers understand such topics as soil composition.

Learning Objective [1]
DESCRIBE THE PURPOSES OF VISUAL AIDS IN WRITTEN AND ORAL COMMUNICATION.

PURPOSES OF VISUAL AIDS

[NOTE 13.3]
Various visual aids accomplish different objectives.

Visual aids can complement your communication by summarizing complex figures in charts and graphs, by identifying your company through the use of a drawing or photograph for a logo, by showing relationships in a chart, by indicating trends in a graph, or by abstracting in a table details that are too cumbersome for written text or oral presentation. Appropriate placement and identification of visual aids will enhance the effectiveness of your communication.

Learning Objective [2]
EXPLAIN WHERE TO PLACE A VISUAL AID WITHIN A REPORT.

PLACEMENT OF VISUAL AIDS IN A WRITTEN REPORT

[NOTE 13.4]
Reports are improved when visual aids are placed in proper locations.

Visual aids (also referred to as *illustrations*) must be placed in appropriate locations to enhance the message of the written report. Illustrations that directly relate to the topic should be placed within the written text. A small illustration, less than one-half page, should be placed after the first reference to the aid, preferably on the same page. A large illustration, one-half to one page, should be placed on the page following the first mention of the illustration. Avoid dividing a visual aid between two pages. It is more desirable to place the entire illustration on one page, separate from the copy, than to divide it.

Illustrations that indirectly relate to the copy may be of interest to only a few readers. These illustrations will add unnecessary bulk to the body of the report and should be placed in an appendix.

You should refer to a visual aid within the written text of the report prior to its appearance. This reference is a powerful tool—it guides the reader to the items you want to stress. The reference may be nothing more than "as shown in Graph 2" or "(see Table 3, page 12)." A reference to a visual aid should be casual and not distract the reader's attention from the material being read.

[NOTE 13.5]
Illustrations should be referred to in a report before they appear.

Learning Objective [3]
LABEL VISUAL AIDS PROPERLY.

IDENTIFICATION OF VISUAL AIDS IN A WRITTEN REPORT

All formal visual aids within a written report should be identified by appropriate titles. The title of a visual aid should describe its contents. The title should contain enough detail so that the reader can understand the visual aid without reading the text of the report, but it should not be extremely lengthy. You should consider the five Ws—who, what, when, where, and why—and use those that will make the title most clear.

[NOTE 13.6]
Illustrations must have titles.

Methods of numbering visual aids vary. One method is to call all visual aids *illustrations* and number them with either Arabic or Roman numerals. A second method is to divide the graphic aids into two categories and use Roman numerals for *tables* and Arabic numerals for *figures* (all illustrations other than tables grouped together). A variation of the second method is to categorize and number each type of figure separately (chart, diagram, graph, etc.) but still use Arabic numerals for identification.

[NOTE 13.7]
The report writer must determine the numbering method for the visual aids.

Visual aids should be numbered consecutively. However, if there is only one visual aid in a report, it need not be numbered. If the report contains more than one section or chapter, the illustrations may be numbered consecutively throughout the report (Figure 1, Figure 2, etc.); or they may be numbered consecutively by sections or chapters (Figure 1.1, Figure 1.2, Figure 2.1, etc.). The most important consideration in numbering illustrations is consistency.

[NOTE 13.8]
Illustrations must be numbered in a consistent manner.

Illustration titles may be printed either in uppercase or in uppercase and lowercase letters. Traditionally, titles were placed above tables and below all other illustrations. Today, businesses use either location. As in the numbering of illustrations, consistency is the important guideline in title placement.

[NOTE 13.9]
Titles may be placed above or below illustrations.

IDENTIFICATION OF VISUAL AIDS SOURCES

The same consideration for acknowledging sources of text material should be used in acknowledging sources of visual aids. A **source note** is used whenever content is obtained from another source. The source note normally consists of the word *source* in uppercase letters followed by a colon and the source. An example of an illustration using material from a report written by Toshi Okano follows:

[NOTE 13.10]
Source notes have to be used for illustrations obtained from others.

SOURCE: *Toshi Okano Report,* January 11, 2000, p. 17.

Although a source note is usually placed a double space below the illustration, it may be placed under the title of the illustration. If the content of an illustration is originated by the writer, no source note is required.

Development of Visual Aids

[NOTE 13.11]
Selecting the right visual aid improves communication.

Effective communication depends in part on the selection of the most appropriate visual aid for a specific situation. You must be knowledgeable about the various types of illustrations so you can select the one that will most effectively convey information under specific conditions. The most frequently used visual aids in business reports are tables, charts, and graphs.

Learning Objective [4]
CONSTRUCT TABLES THAT PRESENT STATISTICAL INFORMATION.

TABLES

[NOTE 13.12]
Tables show data arranged in rows and columns.

A **table** is a typed or printed display of words and numbers arranged in columns and rows. The data in tables should be presented in an orderly arrangement for easy and clear reference. In addition to the title, a table includes headings for the columns and entries in the first column that classify the categories of data in each row. These headings and columnar entries need to identify the data clearly but should be short so they do not detract from the data.

Statistical information can be presented more effectively in a table than in text material. To illustrate this point, consider the following information:

> Oil is a valuable mineral to the Texas economy. More than 20 percent of the oil produced in the United States is produced in Texas. The top 10 Texas counties in crude oil and condensate production in 1997 and 1998 were the following: Andrews—30,554,718 and 29,150,250; Crane—14,332,295 and 13,935,363; Ector—26,719,864 and 25,281,639; Gaines—36,976,256 and 36,016,018; Gregg—16,112,519 and 12,943,293; Hockley—25,546,518 and 25,663,717; Midland—13,225,765 and 13,729,842; Pecos—23,343,542 and 21,397,317; Upton—11,217,533 and 10,248,494; and Yoakum—30,166,705 and 29,398,194. These production statistics were obtained from the *2000–2001 Texas Almanac.*

This statistical information would be communicated more effectively if presented in a table, as shown in Figure 13.1. The statistical information in the 1998 column is listed from high to low. Readers can interpret data more easily when the numbers are listed in some order, high to low or low to high, rather than randomly.

When information to be presented in a table requires numerous columns, the table may be constructed horizontally (lengthwise) on the page rather than vertically. Figure 13.2 is a lengthwise table.

Learning Objective [5]
CONSTRUCT THE THREE TYPES OF CHARTS THAT COMMONLY APPEAR IN BUSINESS REPORTS.

CHARTS

[NOTE 13.13]
Pie charts, flowcharts, and organization charts are commonly used in business reports.

The three types of charts commonly used in business reports are organization charts, flowcharts, and pie charts. None of these charts needs lengthy text interpretation. The first two types, organization charts and flowcharts, clearly present relationships and procedures. The pie chart is used to illustrate the proportion of a part to the whole.

[NOTE 13.14]
An organization chart shows lines of authority and relationships within an organization.

Organization Charts An **organization chart** shows lines of authority among the various positions within an organization. This type of chart illustrates the relationships among departments and of personnel within the departments. The chart may depict the entire organization or a selected portion of it. The senior position is placed at the top of the chart. Other positions are placed on the chart in descending order of

Oil is a valuable mineral to the Texas economy. More than 20 percent of the oil produced in the United States is produced in Texas. The following table shows the top 10 Texas counties in crude and condensate production in 1997 and 1998:

TOP TEN TEXAS COUNTIES IN
CRUDE OIL AND CONDENSATE PRODUCTION

County	**Production in Barrels**	
	1997	**1998**
Gaines	36,976,256	36,016,018
Yoakum	30,166,705	29,398,194
Andrews	30,554,718	29,150,250
Hockley	25,546,518	25,663,717
Ector	26,719,864	25,281,639
Pecos	23,343,542	21,397,317
Crane	14,332,295	13,935,363
Midland	13,225,765	13,729,842
Gregg	16,112,519	12,943,293
Upton	11,217,533	10,248,494

SOURCE: *2000–2001 Texas Almanac*

Figure 13.1
Table

authority. These positions are connected by solid lines if they are line positions with authority over other positions, and by broken or dotted lines if they are advisory or staff positions. An example of an organization chart is shown in Figure 13.3.

Flowcharts A **flowchart** may be used to illustrate step-by-step progression through complicated procedures. Such procedures could include the steps needed to manufacture a product, the route that a form follows when processed in an office, or the steps in a computer program.

[NOTE 13.15]
Flowcharts simplify the interpretation of complicated procedures.

Complicated written instructions are more easily understood when accompanied by a flowchart. Each step of the procedure needs to be included, but the chart should not be so detailed that it becomes difficult to understand. Boxes of various shapes are connected by arrows to illustrate the direction that the action flows during the procedure. The size of a box is determined by the number of words in the label and does not indicate the importance of that particular portion of the procedure. A flowchart displaying the procedure used to take blood pressure is shown in Figure 13.4.

Pie Charts A **pie chart** can be used to show how the parts of a whole are distributed and how the parts relate to each other. To make the chart easy to read, you should begin slicing the pie at the twelve o'clock position and continue in a clockwise direction. The pieces should be arranged in descending order of size. If several smaller pieces are combined into an "Other" category, this piece should be placed last. "Other" should never be the largest segment. Label individual pieces by showing the quantity, or percentage, of each piece. The 1996 U.S. presidential election results are illustrated by the pie chart in Figure 13.5.

[NOTE 13.16]
A pie chart is a circle; its slices show the relationships of the parts to a whole.

[NOTE 13.17]
Certain design principles should be followed when constructing pie charts.

Pie charts are easy for most readers to understand, but there are certain considerations to remember when constructing them. All the pie charts within a report

Figure 13.2
Lengthwise Table

AUTOMOBILES SOLD BY ELAM MOTORS
IN 200–

Employee	Jan.	Feb.	Mar.	Apr.	May	June	July	Aug.	Sep.	Oct.	Nov.	Dec.	Total
Jerry Ahrens	4	5	3	4	5	4	1	6	4	7	4	6	53
Sheri Blackstone	9	4	7	5	4	5	7	5	8	9	11	8	82
Lynn Decker	0	0	0	0	0	0	0	0	4	6	5	5	20
Dustin Easley	6	3	3	6	4	5	2	4	0	3	6	4	46
Eric Elam	1	2	2	1	0	1	1	2	1	1	2	3	17
Paul Hampton	6	5	5	6	3	0	4	5	4	8	6	5	57
Ryan Jackson	0	0	0	2	1	3	1	0	0	0	0	0	7
Yuhong Jung	4	6	4	3	5	4	2	3	4	5	6	2	48
Jeremy Miller	2	1	5	3	4	2	1	3	3	4	5	3	36
Ashley Rankin	5	3	4	2	3	4	2	1	0	0	5	2	31
Alan Sprouse	4	7	5	2	0	4	3	1	2	3	4	6	41
TOTALS	41	36	38	34	29	32	24	30	30	46	54	44	438

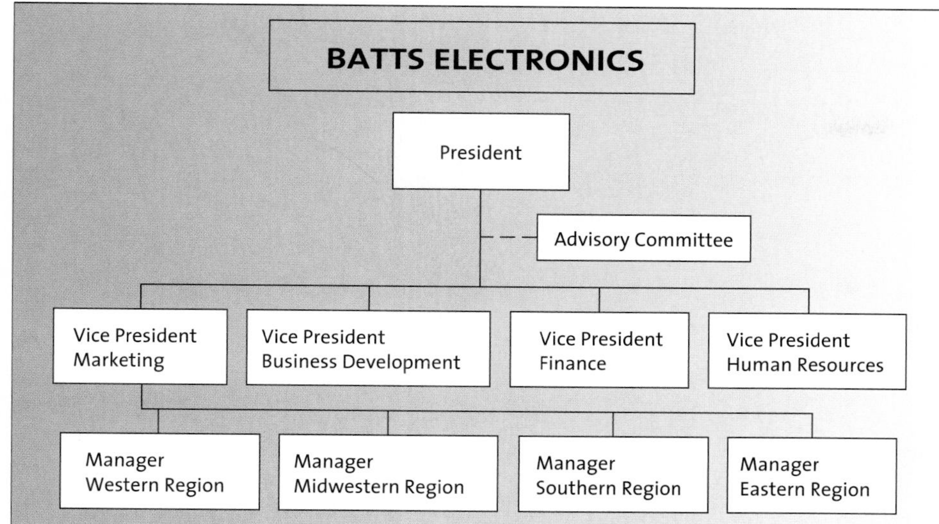

Figure 13.3
Organization Chart

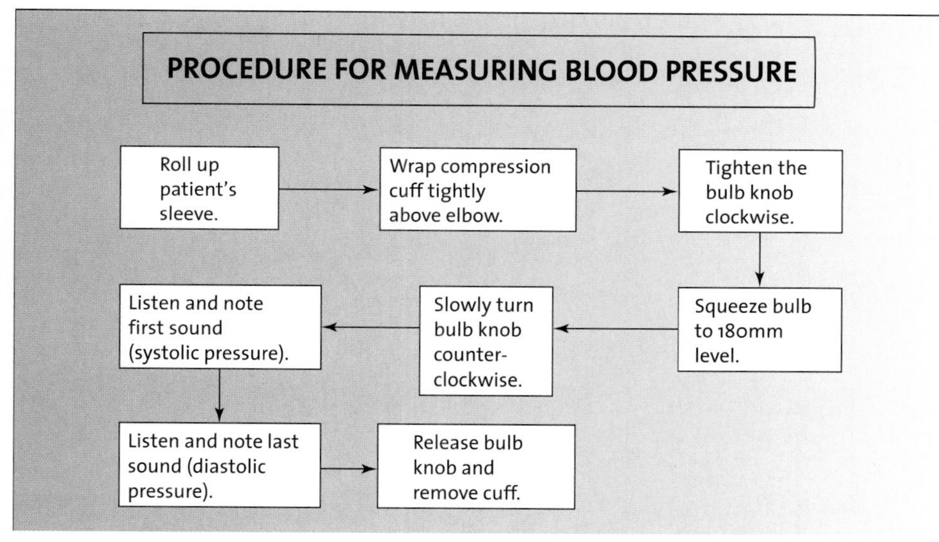

Figure 13.4
Flowchart

should be the same size. A pie chart should contain from two to eight pieces. When more than eight pieces are used, a pie chart becomes unclear. The percentages shown in a pie chart need to total 100 percent.

When a writer wants to emphasize a specific segment, an exploded pie chart may be used. In an exploded pie chart, one segment is separated from the rest of the chart for emphasis. Figure 13.6 shows the same data as Figure 13.5, with the category "Dole" being emphasized.

[NOTE 13.18]
An exploded pie chart is used to emphasize one segment.

Learning Objective [6]
CONSTRUCT THE VARIOUS TYPES OF BAR GRAPHS AND LINE GRAPHS.

GRAPHS

A **graph** is a drawing that represents the relationships of quantities or qualities to each other. A graph provides a convenient medium through which data can be compared. Graphs should use a simple design so that the reader can easily interpret

[NOTE 13.19]
Graphs show relationships among variables and should not have a complex design.

Figure 13.5
Pie Chart

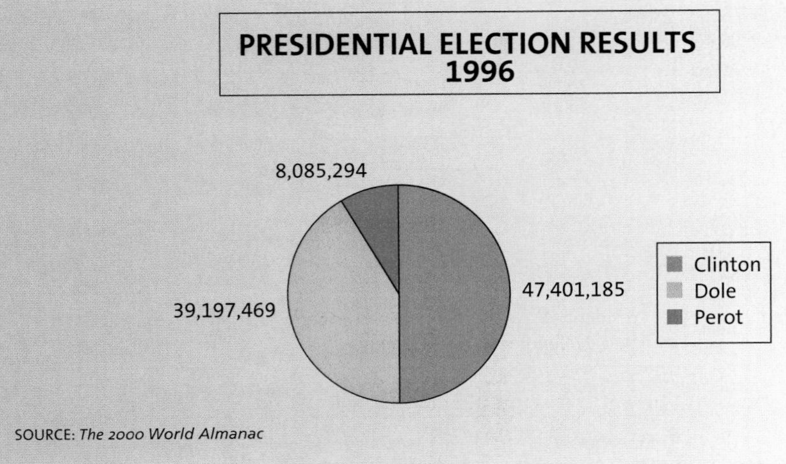

Figure 13.6
Exploded Pie Chart

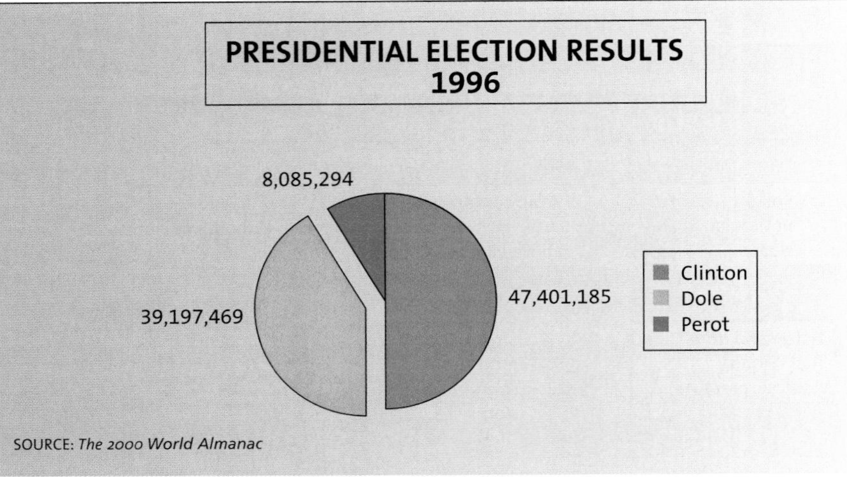

the information. Using complex graphs to impress readers will only confuse them. The most frequently used graphs in business organizations are bar and line. These types of graphs have several variations.

[NOTE 13.20]
Comparisons of quantitative differences can be shown in bar graphs.

Bar Graphs A **bar graph** can be effective in comparing differences in quantities. These differences are illustrated graphically by changes in the lengths of the bars. Bar graphs may be constructed either horizontally or vertically. The most widely used bar graphs include simple, broken, multiple, stacked, and positive-negative. All bar graphs except a positive-negative one should begin with zero at the bottom or extreme left and use the same increments throughout.

[NOTE 13.21]
The length or height of a bar indicates quantity in a simple bar graph.

In a **simple bar graph**, the length or height of a bar indicates quantity. You should use a bar width that makes a good visual impression. The width of individual bars should be the same throughout a graph. A simple vertical bar graph is shown in Figure 13.7, and a simple horizontal bar graph is shown in Figure 13.8.

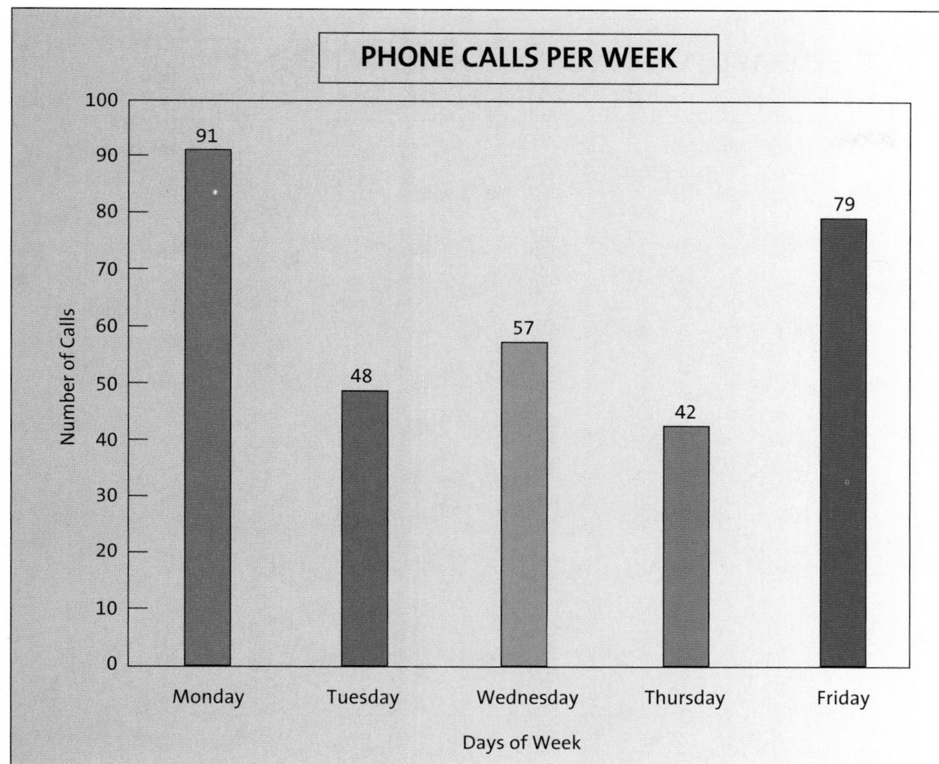

Figure 13.7
Simple Vertical Bar Graph

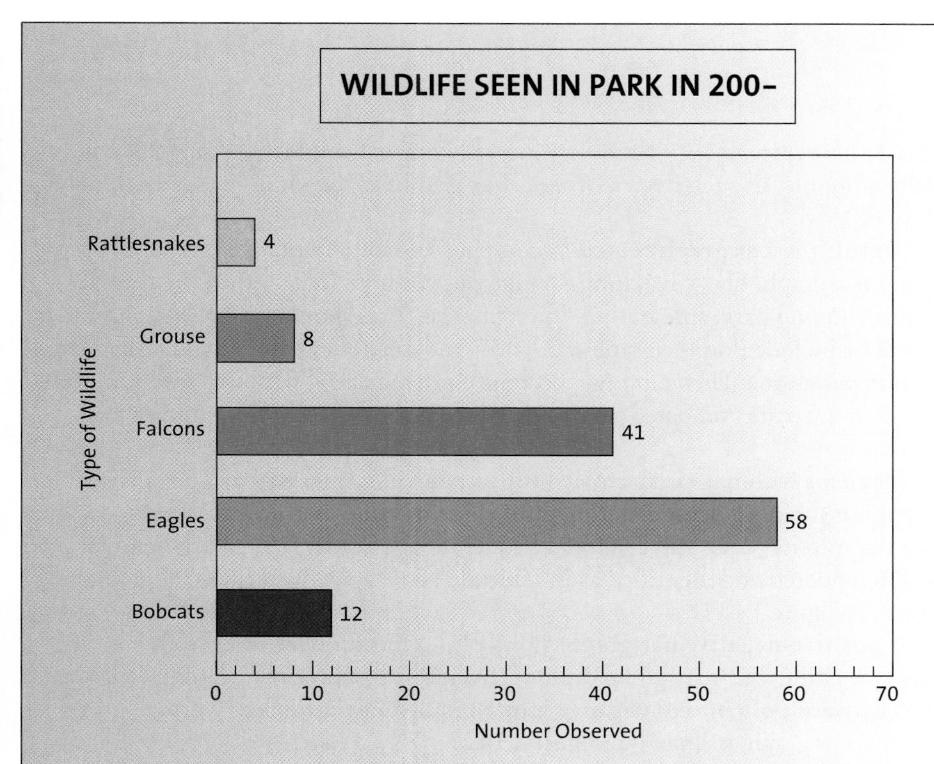

Figure 13.8
Simple Horizontal Bar Graph

Figure 13.9
Broken-Bar Graph

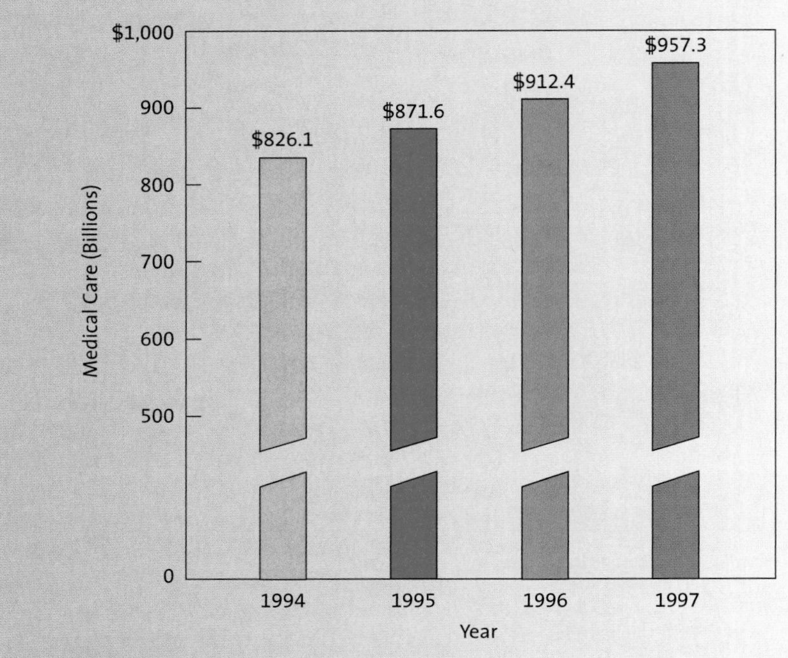

Graphs depicting very large amounts may make it impractical to include the entire amounts. In such cases a **broken-bar graph**, as shown in Figure 13.9, may be used.

[NOTE 13.22]
Several quantitative variables can be compared on one multiple-bar graph.

A **multiple-bar graph** is used to compare several quantitative areas at one time on a single graph. Cross-hatching, shading, or color variation can be used to distinguish among bars representing different areas. Bars should be labeled, or a legend should be included on the graph to identify the different cross-hatching, shading, or color variations. The graph will become cluttered and difficult to read if more than four areas are compared on one graph. Figure 13.10 shows a multiple-bar graph.

[NOTE 13.23]
A stacked-bar graph shows differences in values within variables.

Elements within a variable may be illustrated in a **stacked-bar graph**. This type of graph is useful in demonstrating differences in values within variables by dividing each bar into its parts. Values should be included for each part, and the parts should be differentiated and identified as in multiple-bar graphs. A stacked-bar graph is shown in Figure 13.11.

[NOTE 13.24]
A comparison of variable values that fall above or below a reference point can be shown on a positive-negative bar graph.

A **positive-negative bar graph** shows plus or minus deviations from a fixed reference point. The bars go up or down from this fixed reference point. Relationships between positive and negative values can be illustrated clearly using a positive-negative bar graph as shown in Figure 13.12.

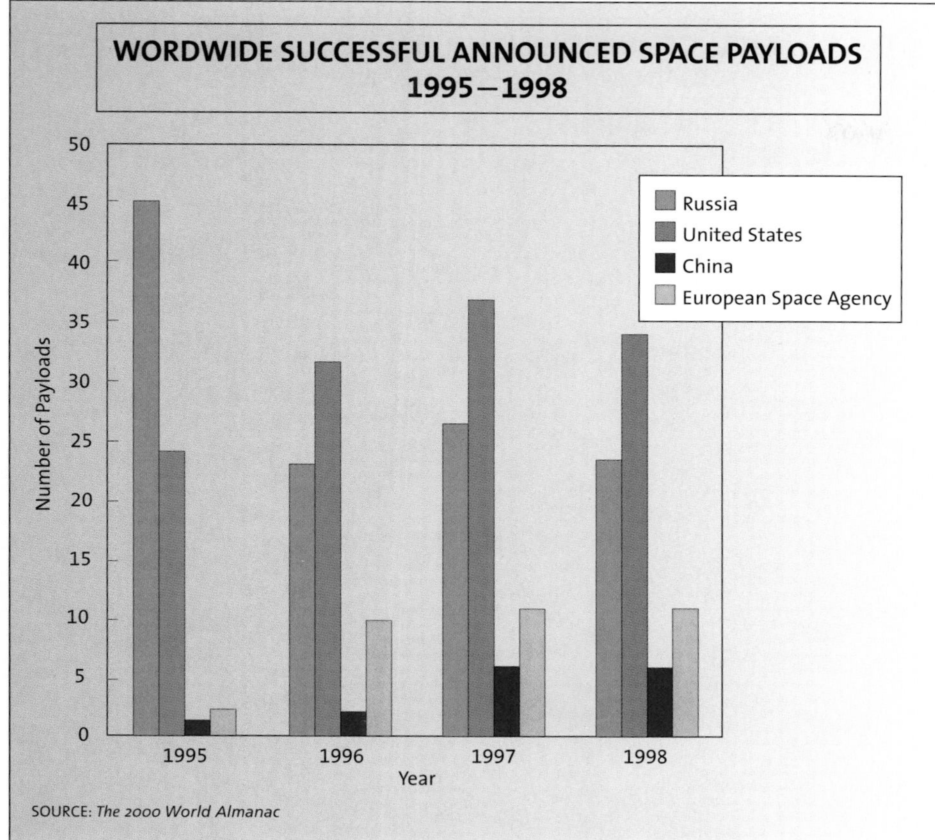

Figure 13.10
Multiple-Bar Graph

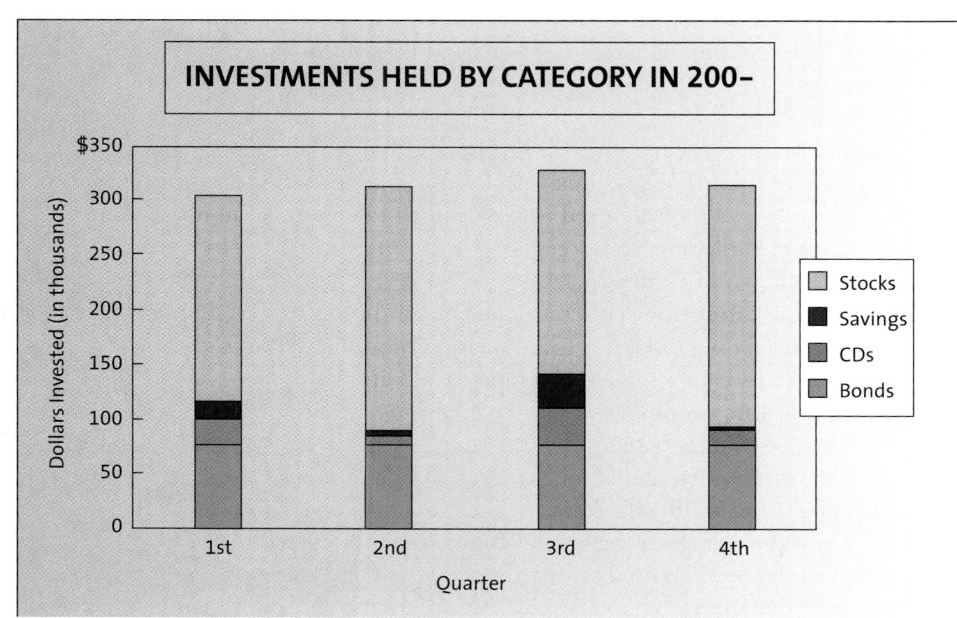

Figure 13.11
Stacked-Bar Graph

Figure 13.12
Positive-Negative Bar Graph

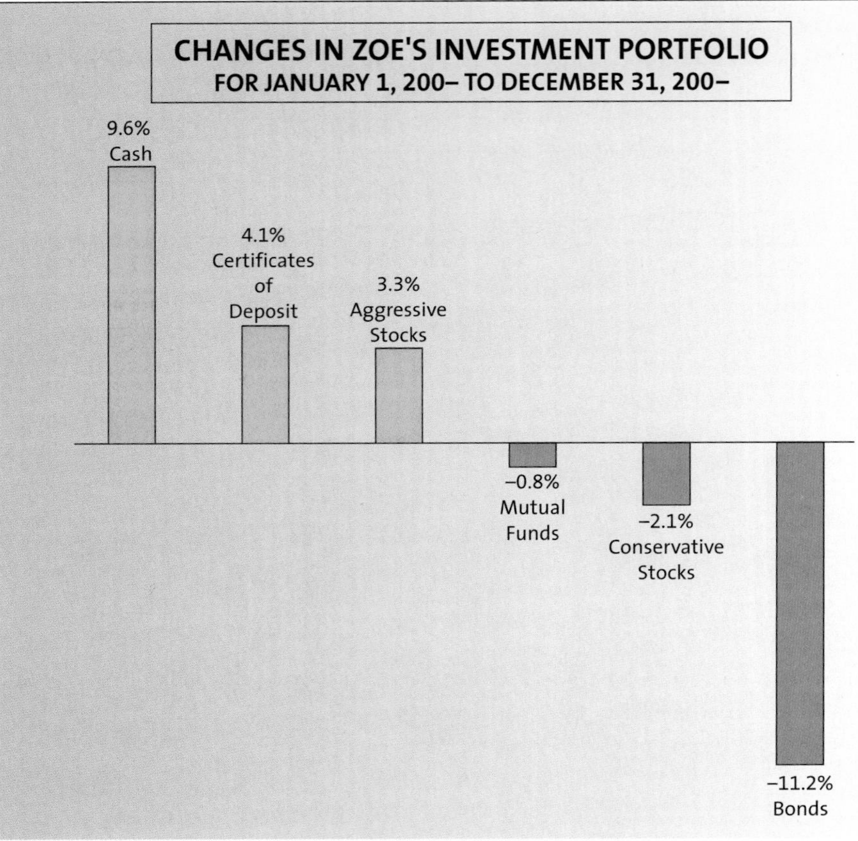

[NOTE 13.25]
Line graphs show changes over time.

Line Graphs A **line graph** is used to illustrate changes over time. Trends can be effectively portrayed by showing variations within each time period.

A line graph is constructed by drawing a line on an equally divided grid, with the horizontal reference line called the *x*-axis and the vertical reference line called the *y*-axis. The interval between each vertical and horizontal line depends on the data being illustrated. The grid lines may or may not appear on the finished version of the line graph. All the data need to be included to give an accurate and informative illustration. If the data are excessive, the grid may be broken by a slash or by wavy lines as shown in Figure 13.13.

A line graph can include either a single line or multiple lines. A **single-line graph,** which is shown in Figure 13.14, depicts movement of one variable. Shading or color may be used in a single-line graph to add emphasis.

[NOTE 13.26]
Changes in several values can be shown at one time on a multiple-line graph.

A **multiple-line graph** is used to illustrate changes in more than one value. The lines can be differentiated easily by using dotted, broken, and solid lines or by changing the symbols (triangle, square, circle, and diamond) for each line. Some writers prefer using a different color for each line; however, this technique requires that the report be printed using several colors, which increases the printing costs. Regardless of the method used to differentiate the lines, a legend should be used to identify lines that are ambiguous or difficult to interpret. A multiple-line graph is shown in Figure 13.15.

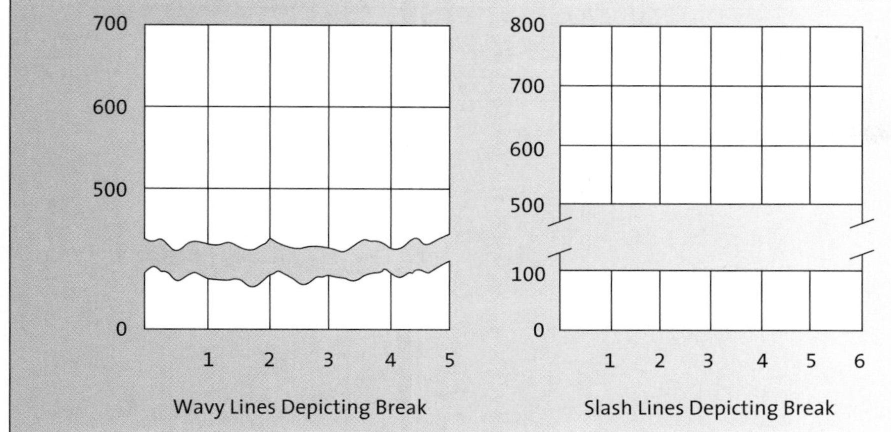

Figure 13.13
Broken Scales on Line Graphs

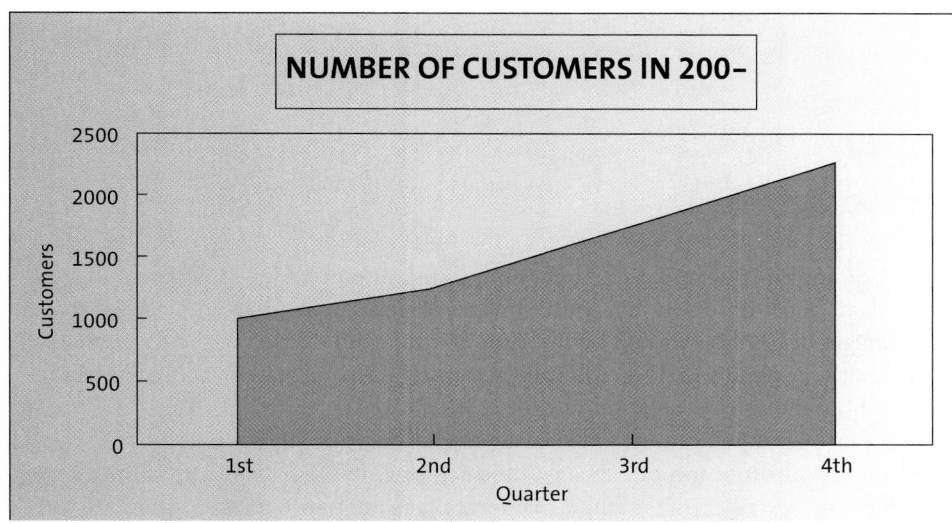

Figure 13.14
Single-Line Graph

Learning Objective [7]
DESCRIBE HOW MISCELLANEOUS VISUAL AIDS ARE USED.

MISCELLANEOUS VISUAL AIDS

Although the most commonly used visual aids are tables, charts, and graphs, these are not the only effective visual aids that can be used in reports. Graphic aids such as maps, photographs, pictographs, and drawings are used infrequently, but they can be extremely effective in conveying specific messages at appropriate times. Many of these visual aids may be obtained from Web sites. Any relevant visual aid that clarifies and strengthens the communication should be considered for use in a report or presentation.

[NOTE 13.27]
Any illustration that complements the written text should be considered for use.

A **map** can be effective in helping a receiver visualize geographic relationships. The complexity of maps ranges from simple sketches to detailed, multicolored presentations. The content of the map determines the size of the visual aid. Notice how the states containing a larger number of Omicron Delta Kappa circles (chapters) are differentiated from the states with only a few circles (chapters) on the map in Figure 13.16.

[NOTE 13.28]
Maps can help the reader understand geographic details.

Figure 13.15
Multiple-Line Graph

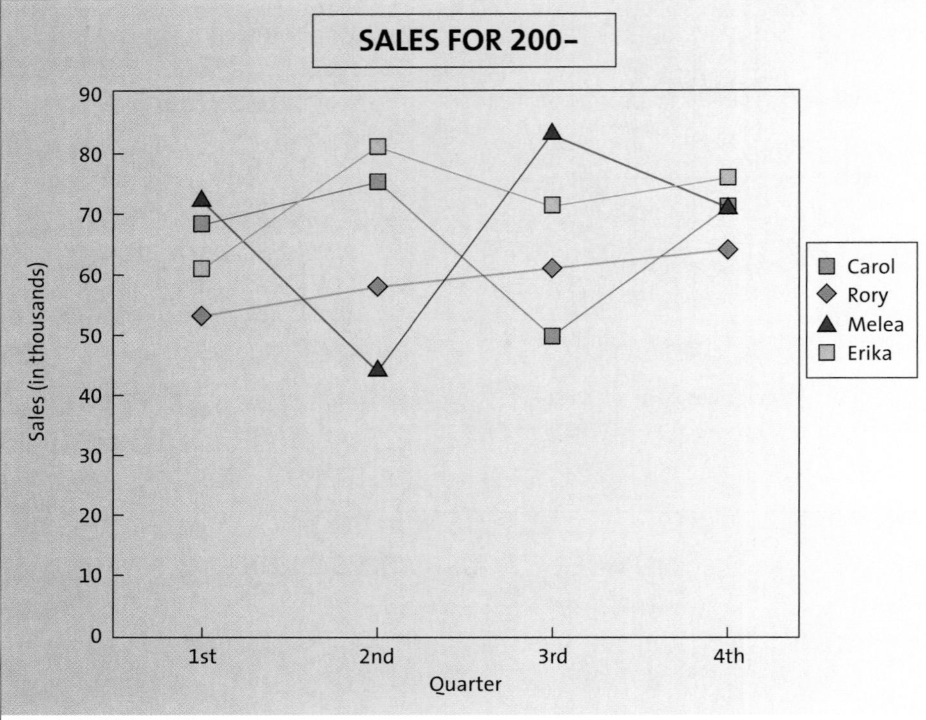

[NOTE 13.29]
Pictographs use images to emphasize differences in quantitative data.

A **pictograph** is similar to a bar graph in that it emphasizes differences in statistical data, but it differs in that it uses images of items or symbols instead of bars. All the images or symbols should be the same size to avoid distorting their values. The pictograph in Figure 13.17 graphically accentuates the increase in cable television use in households over a period of time.

[NOTE 13.30]
Photos used as graphic aids should not contain too much material.

A personal touch can be added to a written report or an oral presentation by including a **photograph** of a facility, product, or employee. The Communication Note below describes one method of effectively using photographs. In order to enhance communication, the photograph must be clear and well planned. A mistake often made in the use of photographs is including too much material. If a photograph shows something extremely large or extremely small, a reference point should

COMMUNICATION NOTE

Using Pictures in a Weight-Loss Program

Dr. Howard Shapiro is the author of *Dr. Shapiro's Picture Perfect Weight Loss: The Visual Program for Permanent Weight Loss*. The book features about 100 food comparisons, including snacks, lunches, and dinners out, and highlights the foods that are the better choices. His patients found that calorie-comparison lists are boring, so he developed a food display program for his patients. Patients who don't know much about portion sizes and high-calorie foods find the photographs in the book very helpful.

Adapted from Nanci Hellmich, "A Picture Is Worth a Thousand Pounds: Visual Aids Are a Slimming Tool," USA Today.com, *April 3, 2000.*

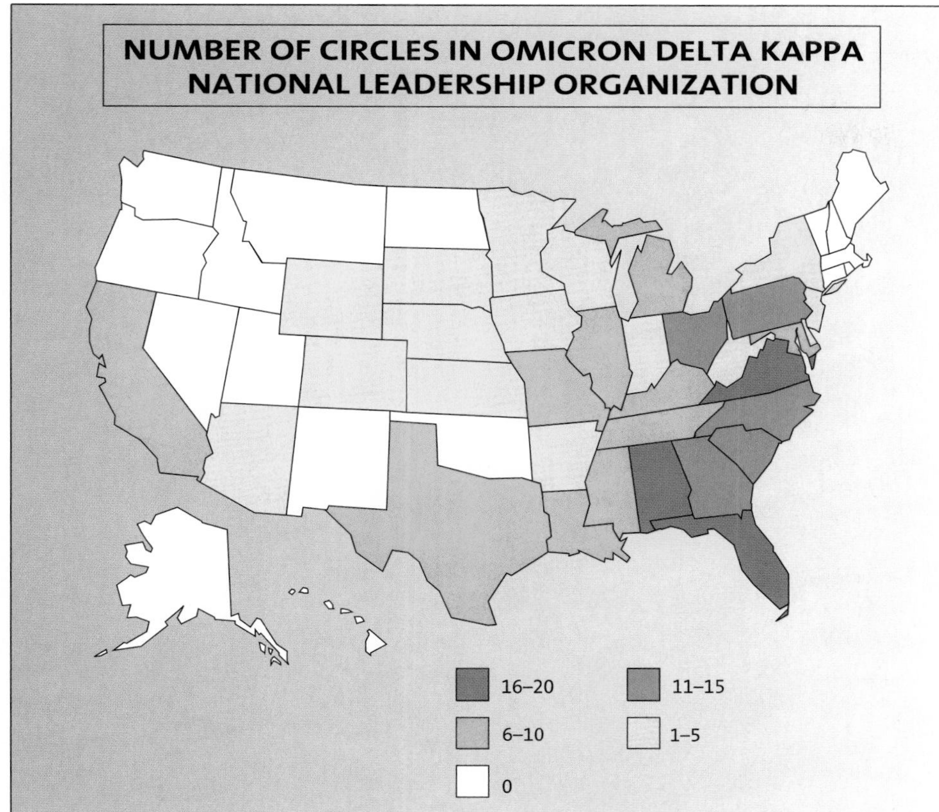

Figure 13.16
Map

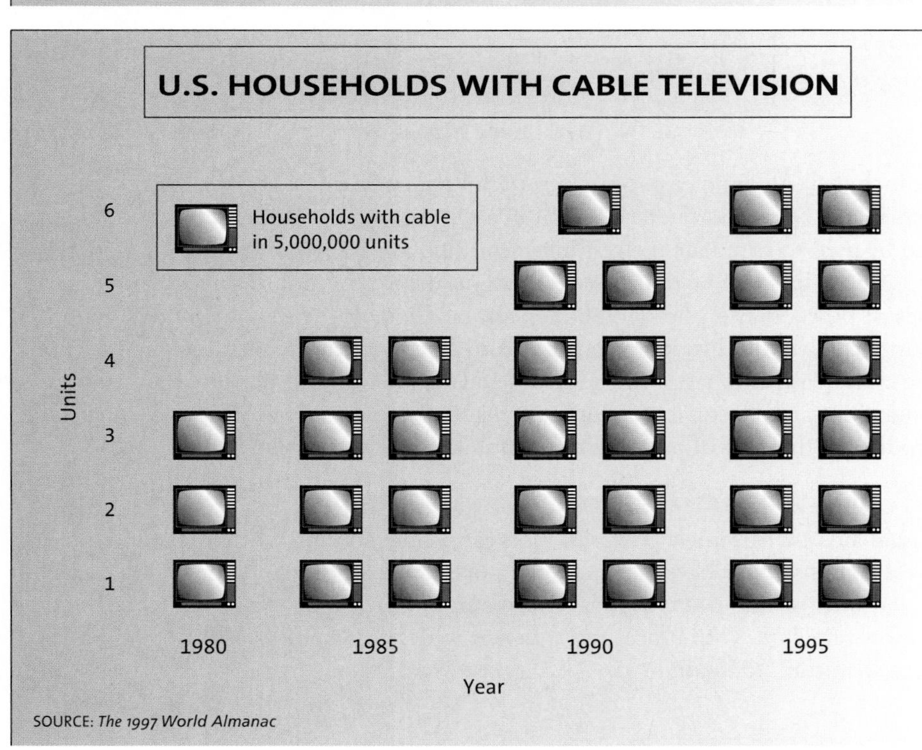

Figure 13.17
Pictograph Showing Cable Television Usage

Photograph used to promote a resort.

be included. A coin or a pin can be a useful reference point for small items, and a person can be a good reference point in a photograph of a large item. A photograph can be used to stimulate interest in vacationing at a resort.

[NOTE 13.31] Drawings can be used to emphasize one point within a procedure.

A **drawing** may be the most effective means of communicating a complicated idea or procedure. A photograph may not be desirable because it would contain clutter that would distract from the idea to be communicated. A drawing can omit the clutter and emphasize the desired details in an idea or procedure. Furthermore, a drawing can reflect parts or components not visible when viewing the "finished" product. A drawing of part of an automobile is shown in Figure 13.18.

COMPUTER-GENERATED VISUAL AIDS

[NOTE 13.32] Computers have simplified the creation of visual aids.

Visual aids are extremely powerful tools for supplementing written text and oral presentations. They have become more popular because technology makes them easier to construct. Many computer programs are available that can integrate graphics software with word processing software to develop an easy-to-understand and informative communication.

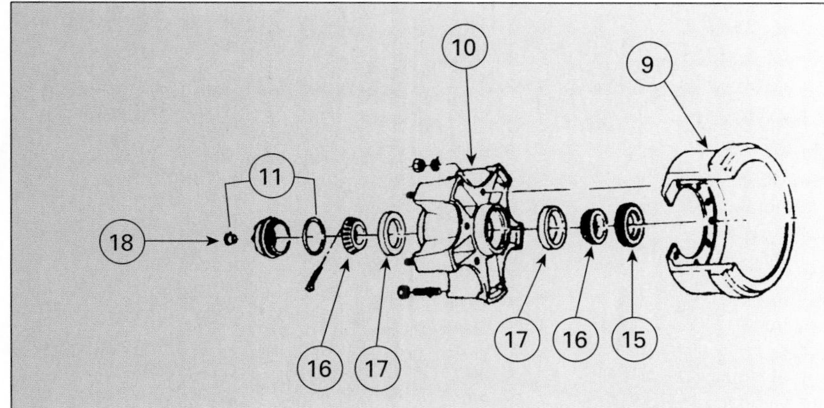

Figure 13.18
Drawing of Part of an Automobile

Graphics software programs are easy to use. The originator needs only to enter the raw data and select the type of visual aid desired. The computer will create the chart or graph selected. These visual aids may be printed using several colors, depending on the type of software and printer.

Using graphics software, the originator can produce visual aids from the simple to the sophisticated. A spreadsheet may be used to display raw data. Current spreadsheet software permits the user to change fonts and to bold or shade data to emphasize selected figures in the spreadsheet. Graphs and tables that are produced using spreadsheet programs can also be imported into word processing or desktop publishing programs. Figure 13.19 shows a spreadsheet prepared using Microsoft Excel.

[NOTE 13.33]
Many types of visual aids may be generated using computer software.

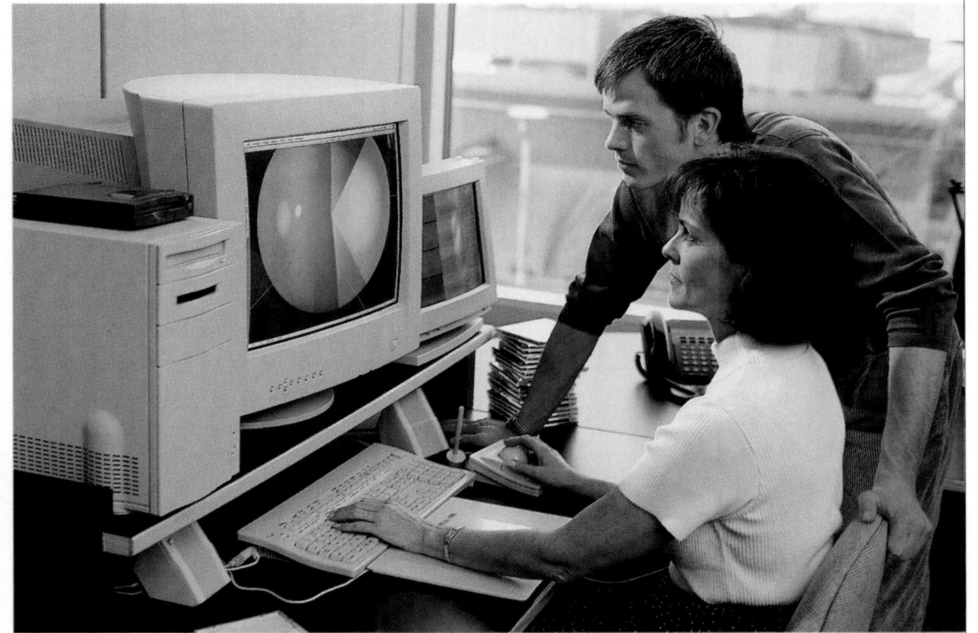

The keyboard and mouse are used to input data. The software uses the data to produce pie charts or other types of graphic aids.

Figure 13.19
Excel Spreadsheet

Maggie Moneybag's Personal Worth

Personal Assets	**Jan. 1998**	**Jan. 1999**	**Jan. 2000**
House	$130,000	$135,000	$137,500
Home Furnishings	5,000	4,500	4,250
Automobile	11,000	10,000	9,000
Truck	14,500	14,000	13,750
Insurance—Cash Value	9,500	10,200	10,500
Total Personal Assets	170,000	173,700	175,000
Investments			
Stocks	215,000	245,000	310,000
Mutual Funds	145,000	155,225	159,825
Undeveloped Land	45,000	70,000	95,000
IRA	60,150	62,325	61,250
Bonds	12,000	13,000	13,520
Art Collection	6,000	6,000	6,000
Savings Account	6,500	5,100	5,750
Total Investments	489,650	556,650	651,345
TOTAL ASSETS	$659,650	$730,350	$826,345
Liabilities			
Loan—Home	$112,750	$110,925	$109,850
Loan—Undev. Land	30,630	28,710	27,450
Loan—Truck	12,840	11,980	11,170
Credit Cards	875	1,120	1,250
TOTAL LIABILITIES	$157,095	$152,735	$149,720
NET WORTH	$502,555	$577,615	$676,625

[NOTE 13.34]
Clip art can make reports more attractive.

The appearance of reports can be improved by the use of **clip art**, prepackaged art images designed to be used with word processing, presentation graphics, or desktop publishing programs. Clip art is included in most word processing, presentation graphics, and desktop publishing programs. It may also be purchased separately and imported. Clip art program files normally are grouped into categories, such as business, travel, history, automobiles, airplanes, or holidays. Examples of clip art are shown in Figure 13.20.

[NOTE 13.35]
Numerous software packages that can produce visual aids are available.

Graphics software packages such as Microsoft Excel, Lotus 1-2-3, Harvard Graphics®, Freelance Graphics®, Aldus® Persuasion®, Corel Draw!®, Claris McDraw®, Charisma®, and GraphShow® can easily produce bar graphs, line graphs, pie charts, area charts, and combination charts. Most software programs permit the creation of several variations of each type of visual aid, such as stacked-bar graphs or exploded pie charts.

[NOTE 13.36]
A variety of visuals can be produced with different software packages.

More sophisticated software programs have additional options: Photographs may be printed in a report; the size of graphic aids may vary; lines, curves, and geometric shapes may be created instantly; main headings and captions with special fonts may be inserted; and color and patterns may be added. The software programs

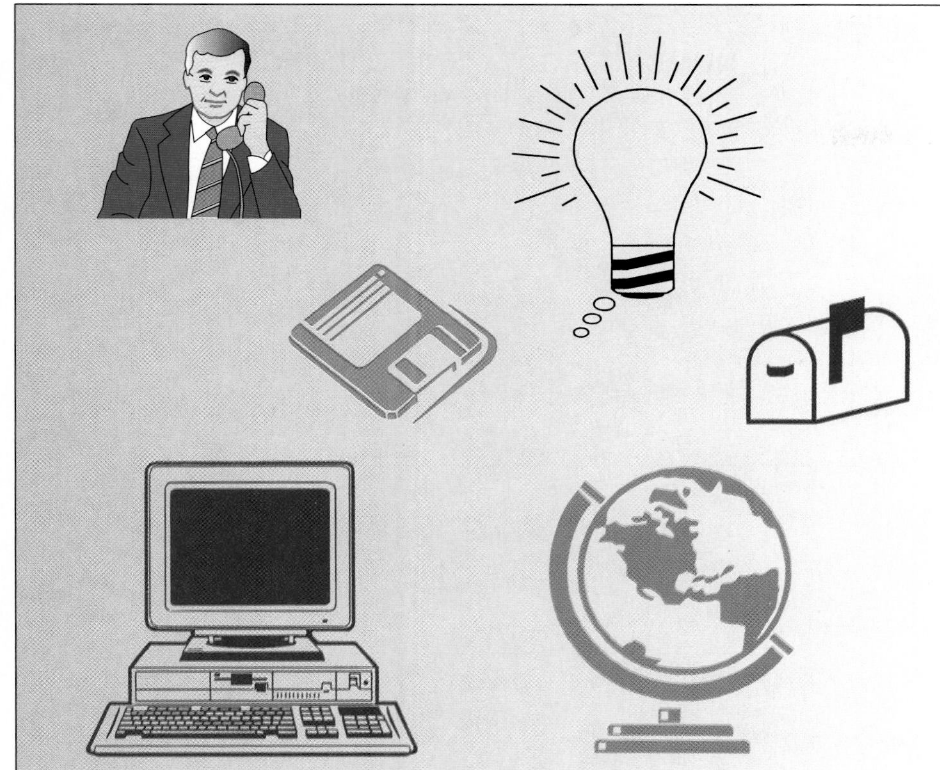

Figure 13.20
Examples of Clip Art

allow the user to size, rotate, flip, recolor, and distort digitally stored drawings or photographs to enhance the written report or oral presentation.

Once data are entered into a software program, different graphs and charts can easily be generated. A spreadsheet was used to generate a line graph for the data in Figure 13.21. An originator using the same data can press a couple of keys to generate a bar graph instead.

[NOTE 13.37]
Different styles of graphs and charts can be created without rekeying data.

Computers can be used to make realistic estimates and to present these estimates in attractive illustrations.

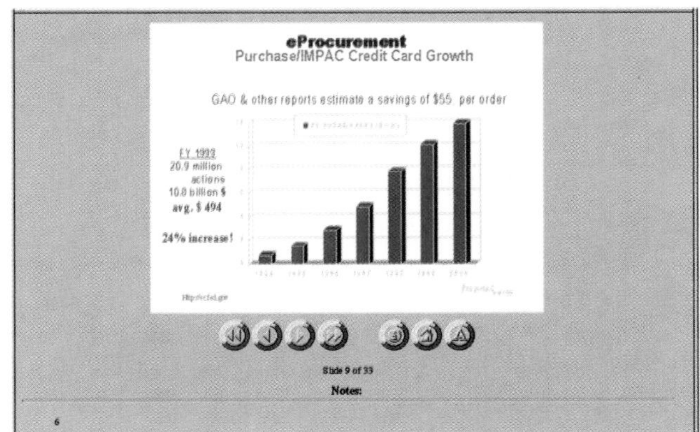

Figure 13.21
Line and Bar Graphs Using Identical Data

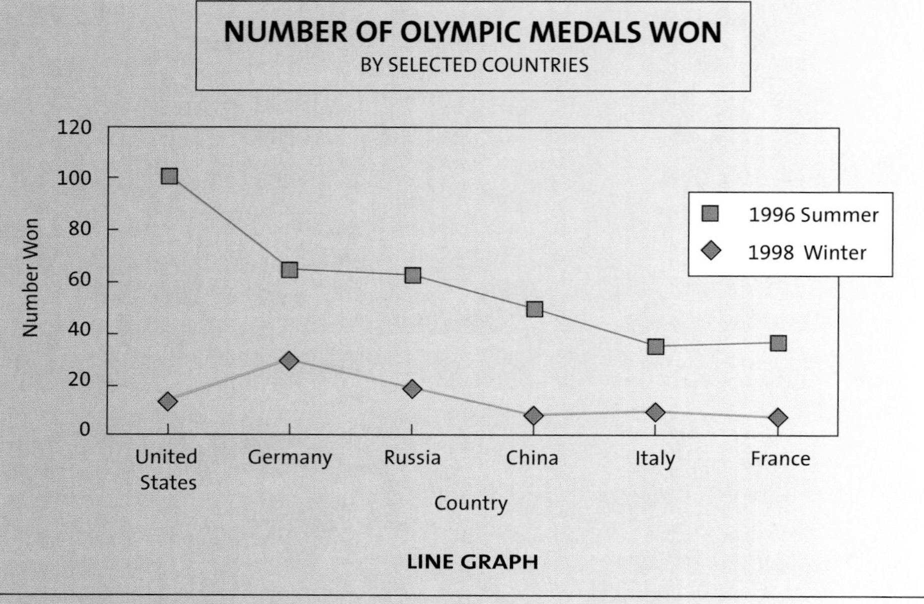

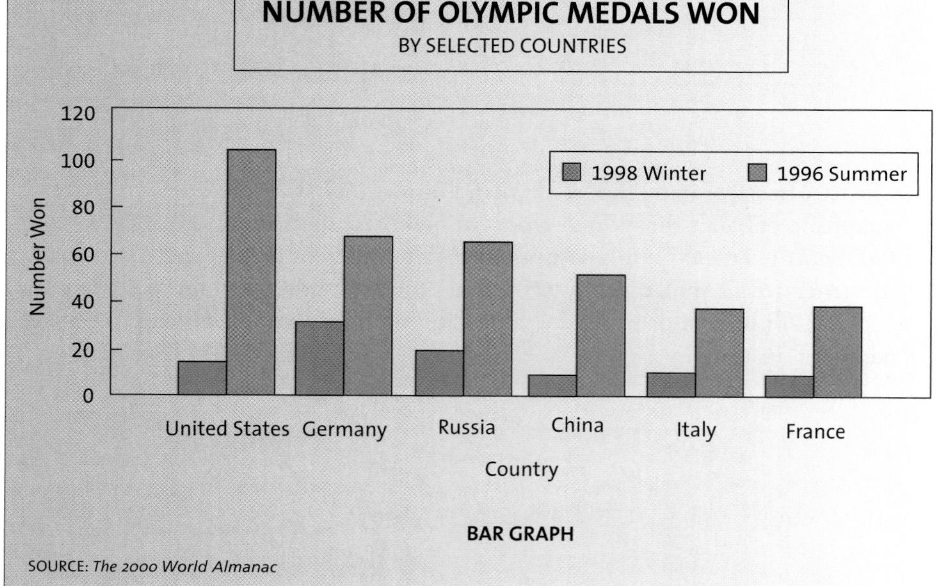

SOURCE: *The 2000 World Almanac*

[NOTE 13.38]
Consideration should be given to the advantages and disadvantages of each program when selecting computer graphics software.

An advantage of using a simple graphics software program is that little training is required to produce a visual aid. A disadvantage of using a simple program is that the visual aid produced may not be exactly what is desired. For instance, some elementary graphics software programs do not begin pie charts with the largest piece at the twelve o'clock position. Also, a simple program may limit the number of characters that may be included in the titles or captions of the visual aids. Care should be taken in selecting a graphics software program so that it will meet the communicator's needs.

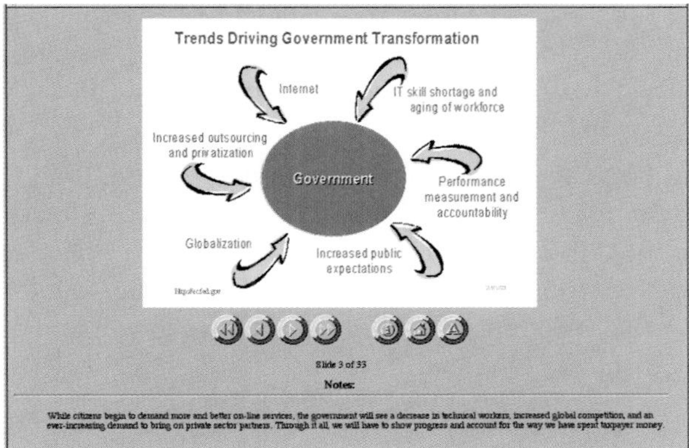

Key points may be projected for emphasis.

Selection of Appropriate Visual Aids

The purpose of a visual aid is to complement the text or presentation by communicating information quickly. Presenting accurate data in a clear and organized manner is important. The receiver will have little difficulty in interpreting the data when the appropriate visual aid is selected.

[NOTE 13.39]
Selecting appropriate illustrations is critical for effective communication in a report.

Comparisons of quantities in data are best illustrated by bar graphs. For instance, a report comparing the various fixed costs with the assorted variable costs can be complemented by the use of bar graphs.

[NOTE 13.40]
Compare quantities in bar graphs.

If a report or presentation discusses trends in quantitative data over a period of time, a line graph would be the most appropriate visual aid. A multiple-line graph is also an effective device for showing changes in two or more related variables. A company comparing the sales trends for its four salespeople can effectively utilize a line graph.

[NOTE 13.41]
Illustrate trends in line graphs.

Pie charts are used to show the relationships between the parts and the whole. Budgets are commonly displayed in pie charts in order to illustrate the proportion each item is to the entire budget.

[NOTE 13.42]
Show relationships with pie charts.

Flowcharts illustrate steps within a procedure. A new employee can easily learn the flow of a work order within an organization by carefully studying a well-designed flowchart.

[NOTE 13.43]
Illustrate steps with flowcharts.

Careful selection of the appropriate visual aid may enhance the effectiveness of a written report or oral presentation. The length of the written text can be reduced by the use of a well-chosen graphic aid. Many times it is easier to interpret a visual aid than to struggle through pages of written text.

Learning Objective [8]
SELECT THE APPROPRIATE TYPE OF VISUAL AID TO COMPLEMENT AN ORAL PRESENTATION.

SELECT APPROPRIATE PRESENTATION AIDS

Unlike a written report, which draws only on the receiver's sense of sight, an oral presentation can draw on sound, sight, touch, taste, and smell. Most speakers will find sound (audio) and sight (visual) most useful. Whether used separately or in combination (multimedia), presentation aids can be an asset in conveying a message. They can make it more understandable. They can spark interest, add variety, and help to hold an audience's attention. See the Tips and Hints on page 415 for guidelines on designing visual aids.

[NOTE 13.44]
Choose presentation aids to strengthen the message.

Visual Presentation Aids The most common and widely used aids are those that require the audience to look at something. Handouts, flip charts, posters, objects, whiteboards, slides, transparencies, and projection devices fall into this category. A brief description of each follows.

[NOTE 13.45]
Distribute simple handouts before and during your presentation and detailed ones afterward.

Handouts Handouts can be used to present an outline of or to illustrate points from your presentation. Handouts that will be referred to during the presentation should be distributed in advance. Handouts containing complex supplementary material should be distributed after your presentation. Although listeners can concentrate better on your comments if they do not have to worry about taking notes, using too many handouts can be distracting.

[NOTE 13.46]
Flip charts are economical and easy to use.

Flip Charts This economical, easy-to-use aid works best with small groups. Charts can be prepared in advance or spontaneously, as part of an interaction with the audience. Their advantage in interactive settings is that each sheet can be posted for reference and serve as a tangible sign of accomplishments. Prepared charts should be designed on paper first, then transferred to the flip chart pad. Penciled notes added when the chart is finished can help remind you of key points you wish to make. Remember that charts require some sort of stand; be sure the pad you select fits the stand.

Posters Posters can be used for text, charts, graphs, and pictographs; they work especially well for blueprints and drawings. Be sure to consider how the posters will be displayed and whether they will be visible during the entire presentation or revealed as they are used. You may also need a pointer to help highlight important items.

[NOTE 13.47]
Models and physical objects can strengthen a presentation.

Objects In many business presentations you will have something to display either in final or model form. If the physical objects or models used as visual aids are not large enough for every member of the audience to see, consider giving each member an object or circulating one or more of the items among audience members. Introducing the sensory dimension of touch into your presentation can reinforce what you have to say, but it does not detract from active listening. Before making objects available to your audience, consider both the benefits and costs to your overall presentation.

[NOTE 13.48]
You can use a whiteboard to develop a concept while you speak.

Whiteboards Whiteboards, either stationary or portable, are the modern-day version of the chalkboards common in most classrooms. The flexibility associated with whiteboards makes them desirable for meetings or other interactive, small-group sessions. Printing legibly is slow and cumbersome, however, and means that the writer's back is to the audience a great deal of the time.

[NOTE 13.49]
Slides can be colorful and professional, but preparation may be time consuming and costly.

Slides Slides can be a colorful and professional-looking presentation aid that works well with groups of various sizes. Depending on the detail of the material to be presented, however, the time and talent necessary to prepare and produce the slides can be substantial. In addition, (1) someone must dim and restore the lights at appropriate times, (2) it is harder to keep the audience attentive, (3) the projector could malfunction, and (4) the speaker could have difficulty using the remote control or communicating with the assistant who will operate the projector. Although not major obstacles to using slides, these factors must be considered.

[NOTE 13.50]
Transparencies are widely used visual aids.

Transparencies Overhead transparencies, also known as foils or acetates, have long been an inexpensive presentation tool for use with groups of various sizes. They can

Designing Visual Aids

TIPS AND HINTS

[1] Display only one idea on each visual. Use progressive disclosure to move through elements of a complex concept.

[2] Select an overall style and use it on all your visual aids. Consistency will help your audience stay focused on what you have to say. Introduce the style in an opening slide that includes the title of your presentation and other information (your name, your organization's name, the date, etc.) the audience might need.

[3] Choose print style and size carefully. Thick, straight characters are easier to read than thin, curved ones. Mixing upper- and lowercase letters saves space and, because it is a familiar style, makes text easier to read. Using the "6 by 6" rule—six lines of no more than six words each—puts font size for keyed material in the 40- to 50-point range.

[4] Use color to emphasize material. Choose a feature color for main ideas; use one or two complementary colors to accent subpoints. Remember that about 10 percent of the male population is red-green color sensitive and that pastels are hard to read, especially from a distance. Background colors must also be considered; a dark background in a darkened room will encourage drowsiness.

[5] Computer graphics (background patterns, clip art, etc.) should be used when they enhance the presentation. Gimmicks are not a substitute for content.

[6] Proofread! Even small errors can embarrass you and portray a poor image of your organization.

[7] Plan ahead. Finish the project well ahead of the presentation date. Allow time to redo visuals that don't satisfy you. If you are relying on in-house or commercial services, respect their schedules.

be prepared in advance using markers, printers, or photocopiers. Markers can also be used to add to or create transparencies as part of a presentation. As with slides, transparencies carry the disadvantages associated with using a projector and operating in a darkened room.

Projection Devices These presentation tools enable images displayed on a computer monitor to be projected for viewing by a larger audience. Some units link the computer directly to the projector; others use a panel placed on an overhead projector. In either case, the user may create or manipulate computer files as the audience watches. This presentation aid works well in meetings where groups attempt to answer what-if questions. However, technical problems with any of the equipment can bring a quick halt to even the most well-prepared presentation.

[NOTE 13.51]
Projection panels are used to display computer images.

Audio Presentation Aids Variety and impact are made possible by supplementing your oral presentation with an audio aid. Cassette tapes are the most common audio aid; CDs also fall into this category. Whatever the medium, the recording quality must be high and the volume sufficient to enable all members of the audience to hear without strain or discomfort. Because audio aids are, in a sense, disembodied

[NOTE 13.52]
Audio aids should be used selectively.

sounds, use them sparingly. An audience can tire quickly of simply listening to sound and not having visual stimuli.

[NOTE 13.53] Multimedia aids require audience members to use more than one sense.

Multimedia Aids Multimedia aids have the capacity to incorporate text, graphics, sound, and animation into a presentation. The most basic multimedia device is a videotape; the most sophisticated device utilizes presentation graphics software on a PC linked to the Internet. Each aid is described in the following paragraphs.

[NOTE 13.54] Videotapes should be not only shown but also discussed.

Videotapes Speakers who use videotapes rely heavily on professionally prepared materials and honor all copyright restrictions. The monitor(s) used during the presentation must be strategically placed and adjusted for appropriate contrast and volume. The speaker must tell the audience the purpose of the tape before showing it and summarize the main points after viewing it. Long tapes should be shown in segments separated by discussions. For the comfort of audience members, keep the lights dimmed during discussions between segments.

[NOTE 13.55] Presentation graphics software offers creation ease and presentation variety.

Presentation Graphics Software This comprehensive aid allows speakers to create, edit, and give presentations using sophisticated computer technology. The ease with which these presentations can be created and the variety they offer make them desirable for small- to medium-sized groups (100 or fewer). The disadvantage of needing a darkened room for clear viewing is often offset by the ability to incorporate sound and motion into the presentation.

[NOTE 13.56] Use presentation graphics software to create

- Slides (images)
- Outlines
- Speaker's notes
- Audience handouts

A number of presentation graphics software programs are available either as separate products or as part of integrated packages. Materials used in the presentation may be keyed directly into the program or copied from another file created, for example, using word processing or spreadsheet software. Although each software program approaches the task differently, all are capable of producing slides, outlines, speaker's notes, and audience handouts.

A **slide** is a one-page visual image. In business, the most common slide format consists of a heading and various levels of subheadings. Each subheading level is marked by a **bullet**, a symbol designed to capture attention and show the beginning of a new item. Different emphasis techniques (font, pitch, color, bold, underscore, italics, etc.) can mark each subheading level. Users may create their own slide format or choose from among many template formats included in the software. Formats may be altered from slide to slide, but a better approach is to select one format, called a **master**, and retain it throughout the presentation. As each item is entered into the slide, the software automatically adjusts it to meet the preset format. Items such as a company logo or the speaker's name may also be imbedded into a master. Figure 13.22 shows a slide created using PowerPoint.

To obtain an overview of the presentation, a speaker can generate an **outline**, a sequential listing of the slides and their content. Because the outline and creation modes are so closely aligned, a user can add, delete, or modify slides while in one function and have them automatically reflected in the other.

A software feature called **speaker's notes** allows the user to add comments to each slide—comments that may be displayed on the screen during rehearsals and removed during the actual presentation. The printed notes will appear either beside or below a copy of the slide. Notes may also be added by hand after printing.

Finally, one or more slides can be printed on a page as an **audience handout** or **take-away**. Distributing your visuals as a handout gives those attending the presen-

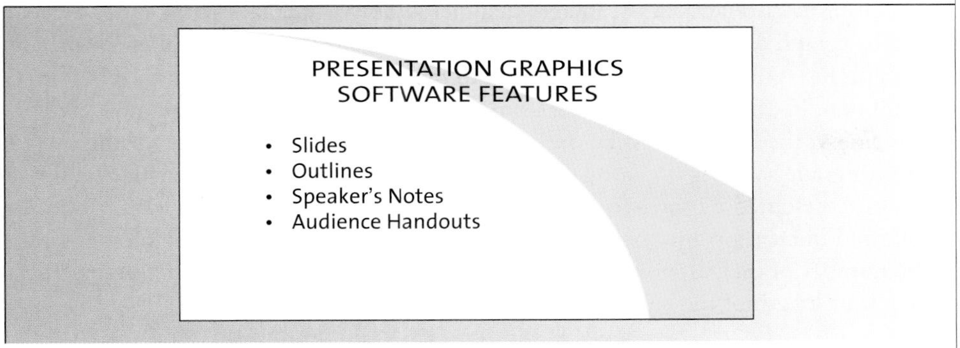

PRESENTATION GRAPHICS
SOFTWARE FEATURES

- Slides
- Outlines
- Speaker's Notes
- Audience Handouts

Figure 13.22
Presentation Graphic Slide

tation an accurate record of the materials that were used and the opportunity to add their own notes about the topic.

[NOTE 13.57]
Sound and animation can be incorporated into a presentation.

Once the basic elements of a presentation have been created, the user can focus on how the software's more powerful features might be used to enhance the presentation. Specifically, the speaker needs to decide whether sound, fades, dissolves, or similar transition techniques will be incorporated into the presentation. A speaker may, for example, decide to use progressive disclosure and reveal the subtopics of a bulleted listing one by one. Sound could be used to signal the addition of an item, or the old item could fade into the background as the new item emerges. When moving from one topic to another, the old image could slowly dissolve. For a lighter effect, a user might choose to have an animated object or character erase the text or to have a gloved hand appear to tear away the old slide. Some software programs offer pre-animated templates. In either case, the user may choose the speed at which a transition takes place. Options are many and varied; creativity and the topic will help a speaker decide which to use without detracting from content.

[NOTE 13.58]
Access to other sources makes interactive sessions possible.

At various points during the presentation, the speaker may wish to draw on other media sources. This can be accomplished by including **hyperlinks**, a method of moving to and immediately accessing another source. The links are displayed as icons (images) on a slide. When clicked (activated), the image causes the computer to point to a different location in its resource base. By using hyperlinks, presenters may access and manipulate a spreadsheet or database, visit one or more Web sites, conduct an Internet search, or engage in any number of other interactive activities.

Although presentation graphics software offers users a host of options, presenters must remember that equipment and software at the presentation site must be compatible with that used to create the presentation. If Internet resources are to be used, for example, a network connection must be available. Speakers must also prepare for unexpected equipment or network failures.

Learning Objective [9]
EXPLAIN HOW RECEIVERS CAN AVOID BEING DECEIVED BY VISUAL AIDS.

Possible Deception in Visual Aids

[NOTE 13.59]
Visual aids can mislead a reader.

Not only should the reader of a report be aware that visual aids can be misleading, but the report writer or presenter should also be careful not to use visual aids to mislead receivers. This misrepresentation may occur if certain principles of construction are violated—intentionally or unintentionally.

[NOTE 13.60]
Bars should be of the same width.

Disproportionate sizes of images in a pictograph or inconsistent widths of bars in a bar graph can deceive the receivers of a message. A receiver scanning the pictograph in Figure 13.23 may interpret it to mean that more wells produced oil in 2000 than in 1999; in fact, there was more production in 1999. Individuals only glancing at the bar graph in Figure 13.23 may perceive the test scores for the twelfth grade as being higher than the eleventh grade test scores; however, the test scores represented by the two bars are of equal value. Specific principles must be followed in creating and interpreting pictographs and bar graphs. In a pictograph, the number of images, not their size, determines the value; and in a bar graph, the height or length of the bar, not the width, determines the value.

Figure 13.23
Deception Caused by Changing Width or Size

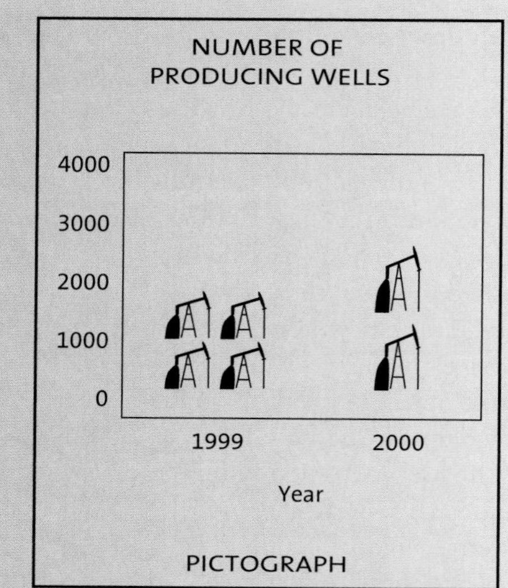

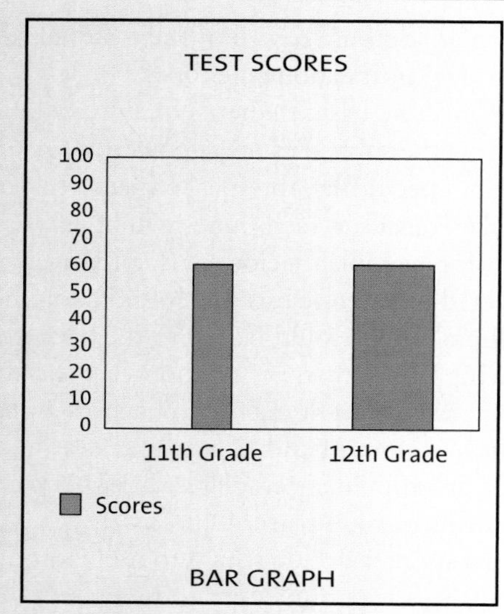

[NOTE 13.61]
Pieces of pie charts need to be drawn to correct proportion.

An originator could deceive a receiver into thinking the administrative costs in Pie Chart A of Figure 13.24 is one-fifth of the whole; it is actually one-third. Pie Chart B in Figure 13.24 displays the proportions correctly. The size of each piece of a pie chart must be in the same proportion to the whole pie as is the value of the part to the total value.

[NOTE 13.62]
The reference point of all bar graphs should be zero.

Another method of deceptive illustration is beginning the bottom of the bars in a bar graph at a point other than zero. This method exaggerates the differences between the individual bars. A company can lead its stockholders to believe that the company has experienced significant growth in sales during the three quarters shown in Graph A of Figure 13.25; Graph B better represents the true sales of the company.

[NOTE 13.63]
Grid increments should be of consistent value throughout a line graph.

Improper construction of a line graph can also deceive the receiver. Inconsistent intervals on the *y*-axis can make changes appear greater or lesser than they actually are. Notice that in Figure 13.26 that the $30,000 increase between 1996 and 2000 appears greater than the $100,000 decrease between 1994 and 1995.

The labels of a visual aid should also be critically evaluated. A receiver looking at the bar graphs in Figure 13.27 should question why the odd years have been

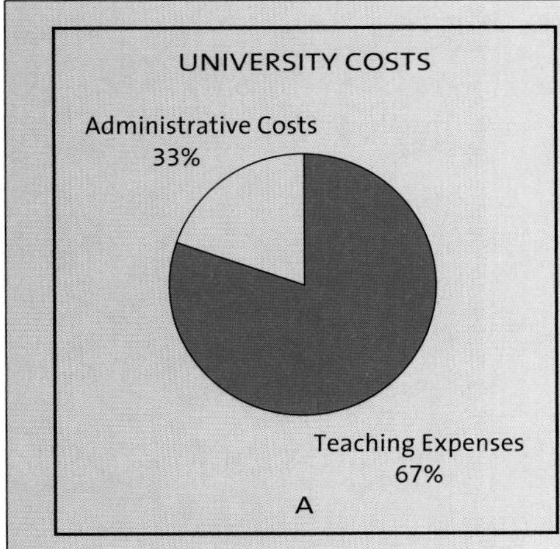

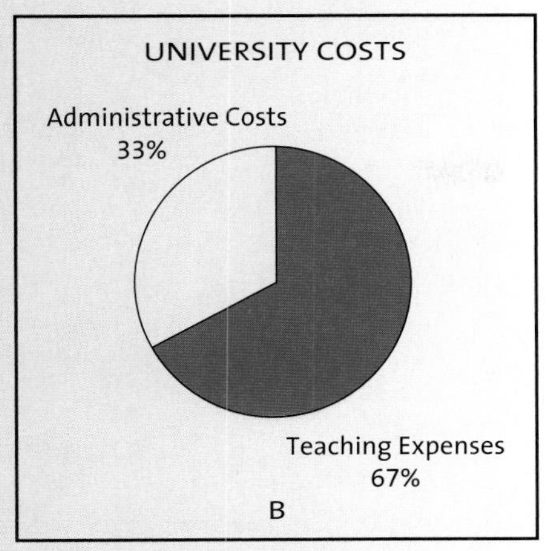

Figure 13.24
Pie Charts Showing Disproportionate and Correct Division

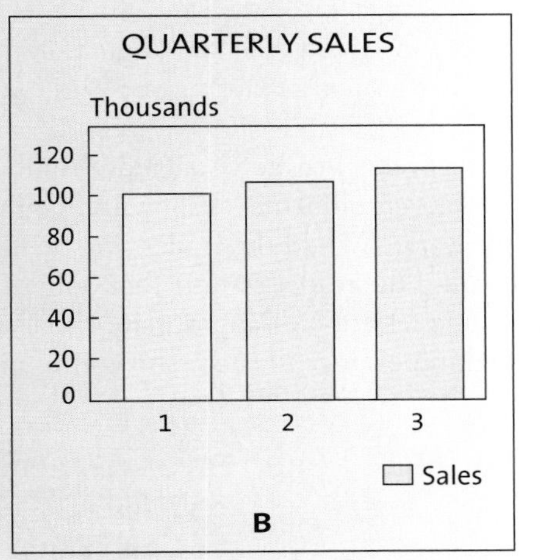

Figure 13.25
Deception Caused by Not Starting Baseline at Zero

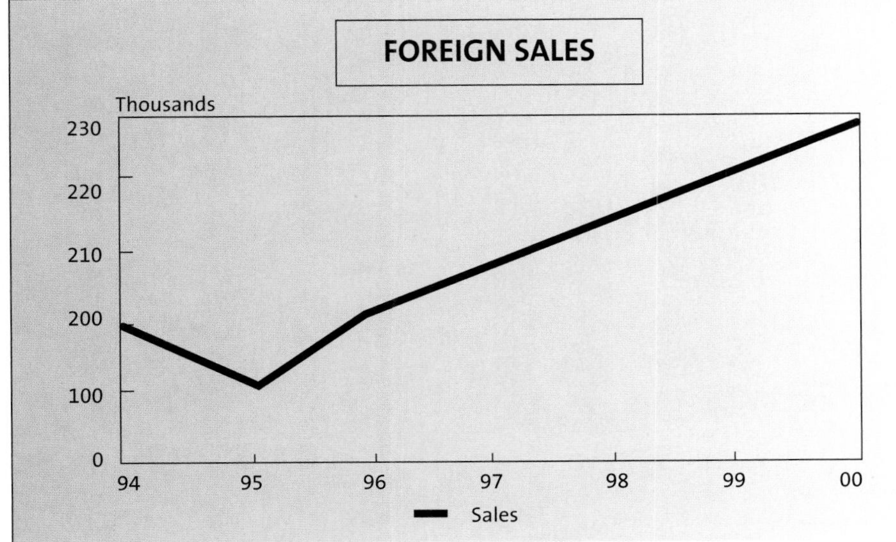

Figure 13.26
Inconsistent Increments on a Line Graph

Figure 13.27
Intentional Omission of Data

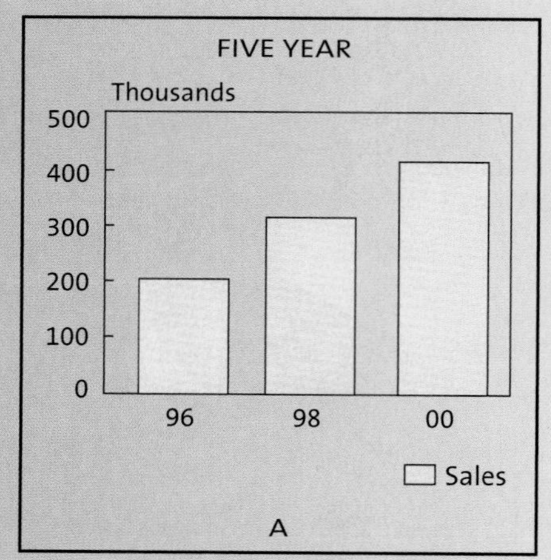

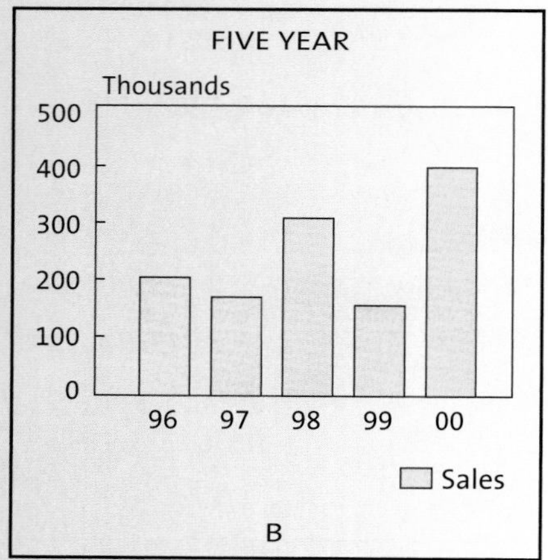

omitted in Graph A. Is the originator attempting to make the receiver believe that there has been a steady increase in the values throughout the period? What happened in 1997 and 1999?

Text references to visual aids should be considered, too. Suppose a report reads, "Student enrollments, as shown in Figure 13.28, have grown steadily during the four years." Would the reader assume that all three types of enrollments have grown or would the reader assume that only MBA enrollments have grown?

[NOTE 13.64] The written text must accurately describe the visual aid.

The selection of appropriate visual aids and accurate descriptions of them are of equal importance to successful communication.

Figure 13.28
Stacked-Bar Graph Showing Student Enrollments

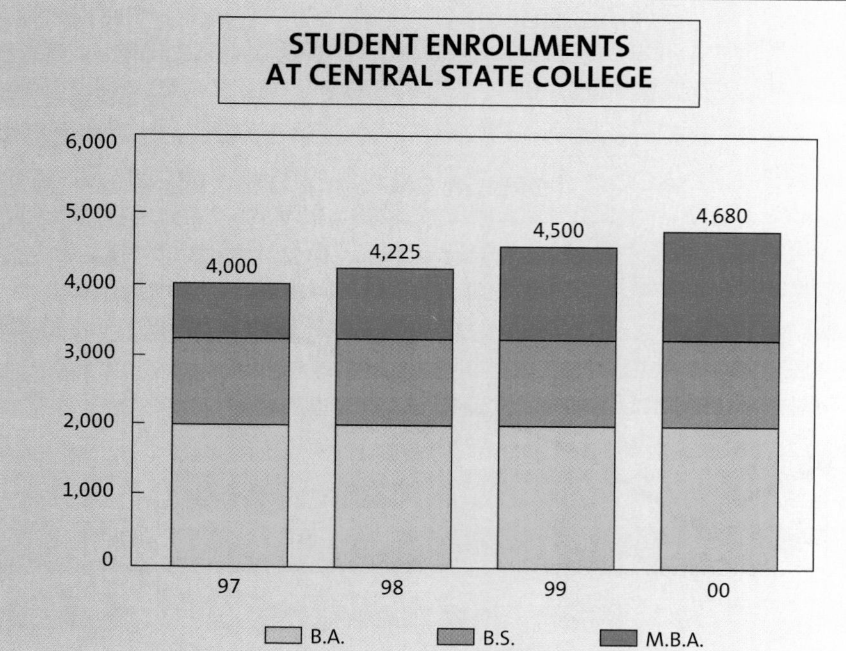

Summary of Learning Objectives

Describe the purposes of visual aids in written and oral communication. Communication can be improved by summarizing complex figures in charts and graphs, by identifying your company through the use of a drawing or photograph for a logo, by showing relationships in a chart, by indicating trends in a graph, or by abstracting in a table details that are too cumbersome. *Learning Objective* [1]

Explain where to place a visual aid within a report. Place illustrations that directly relate to the topic with the written text. A small illustration, less than one-half page, should be placed after the first reference to the aid, preferably on the same page. A large illustration, one-half to one page, should be placed on the page following the first mention of the illustration. Avoid dividing a visual aid between two pages. Place illustrations that are indirectly related to the topic in an appendix at the end of the text. *Learning Objective* [2]

Label visual aids properly. All formal visual aids should be identified by appropriate titles that describe their contents. Consider the five Ws (who, what, when, where, and why) when developing the title. Illustration titles may be printed either in uppercase or in uppercase and lowercase letters and may appear above or below the visual aid. Visual aids should be numbered consecutively, but methods of numbering them vary. When only one visual aid appears in a report, it need not be numbered. The most important consideration in labeling illustrations is consistency. *Learning Objective* [3]

Construct tables that present statistical information. Words and numbers should be arranged systematically in columns and rows in a table. The table should contain a title, a heading for the first column that classifies the categories of data in each row, and a heading for each additional column. *Learning Objective* [4]

Construct the three types of charts that commonly appear in business reports. An *organization chart* depicts the relationships among departments and of personnel within the departments. Positions are connected by solid lines if they are line positions with authority over other positions and by broken or dotted lines if they are advisory or staff positions. A *flowchart* may be used to illustrate step-by-step progression through complicated procedures. Boxes of various shapes are connected by arrows to illustrate the direction that the action follows during the procedure. A *pie chart* can be used to show how the parts of a whole are distributed and how the parts relate to each other. The pie chart should begin at the twelve o'clock position and continue in a clockwise direction. The pieces should be arranged in descending order of size with the category "other" appearing in the last position. *Learning Objective* [5]

Construct the various types of bar graphs and line graphs. A bar graph can be effective in comparing differences in quantities by changing the lengths of the bars. In a **simple bar graph,** the length or height of a bar indicates quantity. Graphs depicting very large amounts may make it impractical to include the entire amounts. In such cases a **broken-bar graph** may be used. A **multiple-bar graph** is used to compare several quantitative areas at one time on a single graph. Cross-hatching, shading, or color variation can be used to distinguish among bars representing different areas. A **stacked-bar graph** can be used to demonstrate differences in values within variables by dividing each bar into its parts. A **positive-negative bar graph** shows plus or minus deviations from a fixed reference point. The bars go up or *Learning Objective* [6] down from this fixed reference point. A **line graph** is constructed by drawing a line on an equally divided grid, with the horizontal reference line called the *x*-axis and the vertical reference line called the *y*-axis. A line graph can include either a single line or multiple lines. A **single-line graph** depicts movement of one variable whereas a **multiple-line graph** is used to illustrate changes in more than one value. The lines can be differentiated easily by using dotted, broken, and solid lines.

Learning Objective [7]

Describe how miscellaneous visual aids are used. A **map** can help a reader visualize geographic relationships. A **pictograph** is similar to a bar graph in that it emphasizes differences in statistical data, but it differs in that it uses images of items or symbols instead of bars. A personal touch can be added to a business report by including a **photograph** of a facility, product, or employee. A **drawing** may communicate a complicated idea or procedure by omitting clutter and emphasizing details in an idea or procedure.

Learning Objective [8]

Select the appropriate type of visual aid to complement an oral presentation. **Handouts** can be used to illustrate points in a presentation. **Flip charts** can be prepared in advance or as part of an interaction with the audience. **Posters** can be developed for most visual aids and work well for blueprints and drawings. Actual **objects** can be displayed during a presentation, and presenters can write on whiteboards. **Slides** can be effective with large audiences while a **transparency** is an inexpensive presentation tool. When a computer is available, **projection devices** can be used effectively. **Multimedia aids** can incorporate text, graphics, sound, and animation into a presentation.

Learning Objective [9]

Explain how receivers can avoid being deceived by visual aids. To avoid being deceived, receivers must remember that in a pictograph, the number of images, not their size, determines the value; and in a bar graph, the height or length of the bar, not the width, determines the value. Receivers also should remember that each piece of a pie chart must be in the same proportion to the whole pie as is the value of the part to the total value. When looking at a bar graph, readers should be aware that the bars must begin at zero to avoid exaggerating the differences between the individual bars. Intervals on the *y*-axis of a line graph must be consistent to avoid changes appearing greater or lesser than they actually are. The labels of a visual aid should also be critically evaluated.

DISCUSSION QUESTIONS

1. List five purposes for which visual aids are used in business reports. (Objective 1)
2. You are writing a report that includes visual aids. Where would you place the visual aids in the report? Explain why you chose these placements. (Objective 2)
3. Describe how and where a title should be printed for an illustration. (Objective 3)
4. You have been hired as a consultant for a restaurant to improve the efficiency of its operation. During your investigation you find that the business serves many more customers on certain days of the week than on other days. In your report you need to illustrate which days are busy and which days are slow. What type of visual aid would best illustrate your findings? Describe how you would construct the visual aid. (Objective 4, 5, or 6)

5. Explain how to present statistical data in a business report table. What parts are necessary to make a table complete? (Objective 4)
6. Monica is constructing a policy manual for her business. She wants to illustrate how a grievance is handled in the organization. She also wants to ensure that everyone knows clearly to whom he or she is responsible. What visual aid(s) would be most appropriate? Justify your selections. (Objective 5)
7. Compare a stacked-bar graph with a positive-negative bar graph. (Objective 6)
8. Describe how graphics software programs can be used to improve a written report. (Objective 7)
9. Name and explain three visual presentation aids a speaker might use when giving an oral presentation. (Objective 8)

10. **Ethics.** Are ethics involved in the construction of visual aids for business reports? Discuss what readers should consider when analyzing visual aids in a report. (Objective 9)

APPLICATION EXERCISES

1. Locate annual reports from three major corporations. Analyze the various visual aids in each of the annual reports. Include in your analysis the placement of the aids, their labels, references to them in the report, and their appropriateness. (Objectives 2 and 3)
2. Prepare a visual aid that will illustrate each step of the procedure you anticipate that you will follow in obtaining a job on graduating. (Objective 4)
3. Construct a visual aid that best illustrates the time you have spent each week studying for each of your classes during the past three weeks. (Objective 6)
4. Select the most appropriate visual aid to illustrate each of the following. Give justification for each of your selections. (Objectives 4, 5, 6, and 7)
   a. Annual change in buffalo population at a state park after their relocation
   b. Arrangement of flowers in a vase
   c. Comparison of the number of students in a school by grade level over a five-year period
   d. Average rainfall for major cities in the United States
   e. Dow Jones Industrial Averages in relation to Dow Jones Bond Averages for a six-month period
   f. Procedure that students must follow to register for classes
   g. Damage to an automobile that was involved in an accident
   h. The number of freshmen, sophomores, juniors, and seniors attending a college
5. Construct the visual aid that best illustrates the data for each of the following situations. Create your own titles and labels. Write the introduction to the aid. Be sure to direct your reader to some aspect of the data and refer to the illustration by number. (Objectives 3, 4, 5, and 6)
   a. The attendance at the Tigers' soccer games in 200–

Game 1	78	Game 4	130
Game 2	121	Game 5	108
Game 3	159	Game 6	98

b. The number of employees in each department at Allan's Electrical

Secretaries	2
Service	8
Residential	6
Commercial	14
Accounting	1
Management	4

c. Income earned in a day at Cherokee Hills Steak House

Appetizers	$1,200
Beverages	5,200
Carryouts	450
Desserts	510
Entrees	11,900
Sandwiches	730

d. Average annual return on Nanci's investments

	Growth & Income	Growth	Aggressive Growth
1997	19.3%	25.4%	31.7%
1998	21.6%	23.8%	21.0%
1999	19.7%	24.6%	24.6%
2000	16.5%	25.1%	19.9%

e. Golf scores for the month of May

May 2	Bob	93	May 23	Bob	97
	Fred	89		Fred	89
	Ralph	98		Ralph	96
May 9	Bob	86	May 23	Bob	89
	Fred	91		Fred	84
	Ralph	103		Ralph	94
May 16	Bob	90			
	Fred	90			
	Ralph	94			

6. Construct a visual aid that most effectively illustrates how the various U.S. tax amounts compare with each other. The receipts of the taxes, in millions, may be the following: (Objective 5)

Individual income	$590,157
Corporation income	157,088
Social insurance	484,474
Excise	97,485
Estate and gift	84,764
Miscellaneous	63,928

7. Construct the most appropriate visual aid to compare the average monthly temperatures for Oklahoma and North Dakota during a typical year: (Objective 6)

	Oklahoma	North Dakota
January	34°	7°
February	38°	12°
March	46°	36°
April	63°	42°
May	73°	50°
June	84°	66°
July	92°	75°
August	97°	74°
September	81°	63°
October	72°	51°
November	68°	47°
December	57°	29°

8. **Global/Multicultural. Teamwork.** Divide into groups of three and perform a library search to determine the five leading wheat-exporting countries for the past year and for ten years ago. Ascertain the principal language that is spoken in each of the countries. Construct a visual aid that could be used in a report discussing languages used in leading agricultural nations. (Objectives 4, 5, and 6)

9. **E-mail.** Send an e-mail to your instructor explaining the use of a source note. Discuss how and where the source note is presented. (Objective 3)

There are Web exercises at **http://krizan.swcollege.com** to accompany this chapter.

MESSAGE ANALYSIS

Rewrite and improve the quality of the following paragraph. Use a visual aid that would be appropriate for the paragraph.

> *Individuals have been going to movies at a fast pace this summer. Many movies have been released this summer. The six newest movies with their gross income are:* Cream Puff Express, *$270,000;* Metroman, *$61,800,000;* Murder After 12, *$51,600,000;* The Perfect Vacation, *$12,325,000;* The Mad Musician, *$70,000,000;* Hounds and Kittens, *$62,500,000. It looks as if* The Mad Musician *will outperform all the rest of the movies this summer.*

GRAMMAR WORKSHOP

Correct the grammar, spelling, punctuation, style, and word choice errors in the following sentences:

1. Unfortunately applications can not be submitted before Wedesday Febuary 1.
2. The entrances to the Trinity Memorial Hospital intensive care unit is located on the 1st floor for patiences convenience.
3. More than 45000 individuals attended the promise keepers conference in Jacksonville, FL.

4. The personal manager wants you to carefully reconsider you're decision to submit your request for retirement.
5. Jon is the slower reader in his class so his instructor cent him to the libary for their speed reading class.
6. The computer programmer is a real smart person that can make a computer do almost anything.
7. Nancy was late in meeting her appointment because she had sat her alarm for 6.00 pm instead of 6.00 am.
8. Either Brian or Bill will leave their car at the airport, when they attend the super bowl at New Orleans.
9. Why did the Administration fire Dr. Fumiko Hayashi Assistant Professor of Foreign Language?
10. The building committee has made it's recommendation for the clubs new building sight.

Oral and Nonverbal Communication

CHAPTER:

CHAPTER

14 Listening and Nonverbal Messages

William Ellis, Personal Trading Specialist, American Express

LET'S TALK BUSINESS Listening is a skill that applies to communication with both internal and external audiences. One of my primary responsibilities as a personal trading specialist in the Compliance Department of American Express is training new employees in SEC personal trading regulations. I use listening to minimize or resolve issues surrounding insider trading. The goal is to prevent insider trading violations, something that is crucial for the individual and the company.

During training sessions, I must listen to questions and read participants' nonverbal cues to determine whether mutual understanding has been achieved. My listening skills are a key factor in determining whether my training sessions are successful. The way in which I listen is essential to creating an environment

(Continued)

[LEARNING OBJECTIVES]

[1] DISTINGUISH BETWEEN HEARING AND LISTENING.

[2] DESCRIBE THE FOUR ELEMENTS OF THE LISTENING PROCESS.

[3] LIST THE GUIDELINES FOR EFFECTIVE LISTENING.

[4] DESCRIBE BARRIERS TO EFFECTIVE LISTENING.

[5] DESCRIBE THE ADVANTAGES OF EFFECTIVE LISTENING.

[6] EXPLAIN THE IMPORTANCE OF NONVERBAL MESSAGES.

[7] IDENTIFY DIFFERENT TYPES OF NONVERBAL MESSAGES AND THEIR IMPACT ON THE COMMUNICATION PROCESS.

in which trainees feel comfortable asking questions. Listening also plays a role in responding to questions that arise after the training session, questions that are often posed via telephone. Based on my experience, I offer these insights about listening.

Telling or talking is the antithesis of listening Team leaders, financial advisors, and colleagues are most successful when they listen to their team members, clients, and peers. Listening to all parts of the message—the emotion, situation, and content—is crucial.

Listening is key in advisory or mentoring relationships Many people have a natural, strong urge to "give advice." Unfortunately, the advice is often given without effective listening. When the need to speak arises, reflecting with empathetic, open-ended questions increases the quality of the communication.

Corporate training is not talking at people One of the key elements in attaining a training course's objectives is the ability of the instructor to listen to participants and assess their readiness. Listening to participants' needs and expectations aids the instructor in realigning the curriculum for increased learning. •

The significant roles of written communication have been stressed in the preceding chapters of this book. However, the importance of listening and nonverbal communication should not be overlooked. Successful businesspeople communicate orally with many different people who have varying abilities to communicate effectively. Chapter 6 introduced speaking, listening, and nonverbal communication as components of interpersonal communication and teamwork. In this chapter, we will explore listening and nonverbal communication in greater depth. Chapter 15 is devoted to oral communication and how to prepare and deliver formal presentations.

Listening

People have various reasons for listening. They listen to enjoy entertainment, to gain information, to receive instructions, to hear complaints, and to show respect. The situations in which listening takes place also vary. Listening can occur (1) in one-on-one telephone or face-to-face conversations; (2) in a small group, such as a few supervisors receiving instructions from their manager; and (3) in a large group, such as an audience listening to a keynote speech at a conference.

[NOTE 14.1]
Information is acquired through listening.

Most people think they are good listeners, and perhaps they are—at least some of the time. But, since listening is more of an art than a science, it's more likely that people have the mixed listening skills described in the following Communication Note.

COMMUNICATION NOTE

Levels of Attentiveness

We often hear the remark "He talks too much" but did you ever hear the criticism "He listens too much"? Although most of us have mixed listening skills and do not fall into convenient categories of classification, there are four basic levels of attentiveness:

[1] *Nonlistener.* This individual is preoccupied with personal thoughts unrelated to the speaker's message.

[2] *Passive listener.* This person hears the speaker's words without really understanding them. This incomplete absorption means the listener lacks a coherent view of the entire message; knowledge is fragmented and vulnerable to distortion.

[3] *Semi-active listener.* The listener attempts to get what the speaker says but still doesn't understand the total intent. Vocal intonation, body language, facial expressions, and intellectual subtleties are missed. He or she forms opinions and draws conclusions before the speaker is finished.

[4] *Active listener.* This person is more effective. The listener pays close attention to the words and their context. He or she listens not only for content but also for applicability to his or her life. The listener will try to see the speaker's point of view and asks appropriate questions.

Adapted from Tom Jenkins, "Prick Up Your Ears," Successful Meetings *48 (12) November 1999, pp. 59–62.*

HEARING VERSUS LISTENING

Learning Objective [1]
DISTINGUISH BETWEEN HEARING AND LISTENING.

[NOTE 14.2]
Hearing is not the same as listening.

Hearing is a physical process; listening is a mental one. For example, you may have attended a class session during which the instructor gave directions for completing a report or project. Later, as you began preparing the assignment, you realized that you could not recall the details needed to complete the work. You *heard* the instructions but did not *listen* to them. Listening involves comprehending and retaining what is heard.

Ineffective listening occurs in the workplace as well as in the classroom. Consider the situation where George, an office manager, is told to develop his unit's budget for the next year by using a 3 percent revenue decrease. George heard the instructions but didn't listen to them and created his budget using a 3 percent increase. His supervisor was not impressed. George needs to learn how to use the entire listening process.

THE LISTENING PROCESS

Learning Objective [2]
DESCRIBE THE FOUR ELEMENTS OF THE LISTENING PROCESS.

The listening process consists of four elements. Hearing is one of these elements; the other three are filtering, interpreting, and recalling. Figure 14.1 shows the four elements of the listening process.

[NOTE 14.3]
Hearing is a physiological process.

Hearing The first element in the listening process, **hearing**, is a physiological process. When we hear, the auditory nerves are stimulated by sound waves. Everyone hears sounds unless he or she has a hearing impairment.

Figure 14.1
The Listening Process

Filtering The second element in the listening process, **filtering**, is the elimination of unwanted stimuli. Filtering allows a listener to focus on stimuli that are of specific interest. Consider an example illustrating both unwanted and wanted stimuli: Suppose someone attending a meeting on insurance benefits is seated near an open window through which the aroma from a nearby fast-food restaurant is wafting, making the listener hungry. The unwanted stimulus is the food aroma, and the wanted stimulus is the speaker's information about insurance. An individual has difficulty concentrating on an oral message when his or her filtering process is unable to eliminate or at least minimize distracting stimuli.

[NOTE 14.4]
Filtering eliminates unwanted stimuli.

Interpreting The third element of the listening process is **interpreting**. When interpreting, the listener's mind assigns meaning to the stimuli. This assignment of meaning is done through the use of the person's mental filters. Listeners tend to consider nonverbal cues as well as verbal cues when interpreting oral messages. In addition, a speaker's prior comments and actions are considered when interpreting present messages. As pointed out in Chapter 1, it is important for the receiver to interpret the stimuli in the way the sender intended.

[NOTE 14.5]
Stimuli are interpreted and assigned meanings by the receiver.

Recalling The fourth element, **recalling**, involves remembering at a later time the information that was interpreted earlier. The success of this element depends heavily on the association (relationship) placed on the stimuli during the interpretation phase.

[NOTE 14.6]
Proper association improves recall ability.

The success of the listening process depends on all four elements. If one of the elements is omitted or fails to function properly, the entire listening process is jeopardized. To ensure that the listening process is carried out properly, certain guidelines need to be followed.

To be a successful listener, you need to take an active role in the listening process.

Learning Objective [3]
LIST THE GUIDELINES FOR EFFECTIVE LISTENING.

GUIDELINES FOR EFFECTIVE LISTENING

[NOTE 14.7]
Listening is an active process and can be improved.

Listening is a process that can be improved if the receiver takes an active role. The following guidelines can help you to improve your listening skills.

Concentrate on the Message People normally speak at 100 to 200 words a minute. Listeners, however, are capable of hearing up to 500 words a minute. This mismatch between speaking and listening speeds makes it necessary for people to concentrate diligently in order to listen effectively. If you do not concentrate, your mind may wander to another topic.

[NOTE 14.8]
Concentrate on the main concepts, but be aware of hidden meanings.

One concentration technique is to summarize mentally the message. This technique is especially important when the speech is not well organized or when the speaker has a heavy accent. Also, you should concentrate on the main points the speaker is trying to convey. Look for hidden messages. Determine whether the speaker is using facts, opinions, or inferences. Do not allow the speaker's physical appearance or vocal qualities to affect your concentration. Focusing on the message will assist you in overcoming barriers that may interfere with your hearing the entire message.

[NOTE 14.9]
The three modes of listening are cautious listening, skimming, and scanning.

Determine the Purpose of the Message Oral messages have purposes, as do written messages. As a listener, you need to determine the purpose of the oral message so that you can decide on the mode that you will use when listening. The three modes commonly used to listen to messages are cautious listening, skimming, and scanning.

[NOTE 14.10]
Cautious listening focuses on concepts and details.

Cautious Listening This mode, **cautious listening**, is used when you need to understand and remember both the general concept and all the details of the message. This mode requires more energy than the others because of the amount or complexity of material on which you must concentrate. When listening in this mode, your mind has no time to relax.

[NOTE 14.11]
You can skim spoken material when you need to remember only general concepts.

Skimming **Skimming** is used when you need to understand only the general concept of the message. When using this mode for listening, your mind has time to relax because you do not need to remember all the details being presented. Think of your mind as a computer. The amount of storage is vast but not limitless. Cluttering your mind with insignificant matter causes it to tire, which could cause you to forget the important points.

[NOTE 14.12]
Scanning is the least careful type of listening.

Scanning When **scanning**, you concentrate on details of specific interest to you instead of on the message's general concept. No energy is wasted trying to retain information that is not of specific value. One shortcoming in using this mode is that your mind may wander; you may miss material that is important.

[NOTE 14.13]
Don't allow biases to influence listening.

Keep an Open Mind The speaker presents the message from his or her viewpoint. Respect this viewpoint by not allowing your own biases to block what is being said. Your listening ability may be impaired when you are not receptive to the message or when you have a strong emotional reaction to the speaker's use of impact words (also called color words). Another obstacle may be your expectation not to understand a speaker with a dialect different from yours. When you listen with an open mind, both you and the speaker will benefit. The speaker will believe that what he or she is saying is worthwhile, and you may acquire valuable information. Evaluate a speaker's message only after hearing the entire message. **Frozen evaluations**—quick, unwavering judgments—benefit no one.

For Better or For Worse

Use Feedback Feedback is important. It is your response to the speaker. The speaker may volunteer more information if he or she receives positive feedback. For instance, a worker describing a problem in the office may expand on his or her comments when you offer feedback such as "Tell me more about . . ." or "Yes, but . . ." or even "Uh-huh." Asking questions to clarify the message also provides feedback. Erika Ludwig comments on the importance of questions and feedback in the following Communication Quote.

[NOTE 14.14]
Positive feedback will improve the communication process.

COMMUNICATION QUOTE

Because Sauer-Sundstrand is aggressively entering new markets to obtain a worldwide presence, communication between coworkers can be difficult. Our employees are often expressing themselves in their second or third language, and it is easy to capture their messages incorrectly. Listening closely, offering feedback, and asking questions are essential to conducting business globally.

Erika Ludwig, Internal Auditor, Sauer-Sundstrand.

Some listening situations are not conducive to giving any type of feedback to the speaker. These situations include radio, television, and video presentations. Small group or one-to-one presentations lend themselves best to oral feedback. Each situation should be analyzed as to its appropriateness for providing feedback.

Minimize Note Taking It may be wise to record complicated presentations for later review. Although your goal should be to have thorough notes, you will not be able to concentrate on listening if you attempt to record everything that is said. Instead, record key words and ideas in an outline. In oral communication situations that are

[NOTE 14.15]
Taking notes may interfere with the listening process.

not complex, record just the major points. Try to remember what is said without using notes.

[NOTE 14.16] Facial expressions and voice tones can change the meaning of a message.

Analyze the Total Message Watch the speaker's actions and facial expressions; listen to his or her tone of voice. A speaker can change the entire meaning of a message by raising an eyebrow or by changing the inflection of his or her voice. Such cues as these enable the listener to understand hidden messages.

[NOTE 14.17] Talking and interrupting interfere with listening.

Do Not Talk or Interrupt An individual cannot talk and listen effectively at the same time. As mentioned in Stephen Duggan's Communication Quote, below, listening should occur more often than speaking. When you are talking, you cannot use all the elements of effective listening. Interrupting a speaker or having side conversations is rude and reduces the effectiveness of the communication. Learn to distinguish between a midthought pause and the end of the speaker's comments.

COMMUNICATION QUOTE

A good friend once told me always to be careful to listen more than I speak. This has been good advice that I always strive to remember. The art of listening is increasingly becoming a key to success in the information age. With the globalization of the marketplace and advances in technology, face-to-face meetings are less common. Business meetings are often conducted via telephone or video conference. As a result, we have to rely more on listening skills as other senses are not available.

Stephen C. Duggan, Publishing Group of America.

BARRIERS TO LISTENING

Learning Objective [4] DESCRIBE BARRIERS TO EFFECTIVE LISTENING.

A **listening barrier** is anything that interferes with the listening process. You should be aware of barriers so that you can avoid letting them interfere with your listening. Some of the more important barriers to listening are discussed here.

[NOTE 14.18] Be aware of physical distractions.

Physical Distractions The individual responsible for setting up the meeting place in which the listening will occur should minimize physical distractions. However, you can take actions to limit this barrier by sitting at the front of the room if you have a hearing impairment, not sitting near a corridor or an open window, or not sitting next to an individual who will talk or whisper during the presentation.

[NOTE 14.19] Don't let your mind wander when listening.

Mental Distractions As a listener, you are responsible for giving your undivided attention to a speaker. You should avoid daydreaming or allowing your mind to wander. You can think approximately four times faster than the speaker can talk, so it is easy to begin thinking about other business or personal interests instead of paying attention to the speaker.

A very common distraction is mentally constructing a comment to make or a question to ask rather than concentrating on what is being said. A related mental distraction is forming an opinion or a rebuttal during a presentation. To listen effectively, keep an open mind—that is, hear *all* of what is said before making judgments.

Health Concerns Good health and well-being play a definite role in effective listening. When a listener is hungry, nauseous, or tired, he or she will find it difficult to listen. When these conditions exist, the speaker may wish to repeat the original message later.

[NOTE 14.20]
Be sensitive to a listener's health.

Nonverbal Distractions A listener may give a speaker negative nonverbal feedback. Facial expressions—frowning, yawning, raising an eyebrow, or closing the eyes—can convey a message of disinterest or disapproval. Glancing at a watch or a clock may tell the speaker that you are ready for the presentation to end. The lines of communication will remain open when these nonverbal distractions are avoided.

[NOTE 14.21]
Give the speaker positive feedback by avoiding negative nonverbal actions.

Inappropriate Timing A listener should ensure that a speaker can present his or her message at an appropriate time. A listener often knows if the time is appropriate. For example, a manager going through a plant may casually ask a worker, "Any problems?" If a supervisor is standing nearby and the manager knows the worker would be reluctant to speak in front of the supervisor, the worker might think the manager really does not want to listen. A more appropriate comment from the manager would be, "If you have any problems, I have an open-door policy and have reserved Wednesday afternoons to listen to employees." This would allow the speaker (the worker) to present his or her message at an appropriate time.

[NOTE 14.22]
The timing of the communication is important.

An individual presenting a message should be given adequate time so that he or she does not have to rush. It is the listener's responsibility to ensure that the speaker will have enough time to present the entire message. For example, if a manager has to leave for a meeting in 5 minutes and a supervisor enters the office to discuss a complex problem the manager should make an appointment to meet with the supervisor at a later time. The manager should not expect the supervisor to condense the presentation into 5 minutes.

[NOTE 14.23]
A listener should give a speaker adequate time to present a message.

Ineffective Speech Characteristics A listener must be able to hear and understand a speaker in order to interpret the message. If the words are spoken at insufficient volume or at such a high pitch that the listener has trouble hearing the words, listening will be difficult, if not impossible. Other characteristic speech barriers include articulation, dialects, unusual pronunciations, jargon, regional speech patterns (accents), vocalization (tongue clicking, "ums"), and speech impairments. These barriers are difficult to overcome because listeners cannot review a spoken message in the same way they can review a written message. A comfortable atmosphere will cause a speaker to set a more relaxed pace and allow his or her message to be understood more easily. In addition, careful concentration may help a listener deal effectively with characteristic speech barriers.

[NOTE 14.24]
Speech barriers are difficult to overcome.

Learning Objective [5]
DESCRIBE THE ADVANTAGES OF EFFECTIVE LISTENING.

ADVANTAGES OF EFFECTIVE LISTENING

One of the best ways to acquire information is through effective listening. Effective listening will help you develop better attitudes. Also, it can improve your relationships with others because they will realize that you are interested in them. Interested individuals will work diligently to communicate with you. This, in turn, will allow you to do a better job because you will have the support of the people around you. Effective listening will encourage individuals to tell you about minor problems before they become major problems. Businesses wishing to be perceived as customer-oriented must make the art of listening an integral part of their employee training.

[NOTE 14.25]
Effective listening will enable you to be more successful.

Nonverbal Communication

[NOTE 14.26] Nonverbal communication is a message without words.

A **nonverbal message** is one that communicates without words. Nonverbal messages are an important part of the communication process because they provide added information the receiver can use in interpreting what is said. The extra information can add to or detract from the meaning of a message.

[NOTE 14.27] Establish a baseline to help interpret nonverbal cues.

People constantly communicate through their conscious or unconscious nonverbal messages. As an example, suppose that every day on your way to work you meet the same person at the same place. Each morning as you pass each other you exchange greetings. Suddenly, one morning your greeting is met with indifference; the person does not acknowledge your presence. Later in the day someone asks whether you saw the passerby that morning and you recall your encounter. Would you be so aware of the encounter if the passerby had spoken to you as usual? Probably not. You were aware of the passerby this time because his or her actions differed from what you had determined to be congruent behavior. You used **benchmarking**—a comparison of "what is" against what you have come to expect as typical. The following Tips and Hints provide more information about benchmarking.

Benchmarking

TIPS AND HINTS

In your first meeting with a client or colleague, discover how he or she looks and sounds when he or she is congruent—when words, tone, and actions match. Open your conversation with discussion of a topic dear to the person's interests and ask questions to elicit a story or opinion demonstrating a strong, positive experience. Watch facial expressions, posture, and gestures; store the information in your mind for future comparison. When presenting a proposal, watch for the same congruence. If it isn't present as fully as before, ask what questions, reservations, or hesitations he or she may have. Respond to incongruence at the beginning of the relationship in order to reduce the potential for disappointment along the way.

Adapted from Judith Light, "Keys to Successful Communication: More Than Words," *Journal of Management Consulting* 10 (1) May 1998, pp. 28–32.

Here is another example of how nonverbal messages affect other forms of communication: A prospective customer receives a poorly printed letter announcing a furniture sale. The poor printing is a nonverbal message suggesting carelessness. How quickly will the customer rush to the store for the sale? Which message is more effective—the written or the nonverbal?

Learning Objective [6]
EXPLAIN THE IMPORTANCE OF NONVERBAL MESSAGES.

THE IMPORTANCE OF NONVERBAL COMMUNICATION

[NOTE 14.28] Be aware of the impact of nonverbal communication.

A person should be aware of the impact of nonverbal communication. Nonverbal messages may not always be intended; nevertheless, they clearly communicate with and influence people. In fact, as cited in the following Communication Note, nonverbals provide the majority of what a receiver interprets as the message.

COMMUNICATION NOTE

How We Communicate

Though we depend heavily on what we hear, especially when what is said matches what we want to hear, only about 7 percent of our communication is verbal. Greater meaning is to be found in the richness of tonalities and of nonverbal behavior. Tonal information accounts for 3 percent of meaning. Nonverbals—including posture, gestures, expressions, breathing patterns, and the actions following a conversation—provide 58 percent of the message.

Judith Light, "Keys to Successful Communication: More Than Words," Journal of Management Consulting *10 (1) May 1998, pp. 28–32.*

Nonverbal messages may aid or hinder communication. The following summarizes the more important characteristics of nonverbal communication:

[NOTE 14.29] Nonverbal communication has several important characteristics.

[1] *The nonverbal communication can be unintentional.* The sender may be unaware that he or she is sending a nonverbal message and, consequently, may not be aware of the impact that message may have.

[2] *A nonverbal communication may be more honest than a verbal one.* Since the message may be transmitted unconsciously, the sender will not have planned it. Therefore, a nonverbal message can be more reliable than an oral or a written one that had been thought out ahead of time.

[3] *Nonverbal communication makes, or helps to make, a first impression.* First impressions are powerful. They often result in frozen evaluations, images that can be very difficult to alter.

[4] *Nonverbal communication is always present.* Neither oral nor written communication exists without nonverbal communication. Examples of nonverbal messages being sent even when the communication may not be face-to-face include tapping the phone receiver, loudly rearranging papers, or silence.

Although nonverbal messages are powerful, a listener should not become so intent on interpreting them that he or she fails to listen to the speaker's words.

TYPES OF NONVERBAL COMMUNICATION

Learning Objective [7]
IDENTIFY DIFFERENT TYPES OF NONVERBAL MESSAGES AND THEIR IMPACT ON THE COMMUNICATION PROCESS.

Nonverbal messages come in various forms. Some of the common types of nonverbal communication follow.

Physical Appearance Physical appearance is an important type of nonverbal communication. An individual will form a first impression from a letter's envelope, stationery, letterhead, format, and neatness. This first impression will definitely influence the receiver's reaction to the letter.

[NOTE 14.30] The physical appearance of a written message influences the first impression of the receiver.

The physical appearance of a speaker influences an oral message as much as the appearance of a letter influences a written message. Listeners use physical appearance as a clue to the speaker's credibility. That is why a sloppily dressed salesperson will find it difficult, if not impossible, to sell expensive clothing.

[NOTE 14.31] Manner of dress communicates a nonverbal message.

Physical appearance also influences a receiver's perceptions of a speaker's socioeconomic status and judgment. For example, an individual who wears designer clothes, custom-made shoes, and expensive jewelry will transmit a nonverbal message. This nonverbal message will be perceived differently by receivers, depending on the occasion for which the individual is dressed. If the individual is going to lunch or dinner at an elegant restaurant, most people would perceive the person to be wealthy and successful. If the individual is washing a car or mowing a lawn, many people would perceive the person to be eccentric or to lack common sense.

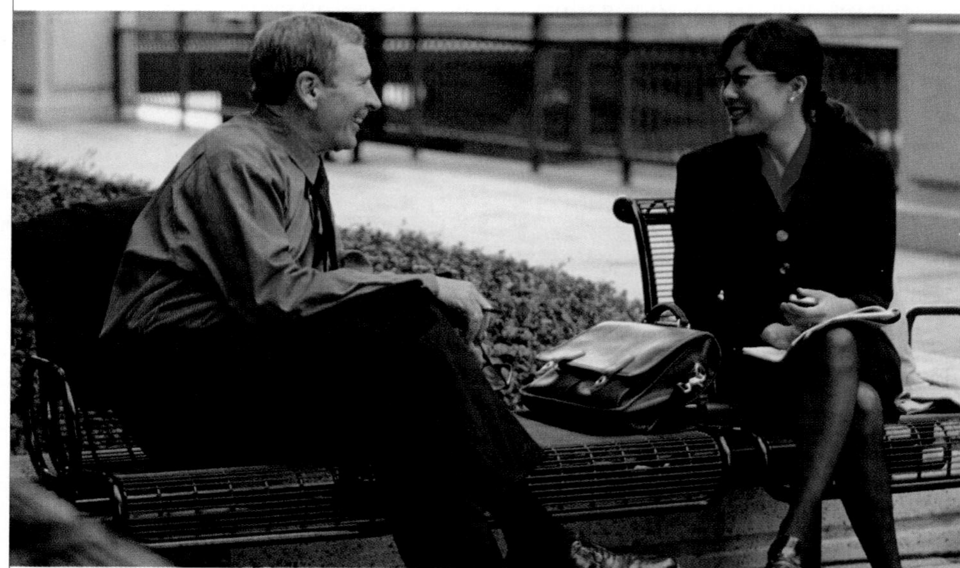

People transmit nonverbal messages through the actions of their bodies.

[NOTE 14.32] The meaning of verbal messages may be changed by body language.

Body Language Body language, whether intentional or unintentional, can change the meaning of a verbal message. The same gesture may be interpreted differently in different cultures. For instance, in the United States crossing the arms over the chest usually means that one's mind is made up and is not open to change. In Finland, however, folded arms are a sign of arrogance. Researchers have studied body language extensively in recent years and have developed body language dictionaries such as Bèuml and Bèuml's *A Dictionary of Gestures* or *The Nonverbal Dictionary of Gestures, Signs & Body Language Cues* found online at **http://members.aol/com/nonverbal2/diction1.htm**.

[NOTE 14.33] Body language may give instant feedback.

An advantage of using body language to respond to a message is that it conveys instant feedback to the sender. A smile is interpreted almost universally as an expression of friendliness and approval. A smile indicates satisfaction, but a frown shows disagreement. The eyes are also a powerful indicator. Failure to look a person in the eye when speaking may indicate shyness, dishonesty, or embarrassment. Eye contact may indicate confidence, agreement, or interest in the subject of a conversation. A raised eyebrow communicates the receiver's uncertainty. An individual who glances around while speaking is exhibiting nervousness or lack of interest.

[NOTE 14.34] Nonverbal messages are communicated through a person's posture.

Other forms of body language include posture and gestures. The way a person sits or stands communicates a nonverbal message. An individual standing or sitting erectly conveys confidence and pride, whereas a person slumping over may be perceived as being tired or depressed. If an individual leans toward another person during a conversation, body language indicates that the person likes or is interested in the other communicator. If the person leans away from the other person, the posture shows a dislike or disinterest in the other individual. Gestures and posture are two items to consider in mirroring, which is explained in the following Tips and Hints.

TIPS AND HINTS

Mirroring

People feel more comfortable when they share a kinship and common values with those around them. The comfort judgment is made quickly—within 2 to 30 seconds—and is based on what is seen. The more differences they perceive in each other, the more difficult it is to create a rapport. Mirroring helps overcome those differences. You can mirror another person by being *similar* to him or her in the following areas:

- Clothing
- Head position and facial expressions
- Stance, posture, and body position
- Voice, vocabulary, and breathing
- Energy

Mirroring is about creating similarity and trust with another person; it is not mimicking. It must be honest, natural, spontaneous, and appropriate to the situation. Anger, for example, should never be mirrored. Practice with friends and relatives before you try the technique in a business setting.

Adapted from Eileen O. Brownell, "Mirror Mirror on the Wall . . . Help Me Communicate With Them All," *The American Salesman* 44 (12) December 1999, pp. 9–15.

A handshake also communicates a nonverbal message. A person who firmly grips your hand demonstrates confidence, whereas an individual who squeezes your hand so tightly that it causes pain gives the impression of being overly aggressive or inconsiderate. The Communication Note on page 440 about handshakes describes several types and what the receiver may interpret them to mean.

[NOTE 14.35]
Handshakes communicate.

It is practically impossible to communicate without some use of gestures. A gesture may be as simple as a thumbs-up to signify approval or a thumbs-down for disapproval. A gesture may be used to emphasize a critical point in an oral presentation. How interesting would a speech be if the only communicative motion was the opening and closing of the speaker's mouth?

[NOTE 14.36]
Gestures are an integral part of nonverbal communication.

Care should be taken in using gestures because, as pointed out in Chapter 2, different cultures interpret gestures in different ways. For instance, if a woman in southern Germany tilts her head to the side and leans forward to listen, she is considered attentive; but in northern Germany, she would be perceived as cringing and timid. To be considered attentive in northern Germany, she would sit up straight and look the speaker directly in the eye; in southern Germany, these actions would indicate that she is angry. Similar cultural differences apply to other nonverbal messages.

COMMUNICATION NOTE

Handshakes

Handshakes can take many forms, and each can convey a different meaning. Consider the following as you develop your personal handshake style:

- *Flabby.* A limp, soft paw that feels like overcooked pasta. These people are pessimists who need reassurance before anything else.
- *Squeeze.* A bench vise. These people, usually men, want to show strength and power, possibly to cover up an inferiority complex. Meet their needs with flattery.
- *Next-to-the-body.* The arm and elbow are bent and the right hand stays close to the side. Politicians and others who hesitate to take risks favor this handshake. Use caution.
- *Impelling.* A vigorous style used by people who never miss an opportunity to shake hands. They seem insecure, so use more insistence than usual.
- *Nongripping.* The hand is thrust forward and the fingers do not move. Approach slowly; these folks don't want to get involved.
- *Robot.* The hand is offered quickly and automatically. When dealing with these indifferent, self-interested people, show that what you have to offer is indispensable to their needs.
- *Jackhammer.* A hand-pumping shake used by people who are strong willed and inflexible. Be more determined than they are.
- *Prison.* A grip that won't be let loose until you give your full attention to the person using it. The user may be an opportunist, so emphasize what good fortune it is that you've met and pursue your objectives.
- *Normal.* An open, honest handshake that means you can trust your instincts with the person who gives it.

Adapted from "Sometimes a Handshake Is Just a Handshake," IIE Solutions *31 (8) August 1999, p. 66, Based on J. T. Auer's* The Joy of Selling.

A nonverbal message can be communicated by the way a person shakes hands. Confidence, aggression, or insecurity may be conveyed.

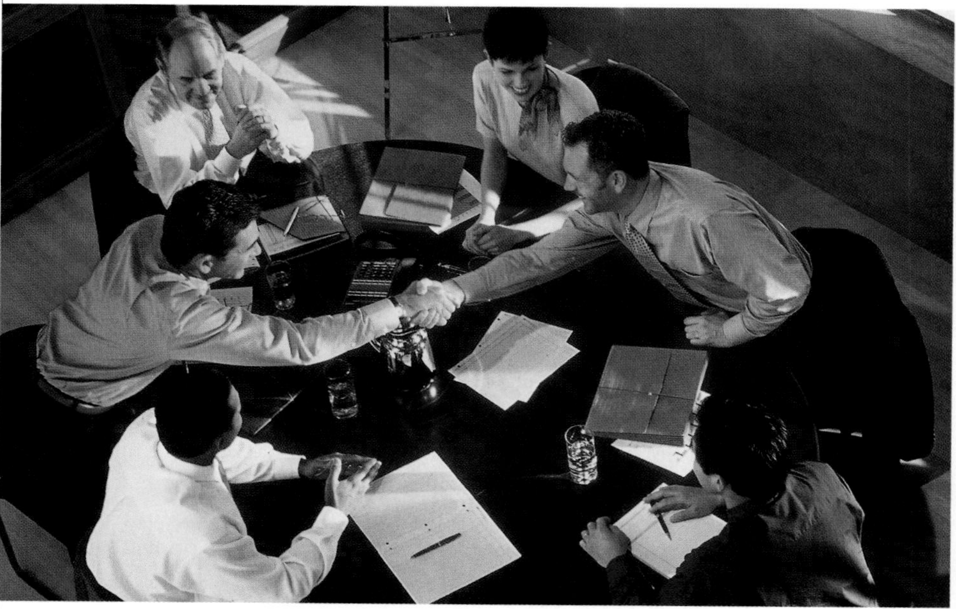

Space Communication is influenced by space. Space, as used in nonverbal communication, includes the size of a physical area, proximity to another person, and obstacles between you and the person with whom you are speaking.

The size of a person's office is an indication of importance within the hierarchy of an organization. The larger the office, the higher the position. The amount of space people possess influences our attitudes and, therefore, inadvertently is a form of nonverbal communication.

[NOTE 14.37]
The amount of space in an office or home indicates the status of the occupant.

A person in charge wants to keep his or her most trusted aide nearby. Therefore the proximity of an employee to a supervisor communicates nonverbally the importance of the employee within the organization. The employee's importance also may be indicated nonverbally by parking space location, by office size and location, or by seating location at meetings.

[NOTE 14.38]
Space transmits a nonverbal message.

Research has shown that eliminating obstacles such as desks, chairs, and tables will improve oral communication between individuals. The communication will improve if both communicators are on the same level—sitting or standing. The distance between the communicators will also affect the communication. This distance will vary with individuals from different cultures. The purpose of the communication will determine the appropriate personal space between communicators. The table in the following Communication Note shows acceptable distances for personal space in the United States.

COMMUNICATION NOTE

Distances for Personal Space in the United States

Distance	Purpose of Communication
½ to 1½ feet	Intimate communication with friends
1½ to 4 feet	Casual conversation with friends and coworkers
4 to 12 feet	Formal conversation with business associates
More than 12 feet	Speeches and presentations to groups

Time Communicators must be aware that the amount of time devoted to a subject transmits a nonverbal message. If the president of a company, for instance, meets with one manager for ten minutes and another manager for two hours, a nonverbal message is being transmitted.

[NOTE 14.39]
Emphasis on time transmits a message.

Punctuality relays a nonverbal message. A person who is always on time is perceived as being well organized. A person who is always late transmits a message that he or she is disorganized or that the appointment is unimportant. For instance, if two people of equal credentials were interviewing for a job and one arrived 15 minutes late for the interview, it is more likely that the punctual applicant would be hired.

The importance of time will vary among cultures. Punctuality is very important with individuals from most European countries; however, a 30-minute delay is customary in most Latin-American countries. Asians expect others to be punctual, but they themselves often will be late.

Summary of Learning Objectives

Learning Objective [1] **Distinguish between hearing and listening.** Hearing is a physical process; listening is a mental one. A person can hear something without listening to it. Listening involves comprehending and retaining the message.

Learning Objective [2] **Describe the four elements of the listening process.** The four elements of the listening process are hearing—the physiological process of the auditory nerves being stimulated by sound waves; filtering—the elimination of unwanted stimuli; interpreting—the listener's mind assigning meaning to the stimuli; and recalling—remembering at a later time the information that was interpreted earlier.

Learning Objective [3] **List the guidelines for effective listening.** Guidelines that may be followed to improve your listening are (1) concentrate on the message, (2) determine the purpose of the message, (3) keep an open mind, (4) use feedback, (5) minimize taking notes, (6) analyze the total message, and (7) do not talk or interrupt.

Learning Objective [4] **Describe barriers to effective listening.** Anything that interferes with the listening process is a barrier to effective listening. A physical distraction is any diversion that interferes with the listener's concentration on what is being said. A mental distraction occurs when a listener daydreams or permits his or her mind to wander from the subject being discussed. Health concerns that may affect listening include being hungry, sick, or tired. Nonverbal distractions include the listener looking at his or her watch, yawning, or frowning. Attempting to present a speech or hold a conversation at an inappropriate time can create a barrier to listening. A listener's understanding can be hindered by a speaker's heavy accent or dialect.

Learning Objective [5] **Describe the advantages of effective listening.** Effective listening will help to develop better attitudes, improve relationships with others, gain support from others, and enable you to learn about minor problems before they become major ones.

Learning Objective [6] **Explain the importance of nonverbal messages.** The sender of a nonverbal message may be unaware that a message is being sent and, therefore, be unaware of its effect on the receiver. Nonverbal messages may be more reliable than written or oral messages because they are usually unplanned. Nonverbal messages often cause the receiver to form a frozen evaluation of the sender. Nonverbal communication is always present.

Learning Objective [7] **Identify different types of nonverbal messages and their impact on the communication process.** The physical appearance of a written message influences a receiver by causing the receiver to form a first impression of a message before reading it. The physical appearance of an individual sends a nonverbal message—the way a person is dressed often influences the opinions of others. Body language—facial expressions, gestures, handshakes, and posture—also communicates nonverbal messages. Communication through body language is instantaneous. The size of the physical area, proximity to another person, and obstacles between you and the person to whom you are speaking are all examples of how space can be used to communicate messages. The amount of time spent with an individual and punctuality are examples of how time communicates nonverbal messages.

DISCUSSION QUESTIONS

1. Distinguish between hearing and listening. Cite a personal example of an occasion when you heard but did not listen. (Objective 1)
2. Describe the four elements of the listening process. (Objective 2)
3. Name and explain the three modes of listening. (Objective 3)
4. How can a listener keep an open mind about the topic? (Objective 3)
5. Describe six barriers to listening. (Objective 4)
6. What can be gained from effective listening? (Objective 5)
7. List and explain the four characteristics of nonverbal messages. (Objective 6)
8. Explain how physical appearance can affect written and oral messages. (Objective 7)
9. What is a "frozen evaluation"? How does it relate to listening and nonverbal communication? (Objective 7)
10. Discuss five ways nonverbal messages could be presented in a positive manner when interviewing for a supervisory position in a business organization. (Objective 7)

APPLICATION EXERCISES

1. **Teamwork.** As directed by your instructor, meet in a small group to discuss the following questions: (Objective 2)
   a. How do you feel when a teacher, manager, colleague, or service representative doesn't seem to be listening to you?
   b. How do you feel when these same people seem to be listening well?

   Make a list of the feelings your group identifies and share them with the class.

2. **Teamwork.** Bring a newspaper, magazine, or book to class. Working in a group of four, have one member read aloud for five minutes while the other three members listen—one using cautious listening, one skimming, and one scanning. Compare the results of the three listening efforts and report your results to the class. (Objective 3)

3. **E-mail.** Send an e-mail message to your instructor explaining how relationships can be improved through more effective listening. (Objective 3)

4. **Teamwork.** Repeat Exercise 2 using different material. Have a fifth person make noise or cause some other distraction. Discuss how the distraction affected each person's ability to listen to the message. (Objective 4)

5. **Teamwork.** Conduct the following exercise with five people:

   Raise your right hand and touch your pointer finger to your thumb to form a circle. Ask your listener to do the same. After he or she has done so, tell him or her to touch that circle to his or her chin. As he or she starts to do so, place your own finger-thumb circle on your right cheek.

   How many of your listeners followed your nonverbal lead as opposed to your verbal instructions? Report your results and interpretation of them in a memo to your instructor. (Objective 6)

6. After the class has been divided into at least two teams, take turns acting out, without speaking, roles presented by the teacher. (Objective 7)

7. **Global/Cross-Cultural.** Interview a foreign student or faculty member and ask him or her to indicate differences in interpretations of nonverbal messages that he or she has observed between Americans and people of his or her culture. Report your findings to the class. (Objective 7)

8. Go to a shopping mall or large store and observe different types of nonverbal messages. Record and report five unusual communication messages that you saw transmitted. (Objective 7)

9. Observe students' and instructors' body language early in the week and late in the week. Record the differences in nonverbal communication. Are the differences easily apparent? (Objective 7)

There are Web exercises at **http://krizan.swcollege.com** to accompany this chapter.

MESSAGE ANALYSIS

Rearrange the following items into a three-column table with *Ten Keys to Effective Listening, The Good Listener*, and *The Bad Listener* as column headings. Each of the ten keys will have one good listener trait and one bad listener trait. Give the document an appropriate title. Be sure to proofread carefully before submitting your work. (Based on material published by Sperry Corporation and referenced at **http://www.tufts.edu/as/stu_act/leadership/listening.html**).

Find areas of interest. Shows no energy output; fakes attention. Keeps mind open to all possibilities. Listens for facts. Capitalize on fact thought is faster than speech. Tends to enter into argument. Be flexible. Resists difficult expository material; seeks light, recreational material. Works hard; exhibits active body state. Opportunizes; asks "what's in it for me?" Judge content, not delivery. Resist distractions. Hold your fire. Reacts to emotional words. Fights or avoids distractions, tolerates bad habits, knows how to concentrate. Tunes out dry subjects. Listen for ideas. Work at listening. Tends to daydream with slow speakers. Interprets color words; does not get hung up on them. Uses heavier material as exercise for the mind. Tunes out if delivery is poor. Doesn't judge until comprehension is complete. Listens for central themes. Resist distractions. Challenges, anticipates, mentally summarizes, weights the evidence, listens between the lines to tone of voice. Exercise your mind. Takes fewer notes; uses from four to five different systems, depending on the speaker. Judges content, skips over delivery errors. Takes intensive notes using only one system. Keep your mind open.

GRAMMAR WORKSHOP

Correct the grammar, spelling, punctuation, style, and word choice errors in the following sentences:

1. John and Becky Pearson was assisted by the blue blazers in cutting the ribbon at the J and B Electric grand-opening celebration last week.
2. Should aaron return the faulty ink cartridge back too the story, ore the manufacturer.
3. The annual Civic Art contest will award a prize for the most perfectly decorate egg created by area children.

4. I just finish reading you're book from cover-to-cover and I think its a great guide to french cooking.
5. Bob were borne in the midwest, but razed in the south.
6. Walter spend the day washing and waxing his car, vacuuming his house, and fed his dog, cat, and bird.
7. When the painter finishes floating and painting the walls and the installers complete lying the carpets the Saxton's will move into its new home.
8. Wendell was not at home when Suzy phone cause he had went to the library.
9. The Store was unabled to make a profit, because much merchandise was stole.
10. Because Sallys'“to Do list was not on her desk she assumed it had bin throne away accidently.

CHAPTER

15 Oral Communication Essentials

Amy Rosvold, Accenture

LET'S TALK BUSINESS As a consultant with Accenture, I make presentations to both internal and external audiences.

Internally, my presentations involve updating my peers about industry trends and sharing lessons learned with different clients at different projects. Externally, the range of topics varies widely, depending on my current project. For example, while working to overhaul Web site products and services for a client, my team makes high-level status reports directly to the client's top managers. This involves analyzing a great deal of information from a variety of sources and filtering out extraneous or minute details. The team also

(Continued)

[LEARNING OBJECTIVES]

[1] IMPROVE THE BASIC QUALITY OF YOUR VOICE.

[2] USE YOUR VOICE EFFECTIVELY.

[3] STRENGTHEN YOUR PERSONAL PRESENCE.

[4] CLASSIFY DELIVERY STYLES BY TYPE.

[5] IDENTIFY THE STEPS TO FOLLOW IN PREPARING AN ORAL PRESENTATION.

[6] DEMONSTRATE THE TECHNIQUES TO BE USED WHEN DELIVERING AN EFFECTIVE PRESENTATION.

[7] IDENTIFY TASKS AND PROCEDURES ASSOCIATED WITH SPECIAL PRESENTATION SITUATIONS.

reports on issues that may prevent a project from implementing on time, makes recommendations for new projects, and suggests ways to manage the entire initiative more effectively.

These experiences have proven to me that you cannot underestimate the importance of oral presentations in the business world. Presentations are an opportunity to demonstrate knowledge, competence, and composure while making an impression on both superiors and subordinates.

Although oral presentations are extremely important, they generally strike fear in the hearts of those who give them. This does not need to be the case. Everyone has heard the adage about picturing audience members in their underpants. However, there is a more important component to giving a successful formal presentation and keeping your wits about you while doing it. That component is *preparation*. Preparation alleviates apprehension and helps identify potential stumbling points in the presentation.

Find an audience to listen to the presentation—a friend, a mirror, or even an attentive pet. Another option is to tape-record yourself, then play back the presentation and analyze it. Go through your entire presentation from beginning to end without stopping. If you reach a section where you stumble, keep going. During analysis, you will discover any weak areas in your delivery; during subsequent practice sessions, you can work to correct them for the actual presentation.

Never stop working to improve your oral presentation skills. Everyone can find something to improve upon, and even the best speakers are always seeking ways to develop their ability further.

Both written and oral communication are vital to your personal success and to the success of the business or organization where you work. Other parts of this text have been devoted to general foundations and principles of business communication and their application to written, interpersonal, and teamwork communication situations. In this chapter, you'll learn how those foundations and principles relate to oral communication. Specifically, you will learn how to improve your voice and presence and how to prepare and deliver a formal oral presentation.

Depending on your position and level of responsibility within an organization, the amount of time you spend giving presentations will vary widely. Certain jobs require extensive oral communication. Amy Rosvold routinely makes presentations in conjunction with her job as a consultant. Sales representatives must make informative and persuasive presentations to prospective customers. Union negotiators must present convincing arguments for their proposals to management. Public relations specialists must organize and moderate news conferences. The list could go

[NOTE 15.1]
Some jobs involve extensive oral communication.

on, but the jobs listed illustrate the fact that effective presentations are a thread common to many careers. Your success in those careers will depend not only on *what* you say, but also on *how* you say it—on the quality of your voice and the strength of your presence. You must speak clearly, intelligently, and confidently.

Improving Your Voice Qualities

Learning Objective [1]
IMPROVE THE BASIC QUALITY OF YOUR VOICE.

The starting point for enhancing your oral communication is to improve your speaking voice.

PROPER CONTROL OF BREATHING

[NOTE 15.2] Quality sound depends on proper use of air.

High-quality sound with adequate volume depends on the proper use of one raw material—air. By taking a few deep breaths, you can relax your sound-producing organs and prepare them for speaking. By controlling the amount of air you inhale and exhale while speaking, you can improve the quality of the sounds you make.

[NOTE 15.3] Controlled breathing helps produce rich, full sounds.

Controlled deep inhalation of air—called **abdominal** or **diaphragmatic breathing**—fills your lungs and provides ample air for speaking. Good posture controls the balance between your vocal cords and helps enrich your voice. When you inhale deeply, keep your shoulders low and level; expand your abdomen, lower back, and sides. The air should go all the way to the diaphragm—a muscle between the chest and the abdomen. When you are nervous, you may breathe shallowly and not fill your lungs. When this happens, you do not inhale enough air to produce rich, full sounds.

When you exhale to speak, the air should come from your diaphragm, pass your vocal cords, and fill the orifices in your head with enough force to cause the sounds to be rich and full. The orifices in your head—mouth, nose, and sinuses—are like echo chambers; they enrich the sound of your voice.

PROPER CONTROL OF JAW, TONGUE, AND LIPS

[NOTE 15.4] Avoid the troublesome t's.

The "troublesome t's" of tight jaw, tight tongue, and tight lips cause mumbled, muffled speech sounds that are hard to hear and difficult to understand. Pronunciation, enunciation, and clarity of sound depend on your jaw being flexible and your tongue and lips being loose and alive.

[NOTE 15.5] Keep a flexible jaw for clear sounds.

Practice freely flexing your jaw by saying *idea*, *up and down*, and *the sky is blue*. Now say those same expressions with a tightly clenched jaw. Notice how clenching your jaw muffles the sounds. For more jaw-flexing practice, count from 91 to 99, and say *fine*, *yes*, *no*, *pay*, *buy*, and *like* over and over.

[NOTE 15.6] Keep your tongue free and alive for good enunciation.

For practice in freeing your tongue and making it come alive, say *either*, *left*, and *wealth*. Try to say the same words holding your tongue still. Now count from 21 to 29 and let your tongue move freely and loosely. Say *health*, *thin*, *think*, *alive*, and *luck*. Practicing these and similar words will increase the flexibility and mobility of your tongue.

[NOTE 15.7] Good enunciation also depends on freely moving lips.

To free your lips—important controllers of voice quality—say *when*, *where*, *be*, and *back*. See what happens to your enunciation when you try to say these words without moving your lips. Other words to practice that will help to free your lips are *west*, *window*, *puff*, *lisp*, and *lips*.

Deep breathing and controlled use of your jaw, tongue, and lips will enable you to achieve full, round tones—the voice quality displayed by announcers and broadcasters in the radio and television industries. Practice until deep breathing and keeping your jaw, tongue, and lips flexible come naturally.

[NOTE 15.8] Practice breath control; keep your jaw, tongue, and lips flexible.

Using Your Voice Effectively

Learning Objective [2] USE YOUR VOICE EFFECTIVELY.

Once you have control of the basic sound-making mechanisms, you are ready to improve the use of your voice. The important considerations in this improvement are pitch, volume, speed, tone, emphasis, enunciation, and pronunciation. These aspects of using your voice effectively can each be improved by using a tape or video recorder for self-analysis or by obtaining feedback from a family member, a friend, or others.

PITCH

Pitch refers to the highness or lowness of your voice. A voice that is too high or too low may be distracting to your listener or audience. Pitch has two important aspects:

[NOTE 15.9] Pitch is the highness or lowness of a voice.

- Finding your natural pitch and, assuming it is not too shrill or too deep, using it
- Varying your pitch while speaking to provide interest and emphasis

Find Your Pitch and Use It To determine your natural pitch, yawn deeply three times. Then say aloud, "My natural pitch is. . . ." Yawn deeply, and say the words again. Your pitch should have become deeper, richer, and fuller. Yawn and repeat the words a third time. Let your voice rest for at least one minute. Now, once again say, "My natural pitch is. . . ." With this exercise you will have found your natural pitch.

[NOTE 15.10] Determine your natural pitch.

To avoid damaging your vocal cords, find and use your natural pitch. If nervousness causes you to speak in a pitch higher than your natural one, you could strain your vocal cords. Speaking in a pitch that is artificially lower than your natural one could also cause you to strain your vocal cords. Strained vocal cords can result in a hoarse, raspy voice or a temporary voice loss.

[NOTE 15.11] Use your natural pitch to avoid damaging your vocal chords.

If you think your pitch is too high or too low, consult a speech correction specialist. Most colleges have or can refer you to a speech correction specialist. With exercises prescribed by a professional, your natural pitch can be brought to a more attractive, pleasant level.

Vary Your Pitch While Speaking The second aspect of improving the use of your voice is to learn to vary your pitch while speaking. The sparkling, interesting, enthusiastic speaker varies the pitch of his or her voice and avoids the dullness of a monotone voice—a voice with a sameness in pitch level. Nothing will lose an audience faster than a monotonous voice, regardless of the quality of the content of the message.

[NOTE 15.12] Avoid being monotonous by varying your pitch.

[NOTE 15.13] Varying your pitch adds life to your voice.

You can make your presentation style interesting and even exciting by using pitch variations effectively. Indicate comparisons by using the same pitch level; indicate contrasts by using varied pitch levels. "The market is up (moderate pitch), and

[NOTE 15.14] Pitch can be used to give meaning to what you say.

its gains are solid (moderate pitch)" shows equal emphasis. "The market is up (high pitch), but its gains are not solid (low pitch)" shows contrast. Make a question clear and forceful by raising your pitch at the end. Emphasize the ending of a declarative sentence with a definite drop in pitch. When a speaker's voice rises at the end of a declarative sentence, he or she sounds tentative rather than confident.

Consciously varying your pitch while speaking is one of the most important ways to improve the effectiveness of your voice. Pitch variety holds your listeners' attention and helps them understand your messages.

VOLUME

[NOTE 15.15]
Improve your voice through proper volume control.

A major aspect of using your voice effectively is **volume**—the intensity of sound. Proper volume control enables you to be heard appropriately by your listeners. Volume control also enables you to vary your emphasis to achieve dynamic, forceful oral communication.

[NOTE 15.16]
Be sure you are being heard, but do not shout.

Use the Appropriate Volume Level The first goal of volume control is to be heard by every member of the audience. You want to project your voice, not shout. If your audience thinks you are shouting, you will have created a communication barrier.

Feedback is an important part of the communication process. You can obtain feedback about your volume level by asking whether you are being heard clearly. Another source of feedback is the nonverbal signals you get from your listeners. Does your audience seem to be getting restless? Are people straining to hear you? Is anyone cupping a hand behind an ear or covering both ears? If feedback indicates your volume level needs to be adjusted, do so immediately.

[NOTE 15.17]
Give emphasis by varying your volume.

Vary Your Volume for Emphasis The second goal of voice volume control is to vary your volume level for emphasis. You can communicate strength, power, forcefulness, and excitement through louder speech. You can create a mood of sorrow, seriousness, respect, and sympathy by lowering the volume of your voice. Both methods can be used to attach importance and emphasis to what you are saying.

You can maintain the attention of an audience, regardless of its size, by varying the volume of your voice. In a one-to-one situation, your voice should be conversational; with a larger group, volume can show a wide range depending on your communication goals.

SPEED

[NOTE 15.18]
Improve your speech through speed control.

Changing the speed of your oral communication provides interest and emphasis. The monotone voice we all try to avoid uses not only the same pitch and volume level but also the same speed.

The rate at which you speak will vary with your topic and the size of your audience. Complex or technical material commands a slower pace than does routine or entertaining material. The slower pace allows the receiver time to concentrate on and absorb what is being said. Interactive communication will generally have a wider range (75 to 250 words a minute) than will one-way communication (75 to 150 words a minute). Rapid speech may impair enunciation and pronunciation. Try to achieve a balance between speed and clarity.

Speed can also be used for emphasis and to convey emotion. Stress selected parts of your message by speaking slowly. Convey excitement with a high rate of speed, seriousness with a slow rate. The important point is to vary your rate as you speak. Learning to phrase well will help with pacing and will make the message easy to understand.

[NOTE 15.19]
Vary your rate of speaking for emphasis.

TONE

Tone is possibly your most important voice quality. **Tone** is the way the message sounds to a receiver. Your tone can convey concern, irritation, confidence, tentativeness, excitement, calmness, disrespect, courtesy, detachment, and so forth. The same sentence, spoken with a different tone, can have a dramatically different meaning. The words, *I know what you mean*, can be said with a concerned tone, conveying understanding; with an irritated tone, conveying frustration; or with a skeptical tone, conveying mistrust.

[NOTE 15.20]
Tone conveys meaning.

Most business communication situations call for a friendly, objective, businesslike tone that conveys warmth, strength, and respect. You will not want to sound negative, overly formal, insincere, condescending, prejudiced, weak, or disrespectful. You should consciously determine the tone you use when you speak.

EMPHASIS

You can give emphasis to your oral communication by varying your pitch, volume, speed, and tone. The following exercise will help you vary your emphasis and give different meanings to the same words. Say each of the following sentences aloud, giving emphasis to the bold italicized word:

[NOTE 15.21]
Practice giving emphasis.

You can improve your voice. (Stresses who)
You ***can*** improve your voice. (Stresses ability)
You can ***improve*** your voice. (Stresses action)
You can improve ***your*** voice. (Stresses ownership)
You can improve your ***voice***. (Stresses what)

Did you vary the emphasis in each sentence by using different pitches? volumes? speeds? Probably you used a combination of these techniques. Now, repeat each sentence in the exercise and emphasize the italicized word by varying your pitch. Next, say the sentences and vary your volume by saying the italicized words more loudly. Then, repeat the sentences and vary your rate by saying the italicized word slowly and the rest of the words quickly. Finally, say the sentences and vary your tone from a disinterested to a caring quality.

From your use of the different emphasis techniques, you can easily see how powerful voice variety can be. You can generate interest and communicate different meanings. You can strengthen the force, power, and effectiveness of your oral communication by using variations in your voice.

ENUNCIATION

Enunciation refers to the manner in which you sound the parts of words. Sound each part of a word clearly and accurately. An example of correct enunciation is sounding clearly the *g's* in words ending in *ing*. Say *talking* instead of *talkin, going to* instead of *gonna,* and *studying* instead of *studyin.*

[NOTE 15.22]
Sound each word part clearly and accurately.

Slowing the rate at which you say individual words will help to correct errors in enunciation. Give each word its fair share of time so that each part can be sounded properly and each can be heard distinctly. Listeners should be able to recognize "Next we will examine" as four words, not one (*nextwewillexamine*). High-quality enunciation reflects favorably on your intelligence and credibility.

PRONUNCIATION

[NOTE 15.23] Join sounds correctly for proper pronunciation.

The way in which you join sounds to say a word is called **pronunciation**. You can make sounds distinctly (enunciate clearly) but still not pronounce a word correctly. The dictionary is your best source of information for correct pronunciation of individual words. The first pronunciation given in a dictionary is usually the preferred one. The second pronunciation is acceptable but less common.

As in the case of high-quality enunciation, the correctness of your pronunciation reflects on your intelligence and credibility. Your listeners expect you to speak correctly. Doing so minimizes the potential for a communication barrier and helps receivers focus on the content of your message. Good oral communicators pronounce words correctly. They say *library* instead of *libary*, *February* instead of *Febuary*, *was* instead of *wuz*, *again* instead of *agin*, *just* instead of *jist*, *because* instead of *becuz*, *to* instead of *ta*, *the* instead of *da*, and *our* instead of *ar*. If you are not sure how to pronounce a word, do not use it until you check a dictionary or learn from another person how to pronounce it correctly.

ANALYSIS

[NOTE 15.24] Analyze your voice to improve its effectiveness.

You can improve the effectiveness of your voice by analyzing its qualities and the way in which you use it. You can perform this analysis in several ways. You can record your voice on a tape recorder for self-analysis. You can ask a family member who speaks effectively and correctly to analyze your oral communication. You can ask an instructor at school for feedback, or you can seek the advice of a speech correction professional. Regardless of the method you choose, taking the time to analyze your voice qualities and to improve them where necessary will help make you a better oral communicator.

Strengthening Your Presence

You can further improve your oral communication by strengthening your personal presence. Your **presence** consists of your poise and bearing. It includes your tangible and intangible nonverbal communication. The important aspects of presence are confidence, enthusiasm, sincerity, friendliness, eye contact, body actions, and appearance.

Learning Objective [3]
STRENGTHEN YOUR PERSONAL PRESENCE.

CONFIDENCE

Whether you are talking to one person or several, your receiver(s) will sense the level of confidence you possess. For a strong presence, you need the right amount of confidence—neither too little nor too much.

[NOTE 15.25]
Your listeners sense your self-confidence.

Too Little Confidence In one-on-one situations, too little confidence is referred to as *nervousness*; when speaking to larger groups, it is called *stage fright*.

[NOTE 15.26]
Lack of confidence causes stage fright.

Speaking with too little confidence causes discomfort for both a speaker and an audience. A speaker's discomfort may be reflected in a quivering voice; shaking hands; perspiration; inability to think clearly; inability to respond to questions; or other unpleasant mental, emotional, or physical symptoms. Listeners will exhibit their discomfort through nonverbal cues or through side comments to others in the audience. Speakers who lack self-confidence may not be able to say what they want to say in the way they want to say it. As a result, they may lose credibility with their audience and reduce the effectiveness of the communication. Neither the speaker nor the audience will find the communication experience pleasant or productive.

For some individuals, too little confidence is caused by negative thinking and unrealistic expectations. Speakers should accept that they do not necessarily have to be admired or respected by everyone in the audience. In addition, they must realize that it is normal to misspeak occasionally; they must not allow such errors to reduce their confidence level.

[NOTE 15.27]
Have realistic expectations.

Too Much Confidence Too much confidence can also inhibit oral communication effectiveness. The overconfident speaker projects a know-it-all attitude and a lack of concern for the audience. Your audience will respond negatively to overconfidence by rejecting you and your message.

[NOTE 15.28]
Too much confidence conveys a lack of concern for your audience.

An Effective Level of Confidence Self-centeredness causes *both* underconfidence *and* overconfidence. Speakers who concentrate exclusively on themselves and do not consider their receivers will be perceived as having either too little confidence or too much. To achieve an effective confidence level, keep the emphasis on your listeners and use the you–viewpoint. You won't be too concerned about yourself if you are thinking about the needs, concerns, and interests of others.

[NOTE 15.29]
Concentrate on the audience and use the you–viewpoint.

Other ways of developing an effective level of confidence include careful preparation, diligent practice, and attention to your personal appearance. Sustain confidence by maintaining eye contact with your audience; talking in a strong, clear voice with sufficient volume; and observing and reacting to audience feedback.

ENTHUSIASM

[NOTE 15.30] An enthusiastic speaker holds the listeners' attention.

Enthusiasm is contagious if it is genuine. When you are enthusiastic, your audience will become enthusiastic and positive about the ideas you express. Dullness can cause receivers to let their minds wander; it can even put some to sleep. Enthusiasm can excite listeners, spark their interest, and keep them alert.

[NOTE 15.31] Speak with energy and animation.

You can project your enthusiasm by speaking with energy and animation. Variations in pitch, volume, and speed will assist in showing enthusiasm. Facial expressions such as smiles and raised eyebrows indicate enthusiasm. Eyes that are wide open, alive, and sparkling also show enthusiasm. Energetic and definite gestures and body movements help, too. Recognize the importance of building a positive, enthusiastic presence; practice every time you have an opportunity—in conversations, oral reports, discussions, and speeches.

SINCERITY

[NOTE 15.32] Being sincere strengthens credibility.

Effectiveness is enhanced if the audience perceives the speaker to be sincere. Inappropriate gestures or facial expressions reflect insincerity and an apparent lack of concern for an audience. In addition, an insincere speaker may have difficulty gaining or maintaining credibility. You communicate sincerity when the general tone of your oral presentation conveys that your message is important. Your message should be presented in a warm, friendly, and caring manner.

FRIENDLINESS

[NOTE 15.33] Friendliness builds positive relationships with listeners.

The speaker who can project a congenial, pleasant, cordial, caring image—a warm friendliness—can relate more effectively to a listener or to an audience. Knowing that friendliness can significantly increase your effectiveness should motivate you to develop your ability to be gracious. A smiling face, a well-paced approach, and a genuine concern for feedback exhibit friendliness and an honest interest in your receivers. Concentrating on the needs and interests of your audience will help convey your friendliness.

EYE CONTACT

[NOTE 15.34] Good eye contact reflects confidence, interest, honesty, and sincerity.

Appropriate eye contact reflects confidence, interest, honesty, and sincerity. Failure to establish eye contact reflects a lack of confidence and may cause you to project an image of weakness, insincerity, fear, and dishonesty.

Be sure the amount of eye contact you have with your audience is appropriate for the cultural mix in that audience. American audiences expect more eye contact (75%) than do Asians (10%) but less than French (100%). Refer to Chapter 2 for more information about eye contact with receivers from various cultures.

[NOTE 15.35] Make every receiver feel important.

When making a presentation, be sure to engage receivers in all areas of the room. Make each person feel that he or she is having a one-on-one conversation with you. Convey the impression that, although you need to talk to others in the audience, you will return to the individual again.

BODY ACTIONS

[NOTE 15.36] Body actions are important nonverbal signals.

Some nonverbal signals that occur during oral communication fall under the heading of body actions. These nonverbal signals include facial expressions, posture, gestures, and body movements. Each of these topics will be reviewed briefly here. They are discussed in more detail in Chapter 14.

Facial Expressions Regardless of the words you say, your eyes and your face will convey your true feelings. Show your sincerity and friendliness in your facial expressions. As you practice for a presentation, look in the mirror to see whether you appear to be interested, enthusiastic, and friendly. If not, practice the necessary facial expressions until your nonverbal signals match your verbal message.

[NOTE 15.37] Facial expressions will be read as your true feelings.

Gestures Your hands, arms, shoulders, and head can convey important supporting nonverbal signals. Sitting stiffly behind a desk or standing immobile behind a lectern results in a dull, uninteresting appearance. Use gestures to strengthen your verbal messages.

[NOTE 15.38] Show that you are interested, enthusiastic, and friendly.

Gestures should be natural, not contrived. Raising the arms with palms facing upward, for example, can accent a verbal message that asks the rhetorical question, *What is the answer?* Pointing to an item on a visual aid helps stress the point being made.

[NOTE 15.39] Use natural gestures to strengthen your nonverbal message.

Gestures should be varied, not repetitious. To develop gestures appropriate for you and the situation, practice in front of a mirror until you find movements that are natural and comfortable for you.

Posture An upright, correct posture will improve your appearance and give you a feeling of confidence. You do not want to appear pompous or stiff but rather natural and comfortable. While standing, keep your weight evenly distributed on your feet. Do not lean on a lectern, table, or chair. When seated, keep your back straight. Do not slouch or hang one leg over a chair arm. Correct posture reflects self-confidence and shows respect for your listener.

[NOTE 15.40] Good posture improves your appearance and gives you confidence.

Other Body Movements Some body movement is important to hold attention and to relax your muscles. These movements should be graceful, unhurried, and natural. You can draw an audience's attention to a visual aid by turning your body toward it or walking to it. As with facial expressions and gestures, you can observe and practice your body movements in front of a mirror until they feel comfortable and convey the correct nonverbal message.

[NOTE 15.41] Other body movements can be useful.

APPEARANCE

The final aspect to consider in strengthening your presence is your appearance. Your personal appearance can be either a barrier or an asset to effective oral communication. Appearance is an important part of the total communication environment, particularly as a first impression.

[NOTE 15.42] Strengthen your presence with a good personal appearance.

You have to accept and work with the raw material of your own basic appearance. What you do with what you have is what will influence your audience. Choose tasteful clothing. Be sure both your clothing and your accessories are appropriate for the occasion and the audience. You should be neatly groomed. Good appearance not only sets a favorable stage for oral communication, but it also serves to increase your confidence.

[NOTE 15.43] Use what you have to your best advantage.

Presentations

Business professionals often find it necessary to make oral presentations. The purpose of most oral presentations will be either (1) to inform the audience of certain facts, or (2) to persuade the audience to accept a point of view or take a certain action. Occasionally, you may be asked to deliver a presentation designed solely to entertain. Regardless of the purpose of a presentation, your career and your organization will benefit when you prepare and deliver it effectively.

Learning Objective [4]
CLASSIFY DELIVERY STYLES BY TYPE.

TYPES OF ORAL PRESENTATIONS

[NOTE 15.44]
Business presentations include briefings, reports, introductions, award presentations, and speeches.

Oral presentations in business take many forms. Depending on your position, you may be asked to brief a group of employees on the status of union negotiations or be asked to report to company officers on the market research your department has been conducting. You might be called on to introduce a speaker, present an award, speak to a class or student group, or give a presentation at a professional meeting. Generally, making such presentations will serve you and your organization well.

Oral presentations are common in business.

[NOTE 15.45]
Choose a delivery style appropriate for the situation.

Business presentations may be formal or informal, internal or external, short or long, delivered to small groups or to large ones. The situation will help guide you in selecting a delivery style. The four delivery styles from which you may choose are manuscript, memorized, impromptu, and extemporaneous. The features of each are described in the following paragraphs.

[NOTE 15.46]
A manuscript presentation is read to the audience.

Manuscript A manuscript oral presentation is written word for word and then read to the audience. Used frequently in broadcast journalism, in high-level politics, or in situations where the audience is extremely large, this style is rare in business. Exceptions occur when precise wording is required, as during a crisis, or when a speaker must give several different presentations to various audiences within a short time frame. One of the difficulties associated with this presentation style is maintaining eye contact with the audience without losing your place in the text. Speakers who read their manuscripts also risk having the pages become disordered. Finally, it is very difficult to prepare a manuscript that sounds conversational; writing for the ear is very different from writing for the eye.

Memorized As the name implies, a memorized oral presentation is one in which the speaker has memorized the content verbatim. This style virtually eliminates the need for notes, but the delivery may appear "canned." In addition, a speaker risks forgetting parts of the presentation or having his or her concentration broken by a question from the audience. A better method is to memorize parts (for example, the opening and closing) rather than the entire presentation.

[NOTE 15.47]
A memorized presentation is learned verbatim.

Impromptu A presentation given without the benefit of time to prepare is referred to as an impromptu oral presentation. For example, in a meeting of the company's sales force, a representative might be asked to say a few words about his or her experience in a specific territory. Remaining calm and thinking quickly are keys to doing a good job in an unexpected speaking situation.

[NOTE 15.48]
An impromptu presentation is one that has to be given with little or no preparation.

Extemporaneous An extemporaneous oral presentation is prepared and delivered from notes or an outline. The extemporaneous style works well in interactive small-group settings as well as in predominantly one-way large-group settings. It is a spontaneous, natural way to relate to an audience. It permits good eye contact, allows free movement, and enables the speaker to respond to audience feedback. This presentation method is the basis for the discussion in the rest of this chapter. The following Tips and Hints provide advice for speakers who work from note cards.

[NOTE 15.49]
An extemporaneous presentation is prepared and given from notes.

TIPS AND HINTS

Working With Note Cards

[1] Use 3×5 note cards.
[2] Write each point or subpoint on a separate card. Include reminders or supporting information you need to explain or reinforce your point.
[3] Type or print only in uppercase letters; leave two or more blank lines between items.
[4] Use color-coding to signal the transition to a new point or to a visual aid.
[5] Number the cards sequentially.
[6] Punch a hole in the upper right corner if you are left-handed or in the upper left corner if you are right-handed. Insert a 1- or 1½-inch O-ring into the hole. Place the ring on the index finger or thumb of your nondominant hand. The cards should fit comfortably into the palm, and you should find it easy to move from one card to another without fear of dropping the set.

Learning Objective [5]
IDENTIFY THE STEPS TO FOLLOW IN PREPARING AN ORAL PRESENTATION.

KEYS FOR SUCCESSFULLY PREPARING AN EFFECTIVE ORAL PRESENTATION

[NOTE 15.50]
Preparation is the key to success.

The foundation for a successful oral presentation is preparation. Speakers who do not prepare are telling the audience members they are unimportant, unworthy of the speaker's best effort. Thorough preparation builds a speaker's confidence and assures the audience of an interesting and informative presentation.

How much time does it take to prepare for a presentation? Although some speakers say they spend 40 hours preparing for each hour of oral presentation, no one formula works in every situation. The audience and the speaker's familiarity with the topic will influence preparation time. The steps in planning an oral presentation are described in the following sections.

[NOTE 15.51]
Determine your purpose and state it clearly.

Determine Your Purpose The first step in preparing for an oral presentation is to determine the purpose of the message. Stating the purpose in terms of the expected result will help to narrow your focus. When the primary purpose of an oral presentation is to inform, you want the audience to learn, to understand, or to know more about the topic. That is the expected result. When the primary purpose is to persuade, you want the audience either to adopt your viewpoint or to take specific action. That is the expected result. Here are some example purpose statements:

- To inform those attending Leigh Acala's retirement dinner about the contributions she made during her 20 years of service
- To inform the audience about recent market research for a product line
- To persuade employees to register as organ donors
- To persuade management to increase the employee discount from 10 to 15 percent

Analyze Your Audience The second step in preparing an oral presentation is to decide exactly who will be in the audience and why. A captive audience is generally less receptive than one that attends voluntarily. Consider how the time of the presentation will affect the audience. People often get lethargic after a meal, can be tardy or slow to tune in for an early morning session, and become preoccupied near the end of the day. Speaking to an international audience outside the United States requires additional analysis, as noted in the Communication Note, opposite.

[NOTE 15.52]
Analyze your audience for a you–viewpoint presentation.

Analyze each member's knowledge, interests, attitudes, and emotional reaction regarding your topic. For large audiences, you may need to examine these factors in categories such as receivers' age, gender, profession, and so on. When speaking to an established small group within your organization, consider not only demographics but also politics. Learn the history of the group. Does the group interact formally or informally? Are members generally conservative or are they open to change? Who are the key decision makers? Who are the informal leaders? What concerns or objections might participants have? Build the oral presentation on your analysis of the audience.

[NOTE 15.53]
Gather information from a variety of sources.

Gather Supporting Information When you have stated your purpose and analyzed the audience, you are ready to gather ideas and materials to support the development of your oral presentation. A good presentation typically has three to five main points; you will want to locate materials that support them. Conduct your research for an oral presentation in the same manner that you would if preparing for a written report. When preparing your speech use primary sources, print and electronic secondary sources, and/or personal experience for examples, illustrations,

COMMUNICATION NOTE

Speaking Outside the United States

When developing a presentation and materials for an international audience, you must consider the customs of the host country, the expectations of the audience, and possible language and cultural barriers. The following suggestions and sources may be helpful:

[1] Do most of your research before leaving the United States. The embassy or consulate of the country to which you will travel is a good starting point. The State Department, the World Bank, the American Chamber of Commerce, and Voice of America are other possible sources. When you phone, introduce yourself and explain your situation. Ask about appropriate dress and greetings. Be sure to say your presentation will be given in English. If you have concerns that certain terms in your presentation may be misunderstood, ask about them. If you plan to use a foreign phrase, triple-check to be sure it means just what you want it to mean.

[2] Verbal humor doesn't translate well. Some cultures view humor as inappropriate in meetings or seminars. Visual humor such as cartoons and comic strips is much more widely acceptable as long as it does not have political overtones. If you use such a visual, read the caption for the audience and give them time to translate what you say.

[3] If you leave the stage during your presentation, remember that interpersonal space varies among cultures. You may want to interact with audience members, but they may view your proximity as an invasion of their personal space. The same caution applies to times when you share the stage with presenters from other cultures.

[4] Remember that the listener's culture will influence whether he or she asks questions. In some cultures, asking a question would imply that the speaker didn't explain the material well enough.

[5] If possible, arrive in the country early so you will have time to solicit a native's comments about your presentation.

Taken from Tom Antion, "There's More Than One Way," Successful Meetings *48 (11), October 1999, pp. 74–76.*

explanations, quotations, statistics, testimonials, comparisons, and analogies related to your topic. Use only credible sources and realistic examples. Be sure to record citation information for material drawn from copyrighted sources.

As stated in the Communication Note on page 460, content has three levels. Your research will provide information; your analysis of that information will lead to knowledge and perhaps to wisdom.

[NOTE 15.54]
Organize your presentation based on your analysis of the audience.

Organize Your Presentation As you gather information, you are apt to find that you have far more material than can be conveyed in the time you have available. Begin to organize your presentation by returning to your purpose and sorting your materials into three sets:

- Materials you **must** include (those closely related to your main idea)
- Materials you **should** include (those that support your main idea)
- Materials you **could** include (related background materials)

The "must" items will definitely be in your presentation, as will some from the "should" set. Information you don't use in your oral presentation will be helpful

COMMUNICATION NOTE

Levels of Content

There are three levels of content: information, knowledge, and wisdom. Wisdom is the most valuable, most needed, and most interesting part of a presentation.

Information consists of facts. For example, data, statistics, and news are information. Since information is basic and common, it is also the least interesting form of content.

Knowledge consists of conclusions that result from interpreting information. Use knowledge to explain and support wisdom.

Wisdom consists of directions that come from interpreting knowledge. It is also the most difficult to obtain. It requires genius to convert knowledge into valuable wisdom.

Taken from Steve Kaye, "It's Showtime! How to Give Effective Presentations," Supervision *6 (3), March 1999, pp. 8–10.*

when responding to questions or during informal discussions that may occur as a result of the presentation.

Once the material is organized, you can determine which, if any, presentation aids to use.

[NOTE 15.55] Choose presentation aids to strengthen your message.

Select Appropriate Presentation Aids Unlike a written report, which draws only on the receiver's sense of sight, an oral presentation can draw on sound, sight, touch, taste, and smell. Most speakers will find sound (audio) and sight (visual) most useful. Whether used separately or in combination (multimedia), presentation aids can be an asset in conveying a message. They can make it more understandable. They can spark interest, add variety, and help to hold an audience's attention. The Tips and Hints below suggest questions to be asked when deciding to use a presentation aid. Selection and preparation of presentation aids is covered in Chapter 13.

[NOTE 15.56] Each part of a presentation must be prepared carefully.

Prepare Your Presentation You know your purpose. You have analyzed your audience. You have gathered supporting data and have prepared your presentation aids. You are now ready to put all this information together in a coherent oral presentation.

Some speakers write a full-text manuscript and then discard it after making notes from it. Other speakers work exclusively from an outline recorded on note

Deciding to Use a Presentation Aid

When deciding whether to use presentation aids, ask yourself the following questions:

- Will this aid make my message clearer?
- Will it be simple enough to be understood?
- Will it be worth the time it will take to develop?
- Will it enhance my message?

If your answer to any of these questions is no, you should not use the aid.

cards or sheets of paper. However you arrive at your fully developed presentation, remember that it will have three parts:

[1] Opening

[2] Body

[3] Closing

The Opening An effective opening is crucial. The audience evaluates your credibility and capability as a speaker in the first few minutes and, regardless of what you do later, it is almost impossible to change that evaluation. A good first impression will serve you and your audience well throughout a presentation.

Use your opening to get audience attention and interest. Effective ways to open a presentation include a surprising statement, a quotation, an anecdote, a humorous story, a question, a problem statement, a historical reference, an impressive statistic, a visual aid, a reference to the situation, or an illustration. A humorous personal story may help you bond with an audience. Remember, though, *never* to make a joke at the expense of an audience member. Regardless of the method you choose, be sure the opening is brief and relates closely to your topic.

View the opening as an opportunity to show your audience why the topic is important, to give an overview of the talk, and to lead into the body of your presentation. Set the mood for the presentation and establish rapport between you and the audience. If the person who introduces you has not done so, tell the audience whether you will take questions during or after the presentation.

[NOTE 15.57]
The audience evaluates the speaker during the opening.

[NOTE 15.58]
Use the opening to capture interest, preview your topic, and establish rapport with the audience.

The Body Most of the information you present to the audience will be contained in the middle of the presentation—in the body. Plan this portion of your oral presentation carefully. Decide which organizational pattern(s) work best for your topic and audience. As shown in the Tips and Hints on page 461, "Selecting an Organizational Pattern," you have several organizational patterns from which to choose.

Follow the selected organizational pattern and make final decisions on how you will present and use the presentation aids. The Tips and Hints on page 461, "Developing the Body of an Oral Presentation," offer guidelines for developing the body of a presentation.

[NOTE 15.59]
The body contains most of the information.

The Closing In the closing, definitely let the audience know that you are ending. Summarize the main points of your presentation; specify what the audience should do; and part with the audience on a positive, professional note.

Use both verbal and nonverbal signals to let the audience know you are ending the oral presentation. Say, "In summary," "In closing," "To review," or "In conclusion." A more subtle way to signal closure is to pause and lower the pitch of your voice. Making a significant change in your stance relative to the lectern is another way.

The summary should be a very simple statement designed to recap the main points of your presentation. It may be followed by advice on how to use the information or by a clear statement of action the audience should take based on your presentation.

[NOTE 15.60]
Summarize your main points in the closing and specify what the audience is to do.

Your presentation should end on a positive, professional note. The techniques suggested for opening a presentation—a surprising statement, a quotation, an anecdote, a humorous story (carefully used), or an illustration—also work well for closing it, but be sure to choose a different technique. The closing is an important point of emphasis for your presentation. Be positive and optimistic. Be professional. Most important of all, use the you–viewpoint.

[NOTE 15.61]
End positively and professionally.

Selecting an Organizational Pattern

TIPS AND HINTS

Speakers have several patterns from which to choose when they organize their presentations. Here are some frequently used patterns:

[1] **Cause and effect.** Show the relationship between events. Use this technique when attempting to persuade.

[2] **Comparison or contrast.** Show the similarities and dissimilarities of the subject matter on a category-by-category basis. This pattern can be used with informative, entertaining, or persuasive presentations.

[3] **Direct or indirect.** Start or end with the main point, depending on whether your receiver will perceive the message as good or bad news.

[4] **Problem and solution.** Describe the problem(s), then present the solution(s). This pattern is appropriate for persuasive messages.

[5] **Spatial relation.** Describe from top to bottom, bottom to top, left to right, right to left, inside to outside, outside to inside, room to room, desk to desk, or follow some other spatial flow pattern. Consider this pattern when making informative or entertaining speeches involving space.

[6] **Time sequence.** Review pertinent material from oldest to newest or from newest to oldest. This pattern works well for informative and persuasive messages because it allows the speaker to integrate valuable background information.

[7] **Topics and subtopics.** Organize the subject according to its logical parts. This pattern is especially useful for presentations designed to inform or entertain.

Developing the Body of an Oral Presentation

TIPS AND HINTS

As you develop the body of an oral presentation, consider these guidelines:

[1] *Hold the listeners' attention.* Use short (less than 25 words) sentences built around active, present tense verbs. Keep your presentation audience-centered by using the you–viewpoint. Use examples and illustrations to create images for your listeners.

[2] *Emphasize your main points.* Use repetition, specificity, and mechanical means. Tell your listeners what is important by saying, "This is my most important point . . ." or "This, then, is the critical issue." You can also use audiovisual aids to give emphasis. Use statistics and examples to support main points. Make descriptions vivid.

[3] *Keep your presentation simple.* Audiences cannot comprehend complex, detailed information presented only orally. That kind of information should be presented in written form so that it can be studied and reread. Match your vocabulary to that of your audience. Avoid jargon and acronyms. Provide a smooth transition from one point to the next within the body. Limit uninterrupted talking (talking without any audience activity) to no more than 20 minutes.

[4] *Involve your listeners in the presentation.* Help them form images that support your points. Have the audience participate in small group discussions, exercises, and demonstrations.

Rehearse Your Presentation Using the notes and presentation aids you have developed, rehearse your oral presentation. Some speech authorities recommend that you rehearse a presentation aloud at least six times, on your feet, as though you were in the real-life situation. Plan your hand gestures and walking patterns. Practice how, when, and where you will move. Rehearsals will help you identify and correct distracting mannerisms such as those listed in the following Communication Note. Anticipate questions that might be asked. Identify three to five questions you hope will be asked and three to five that you hope won't be asked. Prepare to answer both sets.

[NOTE 15.62]
Rehearse your presentation aloud using your notes and audiovisual aids.

COMMUNICATION NOTE

Mannerisms That Distract

Use rehearsals to identify and eliminate these and other mannerisms from your delivery:

- Tightly grasping the lectern.
- Tugging at or playing with clothing or jewelry.
- Touching your hair or brushing it away from your face.
- Tapping the lectern or projector with a pen, pencil, or pointer.
- Shaking your finger at the audience.
- Picking at your fingernails.
- Adjusting your glasses.
- Tapping your feet.

If you will be speaking into a microphone, be sure you know how to use it effectively. Follow the suggestions in the Tips and Hints on page 464. Microphones come in four styles: platform, handheld, lavaliere (clip and hanging), and remote. Platform microphones are the most restrictive; remote units are the least restrictive.

[NOTE 15.63]
Know how to operate the equipment you will use.

To get feedback on your presentation, rehearse in front of a mirror or before friends, relatives, or colleagues. You can use an audio or a video recorder for this purpose as well. This practice will help you to decide which parts of your content and delivery need to be modified or fine tuned. It also gives you experience in handling your audiovisual aids efficiently. It is the only way you can be sure of the length of your presentation.

[NOTE 15.64]
Get feedback on your content and delivery.

Rehearsing your oral presentation is essential to its success. Practice will increase your familiarity with the material and your confidence in delivering it.

KEYS FOR SUCCESSFULLY DELIVERING AN EFFECTIVE ORAL PRESENTATION

Learning Objective [6]
DEMONSTRATE THE TECHNIQUES TO BE USED WHEN DELIVERING AN EFFECTIVE PRESENTATION.

All the material you studied earlier in this chapter applies to the delivery of an oral presentation. You will want to use your voice effectively and project a strong presence. You will want to vary your pitch, volume, and speed for emphasis while speaking. You will want to enunciate sounds clearly and pronounce words correctly. Your poise and bearing should convey confidence, enthusiasm, sincerity, and friendliness. Establish appropriate eye contact with your audience, and use natural gestures. Your appearance should be appropriate for the audience and the situation.

TIPS AND HINTS

Working With a Microphone

Follow these suggestions when using a microphone during a presentation:

[1] Adjust the mounting of a platform microphone to give 6 to 12 inches of space between it and your mouth. Stay within this range or sounds will be lost or distorted. Speak over rather than into the microphone. Remember that each time you turn your head to the right or left, sounds will be lost.

[2] Lavaliere microphones should be clipped or hung at midchest or above, but they should not touch the larynx. Remove pins, tie tacks, necklaces, or other items the microphone might brush against.

[3] Sound levels should be checked in advance and set to compensate for sounds absorbed by a room full of people. If you must check the microphone at the start of a presentation, do so by asking audience members to raise their hands if they cannot hear you well. You may also ask an audience member to stand or otherwise let you know of a sound problem. Blowing into the microphone, tapping on it, or asking, "Can you hear me?" are signs of amateurism.

[4] Remember to step away from, turn off, or remove the microphone after you have finished. Forgetting to do so may mean that your off-the-cuff remarks are heard by the entire audience.

Blondie

You have prepared your oral presentation and now you are ready to deliver it. Here are keys to guide you in successfully delivering your oral presentation.

[NOTE 15.65] Ensure a positive start by checking the facility; being fully prepared; and opening with a clear, confident voice.

Start Positively When you are scheduled to speak in an unfamiliar facility, visit it at least an hour in advance of your presentation. Acquaint yourself with the room arrangement, and determine whether everything you need is or will be in place before your presentation. Check the lectern and make sure it is the right height for you. Learn how to operate the equipment controls and the power supply and locate the room thermostat. Determine who can help if things go wrong.

Whether speaking in a new setting or in a familiar one, arrive five to ten minutes prior to your scheduled speaking time. Make a final check to ensure that the lighting, temperature, public address system, audiovisual equipment, lectern, and seating arrangement support and strengthen your presentation. Be sure your notes and visual aids are with you and in correct order.

When the program starts and you await your turn to speak, look pleasantly and confidently at the audience. At the appropriate time, move to the position designated for the speaker. If speaking in an auditorium or classroom-style setting, walk to the lectern with authority. If making a presentation in a conference room, follow the protocol of the group (move to the head of the table, stay seated, etc.). Whatever the setting, use your body language to tell the audience there is no place you would rather be than there with them. Take a moment to collect yourself. Arrange your notes and presentation aids.

Once you have begun building rapport with your audience by establishing eye contact with them, begin your presentation. It is good to memorize the first part, if not all, of the opening. In this way you can concentrate on the audience and your delivery and not have to worry about checking your notes.

Remember that your delivery is part performance and part content. Both must be well prepared for a successful delivery.

Remain Calm One way to handle nerves is to realize that even the most practiced and professional speakers have some apprehension about speaking to an audience. Don't be surprised if your heart rate accelerates or your palms become sweaty. Learn to relax. Sit comfortably, but keep your back straight.

[NOTE 15.66]
Handle stage fright by thinking positively and concentrating on the you–viewpoint.

A second way of dealing with the stage fright that threatens to detract from a successful delivery is to use imagery. Picture yourself rising and moving to the speaking area. Hear yourself speak in a loud, clear, confident voice. See yourself using natural gestures. Picture the audience responding positively to your message. Remind yourself that you have prepared thoroughly.

Calm can be achieved once you have risen and moved to the area from which you will speak. Just before you begin, inconspicuously take a few deep breaths. Inhale slowly, hold your breath for four or five seconds, then exhale. Finally, concentrate on the you–viewpoint. Focus on the audience's needs, interests, and concerns. Remember that you are there to benefit your listeners and that they want you to succeed. Additional suggestions for controlling stage fright are presented in the Communication Note on page 466.

Use Presentation Aids Effectively You have chosen aids that complement your presentation and have designed them so that the audience can read or hear everything in them. You have practiced handling them efficiently. To use them effectively during your delivery, simply take advantage of your careful preparation. The two sets of Tips and Hints on page 467 contains advice for using presentation aids.

[NOTE 15.67]
Use presentation aids with poise and confidence.

Evaluate Audience Feedback Maintain good eye contact with the members of the audience so that you can secure feedback on how the presentation is progressing. Assess your listeners' changing reactions and make necessary adjustments to keep their attention and interest. Are you sure they can all hear you? If not, speak louder. Can they all see the visual aids? If not, make adjustments. Is their interest waning? If so, change your pace, pick up your enthusiasm, and start involving them in some way. Do they seem not to understand a point? If so, ask them questions, paraphrase, or ask a volunteer to explain his or her understanding of the point. Do members of the audience show signs of physical discomfort? If so, ask them about

[NOTE 15.68]
Adjust your presentation based on audience feedback.

COMMUNICATION NOTE

Stage Fright Symptoms and Cures

Stage fright is really a misnomer because once you step on stage, the fright usually goes away. It's the feeling before you get on stage that can be nerve-wracking.

Try to think of stage fright in a positive way. It makes your reflexes sharper, heightens your energy, adds a sparkle to your eyes, and brings color to your cheeks. When you are nervous about speaking, you are more conscious of your posture and breathing.

Being prepared helps ease nerves. Arriving early to triple-check everything in the presentation room helps. Shaking hands with and smiling at attendees before the program will help to build a rapport with the audience. If stage fright persists, try the techniques in the following table:

Symptom	Cure
Nervous energy	Take a walk.
Trembling legs	Gently and imperceptibly lean on the lectern or a table.
Shaking hands	Use a handheld microphone.
	Avoid holding anything flexible (e.g. sheets of paper) until you are calm.
	Avoid alcohol and caffeinated beverages.
Dry mouth; tight throat	Take small drinks of warm water to loosen your vocal cords.
Feeling isolated	Make eye contact with the friendliest faces in the audience.

Taken from Tom Antion, "When the Tables Are Turned . . . And You Are the Speaker," Successful Meetings *48 (3), March 1999, pp. 94–95.*

it and have the necessary adjustment made. Using the feedback you get from an audience can strengthen the effectiveness of an oral presentation.

[NOTE 15.69] End positively using a clear, strong voice.

End Positively Endings, like beginnings, are important points of emphasis. Deliver the closing with a clear, strong voice. Your poise and bearing should be at their best even if the body of your presentation did not meet your highest expectations. At this point, eye contact with the audience should be 100 percent. You should be focusing exclusively on your audience and using the you–viewpoint.

[NOTE 15.70] Use question-and-answer sessions to strengthen your relationship with the audience.

Respond to Questions Question-and-answer sessions are common in business presentation settings. In a large-group setting, questions are generally posed after the presentation has ended. In a small-group setting, questions may arise during or after the presentation depending on the audience or on the speaker's preference. When speaking to an audience of clients or to people holding positions higher than yours within your organization, it is best to answer questions as they are asked. In other settings, specify as part of your introduction or opening whether you will take questions during the presentation, after the presentation, or both.

Answering questions gives speakers an excellent opportunity to relate positively to the audience, to clarify and reemphasize points, and to alleviate any concerns the audience may have. Following the guidelines in the Tips and Hints on page 468 will help your sessions go smoothly.

When you have finished, smile and graciously accept the applause or thanks the audience offers you. Later, reflect on the experience. Note what worked well and what you would like to improve.

Using Transparencies

These suggestions will help you to use transparencies effectively:

TIPS AND HINTS

[1] *Check equipment in advance.* Be sure the projector is at a comfortable height and placed on a vibration-free base. The projector lens and surface should be clean and dust-free. Locate the spare bulb. Be sure the power cord isn't a hazard to you or your audience. Focus and center the picture; be sure the image is readable from all parts of the room.

[2] *Place the screen on a diagonal, not directly behind you.* Tilt the screen toward the projector to ensure that the image is not larger on the top than on the bottom.

[3] *Face the audience, not the screen.* Be sure nothing comes between the projector and the screen, including you. Place the projector to your right if you are right-handed, to your left if you are left-handed. Be sure you have a surface on which to set your transparencies before and after you use them.

[4] *Place transparencies in sturdy frames.* Write notes on the frame to remind you of key points.

[5] *Use a pen, pencil, or similar device other than your finger to point to items on the transparency.* Movements are exaggerated by projection and may cause a distraction. Set the pointer down when not using it so that it does not distract the audience.

[6] *Darken the screen when nothing is being projected.* Turning off the projector can shorten the life of the bulb, so cover either the projection surface or the lens. Taping a small piece of cardboard above the lens makes darkening the screen convenient and inconspicuous.

Using Presentation Graphics Software

Following these guidelines will help you effectively use presentation software:

TIPS AND HINTS

[1] *Know your equipment and software.* Be sure cords do not present a hazard to you or your audience. Try to rehearse with the equipment you will use when giving your presentation. Audiences get impatient with delays and feel their time is being wasted. Always have a backup plan in case equipment fails.

[2] *Position equipment so that you can see the monitor and use the computer while facing the audience.* Better yet, use a remote mouse. Doing so will free you to interact with your audience and minimize the need to move back to the computer every time you want to change a slide. Such movement interrupts the flow of your presentation and distracts your audience.

[3] *Don't just read the slides.* Provide more information than what appears on the screen.

[4] *Move slowly from slide to slide.* Electronic presentations tend to make you speak more quickly than usual.

[5] *The slide show should not be a distraction.* Remember, the audience should concentrate on you and your message.

[6] *Use blank screens where ideas will pause.* Begin with a blank or title screen; end with a blank screen.

Question-and-Answer Sessions

TIPS AND HINTS

During a question-and-answer session, you may encounter four types of questions: (1) information-seeking, (2) opinion-seeking, (3) hostile or negative, and (4) off-target. The following tips will help you make the experience a positive one for you and your audience:

[1] If time is limited, let your audience know in an inviting manner such as "We have about 25 minutes before this session ends; this would be a good time to ask questions."

[2] If no one asks a question, start the process yourself. Set the tone for a stimulating exchange by posing a clearly worded, concise question and then giving a brief (less than 30-second) direct response.

[3] When a question is asked, listen carefully. If necessary, repeat the question so that all may hear it. Determine the type of question, then formulate and give your answer.

[4] When answering, use a conversational style and look primarily at the person who asked the question.

[5] Deflect hostile or negative questions by rephrasing them before answering. Never argue with a questioner. Becoming defensive, hostile, or sarcastic not only tarnishes your image but also causes the audience to sympathize with the questioner. If someone asks a question unrelated to the topic, offer to meet with him or her after the presentation to discuss it.

[6] When answering a question, try to refer to topics covered during your presentation. This will reinforce and clarify.

[7] Be conscious of the nonverbal messages your gestures and body language convey as you respond to a question.

[8] Be prepared to end the session with a few brief remarks related to your presentation.

Using the keys that have been presented in this section and in the Communication Quote (opposite) will help you to prepare and deliver effective business presentations in traditional settings. Not all speaking situations you encounter, however, will be traditional. Several such situations are described in the next section.

Learning Objective [7]
IDENTIFY TASKS AND PROCEDURES ASSOCIATED WITH SPECIAL PRESENTATION SITUATIONS.

Special Presentation Situations

[NOTE 15.71]
You may encounter other speaking situations.

Two additional speaking situations you may encounter during your career are discussed in this section—emceeing an event and introducing a speaker.

EMCEEING AN EVENT

[NOTE 15.72]
Emcees are responsible for setting and maintaining the flow of an event.

The master of ceremonies, known informally as the **emcee**, plays a significant supporting role in the success of an event. It is his or her responsibility to ensure that the event begins, moves along, and ends in a timely fashion. He or she sets the tone for and maintains the continuity of the event.

The specific duties performed by an emcee will be determined by those who plan the program. At the very least, an emcee will be expected to welcome the audience, introduce a series of speakers in a predetermined sequence, and end the program. Additional responsibilities may include introducing those seated at a head

COMMUNICATION QUOTE

Preparation for a Formal Presentation

In my work with the American Lung Association, I make presentations once or twice a month. The audiences range from preschoolers to senior citizens; I've even spoken to workers in the field at 6 a.m. before they pick pineapples!! Here are some things I've learned that may help you when you have to make a formal presentation:

[1] Have your notes typed in LARGE print on note cards; use only one side.
[2] Visuals help, but don't be totally dependent on them because equipment can fail.
[3] If you are using handouts, don't give them out until you really want your audience looking at them rather than paying attention to you.
[4] Always arrive 15 minutes or so before you are scheduled to speak (as a courtesy to the program director and to help get your butterflies all flying in formation).
[5] Remember, your audience is watching you long before you start to speak.
[6] Organize your presentation so that it's easy for your audience to follow your points.
[7] Have fun! Tell a joke or compliment the audience.

Colleen Welty, Branch Director, Maui County, American Lung Association.

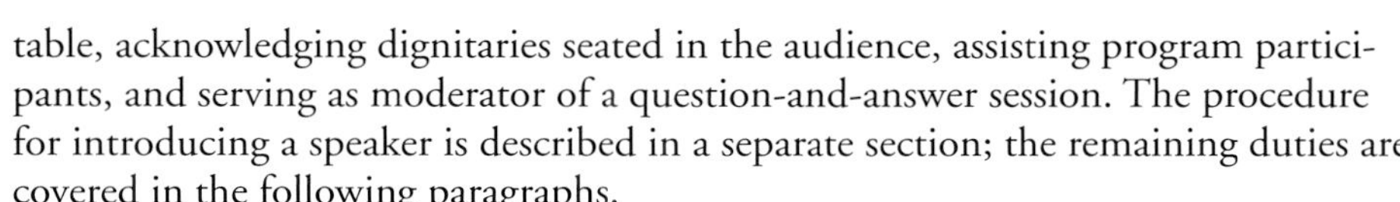

table, acknowledging dignitaries seated in the audience, assisting program participants, and serving as moderator of a question-and-answer session. The procedure for introducing a speaker is described in a separate section; the remaining duties are covered in the following paragraphs.

Welcoming the Audience The welcome, more than any other factor, will set the tone for the event. Begin by greeting the audience and then pausing briefly to allow conversations and activity to cease. Once you have gained the attention of the audience, give your name and welcome the group to the event. You might say, for example, "Good evening ladies and gentlemen. (pause) I'm Rita Rupert, your host for this year's Employee Recognition Dinner. Thank you for sharing this special night with us." Be sure to smile; scan the entire room; and speak in a clear, confident voice. Next, provide a brief overview of the agenda for the event. The entire welcome should take less than two minutes—no longer than five if you are also expected to prime the audience with a few humorous comments.

[NOTE 15.73]
Remember to introduce yourself.

Introducing the Head Table Although an emcee does not determine who sits where at a head table, he or she should follow a standard pattern for introducing those seated there. The pattern calls for moving from the emcee's far right to center, where the lectern is typically placed, then from the emcee's far left to center. Before beginning, the emcee should specify what each individual should do (rise, then be seated; rise, remain standing), and tell the audience to hold applause until all head table guests have been introduced. Correct pronunciation of each name is essential. The emcee should have good eye contact with the audience and occasionally look or gesture toward the people being introduced. The introductions should be simple

[NOTE 15.74]
Pronounce names carefully and correctly.

and brief—name and title, role in the organization, or reason for being seated at the head table. If appropriate, the emcee could also make a lighthearted remark or tell an anecdote about each person. Format consistency is the key.

[NOTE 15.75]
Recognize prominent attendees.

Acknowledging Dignitaries Those who plan the program may wish to have the emcee introduce some attendees not seated at the head table. These individuals may play a prominent role in the community or have some past, special tie to the group. Knowing in advance that each dignitary is actually at the event and where he or she is seated will make the process flow smoothly. Once again, the emcee should specify the actions to be taken by the audience and those being introduced. Names should be pronounced correctly. If several guests are to be introduced, decide how you will achieve smooth transition without being wordy. "Also with us tonight" and "Another special guest" are examples of introductory phrases that can be used as transitions.

[NOTE 15.76]
Prepare for your role as an emcee.

Assisting Program Participants The emcee should introduce himself or herself to each program participant before the event begins. She or he should clarify seating arrangements, explain the sequence of events, verify the time the participant has been allocated, tend to special requests, and confirm the accuracy of personal information such as name pronunciation and title. In addition, the emcee should be sure that the sound system and other equipment are working properly. Also, he or she should be sure that a pitcher of water and several glasses are at or near the lectern. The emcee is responsible for assisting or knowing who has been assigned to assist the speaker with tasks such as distributing materials and operating equipment.

[NOTE 15.77]
Keep to the schedule.

By keeping on schedule, the emcee assists not only those who participate in the program but also those who attend. If the participant exceeds the allotted time, the emcee must ask him or her to stop. Since the emcee is typically seated next to the lectern at a head table, passing a note saying "Your time has expired; please end now" should be sufficient. If the emcee is seated elsewhere, another method of signaling time must be devised. The emcee should select a method based on room and seating arrangements and then inform each participant of it.

[NOTE 15.78]
Extend thanks personally and on behalf of the group.

After the speaker finishes his or her presentation, the emcee should rise, extend personal thanks to the speaker, and then thank the speaker for the entire group. The personal remarks are made privately, as the emcee shakes the speaker's hand; formal thanks are given so the entire audience can hear. The formal thanks should identify the speaker by name and relate in some way to the topic. "Thank you, Dr. Fitzgerald, for sharing with us your ideas about the role of Internet commerce in today's global economy" completes the task in one sentence. Depending on the speaker and topic, a longer, perhaps humorous, statement would be appropriate.

Moderating a Question-and-Answer Session The primary tasks of an emcee during a question-and-answer session are to call for questions, repeat the questions after they have been asked, keep time, and thank the speaker.

[NOTE 15.79]
Ask the first question.

After the presentation has ended and the speaker has been thanked for giving it, the emcee informs the audience of the time available and asks for questions. Often, this request will be met with silence. Audience members may need time to formulate their questions and summon the confidence to ask them. The emcee should give them this time by asking the first question. Doing so relieves the pressure that silence can place on both the audience and the speaker.

As audience members stand or raise their hands to be recognized, the emcee should acknowledge them, listen carefully to the question, and then repeat the question to ensure that all in the audience know what was asked. If the question is long, the emcee should paraphrase. If the question is complex, the emcee should divide it into logical subquestions and pose each separately.

In some settings, audience members are asked to write their questions on cards. The cards are collected and given to the emcee, who then reads them on behalf of the audience members. When this protocol is followed, the emcee should quickly scan the questions and select a fairly simple one as the first. While the speaker is responding, the emcee can decide which of the remaining questions will be asked and in what order. Similar questions may be paraphrased. Several questions should be thought-provoking. Of course, all questions should be in good taste.

When the allotted time has expired, the emcee thanks audience members for their questions and the speaker for responding to them.

Concluding the Event Once all parts of the program have been completed, the emcee issues a general thanks to the entire group and bids them farewell. The remarks may include a brief summary of the events or a reference to the featured speaker's presentation. The emcee allows program participants to leave the stage area first and remains in the room until the majority of guests have left or are clearly engaged in conversation.

[NOTE 15.80]
Give closing remarks.

The emcee at a formal event serves the same purpose the host or hostess serves at a social event. He or she is responsible for ensuring that those who attend feel welcome and have an enjoyable time. That can occur only if the emcee recognizes that his or her role is important to the success of the event but that he or she is not the focus of the event. In other words, the emcee must maintain the you–viewpoint. This same unselfish approach must be used by the emcee or whoever introduces a speaker. Specific techniques for that task are covered in the following section.

INTRODUCING A SPEAKER

When you are asked to introduce a speaker, accept the invitation with enthusiasm. The experience will give you a chance to enhance your own speaking ability and provide a valuable service to the speaker and the audience.

[NOTE 15.81]
Graciously accept invitations to introduce a speaker.

The process you follow in preparing for and delivering a speaker's introduction will parallel that used for a longer presentation. You must identify your purpose, gather information, develop the presentation, rehearse, and deliver the introduction with skill and confidence. Although you might do so in an entertaining fashion, the primary purpose of an introduction is to inform audience members of who the speaker is, what the topic will be, why the topic is important to them, and what credentials qualify the speaker to make the presentation.

[NOTE 15.82]
Speaker introductions must be prepared carefully and thoroughly.

In some cases, the speaker will write his or her own introduction. When this occurs, the person designated to introduce the speaker should practice the introduction and give it with style and enthusiasm. When you are responsible for preparing the introduction, remember that the best source of information about a speaker is the speaker. As soon as you learn you will be making the introduction, obtain a copy of the speaker's resume. Review it and make a few notes to be used in your introduction. Consider consulting secondary sources for information about the topic. Ask program planners whether a formal question-and-answer session will be conducted

[NOTE 15.83]
Draw material for the introduction from a variety of sources.

and, if so, determine whether you or the emcee will serve as moderator. If program planners are flexible, ask the speaker to indicate whether questions should be asked as they arise or held until the presentation is completed. Include the information as part of your introduction.

Several days prior to the event, phone or meet with the speaker to gather additional information and to verify the accuracy and appropriateness of items you intend to use. Try to include more than facts and figures in your introduction. You'll make the speaker seem more real if you include some personal information or an anecdote about the speaker. Such information can be obtained from the speaker, from a friend or colleague of the speaker, or from your conversations with him or her.

[NOTE 15.84] Rehearse the introduction to be sure it is brief, informative, and inviting.

As you prepare your introduction, remember that you have very little time—generally no more than two minutes—to make the audience eager to hear the speaker. Because your time before the audience will be brief, you could either memorize your presentation or give it extemporaneously. Whichever style you choose, be sure to practice. Do not, however, rehearse so much that you destroy the professional, self-confident, and friendly demeanor you wish to achieve.

[NOTE 15.85] Use nonverbal communication to acknowledge the speaker during your introduction.

On the day of the presentation, introduce yourself to the speaker long before you are to make the introduction. Confirm whether the speaker will remain seated or stand at your side while you make the introduction. When it is your turn to speak, rise, face the audience, smile, and begin to speak. Establish good eye contact with your audience. At some point during your introduction, look or gesture toward the speaker.

When you've finished your introduction, lead the applause (if appropriate), step to the side, greet the speaker with a handshake, and inconspicuously return to your seat. If applause is appropriate at the conclusion of the presentation, be the one to lead it. Convey your thanks to the speaker either as part of the program or in a more informal setting after the presentation ends.

Good preparation and attention to the basics of oral communication will help you lead and participate in meetings and deliver effective oral presentations.

Summary of Learning Objectives

Learning Objective [1]

Improve the basic quality of your voice. Speakers who want to improve the quality of their voice pay attention to the way in which they breathe. Inhaling deeply and exhaling so that air is forced from the diaphragm cause deep, rich sounds. Controlling the jaw, tongue, and lips relates to speaking clearly. The jaw should be flexible, the tongue and lips should be loose.

Learning Objective [2]

Use your voice effectively. Finding, using, and varying the natural pitch of your voice will protect your vocal cords from damage and will help to make your speech patterns interesting. Vary volume to be heard and to emphasize important points. Interest and emphasis are achieved by varying the speed at which a message is delivered. Tone is used to convey meaning; a businesslike tone that conveys warmth, strength, and respect is desirable. Speaking clearly and pronouncing words correctly are also important factors.

Learning Objective [3]

Strengthen your personal presence. Speakers who have good personal presence concentrate on their receivers, not on themselves. They are genuinely enthusiastic about the message they convey. They exhibit their friendliness and sincerity through their words and through nonverbal cues involving posture, eye contact, facial expressions, and gestures. Effective speakers choose clothing and accessories appropriate to the occasion and the audience.

Classify delivery styles by type. Presentations may be delivered in any of four styles: manuscript, memorized, impromptu, or extemporaneous. Manuscripts are written in full and read to the audience. Memorized presentations are written in full and delivered without notes. Impromptu presentations arise from situations; there is little or no time to prepare. Extemporaneous presentations are delivered from notes. Extemporaneous is the style preferred for business. *Learning Objective* [4]

Identify the steps to follow in preparing an oral presentation. Determining the purpose of a presentation and analyzing the audience are the first two steps in preparing for an oral presentation. Gathering materials, organizing the presentation, and deciding whether to use presentation aids are additional steps. The presentation consists of an opening, a body, and a closing. Once the speaker has prepared the notes or outline from which the presentation will be given, he or she rehearses to get feedback about how to refine both content and delivery. *Learning Objective* [5]

Demonstrate the techniques to be used when delivering an effective presentation. When the actual presentation occurs, the speaker should remain calm, begin positively, use presentation aids effectively, make adjustments based on audience feedback, end positively, and respond to questions from listeners. *Learning Objective* [6]

Identify tasks and procedures associated with special presentation situations. Emceeing an event and introducing a speaker are among the special speaking situations a business professional might encounter. Emcees are often called on to welcome participants and guests, introduce those seated at a head table, acknowledge special guests, assist program participants, serve as question-and-answer session moderator, and close an event. Sometimes an emcee introduces the featured speaker; at other times another participant has this privilege. Introductions must be brief yet informative. *Learning Objective* [7]

DISCUSSION QUESTIONS

1. What are the "troublesome t's"? How can they be managed? (Objective 1)
2. How does being nervous affect a speaker's ability to produce rich, full sounds? (Objective 2)
3. Explain how pitch can be used to show comparisons and contrasts. (Objective 2)
4. Why is tone so important to successful oral communication? (Objective 2)
5. Define personal presence and explain the role it plays in effective oral communication. (Objective 3)
6. Describe how an audience might react to a speaker who has (a) too little confidence and (b) too much confidence. (Objective 3)
7. Draw from your experience in class, in a student organization, or in another group and discuss situations in which you have been called upon to make presentations using each of the four delivery styles identified in this chapter. (Objective 4)
8. Discuss the keys for successfully preparing and delivering an oral presentation. (Objective 5)

9. What organizational patterns could be used when preparing the body of a presentation to be given to a group of 40 support staff members who are interested in learning more about how to provide customer-centered service? (Objective 5)
10. What advice would you give to a coworker who declines invitations to speak to professional and community groups because he or she is too scared? (Objective 6)
11. Why is the opening of an oral presentation important? (Objective 6)
12. Discuss the role an emcee plays in the success of an event. (Objective 7)

APPLICATION EXERCISES

1. **Teamwork.** Work with one other student. Select a page from this text or some other source and have your partner read it aloud. After he or she finishes reading, comment on the volume, speed, pitch, and tone of the communication; note any enunciation or pronunciation errors that were made. Repeat the process with a different speaker and different material. (Objective 1)
2. Practice keeping your jaw, tongue, and lips flexible by saying the following sentences aloud three or more times each: (Objective 1)

Loose lips sink ships.

Shave a single shingle thin.

Peter Piper picked a peck of pickling peppers.

Hickory dickory dock, the mouse ran up the clock.

She sells seashells by the seashore.

3. **E-mail.** Record your voice on a cassette tape recorder. Listen carefully to the recording and analyze your voice qualities in regard to pitch, volume, and speed. Summarize your findings in an e-mail to your instructor. Your message should include the following: (a) the way your voice sounds to you, (b) the strengths of your voice, (c) the weaknesses of your voice, and (d) a plan for improving your voice. (Objectives 1 and 2)
4. Give emphasis to the important points in the following paragraph by varying (a) your pitch; (b) your volume; (c) your speed; and (d) your pitch, volume, and speed in appropriate combinations: (Objective 2)

Your degree of success in providing leadership to others relates directly to your ability to speak clearly, intelligently, and confidently. Your effectiveness will depend on the quality of your voice and the strength of your presence.

5. Read the paragraph in Exercise 4 three times. Each time, vary your posture so you are (a) standing, head low, shoulders curved forward; (b) seated, almost reclining, with legs extended and crossed at the ankles; and (c) standing, shoulders squared, back straight. Which posture felt most comfortable? Which made you feel most confident? (Objective 3)

6. **Teamwork.** Sit back-to-back with another student in the class so that neither of you can use nonverbal cues to complete this exercise. Take turns saying the following sentence aloud three times: "Why were you late for the meeting?" Each time you speak the sentence, change your tone to reflect one of the following sentiments: concern, irritation, detachment. See whether your partner is able to determine which emotion you are conveying through your words. (Objective 3)

7. **Teamwork.** Form groups of five to seven students each. Have each person in the group speak for one minute about a hobby or personal interest he or she has. The

speakers should practice trying to show a strong, positive personal presence. Listeners should provide constructive feedback. (Objective 3)

8. **Teamwork./E-mail.** Each member in a group of three should locate an article related to some aspect of business communication. Randomly assign the style (manuscript, memorized, or extemporaneous) by which each member will deliver a two-minute summary of the article. After all presentations have been given, discuss the strengths and weakness of each method from the perspective of the speaker and the audience. Summarize your conclusions in an e-mail to your instructor. (Objectives 4, 5, and 6)

9. **Teamwork.** Work in groups of five to seven students. Each group member should prepare and deliver a two- to three-minute presentation about why he or she chose his or her major. During each presentation, various listeners should give nonverbal cues for the speaker to interpret and respond to. After all group members have spoken, the listeners should provide constructive feedback. (Objectives 5 and 6)
10. Prepare and deliver a five-minute presentation on a topic approved by your instructor. Include one quote and one visual aid. (Objectives 5 and 6)
11. Identify a new development in your field. Prepare and deliver a presentation to brief your coworkers about the development. (Objectives 5 and 6)
12. Locate the annual report of a corporation in which you are interested. Use presentation software, or another method as your instructor directs, to present some aspect of the report to your class, who will act as the company's shareholders. Respond to questions from the audience. (Objectives 5 and 6)

13. **Teamwork./Cross-cultural.** Work with six of your classmates to research the appropriate way to introduce people from a culture other than your own. Demonstrate for the class how you would introduce a head table that included political and business leaders from the United States and the country you selected. One group member should act as emcee; the others should be the head table guests. (Objective 7)
14. Assume that a prominent individual of your choice will deliver the address at your school's commencement exercises and that you have been invited to introduce him or her. Do the necessary research, prepare an appropriate introduction, and deliver it to your class. (Objectives 5, 6, and 7)

15. **E-mail.** Project five years into the future and assume that you have accepted an invitation to speak about some aspect of your profession at a national meeting of one of its organizations. Write the introduction you would like given before your presentation. E-mail the text of the introduction to your instructor. (Objective 7).

There are Web exercises at **http://krizan.swcollege.com** to accompany this chapter.

MESSAGE ANALYSIS

Revise and edit the following memo to reflect good organization and to ensure that its format and mechanics are accurate:

TO: *Managers*
FROM: *Alec Jacobs*
DATE: *March 12, 200–*
SUBJECT: ***Making Effective International Presentations***

In effective international presentations can results in misunderstandings, misinterpretations, and missed sales. To ensure that we make the most of our international opportunities, please follow these guidelines and share them with those in your units who make international business presentations.

1. *Use simple, clear content. Word choice variety appeals to an American audience but can confuse a listener for whom English is a second language. If you use the team* suggestions *early in your presentation, stick with it rather than changing to advice or recommendations.*
- *Repeat your message several times during the presentation. Repeat—don't paraphrase. The extra time it takes will pay big dividends in audience retention and you'll reap the rewards of your efforts.*

☞ *Don't use, omit jargon, idiomatic expressions, and acronyms. That could confuse or insult your audience. Choose metaphors appropriate for the culture of your audience. Sports comparisons for baseball and golf may work well in Japan but flop in France.*

3. *Be deliberate in the way you use your voice. Speak in a normal presentation volume and us frequently and enunciate clearly but don't patronize.*

5. *When crating visuals, be aware of the way in which the colors and symbolls—including clip art—your select select will effect your audience.*

Barb Schmidt will be creating a web site to address this topic. If you or your staff have personal suggestions or know of resources that should be included at the site, e-mail her at bschmidt.

GRAMMAR WORKSHOP

Correct the grammar, spelling, punctuation, style, and word choice errors in the following sentences:

1. Barbara Stewart asked whether we plan to re-place hour currant computer monitors with flat screens
2. After useing Clear away for 6 weeks you will both notice that rinkles disappear and age spots fading
3. A mix of stocks bonds and short term reserves will help you achieve a secure financial future.
4. Built in 1997 fore approximately $15.9 million dollars the River Road development contains 224 one, two, and three-bedroom apartments in seven three-story bldgs..
5. Everybody whom attended the demonstration were able to get their questions answered during the ten minute question:answer section that followed the 20 minute presentation.
6. For your convienence I have inclosed a coupon good for a ten % discount which means you'll pay only 13.95 for a full-year of "the Money Manager's Guide'.
7. Known for service that is quick and quality repair work you're car will get the attention it deserves.
8. 4,400 companies-about 1/3 of those operating within the State has less then 5 hundred employees.
9. As the summer season approaches and the Mercury rises, youll wont to keep cool with a knew Feel fresh air-conditioner.
10. When you visit any of the sights discribed on the enclosed brochure the civil war will come alive.

PART 6

Employment Communication

CHAPTER:

CHAPTER

16 The Job Search and Resume

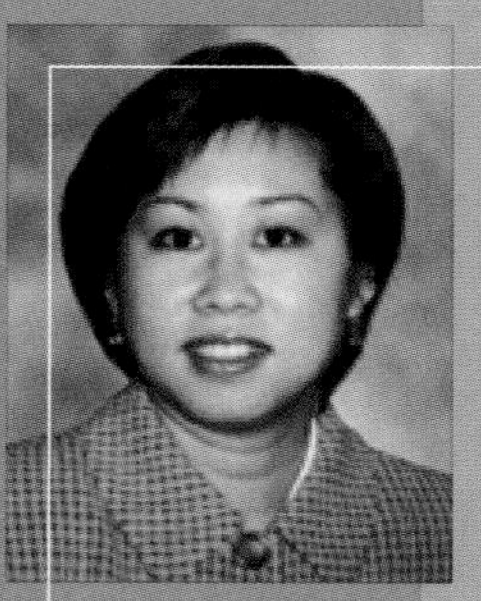

Lulu Fou, Manager, Accenture

LET'S TALK BUSINESS As a senior executive at Accenture, I have spent many years recruiting talented individuals to our consulting firm. The best applicants I have seen are high achievers. These qualities are demonstrated by good grades, work experience, and leadership activities. Good grades indicate that the applicant has the aptitude to learn and the potential to be a quick study. Work experience validates the applicant's sense of responsibility and discipline. Active participation in a student organization or community service provides the applicant the environment to build communication, leadership, and networking skills. Yet, even with all these excellent qualities, the best applicant can be hindered by a poor presentation of her or his resume.

(Continued)

[LEARNING OBJECTIVES]

[1] ANALYZE YOUR QUALIFICATIONS FOR EMPLOYMENT.

[2] DESCRIBE THE SOURCES OF INFORMATION ABOUT JOB OPPORTUNITIES AND JOB REQUIREMENTS.

[3] PREPARE TRADITIONAL RESUMES IN EITHER CHRONOLOGICAL, FUNCTIONAL, OR COMBINATION FORMAT.

[4] PREPARE AN ELECTRONIC RESUME.

Presentation is an expression of the applicant. Content may qualify her or him as an applicant, but if I am turned off by her or his lack of professionalism in her or his presentation, I won't bother to read what she or he has to offer.

Resumes should be kept to one page in length; busy people don't have time to read more than one page. And, most college graduates and many professionals do not have sufficient substance that cannot be summarized in one page. Resumes should be well typeset. With the accessibility of technology and word processing, there is no excuse not to have a well typeset resume. The information should be well organized in some logical sequence that I can easily follow. Lastly, the worst mistake that I have seen is where the applicant misspells the company name. Some highly qualified applicants have lost an opportunity for an interview for this simple but unfortunate oversight.

Once the applicant successfully passes through the resume selection process, the next step is the interview. During the interview, I am validating the resume for its content. In addition, I am evaluating the applicant's understanding of my organization, capabilities, intentions, and ambitions through her or his appearance, communication skills, and responsiveness. The applicant with a neat and professional appearance gives the image that she or he takes the interview seriously. It is equally important that she or he has done proper research to learn about the company. Coming prepared with good and appropriate questions will demonstrate that the applicant has done her or his homework.

The applicant that is enthusiastic and engaged in the interview will score favorably. The bottom line is whether the applicant will be able to integrate well with the team. Is this person reliable, trustworthy, and someone that I would like to work with? The successful applicant will be able to communicate those qualities verbally and nonverbally. •

Your most important business communication will be about your employment. During your life, you will spend most of your waking hours at work. Your work should be enjoyable, challenging, and rewarding. After completing this chapter and Chapter 17, on employment communication and interviewing, you should have a plan for successfully obtaining employment—employment that best matches your interests, values, and qualifications. In these chapters you will also discover how to use the Internet to find a job and launch your career.

[NOTE 16.1]
Employment communication is your most important communication.

[NOTE 16.2] The job campaign involves several steps.

To obtain employment, you will need to conduct a job campaign. This campaign will include

[1] Analyzing your qualifications

[2] Obtaining information about employment opportunities

[3] Developing resumes

[4] Writing application letters

[5] Interviewing for a job

[6] Preparing other employment communication

The first three steps in the job campaign are discussed in this chapter; the last three steps are discussed in Chapter 17.

Analyzing Your Qualifications

Learning Objective [1] ANALYZE YOUR QUALIFICATIONS FOR EMPLOYMENT.

Because *you* are the product you are selling in your job campaign, you need to know yourself well. While you will want to sell yourself honestly and fairly, concentrate on your most positive features—your accomplishments, education, experience, positive attitudes, and potential. You may want to consider going to your campus career center and taking an interest inventory or career decision-making test to assist you in focusing your job campaign. These career decision-making tests or assessment tools are designed to identify your strengths and weaknesses; pinpoint your interests and match them with your strengths; clarify your values and what matters to you, such as making money or feeling you make a difference in the world; and look at the overlap among your strengths, interests, and values and determine appropriate careers.[1] A few examples of assessment tools include the following: *Myers-Briggs Type Indicator,* which can be used to determine your personal strengths and preferences; the *SIGI Plus,* a computerized test used to evaluate your values, interests, and activities; and the *Strong Interest Inventory,* which compares your likes and dislikes to those of other individuals to determine if you might value the same kinds of careers.[2]

[NOTE 16.3] Analyze your qualifications.

Analyzing your qualifications is an important part of your job campaign. The results of your analysis will prepare you to gather information about jobs for which you are qualified. The results will also be valuable as you construct your resume. Your resume will be your primary tool in securing interviews. The top ten personal characteristics employers are seeking in job candidates are shown in the Communication Note, opposite.

[NOTE 16.4] The job requirements are the framework for your analysis.

From your examination of the job market, you will know the kinds of jobs available in your field and their requirements. You will know the type of job you want. Your job campaign may be aimed at one particular solicited job—salesperson for Safeco Insurance Agency, for example—or it may involve sending

[1] Robin Lipkin and Michelle Watson, "Unlock the Door to Your Future—Use This Key," *Planning Job Choices 2000,* pp. 8–9.

[2] Robin Lipkin and Michelle Watson, "Unlock the Door to Your Future—Use This Key," *Planning Job Choices 2000,* pp. 8–9.

COMMUNICATION NOTE

Top ten Personal Characteristics Employers Seek in Job Candidates

[1] Communication skills
[2] Work experience
[3] Motivation/initiative
[4] Teamwork skills
[5] Leadership abilities
[6] GPA/academic credentials
[7] Technical skills
[8] Interpersonal skills
[9] Analytical skills
[10] Ethics

Source: Job Outlook '99, *National Association of Colleges and Employers, Bethlehem, Pennsylvania.*

unsolicited applications to a large number of potential employers. In either case, you will need to analyze your qualifications in relation to each job and its requirements.

In analyzing your qualifications, start by brainstorming (alone or possibly with friends and relatives) a list of facts about yourself. The most important facts are evidence of your accomplishments—your achievements, honors, and knowledge. Think of your accomplishments as you list the facts about your education and experience. In addition, you should list special qualities that you have that could benefit a company. For example, if you are applying for a job as a sales representative for a surf wear company, you may want to list the fact that you are a surfer. Finally, list persons who can serve as your references.

[NOTE 16.5]
Start the analysis of yourself by brainstorming.

Here is one way to brainstorm. Take four blank sheets of paper and label them at the top as follows: "Individual Profile" at the top of the first page, "Education" on the next, "Experience" on the third, and "References" on the last. At a good time of the day for you, find a quiet place and start thinking of facts about yourself. Suggestions for the kinds of facts to list are in the following sections.

INDIVIDUAL PROFILE

Start with your individual profile because it will be the easiest category. Do not try to organize or evaluate the information at this point. The information on this individual profile sheet should include your name, temporary and/or permanent address, telephone number(s), and e-mail address. If you have the ending date for your temporary address, be sure to include that on your resume. You may want to include your fax number; and if you have an online resume, include your Web site address.

[NOTE 16.6]
Develop your individual profile sheet.

Your individual profile should include a list of your interests and hobbies, community service activities, public-speaking experience, church activities, volunteer work, and organization memberships. As appropriate, include your accomplishments, offices held, experience gained, and honors or awards received. On this individual profile sheet do not list your height, weight, birth date, marital status, number of children, or religious affiliation: It is illegal for recruiters to request this information unless it is a requirement of the job. For example, to market or sell liquor you must be at least 21 years of age in most states. Do not include a photograph unless you are applying for a modeling position.

[NOTE 16.7] Stress facts and accomplishments.

In addition, list your special talents or skills, such as an ability to use software, write computer programs, or speak or write foreign languages, and personal attributes, such as enthusiasm, positiveness, initiative, drive, sincerity, dependability, sense of humor, or adaptability. Include in your individual profile any personal information that might be of interest to an employer. For example, list your salary expectations, career objective(s), and willingness to relocate.

[NOTE 16.8] Some information will be used for your resume; some for other purposes.

Some of the information from your individual profile will be used in preparing your resume. Other parts of it will assist you in choosing specific jobs, writing application letters, answering questions during interviews, and completing employment forms.

EDUCATION

[NOTE 16.9] List education information.

[NOTE 16.10] List all your schools, key facts, and achievements.

On the sheet of paper labeled "Education," list the schools you have attended. For each school, list its name, its location, the dates you attended, your major, your minor, your grade point average in your major and overall, and the certificates, diplomas, or degrees you received. Indicate any special groupings of courses such as a series of office technology courses that especially qualify you for the position or positions in your job campaign. Enumerate computer software and hardware skills and specify any special projects you completed, such as a Web page. Describe teamwork experiences and group projects, and list any honors or awards received (such as outstanding student, membership in honorary organizations, dean's honor lists, certificates of recognition or appreciation, or scholarships). Specify any special research reports you have prepared. Indicate all extracurricular activities (such as professional organizations or service organization memberships, fraternity or sorority activities, intramural or intercollegiate athletics participation, community or special service activities, or study/travel abroad experiences). List any other educational information about yourself that might be of interest to an employer.

COMMUNICATION QUOTE

Beyond specific skills for a particular job, I look for indications of a work ethic in a future employee. Two clues to a good work ethic are good grades and extracurricular activities. I believe that if the applicant has been involved in sports or organizations, it is an indication that the person can work as a team member. A new employee's values must be compatible with those of the company—integrity and a respect for other people. And good communication skills are most important. Employees must be able to write and present well-organized and concise reports.

Mike Wiggins, Assistant Vice President, Human Resources, Southwire Company, One Southwire Drive, Carrollton, GA 30119.

EXPERIENCE

List all your work experience—part time and full time—on the third sheet. Keep in mind two basic categories as you reflect on each job you have held:

[1] Responsibilities

[2] Accomplishments, such as achievements, knowledge or skills acquired, and contributions while performing the job

[NOTE 16.11] List all prior job experience.

[NOTE 16.12] For each job, concentrate on responsibilities and accomplishments.

Most persons list only their job responsibilities on their resumes. Although employers are interested in the responsibilities you have had, they are more interested in how successfully you fulfilled those responsibilities. You should list all factual evidence of successful job performances (such as supervised ten employees, increased sales by 25 percent, conducted a presentation skills workshop, or earned a promotion to assistant manager). Remember to use action verbs to show your accomplishments.

List each job held, including any military service. For each, list your job title, name and location of employer, and dates of employment. Indicate your responsibilities and give evidence of your achievements. Specify what you learned while performing the job, any innovations you developed to improve job performance, sales quotas or other goals met, letters or other commendations received regarding your performance, promotions, or increases in responsibilities. List reasons why you held each job, reasons why you left each job, and salaries received.

Add any other work experience information you think might be helpful in your job campaign. You may include jobs held as a volunteer worker. Internships, paid or unpaid, often add a lot to a graduate with little formal work experience. These jobs will be especially important if you have little paid work experience to list.

[NOTE 16.13] Include volunteer work.

REFERENCES

References should be individuals who know you or your work well and who are willing to write letters or talk to potential employers on your behalf. You should have at least three references and may have several more if you have been employed many years. You can select as references those persons who know your character or who are former employers, current employers, professors, and coworkers. Potential employers consider former or current employers the best types of references. At this point, simply list those potential references who will give you a favorable recommendation. Depending on the job you are seeking, you may use all or part of this list.

[NOTE 16.14] List references who will give you favorable recommendations.

[NOTE 16.15] Former and current employers are the most important references.

Before using anyone as a reference, ask him or her for permission. Once the person has agreed to be a reference for you, give him or her one of your current resumes, so that person can be familiar with your recent activities. Although you will need to deal honestly with any unfavorable information in your background, you are not required to list references who will hurt your chances for employment.

[NOTE 16.16] Request permission from references to list them.

For each potential reference, list the person's name, title, position, organization, business (or home) address, and business (or home) telephone number, fax number, and e-mail address. Be sure to ask your references where they would like to be contacted—at their business, home, or other location. A reference list showing this information should be included in your portfolio and available to your potential employers.

[NOTE 16.17] List complete information for each reference.

When you have completed the thorough analysis of your qualifications, you will be ready to seek information about employment opportunities and to prepare your resume—the key written document in your job campaign.

Learning Objective [2]
DESCRIBE THE SOURCES OF INFORMATION ABOUT JOB OPPORTUNITIES AND JOB REQUIREMENTS.

Obtaining Information About Employment Opportunities

[NOTE 16.18]
Determining job availability and requirements is necessary.

Finding positions for which you can apply generally requires an organized effort. You must determine which jobs are available and what the job requirements are for those positions.

[NOTE 16.19]
Positions are either solicited or unsolicited.

Many career-related positions are solicited. A **solicited position** is a specific job for which employers are seeking applicants—jobs listed with campus career centers, advertised in newspapers or journals, announced through private or government placement agencies, or listed on the Web.

A job that is available but is unlisted or unadvertised is called an **unsolicited position**. These positions may be an important part of your job campaign. Unsolicited positions are obtained by direct contact with a company of your choice. You will learn of the availability of many of these positions through your network of friends, relatives, instructors, and acquaintances. Joining a professional association such as SHRM, Society for Human Resources Management (human resources); MISSA, Management Information Systems Student Association (computers); or IFMA, International Facilities Management Association (facilities management), is important for networking with other individuals in your field. This network can help provide you with information on available positions as well as keep you current in your career field.

An effective job campaign requires careful, documented research. You will want to use all appropriate sources of information about the availability of jobs and about their requirements. The following sections discuss possible sources.

CAMPUS CAREER CENTERS

[NOTE 16.20]
Your campus career center is a valuable source of information and services.

The most valuable source of information about jobs will likely be your campus career center. Whether you are an undergraduate student looking for your first career position or a graduate seeking a change in employment, the campus career center can provide many services. According to the 1999 Graduating Student & Alumni Survey conducted by the National Association of Colleges and Employers (NACE), career center staff provided more help with the job search than family, friends, and faculty.[3]

Among the placement services offered by most campus career centers are job-related publications, lists of job openings, arrangements for on-campus interviews with company representatives, maintenance of a credentials file, advice on the preparation of resumes and application letters, and guidance about or training for a job interview. These services are free or offered at minimal cost. The campus career center should be one of the first places you visit as you start your job campaign.

[3] "Who's Most Helpful in the Job Search?" Survey of 1999 graduating students and alumni conducted by National Association of Colleges and Employers, *Planning Job Choices 2000,* p. 8.

Your campus career center is a valuable source of information and services.

Campus career centers may also be located on the Web at **http://www.jobweb.org/**. This Web site is a helpful starting place for information on preparing for the online job search and locating the job.

Of the publications available at the campus career center, the *Job Choices* series is one of the most helpful. This publication contains positions available across the nation. It lists the positions for which employers are seeking applicants and the educational requirements for those jobs. The employers are listed by geographical location, by occupational specialty, and by company name. From this list of employers, you can develop a prospect list of job opportunities in your field. The person to contact within each company is listed; this enables you to develop a mailing list for your job campaign. You can also search online with the new employer directory of *Job Choices* at **http://www.jobweb.org**. This Web site has a database of job postings, employer profiles, career fairs, school districts, and other Web sites for jobs.

[NOTE 16.21]
Job-related publications aid the job campaign.

Several other job-related books such as the *Occupational Outlook Handbook, Dictionary of Occupational Titles,* or job-related periodicals such as *Changing Times, High Technology*, or *Small Business Reporter* may be available at your campus career center. Trade association publications, government publications, and individual company publications may also be available. A CD-ROM software program *Job Power Source* can also help with your job search. This program will help you set career goals, determine your work style, and find jobs.

Two major services of campus career centers are lists of specific job openings and, in larger schools and colleges, arrangements for on-campus interviews with company representatives. Generally, the lists of job openings are published and updated periodically. Campus career centers will post these listings on campus and may mail them to graduates. If you find a position opening that interests you, request that the campus career center assist you with contacting the employer by sending your credentials or by arranging an on-campus interview.

[NOTE 16.22]
Campus career centers provide job listings and arrange interviews.

To take advantage of your campus career center's services, register with that office. This registration will involve the careful, accurate, thorough, and neat

[NOTE 16.23]
Register with the campus career center and complete your credentials file.

completion of your credentials file. The credentials file contains information about your education and experience. In addition, it contains the letters of reference that you request be placed there.

Completing your credentials file will serve you in at least two ways. One, it will motivate you to gather and record important data about yourself; these data will be helpful to you in preparing your resume. Two, the credentials file will be available to be duplicated and, with your permission or at your request, provided to potential employers in a very timely manner.

Many positions are obtained through the services of a campus career center. It should be your first source of information when you initiate a job search.

THE INTERNET

[NOTE 16.24] Access Web sites for job searching on the Internet.

With the advent of the Internet, you now have a new method for seeking your career position and making worthwhile connections. The Web has now opened up a new arena of job hunting for you! The Web can be used for accessing information on how to conduct a job search on the Web, how to develop an online resume, how to learn about the various companies, and which companies have openings in your field. A recent study indicated that the number of job-related Web sites would grow from about 200 sites in 1998 to about 1,200 sites in 2002 and the posting of resumes would increase to more than 16 million by 2002.[4]

To begin the cyberspace job search you must first have a computer and access to the Web. As mentioned earlier, a good place to start your job search is on your campus career center's home page, which will have links to the necessary resources. You may be able to locate your campus career center through the Catapult Career Offices Home Pages: Index at **http://www.jobweb.org/**, or through Jobtrak, which has partnered with over 500 college and university campus career centers nationwide at **http://www.jobtrak.com**. Jobtrak has listings for full-time jobs, part-time jobs, temporary jobs, and internships. Jobtrak has information on career fairs, resume development, job searches, and top recruiters, too.

The Riley Guide Web site, which was developed by Worcester Polytechnic Institute's librarian Margaret F. Riley Dikel (the grandmother of resources for job seekers), has information on employment opportunities and job resources on the Internet. This site, which can be found at **http://www.dbm.com/jobguide/**, has information ranging from basic use of the Internet to incorporating the Internet into your job search, including online job application procedures to recruiting online. This Web site includes all the current information on searching for positions on the Web.

[NOTE 16.25] Explore popular career center Web sites.

Several Web sites that can be helpful with your online job search have been listed in the previous materials. Additional sites that can be accessed on the Web include the following:

- *Career Magazine.* **http://www.careermag.com**. This Web site is an online career magazine with information on job openings, employers, resume banks, and job fairs; it also has various articles on current topics such as diversity in the workplace.
- *JobDirect.* **http://www.jobdirect.com**. JobDirect connects entry-level job seekers with employers who want qualified applicants. This Web site helps students find summer jobs, internships, or career positions.

[4] Bonny L. Georgia, "Resumes Rising," *PC Computing,* November 1999, p. 216.

Search Jobs
Find the job you're looking for from **460,393** job postings now.

My Monster
Job seekers: **post** your resume & **manage** your personal career account.

Featured Employers
NEW Research companies and find out more about today's top employers.

- Airborne Express - Overnight heroes. Find out why...
- Intellution Job Fair Thur Oct 26 Foxboro MA
- PA jobs, employers - iFair Pennsylvania!
- EMAIL YOUR RESUME to 1000's of Recruiters with ResumeZapper NOW
- CT jobs, employers .. iFair Connecticut!

Global Network
Explore the Monster Network

AU BE CA FR DE
HK IE NL NZ SG
ES UK US

About Monster
Check out **66** Monster **job opportunities**.
Use our handy **Site Tools** to learn more about Monster.com

ChiefMonster
Explore senior executive opportunities now.

Monster Talent Market℠
Free Agents start here. Employers search for contract talent.

Monster Moving
Relocating? Visit Monster Moving now.

Site Tools
Help
Alliance Index

CAREER CENTER
Search 2,000 pages of career advice, resumes and salary info.

Job Seeker Communities

Admin	Campus
Internet	Executive
Finance	Healthcare
HR	Mid-Career
NEW Retail	Sales
Technology	Work Abroad
Self Employment	

Check out our
Six Steps program
job tip of the week

Monster Poll
Do you consider yourself loyal to your company?
- Yes, I'm committed to the organization.
- No, I'm only trying to gain experience.
- I'm loyal to the highest bidder.

Results

Share Your Comments
over **18,130** submissions
Previous Poll Results

Presented by:
U.S. Army

Free Career Newsletter!
(Over **449,373** Subscribers)
Subscribe Now

Communicate
Network with thousands of members or ask our experts about dozens of topics.
Chat Schedule

When was the last time

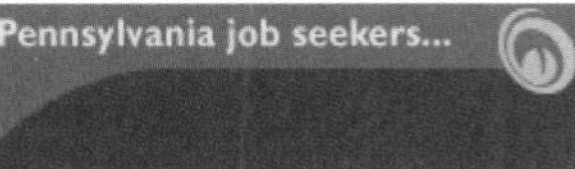

Pennsylvania job seekers...

Privacy Commitment | Terms of Use | Interactive Metrics | The Monster Store | Contact Us
contact: 1-800-Monster
©2000 Monster.com - All Rights Reserved - U.S. Patent No. 5,832,497 - NASDAQ:TMPW; ASX:TMP

For patrons of Monster Cable

Figure 16.1
Web Site for Monster Board at: http://www.monster.com *(Printed with the permission of Monster Board.)*

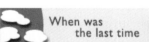

- *Monster Board.* **http://www.monster.com**. One of the most popular Web sites for job seekers, Monster Board offers a variety of hypertext links to job-search resources and connections to job listings. A screen print of this site is shown in Figure 16.1.
- *Tripod.* **http://tripod.com**. This site provides all the tools and resources needed to develop your own online resume. This is a free site and very easy to use.

These are just a few of the Web site addresses for job searching online. You may contact your campus career center staff or Internet directory indexes for additional sites since new ones are added regularly. As you surf the Internet and the many career-related sites, remember to select sites that are current, look out for sales pitches, check the fees for listing your resume, be selective in contacting that potential employer, and ask what type of confidentiality or privacy protection for your resume is offered. The job search on the Web is just another tool to assist you in locating your career position as explained in the following Communication Note.

COMMUNICATION NOTE

Companies Love the Internet as a Cheap and Efficient Way to Fill Jobs

As the Internet revolutionizes the way employers and job hunters find each other, workers may gain the upper hand. That's because the Internet lets workers cast their qualifications to the world, making it easy for companies to find them nestled in their electronic cubbyholes and recruit them away from competitors. Employers, using ever-sophisticated search engines, will comb through millions of resumes.

Where can you post your Internet resume? Workers in many professions use the Web sites of trade associations. State unemployment offices soon will be posting resumes on government Web sites such as America's Job Bank (**http://www.ajb.dni.us**), run by the Labor Department, which lists over 500,000 jobs.

Millions of resumes will be kept on Web sites at universities and newspapers and on dozens of giant private sites such as CareerMosaic (**www.careermosaic.com**) and Monster Board (**www.monster.com**).

As reported by Del Jones, "Casting a Net for Job Seekers," USA Today, *August 26, 1996, p. B1.*

NEWSPAPER AND JOURNAL ADVERTISEMENTS

[NOTE 16.26] Classified ads are sources of jobs.

The classified advertisement sections of newspapers and many trade or professional journals are other sources of information about job openings. You can obtain trade or professional journals for your field at your school library or public library. You may also access classified ads from the *Boston Globe, New York Times, Los Angeles Times, Chicago Tribune, Washington Post, San Jose Mercury,* and several other newspapers at **http://www.careerpath.com**. Classified ads can also be found in *USA Today* at **http://www.usatoday.com**.

[NOTE 16.27] Generally, journal ads are national in scope and newspaper ads are local in scope.

Although journal job advertisements generally are national in scope, newspaper job advertisements are a good source of information about specific positions in a given geographic area. Most classified advertisements of position openings also carry information about the job requirements and salary levels. By studying advertisements, you can determine what jobs are available in a geographic area, what salaries are offered, and whether you can meet the job requirements. Most newspapers have several editions, and the job opening advertisements may vary from edition to edition. If you wish to relocate to Miami, for example, be aware that the edition of the *Miami Tribune* distributed within Miami will likely contain a more comprehensive listing of job openings than the edition distributed elsewhere. If you plan to relocate to a specific area, you may want to subscribe to one or more of the papers published there or access the online edition of the newspaper. If you want to compare salaries and living costs between various states, you can use the Salary Calculator at **http://www.homefair.com/homefair/cmr/salcalc.html**.

PRIVATE OR GOVERNMENT EMPLOYMENT AGENCIES

Private employment agencies bring together job seekers and employers. Their services will be similar to those offered by your campus career center. Private employment agencies are in business both to provide these specialized services and to make a profit. Therefore, either the employee or the employer will have to pay the significant fee charged. Before using a private employment agency, be sure that you understand clearly what services are provided, how much the fee will be, and who is to pay the fee.

[NOTE 16.28] Private agencies can be sources of jobs.

Another category of private employment agency is the nonprofit service of professional organizations. Some professional organizations publish job opening announcements, provide a hotline with recorded job listings, assist in linking job seekers and employers at professional conferences, and maintain a credentials file service. These services are usually offered at low or no cost to members. To determine what services are available to you from professional organizations, ask a professional in your field.

[NOTE 16.29] Some professional organizations can assist in your job search.

Public employment agencies are also found at all levels of government: federal, state, regional, and local. There is usually no charge for their services.

[NOTE 16.30] Government employment agencies can be sources of jobs.

At the federal government level, the U.S. Office of Personnel Management administers an extensive employment service. There are hundreds of area federal employment offices throughout the United States that are sources of job opportunities within the U.S. government. You can locate your nearest federal employment office by contacting any federal government agency in your area. Also, at the federal level, there are job opportunities available in the United States Army, Navy, Marines, Coast Guard, and Air Force. These branches of the military service have recruiters in most local communities. The U.S. government's official Web site for jobs and employment information can be found at **http://www.usajobs.opm.gov/**. America's Job Bank, which also lists jobs that can be found in the 50 states, can be viewed at **http://www.ajb.dni.us**. The home page of the White House is another site for job openings in the United States; the address is **http://www.whitehouse.gov/WH/welcome.html**.

[NOTE 16.31] Federal employment offices provide information on jobs with the federal government.

State governments also provide employment services. These services are more extensive than the employment services provided by the federal government. They include employment opportunities both in the private sector and in the state government. Most states have regional employment offices throughout the state to serve local geographic areas. Usually, you can locate these services by looking under the name of your state in the telephone book, by contacting any state government office, or searching the Web.

[NOTE 16.32] State government employment services list jobs in the private sector and in state government.

[NOTE 16.33] Local and regional employment offices provide information on jobs within their agencies.

Local and regional government agencies provide employment services to link potential employees with positions within their agencies. Cities, counties, and regional service units are all sources of jobs. Usually, you can locate their employment or personnel offices by looking in the telephone book under the name of the government unit, city, county, or region.

Many cities and chambers of commerce publish directories listing the names, addresses, and phone numbers of businesses in their localities. These directories often contain the names of top executives and departmental managers and are a good source for contacting individual businesses for possible unpublished job openings. You may also use a search engine on the Web to locate this information.

OTHER SOURCES

[NOTE 16.34] Friends, relatives, instructors, acquaintances, and past or present employers are important sources for job leads.

Other possible sources of information about available jobs and their requirements are through networks with colleagues, members of your professional associations, friends, relatives, instructors, acquaintances, and past or present employers. In an aggressive, vigorous job campaign, you will want to seek assistance from all sources. It is good to initially throw your net wide and then narrow your search. You may even want to advertise your job interests and qualifications in a newspaper or journal in order to obtain job leads.

Learning Objective [3]
PREPARE TRADITIONAL RESUMES IN EITHER CHRONOLOGICAL, FUNCTIONAL, OR COMBINATION FORMAT.

Resumes

[NOTE 16.35] A resume is a summary of your qualifications.

A **resume** is a summary of your qualifications. It should be a clear, concise, positive review of who you are and what you have to offer an employer. Resumes should be written concisely and clearly because it is estimated that employers spend only about 30 seconds per resume in their first screenings.

[NOTE 16.36] Some job applicants use videotape, CD-ROM, portfolio, or electronic resumes.

While most job applicants use a standard written resume, some use a videotape, CD, portfolio, or electronic resume. Assistance in creating a videotape resume for sales, acting, and other selected job applications is available from some campus career centers and private employment services. Assistance in developing an attractive portfolio of drawings, designs, writing samples, and so forth, for advertising, sales promotion, graphic arts, and other similar positions is available from individual faculty members and other professionals in your field. Particularly good course papers can be edited with faculty assistance and be used in your portfolio. Some applicants place their credentials on file with a resume database service. Employers seeking to fill positions can have direct online access to the database to search for candidates, or the service agency will do it for them. Both the candidate and the employer pay fees for this service.

Practically all applicants, however, must use standard written resumes if they are to be successful in securing job interviews. The rest of this chapter is about how to develop an effective written resume.

[NOTE 16.37] The primary purpose of your resume is to obtain a job interview.

The primary purpose of a resume, along with an application letter, is to obtain a job interview. Fewer than one in ten applications for employment results in an interview. To get an interview, your resume must be better than your competitors' resumes in both appearance and content. If you do not get an interview, you will not be hired.

STYLES OF RESUMES

There are two basic types of traditional resumes: targeted and general. Some applicants use a combination of the two basic types.

[NOTE 16.38] Resumes can be targeted or general.

Targeted Resume A **targeted resume** is prepared for a specific job application. It is individually keyed and printed, and it contains information to show specifically how you qualify for that one job. For example, it may list the courses you had in college that particularly apply to the responsibilities of the specific job.

[NOTE 16.39] Use targeted resumes for specific jobs.

A targeted resume is powerful and should be used for solicited job applications. If you use a word processing program on a computer to prepare your resume, it is easier to personalize and update.

General Resume A **general resume** is a description of your qualifications that can be used for any job and sent to any employer. It is appropriate for use in applying for unsolicited jobs. For example, if you are applying for management trainee positions or a management internship position in several different companies representing different industries, you can use a general resume to send to prospective employers.

[NOTE 16.40] Use general resumes for unsolicited jobs.

FORMATS FOR RESUMES

The three basic formats used for resumes are chronological, functional, and combination. The chronological resume is traditional.

[NOTE 16.41] The basic resume formats are chronological, functional, and combination.

Chronological Format A **chronological resume** is organized by date. Most resumes are organized in chronological order with the most recent information listed within each section. For example, in the section containing your experience, your current or most recent position is described first. The resume then describes each previous position, with the first position you held listed last. The same chronological approach is used in the sections for education, activities, community service, or any other section containing information accumulated over time.

[NOTE 16.42] Most managers prefer chronological resumes.

Most employers prefer the chronological format since it gives the information they need in a familiar sequence and helps them compare resumes. If employers have to search too hard to find a vital bit of information about you, your application may go into the reject pile. Figures 16.2 and 16.3 both show a traditional chronological format for a resume. Figure 16.2 is a targeted resume, while Figure 16.3 is a general resume.

Functional Format A **functional resume** provides information showing qualifications categorized by skills and knowledge and related accomplishments—in other words, by functions. The headings used for functions may include *Management, Marketing* (or *Sales*), *Advertising, Communicator,* or *Trainer.* This format is more creative in a sense and can be used for positions that require more creativity such as advertising, designing, or copy writing. The functional format is appropriate if you have already provided all the standard information to the employer in an application form.

[NOTE 16.43] The functional format can fit some application situations.

The functional format for a resume also works well for an individual who has been out of the job market for a number of years, has little employment experience, or has held several jobs and needs to combine them to make the presentation more

Figure 16.2
A One-Page Targeted Resume in Chronological Format

The opening is complete and balanced.

The chronological format is used in both the Education and Experience sections.

Activities demonstrating leadership skills are important.

LaDanian Childs
710 Anderson Street
Durham, NC 27705-9124
(919) 555-6776
ldchilds2@net.com

Objective To obtain a position in human resources in a company in the computer industry.

Education BA in Business Management—June 2001 (cum laude)
Sierra Nevada College, Incline Village, Nevada
Major emphasized organizational behavior and human resources
Idaho State University, Pocatello, Idaho—June 1998
General Education

Experience **Sales Associate,** Incline Sporting Goods Market, Incline Village, Nevada
September 1998–Present
- Present and explain merchandise.
- Handle customers' complaints and solve problems.
- Price, stock, and order merchandise.
- Train retail sales associates.

Cashier, K-Mart Corporation, Pocatello, Idaho
July 1996–September 1998
- Recorded monetary transactions.
- Performed opening and closing procedures on computer registers.
- Worked efficiently under pressure.

Crewperson, McDonald's, Pocatello, Idaho
June 1995–July 1996
- Served customers quickly and courteously.
- Handled and stocked inventory.
- Supported and augmented the training of 10–15 crewpersons.
- Coordinated special events under the stress of limited time.

Activities Vice President, PIHRA, Sierra Nevada College
Secretary-Treasurer, ISU ASB

concise or more favorable. An example of a resume in functional format is shown in Figure 16.4.

[NOTE 16.44] Combination resumes combine chronological and functional formats.

Combination Format Some applicants use a **combination resume**, which blends the strengths of the chronological format with the strengths of the functional format. Combination resumes work well for individuals with little work experience who are just entering the job market. A one-page combination resume for a recent college graduate is displayed in Figure 16.5.

Figure 16.3
A One-Page General Resume in Chronological Format

Katie E. Parker

451 Peninsula Way, #5B
Erie, PA 16523

E-mail: keparker@net.com
(814) 555-2345

OBJECTIVE An Office Administration Position

EDUCATION Lake Erie Community College, Erie, PA 16523
Degree: Associate of Arts
Major: Administrative Management
Date: June 2000

Pertinent Classes

- Administrative Management
- Principles of Management
- Communication for Management
- Business Telecommunications
- Microcomputer Applications for Administrative Personnel

EXPERIENCE Student Assistant — January 1999–Present
Records, Lake Erie Community College — Erie, PA 16523

- Assist students with transcript questions.
- Assist department with the development and maintenance of a home page.
- File student records.

Volunteer — Summers, 1995–1998
Santa Teresita Hospital — Erie, PA 16523

- Served customers quickly and courteously in gift shop.
- Stocked and counted inventory.

COMPUTER SKILLS

WordPerfect	Lotus 1-2-3	Word
d-Base IV	Eudora E-mail	NetMeeting
PowerPoint	PageMaker	Macintosh

ACTIVITIES Administrative Management Club

The attractive opening is complete.

The Objective is general and would allow the person to be employed in a number of jobs.

Accomplishment is shown in the Education section.

Work experience is provided.

Special section highlights computer skills.

Research indicates that managers who review resumes and make decisions on who will be invited for an interview prefer chronological resumes; therefore, they are more appropriate for most job campaigns. According to the staffing firm Accountemps, of Menlo Park, California, 78 percent of the 150 large-company executives polled prefer chronological resumes compared to 19 percent who preferred the functional format.[5] Three percent of the executives polled gave no preference.

CHOOSING A FORMAT

The format you choose depends on the job you are seeking. If you are applying for a position in a conservative industry or conservative organization, such as banking,

[5] "Reverse the Chronological Order, Please, When Applying for a Job," *The Wall Street Journal,* August 31, 1999, p. A1.

Figure 16.4
A One-Page Functional Resume for a College Graduate With Experience

Complete information is provided in attractive opening.

Career Objective is targeted for a specific position.

Applicant's experience is presented in a functional format.

College education data is presented concisely.

Some campus career centers provide graduates' reference letters to employers on request.

DENNIS HERNANDEZ

Present Address	*Permanent Address* (After 5/15/01)
734 Perrin Drive	Route 5, Box 345
Detroit, MI 22222	Homestead, FL 33030-7123
(888) 555-7843	(305) 555-9215

CAREER OBJECTIVE Human Resource Director for a Fortune 500 Company

EXPERIENCE

Management
- Managed all facets of human resources office.
- Recruited for 300 job positions.
- Administered transfers of personnel.
- Received honors for highest employee retention rates.

Human Resources
- Counseled employees in career decisions.
- Coordinated program for bonuses up to $50,000.
- Helped plan voluntary terminations program.

Training and Development
- Lectured and counseled employees on education benefits.
- Developed cross-training seminars.
- Provided leadership training.

Drug and Alcohol
- Supervised wellness activities.
- Managed accurate urinalysis testing.

EMPLOYMENT
International Business Machines, 1998–Present, Detroit, Michigan
Human Resources Consulting, 1997, Miami, Florida
Martin Fabric Company, 1995–1997, Miami, Florida

EDUCATION
Miami State University, Miami, Florida
B. S. Degree in Business Administration, May 1995
Major: Human Resource Management
Minor: Managerial Computing

REFERENCES
Career Development and Placement Center
MSU Box 17
Miami State University
Miami, FL 33100-5200, Telephone (305) 555-7000,
CarCtr@MSU.edu

public accounting, or manufacturing, you should use the traditional chronological resume. If you are applying for a position in advertising, sales promotion, or entertainment, you may want to choose the nontraditional functional format. If you are a recent college graduate with little work experience, you may want to use the combination format.

Regardless of the type or format of resume you use, your resume should be a carefully prepared, attractive, high-quality representation of you. As has been indicated, it is the primary sales tool you will use to obtain an interview. Through the wording of the content of your resume, convey to employers information about yourself as explained in the following Communication Note.

Javaria S. Vaid
55 Sunkist Circle
San Gabriel, CA 91776
(626) 555-2825
E-mail: jsvaid@hotmail.com

Objective: Seeking a training and development position which will utilize my teaching and organizational skills.

Capabilities and Experiences:

- Developed and presented a workshop on oral presentations at a local high school.
- Coordinated the planning, writing, and presentation of a resume workshop at a state conference.
- Assisted professor with the design, development, and grading of class team projects.
- Supported the trainer in the sales presentation seminar at the University.

Education: Bachelor of Science in Business Administration expected June 2001
Bowling Green State University, Ohio
Major: Human Resource Management
Minor: Communication

Related Courses: Human Resource Management; Training and Development; Staffing, Planning, Recruiting, and Selection; Employee Compensation Plans; Human Resources Information; Organizational Management; Communication for Management

Employment: Teaching Assistant, Bowling Green State University, Ohio 9/99–present
Sales Clerk, Bonnie's Dress Shop, Bowling Green, Ohio 9/95–9/99

Activities: Society for Human Resource Professional Association, President 00–01
American Society of Training and Development, Secretary 99–00
Habitat for Humanity Volunteer

Figure 16.5
A One-Page Combination Resume

Functional format highlights the various skills areas.

Activities show leadership skills and outside interests.

COMMUNICATION NOTE

Resume Talk From Recruiters

The resume is a job seeker's personal document, and many career counselors say that creating a resume is more of an art than a science. Recruiters emphasized that they are not just looking for a particular grade point average or a mother lode of extracurricular activities, but for evidence of leadership qualities, strong communication skills, and the ability to balance outside activities with course work. Recruiters don't just look for work or experiential education experience on the resume—they also look for the descriptive information that will tie an applicant's experience to the needs of the organization.

Valerie Patterson, "Resume Talk From Recruiters," Journal of Career Planning and Employment, *Winter 1996, pp. 37–38.*

Preparing Your Resume

With the information you developed when you analyzed your qualifications and the job market, you are now ready to prepare your resume. While following the principles of business communication, exercise creativity in presenting the best possible picture of yourself. The following are the major sections commonly included in a resume:

[NOTE 16.45] Resumes have commonly used sections.

[1] Opening

[2] Education

[3] Experience

[4] Activities, honors, or special skills

[5] References

You may not need or want all these sections in your resume. Also, you may want to arrange them in some other order. For example, if your experience is your strong point, it should be presented immediately following the opening. If you are a recent college graduate and have limited experience, have the education section follow the opening.

OPENING

[NOTE 16.46] The opening includes a heading and an objective.

The opening of your resume should include a heading, your job and/or career objective, and, if appropriate, a summary of your qualifications. The purposes of the opening are to get potential employers to read the remainder of the resume, to inform them briefly of your interests and qualifications, and to make it easy for them to contact you.

[NOTE 16.47] The heading must include your name, address, telephone number, and e-mail address.

Heading A resume heading with your name, address, telephone number, and e-mail address is essential. You may want to include your fax number, and if you have an online resume, your Web site address. Be sure that your name is in the largest and darkest type. Include both your permanent and temporary school addresses and telephone numbers. Remember to create a voice mail greeting that is professional on your telephone since potential employers will be telephoning your home. Your Web site should also be very professional and businesslike in case employers are assessing it. Remember that the majority of potential employers prefer a conservative, traditional resume. Here are examples:

[1]

MIKE ALVINO
1910 Ginnway Drive
New Castle, DE 19720-2810
(302) 555-1933
(302) 555-1930 Fax
malvino@nc.net

[2]

BRIETTA D'AMORE
bdamore@mind.net

Current Address:	**Permanent Address:**
P.O. Box 826	917 Wellman Drive
Bridgeport, CT 06600-0826	Bridgeport, CT 06600-0826
(203) 555-9173	(203) 555-7845

[3] **SHAWN WATSON**

1234 Dell Way 909.555.1212
Pomona, CA 91768 swatson@email.net

Career Objective Prospective employers like to see a Career Objective, sometimes called a Job Objective, in the opening of a resume so they can tell whether their interests match yours. Your objective can be either specific or general. Use a specific objective for a targeted position and a general objective for a wider variety of positions which would depend on your qualifications and work experience. Remember to read the ad carefully to make sure that the career objective you write matches the job!

[NOTE 16.48]
A Career Objective section can gain you favorable attention.

According to Yana Parker, a resume consultant, the first step in writing a resume is designing your job objective so that it can be stated in about six words. Ms. Parker states that anything longer is probably fluff and indicates a lack of clarity and direction.[6] Remember to use words carefully when preparing the objective. Here are examples:

Specific Career Objectives

[1] ***Objective:*** To obtain an internship in accounting in a Big 8 Accounting Firm.

[2] ***Objective:*** To obtain a position as a human resource director in the health care industry.

General Career Objectives

[1] ***Career Objective:*** Challenging position in sales and marketing.

[2] ***Career Objective:*** To begin a career in an entry-level position leading to a management position in sales management. Long-term goal is to become a manager of a major department store.

Summary of Qualifications This section provides a very brief abstract of your qualifications. The Summary of Qualifications should include *statements* or *phrases* that describe you and your accomplishments. Prepare your Summary of Qualifications section after you have completed the remainder of the resume so that it is comprehensive and high quality. This section is optional; however, some employers like to see a summary statement in the opening of a resume so they can tell whether their interests match yours. Here are examples:

[1] **Summary of Qualifications**

Bachelor of Science in Business Administration with emphasis on computer information systems. Seven years of part-time work in a variety of jobs from janitor to motel night manager-bookkeeper. Work effectively with people and have productive work habits.

[2] **General Qualifications**

- Successful experience in retail sales.
- Promotions for consistently exceeding quotas.
- Associate of Arts degree in retail sales management.
- Dean's Honor Roll last four quarters.

[6] Yana Parker, "Yana Parker's TIPS on Resume Writing," *Knight-Ridder/Tribune News Service,* November 3, 1998, p. K314.

EDUCATION

[NOTE 16.49] Education is the next major section for recent graduates.

Following your resume Opening, present your strongest qualifications. If you are, or will soon be, a recent college graduate and have limited experience, your education and related activities will be your strongest qualifications. If you have been employed for many years and can relate that employment to the job you are seeking, your Experience section should follow the Opening.

If you have or will soon be graduated from a postsecondary institution, it is unnecessary to review your high school record in the Education section. However, if while in high school you developed a job-related skill, you may want to include this skill. For example, if you are applying for a position in international business, you may want to state that while in high school you participated in a foreign exchange program and lived abroad for a year. Listing a high school is also acceptable if you wish to return to an area but no longer have a permanent residence address there.

Titles that you might use for this section are "Education," "Educational Qualifications," "Training for . . . ," "Specialized Education," "Academic Preparation," "Professional Education," "Educational Data," and "Educational Preparation." Remember that all headings at the same level should have parallel construction. If you attended several schools before earning a degree, consider using a statement such as "Degree included courses transferred from . . ." rather than listing each school as a separate entry.

[NOTE 16.50] Remember the most recent information is listed first on a chronological resume.

For the chronological resume, remember the most recent information is listed first. In the Education section list the name and location of each school attended and the dates of attendance. Also, for each school show your degrees, major, and other selected information to reflect your achievements and extent of learning. Here are examples:

[1] *Education*

University of North Dakota, Grand Forks, North Dakota
Degree: Bachelor of Science
Major: Business Administration (IAME Program)
Date: June 2001
Honors: Dean's Honor Roll last five semesters
GPA: 3.3 (4.0 = **A**)

[2] *Educational Qualifications*

Dade County Community College, Miami, Florida (1999–2001)
Degree: Associate of Arts in Office Administration
Courses that especially prepared me for your office coordinator position:

Word Processing	Computer Systems
Keyboarding	Business Communication
Office Administration	Records Management

Marshall High School, Marshall, Florida (1997–1999)
Diploma: College Preparatory
Class Rank: Tenth in class of 100
Activities: Business Club (President), Hi-Y (Treasurer), Student Council (Secretary), Senior Yearbook Editor, Band, Basketball, American Field Service (AFS) Student to Japan

[3] **Central Washington University, Ellensburg, Washington**

B.S: Business Administration—June 2002 expected graduation
Business Education Major and English Minor
GPA: 3.3 (major)

EXPERIENCE

For applicants other than new graduates, employers rate work experience as the most important information in a resume. More decisions to grant or not to grant interviews are based on the quality of work experience than on any other basis.

[NOTE 16.51]
Experience is rated highly by employers.

Although all your work experience is important, the work experience that prepared you for the position you are seeking is especially important and should be highlighted. Your experience indicates your record of responsibility and accomplishments, provides the primary sources for references, and reflects your personality and personal preferences. When analyzing your qualifications, you developed the information needed for the Experience section of your resume. Now you must decide how to present it most effectively.

[NOTE 16.52]
Focus on your accomplishments.

Your accomplishments should be the focal point of your experience presentation, including what you learned from the experience, your achievements, and your contributions to each position. Your responsibilities for each position may also be listed briefly. Use appropriate action verbs in your listings of accomplishments and responsibilities. Remember to use present tense verbs for jobs at which you are currently employed. For each position you should include dates of employment, job title, employer, and employer's address. Remember that for the chronological resume, you should list the most recent information first.

Use Action Words

accomplished	accounted for	accumulated	adapted
administered	advised	analyzed	applied
approved	arranged	assembled	assigned
assisted	attended	budgeted	built
collaborated	communicated	computed	conducted
coordinated	created	decreased	delegated
designed	developed	directed	documented
earned	established	evaluated	executed
gathered	generated	hired	identified
illustrated	implemented	improved	increased
initiated	inspected	installed	instructed
interpreted	interviewed	invented	investigated
led	listened	made	managed
marketed	mastered	mediated	moderated
modified	monitored	motivated	negotiated
obtained	operated	ordered	organized
originated	participated	performed	persuaded
planned	prepared	presented	presided
produced	promoted	published	purchased
recommended	reconciled	recruited	redesigned

(Continued)

Use Action Words (cont.)

reduced	refined	represented	researched
resolved	reviewed	revised	scheduled
secured	selected	set up	simplified
sold	stimulated	summarized	supervised
supported	taught	tested	trained
updated	upgraded	validated	wrote

[NOTE 16.53]
Present your experience using the chronological or the functional format.

Depending on the format of your resume, your experience may be presented using either the chronological, the functional, or the combination format. Examples of how the same information might be presented are as follows:

Chronological Example

[1] EXPERIENCE

Night Manager **Holiday Motel, De Kalb, Illinois (1999–Present)**

Responsibilities
- Supervise four employees.
- Greet and register guests.
- Maintain accounting and guest records.

Achievements
- Learned to work effectively with people.
- Gained skills in meeting difficult customer needs.
- Developed new guest accounting procedures that save an average of two hours of clerical time each night.

Part-time Work **Various employers in the De Kalb area (1996–1999)**

Responsibilities
- Motel auditor, research assistant, appliance salesperson, and janitor.

Achievements
- Promoted from motel desk clerk to night manager.
- Learned research techniques while assisting professor in business communication study.
- Led appliance sales force of four in sales during three of six months of employment.
- Learned to work with a variety of people.

Functional Example

[2] **SKILLS DEVELOPED THROUGH EXPERIENCE**

MANAGERIAL SKILLS — As a motel night manager, developed skills in motivating employees and performing a variety of jobs. Assumed additional responsibilities readily. Improved employee productivity. Observed other managers and practiced their effective behavior.

COMMUNICATION SKILLS — Learned to communicate clearly and concisely with employees and customers in many different situations. Developed ability to provide written and oral reports for financial and customer accounting data.

ACCOUNTING SKILLS — Developed thorough knowledge of double-entry bookkeeping system. Became proficient in completing trial balances, balance sheets, profit and loss statements, and other statements.

ACTIVITIES, HONORS, SPECIAL SKILLS, OR OTHER APPROPRIATE TITLES

Include additional sections in your resume if your background justifies them. Any additional section included should be one that employers would consider positively. For example, if you were involved extensively in extracurricular activities during college, include a separate section on these activities immediately following the education section. Your background may justify a separate section on honors, special skills, computer competence, community services, published works, public presentations, military service, organization memberships, special interests, or any number of other possible categories. If you have a variety of activities, you may combine them into one section labeled simply "Activities." The heading of the section should reflect the contents accurately. The important point is that you should not leave out any vital information that would enhance your resume. For the chronological resume, list the most recent activities first.

[NOTE 16.54]
Special sections may be included if your qualifications and the job justify them.

Special sections should be placed near related information or at an appropriate point of emphasis. For example, a special section on academic honors should follow the Education section. A special interests section, because it is likely less important, should be placed just before the section on references. References are traditionally not listed in the last section of a resume but on a separate sheet. Examples of special sections in resumes follow:

[NOTE 16.55]
Place special sections in appropriate locations in your resume.

[1] HONORS

Outstanding Employee, Bison Excavators, 2000
Boise Citizens' Sparkplug Award, 1999
Outstanding Young Woman in Idaho Award, 1999
Dean's Honor List, Boise State University, 1998–1999
State Academic Scholarship to Boise State University, 1997–2001

[2] EXTRACURRICULAR ACTIVITIES

President, Alpha Kappa Delta	2000–2001
Secretary-Treasurer, Alpha Kappa Delta	1999–2000
Social Chair, Alpha Kappa Delta	1998–1999
NW Representative, Cultural Awareness Program	1998–1999
Coach, Northwood Cross-Country Team	1996–1998
Business Manager, *State College News*	1995–1997

[3] ORGANIZATION MEMBERSHIPS

Executive Board, Management Information Systems Student Association (MISSA) 2000–2002
Coordinator of Marketing, Information Technology 2000
Administrative Management Association (Chapter Secretary, 1999–2001)
Habitat for Humanity 1999–Present
International Facilities Management Association 1998–Present
Civitan Club (Club President 1996–1997, Area Governor 1997–1998)

[4] SPECIAL SKILLS

Proficient in computer software, including PowerPoint, WordPerfect, Microsoft Word, Lotus 1-2-3, and Access. Speak and write Spanish fluently. Speak and understand limited Mandarin and Japanese. Keyboard at 75 words per minute. Know how to use most electronic office equipment.

[5] SPECIAL INTERESTS

Camping, basketball, photography, and cooking.

[6] INTERESTS

Enjoy outdoor activities, including camping, basketball, and photography. Considered a gourmet cook. Energetic. Adaptable. Have sense of humor. Willing to relocate.

Employment laws prohibit employers from discriminating among applicants on the basis of race, color, religion, age, gender, disability, marital status, or national origin. Employers cannot ask for this information, and supplying such information is not recommended.

[NOTE 16.56] Do not include information an employer might prefer not to have.

Omit from your resume any information you think a given employer would prefer not to have. Do not include a photograph of yourself unless you are applying for a position as a model.

[NOTE 16.57] Present only the information that will strengthen your application.

In some job situations, however, your job application can be strengthened if you let a potential employer know your religious affiliation, race, national origin, sexual orientation, marital status, disability, or other special qualification. For example, if you were applying for an administrative position with a Catholic Church headquarters office, letting the employer know that you are a member of the Catholic Church could be helpful. As a way to provide this type of information in your resume, you could list the church as one of your organization memberships, citing accomplishments related to your special qualification. Or, you could include the information in a special section devoted to your status. Another way is to mention the unique qualification in your application letter. Application letters are covered in Chapter 17.

REFERENCES

[NOTE 16.58] References are vital.

A vital part of your job preparation is carefully developing your list of references. Though you want to list only those references who will give you positive recommendations, you should list your most important previous employers. You may also want to list college instructors, possibly high school teachers, and—in special circumstances—coworkers or character references. You may list different references for different job applications. Let the nature of the job and its requirements determine the references you think would be the most helpful to the potential employer.

[NOTE 16.59] Provide full information, including a telephone number and e-mail address.

Instead of taking up valuable space on your resume, develop a separate reference list to accompany your resume. You are encouraged to provide full information on your references on this list including addresses, telephone numbers, and e-mail addresses. For each reference—unless a reference directs you otherwise—list courtesy title, name, position, organization, business address, business telephone number, and e-mail address. In certain areas of the country employers may want you to list the references on the resume; however, it is better to use this extra space for information about yourself. You do not need to list "references available on request" because employers know that you will provide references.

You are encouraged to provide full information on your references on this list including addresses, telephone numbers, and e-mail addresses. If a potential employer finds your qualifications of interest and can easily pick up the phone, call, and receive a favorable recommendation from one or more of your references, you are likely to get an interview. For each reference—unless a reference directs you otherwise—list courtesy title, name, position, organization, business address, business telephone number, and e-mail address. Here is the way a reference list might appear:

REFERENCE LIST
Diane B. Smith
712 Southwood Drive, C-20
Danville, CA 94526
510.555.8873 (Home)
dbsmith@dan.net

Dr. A. D. Ortiz, Professor
Department of Accounting
Middle State College
Danville, CA 94526
510.555.9322 (Work)
510.555.1234 (Home)

Mr. Thomas Hopkins, Manager
Uniform Fitting Inc.
1844 Newport Blvd.
Danville, CA 94526
510.555.1212 (Work)
510.555.6000 (Pager)

Mrs. Rowena Kelsey
Communications Consultant
San Ramon Corporation
2387 Seboyeta Avenue
Danville, CA 94526
510.555.7817 (Work)

Mr. Marion Sandoval, Manager
Sandoval and Sandoval, CPAs
1234 Crownpoint Street
Danville, CA 94526
510.555.7834 (Work)
510.555.7835 (Fax)

Electronic Resumes

Learning Objective [4]
PREPARE AN ELECTRONIC RESUME.

New technology is changing the way you can search and apply for a job. More and more companies are using computers in seeking qualified applicants and selecting qualified personnel. In the new world of hiring, a computer, not a human being, will, more likely than not, do the first read of your resume.[7] Electronic resumes can be classified as either the (1) scannable resume or (2) online resume.

[NOTE 16.60]
Some resumes are scanned by computers.

COMMUNICATION QUOTE

As a human resource specialist, I feel that understanding the format and use of scannable resumes is essential in competitively seeking a job. It is important to have the proper format and content in a scannable resume to provide you with the greatest benefit—an interview. Remember, having an excellent resume is the initial step towards developing your career opportunities.

Sergio Bautista, Recent College Graduate and Human Resource Specialist, Fluor Corporation, 1997.

[7] James Ramage, "New Rules for the Resumes," *Kiplinger's Personal Finance Magazine,* November 1998, v52, n11, p. 78.

[NOTE 16.61] Larger companies rely on applicant tracking systems.

Scannable Resumes Many organizations, including IBM, MCI, Motorola, American Airlines, Citibank, Coca-Cola, Southern California Edison, and UCLA, incorporate applicant tracking computer systems into their human resource departments. With the applicant tracking systems, when a potential employee sends in a resume for either a solicited or unsolicited position, the resume is scanned and placed in an electronic employment folder. The resume is then compared with the job-opening possibilities, and either a letter for an interview or a letter of rejection is generated depending on the final recommendation of the human resource personnel.

Resumes for individuals who are hired are stored in an electronic folder that is periodically updated with their job performance information. This database is used to locate candidates for job advancement. Therefore, if you are hired by a firm with this system, remember to update your resume every six months and date your resume. A word of caution: Since the majority of these computer scanning systems are housed in the human resources department, be careful about sending duplicate resumes, or it will appear that you don't know what position you want or what you want to do! Some companies that do not have their own computer systems for human resources lease the scanning services from providers.

[NOTE 16.62] Keywords should be concrete nouns.

Keywords The scannable resume follows the traditional style but includes a section with a listing of the keywords. Keywords are placed at the top of the resume because many programs will scan only the first 50 words of a resume. Keywords are generally nouns that label you; it is best to have around 20 to 25 keywords for a scannable resume. Examples of keywords are as follows:

Examples of Keywords

Ability to delegate	Accounts payable	Accounts receivable	Accurate
Adaptable	Analytical	Assertive	Associate of Arts
B.S.	Bachelor of Arts	Communication skills	Compensation
Customer support	Creative	Data entry	Detail-minded
Filing	Financial reports	Flexible	Fluent in Spanish
High energy	HTML	Human resources	Industrious
Innovative	Journalism	Leadership	MBA
Medical terminology	Merit pay program	Month-end closing	Multitasking
Open communication	Organizational skills	Presentation skills	Recruitment
Reservations	Results-oriented	Safety-conscious	Salesperson
Team player	Willing to travel	Windows	Written communication

Source: http://www.eresumes.com/tut_keyres_example.html. 2/16/99

[NOTE 16.63] Keywords vary for each position.

Because the keywords mark the electronic trail, you must learn the keywords that are used in the field for which you are applying so that you have a better chance of being selected for a job interview. Each time one of your keywords matches a keyword for the particular position you have a "hit." The more "hits" you receive the better your chance for a job interview. Include only keywords that correctly and honestly describe you and your qualifications. Include job titles, department names, companies and organizations, degrees, skills or knowledge possessed by the applicant, class ranking, skills, and interpersonal traits. An example of a keyword section for an individual working in the human resources area could be as follows:

Keywords

Human resources. EEO regulations. ADA. Merit pay program. Safety coordinator. Certified facilitator and instructor. Communication skills. Organizational skills. Supervisor. Purchasing. IBM. MS Word. PowerPoint. Team player. Self-starter. Willing to train. Enthusiastic. Friendly. Trustworthy. Reliable. Fluent in Spanish and Mandarin. Supportive. Bachelor of Science Business.

Preparing a Scannable Resume Organization and appearance of the scannable resume are essential to the success of your job search. Your name, address, telephone number, fax number, and e-mail address should be centered and be the first lines of the resume since the scanned resume must conform to the client's standardized profile sheet. The type font should be sans serif (such as Arial or Helvetica) and the font size between 10 and 14 points. Boldface is acceptable, but the resume should not have any italic, script, or underlined text. Avoid double columns since scanners will read across the columns and will read the information incorrectly. Some companies do have sophisticated scanning equipment that can read different fonts and styles; however, you cannot be sure of what kind of scanner the company is using unless you telephone them first. Your goal is a plain-vanilla resume. Preferably the scannable resume should be printed by a laser printer with black ink on smooth, white paper. Remember to send your resume to the company in a 9- by 12-inch mailing envelope to avoid folding the resume since the fold may cause the scanner to skip words.

[NOTE 16.64]
A scannable resume is a plain-vanilla resume.

To have your resume selected for human review in this computerized process, you must learn how the computer programming works. If you know your resume will be scanned, find out—from the company or another source—the nature of the computer program so you know what content to include. Figure 16.6 is an example of a scannable resume with a keywords section displayed. This computer-friendly resume can be read easily and accurately by scanners as well as human eyes. Richard Wonder, president of Richard Wonder Associates, gives advice for writers of electronic resumes in the following Communication Note.

COMMUNICATION NOTE

Advice for Electronic Resume Writers

1. Nothing But the Truth—do not lie on the resume or during an interview since you could be fired on the spot. 2. Keep It Simple—avoid script typeface, bold, and italics on your resume. Resumes with fancy graphics can't be scanned electronically and won't be saved into an employer's database. 3. Use Keywords Wisely—Remember to list all the software for which you can claim to be a true expert. Be sure to list the hottest technologies first. 4. Be Reachable—Always include your e-mail address.

Richard Wonder, "Advice for Electronic Resume Writers," Computerworld, *March 22, 1999, p. 44.*

Online Resumes The Internet provides opportunities for accessing online career centers and company Web sites for posting your resume. The online resume is becoming an important tool in the workplace since many human resource departments are conducting searches on the Web for qualified applicants.

[NOTE 16.65]
The Internet plays an important role in the job search process.

Figure 16.6
A One-Page Scannable Resume With a Keywords Section

Complete information is provided in opening.

Keywords highlight the skills, knowledge, and experience of applicant.

The Objective reflects short- and long-range goals.

Education is this applicant's strongest qualification and is presented first.

Job continuity is shown.

Academic achievement and professional commitment are shown.

Mary Carol Chen
301 Palmatum Street
Livermore, CA 94550
Home: 510.555.1751
E-mail: mcchen@net.com

KEYWORDS

Human resources. Management. Organizational skills. ADA. Applicant screening. Applicant tracking. Supervisor. 4+ years experience. Team player. 401K. Training and development. Service award. B.S. IBM. MS Word. PowerPoint. GDSS. Resumix. Communication. Dean's list. SAM. SHRM. Spanish fluency.

OBJECTIVE

Seeking a human resources position which will utilize my management and organizational skills and lead to increased responsibility and advancement.

EDUCATION

California State University, Hayward, California
Bachelor of Science, Business Administration Degree, 2000
Management and Human Resources Major, 3.33/4.0 (Overall) GPA

Chabot College, Hayward, California
Associate in Arts Degree, 1997
Liberal Arts Major, 3.25/4.0 (Overall) GPA

Computer Experience and Training. Hardware: IBM PC, Macintosh, VAX VT120 (UNIX); Software: MS Word 8.0, MS Excel 8.0, MS PowerPoint 8.0, MS Access 8.0, MS Schedule+, Outlook 98, Synchronics, Lotus 1-2-3, Corel WordPerfect 7.0, NetMeeting, Photoshop, GroupSystems v5.0 (GDSS).

Relevant Coursework: Human Resources Principles, Staff Development, Training and Development, Compensation and Benefits Planning, HR Computer Applications, Communications for Management

EXPERIENCE

Tools-R-Us, Livermore, CA 94550
September 1997 to present
Human Resources Specialist and Supervisor

Manage 15 employees in human resources department; coordinate medical, 401K , and pension plans; train employees in human resources hiring procedures; ensure compliance with affirmative action programs.

ACHIEVEMENTS/ACTIVITIES

Dean's and President's Honors List; Community and High School Tennis Coach; BSA Den Leader; Member of Society for the Advancement of Management and Society for Human Resource Managers.

The style of this resume will differ from the traditional or the scannable resume in that the contents may be "linked" to more detailed information about your work. The online resume can be thought of as a targeted home page portfolio with detailed examples of projects, proposals, and reports that you have developed. It is important to keep your Web site professional since employers will be viewing the

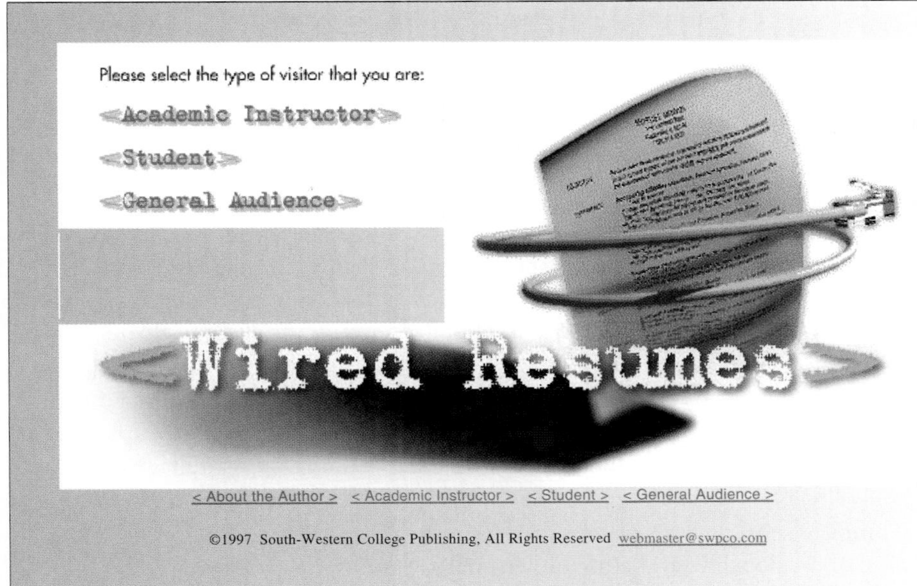

Figure 16.7
Wired Resume Site,
http://www.wired-resumes.com

information that you have provided. Remember to avoid providing personal information on your Web site, including photos, since recruiters are legally barred from using this material in employment decisions.

You may visit the Wired Resumes Web site at **http://www.wired-resumes.com** for information on how to create and post online resumes. Figure 16.7 displays the Wired Resumes site which provides all the tools and resources needed to develop your own online resume. The Joyce Lain Kennedy Web site at **http://www.occ.com/occ/JLK/HowToEResume.html** or Tripod at **http://tripod.com** are good sources for information on developing your online resume.

Remember that when you post your resume to the Internet, your resume may be "shopped" to hundreds of employers at once. This may be good and result in several interviews; however, after you have accepted a position your resume may linger in cyberspace for several months or years.

[NOTE 16.66]
Beware of spiders and salvagers.

Your resume should be dated if it is posted online since it could be snatched by an unscrupulous headhunter, duplicated, and reposted by roving **spiders**. Spiders, automated agents based on online recruiting Web sites, track down the newest resumes on the Internet and automatically e-mail potential candidates.[8] If your savvy Web-smart current employer finds it, you may be called on the carpet and possibly fired. If you have had your resume posted on the Web, it would be good to let the employer know in order to avoid such a misunderstanding. Some corporations are hiring **salvagers** in the human resource department whose job it is to patrol cyberspace and look for wayward employees.[9]

[8] Tim Ouellette, "Technology Snares New Resumes on Web," *Computerworld,* May 4, 1998, v32, n18, p. 20.
[9] Jerry Useem, "Read This Before You Put a Resume Online: Cyberspace Is a Job Jungle," *Fortune,* May 24, 1999, v139, i10, p. 290.

Refining the Resume

You will be judged on the appearance of your resume; it is a potential employer's first impression of you. Though there are many helpful examples available, you should never simply try to make your information fit another resume format.

[NOTE 16.67]
White paper is preferred.

- Your resume should be typed or printed—use a laser printer if possible—on white, buff, or some other light color paper. Remember if your resume is to be scanned, you should use white paper. Use high-quality, clean, 8½ by 11-inch bond paper. Be sure your resume is neat, unwrinkled, and error-free. The quality and clarity of its content will be a potential employer's impression of you.
- You should make effective use of blank space, sometimes called *white space,* and other techniques for emphasis in your resume. Some of these techniques include the use of capital letters, boldfacing, underscoring, italics, lines, and different type sizes. As discussed earlier, your goal is to prepare a plain-vanilla resume for scannable resumes.
- Complete sentences are not required; phrases are appropriate to save space. A note of caution: Avoid the use of personal pronouns; instead begin each phrase with an action word.

[NOTE 16.68]
Show the manager that you fit the position and can do the job.

- Draft your resume carefully to show the employer that there is a clear match between your qualifications and their requirements. Remember it is important that you learn the jargon of the industry and use those words in your resume.
- You may consider giving a draft of your resume to a classmate whom you don't know well and allow that person to scan your resume for two or three minutes. After your classmate has scanned the resume, ask him or her questions about your resume. If the reader can't answer the questions or can't locate the answer quickly, the resume isn't effective.
- Remember to proofread carefully since errors can result in the resume being eliminated from consideration.

[NOTE 16.69]
Employers prefer a one-page resume.

- Many businesspeople prefer a one-page resume for new college graduates with limited experience. If your resume is two pages or longer, a Summary of Qualifications section is essential. If you know that an employer specifies the number of pages in applicants' resumes (such as, "Applicant resumes shall not exceed one page"), be sure to limit your resume length accordingly. Be sure that the information is not overcrowded or does not appear so dense as to discourage its being read.

[NOTE 16.70]
Your objective is to get the job interview.

- Remember your objective is to construct the most powerful resume that you possibly can for each job application so you can convince the employer to give you an interview.

Following the guidelines given in this chapter should enable you to create your own distinctive resume, one that will serve you well in your job search.

Summary of Learning Objectives

Learning Objective [1]

Analyze your qualifications for employment. In analyzing your qualifications, start by brainstorming facts about yourself. The most important facts are evidence of your accomplishments—achievements, honors, and knowledge. In addition, you develop an individual profile about yourself and a list of persons who can serve as your references.

Learning Objective [2]

Describe the sources of information about job opportunities and job requirements. Career positions can be either solicited or unsolicited. Jobs listed with campus career centers, advertised in newspapers or journals, announced through private or government placement agencies, or listed on the Internet are solicited positions. Unsolicited positions are ones obtained by direct contact with a company of your choice.

Learning Objective [3]

Prepare traditional resumes in either chronological, functional, or combination format. A resume is a summary of your qualifications and must be clearly and concisely written. The primary purpose of a resume, along with an application letter, is to obtain a job interview.

Learning Objective [4]

Prepare an electronic resume. Electronic resumes are classified as either scannable or online. The scannable resume follows the traditional style but includes a section with a listing of the keywords. Keywords are nouns that label you; it is best to have around 20 to 25 keywords for a scannable resume. Since the keywords mark the electronic trail, you must learn the keywords that are used in the field for which you are applying so that you have a better chance for being selected for a job interview. The online resume can be developed on your computer and then uploaded to your own home page on the Web. The online computer resume is becoming an important tool in the workplace since many human resource departments are conducting searches on the Web for qualified applicants.

DISCUSSION QUESTIONS

1. Discuss the approach that a person should take in analyzing his or her qualifications. (Objective 1)
2. What are the most important facts about you that you should list when you are analyzing your qualifications? (Objective 1)
3. Define *solicited position*. List where you could find a solicited position. (Objective 2)
4. To prepare yourself to write the Experience section of a resume, what information will you need about your past employment? (Objectives 1 and 3)
5. List the six steps involved in conducting a job search. (Objective 2)
6. Describe the information and services offered by campus career centers. (Objective 2)
7. Describe the role of the Internet in a job search. (Objective 2)
8. How many references should you include on your reference list? What information do you need from each reference? (Objective 3)
9. Explain the term keywords and their importance on your resume. (Objective 4)
10. List and explain the purposes of the five commonly used sections on your resume. (Objectives 3 and 4)

APPLICATION EXERCISES

1. Visit your campus career center and gather information on interests and personality tests they offer or recommend to help an individual determine their career interests. Take the test, have the test evaluated, and write a report to your instructor on the findings. (Objective 1)

2. Interview a prospective employer to learn what qualities he or she would look for in an applicant who is a new college graduate. Design a presentation for your class on your findings. (Objective 1)
3. Analyze the professional organizations in your field of study. List those organizations in which you feel membership would strengthen your job candidacy. (Objective 2)
4. Using the information gained in Exercise 3, attend a meeting of a professional organization in which you feel membership will strengthen your job candidacy. Write a memo to your instructor and make a presentation to your class giving the mission, purpose, and goals of the organization. Give information on the dues and the benefits of membership in the professional organization. (Objective 2)

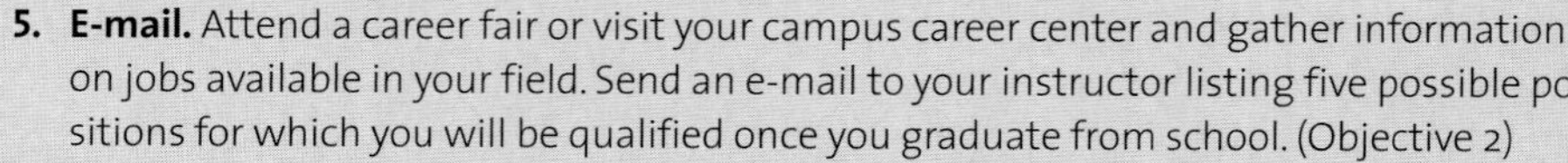

5. **E-mail.** Attend a career fair or visit your campus career center and gather information on jobs available in your field. Send an e-mail to your instructor listing five possible positions for which you will be qualified once you graduate from school. (Objective 2)

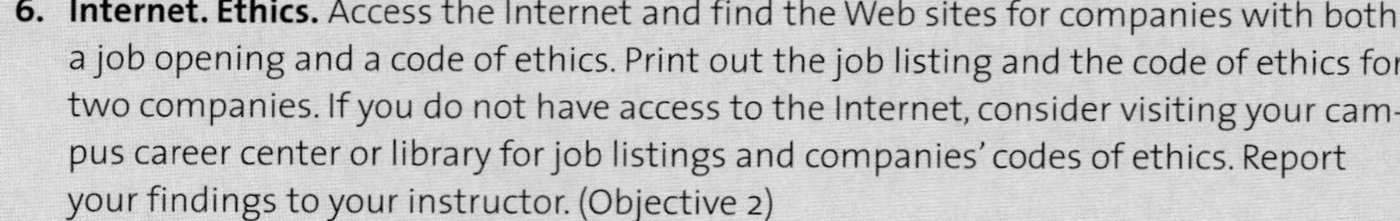

6. **Internet. Ethics.** Access the Internet and find the Web sites for companies with both a job opening and a code of ethics. Print out the job listing and the code of ethics for two companies. If you do not have access to the Internet, consider visiting your campus career center or library for job listings and companies' codes of ethics. Report your findings to your instructor. (Objective 2)

7. **E-mail. Teamwork.** Form a group of two to three students and review the listings in the classified ads section of a local or regional newspaper. Assess the employment opportunities. Summarize your findings in a presentation to your class and an e-mail message or memo to your instructor. (Objective 2)
8. List the names of individuals in your personal network of friends, relatives, instructors, and acquaintances who you think could be valuable to you in a job search and develop a reference list. (Objectives 1 and 3)
9. Assume that you will graduate soon. Using actual information and assuming the course work, activities, and experience you will have between now and then, analyze your qualifications following the recommendations given in this chapter. (Objective 1)
10. Using the information gathered in Exercise 5, prepare a general resume in chronological format. (Objective 3)

11. **Internet.** Access the job opportunities on the Internet or the employment sections of various newspapers, and assess the job opportunities and salaries in your field for positions located in three different states. Using the Salary Calculator at **http://www.homefair.com/homefair/cmr/salcalc.html** or information found at your library or campus career center, compare the salary and cost of living in the three states. Report your findings to your instructor. (Objective 2)
12. Using the information gathered in Exercise 7, prepare a combination resume. (Objective 3)
13. Prepare a targeted resume in chronological format to apply for a job in your field based on an analysis of the job and its requirements and on the information obtained in Exercise 7. (Objective 3)

14. **E-mail.** Develop a scannable resume and e-mail your instructor a copy. (Objective 4)

There are Web exercises at **http://krizan.swcollege.com** to accompany this chapter.

MESSAGE ANALYSIS

Revise and improve the following Experience section for the resume of an individual applying for a human resources management position in an international company that does business in North and South America.

MY EXPERIENCE RECORD

Hayward, Chappel Insurance Agency. Newark, California. 6/95-5/97. Customer Service Representative. Handled new policies and over 100 current policies. Update client files. Recommend improvements in the management of customer policies and translated training manual into Spanish. Train new service representatives. Brunswick Brothers, Inc. South American Division, San Ramon, California. May 1997-present. Financial Analyst and Human Resources. Organize and analyze general and administrative expenses. Update and maintained forecast. Conduct weekly training on worker's compensation reports. Evaluated and completed employment verifications. Use Spanish in working with clients as well as fellow colleagues in Argentina and Chile. 6/94-6/95. Lee and Sons Company. San Jose, California. Human Resources internship through San Jose State University. Recruited employees; developed training program and wrote project on how to train. Designed transfer program.

GRAMMAR WORKSHOP

Correct the grammar, spelling, punctuation, style, and word choice errors in the following sentences:

1. Any one in the class can delegate work to Angela Low or I.
2. The audit report recommended that the fileing procedures are revised; this recommendation makes me eager!
3. One of the new printers in our office are broken.
4. The major advantage for telecommuting are as follows; savings in gasoline; reduction in pollution; and an decrease in traffic congestion.
5. IBM; Xerox; Motorola; and AT&T combined forces, and contributed computer equipment to the 1996 Atlanta Olympic Games.
6. The library of congress in Washington dc is the worlds' largest library.
7. London's Heathrow air port is the busiest air port in Europe.
8. South Africa has a coast line along both the atlantic and pacific oceans.
9. To be a successfull Employee in the Software industry you must work eighty hours per week.
10. The Chinese women interviewed did however feel that things was getting better and she thought their would be lesser problems for their daughter's.

CHAPTER

17 Employment Communication and Interviewing

Pam Hay,
Campus Program Manager,
Agilent Technologies

LET'S TALK BUSINESS In my various staffing and recruiting roles at Hewlett-Packard Company and now at Agilent Technologies, I have had the opportunity to advise candidates on how to prepare for the job search and interview. Companies receive a high volume of inquiries, and students must do certain things to distinguish themselves from the other applicants.

First of all, it's important for you to correspond via the method preferred by the company. For example, many companies today prefer to receive inquiries via the Web or e-mail as opposed to hard-copy letters and resumes. Since much of this information will be scanned at some point, stick with a common format that is easily read and scanned. Limiting letters to one page may also increase your chances that the letter will be read.

(Continued)

[LEARNING OBJECTIVES]

[1] WRITE EFFECTIVE LETTERS OF APPLICATION FOR SOLICITED AND UNSOLICITED POSITIONS.

[2] PREPARE FOR A SUCCESSFUL JOB INTERVIEW.

[3] COMPOSE A VARIETY OF FOLLOW-UP LETTERS AND OTHER MESSAGES RELATED TO EMPLOYMENT.

With regard to content, make sure you are specific with the objective of the letter or message. If you are looking for a position as a computer programmer, say so and mention any experience or training you have had in terms of results. If you are responding to a specific ad, include any information requested in the ad, such as a job title or job number. Also, if someone has referred you, be sure to mention that person early in the message. In addition, although it probably won't be a "make it or break it" item, be sure you have done a thorough review of grammar and spelling. If this is not your best area, ask someone else to help you with it.

One last area is timing. If you are responding to an ad or following up on a call or interview, make sure that you do so in a timely manner, preferably within a few days of the ad or event. This is especially important in cases where employment decisions will be made within days (or even hours).

Today, with the plethora of information available via the Web, interviewees have many tools available to help them prepare for an interview. Since the information is so available, companies may also have higher expectations of interviewees. Prior to your interview, be sure that you have reviewed a company's Web site and can intelligently show that you have done so. Some sites even offer interview tips or sample questions that can help with your preparation. You should also be ready to highlight your accomplishments in terms of measurable results (i.e., time or dollars saved), give examples of team projects focusing on those where you played a leadership role, and be able to talk about key "learnings" from jobs or projects which were especially challenging for you. In addition, being able to talk about your career goals and/or objectives will demonstrate that you have considered the future and where you see your contributions will be. Bring a list of questions to the interview, and prior to leaving, make sure you understand the "next steps" and timeframe/method for follow-up. •

The first three steps in your job campaign were covered in Chapter 16—analyzing your qualifications, obtaining information about employment, and developing a resume. You are now ready for the next three steps: writing application letters, interviewing for positions, and conducting follow-up communications. These steps are covered in this chapter.

Writing Application Letters

[NOTE 17.1]
Sell yourself in an application letter.

Once your resume is completed, you are ready to write a more personal selling tool—an application letter. An **application letter**, which functions as a cover letter in the transmittal of your resume, is a sales letter—with *you* as the product. The application letter is the opportunity to make some important points that you cannot cover in a one-page resume. A strong letter of application will lend support to your resume. Follow the guidelines for persuasive messages given in Chapter 16 for developing application letters. An application letter and resume make up the application package for your job campaign.

Learning Objective [1]
WRITE EFFECTIVE LETTERS OF APPLICATION FOR SOLICITED AND UNSOLICITED POSITIONS.

[NOTE 17.2]
Application letters may be either general or targeted.

Application letters can be either general or targeted, as are resumes. Again, the choice depends on whether you are seeking a solicited or an unsolicited position. If a position has been advertised and you are applying for a specific position, then use the targeted application letter. If you are not sure if an opening or openings in the company are available, then a general letter may be appropriate. In some situations you may be able to combine a general resume and a targeted application letter into an effective application package.

[NOTE 17.3]
The major parts of an application letter are the opening, summary of qualifications, and request for an interview.

There are three major parts in a well-designed application letter:

- An opening that gets favorable attention
- A summary of qualifications that is related to job requirements
- A request for an interview

The primary purpose of an application letter is to motivate a potential employer to read your resume. Then, you hope the employer's reading of your letter and resume will result in your getting an interview. The three major parts of an application letter are discussed in the following sections.

GAINING ATTENTION IN THE OPENING

[NOTE 17.4]
The opening should gain favorable attention and provide transition.

In the opening, you want to gain the favorable attention of your reader—get him or her to read the remainder of the application letter. Also, you want to provide information on why you are writing—provide orientation and transition for the reader.

You can indicate, for example, that you are applying for a position that is listed with your campus career center, is advertised in the newspaper, is recommended by a current employee of the organization, or is unsolicited. Provide for this transition in the first sentence or no later than the second sentence.

There are creative and traditional attention-getting openings for application letters. Your analysis of your reader and the position you are seeking will guide you in determining what kind of opening you should use. If the opening has been advertised, use a direct approach. If you are not sure if an opening in the company is available, then use the indirect approach. Here are examples of openings:

[NOTE 17.5]
Example openings for
- An unsolicited position
- A solicited position

[1] Are you interested in a hard worker with a solid record of accomplishment for your management trainee program?

[2] Please compare my qualifications with the job requirements for the auditor's position that you advertised in the May issue of the *AAA Journal.* Consider me an applicant for the position.

[3] Creative! Knowledgeable! Organized! Just what you want in a new copywriter for Lo's Advertising Agency.

• An unsolicited position

[4] Mr. Bill McMonigle, Manager of your Budget Office, recommended that I apply for the position of assistant budget analyst you have open in the Center for Community Affairs. Please note how well my qualifications, as described in the enclosed resume, match the job requirements of your opening.

• A solicited position

CONVINCING AN EMPLOYER THAT YOU FIT THE JOB

The purpose of the second major part of an application letter is to convince a potential employer that you fit the job requirements of the position you are seeking. This is the most important part of your letter. In it, you should show how employing you will benefit the employer. As in a resume, you will want to emphasize your accomplishments.

[NOTE 17.6]
Show the employer how you fit the job.

In this section of an application letter you should (1) state your education qualifications as they relate to the job requirements; (2) review your work experience as it relates to the job requirements; and (3) specify other qualifications that relate to the job requirements. The order of content may vary in different application letters. The intent, however, is to compose a clear, concise, concrete, and convincing paragraph or two that will motivate the employer to look closely at your resume. Here is an example of the second part of an application letter:

[NOTE 17.7]
Specify job requirements, review qualifications, and refer to your resume.

> I will be graduating with a Bachelor of Science degree in Business Administration with a major in Marketing this June. By choosing this major, I was able to take sales and marketing courses that have prepared me for this position. My senior project, entitled "Developing a Marketing Plan for Small Businesses" has enabled me to develop expertise that will help your firm meet its goals.
>
> Mrs. Duong, the experience I offer Total Quality Staffing complements my education and has prepared me further for sales work. During the summers of 1998 through 2000, I sold encyclopedias door to door. My ranking of first in sales in the Western District (a five-state area) and third in the nation during the summer of 2000 indicates my productivity level. During the academic year, I sold hardware part time, earning a major share of the money I needed to pay my educational expenses.
>
> In addition, I believe I have the personal qualities that would fit your organization. I am an energetic, goal-oriented individual who can work effectively with others in team efforts or alone in sales situations.

PROMOTING ACTION IN THE CLOSE

Now you are ready to try to motivate the employer to take action—to read your resume and invite you to an interview. In practically every application letter, you will be trying to get an interview. The way to get an interview is to ask directly for it. This request should be made in a positive, pleasant manner.

[NOTE 17.8]
Motivate the employer to read your resume.

In the close of your application letter, you should make it easy for an employer to invite you to an interview by providing your telephone number and e-mail address and by offering to be at the employer's office at his or her convenience. Even if you do have some limitations on your flexibility—such as another interview

[NOTE 17.9]
Make it easy to call or write you.

[NOTE 17.10]
Be flexible about your availability.

scheduled for one day next week—you can usually work those things out if the employer calls you. Here are examples of appropriate closings for application letters:

[1] I can contribute to the continuing success of Staples; please call me at (957) 555-1400 or e-mail me at eehew@nds.edu so that we can arrange an interview. I would enjoy meeting with you to discuss the possibility of joining your staff.

[2] May I have an interview to discuss this opportunity with you, Ms. Bartel? The possibility of joining the Lafayette Agency is exciting to me. You can reach me at (510) 555-1122 or e-mail me at ggdickson@wsu.edu. I can arrange to meet with you at your office at your convenience.

[3] I would appreciate the opportunity to talk with you about the accounting position at Salvatore's Agency. You may reach me by telephone at (925) 555-1983 or by e-mail at jsn@srvhs.edu. I will be available for an appointment at your convenience.

ADDITIONAL APPLICATION LETTER GUIDELINES

[NOTE 17.11] Application letters should be high quality and brief—generally no more than one page.

The application letters you use in your job campaign must meet the same high standards as resumes for neatness, clarity, and conciseness. Application letters should be brief, generally no more than one page. Before you write the letter, research the company and learn something about the kind of business it is. Analyze your reader, use the you–viewpoint, use the principles of business communication, and follow the guidelines given in Chapter 10 for persuasive messages and the following Communication Note.

COMMUNICATION NOTE

Tips for Writing and Producing Job-Search Correspondence

[1] Design your letter to be work-centered and employer-centered, not self-centered.
[2] Never delegate responsibility for your job search to anyone else. Do all the writing yourself, and take responsibility for following up with employers.
[3] Always address your letters to a specific individual with his or her correct title and business address.
[4] Use high-quality stationery and envelopes.
[5] Keep the letter to one page.
[6] Produce error-free, clean copy.
[7] Tailor your letters for each situation.
[8] Show appreciation to the employer for considering your application, for granting an interview, and so forth.
[9] Always keep your reader in mind.
[10] Be timely.
[11] Be honest.

"Tips for Writing and Producing Job-Search Correspondence," Planning Job Choices 2000, *p. 55.*

Use 8½- by 11-inch bond paper for application letters. The paper should be the same quality and color as was used for your resume. Use a 9- by 12-inch mailing envelope to avoid folding the letter and resume. Many letters, like resumes, are scanned, and the folds may cause the scanner to skip the words caught in the fold.

An application letter should be addressed to a specific person. You may call an organization and ask for the name and address of the person to whom your letter should be addressed. The letter should be individually prepared; never photocopy a general application letter for distribution to prospective employers. If responding to a blind ad, use the simplified block letter format (see Appendix A); do not address an application letter with "To Whom It May Concern."

If you are sending several letters, a word processing program on your computer can be helpful in preparing them so that variable information may be inserted. Proofread your letter carefully for the correct receiver's name, organization, and address. Remember to refer to your enclosed resume (this reference may be elsewhere in the letter). Be sure to keep copies of the letters and resumes sent to each potential employer.

SAMPLE APPLICATION LETTERS

Figure 17.1 shows a general letter that could be addressed to human resources managers at several companies. It is directed at obtaining an unsolicited job.

Figure 17.2 is an example of a targeted letter sent in response to a solicited job announcement. Targeted letters usually are more powerful than general letters; in a targeted letter you can show specifically how you will benefit the employer.

[NOTE 17.12]
General letters can be designed for unsolicited applications.

[NOTE 17.13]
Targeted letters should be used for solicited applications.

Interviewing for a Job

Learning Objective [2]
PREPARE FOR A SUCCESSFUL JOB INTERVIEW.

The goal of sending your application letter and resume was to obtain a job interview. When you find out you are going to have an interview, start your preparation for it. The interview can be one of the most important experiences in your life because it can determine the course of your career. You will want the interview to go as well as possible.

[NOTE 17.14]
Your goal thus far in your job campaign has been to obtain an interview.

[NOTE 17.15]
The interview is the critical step in your job campaign.

PREPARING FOR A JOB INTERVIEW

You have already done a great deal of preparation for your job interview. You have analyzed your qualifications, examined the job market and job requirements, prepared your resume, and written application letters. Through this process you have learned more about yourself. In addition, you have organized this information so that you can talk about it efficiently and logically.

[NOTE 17.16]
Prepare for an interview.

Be Ready to Answer Questions The next step in your preparation is to anticipate all the questions that might be asked in an interview and to prepare generally the answers you will give. Have a friend or relative ask you the questions to give you practice answering.

[NOTE 17.17]
Anticipate questions.

Since you will not know what kind of interview it will be beforehand, you must prepare for both the traditional style and behavioral style interviews. All this

Figure 17.1
General Application Letter for Management Trainee Position From Applicant With Limited Work Experience

The letter is addressed to the appropriate individual.

The opening gains favorable attention and provides reader information on why you are writing.

The review of qualifications emphasizes accomplishments and positive personal attributes.

Limited work experience is presented positively.

The close motivates employer to offer an interview; it includes a reference to the resume.

71 Crestview Drive
Columbia, MO 65211
June 1, 200–

Ms. Leah Lemmerman
Department of Human Resources
Lorman Engineering Software, Inc.
1004 East 24th Avenue
New York, NY 10011-0786

Dear Ms. Lemmerman:

Is your company looking for a salesperson for your South American market who has a thorough knowledge of marketing and selling engineering computer software, is willing to work hard, is fluent in Spanish, and gets along well with people? If it is, please consider my application for employment.

During my University of Missouri education, I completed a Bachelor of Science degree in International Business Marketing with a minor in engineering. This major, along with my minor, enabled me to take courses in marketing in our global society, business administration, and general engineering. The Department of International Business Marketing at the University of Missouri is rated highly, and its graduates have been successful. My extracurricular activities complemented my college course work. As an active member of the American Marketing Club, I served as chairperson of the Membership Committee. I also served as vice president of the Engineering Software Club. The knowledge I acquired and the work habits I developed in these leadership roles would serve your company well.

My senior project was to design a sales marketing plan for a local company that has begun to market its computer software to China and Mexico. With the assistance of my project advisor, Dr. Iman, and my team members, I developed the plan for the company.

If these highlights of my qualifications and the additional information in the enclosed resume describe what you want in a engineering computer software salesperson, please call me at (573) 555-3311 or e-mail me at rcbrown@um.edu to arrange an interview. I can come to your office at any time convenient to you.

Sincerely,

Russell Craig Brown

Russell Craig Brown

Enclosure: Resume

Figure 17.2
Targeted Application Letter for a Human Resources Position From an Applicant Who Is a Recent College Graduate

111 Claremont Avenue
San Jose, CA 95018
November 3, 2001

This targeted letter is designed for one specific job application.

Mrs. Peggy Read, President
The Capital Group
3300 Dover Street
Cupertino, CA 95015

It is addressed to the appropriate person.

Dear Mrs. Read:

Please accept this letter and resume as my application for the Human Resources position you posted in the Career Center at San Jose State University, San Jose, on November 1, 2001. I believe that my qualifications and experiences match the requirements for the position.

The positive opening provides transition and gains favorable attention.

As shown on the enclosed resume, I will be graduating in December 2001, with a Bachelor of Science degree in Business Administration. The Management and Human Resources major has given me the opportunity to complete courses in employee compensation, benefits analysis, information systems technology, and training and development.

A reference to the resume is included.

My internship in human resources at Tools-R-Us located in Cupertino, California, gave me an opportunity to learn the many facets of a human resources department. While participating as an intern, I was able to assemble a manual for new hires and to conduct a new employee training session. Working for a small business gave me an opportunity to apply the theory from my class work.

As a student, I participated as a member of the cross-country team and was elected team captain. As team captain, my responsibilities included not only leading the team in the championship finals, but also maintaining the scoring sheets and attendance records. The organizational skills learned as the team captain have helped me prepare for the Human Resources position that you have advertised.

The applicant's qualifications that relate directly to the job are reviewed and emphasized.

I would appreciate the opportunity to talk with you about the Human Resources position. You may reach me by telephone at (908) 555-1762 or by e-mail at tja5@net.com. I will be available for an appointment at your convenience.

The close promotes employer action.

Sincerely,

Mr. Tony J. Abulario

Mr. Tony J. Abulario

Enclosure

COMMUNICATION QUOTE

What Do You Look for When You Hire People?

In a small company we need people who are flexible, people who will say, "That wasn't in my job description but it needed to be done." We need people who are willing to accept change. The big thing I look for is a willingness to accept responsibility. When job applicants talk about what was wrong at their old company, I want to know what they did to try to help make things right. It's easy to point out what is wrong, but harder to act to improve things.

I look for communication skills—how well they present themselves, and I expect their writing and speaking skills to be good. I also look for creativity. Are they going to plug along and just do everything I tell them to, or are they going to come up with some good ideas too?

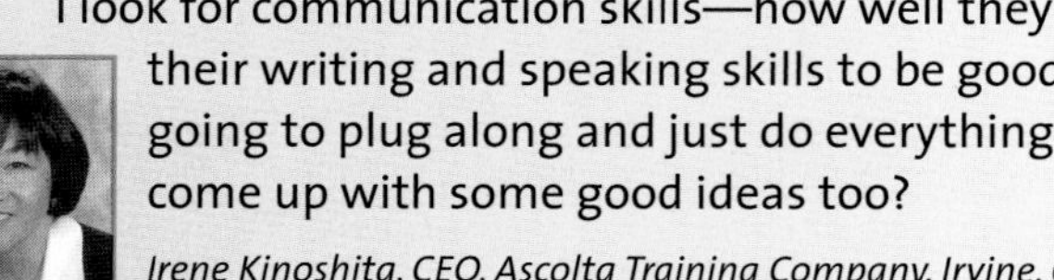

Irene Kinoshita, CEO, Ascolta Training Company, Irvine, California, ***http://www.ascoltatraining.com***.

is important preparation for representing yourself in an interview because both types of questions may be asked of you.

Traditional Style Interviews **Traditional style interviews** are designed to find out about your education and experience. Many companies will use the traditional style interview to determine whether you have the background to fill the position. Have your answers ready for these questions, which will focus on your education and work experiences. Examples of questions that may be asked are as follows:

Traditional Style Interview Questions

Character

[1] Tell me about yourself.

[2] What is your greatest strength?

[3] What is your greatest weakness?

[4] Who are your role models? Why?

[5] Where do you want to be in five years? Ten years?

[6] How does your college education or work experience relate to this job?

[7] Give me three words that best describe you.

[8] What motivates you?

[9] What can you offer us?

[10] Why should we hire you rather than another candidate?

Education

[11] Why did you choose to attend your college or university?

[12] Why did you choose your major? Minor?

[13] Tell me about your education at . . .

[14] What is your GPA?

[15] Tell me about your course work.

[16] Tell me about your extracurricular activities while you were in school.

[17] Tell me about your involvement with your professional organization.

[18] Do your grades accurately reflect your ability? Why or why not?

[19] Were you financially responsible for any portion of your college education?

[20] Do you have plans to get additional education?

Experience

[21] Why did you choose this field of work?

[22] What job-related skills have you developed?

[23] For what kind of supervisor do you like to work?

[24] Do you consider yourself ambitious?

[25] What do you think should determine the progress a person makes in a company?

[26] What does *teamwork* mean to you?

[27] What did you do on your job at ___________?

[28] Have you ever quit a job? Why?

[29] What did you like least in your job at ___________?

[30] Have you ever done any volunteer work? What kind?

Career Goals

[31] How important is money to you?

[32] Do you like to work alone or with other people? Why?

[33] Are you willing to relocate?

[34] You are younger than most of the people you will supervise. What problems might this pose? How will you resolve them?

[35] What salary do you expect to receive in this job?

Behavioral Style Interviews Today more companies are using the **behavioral style interview**, which is designed to focus on an applicant's past actions and behaviors in order to determine how he or she will perform in the future. Employers support this style of interview because they have found that past behaviors predict future behaviors. You can prepare for these interviews by reviewing previous situations at school or at work and how you handled them. Examples of questions that may be asked are as follows:

Behavioral Style Interview Questions

[1] Describe a major problem you had with an employee at work and how you handled it. Describe at what point you decided to confront this employee at work.

[2] Describe a situation where you were working as a team member on a class project and a student on the team was not doing his or her work. Explain how you handled the situation. Explain what happened at the end of the project.

[3] Describe the most difficult challenge you have faced. Explain why you believe you met or failed to meet that challenge.

[4] Describe a situation in which you were successful (or unsuccessful) in motivating someone.

[5] Describe a situation at work or at school where you took the initiative. What was the result? How did you feel?

Remember that the traditional interview will focus on how you *would* handle a particular situation whereas the behavioral interview focuses on how you *did* handle a particular situation.

Answering Questions For all interviews you must be honest, sincere, positive, and enthusiastic when answering. Be yourself, be polite, and be attentive. Relate your answers to the job for which you are applying. Take advantage of the opportunity to show your knowledge of the company and the position. Your answers should be brief, but not just yes or no. For example, in answering the question, "Do you have plans to get additional education" you might say, "Yes, I think it is important to keep up to date. I am interested in taking short continuing education courses and, in a few years, working on an MBA degree." In response to, "What do you consider to be your weaknesses?" you might say after reflecting for a moment, "Well, some people may think I am reserved, but thinking before acting has helped me relate effectively to others." Remember to turn your weaknesses into strengths.

[NOTE 17.18] Be prepared to handle illegal questions.

Handling Illegal Questions Remember that various federal, state, and local laws regulate the questions a prospective employer can ask; the questions must be related to the tasks you would be performing on the job you are seeking. According to Rochelle Kaplan, General Counsel for the National Association of Colleges and Employers, you have three options for handling illegal questions:

[1] You can answer the questions—you are free to do so if you wish.

[2] You can refuse to answer the questions, which is well within your rights.

[3] You can examine the questions for their *intent* and respond with answers as they might apply to the job.[1]

[NOTE 17.19] Discuss salary, if appropriate.

Be Prepared to Discuss Salary The salary question—the last one on the list of traditional style interview questions—is an important one. Be ready to answer it. The employer may have set a salary or a salary range for the position. You should try to get that information before the interview if you can. Also, you should try to learn before the interview what salaries are being paid for similar jobs in the employer's geographic area. Your campus career center or the Salary Calculator Web site at **http://www.homefair.com/homefair/cmr/salcalc.html** are good sources for salary information. Newspaper employment ads sometimes carry this information, too. If pinned down to a specific answer, respond in a straightforward, objective manner. You might say, "Apparently the starting salaries for this kind of position range from $____________ to $____________. In comparing my qualifications with others in or entering the job market, I would hope to start at $____________." If you do not

[1] Rochelle Kaplan, "Handling Illegal Questions," *Planning Job Choices 2000,* pp. 66–67.

Mention your strengths in the interview. If computer capabilities are your strengths, stress these.

feel pressured to give a specific answer, you might say, "I would want a salary that is appropriate for my education and experience."

Be Ready to Ask Questions You should have some key questions of your own for the interviewer. Do not just concentrate on questions of personal benefit to you, such as ones about fringe benefits, retirement programs, vacation policies, and salary. Your questions might be about such subjects as job duties, the employee evaluation system, management philosophy, company progress and plans, promotion policies, and employee development programs. Examples of questions you may ask are as follows:

[NOTE 17.20]
Ask questions.

[1] Please describe the duties of the job for me.

[2] Would you describe the normal routine of this position? Describe a typical day.

[3] What kinds of job assignments might I expect the first six months on the job?

[4] How is job performance evaluated and how often?

[5] How much travel is normally expected? Is a car provided?

[6] Describe your relocation policy.

[7] Do you have plans for expansion?

[8] Does your company encourage further education?

[9] When do you expect to make a decision?

[10] Where do we go from here?

Research the Company Learn as much as you can about the company prior to the interview. Secure descriptive materials on the company and its industry from the company, your campus career center, the library, the chamber of commerce, the Better Business Bureau, a trade association, or the Web.

[NOTE 17.21]
Learn all you can about the company.

The Web has many sources of information. You may check to see if the company has its own Web site by simply keying in www.(company name).com; this site can be a valuable source of company information. The Monster Board at **http://www.monster.com** has company profiles of over 4,000 employers. Another source for company information is Career Path.com at **http://www.careerpath.com**, with mini–home pages for some of the leading employers in the United States. Study these materials carefully. A thorough preparation of this kind will help you in the interview in two basic ways: It will aid your communication with the interviewer, and it will set you apart from the other interviewees who learned nothing about the company prior to an interview. Examples of questions you should ask about the organization are as follows:

[1] What is the size of the organization or company?

[2] Describe growth prospects for the company.

[3] What is the percent of annual sales growth in the last five years?

[4] What type of service or products does the company offer?

[5] What are the strengths and weaknesses of the company?

[6] What is the organizational structure?

[7] Is the company an international company?

[8] What is the corporate culture of the company? Does it match your personality?

[9] What are the typical career paths and advancement opportunities offered by the company in your field?

[10] What is the salary range for the position?

[11] How long has the company been in business?

[NOTE 17.22] Organize yourself personally; build your confidence.

Prepare Yourself Personally Choose your clothes carefully, give attention to personal grooming, and avoid wearing heavy jewelry or strong colognes. The interviewer(s) may be dressed in more casual clothing; however, employers expect that you dress in a conservative business style for an interview. Wear the clothing at least once before the interview to be sure it is comfortable. Appropriate dress is as follows:

Men

- Two-piece conservative suit in a solid color such as blue or gray.
- White shirt with a tie in a plain or simple pattern.
- Polished shoes with socks that match the suit. Remember your belt should match your shoes.

Women

- Two-piece conservative suit with a knee-length or longer skirt in a solid color such as blue or gray. Pants are not recommended for interviews unless you have been told they are appropriate.
- White blouse with modest jewelry.
- Polished shoes with plain hosiery. Remember your belt should match your shoes.

Many companies are now suggesting to students that they dress in business or office casual for one of the interviews at the company. Since business casual can vary greatly from company to company, follow the following guidelines:

Men

- Sport coat and belted slacks
- Collared shirt
- Polished shoes and matching socks
- A tie is optional; however, you may want to carry one in your coat pocket

Women

- Sport coat and belted slacks
- Blouse
- Hosiery and polished shoes

Remember to be modest with the use of jewelry and cologne. Students should always dress very professionally for an interview even if they know the employer will be wearing jeans.

Practice walking, sitting and rising, and shaking hands for the interview. Plan your schedule so that you arrive early. Allow time for heavy traffic, a flat tire, or other delays. Take a portfolio with the following materials: two copies of your resume, a copy of your transcript, examples of your course work and work projects, letters of reference, a reference list, and an application form with all the important details regarding former employers, addresses, phone numbers, and so on. In addition, take a pen and a small notebook to record notes about the position and the names of the people you have met. Ask for business cards so you can send a thank-you letter immediately after the interview.

Talk (mentally) to yourself. Build your confidence by telling yourself that you have done all you can to prepare for the interview. You have anticipated questions and have prepared answers, you have learned about the company, and you have prepared yourself personally. You are ready for the interview.

An effective exchange of information takes place in a successful job interview.

PARTICIPATING IN AN INTERVIEW

[NOTE 17.23] Some nervousness is natural and helpful.

An interview should be viewed as an opportunity to share your qualifications with someone who is interested. View the interview as important, but not so important that you become overly nervous. Some nervousness is natural and helpful to you; but too much nervousness will make a poor impression. Plan to do some practice interviewing; videotape it and evaluate your performance. Before you begin the interview, read the ten steps to a successful interview outlined in the following Communication Note.

COMMUNICATION NOTE

Ten Steps to a Successful Interview

[1] Arrive on time.
[2] Introduce yourself in a courteous manner.
[3] Read company materials while you wait.
[4] Have a firm handshake.
[5] Use body language to show interest.
[6] Listen.
[7] Smile, nod, and give nonverbal feedback to the interviewer.
[8] Ask about the next step in the process.
[9] Thank the interviewer.
[10] Write a thank-you letter to anyone with whom you have spoken.

As reported in "The Successful Job Interview: KNOW the Company," Planning Job Choices: 1997, *1997, p. E65.*

[NOTE 17.24] Greet the interviewer warmly; let the interviewer take the lead.

Greet your interviewer warmly by name, pronouncing the name correctly. Let the interviewer take the lead. If an offer is made to shake hands, do so with a firm grip and a smile. Sit when asked to do so. See your role as primarily responding to questions in a businesslike fashion. Keep appropriate eye contact with the interviewer. The amount of appropriate eye contact with interviewers will vary depending on their cultural backgrounds; 75 percent of the time is a good goal for interviews with Americans. Other cultural variations that are important in interviews include many verbal and nonverbal communication considerations (see Chapter 2 for further information).

[NOTE 17.25] Show your knowledge and interest.

The interviewer may intentionally challenge you by asking difficult questions or by appearing disinterested or even irritated. Be knowledgeable, calm, positive, gracious, and friendly.

[NOTE 17.26] Be friendly, positive, and level-headed.

During the interview avoid appearing

- Overly aggressive or conceited
- Meek and mild
- Negative about past employers or other topics
- Unenthusiastic
- Too interested in money
- Too ambitious
- Humorless

- Too vague with answers
- Unappreciative of the interviewer's time

Don't smoke, chew gum, eat your lunch, lean back in the chair, act immature, or laugh nervously.

Be alert for signals that the interview is ending. The interviewer may slide her or his chair back, stand, or send you verbal signals. When the interview is over, express appreciation for the time and information given you. Indicate that you look forward to hearing from the interviewer. Shake hands and warmly tell the interviewer goodbye.

[NOTE 17.27]
End the interview appropriately.

After the interview, evaluate your performance. Make written notes of those things that went well and those that you will change the next time you interview. Make a record of the information you learned about the job for comparison with other job opportunities. Record the correct spellings of the names and titles of those who interviewed you, and note what you will want to say in your follow-up communication.

[NOTE 17.28]
After the interview, evaluate.

TYPES OF INTERVIEWS

Regardless of the kind of interview, interviews are usually set up at a mutually agreeable time for applicant and employer. One interview may cover two or more interview stages; some businesses only will interview a candidate once, maybe twice. With the increasing use of computers today, some interviews are conducted using a video conferencing or online computer system. Group interviews as well as individual interviews may be used to assess your qualifications and to determine whether you can fill the position adequately.

[NOTE 17.29]
Interviews will be prearranged.

Screening Interviews The **screening interview**, sometimes called a *preliminary interview,* is designed to find out whether you have the required education, work experience, communication skills, and personality needed for the position. Screening interviews may take place in the campus career center or in the employer's office. In some cases, the screening interview will be conducted by the use of a telephone or telephone conferencing system. This interview will start with traditional style interviewing questions and may be followed by behavioral style interviewing questions. Most of these interviews will be conducted by one or two human resource employees. If you make a favorable impression on the interviewer(s), you may be asked to the second interview. Also, note that some employers do not hold screening interviews; the screening of resumes and application letters can suffice.

Subsequent Interviews After you have passed the screening interview, you may be invited to a company's office for an additional one or more interviews. The subsequent interviews may include meeting with several individuals in the company separately and/or as a team on a panel. Panel or team interviews are conducted by a group of employees and may include a human resource person, a potential supervisor, and potential colleagues. When you are involved with a panel interview, eye contact with the questioner is necessary. Be prepared to answer questions from each interviewer. Always bring a paper and pencil with you so that you can write down the various names of the interviewers.

Video Interviews A newer form of interviewing uses a video conferencing system. Video interviews have become more popular because they allow companies to interview new recruits at colleges more economically. If you are to participate in a video interview, your campus career center will provide you with the information on where the interview will take place. Many universities have their own video conferencing centers.

Online Interviews Online interviewing uses a combination of video, camera, computer, and the Internet. Online interviewing may become more popular because of advancing technology. These interviews can be conducted by either an individual or a team. Online interviewing enables employers to screen candidates rapidly and to cut interview costs.

Group Interviews With group interviews several people are interviewed at the same time for the same position(s). Companies use this method to determine how a potential employee will interact in a group situation and to evaluate the potential employee's interactive skills. Disney and various airline companies conduct group interviews.

The decision as to whether you will be offered the job will be made as a result of the interview. Your decision as to whether you will accept an offer may be made at this time. Regardless of the kind of job interview, the interview is a critical juncture in your job campaign.

COMMUNICATION QUOTE

Tapping the Web as an information resource will prove very beneficial in your preparation for an interview, for negotiating job offers, or for preparing your cover letter. Read the organization's Web pages to see how they describe themselves and what new services or products they offer. Check out salary surveys and competitive job listings to see if your salary offer is in the ballpark for the market and your level of experience. Use the

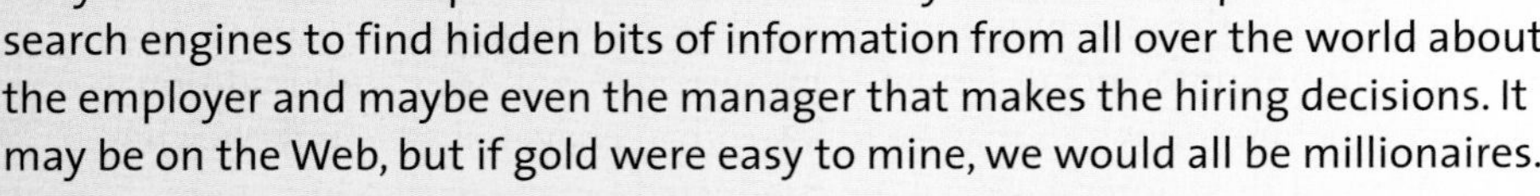

search engines to find hidden bits of information from all over the world about the employer and maybe even the manager that makes the hiring decisions. It may be on the Web, but if gold were easy to mine, we would all be millionaires.

Margaret F. Riley Dikel, Author, The Riley Guide, ***http://www.dbm.com/jobguide***.

Learning Objective [3]
COMPOSE A VARIETY OF FOLLOW-UP LETTERS AND OTHER MESSAGES RELATED TO EMPLOYMENT.

Preparing Other Employment Communications

[NOTE 17.30]
Employment-related communication may involve telephone calls, letters, or in-person contacts.

Employment communication is not limited to resumes, application letters, and interviews. Other employment communication can include telephone calls, letters, e-mail, and in-person contacts. You may need to follow up on a pending application or communicate your acceptance of an invitation for an interview. You may want some kind of follow-up contact after an interview. It will be necessary to communicate your rejection or acceptance of a job offer. If you accept a job, you may need to resign from another job. Finally, you should express appreciation to all those who assisted you in your job campaign. Suggestions for composing these communications are given in the following sections.

FOLLOWING UP AN APPLICATION

If you think it has been too long since you heard about your application with an employer, you may want to initiate a follow-up contact after a couple of weeks. Remember, many unsolicited applications are not acknowledged. Your follow-up contact, depending on the circumstances, can be by letter, in person, or by telephone (be prepared to leave your message on an answering machine or in voice mail). Such a message would be neutral news for the employer; consequently, the direct plan should be used. Here is an example of such a follow-up message:

[NOTE 17.31]
You may want to follow up an application.

> In March I sent you an application for a position in your marketing department. I am still very much interested in employment with Seagate Computer Sales.
>
> Since March, I have completed my Bachelor of Science degree in Business Administration with a major in Marketing. During May, I was selected as the outstanding member of the Marketing Club on campus.
>
> If you need any additional information, please telephone me at (716) 555-2995 or e-mail me at dyknow@ccuicon.edu. I want you to know that I am very much interested in interviewing for the position you have in marketing.

The examples given in this chapter are of the body of the letter only and do not include dates, inside addresses, salutations, and closings. All employment communications need the appropriate format as shown in Appendix A.

ACCEPTING AN INTERVIEW INVITATION

Most of the time interview invitations will be by telephone; however, more companies are using e-mail to contact potential employees for job interviews. Be prepared to receive this kind of call or e-mail any time during your job campaign and to respond logically, clearly, and maturely. Check your voice mail messages on your home telephone and the information on your e-mail account to be sure that it is professional. Your communication accepting an interview should use the direct plan (for positive news) and should (1) express appreciation, (2) indicate availability, and (3) convey a positive and optimistic attitude. Here is an example of the content for either a written or an oral message:

[NOTE 17.32]
Be prepared to accept an interview invitation.

> Thank you for the opportunity to interview for the position in the Accounting Department. I am very much interested in meeting with you to discuss the position and my qualifications.
>
> Because of my work and class schedules, the best dates for me for the interview are March 7, 9, or 10. I appreciate your asking me for three alternative dates. Any one of them will be fine with me.
>
> I am looking forward to visiting your offices and learning more about the auditing position.

FOLLOWING UP AN INTERVIEW

A letter of appreciation is appropriate after an interview. If a company has been corresponding with you using e-mail, then it is acceptable that you send an e-mail thank-you letter. This letter should be sent within one or two days following the interview. If you think you are still interested in the position, you should express

[NOTE 17.33]
Following up an interview is appropriate.

that interest in the letter. If you are definitely not interested in the position, a letter of appreciation for the interview is still appropriate. In the latter case, in fairness to the employer, you should withdraw your candidacy. The letter in which you express your continuing interest should use the direct plan, and the letter in which you withdraw your candidacy should use the indirect plan. These letters should be brief, cordial, businesslike, and typewritten. An example of a follow-up thank-you letter for a position you wish to obtain is shown in Figure 17.3.

Figure 17.3
A Letter of Appreciation for a Job Interview

4810 Dickens Court
Walnut Creek, CA 94596
925-555-2688
Fax: 925-555-6689
rrsherman1@aol.com

May 6, 200–

Mr. David Rice
Oberman's Manufacturing
3909 Maui Terrace
Modesto, CA 95355

Dear Mr. Rice:

Shows appreciation for time spent during interview.

Thank you for taking the time last Monday to interview me for the operations management position. Please extend my thanks to the other members of the interview committee.

Very specific about the contribution the candidate can make for the position.

After spending the morning discussing the operations management position with you, I am very enthusiastic about the possibility of working for Oberman's Manufacturing Corporation. I believe my strong computer skills and previous work experience would make me a valuable member of your company.

The close provides easy access to the candidate.

If you have any questions or need additional information, please telephone me at (925) 555-2688 or e-mail me at rrsherman1@aol.com.

Sincerely,

Rosa Randall Sherman

Rosa Randall Sherman

ACCEPTING EMPLOYMENT

[Note 17.34]
Use the direct plan when accepting employment.

The communications offering employment and accepting employment most likely will be by telephone or in person, followed by confirming letters. A letter accepting employment is a positive communication and should use the direct plan: (1) The offer should be accepted, (2) any essential information about assuming the position should come next, and (3) an expression of appreciation should close the letter. A confirming acceptance letter might look like this:

> I am pleased to confirm my acceptance of the sales position with Mead Packaging Corporation. Enclosed you will find a signed copy of the offer letter.
>
> It is my understanding that this position pays a salary of $2,250 per month and a 10 percent commission on sales. As agreed, I will report at 8 a.m. on June 20, 200– to Mrs. Elaina Mecklenburg in Building F, Room 200.
>
> Thank you for this opportunity. I am eager to begin work with you.

REJECTING EMPLOYMENT

As is the case with accepting employment, the first communication related to rejecting employment most likely will be by telephone. An indirect message following up an oral employment rejection may be appropriate. This letter should be brief, cordial, businesslike, and typewritten. A letter rejecting employment might look like this:

[NOTE 17.35]
Employment rejection messages should use the indirect plan.

> Thank you for offering me the position of customer service representative with Spectrum Laboratory. I appreciate your taking the time to interview me for the position and giving me the time to consider your offer.
>
> The position at Spectrum Laboratory sounds very interesting; however, I have been offered a similar position at Access Laboratory. Since Access Laboratory is located closer to my home and will not involve commuting, I believe it is the best choice for me at this time in my career.
>
> Thank you for this opportunity. It was a pleasure meeting you and your excellent staff.

EXPRESSING APPRECIATION TO REFERENCES AND OTHERS

When you have completed a successful job campaign and accepted an employment offer, share the good news with your references. Also, it will be important to notify any placement service and others who assisted you. These expressions of appreciation for assistance may be by telephone, by e-mail, by letter, or in person.

[NOTE 17.36]
Thank those who helped in your job campaign.

RESIGNING FROM A JOB

Once your job campaign is completed, it may be necessary to resign from your present position. It is best that your resignation not be a surprise for your employer. If you can, let your employer know that you have applied for another position while you are searching. If you think your employer would react negatively to your search for another position, you may want to keep your job search confidential.

Most resignations will be oral and in person. The employer may then request that you put your resignation in writing. Be sure to give your employer the amount of notice required in company policy. In most cases a resignation would be a negative message. Here is an example of a resignation letter written using the direct plan:

[NOTE 17.37]
Most resignations will use the indirect plan.

> Please accept this letter as official resignation from my position as a human resource intern, effective Friday, January 15, 200–.
>
> I have enjoyed working here as an intern. The practical skills I have obtained have made me competitive in the job market as a new college graduate. I really appreciate the experience and support you have provided.
>
> In my new position as assistant human resources manager, I am sure we will have continuing contact. I look forward to that. Best wishes for continued success with your work.

Summary of Learning Objectives

Learning Objective [1] **Write effective letters of application for solicited and unsolicited positions.** An application letter is a sales letter with *you* as the product. The major parts of an application letter are the opening, the summary of qualifications, and the request for an interview. Remember the primary purpose of an application letter is to motivate a potential employer to read your resume and then invite you for an interview.

Learning Objective [2] **Prepare for a successful job interview.** Preparing for an interview includes reviewing information gathered to this point; learning all you can about the company through research at the library, chamber of commerce, or the Web; preparing to ask and answer questions; dressing appropriately for the interview; and participating in the job interview.

Interviews can either be traditional style or behavioral style. Traditional style interviews are designed to find out about your education and experience, and behavioral style interviews are designed to focus on your past actions and behaviors in order to determine how you will perform in the future.

The screening interview is designed to find out whether you have the required education, work experience, communication skills, and personality for the position. Subsequent interviews may include meeting with several individuals in the company separately and/or as a team on a panel. Other kinds of interviews include video, online, and group interviews. The video interview uses a video conferencing system, and the online interview uses a combination of video, camera, computer, and the Internet. Group interviews involve several people being interviewed at the same time for the same position(s).

Learning Objective [3] **Compose a variety of follow-up letters and other messages related to employment.** The other employment messages that you should be able to prepare are as follows: a follow-up to an application letter; an interview acceptance letter; a thank-you letter following a job interview; a job acceptance letter; a letter rejecting employment; and a letter of resignation.

DISCUSSION QUESTIONS

1. Discuss the purpose of developing application letters. Describe the two kinds of application letters. (Objective 1)
2. Describe briefly the purposes of each of the three major parts of an application letter. (Objective 1)
3. Describe how to answer questions during an interview. (Objective 2)
4. How would you answer the question, "What do you consider your weaknesses?" (Objective 2)
5. How should you answer the question, "What salary do you expect for this position?" (Objective 2)
6. What questions should you be prepared to ask during an interview? What questions should you be prepared to answer during an interview? (Objective 2)
7. Describe how you could gather information about a potential employer. Why is it important to have background information on a future employer? (Objective 2)

8. Describe appropriate business casual dress for an interview. (Objective 2)
9. If you were to resign from a job, explain the types of communication you would use. (Objective 3)
10. Is it necessary to send a letter of appreciation after a job interview? Is an e-mail appropriate? Explain. (Objective 3)

APPLICATION EXERCISES

1. Locate an ad in your local newspaper and prepare a targeted application letter to accompany the resume you prepared for Chapter 16. (Objective 1)
2. **Global/Cross Cultural.** Explore business Web sites and find a company with international opportunities for whom you would like to work. Write a general application letter expressing your interest in working for that company. (Objective 1)
3. List your answers to the 35 sample interview questions given in this chapter. (Objective 2)

4. **Teamwork. Ethics.** Form a group of two to three students, and discuss how much salary and the kinds of benefits you could expect if hired as a management trainee. Discuss how you would handle a situation where you were offered a better job with better pay a week after you had accepted another position. (*Hint:* Visit your campus career center for assistance.) (Objective 2)
5. Assume that you submitted an application for a job opening in your field six weeks ago. You are interested in the position and have not heard from the employer since the human resource manager acknowledged receipt of your application letter and resume. Write a letter following up on this application. Assume that since your initial letter you have completed a special course on the Web and have developed an online resume on your own home page. (Objective 3)
6. Assume that you graduated from high school five years ago and have been employed as a teller in a bank while completing your Bachelor of Science degree. Your experience in this position has been excellent, and you have just graduated from college. Your immediate supervisor gave you increasing amounts of responsibility, and you grew professionally. In fact, you did so well that you were the successful candidate for an operations manager position responsible for overseeing tellers in a bank that is a major competitor of your current employer. Your supervisor is aware that you have accepted the new position and has asked that you put your resignation in writing. Write two letters: (a) a letter accepting the new position and (b) a letter resigning from your present position. Create any facts necessary to complete the letters. (Objective 3)
7. Write a letter following up an interview you have had for a job in your field. Assume that you want the position. (Objective 3)
8. Write a letter following up an interview you have had for a job in your field. Assume that you definitely are not interested in the position. (Objective 3)

9. **Teamwork.** Form a group of two or three students, and discuss how you would resign from a job. Draft a letter of resignation. (Objective 3)
10. **E-mail.** Assume your instructor is the manager of the Walmsley Corporation and that you have just completed an interview for a position as computer systems analyst. Send a follow-up thank-you letter to your instructor, via e-mail, expressing appreciation for the interview and letting him or her know you "fit" the position perfectly. (Objective 3)
11. **BusinessLink Video.** *Interviewing: A Study of Hudson's.* As we learned in a previous video, Target Corp., formerly known as the Dayton-Hudson Corporation, with head-

quarters in Minneapolis, is the fourth-largest general merchandise retailer in the United States. The corporation consists of Target, an upscale discount chain; Mervyn's, a middle-market promotional department store; and the Department Store Division, consisting of Dayton's, Hudson's, and Marshall Field's, all upscale department stores. Hudson's is committed to hiring employees with a strong commitment to helping others and serving guests for its new Somerset Hudson's anchor store.

After viewing the video *Interviewing: A Study of Hudson's,* complete the following and submit a memo to your instructor outlining your answers and recommendations:

a. List five skills that Hudson's is looking for in hiring its new employees. Compare your skills to the requirements of Hudson's.

b. Explain how you should prepare for a job interview with Hudson's. Explain positive body language.

c. Describe the characteristics of an effective resume for a position at Hudson's.

d. What is follow-up communication? Explain what Hudson's expects in follow-up communication.

There are Web exercises at **http://krizan.swcollege.com** to accompany this chapter.

MESSAGE ANALYSIS

Rewrite the following application letter. Strengthen the letter's effectiveness.

I am interested in working in your company in any job that you have open. If I can get a job now, I will be ready to go to work now in any position. I am majoring in marketing and minoring in finance at Wake Forest College and hope to graduate in one semester if I pass all my classes. I can do any type of job since I took first line management and supervision. I have been working at Woolworth's Store for two years as a cashier and assistant manager. Before that job I worked three summers as a camp counselor at the YMCA. I also developed training materials for both jobs. If you are interested, please call me. Thanks.

GRAMMAR WORKSHOP

Correct the grammar, spelling, punctuation, style, and word choice errors in the following sentences:

1. Alot of are buisness decisions is empacted by the stockmarket.
2. I appreciated him redecorating my home office already.
3. What affect do you think that the low math test score will have on the quarter' grade.
4. The discount jewelers sell diamond rings real cheap.
5. One of the modems in the 9-201 classroom are broken.
6. Her started teaching english on September 1 1995, and as all ready been promoted to associate Professor.
7. I had worked in swaziland Africa, Yantai china, and Mexico city Mexico.
8. Of the two employers ABC was the most family oriented business.
9. At the department level she was co-advisor of the MBA club; advising students in her office, and she taught job interviewing techniques.
10. Her contributions as a secretary is highly value by the Department.

Business English Seminars

SEMINAR:

A	Parts of Speech
B	Sentence Structure
C	Punctuation
D	Style
E	Word Usage

SEMINAR

Parts of Speech

[NOTE SA.1]
Knowledge of parts of speech will aid you in communicating.

Every word in a sentence has a use or function. Knowing word functions will enable you to select the right word, which in turn will help you communicate your ideas effectively. Your understanding of the parts of speech will aid you in selecting the right word at the right time. The eight parts of speech are as follows:

[1] **Verb**. A word or phrase that describes the action or state of being (or condition) of the subject

[2] **Noun**. A word that names a person, place, or thing

[3] **Pronoun**. A word that takes the place of a noun

[4] **Adjective**. A word that describes or modifies a noun or pronoun

[5] **Adverb**. A word that describes or modifies a verb, an adjective, or another adverb

[6] **Preposition**. A word that connects a noun or pronoun to other words in the sentence

[7] **Conjunction**. A word that joins words, phrases, or clauses

[8] **Interjection**. A word that expresses surprise, emotion, or strong feeling and is not related to other words in the sentence

Verbs

The verb is the most important part of speech in a sentence. It expresses an action or a state of being. Every complete sentence must have a verb. Some sentences—compound and complex—have more than one verb. (Compound and complex sentences are discussed in Seminar B.) When you are constructing sentences, remember that you should build each sentence around the verb.

[NOTE SA.2]
A verb is the most important part of speech.

VERB TYPES

Sentences are constructed using two types of verbs. The two types of verbs are action verbs and state-of-being verbs.

Action Verbs An **action verb** expresses acts. It adds power and precision to your communication. *Audit, invest, join, negotiate, organize, praise, liquidate*, and thousands of other words are action verbs. The action verb is italicized in the following examples:

[NOTE SA.3]
Action verbs are powerful.

Twila *informed* her friends about the accident.

Crude oil prices *rose* nearly $1 a barrel last week.

State-of-Being Verbs A **state-of-being verb** expresses the five senses (*hear, smell, see, taste*, and *touch*). A state-of-being verb is also called a *linking verb*. These verbs join or link one part of a sentence to another. State-of-being verbs are less powerful and less precise than action verbs. Other state-of-being verbs include *is, am, are, was, were, seem, appear, will be*, and *have been*. The state-of-being verbs are in italics in the following examples:

[NOTE SA.4]
State-of-being verbs are used to link parts of sentences.

The stockbroker *saw* her client at the bank.

The new office building *is* the tallest structure in the state.

VERB TENSE

Verb tense indicates the time that action occurs. Six verb tense forms are used to indicate time. The six tenses are categorized into two groups—simple tense and perfect tense.

[NOTE SA.5]
Verb tense indicates the time that action occurs.

Simple Tense Simple tense includes present, past, and future. The time of action or state of being of each simple tense is designated by its name.

[NOTE SA.6]
The three simple tenses are present, past, and future.

Present Tense A **present tense verb** expresses action that is going on at the present time or action that is continuing or habitual. Present tense verbs may also be used to indicate general truths. Verbs showing present tense are in italics in the following examples:

[NOTE SA.7]
Present tense expresses current and continuing action or general truths.

The president *is presenting* his recommendation to the board. (present time)

Nancy *stocks* the fabric department at night. (continuing)

Fax machines *facilitate* communications within organizations. (general truths)

Past Tense A **past tense verb** indicates action that has been completed. Verbs in the past tense have two forms—regular and irregular. The past tense of regular verbs is

[NOTE SA.8]
Past tense expresses completed action.

formed by adding *d* or *ed*. The past tense of irregular verbs is formed by changing the root word. *Regular* and *irregular verbs* in the past tense are shown in italics in these examples:

Robert *learned* to operate the new cash register. (regular—*learn* [root word] + *ed*)

Robert *saved* 10 percent of his pay check each month. (regular—*save* [root word] + *d*)

Karen *taught* Robert to operate the new cash register. (irregular—root word is *teach*)

[NOTE SA.9] Future tense expresses expected action.

Future Tense A **future tense verb** is used to indicate actions that are expected to occur in the future. Future tense is formed by using *will* before the present tense form of the verb. The following sentences show verbs in the future tense in italics:

Rick *will receive* a $100,000 bonus when his company completes the transaction.

Will you *delay* your retirement until next summer?

[NOTE SA.10] The three perfect tenses are present perfect, past perfect, and future perfect.

Perfect Tense A **perfect tense verb** shows action that has been completed at the time the statement is made. The perfect tense requires a form of the verb *have*, along with the past participle of the main verb. (Participles are discussed at the end of this section.) The perfect tenses are present perfect, past perfect, and future perfect.

[NOTE SA.11] Present perfect tense = *has* or *have* + past participle.

Present Perfect Tense A **present perfect tense verb** refers to an action begun in the past and completed in the present. Present perfect tense may also refer to habitual or repeated past action. This tense is formed by adding *has* or *have* to the past participle of the main verb. The following examples show verbs in the present perfect tense in italics:

Mr. Thompson *has served* as the company president for 15 years.

We *have watched* the Super Bowl together since its inception.

Our organization *has donated* time and money to the community's drug center.

[NOTE SA.12] Past perfect tense = *had* + past participle.

Past Perfect Tense A **past perfect tense verb** refers to an action that was completed before another event in the past occurred. This tense is formed by adding *had* to the past participle of the main verb. The verbs in the past perfect tense are in italics in the following examples:

Mr. Thompson *had served* as the company president before his retirement.

We *had watched* the Super Bowl together before Sharon moved to Chicago.

Our organization *had donated* time and money to the community's drug center before it closed.

[NOTE SA.13] Future perfect tense = *shall have* or *will have* + past participle.

Future Perfect Tense A **future perfect tense verb** is used to express an action that will be completed before a stated time in the future. This tense is formed by adding *shall have* or *will have* to the past participle of the main verb. Examples of verbs in the future perfect tense are in italics in the following sentences:

Mr. Thompson *will have served* as the company president for 15 years on January 1, 2000.

We *will have watched* the Super Bowl before we go to the NCAA basketball playoffs.

By the end of the year, our organization *will have donated* time and money to the community's drug center.

VERB VOICE

Voice is the term used to indicate whether the subject is doing or receiving the action. Sentence meaning and emphasis are communicated through the proper use of verb voice. The two voices of verbs are active and passive.

[NOTE SA.14]
The two voices of verbs are active and passive.

Active Voice When the subject of the sentence is performing the action, the verb is in the **active voice**. In business communication the active voice usually is preferred because it is more direct and concise. Sentences that use verbs in the active voice identify the one performing the action. The following examples demonstrate how the verbs, shown in italics, are used in the active voice:

[NOTE SA.15]
The subject performs the action in the active voice.

Yu-lan *spoke* at the annual sales conference.

Echo *is applying* for the sales manager's position.

Passive Voice A verb is in the **passive voice** when the subject of the sentence receives the action. The passive voice is used sparingly in business communication. It is used when the subject is unknown or when the writer wants to soften the message to avoid making an accusation. Another use of the passive voice is to emphasize the action rather than the person who performed the action. The passive voice can also be used to eliminate a gender pronoun.

[NOTE SA.16]
The subject receives the action in the passive voice.

Passive voice verbs require a form of *be* (*am, is, are, was, were, been*) as a helping verb, along with a past participle of the verb. Uses of verbs in the passive voice are shown in italics in the following examples:

Adrian *was informed* of his termination through an e-mail message. (Emphasis is on being informed rather than being terminated.)

The pallet of toys *was lifted* with a forklift. (The main point is what was lifted—the pallet of toys—not how it was lifted—with a forklift.)

New activities *were added* to attract new members. (The desire to attract new members was softened by emphasizing new activities.)

Changing the verb voice from active to passive does not change the verb tense from present to past. The tense in the passive voice is expressed by its auxiliary (helping) verb. The following examples show verbs (in italics) in the passive voice in several different tenses:

Training sessions *are offered* each Thursday and Friday. (*passive voice*, present tense)

The company *offers* training sessions each Thursday and Friday. (*active voice*, present tense)

Training sessions *were offered* last summer. (*passive voice*, past tense)

The company *offered* training sessions last summer. (*active voice*, past tense)

Training sessions *will be offered* during the morning in the spring. (*passive voice*, future tense)

The company *will offer* training sessions during the morning in the spring. (*active voice*, future tense)

VERB MOOD

[NOTE SA.17] The three verb moods are indicative, imperative, and subjunctive.

Communicators use **verb moods** to express facts, commands, or conditions. The three moods are indicative, imperative, and subjunctive.

[NOTE SA.18] Use indicative mood to ask questions or make factual statements.

Indicative Mood The **indicative mood** is used to make statements or to ask questions involving facts. Business writers use verbs in this mood more than in the imperative or subjunctive moods. Examples are in italics in these sentences:

What positions *will be available* in October?
The warehouse *will be demolished* next week.

[NOTE SA.19] Commands, instructions, and requests are in the imperative mood.

Imperative Mood The **imperative mood** is used to give commands, give instructions, or make requests. Sentences in the imperative mood usually have *you* understood as the subject and, therefore, it is omitted. Verbs used in the imperative mood are shown in italics in the following sentences:

Please *submit* your prospectus to the board.
Take this report to Ms. Elam on your way to lunch.

[NOTE SA.20] The subjunctive mood is rarely used.

Subjunctive Mood The **subjunctive mood** is used to express a wish, a doubt, or a situation that is contrary to fact. This mood is rarely used today. Many people find its use difficult because in the subjunctive mood the verb *were* replaces the verb *was* and the verb form *be* replaces *am, are*, and *is*. Here are some examples; the subjunctive mood verbs are in italics:

Should the gas well *be productive*, we will build a new house. (doubt)
I wish the car *were* red. (wish)
Erika insisted that her automobile *be* completely rebuilt. (contrary to fact—*be* is used for *is*)

VERBALS

[NOTE SA.21] The three verbals are the infinitive, the gerund, and the participle.

A **verbal** is a verb form used as a noun, an adjective, or an adverb. Verbals cannot function as verbs and do not express action or state of being. The three verbals are the infinitive, the gerund, and the participle.

[NOTE SA.22] Infinitive = *to* + present tense of verb.

[NOTE SA.23] Infinitives are used as nouns, adjectives, or adverbs.

Infinitive The **infinitive** is formed by placing the word *to* in front of the present tense of the verb. Several examples are *to rent, to program*, and *to hire*. An infinitive can function as a noun, an adjective, or an adverb, but it can never be used as a verb. The infinitive is in italics and its use is in parentheses in each of the following sentences. (Some parts of speech are identified in examples in Seminar A and are discussed in depth in Seminar B.)

To increase profits was the board's main objective. (noun—subject)
Debra plans *to speak* at the annual conference in New York. (noun—direct object)
Natasha's job is *to greet* customers as they enter the store. (noun—predicate nominative)
Carmen's dream *to retire* early hinges on her investments. (adjective)
The tire company has agreed *to replace* defective tires. (adverb)

Gerund A **gerund** is a present tense verb form that can function only as a noun. It is formed by adding *ing* to a verb. *Typing, hiring,* and *manufacturing* are examples of gerunds. Gerunds may be used in phrases consisting of a gerund, an object, and words modifying the object. In the following sentences the phrases are in italics, the gerunds are in bold, and their uses are in parentheses:

[NOTE SA.24]
Gerunds are used only as nouns.

[NOTE SA.25]
Gerund = verb + *ing*.

> ***Interviewing** prospective employees* is the responsibility of the human resources department. (subject)
>
> Ralph's job is ***renovating** old furniture.* (predicate nominative)
>
> They enjoy ***going** to the movies.* (direct object)
>
> He was awarded the prize for ***driving** the longest distance.* (object of preposition)
>
> Mikki, ***performing** in the play*, is the youngest member of the cast. (appositive)

Participle A **participle** is a verb form that can be used as an adjective or as part of a verb phrase. The three types of participles are present, past, and perfect.

[NOTE SA.26]
Participles are used as adjectives or as parts of verb phrases.

Present Participle The **present participle verb** is always formed by adding *ing* to the present tense of a verb. The participial phrase is in italics, and the present participle is in bold in each of the following examples:

[NOTE SA.27]
Present participle = present tense verb + *ing*.

> The sales force has a ***driving** desire* to be number one in its region. (adjective)
>
> Martha is ***saving** her money* for a vacation in Europe. (verb phrase)

Past Participle A **past participle verb** is usually formed by adding *d* or *ed* to the present tense of a regular verb. Irregular verbs form their past participles by changing the spelling of their root words. The past participle is in italics in each of the following examples:

[NOTE SA.28]
Past participle usually = present tense verb + *d* or *ed*.

[NOTE SA.29]
Sometimes the root word is changed.

> The administrative assistant *purchased* five airline tickets for the office staff. (verb—regular verb)
>
> The language seminar will concentrate on *spoken* Spanish. (adjective—irregular verb)

Perfect Participle A **perfect participle verb** is always used as an adjective and is formed by combining *having* with the past participle. The perfect participles are in italics in the following sentences:

[NOTE SA.30]
The perfect participle is always an adjective.

[NOTE SA.31]
Perfect participle = *having* + past participle.

> *Having fed* the animals, the zookeeper locked the cages.
>
> Patsy, *having resided* in Japan for 20 years, will experience difficulty in adjusting to the American culture.

Nouns

A noun is a person, place, or thing. The two main groups of nouns are proper nouns and common nouns.

[NOTE SA.32]
Nouns are words that identify persons, places, and things.

PROPER NOUNS

A **proper noun** is a particular person, place, or thing. Proper nouns are always capitalized. *Washington Monument, Michael Jordan, Chicago,* and *USA Today* are examples of proper nouns.

[NOTE SA.33]
Proper nouns are specific.

COMMON NOUNS

[NOTE SA.34] Common nouns are general.

A **common noun** identifies a general class of persons, places, things, or ideas. Common nouns are not capitalized. Examples of common nouns are *supervisor, table, carpet, sorrow, assets*, and *deposits*. The three classes of common nouns are concrete, abstract, and collective.

[NOTE SA.35] Concrete nouns are precise.

Concrete Nouns A **concrete noun** identifies those things that you can see, touch, hear, taste, or smell. Words such as *examiner, dog, paper, computer, teacher*, and *truck* are concrete nouns. Concrete nouns are precise and easily understood, which makes them effective for business communication.

[NOTE SA.36] Abstract nouns are vague.

Abstract Nouns An **abstract noun** identifies an idea, emotion, quality, or belief. Examples of abstract nouns are *charity, disappointment, joy, love, surprise, attitude*, and *elation*. People's opinions and feelings differ in degree; therefore, abstract nouns are less precise than concrete nouns. Abstract nouns should be used infrequently in business communication because they are more difficult to understand.

[NOTE SA.37] Collective nouns identify a group.

Collective Nouns A **collective noun** is a group of persons or a collection of things. It is normally treated as a singular noun because the group is acting as one; however, a collective noun would be treated as a plural noun if the group members were acting as individuals. Collective nouns include *club, faculty, company, association, crew*, and *band*.

COMPOUND NOUNS

[NOTE SA.38] Compound nouns are multiple words used to name singular nouns.

A **compound noun** is two or more words used to identify one person, place, or thing. A compound noun may be written as one or more words, or it may be hyphenated. When in doubt, consult a dictionary for the correct spelling. Compound nouns can be classified under any of the three classes of common nouns. Examples of compound nouns in each class follow:

Concrete:	flight attendant, vice president, mother-in-law
Abstract:	self-esteem, common sense, goodwill, life cycle
Collective:	booster club, board of directors, civil service staff

PLURAL FORMS OF NOUNS

[NOTE SA.39] A plural noun is normally formed by adding *s* or *es* to a singular noun.

A **plural noun** is used to identify two or more persons, places, or things. The plural of most nouns is formed by adding *s* or *es* to the singular form of the noun. Because there are so many ways of forming plurals, consult a dictionary if a question arises. Examples of different ways that nouns are formed as plurals include computer, *computers*; dress, *dresses*; company, *companies*; portfolio, *portfolios*; sister-in-law, *sisters-in-law*; deer, *deer*; and shelf, *shelves*.

POSSESSIVE FORMS OF NOUNS

[NOTE SA.40] Possessive nouns show ownership.

A **possessive noun** is used to show possession or ownership. The possessive form of a noun is indicated by using an apostrophe. The following general guidelines will help you correctly form possessive nouns in written communication:

[1] The possessive of a singular noun not ending with an *s* or a *z* sound is formed by adding *apostrophe s*.

pilot's plane company's executives

[2] The possessive of a singular noun ending with an *s* or a *z* sound is formed by adding *apostrophe s* to a noun with one syllable and by adding only an *apostrophe* to a noun with more than one syllable.

Jones's automobile Kirkpatz' house

[NOTE SA.41] Placement of apostrophe and addition of *s* to show possession depends on the noun and the ending sound.

[3] The possessive of a plural noun ending with an *s* or a *z* sound is formed by adding an *apostrophe.*

clients' rights players' union

[4] The possessive of a compound noun is formed by placing the *apostrophe* or *apostrophe s* after the final word or word element.

ambassador-at-large's house all major generals' aides

[NOTE SA.42] For compound nouns, possession is shown after the last word.

[5] When two or more people share ownership of an object or objects, add an *apostrophe* or *apostrophe s* to the final name.

Cathy and Angela's apartment Tim and Stewartz' investments

[NOTE SA.43] Joint or individual possession of objects influences placement of apostrophe or apostrophe *s*.

[6] When two or more people each own separate objects, possession is indicated by adding an *apostrophe* or *apostrophe s* to each noun.

Cathy's and Angela's apartments Tim's and Stewartz' investments

Pronouns

Pronouns are used in place of nouns. Pronouns make your writing more interesting because you do not repeat the noun. There are seven types of pronouns: personal, relative, interrogative, indefinite, demonstrative, reflexive, and intensive. Each type of pronoun performs a different function in a sentence.

[NOTE SA.44] Pronouns replace nouns.

[NOTE SA.45] The seven types of pronouns are personal, relative, interrogative, indefinite, demonstrative, reflexive, and intensive.

PERSONAL PRONOUNS

A **personal pronoun** is a substitute for a noun that refers to a specific person or thing. Personal pronouns change their form when they perform different functions and appear in different parts of a sentence. The different forms are called *cases*. The three types of personal pronoun cases are nominative, possessive, and objective.

[NOTE SA.46] Personal pronouns refer to specific people or things.

Nominative Case The **nominative case** is used when the pronoun functions as the subject of a sentence or a clause. The nominative case is also called the *subjective case*. Singular personal pronouns in the nominative case are *I, you, he, she*, and *it*. Plural personal pronouns in the nominative case are *we, you*, and *they*. The nominative case is also used when the pronoun follows a linking verb. The italics in the following sentences illustrate the uses of nominative case pronouns:

[NOTE SA.47] Nominative case is used when the pronoun is the subject.

She translated the document from French to English. (subject of sentence)

When *they* announce the new corporate structure, Shemika may search for another job. (subject of clause)

It was *they* who surveyed the property. (*it*—subject of sentence; *they*—follows linking verb)

[NOTE SA.48]
Possessive case shows ownership.

Possessive Case The **possessive case** is used when the pronoun shows possession or ownership. The possessive case does not need an apostrophe. Singular possessive pronouns are *my, mine, your, yours, his, her, hers*, and *its*. Plural possessive pronouns are *our, ours, your, yours, their*, and *theirs*. Several examples of pronouns in the possessive case are shown in italics in the following sentences:

That house belonged to *my* parents. (shows whose house)
Where are you going on *your* vacation? (shows whose vacation)
If the report is not *yours*, it must be *hers*. (shows whose report)
The employees nominated *their* manager for the award. (shows whose manager)
The company updated *its* logo. (shows whose logo was updated)

[NOTE SA.49]
Objective case is used when the pronoun is an object.

Objective Case The **objective case** is used when the pronoun functions as an object in a sentence, clause, or phrase. Singular pronouns in the objective case are *me, you, him, her*, and *it*. Plural objective pronouns are *us, you*, and *them*. The following sentences show in italics pronouns that are performing these functions:

Monica drove *them* to school every day. (direct object of a sentence)
Troy threw the pass *to him*. (object of preposition)
When we saw *her*, Mary was driving an SUV. (direct object of a clause)

RELATIVE PRONOUNS

[NOTE SA.50]
Relative pronouns link clauses to nouns or pronouns.

A **relative pronoun** connects a group of words containing a subject and verb (a clause) to a noun or pronoun. *Who, whom, whose, which*, and *that* are the relative pronouns. If the word to which the pronoun refers is a person, use *who, whom, whose*, or *that*. Use *who* when the pronoun referring to a person is in the nominative case and *whom* when the pronoun is in the objective case. Use *which* or *that* if the pronoun refers to a thing. Relative pronouns are in italics in the following sentences:

Did you see *who* lit the fire?
To *whom* shall we credit the sales?
In case of a disagreement, *whose* story will you believe?
The ship, *which* we sailed on, is called the Majestic Dragon.
The stock prices *that* were quoted were for Friday.

INTERROGATIVE PRONOUNS

[NOTE SA.51]
Interrogative pronouns ask questions.

An **interrogative pronoun** is used within a question. *Who, whose, whom, which*, and *what* are the interrogative pronouns. Pronouns precede verbs in questions. Like other pronouns within sentences, they function as subjects, objects, modifiers, and subject complements. The italics in the following sentences illustrate how interrogative pronouns are used:

Who canceled JoAnn's hotel reservations? (subject)
Whose department contributed the most to the flood victims? (modifier)
Whom do you think the Cowboys will hire as a placekicker? (object)
Which manuscript was submitted first? (modifier)
What was the basis for selecting the winners? (subject complement)

INDEFINITE PRONOUNS

An **indefinite pronoun** is used to make a general statement about individuals or things. Indefinite pronouns include *each, anyone, one, anything*, and *nobody*. The indefinite pronouns are in italics in the following sentences:

> *Each* accountant is competent with spreadsheets.
> Will *anyone* take a vacation in April?
> *One* of the employees invests 10 percent of his paycheck in the stockmarket.
> Joshua will do *anything* to complete the job.
> *Nobody* can rely on an NFL team remaining in any city for ten years.

[NOTE SA.52]
Indefinite pronouns do not specify a particular person or thing.

DEMONSTRATIVE PRONOUNS

A **demonstrative pronoun** is used to indicate a specific person, place, or thing. The four demonstrative pronouns are *this, these, that*, and *those*. Demonstrative pronouns are in italics in these sentences:

> *This* project will require much work.
> *These* microcomputers will be used ten hours a day.
> Why did they select *that* plan for balancing the budget?
> Are *those* the employees who earned the bonuses?

[NOTE SA.53]
Demonstrative pronouns substitute for specific nouns.

COMPOUND PERSONAL PRONOUNS

A **compound personal pronoun** has the suffix *self* or *selves*. A compound personal pronoun may be an intensive or reflexive pronoun. *Intensive pronouns* are used for emphasis, whereas *reflexive pronouns* reflect the action of the verb to the subject or to a noun or pronoun in the sentence. Examples of intensive and reflexive pronouns, in italics, follow:

> Bob stated that he *himself* would address the shareholders. (intensive—emphasizes a pronoun)
> John will go to the bank *himself*. (intensive—emphasizes a noun)
> The birds saw *themselves* reflected in the stream. (reflexive—refers to the subject, a pronoun)

[NOTE SA.54]
Compound personal pronouns are *intensive* or *reflexive*.

Adjectives

An **adjective** provides additional information about a noun or a pronoun. Adjectives make the meaning of the noun or pronoun more exact by answering such questions as *which one, how many*, and *what kind*. Adjectives also are called *modifiers*.

Adjectives may be regular or irregular. *Regular adjectives* generally are one-syllable words with *er* or *est* added when making comparisons. Irregular adjectives usually contain two or more syllables and use *less, least, more*, or *most* when making comparisons.

[NOTE SA.55]
Adjectives modify nouns and pronouns and make them more precise.

DEGREES OF COMPARISON IN ADJECTIVES

Adjectives change form to show degrees of comparison. There are three degrees of comparison: positive, comparative, and superlative. Examples of the degrees of comparison of adjectives are shown in Figure SA.1.

[NOTE SA.56]
The three degrees of comparison for adjectives are *positive, comparative*, and *superlative*.

Figure SA.1
Degrees of Comparison of Adjectives

Positive	**Comparative**	**Superlative**
sleepy	sleepier	sleepiest
easy	easier	easiest
cheerful	more cheerful	most cheerful
considerate	more considerate	most considerate

[NOTE SA.57]
Positive degree describes one noun.

Positive Degree The **positive degree** is used to describe one item or one group of items. The positive form is the form used in dictionary definitions. The adjective in the positive form is in italics in the following examples:

T'nesha is *wealthy*.
Floyd operates a *good* restaurant.
Her necklace is *expensive*.

[NOTE SA.58]
Comparative degree compares two nouns.

Comparative Degree The **comparative degree** is used to show the difference between two items. The comparative degree is formed by adding *er* to a regular adjective or by adding the words *more* or *less* to an irregular adjective. The adjectives used in the preceding examples in positive degree are shown in the following examples in the comparative degree:

T'nesha is *wealthier* than Deonte.
Floyd operates a *better* restaurant than Mark.
Her necklace is *more expensive* than her bracelet.

[NOTE SA.59]
Superlative degree compares three or more nouns.

Superlative Degree The **superlative degree** is used to compare three or more items. It can also be used for emphasis. The superlative degree is formed by adding *est* to a regular adjective or by adding *most* or *least* to an irregular adjective. The adjectives used in the previous two examples are now shown in the superlative degree:

T'nesha is the *wealthiest* person in town.
Floyd operates the *best* restaurant in the area.
Her necklace is the *most expensive* piece of jewelry that she owns.

ABSOLUTE ADJECTIVES

[NOTE SA.60]
Absolute adjectives are always in the superlative degree.

An **absolute adjective** is always in the superlative degree. Therefore, it cannot be compared. For example, if the design of a building is *perfect*, another building cannot have a *more perfect* design. Some absolute adjectives are *essential, unique, right, final, full, square, round, correct, never, dead*, and *empty*.

COMPOUND ADJECTIVES

[NOTE SA.61]
Two or more adjectives used as one become a compound adjective.

A **compound adjective** is two or more words used together to describe a single noun or pronoun. Often compound adjectives are hyphenated; sometimes they are not. When compound adjectives are shown hyphenated in the dictionary, they are considered *permanent compounds* and should always be hyphenated. Compound nouns used as adjectives and shown as *open compounds* in the dictionary are not hyphenated. Compound adjectives not shown in the dictionary are referred to as *temporary compounds* and are hyphenated when they appear *before* the noun or pronoun they describe but are not hyphenated when they appear after the words they describe. Consult a dictionary for hyphenation of compound adjectives. Compound adjectives appear in italics in the following sentences:

Greg is a *part-time* employee of Gene and Jo's Florist. (permanent compound adjective)

Sylvia opened a *money market* account after she was promoted. (open compound adjective)

City-owned vehicles are maintained by LaRoche Motors. (temporary compound adjective used before the noun)

LaRoche Motors maintains all vehicles that are *city owned.* (temporary compound adjective used after the noun)

Articles

Although classified as adjectives, *a, an*, and *the* are also called **articles.** The article *the* is used to denote specific nouns or pronouns. The articles *a* and *an* are used to denote general nouns or pronouns. The articles are in italics in the following examples:

[NOTE SA.62]
A, an, and *the* are articles. *The* is specific. *A* and *an* are general.

Amy won *the* final tennis match.

Amy won *a* tennis match.

Amy won *an* exhaustive tennis match.

When the word following the article begins with a consonant sound (*s*tore, *b*each, *c*ar, etc.), you use *a*; use *an* if the word begins with a vowel sound (*h*our, *e*gg, *e*xciting, etc.). Examples of articles used with words beginning with consonant and vowel sounds are shown in italics:

A picture of the President hangs in the capitol.

Cassandra is *an* honest individual.

Carolyn did *an* excellent job in conducting the survey.

Adverbs

Adverbs are modifiers that restrict, limit, or describe verbs, adjectives, or other adverbs. They answer questions such as *how, when, where, why, in what manner*, or *to what degree*. Many end in *ly*. Examples of adverbs used as modifiers are shown in italics in the following sentences:

[NOTE SA.63]
Adverbs are used to modify verbs, adjectives, or other adverbs.

The annual report was *well* written. (written *how*?)

A complete audit is conducted *annually*. (conducted *when*?)

The regional conference will be held *here*. (held *where*?)

The value of antique automobiles is increasing *extremely fast*. (increasing *how*? fast; *to what degree*? extremely)

[NOTE SA.64] The placement of an adverb depends on how it is used in the sentence.

PLACEMENT OF ADVERBS

An adverb may be a single word (drive *carefully*), a phrase (drive *in a careful manner*), or a clause (drive *as carefully as you can*). A single-word adverb can be placed before or after the word it modifies. Prepositional and infinitive phrases and clauses that function as adverbs usually follow the word they modify. An **adverbial clause**, which is a dependent clause that acts as an adverb, precedes the independent clause in a sentence. Seminar B contains a detailed discussion of phrases and clauses.

[NOTE SA.65] Adverbs also have *positive*, *comparative*, and *superlative* degrees.

DEGREES OF ADVERBS

Some words that are used as adverbs as well as adjectives have positive, comparative, and superlative degrees of comparison. Examples of the degrees of comparison of adverbs are shown in Figure SA.2.

Figure SA.2
Degrees of Comparison of Adverbs

Positive	Comparative	Superlative
slow	slower	slowest
early	earlier	earliest
delightful	more delightful	most delightful
widely	less widely	least widely

Prepositions

[NOTE SA.66] A preposition is a connector that needs an object.

A **preposition** connects a noun or pronoun to another word in a sentence. The noun or pronoun that follows the preposition is called the **object of the preposition**.

[NOTE SA.67] A prepositional phrase contains the preposition and its object.

A word group containing a preposition and the object of the preposition is called a **prepositional phrase**. The following sentences illustrate prepositional phrases. The prepositions are in italics, and the object of each preposition is in bold.

Sales rose *in* all **segments** *of* the **economy** *during* the first **quarter** *of* the **year**.

Don will be moved *to* the **top** *of* the **list** *for* **promotion**.

Include a letter *of* **recommendation** *with* your **resume** when you send it *to* **employers**.

[NOTE SA.68] Prepositional phrases work as adjectives and adverbs.

FUNCTIONS OF PREPOSITIONAL PHRASES

Prepositional phrases work as units in a sentence. They perform the functions of adjectives and adverbs and provide variety within the sentence. Examples of prepositional phrases that act as adjectives and adverbs are in italics in these examples:

The president *of the company* will arrive tomorrow. (The prepositional phrase as adjective modifies the noun *president.*)

When are we going *to town*? (The prepositional phrase as adverb modifies the verb *are going.*)

LuAnn is going *to the lake with a friend.* (Both prepositional phrases act as adverbs. They modify the verb *is going.*)

OBJECT OF PREPOSITION

As previously mentioned, the object of a preposition is a noun or pronoun that follows the preposition. The object of a preposition can be modified by an adjective; for example, "Belinda was proud of *her* grades."

Personal pronouns and *who* have unique objective forms. The objective form of *who* is *whom*. The personal pronouns are *me, us, you, him, her*, and *them*. The objects of the prepositions are in italics in these sentences:

To *whom* did you deliver the package?

Did you send an e-mail message to *me*?

Charley drove the bus for *us*.

Packages were sent to *him* and *her*.

Yesterday, I received a letter from *you*.

Harry gave tomatoes to *them*.

[NOTE SA.69]
Objects of prepositions are nouns or pronouns and can be modified by adjectives.

UNNECESSARY PREPOSITIONS

Although prepositional phrases can be used effectively to make communication more interesting, a communicator must be careful to avoid unnecessary and, therefore, incorrect prepositions. Effective business communicators avoid inserting extra prepositions within a sentence or ending a sentence with a preposition.

However, ending a sentence with a preposition is acceptable in oral communication if rearranging the sentence is awkward. Use only those prepositions that clarify a sentence. The prepositions *to, of, at, for*, and *up* are frequently used unnecessarily. Examples of these uses are shown in italics in the following sentences:

[NOTE SA.70]
Omit unnecessary prepositions within sentences.

[NOTE SA.71]
Avoid ending a sentence with a preposition.

The team did not say where they were going *to*. (unnecessary preposition)
The team did not say where they were going.

The bird flew off *of* its perch. (unnecessary preposition)
The bird flew off its perch.

The mother did not know where her child was *at*. (unnecessary preposition)
The mother did not know where her child was.

Who is that phone call *for*? (incorrect)
For whom is that phone call?

The tree grew *up* three feet last summer. (unnecessary preposition)
The tree grew three feet last summer.

Do you have any idea about what the meeting is? (awkward)
Do you have any idea what the meeting is about? (preferred)

Conjunctions

A **conjunction** is used to join words, phrases, and clauses. Conjunctions are also used to introduce clauses. Conjunctions are similar to prepositions in that they serve as connectors but are different in that they do not have objects. The three kinds of conjunctions are coordinate, correlative, and subordinate. Coordinate and

[NOTE SA.72]
Conjunctions are connectors without objects.

[NOTE SA.73]
The three types of conjunctions are *coordinate, correlative*, and *subordinate*.

correlative conjunctions join grammatically equal word elements; subordinate conjunctions join grammatically unequal word elements.

COORDINATE CONJUNCTIONS

[NOTE SA.74] Coordinate conjunctions connect elements of equal rank.

A **coordinate conjunction** joins words, phrases, and independent clauses that are of equal importance or rank. Of equal importance or rank means that similar elements are connected; for example, adjectives are connected to adjectives and nouns are connected to nouns. The coordinate conjunctions are *and, but, or, nor, for, as,* and *yet.* The following examples show coordinate conjunctions (in italics) joining words, phrases, and independent clauses:

John *and* Lila are shoveling snow. (joins nouns)

The wolf moved quickly *but* quietly. (joins adverbs)

The children danced *and* sang at the party. (joins verbs)

They walked up one side *and* down the other. (joins prepositional phrases)

The dentist had a difficult time cleaning Jay's teeth, *for* the plaque had accumulated. (joins independent clauses)

CORRELATIVE CONJUNCTIONS

[NOTE SA.75] A correlative conjunction is a pair of connectors that link sentence elements.

A **correlative conjunction** is paired with another correlative conjunction to connect two parallel words, phrases, or clauses. The most common correlative conjunction pairs are *both . . . and, either . . . or, neither . . . nor, not . . . but, not only . . . but also,* and *whether . . . or.* Examples, shown in italics, follow:

Emmit *not only* ran patterns *but also* caught passes. (connects verb phrases)

Lori is a member of *both* the Civic Club *and* the Academic Club. (connects nouns)

Christie informed her mother that she would *either* wash the car *or* mow the yard. (connects clauses)

[NOTE SA.76] Be sure that connected elements are parallel.

A common difficulty with using correlative conjunctions involves *parallelism.* Be sure that connected elements are equal or parallel in grammatical form or rank. A detailed discussion of parallelism is in Seminar B. The following sentences demonstrate a few parallelism errors. The correlative conjunctions are in italics.

Diane should *either* go to college *or* she should get a job. (Incorrect—*either* precedes the verb *go*, but *or* precedes the pronoun *she.*)

Diane should *either* go to college *or* get a job. (Correct—both conjunctions precede verbs.)

Mandy *not only* bought computers *but also* printers. (Incorrect—*not only* precedes the verb *bought* and *but also* precedes the noun *printers.*)

Mandy bought *not only* computers *but also* printers. (Correct—both conjunctions precede nouns.)

SUBORDINATE CONJUNCTIONS

[NOTE SA.77] Subordinate conjunctions connect clauses of unequal rank.

A **subordinate conjunction** joins a subordinate clause to the main clause; that is, a dependent clause to an independent clause. Some subordinate conjunctions are *after, although, because, before, since, when, while, where, if, whether, though,* and *until.* The subordinate conjunctions are in italics and the main clauses are in bold in the following examples:

> *Before you write the proposal,* **read the RFP very carefully**.
> **The bird made strange sounds** *when the light was turned off.*
> **The grass turned green** *after it rained.*

Interjections

An **interjection** expresses strong emotion or feeling. It is not related grammatically to any other word in a sentence. Most interjections do not have any meaning if they are taken out of the message context. An interjection is normally punctuated with an exclamation point. Interjections are seldom used in business writing. They may be used in oral communication and in written advertising material. The interjections are in italics in the following examples:

[NOTE SA.78]
Interjections express strong emotions.

> *My goodness!* That siren startled me.
> *Wow!* Those flowers are beautiful.
> *Oops!* He spilled the tray of food.

APPLICATION EXERCISES

1. Identify each verb and indicate whether it is an action or a state-of-being verb. Also indicate whether the verb is in active or passive voice.
   - **a.** The door was closed last night.
   - **b.** Steve put the proposal on Ginny's desk after he completed reading it.
   - **c.** The hummingbirds were seen for the first time last week.
   - **d.** Antique collectors cherish things from the past.
   - **e.** The cottontail rabbit has an established home range of approximately five acres.
   - **f.** The chairs were recovered in a dreadful color on the advice of the office manager.
   - **g.** The proposed regulation establishes limits on how long an airplane can be exposed to snow or freezing rain before being deiced again.
   - **h.** The manager told the workers to go home early on Friday.
   - **i.** The telecommunication office will be closed for the holidays on Monday.
   - **j.** If their marriage survived this past week, it surely is solid enough for anything the future has in store.
2. Identify each verb or verb phrase and indicate whether it is in the indicative, imperative, or subjunctive mood:
   - **a.** Warren looks at all opportunities to acquire more companies.
   - **b.** The contractors worked together extremely well after the accident occurred.
   - **c.** The forklift damaged the crate containing the antique clock.
   - **d.** Who brought the doughnuts for the morning break?
   - **e.** Come enjoy a glimpse of early Texas in the History Museum which includes a genealogical library.

- **f.** Ted, take the video camera to the repair shop.
- **g.** Market Day is held at the Fairgrounds the first Saturday of each month from March through December.

3. Identify each verbal and indicate its form (infinitive, gerund, or participle):

- **a.** We are happy that you decided to join our organization.
- **b.** Tim asked his boss for an increase in salary.
- **c.** I appreciate your collecting donations for the relief fund.
- **d.** The television network decided to take the lead in limiting pornography in its programs.
- **e.** Talking with friends, Fred missed the results of the race.
- **f.** Investments in mutual funds increased in the rapidly spiraling stock market.
- **g.** Instead of asking for help in unjamming the printer, Mindy broke it.
- **h.** Having finished her term paper, Mary Ann celebrated.

4. Determine the correct verb form and indicate the tense of the verbs that are italicized in the following sentences. Example: The announcement of the resignation *shake* the building. *Shook—past tense*

- **a.** Tomorrow we *went* to the movies.
- **b.** Late last night Candace *answers* the telephone.
- **c.** The price of BCK stock has fallen since it *will merge* with Realway.
- **d.** I *sent* the package to you next week.
- **e.** It *looked* warm outside, but it is cold.
- **f.** By the end of the decade, all of Bill and Cindy's children *will have went* to college.
- **g.** Next month Tari *began* working for Pyramid Grain.
- **h.** Economic numbers *are* pretty gloomy last month.
- **i.** The company *celebrates* its tenth anniversary next Tuesday.
- **j.** I *visited* the museum every week since moving to Chicago.

5. Identify each adjective and adverb in the following sentences, and indicate how the word is used (adjective or adverb). Indicate the word that each adjective or adverb modifies.

- **a.** Gasoline prices have been steadily dropping while oil prices have been rising.
- **b.** Kapland Airlines will resume negotiations with its pilots tomorrow for the first time in nearly three weeks.
- **c.** Profits were rapidly sliding, and stockholders were becoming increasingly alarmed.
- **d.** Officials of tax-exempt groups will soon face stiff new penalties.
- **e.** Networks buy new shows from Hollywood studios and later resell them to local television stations.
- **f.** The economic development plan included tax credits that were more generous than had been expected.
- **g.** The law was carefully designed to prevent discrimination against people with disabilities.
- **h.** It's a good time to consider buying a new car.
- **i.** One good sign is that revenues have picked up dramatically.
- **j.** How can someone qualify for a monthly pension and then not receive it?

6. Common errors occur in the following sentences. Find and correct the errors. Explain each correction.
   a. Do you know where the children are going to.
   b. The runoff from the rain cut deep into the topsoil.
   c. Where are you taking the horse to?
   d. The new restaurant was builded on the corner of Sycamore and Vine.
   e. The workers will either accept the contract or they will strike.
   f. Jill is unable to go to lunch because she has went out of town.
   g. If I was in charge of this operation, we would close on Thursday for the holiday.
   h. The employees of Swift Truck Line hired an auditor to investigate the companies pension plan.
   i. John shaped and molded the image of African Americans worldwide.
   j. Between the NFL teams, the Cowboys have the higher salaries.
7. Identify the part of speech for each word in the following sentences:
   a. The candidates gave speeches throughout the day.
   b. Josh raked the leaves and put them into large bags.
   c. Worldwide, stocks rose in dollar terms.
   d. The government should do a thorough economic analysis of the deal's effect on farmers.
   e. Fantastic! Hog futures quadrupled last month.
   f. Today's hike was longer and required some tricky footwork crossing a beaver dam.
   g. Rebates and other forms of price discounting will continue into the next decade.
   h. Prior to investing in stocks, an individual should have a thorough understanding of economics.
   i. Displaced employees turn to self-employment when other jobs are not readily available.
   j. Nowhere will you find a state with more pride in its history than Texas.

MESSAGE ANALYSIS

Correct all grammatical errors in the following paragraphs:

Paragraph component's include a topic sentence; supporting sentences; descriptive detales, and concluding sentence. Good writers very the lengths of sentences and paragraphs.

The type and purpose of paragraphs determines the organization and sequins of detales. Messages that tell a story, describe, or pursuade follow specific organizational patterns and use direct or indirect approaches too writing.

Opening paragraphs attracts the readers interest; closing paragraphs use memorable statements, look to the future, or call for action. These two paragraphs create the first and last impressions of the message.

SEMINAR

B Sentence Structure

[NOTE SB.1]
A sentence expresses a complete thought.

A **sentence** is a group of related words that expresses a complete thought. A sentence always contains a subject and a predicate. It is the basic unit for organizing messages.

[NOTE SB.2]
Correct grammar provides clarity, precision, and credibility.

You can improve your ability to communicate by becoming familiar with sentence construction and learning how to organize sentences. It is important that you construct grammatically correct sentences for the following reasons: (1) your messages will be clearer; (2) your messages will be more precise; and (3) your credibility will be increased.

Parts of Sentences

[NOTE SB.3]
The main parts of a sentence are the subject and the predicate.

The starting point in developing your understanding of how to structure sentences is to know their two essential parts. These parts are the subject and the predicate.

[NOTE SB.4]
The subject tells who or what is being discussed.

THE SUBJECT

The **subject** is the part of a sentence that tells who or what is being discussed.

The Complete Subject The **complete subject** includes all words related directly to the subject. The complete subject is italicized in the following examples:

Gloria sails.

Athletic, lean Gloria sails.

Cats hide.

The cat, with the stripes, eats every morning.

[NOTE SB.5]
The complete subject includes all words related directly to the subject.

The Simple Subject The **simple subject** is the main noun or pronoun in the complete subject. The simple subject in a sentence is the *who* or the *what* that performs the action or is in the state of being described in the sentence. In the following examples, the simple subject is in bold print and the complete subject is in italics:

Athletic, lean ***Gloria*** sails. (Gloria is the *who* that performs the action of sailing.)

The ***envelope****, which contained the check,* was received on Monday. (The envelope is the *what* that was received.)

The football **game** was exciting. (The game is the *what* that was exciting.)

[NOTE SB.6]
The simple subject is the main noun or pronoun in the complete subject.

The Compound Subject When two (or more) simple subjects are connected by a coordinate conjunction, a **compound subject** is formed. The coordinating conjunctions are *and, or, but, nor, for, yet,* and *so*. The compound subject is in bold print in the following examples of italicized complete subjects:

Lauren and Scott think the price is too high.

The ***doctor and her staff*** work to keep health care costs down.

The ***Horned Frogs or*** *the* ***Banana Slugs*** will play in the bowl game in Alabama.

[NOTE SB.7]
A compound subject is formed when two or more simple subjects are connected by a coordinating conjunction.

THE PREDICATE

The **predicate** is the part of a sentence that tells something about the complete subject. The predicate may be complete, simple, or compound.

[NOTE SB.8]
The predicate tells something about the complete subject.

The Complete Predicate The **complete predicate** includes the verb and all the words directly related to it. The complete predicates are in italics in the following examples:

Gloria *sails.*

Cats *eat daily.*

The package *was sent by overnight express delivery service.*

Were you *comfortable in the 2001 Volvo?*

[NOTE SB.9]
The complete predicate includes the verb and all words directly related to it.

The Simple Predicate The **simple predicate** is the main verb in the complete predicate. The verb expresses action or a state of being. The simple predicate is in bold print in these examples of italicized complete predicates:

We **left** *in a hurry.* (*left* expresses action)

The package **was sent** *by overnight express delivery service.* (*was sent* expresses action)

They **feel** *good.* (*feel* expresses a state of being)

[NOTE SB.10]
The simple predicate is the main verb in the complete predicate.

[NOTE SB.11] A compound predicate is formed when two or more simple predicates are connected by a coordinating conjunction.

The Compound Predicate A **compound predicate** is formed when two (or more) simple predicates are connected by a coordinating conjunction. The compound predicate is in bold print in these examples of italicized complete predicates:

Kathryn ***sails*** *weekly* ***and races*** *monthly.*

The weekly journal ***was prepared, e-mailed, and accepted***.

SUBJECT AND PREDICATE IDENTIFICATION

[NOTE SB.12] Analyze sentences by first locating the simple predicate and then finding the subject.

Practice in recognizing subjects and predicates will strengthen your understanding of sentence structure. It is easier to analyze sentence structure if you start by locating the simple predicate (the verb); then ask *who* or *what* to identify the subject. The following examples illustrate this approach:

The YMCA opened at 5 a.m. (The action *opened* is the verb. What opened? The *YMCA* is the simple subject.)

Tan manages the computer store. (The action *manages* is the verb. Who manages? *Tan* is the simple subject.)

Nikolas Pantuliano is 16 years old. (The state of being *is* is the verb. Who is? *Nikolas Pantuliano* is the subject.)

The J. Paul Getty Trust Museum was interesting. (The state of being *was* is the verb. What was? The *museum* is the simple subject.)

Before leaving, Shanthi and Linda completed the project for the department. (The action *completed* is the verb. Who completed? *Shanthi and Linda* is the compound subject.)

During the week, Carol rises early and runs. (The action *rises and runs* is the compound predicate. Who rises and runs? *Carol* is the simple subject.)

[NOTE SB.13] In the usual sentence arrangement, the subject precedes the verb.

[NOTE SB.14] In inverted sentences, the verb precedes the subject.

The most common sentence arrangement is for the subject to be followed by the verb (e.g., *Chuck rebuilt his Volkswagon*). A sentence in which the subject follows the verb is called an **inverted sentence**. Examples of inverted sentences include sentences beginning with *here* or *there,* some questions, and a few other instances. The following examples, in which the subject is in bold print and the verb is in italics, illustrate this inverted arrangement:

There *are* 20 **employees** in the front office.

Here *is* the **umbrella**.

Why *was* **he** absent?

In back *is* **Khahn**.

To locate the subject and verb more easily in these cases, restate the sentence in the standard order—subject, then verb. For example

Inverted order:	There *are* 20 **employees** in the front office.
Standard order:	Twenty **employees** *are* in the front office.
Inverted order:	Here *is* the **umbrella**.
Standard order:	The **umbrella** *is* here.
Inverted order:	Why *was* **he** absent?
Standard order:	**He** *was* absent why?

Inverted order: In back *is* **Khahn**.

Standard order: **Khahn** *is* in back.

In some of the previous examples, words or groups of words were ignored when the predicate and subject were being located. These parts of sentences will be considered in the next sections.

OBJECTS AND SUBJECT COMPLEMENTS

Objects and subject complements are important parts of sentences. They help to complete the thought expressed by the subject and the simple predicate. Understanding the functions of objects and subject complements will assist you in avoiding grammatical errors.

[NOTE SB.15]
Objects and complements help complete the sentence thought.

Objects An **object** is a noun, a pronoun, or a phrase or clause that is used as a noun. Objects may be direct or indirect.

[NOTE SB.16]
Direct objects receive the action of the verb.

A **direct object** receives the action of the verb and helps complete the thought of the sentence. The direct object answers the *what* or *whom* question raised by the subject and verb. Examples of direct objects are shown in italics in the following sentences:

Cathy teaches the *piano*. (Cathy teaches what?)

If you feel ill, you can go to *bed*. (You can go where? Note that only action verbs can take direct objects; feel is a linking verb [see Business English Seminar A, page 537].)

He ran *track* one semester. (He ran what?)

The recommendation assisted *Kern Kwong*. (The recommendation assisted whom?)

An **indirect object** receives the action that the verb makes on the direct object. The indirect object usually answers the question, "To whom is the action being directed?" Indirect objects are always located between the verb and the direct object. You cannot have an indirect object if you do not have a direct object. Neither the direct object nor the indirect object ever appears as a prepositional phrase. You can locate the indirect object by inverting the sentence and mentally inserting the word *to*. In the following two sentences the indirect object is in bold print and the direct object is in italics:

[NOTE SB.17]
Indirect objects receive the action the verb makes on the direct object.

Kitty gives **Jon** the *saxophone*. (The saxophone was given by Kitty *to* Jon.)

Rob sold the **BYC member** a *laser sailboat*. (A laser sailboat was sold by Rob *to* the BYC member.)

Subject Complements The **subject complement** is (1) a noun or pronoun that renames the subject or (2) an adjective that modifies the subject. In both cases, the subject complement follows a linking verb in the sentence. A **linking verb** (such as, *is, was, has been, am, are*, and *seem*) does not show action. In each of the following examples, the subject and the subject complement are in italics and the linking verb is in bold:

[NOTE SB.18]
Subject complements rename or modify the subject.

[NOTE SB.19]
Linking verbs do not show action.

Peter and Lauren **are** good *friends*. (*Friends* is a noun that renames *Peter and Lauren*.)

The *e-mail* **was** *helpful.* (*Helpful* is an adjective that modifies *e-mail.*)

The *cake* **is** *good.* (*Good* is an adjective that modifies *cake.*)

He **was** *brilliant.* (*Brilliant* is an adjective that modifies *he.*)

PHRASES, CLAUSES, AND FRAGMENTS

Being able to identify groupings of words—referred to as *phrases* or *clauses*—is important for understanding sentence structure. Also, you should know what sentence fragments are and make conscious decisions on whether or not you will use them.

[NOTE SB.20] A phrase functions as a part of speech.

Phrases A **phrase** is a group of related words that functions as a part of speech. Phrases do not contain both a subject and a verb; some phrases contain one or the other, some contain neither. Here are some examples of phrases:

Verb phrases:	will be mailing/have keyed/is considered
Noun phrases:	the home office/a fast car/a fair election
Prepositional phrases:	to the college/during the concert/beneath the desk
Adjective phrases:	cute and sweet/on-time/three dozen
Participial phrases:	having been promoted/seeing clearly/keying rapidly
Infinitive phrases:	to run/to drive/to promote/to elect

[NOTE SB.21] Phrases can strengthen and add life to writing.

Using phrases as parts of speech—as adjectives, adverbs, and nouns—can make your writing more interesting. Phrases can add variety and color. They are a way to add strong words to your sentences and bring power to your writing. Finally, they can strengthen your writing by providing helpful details and showing relationships. Note how the italicized phrases in the following examples add detail, variety, color, interest, power, and liveliness:

Mary Rose sings. (no phrases)

Mary Rose sings songs *in the shower.* (prepositional phrase)

Mary Rose sings *better than the average soprano.* (adjective phrase)

Mary Rose, *a better-than-average soprano*, sings *contemporary songs.* (adjective phrase, noun phrase)

Mary Rose seems *to be a natural soprano.* (infinitive phrase)

A *natural soprano*, Mary Rose sings *contemporary songs.* (adjective phrase, noun phrase)

Serenading softly, Mary Rose sings *contemporary songs.* (participial phrase, noun phrase)

Understanding the purpose of the phrase is also important. For example, prepositional phrases can serve both as adjectives and as adverbs. If a phrase is serving as an adjective, it should be placed close enough to the noun it modifies so that the relationship is clear:

Wrong: The members present were *of the National Business Education Association.*

Right: The members *of the National Business Education Association* were present.

The phrase *of the National Business Education Association* serves as an adjective and modifies the noun *members*. This relationship is more clearly understood if the modifying phrase is close to the noun.

Clauses A **clause** is a group of related words that contains both a subject and a predicate. There are two kinds of clauses: independent and dependent. An **independent clause**, sometimes referred to as the *main clause*, expresses a complete thought. It can stand alone as a separate sentence. In the following examples of independent clauses, the simple predicates are shown in bold print, and the subjects are shown in italics:

[NOTE SB.22]
A clause has both a subject and a predicate.

[NOTE SB.23]
Independent clauses can stand alone.

both *the telephone and the fax* **are** important communication tools
the *environmental nature center* **fought** the change

A **dependent clause**, also called a *subordinate clause*, does not express a complete thought and cannot stand alone. The dependent clause contains both a subject and a predicate; but, because of its construction, it depends upon another clause for the thought to be complete.

[NOTE SB.24]
Dependent clauses are introduced by subordinate conjunctions or relative pronouns; they cannot stand alone as sentences.

The dependent clause is almost always introduced by a subordinating conjunction (such as *because, as soon as, if,* or *when*) or by a relative pronoun (such as *who, which*, or *that*). Look at the subordinating conjunction or relative pronoun (shown in bold), the simple subject (in bold italics), and the simple predicate (in regular italics) in these examples of dependent clauses:

if the ***order*** *arrived* by Monday
that the ***class*** *is* acceptable

The basic difference between dependent and independent clauses is the use of a subordinating conjunction or relative pronoun. If you add a subordinating conjunction to an independent clause, you make it a dependent clause. On the other hand, if you were to omit the subordinating conjunction or relative pronoun at the beginning of the previous illustrations of dependent clauses, those clauses would become independent clauses:

the order arrived by Monday
the class is acceptable

One other point related to clauses is that the word *like* should not be used to introduce a clause. Grammar rules permit using *like* as a verb, adjective, or preposition, but *as* should be used to introduce clauses:

Wrong: The message is short *like* you wanted it to be.
Right: The message is short *as* you wanted it to be.

Sentence Fragments A **sentence fragment** is a group of words that may or may not have meaning. *Sentence fragment* is another name for an *incomplete sentence.* Note the following examples:

[NOTE SB.25]
Sentence fragments are incomplete sentences and may or may not have meaning.

If the vacation is taken early (lacks meaning)
Congratulations! (has meaning in context)
Ernesto, having been promoted (lacks meaning)
Best wishes for success (has meaning in context)

Although the use of sentence fragments that have some meaning in context is fairly common in business communication, the acceptability of their usage is debated. Some business communicators think the infrequent, selective use of

[NOTE SB.26]
Some writers selectively use sentence fragments; others never use them.

meaningful sentence fragments gives life and personality to their messages. Other business communicators do not use sentence fragments because, technically, they are grammatically incorrect. You will need to make your own decision on this issue.

SENTENCE PATTERNS

[NOTE SB.27] A common sentence pattern is subject → verb → object or complement.

A helpful approach to understanding sentence construction for many students is to examine the most common basic sentence patterns. Although the English language is extremely flexible, the following patterns are the most frequently used:

[1] Subject → Verb

Elena → reads.

[2] Subject → Verb → Direct Object

Elena → reads → a novel.

[3] Subject → Verb → Indirect Object → Direct Object

Elena → reads → Cruz → a novel.

[4] Subject → Verb → Subject Complement

Gregory → is → lost.

[5] Here (or There) → Verb → Subject

Here → is → your snow board.

Subject and Verb Agreement

[NOTE SB.28] The subject and verb must agree in number.

One of the basic rules of sentence construction is that the subject and the verb must *agree in number*. If the subject is singular—refers to just one person or one thing—then the verb must be singular. If the subject is plural, the verb must also be plural. Your ability to identify the subject is essential to determining whether it is singular or plural. The subject and the verb are in italics in the following examples:

Singular: The *entrepreneur was* on the program.
Plural: The *entrepreneurs were* on the program.
Singular: The *pilot flies* the helicopter.
Plural: The *pilots fly* the helicopters.

Recall that adding an *s* to most subjects makes them plural and adding an *s* to most verbs makes them singular. If you are not sure whether the subject is singular or plural (for example, a word like *athletics*), look it up in a dictionary. Then use the verb that agrees with the number of the subject.

Words between the subject and the verb (intervening words) must be ignored when determining the correct number of the subject. In the following examples the subject and the verb are in bold, and the word or words to be ignored are in italics:

Singular: The **man** *with the rackets* **is** the tennis player.
Plural: The **men** *with the rackets* **are** the tennis players.

Singular: The **computer**, *as well as the printers*, **was** new.
Plural: The **runners**, *other than Coach Bill*, **were** on time for the track meet.

Recall that a compound subject is two (or more) subjects connected by a coordinating conjunction. Some compound subjects take singular verbs and some take plural verbs. There are four possibilities:

[NOTE SB.29]
Compound subjects may take singular or plural verbs.

[1] When compound subjects are connected by *and*, they are plural and require a plural verb.

[2] When compound subjects are connected by *or* or *nor* and both are singular, they take singular verbs.

[3] When compound subjects are connected by *or* or *nor* and both are plural, they take plural verbs.

[4] When compound subjects are connected by *or* or *nor* and one of the subjects is plural and one singular, the verb should agree with the number of the subject which is closer to it.

The compound subjects are in bold print, and their correct verbs are in italics in these examples:

Plural: **Gloria and Catherine** *are* sisters.
Plural: The **pilot**, the **copilot**, **and** the **navigator** *fly* all the international flights.
Singular: **Either Bob or Joe** *is* to jump the hurdles.
Singular: **Neither Nancy nor Art** *is* going.
Singular: The **tents or** the **cabin** *is* available for camping.
Plural: **Neither** the **cabins nor** the **tents** *are* available for camping.
Plural: **Neither** the **cabin nor** the **tents** *are* available for camping.

Notice in the last two examples that the plural verb sounds better. In sentences with both singular and plural subjects, this is almost always true. It will be best for you, therefore, to try to put the plural subject closer to the verb.

Some words used as subjects are singular even though they may give the appearance of being plural. Examples of these words are *everybody, everyone, anybody, anyone, somebody, someone, nobody,* and *neither*. With these singular subjects, use singular verbs:

[NOTE SB.30]
Some subjects appear to be plural but are singular.

Singular: Anyone is (not *are*) invited.
Singular: Everybody is (not *are*) welcome.
Singular: Each of the participants attends (not *attend*) a conference.
Singular: Neither was (not *were*) late for the meeting.

Also, some words that end in *s* are singular. Use singular verbs with those words:

Singular: Athletics is an extracurricular activity.
Singular: Mathematics is my favorite subject.
Singular: Economics is an important field of study.

The name of one song, book, company, magazine, or article is singular even though the name is plural:

Singular: *People* is an interesting magazine.
Singular: Starving Students, Inc., is located in Ft. Lauderdale.
Singular: "Edelweiss" is an old song.

Subjects in plural form that are considered as a single unit or as a whole take singular verbs. Amounts, distances, and some compound subjects are examples of this:

Singular: Ten feet is the distance to the end of the wall.
Singular: Five to seven pounds is the average weight for a notebook computer.
Singular: Turkey and dressing is a Thanksgiving favorite.

[NOTE SB.31] Some subjects appear to be singular but are plural.

The words *few, both, many*, and *several* are considered plural and take plural verbs. For example

Plural: Few think that the car will be the best-selling convertible.
Plural: Both were hired before graduation.
Plural: Many select the 900MHZ cordless telephone.
Plural: Several are singing in the All American Boys concert.

[NOTE SB.32] Collective nouns may be singular or plural.

Collective nouns such as *board, faculty*, and *audience* may be singular or plural. If the group is acting as one, the verb should be singular. If the group members are acting as individuals, the verb should be plural:

Singular: The committee has written an academic code of honor this year.
Plural: The faculty are testing their students in spite of the upcoming holiday.

Pronoun and Antecedent Agreement

[NOTE SB.33] Pronouns and their antecedents should agree.

[NOTE SB.34] Pronouns are noun substitutes.

[NOTE SB.35] Pronouns replace antecedents.

To be grammatically correct in your communication, you will want to know and use another form of agreement—the *agreement of pronouns and their antecedents*. Recall that pronouns are noun substitutes. The pronouns used as subjects, objects, or complements are *he, she, I, we, you, it, her, him, them*, and *they*. As a possessive, a pronoun is used as a modifier. Examples of possessive pronouns are *my, mine, our(s), your(s), his, her(s), its*, and *their(s)*. An **antecedent** is a word, phrase, or clause that is replaced by the pronoun. An antecedent is most likely to be a noun.

[NOTE SB.36] Pronouns and their antecedents should agree in number.

Pronouns and their antecedents must agree in three ways: (1) in number, (2) in gender, and (3) in clear relationship. In the following examples of agreement in number, the antecedent is in italics and the pronoun is in bold print:

Singular: *Robin* reported on Monday, and **she** said the report is complete.
Plural: *Robin and Dennis* reported on Monday, and **they** said the report is complete.

Singular: *Russell* took **his** chemistry test on Friday.
Plural: *Russell and Andy* took **their** chemistry tests on Friday.

Singular: *Everybody* sat at **his or her** desk.
Plural: The *elephants* roamed **their** reserve.

Singular: *Software, Inc.,* is opening **its** fifth store.
Plural: All Software, Inc., *employees* believe **their** company will continue to grow.

Singular: Either *Michelle* or *Conseulo* will sail **her** sabot in the Stanford Regatta.
Plural: *Both Michelle and Conseulo* will sell **their** sabots in the Stanford Regatta.

Singular: The *number* is high; **it** exceeds 100.
Plural: A *number* of birds have eaten **their** bird seed.

The next set of examples of pronouns and their antecedents shows agreement in gender. The antecedent is in italics and the pronoun is in bold print:

[NOTE SB.37]
Pronouns and their antecedents should agree in gender.

Masculine: *Rudy* will play **his** piano at the concert today.
Feminine: *Lizbeth* cut **her** hair in a pageboy style today.
Mixed: Every *man* and *woman* must send **his** or **her** letter before the meeting on Wednesday.
Neuter: A *meeting* is begun when **its** president calls it to order.

Finally, there must be a clear relationship between a pronoun and its antecedent. Examples of unclear relationships and clear relationships follow:

[NOTE SB.38]
Pronouns and their antecedents should clearly relate.

Unclear: Will attended the Las Vegas convention with his colleague, and he said the convention sales were low. (Antecedent not clear; who said the sales were low?)
Clear: Will attended the Las Vegas convention with his colleague, and Will said the convention sales were low.

Unclear: Walter telephoned Nirmal when he was on a sabbatical. (Who was on the sabbatical?)
Clear: When Walter was on a sabbatical, he telephoned Nirmal.

Parallelism

One other important form of agreement you will want to use in constructing correct sentences is parallelism. **Parallelism** means having balance and consistency between or among parts of sentences that serve the same function.

[NOTE SB.39]
Sentence constructions should be parallel.

Parallelism is achieved by using the same grammatical form for the two or more parts of sentences that serve the same function. Using the same grammatical form means using noun with noun, adjective with adjective, verb with verb, adverb with adverb, phrase with phrase, or clause with clause. Parts of sentences serve the same function if they serve as a part of a series, a contrast, a comparison, a choice, or an expression of equality.

[NOTE SB.40]
The same grammatical form should be used for parts that serve the same function.

Different examples of parallelism are shown in the following illustrations. The parts of these sentences that are not parallel are shown in bold.

[NOTE SB.41] Parts of series should be parallel.

SERIES

Not parallel: The Balboa Bay Club director is accountable for membership development, dues collection, and **to arrange sailing events.** (Two parts of the series, *membership development* and *dues collection*, are noun phrases; one part, *to arrange sailing races*, is an infinitive phrase.)

Parallel: The Balboa Bay Club director is responsible for membership development, dues collection, and sailing events. (All parts of the series are noun phrases.)

Not parallel: Parents must teach values to their children consciously, openly, and **with consistence**. (The parts, *consciously* and *openly*, are adverbs; *with consistence* is a prepositional phrase.)

Parallel: Parents must teach values to their children consciously, openly, and consistently. (All parts of the series are adverbs.)

Not parallel: Club Med has good food, live entertainment, and a pool **that is heated**. (While other parts of the series are adjectives, *that is heated* is an adjective phrase.)

Parallel: Club Med has good food, live entertainment, and a heated pool. (All parts of the series are adjectives.)

[NOTE SB.42] Parts of contrasts should be parallel.

CONTRAST

Not parallel: Mansour speaks clearly but **writes with many errors**. (The part *speaks clearly* is a verb-adverb combination, but *writes with many errors* is a verb-prepositional phrase combination.)

Parallel: Mansour speaks clearly, but writes poorly. (Both parts are verb-adverb combinations.)

[NOTE SB.43] Parts of comparisons should be parallel.

COMPARISON

Not parallel: Your selling season is longer than **the Sandburg RV Center**. (The comparison is not clear—Is the selling season longer than the Sandburg RV Center? The necessary information to complete the comparison is omitted.)

Parallel: Your selling season is longer than the Sandburg RV Center's selling season. (Both parts of the comparison now contain clarifying adjective-noun combinations.)

[NOTE SB.44] Expressions of equality should be parallel.

EXPRESSION OF EQUALITY

Not parallel: Bob Kendall tutored a sophomore girl and **junior**. (The use of the adjective *sophomore* as a modifier for *girl* and *junior* produce the unlikely meaning that the girl is a sophomore and a junior.)

Parallel: Bob Kendall tutored a sophomore girl and a junior boy. (The use of appropriate articles and modifiers in both places clarifies that two people were tutored.)

The parallel constructions in these illustrations are generally shorter, clearer, and stronger than the constructions that are not parallel. Achieving parallelism in your sentences improves their readability and maintains their momentum. Because of their balance and consistency, parallel constructions communicate effectively as well as correctly.

[NOTE SB.45]
Parallel constructions are both correct and clear.

Common Sentence Errors

Dangling modifiers and double negatives are common sentence errors you will want to avoid. You will also want to avoid split infinitives.

[NOTE SB.46]
Avoid common sentence errors.

DANGLING MODIFIERS

A **dangling modifier** exists in a sentence when a phrase that limits or slightly changes the meaning of a word is not placed so that its relationship to that word is clear. In other words, the modifying phrase is *dangling* if it is too far removed from the word it modifies. For clarity in your messages, avoid dangling modifiers. In each of the following examples, the modifier is in italics and the word to be modified is in bold print:

[NOTE SB.47]
Avoid dangling modifiers; modifiers must be placed correctly.

Incorrect: The human resources **manager** hesitated to explain the policy to the employee, *seemingly confused.* (Who is *seemingly confused*?)

Correct: The human resources **manager**, *seemingly confused*, hesitated to explain the policy to the employee. (Moving the modifier closer to **manager** clarifies the relationship.)

Incorrect: *While participating as a cheerleader for Northwood High,* the teacher gave **me** a new cheer. (Who was participating as a cheerleader?)

Correct: *While participating as a cheerleader for Northwood High,* **I** was given a new cheer by my teacher. (Modifier *When participating as a cheerleader for Northwood High,* now clearly modifies the subject, **I**, in the rephrased sentence.)

DOUBLE NEGATIVES

A **double negative** is formed when a negative adverb (*no, not, hardly, barely, scarcely,* etc.) is used in the same sentence with a negative verb (can't, couldn't, won't, didn't, etc.). Such constructions are illogical because their use actually forms a positive. Double negatives are grammatically unacceptable and should be avoided. In the following examples the negative adverbs are in bold print and the negative verbs in italics:

[NOTE SB.48]
Avoid double negatives; do not use negative adverbs and negative verbs together.

Incorrect: I *don't* **hardly** know how to tell her. (The negative adverb **hardly** and the negative verb *don't* are used in the same sentence.)

Correct: I *don't* know how to tell her. (The negative adverb **hardly** has been removed from the sentence.)

Incorrect: It *won't* do **no** good to continue membership in the club. (The negative verb *won't* and negative adverb **no** are used in the same sentence.)

Correct:	It *will* do **no** good to continue membership in the club. (The negative verb *won't* has been changed to the positive verb *will.*)

SPLIT INFINITIVES

[NOTE SB.49] Avoid split infinitives when possible; do not place adverb between *to* and a verb.

An infinitive is formed by placing the word *to* before a present tense verb (*to accept, to agree, to feel,* etc.). A **split infinitive** is formed when an adverb is placed between the *to* and the verb (to *bravely* accept, to *barely* agree, to *warmly* feel, etc.). Although the trend is toward accepting split infinitives, many receivers still believe they are ungrammatical. It is best to avoid them when possible. Also avoid using several words to divide the infinitive. In the following examples, the infinitives are in bold print and the adverbs or other words that split the infinitives are in italics:

Incorrect:	Pamela was selected **to** *exclusively* **represent** the human resources department at the company's annual conference. (The infinitive **to represent** has been split by the adverb *exclusively*.)
Correct:	Pamela was selected **to represent** exclusively the human resources department at the company's annual conference. (The adverb *exclusively* has been placed after the infinitive.)
Incorrect:	Tina was asked **to** *quickly as possible* **design** a presentation for ABC. (Several words, *quickly as possible*, split the infinitive **to design**.)
Correct:	Tina was asked **to design** a presentation for ABC *as quickly as possible*. (The words *as quickly as possible* have been moved to the end of the sentence so they do not split the infinitive.)

[NOTE SB.50] Some business communicators choose to use selected split infinitives because they sound better.

Some split infinitives seem to sound better than do technically correct versions. In these cases you should either use the split infinitive or reword the sentence to avoid the problem. For example

Technically correct:	He decided to change gradually the procedures. (The wording *to change gradually* is awkward.)
Split infinitive:	He decided to gradually change the procedures. (When the infinitive *to change* is split with the adverb *gradually*, the sentence sounds better.)
Revision:	He decided to change the procedures gradually. (The revision avoids the problem of a split infinitive.)

Functions of Sentences

[NOTE SB.51] Sentences can serve as statements, questions, commands, or exclamations.

Sentences can serve one of four basic functions. These four functions are:

[1] *To state a fact.* A statement or **declarative sentence** is followed by a period. For example

The executive board will meet on November 5.

Gray spoke with Matt about the wedding.

[2] *To ask a question.* A question or **interrogative sentence** is followed by a question mark. For example

Have you written the article?

Are you going to Westmont College?

[3] *To issue a command or to make a polite request.* A command or request, also known as an **imperative sentence**, is followed by a period. Usually *you* is understood as the subject in a command or request. For example

[You] Please bring the file to our next meeting.

[You] Send the medical form to David Wu.

[4] *To express strong emotion.* An exclamation or **exclamatory sentence** is followed by an exclamation point. For example

Congratulations on your acceptance into the MBA program!

Ouch! I hit my toe!

Types of Sentence Structures

Finally, for you to know how to construct correct sentences, it is essential that you know the four basic sentence structures. The technical names of these sentence structures are *simple sentence, compound sentence, complex sentence,* and *compound-complex sentence.* Sentence structures are classified on the basis of the number and kinds of clauses they have. The two kinds of clauses—independent (main) and dependent (subordinate)—were discussed earlier in this chapter.

[NOTE SB.52]
There are four sentence structures.

Your messages will be more interesting if you vary the sentence structures you use. You can also emphasize an idea by placing it in an independent clause or de-emphasize it by placing it in a dependent clause. The effective communicator understands and uses all four sentence structures.

THE SIMPLE SENTENCE

The **simple sentence** contains one independent clause and no dependent clauses. You will recall that independent clauses contain both a subject and a predicate and are not introduced with a subordinate conjunction or a relative pronoun. Also, simple sentences can have compound subjects or compound predicates and can include phrases. Here are some examples of typical simple sentences:

[NOTE SB.53]
Simple sentences contain one independent clause.

Tito swims. (simple sentence)

Miss Hanson and Miss Bloom competed on the golf team. (simple sentence with compound subject)

Sales of scanners doubled last year. (simple sentence with prepositional phrase)

Because of the extension of the reporting date, we can edit and proofread our report again. (simple sentence with introductory prepositional phrase and compound predicate)

Mr. Manrique is the second executive director of Ukropina Delivery. (simple sentence with prepositional phrase)

[NOTE SB.54]
Simple sentences are businesslike, but their overuse results in choppy speaking or writing.

You can make your communication of an idea more powerful by using a simple sentence. This sentence structure gives the greatest emphasis to the idea because there are no distracting dependent clauses. The simple sentence is especially effective in composing business messages. It is a clear, concise, and efficient way of communicating—the simple sentence is businesslike. Overuse of simple sentences in a message, however, can result in choppy, singsong monotony—particularly if the sentences are all short. Note the choppiness in the following paragraph:

> The computer was started. The AOL account was accessed. The MetaCrawler search engine was launched. The listing of Web sites was given. The URL for LOT Airlines' Web site was located. The AOL connection was lost. The computer was started again. The AOL account was accessed again. The URL for the LOT Airlines' Web site was located again. The URL for the LOT Airlines' Web site was entered. The airline schedule for New York to Warsaw, Poland, was given. The ticket was booked.

To make your writing more interesting and possibly to de-emphasize some ideas, you will want to use sentence structures other than simple sentences.

THE COMPOUND SENTENCE

[NOTE SB.55]
Compound sentences contain two or more independent clauses.

The **compound sentence** contains two or more independent clauses and no dependent clauses. In this sentence structure, two or more ideas share equal emphasis. By pairing the ideas in one sentence consisting of independent clauses of similar strength, the ideas receive somewhat less emphasis than they would in separate simple sentences.

In the following examples, the subjects are in italics and the verbs are in bold. Note in these examples that the independent clauses in each compound sentence are joined with a coordinating conjunction, a conjunctive adverb, or a semicolon:

> *Ronalee* **will take the train** to the conference, and *she* **will speak** on cellular biology at the 9 a.m. session.
>
> *Kevin* **worked** for Blockbuster Video for three years; *Craig* **worked** for Boys Scouts of America for two years.
>
> *Mr. March* **was offered** the position, but *he* **did not accept** the offer.
>
> The *applicants* **appeared** to be equally qualified; however, *most of the managers* **chose** Mr. March.

Here is the example paragraph to show the use of compound sentences:

> The computer was started, and the AOL account was accessed. The MetaCrawler search engine was launched, and the listing of Web sites was given. The URL for the LOT Airlines' Web site was located, and the AOL connection was lost. The computer was started again, and the AOL account was accessed. The URL for the LOT Airlines' Web site was entered, and the airline schedule for New York to Warsaw, Poland, was given and the ticket booked.

The use of the compound sentence structure enables you to show that two or more ideas are of equal importance. By putting them together in one sentence, you indicate a close relationship which constitutes another, larger idea.

[NOTE SB.56]
Compound sentences can convey a close relationship of two or more ideas.

THE COMPLEX SENTENCE

The **complex sentence** contains one independent clause and one or more dependent clauses. Remember that a dependent clause depends on the independent clause to make a complete thought—hence, the term *dependent clause.*

[NOTE SB.57]
Complex sentences contain one independent clause and one or more dependent clauses.

In the *complex sentence* structure, one or more ideas are subordinate to the main idea. The less important or negative ideas can be de-emphasized by placing them in dependent clauses; the main idea can be emphasized by placing it in the independent clause. Another advantage of the complex sentence is that the dependent clause can be used to explain, clarify, and strengthen the main idea. The dependent clauses commonly used in complex sentences are the following:

[NOTE SB.58]
Ideas can be emphasized and de-emphasized in complex sentences.

- Noun clauses—used as subjects and objects
- Adjective clauses—used to modify nouns and pronouns
- Adverb clauses—used to modify verbs

As you know, a dependent clause contains both a subject and a verb and is introduced with a subordinating conjunction (such as *because, although, while, as soon as, if, whether*, or *when*) or a relative pronoun (such as *who, which*, or *that*). In the following examples the dependent clauses are in italics:

> *Although 99 percent of American retail stores stay open all year*, most of them make more than half their profit during the November-December holiday season.
>
> *While it is important that you be on time for work*, "flextime" permits you to choose your starting time.
>
> You will want to know *that many call the independent clause the main clause.*
>
> The independent clause is either preceded or followed by the dependent clause *which may be referred to as the subordinate clause.*
>
> All *who are being promoted* will receive raises.
>
> *When new graduates seek employment*, they should be sure to use their networks of friends, acquaintances, and relatives.

Here is the example paragraph using complex sentences:

> The AOL account was accessed after the computer was started. When the MetaCrawler search engine was launched, the URL for the LOT Airlines' Web site was listed. Since the AOL connection was lost, the computer was restarted and the AOL account accessed again. After the URL for the LOT Airlines' Web site was entered, the schedule for New York to Warsaw, Poland, was given and the ticket booked.

Complex sentences are more complicated than simple sentences in that they carry more than one idea. By its design, this structure causes some ideas to be de-emphasized and some ideas to be emphasized.

OAK WEST
EDUCATIONAL SERVICES
32 Arlington Square
Arlington, TX 76013
(817) 555-2324
(817) 555-2325 FAX

To: Michael Wang
From: Kristina Porter, Associate Director
Date: December 30, 2001
Subject: OAK WEST SAT I Course

Subject and predicate do not agree.

Thank you for your interest in OAK WEST. The OAK WEST SAT I course is unique since it were designed as a one-on-one program. By focusing on the individuals needs of each student, our tutors are able to provide the most effective SAT instruction.

Sentence is incomplete.

Are one-on-one tutoring provides. The tutors come right to the home. The lessons are scheduled directly with the student. OAK WEST's instructors is available seven days a week. The students is never locked into a set schedule.

Short, choppy, simple sentences; verbs are incorrect.

Series is not parallel.

The OAK WEST SAT program consists of five math sessions, ten sessions are given in verbal lessons, and one writing session. The materials included the $845 fee for the program are as follows:

1. OAK WEST math and verbal course books.
2. Specially designed OAK WEST homework drills.
3. OAK WEST series of computer-analyzed SAT tests.

List is not parallel.

We are very proud of our private tutorial program. If we can answer questions. Please feel free to call us at (817) 555-2324 for more information.

Sentence is incomplete.

Figure SB.1
Example of Poor Memo—Lacks Credibility Because of Grammatical Errors and Poor Sentence Structure Choices

To help you more fully realize the importance of correct grammar and sentence structure in your communications, review two examples of messages. Figure SB.1 is an example of a **poor** memo. Its writer will lose credibility because of the grammatical errors and poor sentence structure. Figure SB.2 is a **good** version of the same memo, a message that will gain credibility because of its correctness.

OAK WEST
EDUCATIONAL SERVICES
32 Arlington Square
Arlington, TX 76013
(817) 555-2324
(817) 555-2325 FAX

To: Michael Wang
From: Kristina Porter, Associate Director
Date: December 30, 2001
Subject: OAK WEST SAT I Course

Thank you for your interest in OAK WEST. The OAK WEST SAT I course is unique since it was designed as a one-on-one program. By focusing on the individual needs of each student, our tutors are able to provide the most effective SAT instruction.

Our one-on-one tutoring provides more interaction than can be found in any classroom-based course. The tutors come right to the home, and the lessons are scheduled directly with the student. OAK WEST's instructors are available seven days a week so that the student is never locked into a set schedule.

The OAK WEST SAT program consists of five math sessions, ten verbal sessions, and one writing session. The materials for the program are as follows:

1. OAK WEST math and verbal course books.
2. OAK WEST specially designed homework drills.
3. OAK WEST series of computer-analyzed SAT tests.

We are very proud of our private tutorial program which costs $845. If we can answer questions, please feel free to call us at (817) 555-2324 for more information.

Sentence is complete and shows relationship of ideas.

Sentence combines related ideas; pronouns agree with antecedent.

Series is parallel; all parts are adjective-noun combinations.

List is parallel; item No. 2 changed to be compatible.

Sentence is complete and shows relationship of ideas.

Figure SB.2
Example of a Good Memo—Gains Credibility Because of Grammatical Correctness and Appropriate Sentence Structure Choices

THE COMPOUND-COMPLEX SENTENCE

The **compound-complex sentence** contains two or more independent clauses and one or more dependent clauses. The compound-complex sentence structure offers a business communicator the advantages of both the compound and complex sentences. Ideas can be related, emphasized, and de-emphasized in this complicated structure.

[NOTE SB.59]
Compound-complex sentences contain two or more independent clauses and one or more dependent clauses.

[NOTE SB.60] Compound-complex sentences are used infrequently in business messages because of their length.

The compound-complex sentence structure, however, can become long and cumbersome. Business readers want to be able to understand a sentence on the first reading. For this reason, this sentence structure is used infrequently in business messages. In the following examples of compound-complex sentences, the dependent clauses are in italics and the independent clauses are in bold print:

> *Because many businesses are in isolated areas,* **volunteer fire fighting organizations are important to them**; *in addition to fighting fires effectively,* **these volunteer organizations help keep insurance rates low**.
>
> *Although the touring chorus goes to Canada with Tony and David,* **the concert chorus must continue to sing at home**; *however,* **the concert chorus is capable of putting on a good concert.**

Here is the example paragraph using compound-complex sentences:

> The computer was started, the AOL account accessed, the MetaCrawler search engine launched, and the URL for the LOT Airlines' Web site listed. When the AOL connection was lost, the computer had to be restarted and the AOL account accessed; after the URL for the LOT Airlines' Web site was entered, the schedule for New York to Warsaw, Poland, was given and the ticket booked.

APPLICATION EXERCISES

1. On a separate sheet of paper write each of the following sentences. Identify the complete subject by underlining it once and the complete predicate by underlining it twice.
   - **a.** Women shop with lists.
   - **b.** Boys and girls take the SAT tests for college admission.
   - **c.** Bonnie introduced the foreign students at the convention.
   - **d.** Mrs. Honeycutt, the English teacher, was responsible for the high school newspaper.
   - **e.** Don, who received the outstanding principal award, is now the assistant superintendent for the high school district.
   - **f.** All English tests were administered on the same day.
   - **g.** Fort Worth and Dallas are large cities with good universities.
   - **h.** A summer sports camp is designed for kids.
   - **i.** There were students who wanted to pursue an elementary teaching credential.
   - **j.** Why can't you install the computer memory?
2. Circle the simple subject and the simple predicate in each sentence in Exercise 1.
3. List the letter for each sentence in the following paragraph. Write the complete subject for that sentence beside the letter.

(a) Many types of businesses can be profitable. (b) Among the most profitable are restaurants. (c) But there can also be business failures. (d) It comes down to quality—quality food and quality management. (e) Cynthia and Andrea opened a Greek restaurant. (f) The two of them bought only the best food, and they oversaw its careful preparation. (g) Al-

though Cynthia and Andrea charged high prices, many customers were served; and excellent profits were made.

4. List the letter for each sentence in Exercise 3. Write the complete predicate for that sentence beside the letter.

5. List the letter of each of the following sentences. Write the direct objects and any indirect objects for that sentence beside the letter.

a. Jeannie sent the e-mail to Juan's account.

b. Gordon gave Allen a haircut.

c. Kathy Hath wrote a letter for the student.

d. Lester Freemon offered the football player a scholarship.

e. Every parent donated money to the Corona del Mar Foundation.

6. List the letter for each of the following sentences. Identify and explain the purpose of the italicized phrases in each sentence.

a. Anton *is definitely* on his way to be named the manager of Crate & Barrel.

b. Jane likes *to conduct* meetings for the Foundation.

c. Why is the office *closed so early*?

d. The principal is *an understanding person*.

e. All the boys were tired, *having sung 30 days straight*.

7. Identify the linking verbs in the following sentences:

a. We looked frightened.

b. You appeared nervous.

c. I feel cold.

8. List the letter for each of the following sentences. Beside each letter, write any dependent clause the sentence may contain, and indicate the sentence structure (i.e., simple, complex, compound, or compound-complex).

a. When the question of ethics arose, the supervisor stated clearly that all the accurate information would be provided.

b. Overseas shipments of freight are to be insured for full value.

c. Fair pay for women needs to be resolved; one would argue the sooner the better.

d. Esther is well liked because she is a good listener when students need her.

e. If you can, please let me know when the pizza will be ready.

f. The College of Business Faculty Support Center is a full-service communication facility; when you need word processing, e-mail, fax services, and other services, all you have to do is request them.

g. I am steadily making progress because I am continually improving my ability to give speeches.

h. Angel was glad she attended the class; she learned how to speak Spanish, which is knowledge she needs for international business.

i. Graphic aids are an important way to make complex information understandable.

j. Although not all the sales agents agreed, the home office changed the structure of the sales commissions.

9. List the letter for each sentence in Exercise 8. Write the independent (main) clause(s) beside each letter.
10. Circle the correct verb form for each of the following sentences:
    a. Forensics (is, are) required for the study of debate.
    b. Either Nancy or Peggy (is, are) going.
    c. *Communication Notes* (contain, contains) articles helpful to business writers.
    d. The committee (agree, agrees) with the new procedure.
    e. The board, rather than the officers, (vote, votes) on increasing fees.
    f. Neither Tien nor Michael (is, are) ready to report.
    g. The committee (has, have) decided to proceed with the project.
    h. Each member of the group, however, (think, thinks) the project should be done a different way.
    i. Most of the guys (is, are) in the jazz band.
    j. The police (has, have) spoken to the students last quarter.
11. Circle the correct pronoun in each of the following sentences:
    a. All of the students had (their, his or her) lunches.
    b. Either Christina or Lucy left (their, her) coat at Julio's house.
    c. Texas Christian University opened (their, its) school year on August 20.
    d. Each of the students introduced (their, his or her) dorm roommates.
    e. Every woman and man must introduce (their, her or his) parent.
12. Explain how each of the following sentences lacks parallelism. Rewrite the sentence correcting the lack of parallelism.
    a. CostCo's prices were lower than the Corner Store.
    b. The manager encouraged the plant employees, and the office employees were motivated by her.
    c. Shahz was strong, optimistic, and a woman of courage.
    d. Alex performs as a pianist and is running the marathon.
    e. The student's paper was brief and clearer.
13. Examine the following sentences for the common sentence errors of dangling modifiers, double negatives, and split infinitives. List the letter of each sentence and write a corrected version of that sentence beside the letter.
    a. He wouldn't never deny that he had a good time.
    b. Sailing on the ocean, a beautiful sunset filled the sky.
    c. The attendance clerk wrote the note to specifically excuse the boy from class.
    d. Kathryn and Andy wanted to really work hard at winning the election.
    e. Running through the park, a coyote crossed the path.
14. Write a short paragraph that includes an example of each of the four functions of sentences—statement, question, command or request, and exclamation.
15. Write a short paragraph that includes an example of each of the four basic sentence structures—simple sentence, compound sentence, complex sentence, and compound-complex sentence.

MESSAGE ANALYSIS

Examine the following message. Rewrite the message and correct any grammatical errors you find.

As we knows, a birth day are a very special day in our life, a celebration of life and future possibility. Theirfor, I want to invite you too a reception for all those in Academic Affairs whom will bee celebrating a birthday dureing the months of November and December. The reception will be held on Friday, December 10th, from 12-1:00 p.m. in the Academy Lodge.

This celebration will also give all off us a oppurtunity to meat knew persons through out our division. This unity can help promote a better sence of community.

Please RSVP to Carmen Ductoc at Ext. 257 by Monday, December 6th, so that we will be able to plan our refreshments. I look foreward to see you on December 10th.

SEMINAR

Punctuation

[NOTE SC.1]
Punctuation marks add emphasis and clarity to a message.

When you speak, the tone of your voice, the gestures you make, and the pauses you insert help your listeners understand what you are saying. When you write, punctuation helps your readers understand your message. Punctuation tells your readers where one thought ends and the next begins. Punctuation adds emphasis and clarifies meaning. Writing without punctuation is comparable to building a house without a blueprint.

[NOTE SC.2]
Check reference sources when you are uncertain about punctuation.

This seminar reviews the punctuation that occurs most often in business writing. The material is not designed to eliminate the need for reference manuals. When you have a question about punctuation, do not leave the answer to chance. Take the time to check this seminar, a reference manual, or a similar source. Using incorrect punctuation can cause your reader more confusion and frustration than using no punctuation at all.

Terminal Punctuation

[NOTE SC.3]
Periods are used to end
- Declarative and imperative sentences
- Polite requests that require action
- Indirect questions

The three punctuation symbols that are used to signal the end of a complete thought are the period, the question mark, and the exclamation point.

THE PERIOD

The **period** is the most frequently used ending mark of punctuation. It signals the end of a declarative or an imperative sentence. A declarative sentence makes a statement; an imperative sentence gives a command:

Miller's Hardware Store sustained nearly $500,000 in damage from the fire. (declarative)

You may have the gift wrapped at no extra charge. (declarative)

Lock the door when you leave. (imperative)

Take the package to the post office. (imperative)

A **polite request**, sometimes called a *courteous request,* requires action rather than an oral or written response. The writer would rather have the reader devote time to doing what has been requested than to writing or calling to say yes or no. A polite request ends with a period:

Won't you take a few moments now to complete and return the survey.

Will you please return my call before 3 p.m. today.

The period is also used when the writer asks an **indirect question**—a statement about a question:

I wonder when the copier will be repaired.

Manuel asked whether you and I are related.

THE QUESTION MARK

A **question mark** should be used with an interrogative sentence. An interrogative sentence asks for or requires a definite response. The response may be a single word, or it may be one or more sentences:

[NOTE SC.4]
Question marks are used to end direct questions.

Was the carton damaged when it arrived? (one-word response)

What arrangements have you made for your trip to Seoul? (a response of one or more sentences)

When a series of questions has a common subject and predicate, each question is followed by a question mark. Unless the questions in a series are proper nouns or complete thoughts, capitalize only the first letter of the sentence:

Have we determined when? where? why?

Do you golf? play tennis? swim?

Will you visit Paris? London? Berlin? Stockholm?

THE EXCLAMATION MARK

An **exclamation mark** is used with an exclamatory sentence—one that shows strong emotion. Because of the dramatic effect it creates, the exclamation mark is used sparingly in business correspondence:

[NOTE SC.5]
Exclamation marks show strong emotion.

Yes! We submitted the low bid.

Hurry! Make your reservation today.

Congratulations!

Sharp's will not be undersold!

CHOOSING TERMINAL PUNCTUATION

When deciding which terminal punctuation mark to use, ask these questions:

- Am I expressing a strong emotion? (If yes, use !)
- Am I asking the reader to give me a response? (If so, use ?)
- If you answer no to both questions, use the period.

Primary Internal Punctuation

Terminal punctuation marks help guide your reader through your message. Internal punctuation marks help him or her through each sentence. The comma and the semicolon are the most frequently used internal punctuation marks.

THE COMMA

[NOTE SC.6] Commas separate items in sentences.

[NOTE SC.7] Too few or too many commas can hamper message clarity.

The comma plays an important role in business writing. A **comma** separates items in a sentence and helps the reader correctly interpret each thought. By learning how commas are used and by mastering the rules for their placement, you will become a more effective business writer. Using commas incorrectly—omitting them where needed or adding them where they are not needed—can hamper communication. Consider these examples:

> After you have eaten the leftover meat the vegetables and the dairy products should be placed in the refrigerator. (commas have been omitted)

In this sentence, the absence of commas makes the reader wonder what is to be eaten and what is to be put into the refrigerator. Confusion results, and additional communication is necessary. The message becomes clear when a comma is inserted after the word *eaten* and between each item in the compound subject:

> After you have eaten, the leftover meat, the vegetables, and the dairy products should be placed in the refrigerator.

In the following sentence, message clarity is lost because four commas are used where none are needed:

> This afternoon, we will meet with the chair of the board, while her staff members, tour the new addition, to the factory. (commas are used where they are not needed)

The sentence should read as follows:

> This afternoon we will meet with the chair of the board while her staff members tour the new addition to the factory.

[NOTE SC.8] Be sure to justify each comma you use.

Although the original versions of these sentences are extreme examples of comma omission and misuse, they illustrate the need for caution in using commas. The best way to ensure correct use of commas is to be able to justify their placement.

[NOTE SC.9] Use commas with complete calendar dates.

Calendar Dates A complete **calendar date** consists of a month, a day, and a year. Whenever a complete calendar date occurs within the body of a sentence, the year is set apart from the rest of the sentence by commas. When a complete calendar date occurs at the end of an independent clause or a sentence, the final comma is replaced by a semicolon or terminal punctuation. If the military or international date form is used, however, no commas are needed:

> On *June 17, 1932,* Carlson College held its first commencement ceremony. (Calendar date is complete.)
>
> In *June 1932* Carlson College conducted its first commencement ceremony. (Commas optional when date consists only of month and year. *June, 1932,* is also correct.)

Carlson held its first commencement ceremony on *June 17, 1932*. (The calendar date is complete and ends the sentence.)

On *17 June 1932* Carlson College conducted its first commencement ceremony. (The military or international date form does not need commas.)

When a weekday is used with a calendar date, the date is set off by commas. The calendar date may be complete or incomplete:

On *Monday, October 23,* the Bloodmobile will be at Village Mall. (Weekday with incomplete calendar date.)

Spring semester classes will begin on *Friday, January 18, 2002*. (Weekday with complete calendar date.)

Geographic Locations A complete **geographic location** consists of a city and a state, province, or nation. When such a geographic location occurs within a sentence, the name of the state, province, or nation is set apart from the rest of the sentence by commas. When an incomplete geographic location is named in a sentence, no commas are necessary:

[NOTE SC.10]
Use commas with complete geographic locations.

The Olympic Games were held in *Atlanta, Georgia,* during the summer of 1996. (*Atlanta, Georgia,* is a complete geographic location.)

We will close our *Seattle* warehouse in August. (The geographic location is incomplete.)

Have you ever visited *Acapulco, Mexico*? (The geographic location is complete; the question mark replaces the ending comma because the name of the country is the last item in the interrogative sentence.)

Independent Adjectives When two or more adjectives in a series independently modify the same noun, they are called **independent adjectives**. Commas are used to separate independent adjectives:

[NOTE SC.11]
A comma replaces the word *and* between independent adjectives.

Avery is a patient, caring, sincere foster parent; Dyanne is a well-known, well-respected office automation consultant.

The adjectives in the first series independently describe Avery as a foster parent; those in the second series independently describe Dyanne as a consultant. The writers could have stated it this way:

Avery is a patient and caring and sincere foster parent; Dyanne is a well-known and well-respected office automation consultant.

Combining the adjectives, however, is more efficient for the writer and more pleasing to the reader. A good test of the need for commas and where they should be placed is to insert the word *and* between the adjectives. If the word *and* can be inserted without altering the meaning of the sentence, a comma should be used:

Sentence without punctuation: Reo gave a brief emotional acceptance speech.

Test: Reo gave a brief (and) emotional acceptance speech.

Correctly punctuated: Reo gave a brief, emotional acceptance speech.

The following example needs no commas. If we try to insert the word *and* between the adjectives, the sentence becomes awkward.

Sentence without punctuation: Roberto drives a shiny blue sports car. (The words *shiny*, *blue*, and *sports* describe the car, but they do so collectively, not independently.)

Test: Roberto drives a shiny (and) blue (and) sports car.

Correctly punctuated: Roberto drives a shiny blue sports car.

[NOTE SC.12] When two independent clauses are joined by a coordinating conjunction, place a comma before the conjunction.

Independent Clauses When the independent clauses in a compound sentence are joined with a coordinating conjunction (*and, but, or, nor*), use a comma before the conjunction:

The car handles well, *and* it gets good mileage. (The coordinating conjunction joins independent clauses.)

The trees and wild flowers in the forest were beautiful and created a peaceful atmosphere, *but* Leona and Signe longed for the noise and activity of the city. (The coordinating conjunction joins the independent clauses.)

Maddie and Katy sing in the choir. (No comma is needed because the coordinating conjunction *and* does not connect two independent clauses.)

[NOTE SC.13] Use a comma after a dependent clause that introduces an independent clause.

Introductory Clauses When a dependent clause *introduces* an independent clause in a complex sentence, a comma is used to separate the clauses. Introductory clauses commonly begin with one of the following words:

after	before	until
although	if	when
as	since	whenever
because	unless	while

When the dependent clause does not introduce the independent clause, a comma is not used:

If you join, you will receive a free calculator. (The dependent clause introduces the independent clause.)

After we receive your check, we will process your order. (The dependent clause introduces the independent clause.)

Let's go to the mall *after we work out at the gym*. (No comma is needed; the dependent clause does not introduce the independent clause.)

Nonessential Elements Words, phrases, or clauses that are not necessary to the meaning or structure of a sentence are considered **nonessential elements**. Appositives, introductory words, introductory phrases, nonrestrictive clauses, parenthetical expressions, and transitional expressions are all nonessential elements.

[NOTE SC.14] Nonessential elements require one or more commas.

Each nonessential element requires one or more commas. A nonessential element that begins a sentence is followed by a comma. A nonessential element that ends an independent clause is followed by a comma or a semicolon; one that ends a sentence is followed by the appropriate terminal punctuation mark. A nonessential element that does not end an independent clause or a sentence is preceded and followed by a comma. To determine whether an item is nonessential, omit it from the sentence. If the meaning and structure of the sentence are complete, the item is considered nonessential.

Appositives An **appositive** is a word or a phrase that immediately follows a noun and either explains or provides additional information about it. When this additional information is not necessary to the meaning of the sentence, it is separated from the rest of the sentence by commas:

> [NOTE SC.15]
> Use commas with nonessential appositives.

My oldest sister, Sarah, serves on the City Council. (The name Sarah is not essential to the meaning of the sentence; only one of the writer's sisters may be the oldest.)

My sister Sarah serves on the City Council. (The name is needed to indicate which of the writer's sisters serves on the Council.)

Introductory Words An **introductory word** is the first word in a sentence; it leads the reader to the independent clause and is separated from the clause by a comma. *Obviously*, *generally*, and *unfortunately* are examples of introductory words; others are used in the following examples:

> [NOTE SC.16]
> An introductory word is followed by a comma.

Yes, Ms. Armandoza was employed as a clerk in our office. (The introductory word is not essential to the meaning or structure of the sentence.)

Currently, I am coaching a youth softball team. (The introductory word is not essential to the meaning or structure of the sentence.)

When the receiver is named as the opening word(s) of a sentence, the writer has used a **direct address**:

Mr. Wilson, you'll receive many hours of enjoyment from your new treadmill.

Paula, do you know Jarrod's e-mail address?

Introductory Phrases An **introductory phrase** is a group of words that begins a sentence and introduces an independent clause. Introductory phrases may or may not be separated from an independent clause by a comma; the deciding factor is readability. If omitting the comma could cause reader confusion, include it. Some writers use a comma after an introductory phrase that has five or more words. You, too, may find this technique helpful:

> [NOTE SC.17]
> Commas are optional after introductory phrases.

To earn a bonus you must exceed your sales goal by at least 20 percent. (No comma is necessary; the message is clear without the comma.)

By paying now you will avoid finance charges. (No comma is necessary; the message is clear without the comma.)

Without warning, Juan turned and walked away. (Message clarity is improved by placing a comma after the introductory phrase.)

After entering your five-digit authorization code and hearing the progression tone, enter the area code and number. (Message clarity is improved by placing a comma after the long introductory phrase.)

Nonrestrictive Clauses Earlier in this section, you learned that an appositive provides additional information about a noun; a **nonrestrictive clause** has the same function. One feature distinguishes an appositive from a nonrestrictive clause: An appositive is a word or a phrase—not a clause.

> [NOTE SC.18]
> Nonrestrictive clauses provide additional information; use a comma before and after them.

Nonrestrictive clauses frequently begin with *who* or *which*. They are separated from the rest of a sentence by commas. Some writers prefer to use the word *which* to begin a nonrestrictive clause and the word *that* to begin a restrictive (essential) clause:

> The sculpture, *which was commissioned by the council*, will be displayed in the courtyard of City Hall. (The clause is not essential to the meaning of the sentence.)
>
> The payment *that was due March 15* is now three weeks late. (The clause is essential to the sentence.)
>
> The people *who want to speak with you* are seated in the lobby. (The clause is essential to the sentence.)
>
> Please inform Senator Barjo that, *although we have supported him in the past*, we will oppose him on the sales tax issue. (The clause is not essential to the meaning of the sentence. Note that this nonrestrictive clause does not begin with who or which.)
>
> Sally, *who visited Mexico City last spring*, plans to vacation in Toronto this fall. (The clause does not restrict the meaning of the sentence.)

[NOTE SC.19] Parenthetical expressions interrupt the flow of a sentence; they should be preceded and followed by a comma.

Parenthetical Expressions When one or more words interrupt the flow of a sentence, a **parenthetical expression** is created. The expression is separated from the rest of the sentence by commas:

> If you delay, *however*, all the good seats will be gone. (The word *however* interrupts the flow of the sentence.)
>
> The white blossom, *although less common*, is as beautiful as the red. (The words *although less common* interrupt the flow of the sentence.)
>
> The film is, *to quote the reviewer*, "extraordinary." (The words *to quote the reviewer* interrupt the flow of the sentence.)

[NOTE SC.20] Transitional expressions link independent clauses.

Transitional Expressions A word or phrase that links sentences or independent clauses is a **transitional expression**. When a transitional expression links two independent clauses, it is preceded by a semicolon and followed by a comma. When a transitional expression links two sentences, it is followed by a comma:

> The wallpaper was printed in two different lots; *therefore*, the colors did not match. (A transitional expression links two independent clauses.)
>
> Your newest catalog had not yet arrived when we placed our order. *As a result*, we were unable to use the new price in calculating the total cost of our order. (The transitional expression links two sentences.)

Words such as *however* and *therefore* and phrases such as *of course* and *as a result* may be either parenthetical or transitional. The key is how they are used in the sentence:

> The invoice, *therefore*, has been approved for payment. (The word *therefore* interrupts the flow of the sentence—it is parenthetical.)
>
> The remaining items in the order were delivered yesterday; *therefore*, the invoice has been approved for payment. (The word *therefore* is used as a transitional word linking two independent clauses.)

[NOTE SC.21] Commas separate items in a series.

Series When three or more words, phrases, or clauses are to be taken as one unit to form a subject, a verb, or an object, a **series** is formed. Items in a series should be separated by commas. The final item is usually set apart from the others by the word *and* or the word *or.* For clarity, a comma should be used before the conjunction as well as between each of the items:

> *Kevin, Harold, and Rich* are fraternity brothers. (The three names are part of a compound subject.)
>
> Jason plays *bridge, chess, and backgammon.* (The items are the direct object of the verb plays.)
>
> The campers will *canoe, hike, and swim.* (The verbs describe the actions of the campers.)
>
> *Up/down, near/far,* and *thick/thin* are pairs of antonyms. (Each pair of words in the series is part of a compound subject.)

[NOTE SC.22]
The final item in a series follows a conjunction.

THE SEMICOLON

The **semicolon** is used to separate. It may also be used to join.

[NOTE SC.23]
Semicolons may be used to separate and to join.

Independent Clauses Without Coordinating Conjunctions A semicolon is used to join two independent clauses not joined by a coordinating conjunction. The semicolon makes the reader aware of the close relationship between the independent clauses. Although each clause could be written as a separate sentence, joining them with a semicolon creates a smoother writing style:

[NOTE SC.24]
Semicolons join independent clauses when no conjunction is used.

> Please sign and return the enclosed card; it requires no postage. (The clauses are closely related; no conjunction is used.)
>
> Marilyn has agreed to chair the meeting; please send your agenda items to her. (The clauses are closely related; no conjunction is used.)

When a comma is mistakenly used to join independent clauses where no conjunction is present, a *comma splice* is created. Writers should be careful to avoid this error:

> Larry has asked for a one-month leave of absence, he and his wife plan to tour the Orient. (incorrectly punctuated; comma splice)
>
> Larry has asked for a one-month leave of absence; he and his wife plan to tour the Orient. (correctly punctuated; semicolon joins independent clauses)

Independent Clauses With Coordinating Conjunctions When independent clauses are joined by a coordinating conjunction and either or both of the clauses contain commas, clarity is achieved by using a semicolon (rather than a comma) before the conjunction that joins the two independent clauses. In the example that follows, the second sentence uses a semicolon and is clearer and easier to read:

[NOTE SC.25]
Semicolons should be used to join independent clauses that contain commas.

> Mr. Abelson, Ms. Skurla, and Mrs. Newstrom will leave for Detroit on September 10, but Mr. Yukita, Mrs. Zollar, and Mr. Nelson will not leave until September 12.
>
> Mr. Abelson, Ms. Skurla, and Mrs. Newstrom will leave for Detroit on September 10; but Mr. Yukita, Mrs. Zollar, and Mr. Nelson will not leave until September 12.

Series Items Containing Commas Using commas to separate items in a series could result in confusion when one or more items within the series contain a comma. By

[NOTE SC.26]
Use semicolons to separate long, complex series items that contain commas.

using semicolons to separate the items in this type of series, the message is easier to interpret. In the example that follows, the second sentence—the one that uses semicolons to separate the series items—is much clearer:

> While in Europe, they will visit Vienna, Austria, Paris, France, Munich, Germany, and Naples, Italy. (Unclear)
>
> While in Europe, they will visit Vienna, Austria; Paris, France; Munich, Germany; and Naples, Italy. (Clear)

The comma and the semicolon are two punctuation marks that influence the clarity and readability of a message. Use them effectively to help your reader better understand your message.

Secondary Internal Punctuation

Several other punctuation marks are used within sentences to bring clarity, emphasis, and variety to writing. Those punctuation marks are discussed in this section.

THE APOSTROPHE

[NOTE SC.27] Apostrophes are used to form possessives and contractions.

As you write letters, memos, and reports, you will use the apostrophe in three ways: to form possessives, to form contractions, and to form plurals.

Possessives A **possessive** shows ownership. Both nouns and pronouns may be expressed as possessives. Figure SC.1 shows the possessive form of several nouns and pronouns. Recall that only nouns use an apostrophe in their possessive form. The apostrophe is placed either before the *s* ('s) or after the *s* (s') depending on the noun. The context of the sentence will often provide a clue to placement of the apostrophe. Seminar A contains detailed information about forming possessives.

Figure SC.1
Possessive Forms

Word	Possessive	Word	Possessive
she (pronoun)	her car	employee (noun)	employee's file
we (pronoun)	our house	employees (noun)	employees' lounge
they (pronoun)	their class	Mike (noun)	Mike's office
he (pronoun)	his computer	window (noun)	window's reflection
month (noun)	a month's data	Chris (noun)	Chris' report

[NOTE SC.28] Contractions are seldom used in business correspondence.

Contractions A **contraction** is a combination of two words in a shortened form. An apostrophe signals the omission of one or more letters in the contraction—*you're* for *you are, wouldn't* for *would not,* and *let's* for *let us.* Contractions are seldom used in business writing because they lack the formality desired in a permanent record. The opposite is true of *o'clock*; this contraction for *of the clock* is used when writers want formality.

When spoken, several contractions sound the same as possessive pronouns. These potentially confusing words are listed in Figure SC.2. If you are unsure about whether to use an apostrophe, remember this: A contraction *always* has an apostrophe.

Word	Meaning
its	possessive form of pronoun *it*
it's	contraction of *it is*
their	possessive form of pronoun *they* (before noun)
they're	contraction of *they are*
theirs	possessive form of the pronoun *they* (not before noun)
there's	contraction of *there is*
whose	possessive form of pronoun *who*
who's	contraction of *who is*
your	possessive form of pronoun *you*
you're	contraction of *you are*

Figure SC.2
Possessive and Contraction Soundalikes

Plurals For clarity, use an apostrophe to form the plural of a lowercase letter. Also use the apostrophe to form the plural of the uppercase letters A, I, M, and U. Without an apostrophe, these uppercase letters could be misread as words (As, Is, Us) or as an abbreviation (Ms):

Place x's before all items that apply.

How many A's did you earn last term?

THE COLON

The colon is often used as a clue to the reader that a *list*, an *explanation*, or an *example* will follow. The words that introduce the list should contain a subject and a predicate. The items following the colon may be words, phrases, or complete sentences. They may be displayed as part of the paragraph text or as a vertical list. The writer makes the placement decision based on the space available and the amount of emphasis to be placed on the items. A list will receive more attention than items presented in paragraph form. When displayed in paragraph form, items following a colon begin with a capital letter only when they are complete sentences; items in a list always begin with a capital letter. Items may be numbered in either style, but only one form should be used in the list:

[NOTE SC.29]
Colons alert the reader that something of importance will follow.

Bretta's reason for missing the meeting was simple: She was one of three passengers in the elevator when it stopped between the sixth and seventh floors. (explanation in paragraph form)

Several factors influenced our decision: personnel, space, and equipment. (listing in paragraph form; common nouns)

Three factors influenced our decision: (1) Additional personnel would be needed. (2) Space for expansion does not exist. (3) Our equipment is old and fragile. (explanatory list in paragraph form with numbered sentences)

[NOTE SC.30]
Paragraph form.

The decision was influenced by the following factors:

1. The need for additional personnel
2. The lack of space for expansion
3. The condition of our equipment

[NOTE SC.31]
Vertical list form.

Our decision was influenced by personnel, space, and equipment factors. (No colon is used because the portion of the sentence before the series is not an independent clause.)

The colon has several other applications that occasionally occur in business writing. Those uses and an example of each are presented in Figure SC.3.

Figure SC.3
Other Uses of the Colon

Use	Example
ratio	3:1 (3 to 1)
references	17:55–62 (volume: page numbers)
reference initials	SLP:gg (author: keyboarder)
salutations	Dear Ms. Wilcott: (mixed punctuation)
times	4:45 p.m. (hour: minutes)

THE DASH

[NOTE SC.32]
Dashes separate.

A **dash** is used to separate. It shows a sudden change in thought or places emphasis on what follows. A dash has no space before, between, or after the two hyphens that form it. Because of its strength and impact, the dash should be used less frequently than other marks of punctuation:

Only one product sold better than we predicted—the portfolio. (emphasis)

She must decide soon—the offer expires Monday. (emphasis)

Bilin—a B+ student—plays catcher for the softball team. (sudden change of thought)

THE DIAGONAL

[NOTE SC.33]
The diagonal has several uses.

The **diagonal** (also called the *slant* or *slash*) frequently indicates a choice or an alternative. The diagonal is also used in creating fractions and may be used with some abbreviations. No space is used before or after the diagonal:

Do you want bagels and/or muffins at the meeting? (Either or both may be served.)

The individual we hire will prepare our annual report; his/her workstation will be equipped with a computer and a color printer. (The gender of the new employee is unknown.)

S/he will replace Arturo, who retires in May. (S/he is used to mean she or he and to eliminate gender bias.)

Tell them to proceed w/o delay. (without)

4/5 (fraction)

33 1/3 (mixed number; space before fraction)

[NOTE SC.34]
In correspondence, avoid using the diagonal with a date.

When completing business forms, writers often use the diagonal as part of a date. The standard format is month/day/year; two character positions are allocated to each part. The emerging popularity of the international date style (day/month/year) and the confusion that could result make this format inappropriate for use in correspondence:

02/03/03 (February 3, 2003? March 2, 2003?)

THE ELLIPSIS

[NOTE SC.35]
Ellipsis points indicate that words have been omitted.

An **ellipsis** is an intentional omission of words. An ellipsis is signaled by **ellipsis points**, a series of three periods separated from each other and from what precedes or follows them by one space. Ellipsis points are used for emphasis in advertising. In other forms of business writing, ellipsis points are used to indicate that words have been omitted from a direct quotation. When the ellipsis occurs at the end of a sentence, add the terminal punctuation:

> The fluctuations in currency exchange rates are interesting . . . and worth watching.
>
> The recipe says the batter should be ". . . light and fluffy."
>
> Ethel choked back tears as she began her acceptance speech by saying, "I am truly honored. . . ." (end of sentence)

THE HYPHEN

The **hyphen** is used to bring things together, to show that two items are related. Because the purpose is to join, there is no space before or after a hyphen. Hyphens are commonly used in four ways: (1) to form compound words, (2) to join prefixes and suffixes to root words, (3) to join numbers or letters in a range, and (4) to indicate where a word has been divided. The first three uses are more common and are explained in this section.

Compound Words The most frequent use of the hyphen is to form compound words. A **compound word** is two or more words used as one. Compound words may be nouns, verbs, or adjectives. Writing experts do not always agree on whether compound words should be hyphenated, written as two words, or written as one word; style preferences are continually changing. The best source of information about compound nouns and verbs is a current dictionary. The information presented in this section will help you determine when and how to hyphenate compound adjectives.

[NOTE SC.36]
Hyphens form compound words.

Compound adjectives may be permanent or temporary. Permanent compound adjectives include a hyphen as part of their dictionary entry; temporary compound adjectives do not. Permanent compound adjectives use a hyphen all the time; temporary compound adjectives contain a hyphen only when they come before a noun. Compound adjectives formed using an *-ly* adverb are never hyphenated:

[NOTE SC.37]
Compound adjectives may be permanent or temporary.

> Patricia Cornwell is a *well-known* author. (permanent compound)
>
> Patricia Cornwell is *well-known* as an author. (permanent compound)
>
> They are a *well-organized, highly motivated* team. (temporary compound; *-ly* adverb compound)
>
> The tasks are simple but *time consuming*. (temporary compound not before noun)

Dictionaries may vary. Always consult the current edition of a well-known dictionary.

Sometimes two or more hyphenated compound words with the same base word appear in a series. In this case the hyphen is used, but the base word may be omitted in all except the last item of the series. This procedure is called suspending a hyphen:

> Be prepared to discuss your *short-* and *long-range* goals. (The word *range* is omitted in the first compound word.)
>
> The announcement can be repeated at *5-*, *15-*, or *30-minute* intervals. (The word *minute* is omitted in the first two compound words.)

Prefixes A **prefix** is one or more syllables added to the beginning of a word. Prefixes are followed by hyphens in a variety of situations. Figure SC.4 lists those situations and gives an example of each.

Figure SC.4
Hyphenating Prefixes

Prefix/ Prefix Ending	Hyphenated	Example
prefix ending in *i*	before word beginning with *i*	quasi-intellectual
prefix ending in *a*	before word beginning with *a*	ultra-ambitious
prefix ending in *e*	seldom; consult a dictionary	de-emphasize, deactivate, prerecorded, vice president, vice-consul
prefix ending in *o*	seldom; consult a dictionary	coworker, co-author, microchip, microorganism
ex (former)	always when a prefix	ex-member, ex-spouse
non	seldom; consult a dictionary	nonessential, nonurgent
re (to do again)	to distignuish from word with different meaning	re-form/reform
self	always when a prefix	self-assured, self-addressed

Whenever a prefix is added to a proper noun, the prefix is separated from the word by a hyphen:

mid-May   trans-Alaska

[NOTE SC.38]
Hyphens are used between points in a range.

Ranges A hyphen connects the high and low numbers or first and last letters in a range. The hyphen indicates the relationship between the items by taking the place of *to* or *through:*

The range of temperatures during July was 89-101.

Items 1-5 focus on demographics; items 6-10, on opinions.

When main floor seating is nearly full, open balconies A-C.

The reception will be Saturday, 7-9 p.m.

PARENTHESES

[NOTE SC.39]
Items that are unimportant may be placed in parentheses.

Parentheses, like commas, may be used to separate nonessential information from the rest of a thought. If parentheses and commas were compared according to their strength, however, parentheses would be rated as weaker marks of punctuation. The information they contain may be so unimportant that the writer should consider eliminating it entirely. Names, dates, times, amounts, reference citations, abbreviations, area codes, phone numbers, addresses, and editorial comments are just a few of the items that may be enclosed within parentheses. If a writer chooses to use parentheses, certain requirements must be met:

[1] Both left and right parentheses must be used.

Baron Clothiers, Inc. (BCI) accepts telephone orders between 7 a.m. and 4 p.m. (EST) Monday through Friday.

[2] Commas, semicolons, periods, or other punctuation marks should be used as needed within the parentheses.

The entree (salmon) will be served with a baked potato, broccoli with cheese sauce (or, if you prefer, lemon butter), and a colorful fruit garnish.

[3] The presence of parentheses should not affect the use of punctuation elsewhere in the statement or question.

After she retired (lucky woman!), Elsa moved to Idaho.

THE PERIOD

Earlier in this chapter, you reviewed the use of the period as a mark of terminal punctuation. While that use of the period is certainly the most common, it is by no means the only use. This section focuses on other uses.

[NOTE SC.40]
Periods are used with
- Abbreviations
- Decimals
- Lists

Abbreviations **Abbreviations** are shortened forms of words, names, or phrases; their primary purpose is to save time and space. As a general rule, business writers restrict their use of abbreviations to those they believe their receivers will recognize.

The capitalization, punctuation, and spacing of abbreviations vary widely. Seminar D covers some of these issues. The most comprehensive source of information about abbreviations is a reference manual.

Decimals A **decimal** is one method by which writers may express fractional components of a whole number. In business writing, use decimals when expressing money or measurements. Do not use a space before or after the decimal:

> Safeway's rate for a 47-passenger coach is $1.10 a mile.
>
> Each package should contain 14.5 ounces of cereal.
>
> The second portage is the longest, 2.8 miles.
>
> All units that vary from specification by more than .0025" must be rejected.

Lists When items in a list are identified by numbers or letters, a period is used. Lists may be formatted in three ways; all three apply to either numeric or alphabetic listings:

[NOTE SC.41]
List formats vary.

[1] In one format, the number is indented and the text wraps to the left margin. This is true whether the text runs over one line or many.

[2] In another format, both the number and any runover lines of the text begin at the left margin. This, also, is true whether the text runs over one line or many.

[3] Still another option is to key the number at the left margin and hang indent the text. This is true whether the text runs over one line or many.

A minimum of two spaces should follow the period. When using word processing software, simply tab to the next position on the preset tab grid.

THE QUOTATION MARK

A **quotation mark** serves three different purposes in written messages: (1) to indicate that the writer is using the exact words of another individual, (2) to emphasize words that are unique or have a special meaning in a particular message, or (3) to identify literary or artistic works. In all cases, quotation marks are used in pairs—one is placed at the beginning of the quote or item of information, while the other is placed at the end.

[NOTE SC.42]
Quotation marks show exact wording, give special emphasis, or identify literary or artistic works.

Exact Words Quotations may be indirect or direct. An **indirect quotation** paraphrases the words of a writer or speaker. A **direct quotation** uses the exact words of a writer. Quotation marks are used only with a direct quotation:

> Mrs. Gotto said, "Expenditures must be reduced by 10 percent."
>
> Mrs. Gotto said that we need a 10 percent reduction in expenditures.

[NOTE SC.43] The length of a quote influences its display.

Using quotation marks to highlight someone's exact words works well if the quote is brief. When the quote is long, however, another display technique is more emphatic. If a direct quotation occupies less than four lines of type, place the text in quotation marks but do not indent the material:

> In his inaugural address, Governor Snellgrover told the citizens of the state, "Education, jobs, and the environment are high-priority items." (Short direct quotation)

If the quoted material occupies four or more lines of type, display it as a separate, single-spaced paragraph and indent the material from both the left and right margins. This indented format, together with information about the source of the material, makes quotation marks unnecessary:

> In his inaugural address, Governor Snellgrover told the citizens of the state
>
> > During my campaign I promised to work to maintain the quality of life that has made this state such a fine place in which to live. Education, jobs, and the environment are high-priority items. We must not lose what we have worked so hard to achieve; we must strive to make further gains.

[NOTE SC.44] Words in quotation marks receive emphasis.

Emphasis Whenever you wish to emphasize a word or phrase, even if it is not part of a direct quote, consider displaying it in quotation marks. Humorous items, definitions, slang words or phrases, and technical terms used in nontechnical ways are good candidates for this type of emphasis. If words are emphasized with quotation marks too frequently, however, the benefits of this display are lost:

> Mickey named his turtle "Speedy."
>
> Etc. is the abbreviation for the Latin phrase meaning "and so forth."

Literary and Artistic Works Use quotation marks to set off the title of any section of a published work:

> Martin's article, "Bigger Isn't Always Better," has been accepted for publication in *The Entrepreneur*. (article in a magazine)
>
> "Houseplants" is the second chapter of Beth Bretaglia's book, *The Green Thumb Gardener*.
>
> "Memory," a well-known song from the Broadway musical *Cats*, is one of the selections contained in *The Andrew Lloyd Webber Collection*. (song, musical, album)

With Other Punctuation Marks Because quotation marks may be used to begin, end, or set off material within a statement or question, some guidelines must be set regarding the use of other punctuation when quotation marks are present. Figure SC.5 will be a helpful reference.

Three additional rules concerning the use of punctuation and quotation marks should be remembered in writing business letters, memos, and reports:

[1] Punctuation may be included in a quotation. If the quote is taken from a printed source, the punctuation should be included where the original author inserted it—even if it is incorrect.

[2] Ending punctuation may be placed before or after the quotation marks but never in both places. When a conflict exists, use the stronger mark of punctuation. Exclamation marks are stronger than both question marks and periods.

Punctuation mark	Placement
period	inside quotation marks
comma	inside quotation marks
colon	outside quotation marks
semicolon	outside quotation marks
question mark	inside when quotation is a question; outside when the entire item is a question
exclamation point	inside when quotation is an exclamation; outside when the entire item is an exclamation

Figure SC.5
Quotation Marks With Other Punctuation Marks

[3] Direct quotes that occur in the middle or near the end of other statements or questions are introduced by either a colon or a comma.

The following items illustrate how the placement guidelines and rules may be applied:

Did the performance appraisal contain this statement: "Sandra has become the department's expert in database management"? (The entire item is a question.)

One of the golfers in the foursome behind us yelled "Fore!" (Only the quote is an exclamation.)

This badly damaged package was marked "Fragile"! (The entire sentence is an exclamation.)

THE UNDERSCORE

The **underscore** is used to give special emphasis. When preparing a manuscript for typesetting by a printer, for example, the underscore signals that what is above it should be set in italics. Because typewriters and computer printers may not be able to print italicized characters easily or well, the underscore has become an acceptable substitute.

[NOTE SC.45]
Underscores show special emphasis.

[NOTE SC.46]
Underscores may be used as a substitute for italics.

The underscore is used to emphasize the titles of complete literary and artistic works. Literary works include books, magazines, and newspapers; artistic works include movies, plays, paintings, and sculptures. Displaying the titles of complete works in uppercase letters is also acceptable. As noted earlier in this chapter, titles of sections of these works are displayed in quotation marks:

For faster service, call <u>1-800-555-CASH</u>. (printing instructions)

For faster service, call *1-800-555-CASH.* (after printing)

When will <u>Treasures of the Heart</u> be available in paperback? (book title)

"Art in the Workplace" is the lead article in this month's issue of <u>Pizazz!</u> (magazine)

<u>Window on the World</u> is just one of the watercolors in Calley's show. (painting)

Other Uses for Punctuation

Punctuation marks may be used in a number of other ways, among them as delimiters or dividers within mathematical formulas, telephone and fax numbers, e-mail addresses, and Internet URLs:

[NOTE SC.47]
Punctuation may be used as a delimiter or divider.

$x = 3/(2y \bullet 4)+5$	(707) 555-1234	707/555-2468
1.800.555.9876	jp@tophat.org	http://www.vqun.com

APPLICATION EXERCISES

1. Carefully read each of the following items. Insert the terminal mark of punctuation that would be best in each situation. Choose periods, question marks, or exclamation marks.
   - **a.** The customer asked why we denied her application for a car loan
   - **b.** You're our *best* sales representative
   - **c.** Have you created a Web page for your business
   - **d.** The fire alarm is sounding
   - **e.** When will R. J. be released from the hospital
   - **f.** Will you please insure the package before mailing it
   - **g.** Elevator 2 will be out of service for three days
   - **h.** Do you offer a discount to children and senior citizens
   - **i.** The company manufactures bath and bedding products for major department store chains
2. Locate the dates and geographic locations in the following sentences. Determine whether commas are needed, insert them where necessary, and give the reason for their use.
   - **a.** Barbara lives and works in Calgary Alberta but often travels to Winnipeg Manitoba to consult with personnel at the corporate headquarters.
   - **b.** We depart on Wednesday January 5 and return Sunday January 16.
   - **c.** Travel must be completed between February 15 and March 10.
   - **d.** The store opened for business on Monday June 7 1958.
   - **e.** The restaurant will be closed for remodeling from June 28 through July 9.
   - **f.** In June 2003 Richard will retire and move to the home he and Phoebe are building in Lakeland Florida.
   - **g.** The contract must be signed and returned by May 26.
   - **h.** Their journey began in Seattle Washington on August 17.
   - **i.** In September 1990 Naples Florida formalized its Sister City agreement with Piemonte Italy
3. Read each of the following sentences and insert commas where necessary between independent adjectives. Some items may be correct.
   - **a.** The Lunar New Year is the longest most important Chinese festival.
   - **b.** The book includes maps as well as a wealth of interesting helpful information about things to see and do in San Juan.
   - **c.** Wooden furniture treated with dark mahogany stain helps create a warm welcoming atmosphere.
   - **d.** The veterinarian described the dog as a neatly groomed healthy animal.
   - **e.** Chuck's vintage motorcycle drew the attention and admiration of parade watchers.
   - **f.** The clean basic lines of the design make the building distinctive.
   - **g.** The consultant provided us with a very clear picture of what needs to be done.
   - **h.** The soft soothing music playing in the waiting room calmed the patients.
   - **i.** The laundry was unable to remove the stain from Sarah's dark blue wool suit.
4. Insert commas where needed in the following sentences, which may or may not contain independent or introductory clauses:

a. Although the agenda was distributed in advance three committee members forgot to bring it to the meeting.

b. Take the forms to Personnel when you go to lunch.

c. The visitors' center manager has requested both a photocopier and a fax machine but I think we should buy one unit that performs both functions.

d. After you decide what software you need we'll discuss which scanner to buy.

e. The efficiency apartment is more affordable but I prefer the view and space in the studio unit.

f. As we discussed yesterday your account will be credited for $57.

g. When Martin arrives please page Wilbur.

h. Please verify the time and date of the next negotiation session.

i. When you join our management team you will have the opportunity to travel to both Europe and Asia.

5. Locate the nonessential elements in each of the following sentences and insert punctuation where needed. Indicate whether the nonessential element is an appositive, an introductory word, an introductory phrase, a nonrestrictive clause, a parenthetical expression, or a transitional expression.

a. The package was damaged during shipment therefore you are entitled to a full refund.

b. Mo said that he would be working late every night this week; he indicated however that he will not be working this Saturday.

c. Mr. Winston I look forward to meeting with you and your staff on the 19th.

d. In the interest of customer safety we are recalling the Model 12.

e. Interstate 94 which passes through Chicago is the best way to reach your destination.

f. You will of course be fully vested in the retirement program.

g. Yes two pedestrians witnessed the accident.

h. Brad Isobe our tax attorney will represent us in this matter.

i. Fortunately the negatives were not destroyed in the fire.

6. Insert commas where necessary to separate series items in the following sentences:

a. Corporations must begin to address social issues such as diversity work-family balance equal rights and the environment.

b. People attending the concert may park in lot A D or F.

c. Your resume should include information about your work experience your educational qualifications and your activities.

d. The store in the lobby sells newspapers from Los Angeles Chicago Dallas and Miami.

e. The lease specifies that we must shampoo the carpets wash the windows and clean the oven before we vacate the apartment.

f. ABC FOX NBC and CBS have reporters on the scene.

g. Be sure to print your name address and phone number on the form.

h. Rooms 316 317 and 318 will be remodeled next month.

i. The cafeteria is open for breakfast lunch and dinner.

7. Insert commas and semicolons where necessary in each of the following sentences. Explain the reason for each punctuation mark.

a. Computers were large and cumbersome in the 60s today they are small and manageable.
b. Sessions will be held on Monday Tuesday and Wednesday but too few people registered to justify offering sessions on Thursday and Friday.
c. Will the next convention be in Dallas Texas Seattle Washington or Orlando Florida?
d. Once the logo has been redesigned we'll reprint our stationery internal forms however will not be reprinted until our current inventory is depleted.
e. Your representative sensed my anxiety and he responded with patience and concern.
f. Thanks to you Sandy the project was a success we appreciate your efforts.
g. Sharon was angry when she learned of the defect she relaxed when she learned it would be repaired without cost.
h. The chairs were the wrong color the style was ideal.
i. The conference center is 27 miles from town so be sure to rent a car.

8. Insert terminal punctuation marks, commas, and semicolons where appropriate; some items may be correct:
a. Your continued support of the Heritage Museum makes good business sense.
b. Sam Barker a freelance photographer raises roses as a hobby.
c. The Bookworm Club offers a wide selection of mystery novels: thrillers chillers and whodunnits
d. The first part of the test went fairly well I think but I will need to review my English spelling and mathematics before returning for the next section of the examination.
e. After reading ARE YOU UNDERINSURED? in your December issue I immediately phoned my agent and asked for a policy review.
f. Robert Brown president of Brown Brothers Albert Pyroz personnel director at Dataform Sylvia Jacobsen owner of a consulting firm and Amanda Newel records manager at BZP Corporation were all members of the panel discussing mid-life career changes.
g. You must use a pencil to record your responses otherwise the scanner will not be able to read them.
h. If you want to explore the Internet without investing in a full-scale computer system consider purchasing a WebTV terminal.
i. Welcome Barbara
j. The Bailey study which was conducted in California in 1998 challenges the results of earlier research.
k. You must get the data to Olivia by noon on Friday or a decision on the waiver will be delayed until next week.
l. Meteorologists do not control the weather they simply predict what is likely to occur.
m. The contract calls for a bonus of 10 percent if construction is completed by June 23 2004.
n. Your request for permission to convert to a month-to-month lease must therefore be referred to the Residents' Council.
o. Unfortunately that model has been discontinued.

9. Decide whether the secondary internal punctuation marks have been used correctly in the following sentences. Make all changes that are necessary.

a. Ms. Wilkins asked me, "Why more of our workers don't take advantage of flexible work hours"?
b. The visitors from abroad had difficulty understanding what Marvin meant by a "rock bottom price".
c. Three options are available. 1 Enter into a contract with a service bureau. 2. Hire temporary workers. (3). Ask our employees to work overtime.
d. The components were broken and had to be refused before shipping.
e. Birchwood offers one two and three bedroom condominiums for senior citizens.
f. The sign on the boat read, For Sail.
g. From 7 ... 9 p.m. Thursday, each student who brings his:her ID card to the theater will receive $1 1_2 off the posted ticket price and a coupon for a free box of popcorn.
h. Hans Jensen is best known for the spine tingling mysteries he has written.
i. Chapter 2, Sinks and Faucets, can be found on pages 126/134 of "Home Improvement Hints".

MESSAGE ANALYSIS

Make the changes needed to ensure that the following letter is punctuated correctly. If you think that two sentences are closely related, replace the period and the capital letter that follows it with a semicolon and a lowercase letter.

Dear Mrs. Zylen:

Thank you for speaking at the March meeting of the Lakeview Garden Club. Your presentation was excellent.

After the meeting several members commented on how much they enjoyed your discussion of perennial gardening and the slides you used to emphasize your points. You certainly have been successful in blending size color and seasonality into your designs. Each garden reflects the unique personality of the home's owner while accommodating the ever present natural constraints of drainage light and soil richness.

Ms. Zylen please accept the enclosed gift certificate as a token of our appreciation for sharing your insight and experience with us. You can be sure that our knowledge 'grew' as a result of your presentation.

SEMINAR

D Style

[NOTE SD.1] Style refers to rules for correct usage.

The word *style* is used in several different ways in business writing. A person's ability to organize and express ideas is called style. The format of a letter, memo, or report may be referred to as style. Reference manuals are sometimes called style manuals. In this seminar, **style** is used to mean the basic rules for number display, capitalization, word division, and abbreviation that apply to business writing.

Writers should be as concerned about correct usage as they are about their basic writing skills. Correct usage—usually called mechanics—and good writing skills work together to

- Minimize the number of distractions in a message
- Bring consistency to communication
- Reflect well on the writer
- Have a positive effect on the reader

Reference manuals differ in the way they approach style items. Materials in this seminar are based on the ninth edition of *HOW 9, A Handbook for Office Workers,* by Clark & Clark.

Numbers

Numbers play a major role in our lives. They represent, describe, and locate people and objects. Because numbers are used so widely, attention must be given to expressing them correctly in business writing.

Business writers use general style when expressing numbers. **General style** is a blend of two styles known as *formal* and *technical*. In general style, numbers are represented in words when formality is needed and in figures when clarity is desired.

[NOTE SD.2]
General style is used for expressing numbers in business writing.

GENERAL GUIDELINES

Several guidelines relate to the way numbers are expressed. Some of these guidelines are used frequently in business writing, others are used rarely. This section describes those guidelines that have frequent application in business correspondence and reports.

Writing Whole Numbers Whole numbers greater than ten are written in figures. This guideline applies only to whole numbers—those that have no decimal or fractional parts:

[NOTE SD.3]
Write whole numbers greater than ten in figures.

The bill shows that Art made *three* long distance calls last month.

If no one claims the package in *five* days, return it to the sender.

The manufacturer predicts that the van will get *19* mph in city driving conditions.

Writing Round Numbers Round numbers may be expressed in figures, in words, or as a combination of the two. To reduce the emphasis placed on a round number, use words. When emphasis is desired, use figures. Figures are often used in advertising for emphasis. Because numbers greater than a million may be difficult to read when expressed in figures, a writer may combine words and figures to achieve greater clarity:

[NOTE SD.4]
Using figures draws attention to large numbers.

The Toronto plant produced *347,000* units this quarter.

The band spent more than *three hundred* days on the road last year.

The population of the country exceeds *15 million.*

Beginning a Sentence With a Number Numbers that begin a sentence are expressed in words. If the number is large, rewrite the sentence:

[NOTE SD.5]
Use words for numbers that begin sentences.

Five managers have requested early retirement.

Four thousand tickets have been printed.

Thirteen thousand two hundred seventy-seven people attended the convention. (Awkward. See the following sentence.)

The convention attendance was *13,277*. (improved version)

Writing Numbers Consistently Be consistent in expressing numbers, and strive for easy reading. When *related* numbers greater than and less than ten appear in the same sentence, use figures for all numbers. When *unrelated* numbers greater than

[NOTE SD.6]
Make numbers easy to read.

and less than ten appear in the same sentence, follow the general guideline for writing whole numbers:

> A discount is offered for payment made within *10 days*, and the full amount is due within *30 days*. (related numbers)
>
> The tour group consisted of *15 people* each of whom had at least *two suitcases*. (unrelated numbers)

If two numbers are adjacent to one another, as in a series, punctuation and spacing enhance readability. When one of two adjacent numbers is part of a compound modifier, the first number is written in words. If the first number cannot be written in one or two words, display it as a figure also:

> The performance schedule includes *two 15-minute* intermissions. (adjacent numbers; compound modifier)
>
> The shipment included *125 36-inch* televisions. (large number as part of adjacent number; compound modifier)

When two unrelated numbers are adjacent to one another in a sentence, place a comma between them to make them easy to read:

> By *1998, 15* of the franchises had been remodeled. (easy to read)

[NOTE SD.7] Use commas in numbers with four or more digits.

Punctuating Numbers In numbers with four or more digits, a comma is usually used. The comma is omitted in identification, model, serial, house, page, and telephone/fax numbers. It is also omitted in ZIP Codes, decimal fractions, and metric measurements:

1,113	1,250,671	ID No. 10558
2112 Shore Drive	Serial No. 8512-C	page 1036
Cleveland, OH 44122-1856	1999	(715) 555-3821
.25901	3000 meters	Model 3700

SPECIFIC GUIDELINES

[NOTE SD.8] Ordinals show position in a series.

The general guidelines just presented will help you through many writing situations involving numbers. There are some specific guidelines, too, that should be mastered. As you read the material, you will encounter the term *ordinal*. **Ordinal** words or numbers show position in a series. *First*, *second*, *third*, *tenth*, and *seventy-fifth* are examples of ordinal words; *1st*, *2nd*, *3rd*, *10th*, and *75th* are examples of ordinal numbers.

[NOTE SD.9] Use figures for house and building numbers in mailing addresses.

Addresses House or building numbers except *one* are written in figures when used within the text of a message. As part of the mailing address in a letter or on an envelope, *all* house and building numbers are displayed in figures; *one* is no longer an exception. Numbered streets are written as words if ten or below and as figures in all other cases. When figures are used for both house number and street name, use an ordinal for the street name:

[NOTE SD.10] Use words for street names ten and under; otherwise use figures.

> One Salem Blvd. (when used in text)
>
> 1 Salem Blvd. (when on an envelope)
>
> 906 West Third Avenue

1477 81st Street
10 North 125th Avenue

Dates Figures are used for the day and the year. If the day is used without a month or if the day precedes the month, ordinal numbers or words may be used:

[NOTE SD.11]
Use figures for the day and the year.

April 1904 August 17 January 1, 2005
the 1st and 15th (ordinal without a month)
the 2nd of October (ordinal number)
the fifth of September (ordinal word)

Some writers use the international (military) date form, but it has not received widespread acceptance in American business correspondence. The international date form should be used in correspondence sent to receivers outside the United States. Select the form used in the country to which you are writing. Here are two common international date forms:

23 March 2002 2002.3.23 (year/month/day)

Fractions When a fraction appears alone, it is written in words. Use a hyphen between the numerator (top number) and denominator (bottom number) of a fraction written in words when the fraction is used as a compound adjective. When a fraction is part of a mixed number, express it in figures:

[NOTE SD.12]
Use words when a fraction stands alone; use figures when a fraction is part of a mixed number.

one fourth of the proceeds	a one-third share (adjective)
one twenty-fifth	9 2/3

Notice the space in the mixed number between the fraction and the whole number. Unless a typewriter or keyboard has a special key for fractions, this space is necessary for readability. Without the space the figure could be misread as 92/3 (ninety-two thirds).

Money Money amounts are expressed in figures. If the money amount is a whole number, the decimal and zeros are omitted—even when whole and mixed dollar amounts occur in the same series. A comma is used in most money amounts of four digits or more. An indefinite amount of money should be written in words:

[NOTE SD.13]
Express money amounts in figures.

[NOTE SD.14]
Indefinite money amounts are written in words.

$7,093.32 $688 $8,000 several thousand dollars
The missing checks were for payments of $127.63, $250, and $325.50.

For amounts of money less than a dollar, use figures and spell the word *cents:*

1 cent 79 cents

On orders, invoices, and other business forms, the symbol ¢ may be used. If definite amounts of money greater and less than one dollar occur in the same sentence, use the $ symbol and a decimal where necessary:

The three lowest bids were $1.19, $1.03, and $.96 per unit.

Ordinals If an ordinal can be expressed in one or two words, spell it in full. If the ordinal exceeds one or two words, rewrite the sentence to avoid the need for an

[NOTE SD.15]
Use only one- or two-word ordinals; in other cases, rewrite.

ordinal. This restriction applies only to ordinals that appear within the body of a sentence. Refer to the sections on addresses and dates under the Specific Guidelines heading in this seminar for the proper use of ordinals in those items:

The *first* annual Outstanding Citizen award was presented to Thomas Doi.
The President gave a gold watch to Fred Benson, who was celebrating his *thirtieth* anniversary with the company.
Dilton's *one-hundred seventeenth* Customer Appreciation Sale will begin Monday, August 12. (Long ordinal; hard to read when written in words.)
Dilton's has held a Customer Appreciation Sale for *117* years; this year's sale will begin Monday, August 12. (Improved version; sentence has been rewritten to avoid the need for an ordinal.)

[NOTE SD.16] Use the word *percent* within text.

Percentages In nontechnical business communication, write *percent* as a word, and express the number as a figure:

33 percent   18½ percent   76.2 percent

At the beginning of a sentence, spell the number or reword the sentence:

Six percent of our budget is targeted for equipment purchases.
We have targeted *6 percent* of our budget for equipment purchases.

[NOTE SD.17] Designate time in figures or words based on content.

Time To designate time with a.m. (midnight to noon) or p.m. (noon to midnight) use a figure; zeros are not needed for on-the-hour times. For formality, use a word before *o'clock*; for emphasis, use a figure before *o'clock*. Approximate time and time on the half hour are expressed in words:

On weekends, the stores in the mall close at *9 p.m.*
The flight is scheduled to arrive at *8:30 p.m.*
The reception will begin at *eight o'clock* this evening. (formality)

In all cases, be sure the time of day is clear:

The train will arrive at *5:30.* (in the morning or in the afternoon?)
The train will arrive at *5:30 this afternoon.* (clear)

To avoid confusion, writers usually use *midnight* rather than 12 a.m. and *noon* rather than 12 p.m. Omit *a.m.* when using *noon* and omit *p.m.* when using *midnight:*

The doors will be opened at 6 *a.m.* and locked at *midnight.*

Capitalization

Early in your education, you were taught to capitalize the first letter of a word that begins a sentence and the first letter of a proper noun. Few, if any, writers have difficulty with these practices. This section, therefore, will present other accepted rules for capitalization.

[NOTE SD.18] Capitalize specific academic courses and languages.

ACADEMIC COURSES

When referring to a specific course, capitalize the first letter of the main word(s). Do not capitalize general subjects other than languages:

Issues in Global Ecology is a very popular course on this campus.
Are you taking an *ecology* course this term?
Dr. Harwood teaches *Finance* 200, 315, and 450.
Dr. Harwood teaches *finance* courses.
Norma enrolled in *German*, *business,* and *history* classes this term.

COMPASS DIRECTIONS

Names of specific geographical regions are capitalized. Do not capitalize general directions:

[**NOTE SD.19**]
Compass directios that refer to a specific region should be capitalized.

She was born in the *South* but raised in the *North*.
Their business will expand to the *Midwest*.
The parking lot on the *east* side of the building is being repaired. (a direction)
Drive three miles *south* on Highway G, then turn *west* on Route 12. (directions)

GOVERNMENT

Principal words in the names of domestic and foreign government agencies, units, and organizations are capitalized:

[**NOTE SD.20**]
Full names of governments and their subsections are capitalized.

Securities and Exchange Commission
Royal Canadian Mounted Police
United States Air Force

Short forms of the names of national and international government bodies and their major divisions are generally capitalized. Writers should use short forms only when they are certain their readers will understand them:

the Court (United States Supreme Court)
the Senate (United States Senate)
the Corps (United States Corps of Engineers)

The short forms of the names of state and local government bodies are not capitalized unless used in formal communication:

My parents were born and raised in this county. (general reference)
A city ordinance prohibits burning trash outdoors.

When in doubt about the capitalization of government and judicial body names, consult a reference book such as *HOW 9,* published by South-Western ITP.

INSTITUTIONS AND ORGANIZATIONS

The full names of institutions (churches, libraries, hospitals, and schools) and organizations (associations, companies, and clubs) and their divisions or departments are capitalized. The word *the* is capitalized only when it is part of the official title. Follow the style established by the organization or institution as shown on its letterhead stationery or in other written communication:

[**NOTE SD.21**]
Capitalize the full name of an institution or organization according to its preference.

Memorial Hospital has released the plans for its new addition.
Temple Israel has been selected as the site for the dinner.
Have you accepted the invitation to join Pi Sigma Epsilon?

Selina has accepted a job offer from The Prudential Insurance Company.

Hospitality Committee	but	the committee
Intensive Care Unit	but	the unit
Finance Department	but	the department

TIME

[NOTE SD.22] Dates are only one way to express time.

[NOTE SD.23] Capitalize most references to time.

The most common reference to time in business writing is a date, but time can also be a reference to seasons, holidays, or events. The names of days, months, specific special events, holidays, religious days, and historical events are always capitalized. The names of decades and centuries are generally not capitalized; season names, however, are capitalized when combined with a year:

Tuesday, April 15	Martin Luther King Day
Rosh Hashanah	Moonlight Madness Sale
twenty-first century	the late seventies
Fall Festival	Spring 2002

TITLES

[NOTE SD.24] Capitalization of personal titles depends on how they are used.

Titles are divided into two categories—occupational and official. Both titles are capitalized when used in a signature line or a mailing address. An occupational title is capitalized only when it is a specific job title. In correspondence text, however, the two are treated differently. An official title is capitalized when it comes before a personal name, unless the personal name has been added to clarify or describe (nonessential element set off by commas). An official title is generally not capitalized when it follows a personal name or replaces a personal name. The titles of state, national, and international officials are an exception; these titles are capitalized when they come before, come after, or are used in place of personal names:

The maintenance manager, P. J. Perkins, described the changes in the safety code. (name clarifies)

Marketing Director Ellen Francis has announced her resignation. (specific job title)

Josefina Ortiz, city manager, reported on economic development activities. (title following name)

After vacationing in Florida, Ambassador Portor returned to France. (national title before a personal name)

The Emir hosted the dinner. (international title used in place of name)

Word Division

[NOTE SD.25] Word division is an option.

When traditional typewriters are used to produce business documents, it *may* be necessary to divide a word at the end of a line of type in order to achieve a balanced right margin. Note the emphasis on the word *may*. Word division is an option—not a requirement.

Computers and word processing software have minimized a writer's need to decide when and how to divide words. Even with word processing software, however, a writer may elect to divide a word. Therefore, it is important for all business writers to know how to divide words properly.

Two reference books that help writers decide where to divide a word are a word book and a dictionary. A **word book** is a better reference because it shows not only syllables but also preferred word division points. A **dictionary** will indicate only syllables; writers must then determine where the word is best divided.

[NOTE SD.26]
Use a dictionary or word book when you need help in deciding where to divide a word.

If you decide to divide a word, use the following guidelines. Note that the guidelines are for those who write business correspondence and reports. The rules are not as strict for typesetters, that is, those who produce such things as books and magazines.

[1] Divide a word only between syllables.

[2] Divide between two vowels if they are pronounced separately (e.g., gradu-ate, cha-otic, evalu-ation).

[3] Divide after a one-syllable vowel unless the vowel is part of a suffix. When this occurs, the suffix should be carried to the next line (e.g., mechan-ical).

[4] Divide before a suffix (e.g., announce-ment).

[5] Divide between two parts of a compound word (e.g., book-keeper; easy-going). If the word is hyphenated, divide at the hyphen.

[6] Avoid dividing names, dates, and addresses. If these items must be divided, follow these guidelines:
   a. Do not use a hyphen to show that the item has been divided.
   b. Keep a personal title with the name (e.g., Mrs. Sarah/Jones).
   c. Divide a date between the day of the month and the year (e.g., June 20, /2004).
   d. Divide an address between the street name and the street designation or between the city and the state (e.g., 103 Edgar/Road; Miami/FL).

[7] No fewer than two letters of the word should be left on the first line, and no fewer than three letters should be carried to the next line. The goal is to give the reader an idea of the word before it is divided. Therefore, if it is possible to divide a word in more than one place, select the division point that places the larger part of the word on the upper line. The previous guidelines refer to what should be done when words are divided. Some words, however, should not be divided:
   - Words of six or fewer letters should not be divided even if they have two or more syllables.
   - The last word on a page should not be divided. Avoid dividing a word at the end of the first or last line in a paragraph.
   - Divide as few words as possible; avoid ending two consecutive lines with divided words.
   - Do not divide figures, abbreviations, contractions, or items containing symbols.

[NOTE SD.27]
Use only those abbreviations your reader will understand.

Abbreviations

Abbreviations save space and time in business writing. Their use should be limited, however, to those that the reader will recognize and understand. If an abbreviation is to be used several times within a letter or report, the complete form—followed by the abbreviation in parentheses—should be used at the first instance. The reader will then understand the abbreviation when it occurs again:

The Student Conduct Committee (SCC) has filed its report. After the vice president has reviewed the SCC report, she will submit it to the Board of Governors.

Generally, an abbreviation follows the full-text format with respect to whether it is displayed in uppercase or lowercase letters—abbreviations for proper nouns use uppercase letters; abbreviations for common nouns use lowercase letters. Guidelines about whether to use or omit periods within the abbreviation are less clear. To be sure, consult a reference manual.

ACRONYMS AND INITIALISMS

[NOTE SD.28] Acronyms are pronounced as words; initialisms are not.

Acronyms and initialisms are special forms of abbreviations. **Acronyms** are words formed by using the first letter of each major word of a compound item. When abbreviations are formed from the first letter of majors words in a compound item but the outcome is not pronounced as a word, the abbreviations is called an **initialism**. Business firms, government agencies, and professional groups are often known by their initialisms:

Cost-of-living adjustment	becomes	COLA
Initial public offering	becomes	IPO
Beginners All-purpose Symbolic Instruction Code	becomes	BASIC
Consolidated Omnibus Budget Reconciliation Act	becomes	COBRA
America Online	becomes	AOL
Central Intelligence Agency	becomes	CIA
American Medical Association	becomes	AMA

BUSINESS AND ASSOCIATION NAMES

[NOTE SD.29] Spell generic business names when used alone in a sentence.

Abbreviated words are often part of the name of a business firm. *Assn.* for Association, *Co.* for Company, *Corp.* for Corporation, *Ltd.* for Limited, and *Inc.* for Incorporated are just a few examples. Abbreviate these items only when they are part of a business name; spell them in full when used independently within a sentence:

Brown and Bowen *Co.*

Financial analysts report that the *company* is sound.

COURTESY AND PERSONAL TITLES

[NOTE SD.30] Courtesy titles should be abbreviated when they occur before a name.

Courtesy title abbreviations such as *Mr.*, *Mrs.*, *Ms.*, and *Dr.* are used before a personal name:

Mr. Juan Estrada   *Ms.* Rose Pardue

Mrs. Renee Grand   *Dr.* Victor Cruz

[NOTE SD.31] The individual's preference should be respected when using titles.

Unless a woman's specific title is known, use *Ms.* A woman should tell her correspondents the title she prefers. When the person's preference is known, that title should be used. If a writer's first name may be used by members of either gender (Pat, Terry, Lee), the writer should include a personal title in the signature line. This procedure should also be followed if a writer uses only initials (A. K. Jones; B. W. O'Brien). This technique, as well as other options, is illustrated in Appendix A.

The personal titles *Junior* and *Senior* are abbreviated when they follow a name:

Kenneth Langford, *Jr.*   Mark Shane, *Sr.*

MEASUREMENTS

Measurements may be abbreviated when they occur frequently in tables or business forms. When used, they are displayed in lowercase letters, with periods if they represent one word and without periods if they represent more than one word. In most business writing, measurements are spelled in full rather than abbreviated. Metric units of measurement are always written without periods. Common measurements and their abbreviations are shown in Figure SD.1.

[NOTE SD.32]
Spell measurements in general correspondence.

Measure	Abbreviation	Measure	Abbreviation
centimeter	cm	miles per hour	mph
foot	ft.	pound	lb.
gallon	gal.	pages per minute	ppm
kilogram	kg	words per minute	wpm

Figure SD.1
Measurement Abbreviations

MONTHS/DAYS

Each of the months of the year and days of the week has a standard abbreviation:

Jan.	Apr.	July	Oct.			
Feb.	May	Aug.	Nov.			
Mar.	June	Sept./Sep.	Dec.			
Sun.	Mon.	Tues. (Tue.)	Wed.	Thurs. (Thu.)	Fri.	Sat.
Su	M	Tu	W	Th	F	Sa

These abbreviations should be used only to save space on business forms; they should not be used in business reports or correspondence.

[NOTE SD.33]
Use abbreviations sparingly for months and days.

PERSONAL NAMES

Abbreviations for personal names may take the form of an initial or a shortened form of the name:

D. L. Falk C. Luisa Diaz
Ilene F. Jensen Wm. Baxter

[NOTE SD.34]
Names may be abbreviated by using initials or a shortened form of the name.

An abbreviation is different from a nickname. An abbreviation is always shorter than its given name; it always ends with a period. Nicknames may be modifications of a given name (Vicky for Victoria) or may be totally unrelated to the given name (George Herman "Babe" Ruth). Personal names should not be abbreviated unless space is limited, as in tabulations or enumerations. In business writing, restrict the use of nicknames to those that are modifications of given names (e.g., Bill for William). Before abbreviating a person's name, be sure that the individual will not object to the use of the abbreviated form.

[NOTE SD.35]
Nicknames differ from abbreviations.

PROFESSIONAL TITLES, DESIGNATIONS, AND DEGREES

Many people choose to use their professional titles, designations, or degrees when conducting business. Whenever possible, write professional titles in full. Abbreviate designations and academic degrees:

Professor Bernard Lomax Reverend Elizabeth Torvick
Tamara J. Webster, C.P.A. J. J. Alvarez, R.N.
Pamela Poe, D.D.S. Richard Beckett, M.D.

[NOTE SD.36]
Abbreviate designations and academic degrees.

[NOTE SD.37]
Use either a title or an academic degree abbreviation, not both.

When referring to a person who has the academic or medical credentials to be addressed as doctor, use either the title or the abbreviation for the degree, but not both. If the title is used, place the abbreviation *Dr.* before the name. If the abbreviation for the degree is used, place it after the name, and use a comma to separate the name from the abbreviation:

Dr. Jane Alexander   Jane Alexander, D.D.S.

STATES/TERRITORIES/PROVINCES

[NOTE SD.38]
Abbreviate names of states, territories, and provinces when they are part of a complete address.

The official two-letter postal abbreviations for state, territory, and province names should be used when part of a complete address. In all other cases, the name of the state, territory, or province should be spelled in full. A complete list of the two-letter postal abbreviations used in the United States and Canada is on page 623. Be sure to secure the postal address requirements of other countries to which you write.

SYMBOLS

[NOTE SD.39]
Symbols are a form of abbreviation.

[NOTE SD.40]
Use only those symbols that your receiver will interpret correctly.

Symbols are a form of abbreviation. Figure SD.2 includes several standard symbols. A brief definition and an example of each are also provided. Symbols should be used sparingly in business writing. Include only those symbols that your readers will interpret correctly.

Figure SD.2
Frequently Used Symbols

Symbol	Definition	Example
&	ampersand (meaning *and*)	Mr. & Mrs. Lee
*	asterisk (refers reader to a note)	Price* *subject to change without notice
@	at, each, per	17 @ $2.25 each
©	copyright	© South-Western College Publishing
®	registered trademark	Compaq®
°	degree	77°
/	diagonal, slash	and/or, s/he, http://, 12/31/99
¢	cents	59¢
$	dollars	$126.99
'	feet (apostrophe)	6'
"	inch (quotation mark)	9"
:	ratio (colon)	4:1
#	number (before figure)	#10
#	pounds (after figure)	100#
%	percent	66%
x	by or times (lowercase *x*)	2 x 4, 3 x 5
K	thousand	640K, $20K
<, >	less than, greater than	< 20, >75

TIME ZONES

[NOTE SD.41]
Time zones for both standard and daylight savings time are abbreviated.

The world is divided into time zones. In Canada and the United States, each zone has its own abbreviation. In addition, one character in that abbreviation is changed to indicate whether those residing in the region are observing standard or daylight saving time:

EST	Eastern Standard Time	EDT	Eastern Daylight Time
CST	Central Standard Time	CDT	Central Daylight Time

MST Mountain Standard Time	MDT Mountain Daylight Time
PST Pacific Standard Time	PDT Pacific Daylight Time

Telephone directories typically include a map of North America and show the areas covered by each zone. When writers ask receivers to phone them, they often include the time zone in the message. Typically, the time zone is displayed in parentheses following the hours during which telephone calls are received—for example, 9 a.m. to 4 p.m. (EST).

OTHER ABBREVIATIONS

So many abbreviations are used in business that it is impractical to include all of them in this seminar. A brief list of some of the most commonly used terms is included in Figure SD.3.

[NOTE SD.42]
Consult references before abbreviating unfamiliar terms.

Figure SD.3
Other Commonly Used Abbreviations

Term	Abbreviation	Term	Abbreviation
account	acct.	manager	mgr.
additional	addnl., add'l	merchandise	mdse.
also known as	a.k.a.	money order	MO
amount	amt.	month, months	mo., mos.
as soon as possible	ASAP	national	natl.
attached	att.	net weight	nt. wt.
average	avg.	not applicable	NA
balance	bal.	not available	NA
care of	c/o	optional	opt.
charge	chg.	organization	org.
collect on delivery	COD	original	orig.
continued	cont.	out of stock	OS or o.s.
courtesy copy	cc	over-the-counter	OTC
credit	cr.	package	pkg.
depreciation	depr.	page, pages	p., pp.
destination	dstn.	paid	pd.
discount	disc., dis.	parcel post	PP
division	div.	part, point	pt.
extension	ext., Ext.	port of entry	POE or p.o.e.
fiscal year	FY	prepaid	ppd.
for example	e.g.	purchase order	P.O., PO
forward	fwd.	quantity	qty.
freight	frt.	quarter, quarterly	qtr.
gross weight	gr. wt.	received	recd.
headquarters	HQ, hdqtrs.	requisition	req.
hour	hr.	respond, if you please	R.S.V.P., RSVP
institute	inst.	self-addressed, stamped envelope	SASE
international	intl., intnl.	standard	std.
inventory	invt.	statement	stmt.
invoice	inv.	wholesale	whsle.

Notice that some of the abbreviations use capital letters; others use lowercase letters. Some of the abbreviations use periods, others do not. Because abbreviations are often associated with particular fields (e.g., education, law, medicine, transportation), you may encounter abbreviations with which you are unfamiliar. When this situation arises, consult a dictionary or reference manual.

APPLICATION EXERCISES

1. Circle the appropriate expression(s) for each number in the following items:
   - **a.** The (first/1st/1) (100/one hundred/1 hundred) people to enroll will receive a ($10/$10./ten dollar/$10.00) discount.
   - **b.** The auto dealer reported that there were (fifteen/15) (two-door/2-door) sedans left in stock.
   - **c.** Mail my reimbursement check to (523/Five Twenty-three/Five Hundred Twenty-three) (Second/2nd/2) Street South.
   - **d.** The serial number on the Model (1222/1,222/twelve 22/twelve twenty-two) laser printer is (736,921-G/736921-G).
   - **e.** PQG declared a (38 cent/thirty-eight cent/$.38) dividend.
   - **f.** Officials estimate that more than (2,000,000/2 million/two million) people will attend the (three-/3-) day event.
   - **g.** Please change my address from (763 - Fifth Avenue/763 - 5th Avenue/763 5th Avenue/763 Fifth Avenue) to (376 - Fifth Avenue/376 - 5th Avenue/376 5th Avenue/376 Fifth Avenue).
   - **h.** The stock rose (1 1/4 / 11/4 / 1 and one-fourth) points in (two/2) days.
   - **i.** By subscribing now, you'll get (15/fifteen) issues for the price of (10/ten), a savings of (50%/50 percent/fifty percent).
   - **j.** We are a ($5 billion/five billion dollar/5 billion dollar) company that employs a total of (4,000/4 thousand/four thousand) people in (six/6) states.
2. Each of the following sentences requires corrections in capitalization. Some words shown in lowercase should be capitalized; some shown in capital letters should be in lowercase. Correct the errors.
   - **a.** The Internal Revenue service has pledged to improve customer service.
   - **b.** The centers for Disease Control (cdc) reported an outbreak of german measles in the Western Suburbs of Dallas.
   - **c.** Paulette Bowman, who works for Rybert company in st. Paul, has completed the requirements for the cpm.
   - **d.** according to a recent Report from the American Council on Science and Health, fluoridation of drinking water is a very effective weapon against tooth decay.
   - **e.** to meet a requirement for our film in society class, Matt and I went to a french film with English Subtitles.
   - **f.** The vice president will represent the President at the Nato meeting.
   - **g.** the director's comments were well received; her Staff applauded.
   - **h.** Each Summer, the residents of smithville gather at City park for a founder's day Picnic.
   - **i.** After the election, mayor Bennett removed the door on his Office to show the citizens of parker that she had an "open door" policy.
   - **j.** After earning her bachelor of arts degree in english, Louisa began working as a copy editor for the westport Daily News.
   - **k.** The Accounting department recently installed four apex computers.
3. Indicate if and where each of the following items should be divided. Some items may be divided in more than one place; indicate all acceptable dividing points.
   - **a.** advisement
   - **b.** enviable
   - **c.** Honolulu, HI
   - **d.** willing

e. favor
f. well-known
g. strenuous
h. whenever
i. quantity
j. proposition

4. Several company, organization, agency, and program names are listed here. By what abbreviation is each name most commonly known?
   a. Federal Deposit Insurance Corporation
   b. Organization of Petroleum Exporting Countries
   c. Individual Retirement Account
   d. Occupational Safety and Health Administration
   e. American Automobile Association
5. Each of the following items contains at least one abbreviation. Decide whether each has been used correctly. If the abbreviation is incorrect, change it.
   a. Dr. Timothy Ordean, Dv.M., volunteers with the Omaha Zoo.
   b. Mr. @ Mrs. Harvey Wilcox, Jun., spent Sun. afternoon planning their Aug. trip to London.
   c. Fitness centers were recently opened in Seattle, WA; Oxford, Mississippi; Reno, Nevada; and Regina, Saskatchewan.
   d. Bagley # Sons, the co. for which Emi works, offers its employees a 10 percent disc. on the glassware it makes.
   e. MS Edith Port has been named ceo at Player, ltd.

MESSAGE ANALYSIS

Edit the following message to reflect correct use of numbers, capitalization, abbreviations, and symbols:

7.March.00

MS. Wan-ying Chu
One West Maple Court
Atlanta, GA 30321-4822

Dear Miss Chu:

TY for you're recent ltr re. your app. for employment as a Jr. Accts. Specialist with Bellows @ Magee, inc.

your app. is one of over 100 we rec'd in response to our 2/3 ad in The gazette. Because the no. of applications we received is > we expected, the screening process has been delayed. The selection Committee is scheduled to meet on Tues., 3/12; once they have narrowed the # of candidates, we will contact references and arrange for interviews with the finalists.

*We appreciate your cont. int. in Bellows * Magee, inc.*

Yours truly,
(Mrs.) Terry Mercado
Personnel Administrator

SEMINAR

E Word Usage

The words listed in this seminar are among those that can pose problems for writers. Some words are included because they are misused; some are included because they are often confused with other words. The words are listed alphabetically according to the first word in each set:

ABOVE **BELOW**	Avoid using these words in business writing. Instead, use *preceding* to indicate what came before and *following* to indicate what will come after.
ADVICE **ADVISE**	*Advice* is a noun; *advise* is a verb. When you advise, you give advice.
AFFECT **EFFECT**	Although both words may be either a verb or a noun, *affect* is is most often used as a verb showing change or influence; *effect* is most often used as a noun denoting a result or an outcome.
ALL READY **ALREADY**	Refers to a state of complete readiness. Refers to time.
ALL RIGHT **ALRIGHT**	The word *alright* is considered inappropriate for business writing; use *all right*.

ALL TOGETHER **ALTOGETHER**	Refers to physical or figurative unity or closeness. Means entirely or wholly.
AMONG **BETWEEN**	When referring to three or more, use *among*; when referring to two, use *between*. The appropriate conjunction to use with *between* is "and."
AMOUNT **NUMBER**	*Amount* is used with "mass" nouns—things that can be measured but cannot be counted; *number* is used with "count" nouns, such as "people."
ANXIOUS **EAGER**	Use *anxious* when you wish to show anxiety or great concern. *Eager*, which has a positive connotation, is usually a better choice.
ANY ONE **ANYONE**	Stresses *one* of a group of persons or things. Stresses *any* and refers only to persons.
ANY WAY **ANYWAY**	Emphasizes *any*; no preference for method. Means "in any case."
ARBITRATE **MEDIATE**	To decide between two disagreeing people or groups, such as an employer and a union. To work to gain agreement between two disagreeing people or groups.
ASSURE **ENSURE** **INSURE**	All three refer to making something certain. Use *assure* when indicating you are placing a person's mind at rest by removing doubt; use *ensure* when indicating you are making something safe; and use *insure* when indicating you are taking steps beforehand to guarantee the safety of life or property.
BAD **BADLY**	*Bad* is used with "sense" verbs (feel, hear, see, smell, taste, touch, etc.) and is an adjective—it modifies a noun. *Badly* is an adverb; it modifies a verb, adjective, or another adverb.
BIANNUAL **BIENNIAL**	Twice a year. Every two years.
BIMONTHLY **SEMIMONTHLY**	Every two months. Twice a month.
BRIEF **SHORT**	Used only when referring to time. Used when referring to time or to measurement.
BRING **TAKE** **GET**	*Bring* denotes movement toward the speaker or writer or the place she or he occupies; *take* denotes movement away from the person or place; and *get* refers to gaining possession.
CALL/WRITE **CONTACT**	*Contact* is abstract and should be avoided in business communication. Writers should use specific words, such as *call* and *write*, or the more general "let us know."

CAN **MAY**	Refers to the ability to do something. Refers to permission to do something.
CAN NOT **CANNOT**	Unacceptable in business writing. Unable to do otherwise.
CAPITAL **CAPITOL**	Use the *al* ending when referring to assets or uppercase letters; use the *ol* ending when referring to a state or national government building.
CITE **SIGHT** **SITE**	Means to refer to or quote; is the root of the word citation. As a noun, *sight* relates to vision; it is also used to refer to a spectacle or view. As a verb, *sight* means to see, observe, or perceive. Refers to a place, an area, or a location.
COMPARE **CONTRAST**	Refers to an examination of similarities and differences. Refers to an examination of differences.
COMPLEMENT **COMPLIMENT**	Means to complete or to enhance. Means to praise.
COMPOSED **COMPRISED**	Is used when referring to the parts or components of something. Is used when referring to things included within something.
CONSUL **COUNCIL** **COUNSEL**	Refers to a government official who resides in a foreign country for the purpose of representing the citizens of his or her home country. Refers to an advisory group. Refers to advice or one who gives it.
CONTINUAL **CONTINUOUS**	Means recurring activity with pauses or breaks. Means uninterrupted activity.
DATA **DATUM**	*Data* is the plural form of *datum*, a noun meaning "fact." In business writing, *data* may be followed by either a singular or a plural verb form.
DECENT **DESCENT** **DISSENT**	Means in good taste. Means a movement downward. Means to disagree or to hold a different opinion.
DISBURSE **DISPERSE**	Means to pay. Means to break up or spread.
ELICIT **ILLICIT**	Means to bring out. Refers to something unlawful or not permitted.
EMINENT **IMMINENT**	*Eminent* is used when referring to someone or something that stands out about others in quality or in position. *Imminent* refers to something that is threatening, such as a storm.

FARTHER **FURTHER**	Refers to distance—*far* ther. Means additional or advanced.
FEWER **LESS**	*Fewer* applies to things that can be counted; it is used with references to people and to modify other plural nouns. *Less* is used most often to modify plural nouns involving time, distance, weight, and money.
IF **WHETHER**	Used to establish or describe a condition. Used with implicit or explicit alternatives.
INVALUABLE **VALUABLE**	Things that are *invaluable* are priceless. *Valuable* things have a desirable monetary value.
IT'S **ITS**	The contraction for *it is.* The possessive form of the pronoun *it.*
LAST **LATEST**	*Last* refers to something final, something at the end. *Latest* refers to something recent, the most current of a series.
LAY **LIE**	Means to put or to place. Means to recline or to rest.
LED **LEAD**	Past tense of the verb *lead.* When pronounced as *led,* this noun refers to a type of metal used when making pipes.
LOOSE **LOSE**	An adjective used to describe fit; it is the opposite of tight. A verb; it is the opposite of find.
ME **MYSELF**	*Me* is the objective case of the personal pronoun I. *Myself* is a reflexive pronoun. It should be used in business writing only when you have been identified earlier in the sentence.
MEDIA **MEDIUM**	*Media* is the plural; it refers to several mass communication methods. Each mass communication method (TV, radio, etc.) is a *medium.*
PERPETRATE **PERPETUATE**	Means to bring about or commit an act, such as a crime or injustice. Means to continue something indefinitely.
PERSONAL **PERSONNEL**	Means private or relating to a person. Refers to a group of workers or employees.
PRECEDE **PROCEED**	Means to go or to come before. Means to go forward with or to continue some action.
PRINCIPAL **PRINCIPLE**	Refers to a leader or to something *chief* or *primary.* Refers to a rule or a basic truth.
SET **SIT**	Means to place or to put. Means to lie or to rest.

SOME TIME **SOMETIME**	Refers to a specific time. Refers to an indefinite time.
STATIONARY **STATIONERY**	Means in a fixed position. Means writing paper.
STATUE **STATUTE**	Refers to a three-dimensional figure. Refers to a law or permanent rule.
THAN **THEN**	Used as part of a comparison. Used with reference to time.
THAT **WHICH** **WHO**	*That* is used to refer to persons, animals, or things; it introduces restrictive clauses. *Which* is used to refer to animals or things; it introduces nonrestrictive clauses. *Who* is used to refer only to persons; it may be used to introduce either a restrictive or a nonrestrictive clause.
THOROUGH **THROUGH** **THRU**	*Thorough* refers to the fullest level of detail. *Through* is used to show movement into and out of, to specify methods, or to show completion. *Thru* is informal and should not be used in business writing.
TO **TOO**	Indicates movement or direction. Means also or to an excessive degree.
TRACK **TRACT**	Means a path. Refers to a defined piece of land.
WHO **WHOM**	*Who* is a pronoun used in questions to indicate what person or which persons. *Whom* is an objective case pronoun; it is used as an object of a verb or a preposition.

APPLICATION EXERCISES

1. Select the appropriate word(s) in each of the following sentences:
   a. The speaker (complemented/complimented) the audience on (it's/its) ability to recognize the (principal/principle) idea of his speech.
   b. Wil has taken Gerry's (advice/advise) and offered to (arbitrate/mediate) the disagreement (among/between) Alex and Jamal.
   c. The (last/latest) issue of *Modern Textiles* is (laying/lying) on the table; the next issue will be available in two weeks.
   d. Let me know (if/whether) you plan to attend the groundbreaking ceremony at the construction (cite/sight/site).
   e. Unless we (bring/take/get) the manual to the printer today, we (can not/cannot) be sure it will be ready by our deadline.

f. Maynard (continually/continuously) tries to (elicit/illicit) a positive response from the (stationary/stationery) company.

g. (Some time/Sometime) next month, I will seek the (consul/council/counsel) of a (personal/personnel) trainer and try to (affect/effect) a change in my exercise pattern.

h. Sarah (can/may) (call/contact/write) Adam and suggest he invite (fewer/less) people to this year's seminar (than/then) were invited last year.

i. The legislature passed a (biannual/biennial) budget that includes money for (capital/capitol) expenditures.

j. Please (assure/ensure/insure) the (invaluable/valuable) (statue/statute) in case the movers (loose/lose) it.

k. Edith said she had never seen (any one/anyone) as (anxious/eager) to (perpetrate/perpetuate) a bad habit as Milton.

l. Let me know when you are (thorough/through/thru) with Part A; we can (than/then) (precede/proceed) with Part B.

m. The (farther/further) we drove along the rutted dirt road, the more sure we were that the (track/tract) of land we bought was (bad/badly) overpriced.

n. The (consul/council/counsel) was (composed/comprised) of (eminent/imminent) scientists.

o. Be sure to (cite/sight/site) the source of the (data/datum) you use in preparing the (bimonthly/semimonthly) report for January and February.

2. Find and correct the word use errors in the following sentences. If a sentence has no errors, write correct.

a. The crowd was composed of a large amount of people whom had driven a brief distance to attend the concert.

b. The treatment, that began just two weeks ago, has already begun to show positive affects.

c. My schedule for Tuesday is full, but I'm sure we can find some time to meet on Wednesday or Thursday to discuss the consultant's advice.

d. Did anyone question whether we have the authority to precede with plans to remodel the facility?

e. The report contrasts our current method with that proposed by the technology team and illustrates the strengths and weaknesses of each.

f. We are anxious to see how well the furnishings in the outer office complement the decor of the conference room.

g. Manny has assured us that the new server will permit us to rely on e-mail as our principle internal communication media.

h. Sally has tract down the problem—its a lose wire.

i. If we had to choose between the options, I would select A over B because of it's relationship to continuous process improvement.

j. Please bring the package to the Capital by noon so that Senator Billings may review it before this afternoon's hearings.

k. ABC has led the industry by providing top-quality products and high-quality service while earning a descent profit.

l. After you have analyzed the data, summarize your results and send a copy to Bill and myself.

m. Any one of the three applicants is imminently well qualified for the job; choosing between them will be a difficult task.

n. The goal we have set for next year is to achieve greater balance between our desire for profit and our principals.

o. Although we will have less opportunities to work together, we may keep our friendship alive thorough social and recreational outlets.

Appendices

Appendices:

A Formats of Letters and Memos

B Document Format—APA and MLA

C Formal Report

APPENDIX

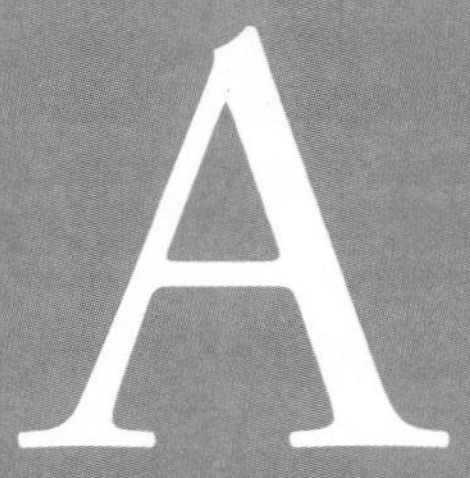

Formats of Letters and Memos

[LEARNING OBJECTIVES]

[1] DESCRIBE THE SEVEN STANDARD PARTS OF A LETTER.

[2] DESCRIBE THE APPROPRIATE USE OF SUPPLEMENTARY PARTS OF A LETTER.

[3] FORMAT BUSINESS LETTERS USING THE FULL BLOCK, MODIFIED BLOCK, AND SIMPLIFIED BLOCK STYLES.

[4] ADDRESS AN ENVELOPE PROPERLY.

[5] FORMAT A MEMO PROPERLY.

[6] DISCUSS THE CHARACTERISTICS OF APPROPRIATE STATIONERY FOR LETTERS, MEMOS, AND ENVELOPES.

Your letters or memos should make an initial impression that will have a lasting effect on the receivers of your messages. The energy expended in writing good letters and memos is well spent when you select appropriate stationery and formats. The receiver will assume that you care and that you are knowledgeable about letter and memo writing when you use proper grammar, punctuation, spelling, stationery, and formats.

Letters

A **letter** is used to communicate a formal written message. The appearance of a letter is important because it makes the first impression on the reader; the content is important because it ensures that the reader understands and fully accepts your message. The appearance of a letter depends on the parts of a letter, punctuation style, letter format, and stationery. In this appendix, you will learn how to improve the appearance of a letter; you will be taught how to organize and write the content of a letter in Chapters 7, 8, 9, 10, and 16.

USES OF LETTERS

Letters are used to communicate written messages to individuals outside an organization. Letters are also used to communicate formal written messages to employees within an organization.

STANDARD PARTS OF A LETTER

Learning Objective [1]
DESCRIBE THE SEVEN STANDARD PARTS OF A LETTER.

The number and location of letter parts depend on the format you select. As shown in Figure APA.1, most letters contain seven standard parts: heading, inside address, salutation, body, complimentary close, signature block, and reference initials.

Heading The first standard part of a letter is the **heading**, which consists of the letterhead and the dateline or the return address and a dateline. All business organizations should use letterhead stationery for the first page of a letter. A **letterhead** contains the name of the company and its complete address. It may contain a phone number; fax number; e-mail address; originating department; originator's title; founding date; organizational slogan, emblem, or logo; and other information that the organization deems appropriate. The amount of information in a letterhead will depend on the type of organization sending the letter. However, a letterhead should use no more than two vertical inches of stationery space. Although a letterhead usually is placed at the top of the page, part of the information may be at the bottom of the page. For example, the street address and telephone number or another location may be shown at the bottom of letterhead stationery. The letterhead may be printed in more than one color. Examples of letterheads are shown in Figure APA.2.

The **dateline** contains the month, day, and year that the letter is written. The month should be spelled in full. Figures are not used for the month (e.g., 6/09/00) because there is no universal agreement as to whether the day or month appears first. Dates may be in one of the following two styles:

June 9, 200–
9 June 200–

Figure APA.1
The Seven Standard Parts of a Letter

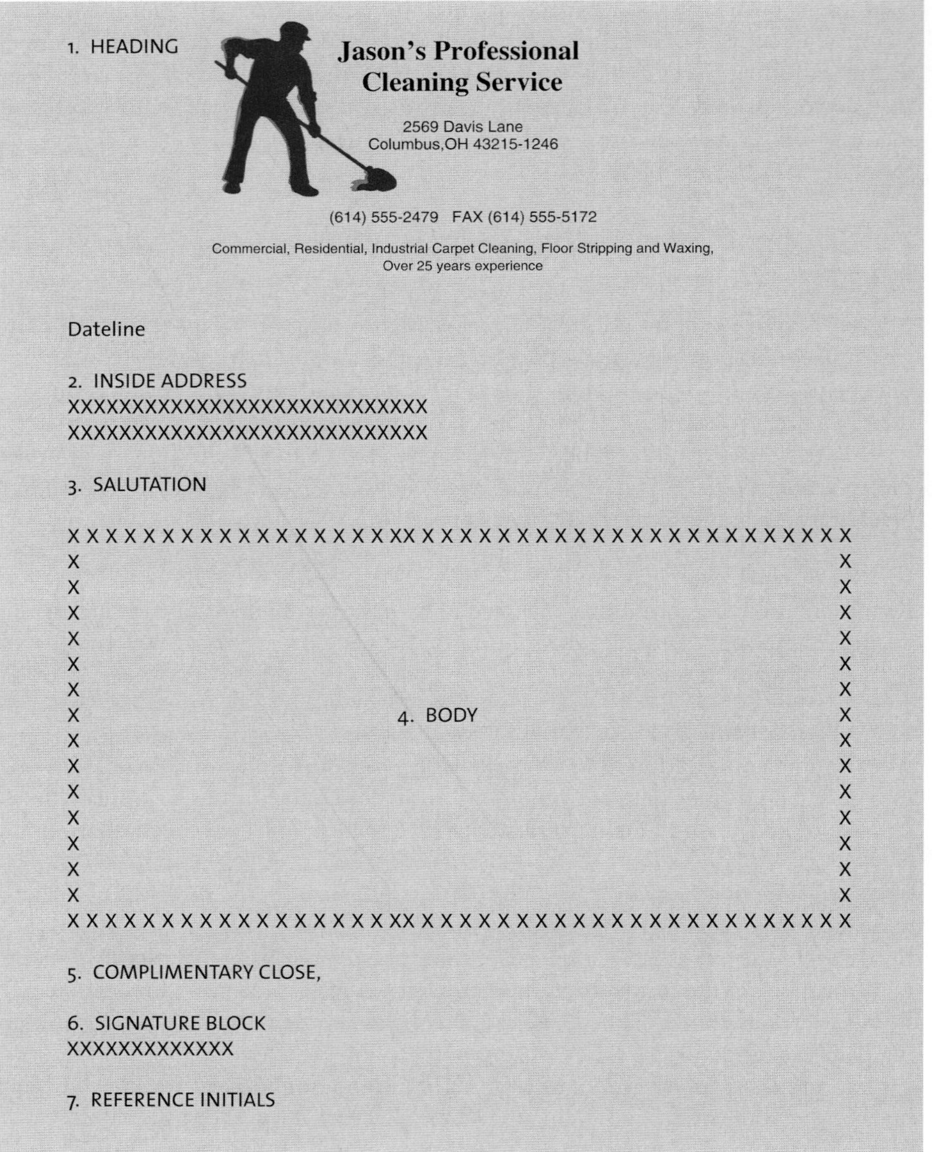
1. HEADING

Jason's Professional
Cleaning Service

2569 Davis Lane
Columbus,OH 43215-1246

(614) 555-2479 FAX (614) 555-5172

Commercial, Residential, Industrial Carpet Cleaning, Floor Stripping and Waxing,
Over 25 years experience

Dateline

2. INSIDE ADDRESS
XXXXXXXXXXXXXXXXXXXXXXXXXXXX
XXXXXXXXXXXXXXXXXXXXXXXXXXXX

3. SALUTATION

4. BODY

5. COMPLIMENTARY CLOSE,

6. SIGNATURE BLOCK
XXXXXXXXXXXXX

7. REFERENCE INITIALS

Notice that there is no punctuation when the day appears before the month in the dateline. Placing the month before the day is the style used by most American business organizations. Placing the day first is the preferred style for international and military use.

The horizontal placement of the dateline (or the keyed return address and dateline) depends on the letter format. The vertical placement of the dateline varies depending on the length of the letter. The dateline usually is keyed two or more lines below the printed letterhead or is keyed two inches from the top edge of the page.

When a return address is keyed at the top of a personal business letter, the dateline is keyed on the line below it. When the return address appears below the signa-

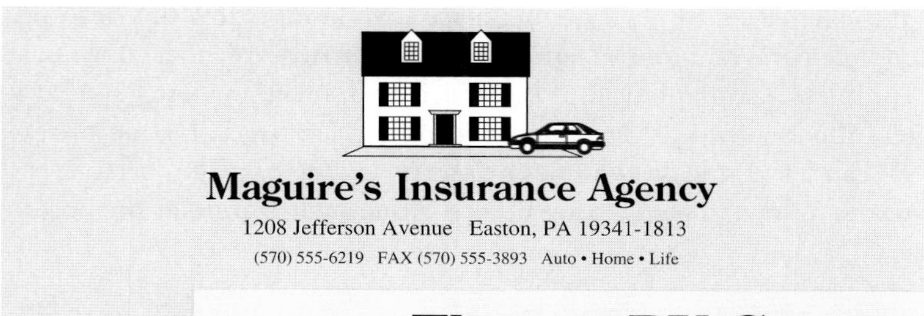

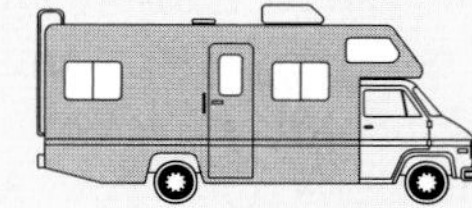

Figure APA.2
Examples of Letterheads

ture block of a personal business letter, the date usually is placed between lines 10 and 15.

Letterhead stationery is used only for the first page of a letter. Stationery of the same color and quality, but without the letterhead, is used for continuation pages. The heading on each additional page begins on line seven, leaving a top margin of one inch (six lines). The continuation page heading should contain the first line of the inside address, the page number, and the date. Two popular formats for continuation page headings are

Mr. Herbert Hughes   3   July 22, 200–

or

Mr. Herbert Hughes
Page 3
July 22, 200–

The body of the letter continues a double space (two lines) below this heading. At least one complete paragraph of the letter should be carried over to a continuation page. If a complete paragraph cannot be carried over, revise the letter so that it is only one page. Individual words are never divided between pages. Divide a paragraph only if you can leave at least two lines on the preceding page and carry over at least two lines to the following page. Leave at least a one-inch margin at the bottom of the first page.

Inside Address The **inside address** includes the receiver's courtesy title (Ms., Miss, Mrs., Mr., Dr., etc.), name, street number and name (or some other specific mailing designation, such as post office box number), city, state, and ZIP code. Abbreviations should be avoided in street addresses (e.g., use *Avenue* instead of *Ave.*; use *Road* instead of *Rd.*). The two-letter U.S. postal abbreviation should be used in complete mailing addresses. United States and Canadian two-letter postal abbreviations are shown in Figure APA.3. The ZIP code is keyed one space after the postal abbreviation.

The **ZIP code** is a five-digit code that identifies areas within the United States and its possessions. In 1985 the U.S. Postal Service introduced the **ZIP + 4** system. This system uses the original ZIP code plus a hyphen and four additional numbers. This expanded code should be used when it is known because it speeds the delivery of mail. It enables the Postal Service to sort mail on high-speed automated equipment for specific streets, specific buildings, or even to specific floors within buildings. The ZIP code for an address can be obtained from a ZIP code directory provided by the U.S. Postal Service.

Other countries, such as Canada and Germany, also use mail codes. Canada's six-character codes use alternating numbers and letters (e.g., T2K5S3). In Germany the city identification code is keyed prior to the name of the city (e.g., 53105 Bonn).

The inside address is always keyed flush with the left margin and usually follows the date. The length of the letter determines the number of blank lines between the date and the inside address. Normally, the first line of the inside address is keyed three to five lines below the date.

Salutation The **salutation** is the greeting that begins the message. Examples of correct and incorrect salutations for letters to specific individuals include the following:

Correct	Incorrect
Dear Ms. McCuan:	Dear LaDonna McCuan:
Dear LaDonna:	Dear Ms. LaDonna:
Dear Jack and Edna:	Dear Vaughns:

Examples of correct and incorrect salutations in writing the same letter to many people include the following:

Correct	Incorrect
Dear Customers:	Dear Gentlemen:
Ladies and Gentlemen:	Dear Ladies and Gentlemen:

Figure APA.3
Two-Letter Postal Abbreviations

TWO-LETTER POSTAL ABBREVIATIONS

U.S. State, District, and Territory Names

Name	Two-Letter Abbreviation	Name	Two-Letter Abbreviation
Alabama	AL	Montana	MT
Alaska	AK	Nebraska	NE
Arizona	AZ	Nevada	NV
Arkansas	AR	New Hampshire	NH
California	CA	New Jersey	NJ
Colorado	CO	New Mexico	NM
Connecticut	CT	New York	NY
Delaware	DE	North Carolina	NC
District of Columbia	DC	North Dakota	ND
Florida	FL	Ohio	OH
Georgia	GA	Oklahoma	OK
Guam	GU	Oregon	OR
Hawaii	HI	Pennsylvania	PA
Idaho	ID	Puerto Rico	PR
Illinois	IL	Rhode Island	RI
Indiana	IN	South Carolina	SC
Iowa	IA	South Dakota	SD
Kansas	KS	Tennessee	TN
Kentucky	KY	Texas	TX
Louisiana	LA	Utah	UT
Maine	ME	Vermont	VT
Maryland	MD	Virgin Islands	VI
Massachusetts	MA	Virginia	VA
Michigan	MI	Washington	WA
Minnesota	MN	West Virginia	WV
Mississippi	MS	Wisconsin	WI
Missouri	MO	Wyoming	WY

Canadian Provinces and Territories

Name	Two-Letter Abbreviation	Name	Two-Letter Abbreviation
Alberta	AB	Nova Scotia	NS
British Columbia	BC	Ontario	ON
Manitoba	MB	Prince Edward Island	PE
New Brunswick	NB	Quebec	PQ
Newfoundland	NF	Saskatchewan	SK
Northwest Territories	NT	Yukon Territory	YT

The content of the salutation depends on the first line of the inside address. When a letter is addressed to a company and contains an attention line (discussed on page 625), the salutation is directed to the company and not to the person in the attention line. The formality of the salutation depends on the relationship between the sender and the receiver of the letter. A general guide is to use the name that you would use if you met the person or persons face to face. If the first line of the inside address is singular, the salutation must be singular; if the first line is plural, the salutation must be plural.

The salutation is keyed flush with the left margin and placed a double space below the last line of the inside address or attention line, if used. A colon follows the salutation in a business letter if mixed punctuation is used; no punctuation follows the salutation if open punctuation is used. Mixed and open punctuation styles are discussed on pages 627–628. The salutation is omitted in the simplified block format (see page 628).

Body The **body** is the message section of the letter. It begins a double space below the salutation. The body is single-spaced within paragraphs and double-spaced between paragraphs. The paragraphs may be indented or blocked, depending on the letter format selected. Normally, the first and last paragraphs of a letter are shorter than the other paragraphs.

Complimentary Close The **complimentary close** is a phrase used to end the message. Frequently used complimentary closes include the following:

Sincerely, Sincerely yours, Cordially,

The complimentary close is keyed a double space below the last line of the body of the letter. The first character of the close should begin at the same horizontal point as the first character of the date. Only the first character of the first word in the complimentary close is capitalized. The complimentary close is followed by a comma if mixed punctuation is used and by no punctuation if open punctuation is used. The simplified block letter omits the complimentary close.

Signature Block The **signature block** contains the writer's signed name, keyed name, and title. The name is keyed four spaces (lines) below the complimentary close. A courtesy title in the signature block is optional. It may be included, in parentheses, when the gender of the writer is unclear (e.g., Pat, Kim, or Lynn). The position title of the sender is keyed a single space (line) below the keyed name. If the name and position title are on the same line, a comma separates them. The sender of the message signs the letter in the space between the complimentary close and the keyed name. The signature normally does not include the courtesy title even if it is keyed in the signature block.

Reference Initials The initials of the message originator and the keyboard operator make up the **reference initials**. If the originator is the same person who signs the letter, his or her initials are optional. When the message originator keys the letter, no reference initials are necessary. If the originator's initials are given, they are separated from those of the keyboard operator by a colon or a diagonal. The originator's initials should be uppercase and the keyboard operator's lowercase. The reference initials are flush with the left margin on the line below the sender's title. Examples of reference initials are the following:

ev

NRE:pd

JHT/ras

SUPPLEMENTARY PARTS OF A LETTER

Learning Objective [2]
DESCRIBE THE APPROPRIATE USE OF SUPPLEMENTARY PARTS OF A LETTER.

In addition to the seven standard parts, letters may contain one or more supplementary parts. These parts include the attention line, subject line, company name in signature block, enclosure notation, copy notation, and postscript.

Attention Line When a company name is used as the first line of the inside address, the **attention line** can be used to direct the letter to a person, position title, or department within the company. Using a person's name in the first line of the inside address is preferred over using an attention line.

When used, the attention line should be a double space below the last line of the inside address. It may be keyed with all capital letters or a combination of initial capital and lowercase letters. The word *Attention* should not be abbreviated. Separating the word *Attention* from the rest of the attention line with a colon is optional. The salutation agrees with the first line of the address and not the attention line. An example of an inside address with an attention line follows:

First National Bank
358 Chestnut Drive
Red Cloud, NE 68970-4224

Attention: Loan Officer

Ladies and Gentlemen:

Subject Line The **subject line** identifies the main topic of the letter. It is considered part of the body of the letter. The subject line should be short—less than one line—and it should not be a complete sentence. The key words contained in a subject line help office personnel to sort and route incoming mail and to code documents for storage and retrieval.

The subject line is keyed a double space below the salutation. It may be centered, flush with the left margin, or indented the same number of spaces as the paragraphs. It may be keyed in all capitals or keyed with initial capitals and lowercase letters—and underlined. If the word *Subject* is used, a colon follows it. If an attention line appears in the same letter, use the same format for both lines. A letter that includes a subject line is shown in Figure APA.4.

A **reference line** is sometimes used instead of a subject line (Re: Contract 1065-940). It is used to direct the reader to source documents or files. A reference line is keyed a double space below the inside address.

Company Name in Signature Block The name of the company may be keyed in all capital letters a double space below the complimentary close. The company

Figure APA.4
Full Block Letter Format, Mixed Punctuation

Heading

2435 Bridge Street, Stafford, VA 22554-5272 (703) 555-5549 • FAX (703) 555-3198

April 17, 2001

Inside Address

Ms. Teri Prince
Lourdes Center for Aging
427 Haymarket Road
Burke, VA 22015-4212

Salutation

Dear Teri:

Subject Line

LETTER USING FULL BLOCK FORMAT

Body

This letter is in full block format which is the most streamlined letter style because all parts and all lines begin at the left margin. The letterhead uses less than two vertical inches of stationery, and the date is placed approximately a double space (two lines) below the letterhead.

The inside address is keyed flush with the left margin and is the same as the address on the envelope. Depending on its length, the position title may be keyed after the name on the first line or on the line below the name.

The salutation is on the second line below the inside address. The name used in the salutation should be the same as would be used if the sender met that person on the street. Notice the colon after the salutation (mixed punctuation).

The subject line is keyed flush with the left margin a double space below the salutation and is considered part of the body. The body is single-spaced within paragraphs and double-spaced between paragraphs.

The complimentary close is keyed a double space below the body and is flush with the left margin. A comma follows the close (mixed punctuation). The signature block (writer's name and title) is keyed four lines below the complimentary close.

Complimentary Close

Sincerely,

Shannon Willard

Signature Block

Shannon Willard
Communication Specialist

Reference Initials

vfr

name is placed in the signature block when the letter is in the nature of a contract or when plain paper is used rather than letterhead stationery. The first character of the company name is aligned with the first character of the complimentary close. An example of a company name in the signature block follows:

> Sincerely,
> THURMAN FURNITURE
>
> Gail Hendon, Manager

This addition is not commonly used with letterhead stationery.

Enclosure or Attachment Notation Any item included in the envelope other than the letter, such as a check, invoice, or photograph, is considered an **enclosure**. When something is included with a letter, an enclosure notation should be keyed a single or double space below the reference initials (flush with the left margin). The enclosures may be identified, or the number of enclosures may be put in parentheses. When an enclosure is attached to the letter, use *Attachment* or *Att.* in place of the enclosure notation. Examples of enclosure and attachment notations are as follows:

Enclosure: Abstract
Enclosures (3)
Enc. 3
Attachment
Attachment: Donation receipt

Copy Notation A **copy notation** is used when a copy of a letter is being sent to someone other than the addressee. The copy notation is keyed as a "cc" flush with the left margin and a double space below the reference initials (or enclosure notation if used). Some companies prefer to note copies made on a photocopier with a "pc" flush with the left margin. The names of the individuals or groups to receive the copies should be keyed after the notation. Examples of copy notations include the following:

cc: Tim Miller

cc: Roger Schoenfeldt
Holly Rudolph

pc: Accounting

A **blind copy notation** is used when it is unnecessary or inappropriate for an addressee to know that a copy of the letter is being sent to other individuals. The blind copy notation is indicated only on copies of the letter or memo, not on the original. Place the blind copy notation where the regular copy notation normally appears. An example of a blind copy notation is

bcc: Suzie McReynolds

Postscript A **postscript** may be used to add a personal comment or to emphasize an important point discussed in the body of the letter. It should *not* be used to add an important point omitted from the body of the letter. The postscript should follow the last notation and be formatted in the same style as the paragraphs of the message. If the paragraphs are indented, the postscript should also be indented. A postscript may be handwritten. The notation "P.S." is usually omitted.

PUNCTUATION STYLES

The two styles of punctuation commonly used in business letters are mixed and open. The most popular style is mixed punctuation. **Mixed punctuation** requires a colon after the salutation and a comma after the complimentary close.

Letters using **open punctuation** omit the colon after the salutation and the comma after the complimentary close. Open punctuation is becoming more accepted but is still less popular than mixed punctuation.

LETTER FORMATS

Learning Objective [3]
FORMAT BUSINESS LETTERS USING THE FULL BLOCK, MODIFIED BLOCK, AND SIMPLIFIED BLOCK STYLES.

The format helps create the reader's first impression of your letter. Organizations usually designate the format of their letters, but in some circumstances they may permit the originator to select the format. The most frequently used formats are full block, modified block, and simplified block.

Full Block The **full block format** is becoming very popular. It can be keyed rapidly because none of the parts of the letter are indented. Figure APA.4 shows a full block format letter.

Modified Block The date (or the return address and date), complimentary close, and signature block begin at the horizontal center of the page in the **modified block format**. There are two versions of the modified block format: (1) body of the letter with block paragraphs and (2) body of the letter with indented paragraphs. Letters using the modified block format are shown in Figures APA.5 and APA.6.

Simplified Block The **simplified block format** is a modern, efficient letter format similar to the AMS simplified letter that was developed several years ago by the Administrative Management Society. The simplified block letter eliminates the salutation and complimentary close. It is often used when the gender or marital status of a female receiver is unknown. Figure APA.7 shows a letter in the simplified block format.

PLACEMENT

A carefully arranged letter resembles a picture in a frame. The letter should have a border of blank space to form a frame. The width of this frame will vary with the length of the letter, but it should normally be at least one inch on each side. Today, with most offices using word processing software, a letter can be adjusted easily to give it an attractive appearance. Some organizations are justifying their line lengths (making the right margin even). This gives the letter an attractive and somewhat more formal appearance.

PERSONAL BUSINESS LETTERS

A **personal business letter** is written by an individual when conducting business of a personal nature. An application for employment, a request for information, and a comment about services received are examples of personal business letters. A good grade of paper should be used for this type of letter. A full block style or modified block style with mixed or open punctuation is suitable. The return address of the sender should be placed two inches from the top edge of the paper. The date should be keyed on the line below the return address; however, the date is not considered a part of the return address. The simplified block format is not recommended for application letters because many individuals interpret the lack of a salutation as being impersonal. Figure APA.8 shows a personal business letter.

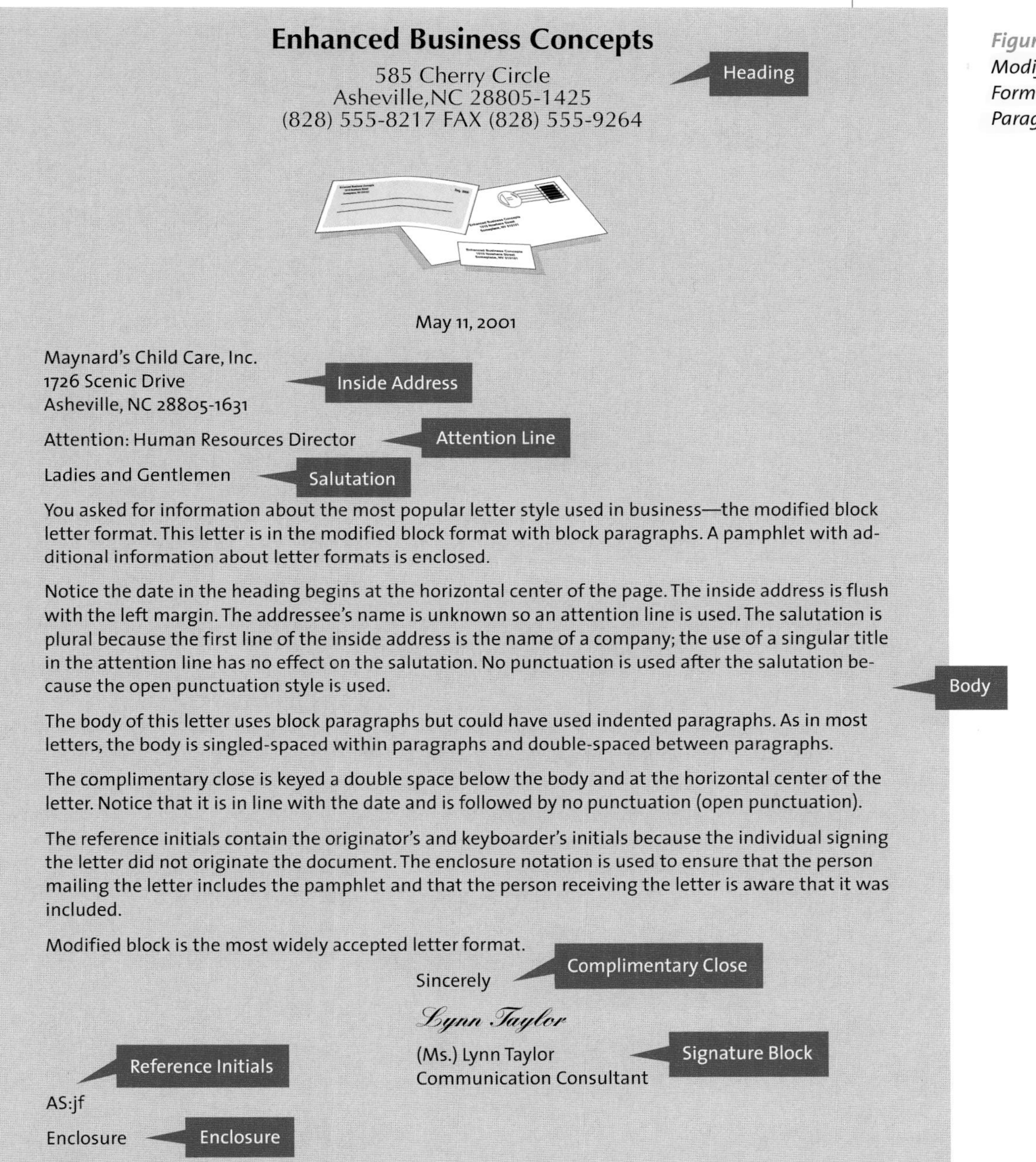
Enhanced Business Concepts
585 Cherry Circle
Asheville,NC 28805-1425
(828) 555-8217 FAX (828) 555-9264

May 11, 2001

Maynard's Child Care, Inc.
1726 Scenic Drive
Asheville, NC 28805-1631

Attention: Human Resources Director

Ladies and Gentlemen

You asked for information about the most popular letter style used in business—the modified block letter format. This letter is in the modified block format with block paragraphs. A pamphlet with additional information about letter formats is enclosed.

Notice the date in the heading begins at the horizontal center of the page. The inside address is flush with the left margin. The addressee's name is unknown so an attention line is used. The salutation is plural because the first line of the inside address is the name of a company; the use of a singular title in the attention line has no effect on the salutation. No punctuation is used after the salutation because the open punctuation style is used.

The body of this letter uses block paragraphs but could have used indented paragraphs. As in most letters, the body is singled-spaced within paragraphs and double-spaced between paragraphs.

The complimentary close is keyed a double space below the body and at the horizontal center of the letter. Notice that it is in line with the date and is followed by no punctuation (open punctuation).

The reference initials contain the originator's and keyboarder's initials because the individual signing the letter did not originate the document. The enclosure notation is used to ensure that the person mailing the letter includes the pamphlet and that the person receiving the letter is aware that it was included.

Modified block is the most widely accepted letter format.

Sincerely

Lynn Taylor

(Ms.) Lynn Taylor
Communication Consultant

AS:jf

Enclosure

Figure APA.5 *Modified Block Letter Format, Blocked Paragraphs*

INTERNATIONAL BUSINESS CORRESPONDENCE

Business letter formats used by writers in other countries are similar to those used by business letter writers in the United States. When corresponding with someone in a foreign country, you must be knowledgeable about differences in letter formatting that may cause misunderstandings. For instance, the month should be spelled out because in the United States the date March 9, 2000, would be written

Figure APA.6
Modified Block Letter Format, Indented Paragraphs

Heading

Enhanced Business Concepts
585 Cherry Circle
Asheville,NC 28805-1425
(828) 555-8217 FAX (828) 555-9264

May 11, 2001

Inside Address

Maynard's Child Care, Inc.
1726 Scenic Drive
Asheville, NC 28805-1631

Attention Line

Attention: Human Resources Director

Salutation

Ladies and Gentlemen

Body

You asked for information about the modified block letter format. This letter is in the modified block format with indented paragraphs. You will notice that it is identical to the modified block except that the first word in each paragraph is indented one-half inch. When a subject line is used, it may be centered or indented one-half inch to match the paragraphs. A pamphlet with additional information about letter formats is enclosed.

The date in the heading begins at the horizontal center of the page, whereas the inside address is flush with the left margin. No punctuation is used after the salutation because the open punctuation style is used.

The body of this letter uses indented paragraphs but could have used blocked paragraphs. As in most letters, the body is singled-spaced within paragraphs and double-spaced between paragraphs.

The complimentary close is keyed a double space below the body and at the horizontal center of the letter. Notice that it is in line with the date and is followed by no punctuation (open punctuation).

The reference initials contain the originator's and keyboarder's initials because the individual signing the letter did not originate the document. The enclosure notation is used to ensure that the person mailing the letter includes the pamphlet and that the person receiving the letter is aware that it was included.

Modified block is a well-accepted letter format that is popular in many organizations.

Complimentary Close

Sincerely

Lynn Taylor

Signature Block

(Ms.) Lynn Taylor
Communication Consultant

Reference Initials

AS:jf

Enclosure

Enclosure

9.3.2000 in Germany. Figure APA.9 shows a sample business letter written in German, and Figure APA.10 shows the same letter written in English.

There are other differences between German and American letter formatting: The street name comes before the house number, the city name follows the mailing

2175 Bonnie Castle Lane
Louisville, KY 40204-4372
(502) 555-5218 FAX (502) 555-8326

10 June 2001

Ms. Teresa Underhill
24718 Wellford Drive
Paducah, KY 42086-2184

SIMPLIFIED BLOCK FORMAT

This letter, Teresa, is in the simplified block format. It is modern and time saving. The letter should be constructed using these guidelines:

1. Use full block format.

2. Omit the salutation and complimentary close. Use the addressee's name in the first sentence to personalize the message.

3. Use a subject line keyed in all capital letters. The subject line is keyed a double space below the address; the body is keyed a double space below the subject line.

4. Key all enumerations at the left margin.

5. On the fifth line (leave four blank lines) below the body of the letter, key the writer's name and title in all capital letters flush with the left margin.

6. Key the keyboard operator's initials in lowercase letters a double space below the writer's name. Enclosure notations and copy notations are keyed a double space below the keyboard operator's initials.

Teresa, you will enjoy using this format once you become familiar with it. An enclosed brochure describes future writing workshops that will give you practice in creating letters in different formats.

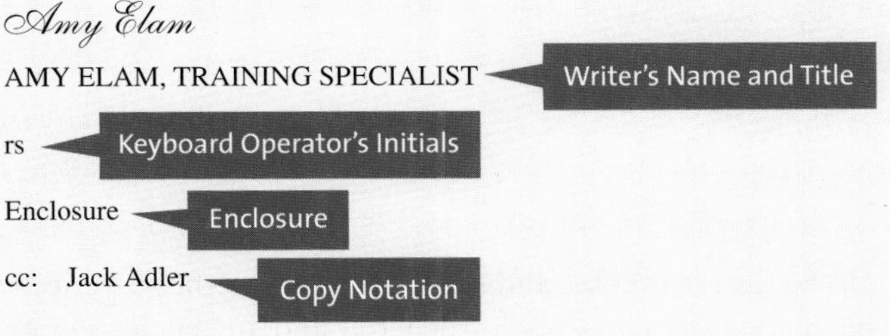

AMY ELAM, TRAINING SPECIALIST

rs

Enclosure

cc: Jack Adler

Figure APA.7
Simplified Block Format

code, the dateline is always flush right, and the salutation is a double space below the subject line. Germans are more formal than Americans in their communication; writers include titles such as Dr., Mr., Mrs., or Ms. in the salutation and rarely address someone by his or her first name.

Figure APA.8
Personal Business Letter

Heading

536 Moss Road
Fargo, ND 58102
October 6, 2001

Inside Address

Mr. Tom Seymour
875 Bailey Road
Minot, ND 58701

Salutation

Dear Tom:

Body

This is a personal business letter keyed in modified block format with indented paragraphs. The personal business letter may use any of the three accepted formats.

The heading contains the sender's address immediately above the date. This address is keyed and not printed, as it would be in letterhead stationery. Notice that the individual sending the letter omits his or her name in the heading. A general guide is to place the heading two inches from the top edge of the paper, but this varies with the length of the letter.

The inside address is flush with the left margin about four to six lines below the dateline. The inside address is the receiver's address, which also appears on the envelope.

The salutation is a double space (two lines) below the inside address. When mixed punctuation is used, key a colon (not a comma) after the salutation because this letter is business and not personal in content.

Supplementary parts (attention lines, subject lines, enclosures, etc.) are used as in regular business letters. The body of the letter contains the message that the sender is transmitting to the receiver. The body should be single-spaced within paragraphs and double-spaced between paragraphs.

The writer signs in the space between the complimentary close and the signature block. Normally, a personal business letter does not contain reference initials because the sender keys the letter.

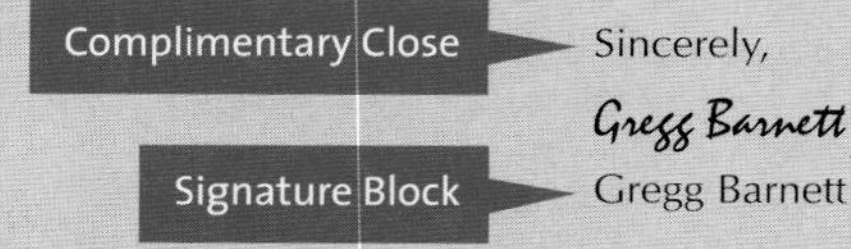

Envelopes

Learning Objective [4]
ADDRESS AN ENVELOPE PROPERLY.

Envelope paper should be the same color and quality as the letterhead stationery. The envelope must be of adequate size to hold the letter and any enclosures or attachments without unnecessary folding. The return address, mailing address, and envelope notations are the three things that may be included on an envelope. Correctly addressed envelopes are shown in Figure APA.11.

RETURN ADDRESS

The **return address** is the sender's address. It is keyed in capitals in the upper left corner of the envelope. It should contain the sender's address as shown on the

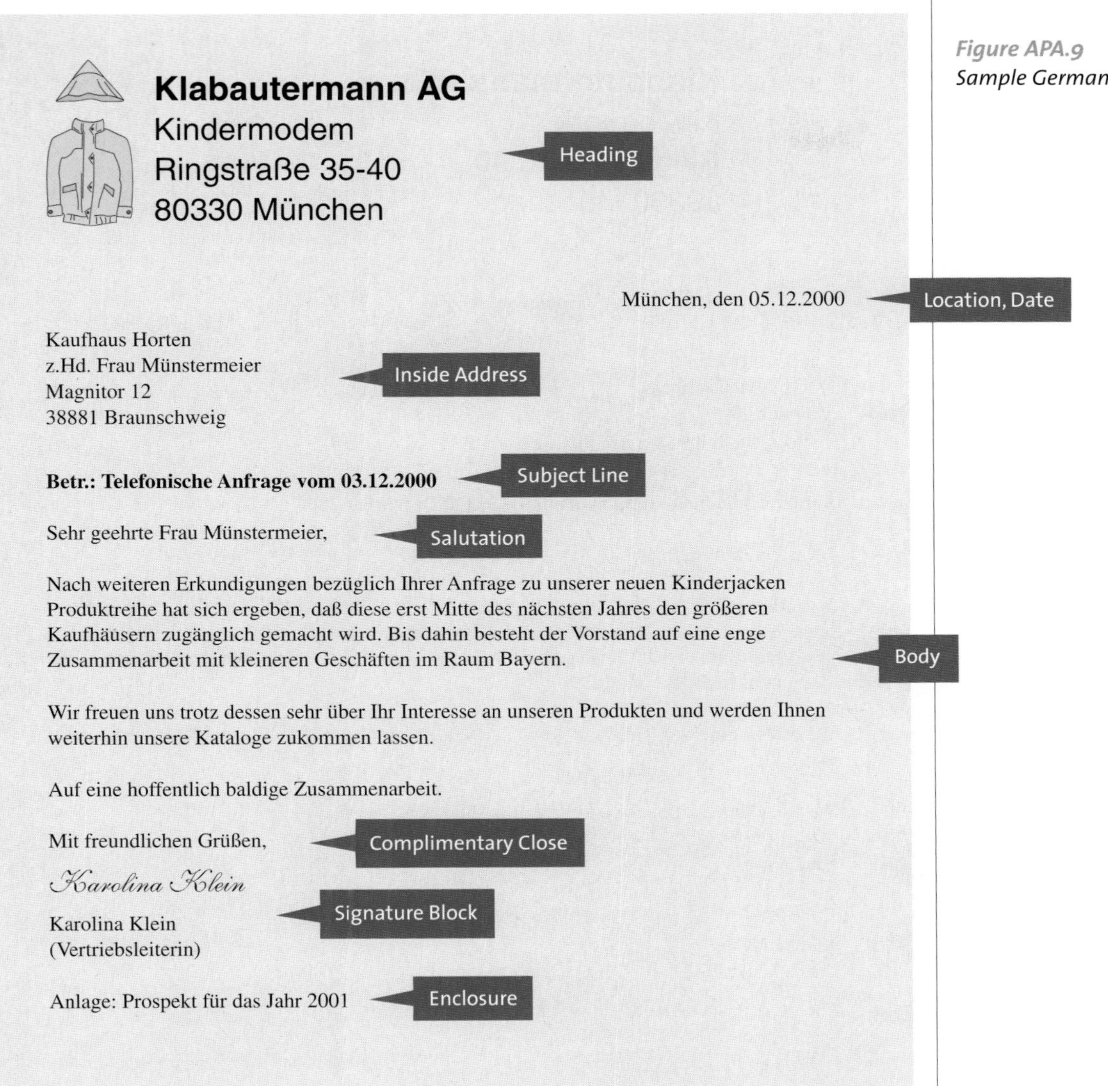

Klabautermann AG
Kindermodem
Ringstraße 35-40
80330 München

München, den 05.12.2000

Kaufhaus Horten
z.Hd. Frau Münstermeier
Magnitor 12
38881 Braunschweig

Betr.: Telefonische Anfrage vom 03.12.2000

Sehr geehrte Frau Münstermeier,

Nach weiteren Erkundigungen bezüglich Ihrer Anfrage zu unserer neuen Kinderjacken Produktreihe hat sich ergeben, daß diese erst Mitte des nächsten Jahres den größeren Kaufhäusern zugänglich gemacht wird. Bis dahin besteht der Vorstand auf eine enge Zusammenarbeit mit kleineren Geschäften im Raum Bayern.

Wir freuen uns trotz dessen sehr über Ihr Interesse an unseren Produkten und werden Ihnen weiterhin unsere Kataloge zukommen lassen.

Auf eine hoffentlich baldige Zusammenarbeit.

Mit freundlichen Grüßen,

Karolina Klein

Karolina Klein
(Vertriebsleiterin)

Anlage: Prospekt für das Jahr 2001

Figure APA.9
Sample German Business Letter

letterhead. Often the sender's name will be keyed immediately above a preprinted business return address. For personal business letters, return addresses should be printed on labels or keyed on plain envelopes.

MAILING ADDRESS

The mailing address contains the receiver's name and address as shown in the inside address. The address should not exceed five lines, and all lines should be blocked. The ZIP code or ZIP + 4 (preferably) should be used in all addresses. The Postal Service recommends using all capital letters and no punctuation on the envelope to facilitate use of optical scanning equipment. The last line of the inside address must contain only the city, state, and ZIP code.

Figure APA.10
English Translation of German Business Letter

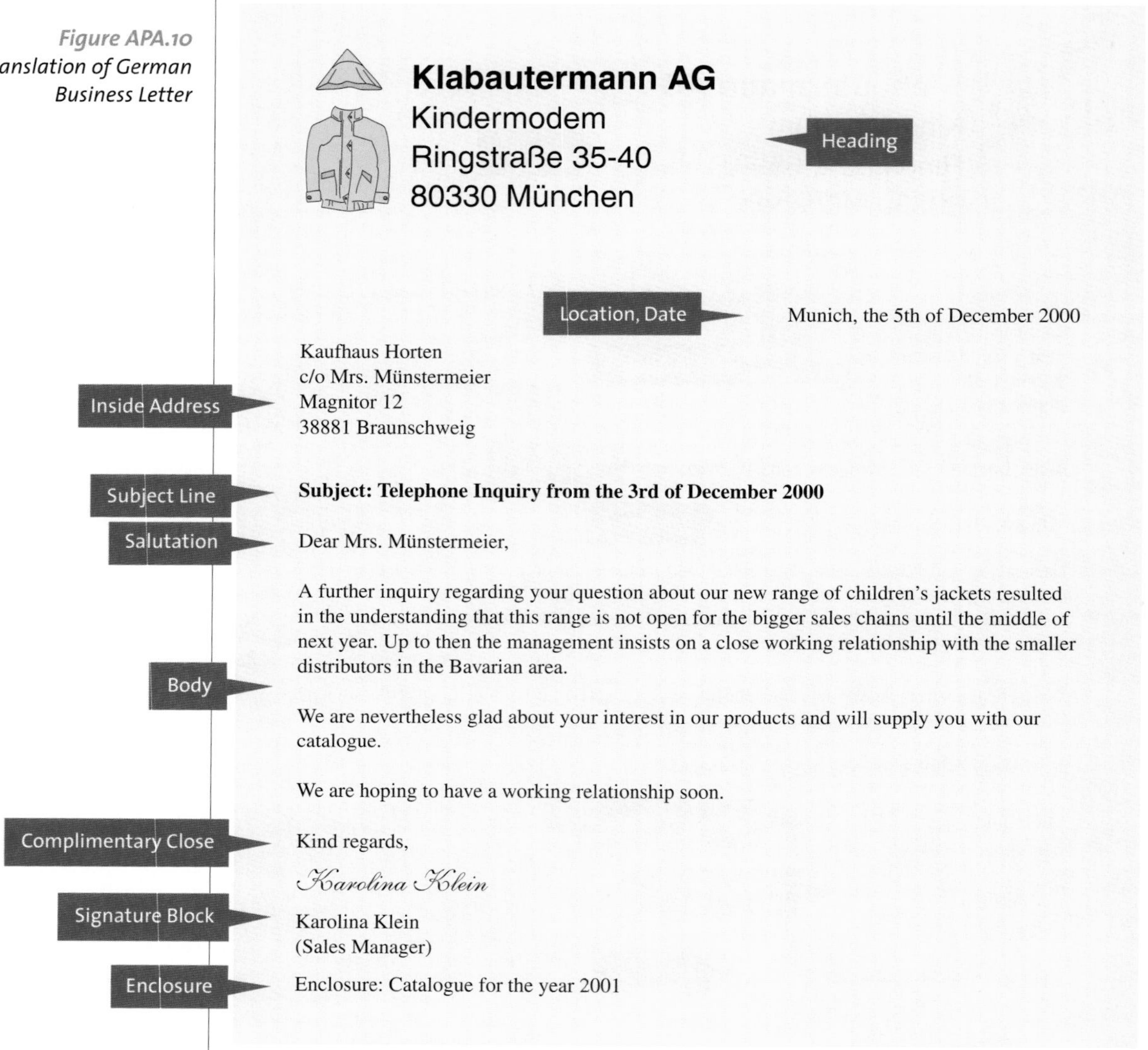

Heading

Klabautermann AG
Kindermodem
Ringstraße 35-40
80330 München

Location, Date — Munich, the 5th of December 2000

Inside Address

Kaufhaus Horten
c/o Mrs. Münstermeier
Magnitor 12
38881 Braunschweig

Subject Line

Subject: Telephone Inquiry from the 3rd of December 2000

Salutation

Dear Mrs. Münstermeier,

Body

A further inquiry regarding your question about our new range of children's jackets resulted in the understanding that this range is not open for the bigger sales chains until the middle of next year. Up to then the management insists on a close working relationship with the smaller distributors in the Bavarian area.

We are nevertheless glad about your interest in our products and will supply you with our catalogue.

We are hoping to have a working relationship soon.

Complimentary Close

Kind regards,

Karolina Klein

Signature Block

Karolina Klein
(Sales Manager)

Enclosure

Enclosure: Catalogue for the year 2001

The first line of the address should be keyed one-half inch to the left of the horizontal center of the envelope and on line 14 or 15 of a No. 10 envelope or on line 12 of a No. 6¾ envelope.

ENVELOPE NOTATIONS

Two types of envelope notations are used. Special mailing instructions should be keyed in all capital letters a double space below the postage stamp or meter mark. These Postal Service requirements permit electronic scanning and sorting of mail. Mailing instructions include SPECIAL DELIVERY, SPECIAL HANDLING, REGISTERED, and CERTIFIED.

Instructions to individuals handling the receiver's mail are keyed in all capital letters a double space below the return address. These notations include CONFIDENTIAL, HOLD FOR ARRIVAL, PERSONAL, and PLEASE FORWARD.

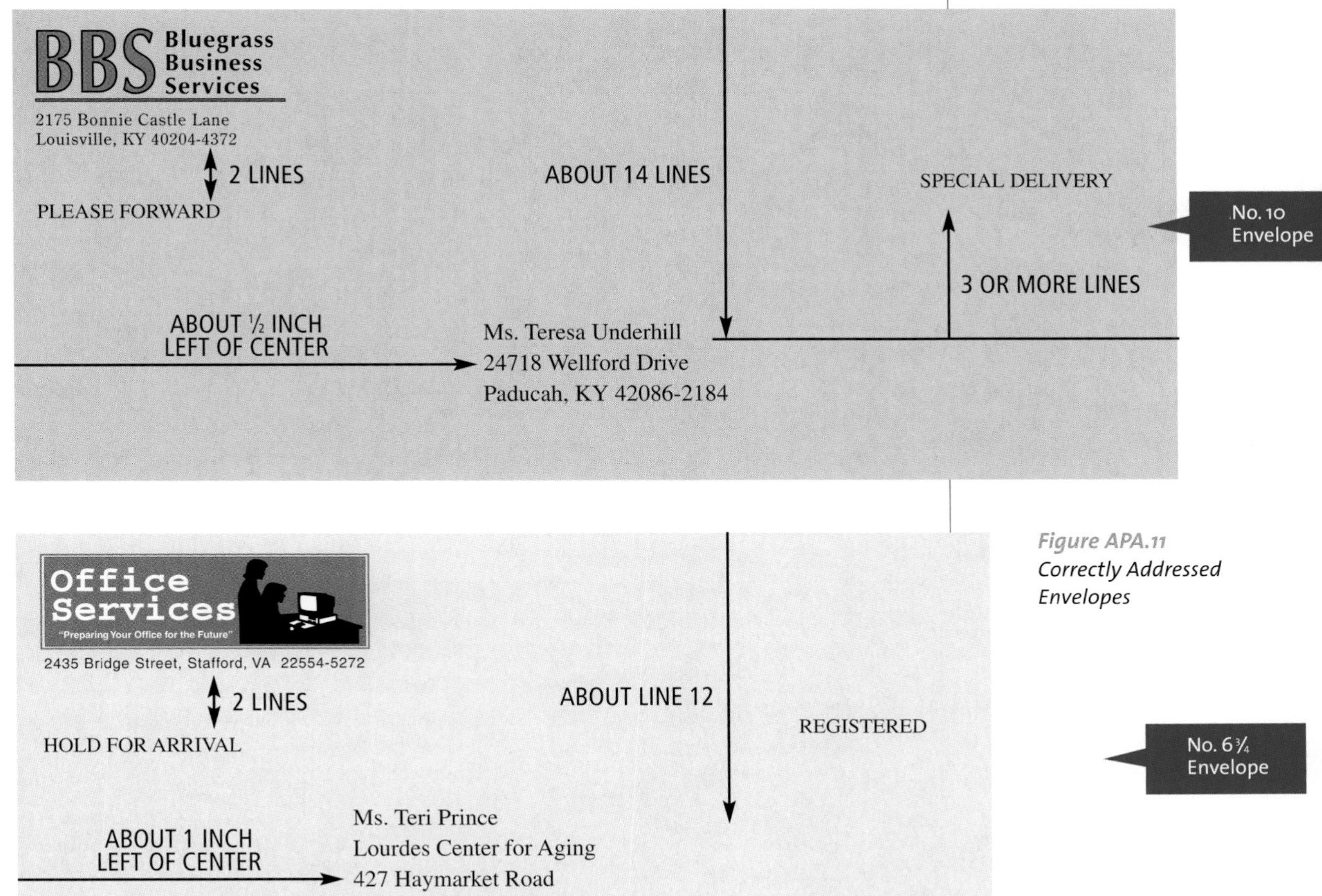

Figure APA.11
Correctly Addressed Envelopes

Memos

Learning Objective [5]
FORMAT A MEMO PROPERLY.

The most common form of written message for communication within an organization is the **memorandum**, or *memo* as it is usually called. Memos have grown in popularity as organizations have become larger and as communications within organizations have become more complex. Memos are normally less formal and shorter than letters.

USES OF MEMOS

Memos are used in a variety of ways. They may be used to communicate upward to superiors, downward to subordinates, laterally to peers, and diagonally to other members of a network. Information of all kinds can be conveyed from one department to another through the use of memos. They are used to announce such things as times and dates of upcoming meetings as well as results of previous meetings, proposed or actual changes in policies or procedures, reports of activities, and instructions.

ADVANTAGES OF MEMOS

Using memos has several advantages. One advantage is that the same memo can be addressed to several individuals. If you want to send the same memo to specific employees, you can list all the names and place a check mark after a different name on each copy. Or, you can list all the names and request that the memo be routed from the first-named person through the last-named person. Entire groups can be addressed in a memo and individual copies can be given to each member of the group, or the memo may be placed on a bulletin board. Examples of ways to address memos properly follow:

Specific Individuals	**Entire Groups**
TO: Jim Thomas Teresa Underhill George Williams	TO: Human Resources Department Employees

TO: See Distribution List Below

In the last example, See Distribution List Below, the names on the distribution list would be listed at the left margin two lines below the text of the memo under a section entitled Distribution List.

A second advantage of using memos is that they are less formal than letters and may require less time to compose. Memos should be clear and accurate, but they usually do not have to be as polished as letters. Memos may be handwritten to save time.

Another advantage of using a memo is that it provides a written record of the message. Written messages make a more lasting impression than do oral messages.

FORMATS OF MEMOS

Memos may be prepared using a formal or a simplified format. The same organization may use more than one format for its memos, or it may specify the format that will be used throughout the organization.

A formal memo may be prepared on a preprinted form that contains the headings TO:, FROM:, DATE:, and SUBJECT:, or on letterhead stationery with headings keyed when the memo is keyed. In addition, most word processing software packages permit the user to select a preformatted memo form from a built-in template or macro. A simplified memo may be keyed on plain paper or letterhead stationery. The format of a simplified memo is the same as a simplified block letter, except that the address is omitted. A formal memo prepared using a Microsoft Word memo template is shown in Figure APA.12; a simplified memo appears in Figure APA.13.

SPECIAL FORMS OF MEMOS

Business firms have developed various kinds of memo forms to perform specific functions within an organization. One is a **round-trip memo**, which is also called a *message-reply memo.* It usually consists of multiform paper, carbon or carbonless, on which the sender can complete the heading and the message portion. The sender can then remove a copy for her or his files before sending the memo. The receiver may add a reply and remove a copy before returning the memo to the original sender. An example of this kind of memo is shown in Figure APA.14.

Hughes & Associates

Memo

To: All Employees
From: Herbert Hughes, Office Manager HH
Date: 12/29/01
Re: Characteristics of Formal Memos

Heading

Many questions have arisen concerning proper construction and use of formal memos. The following guidelines should answer these questions.

Formal memos contain several unique characteristics. Some of these characteristics follow:

1. A preprinted or keyed memo heading consisting of **TO:**, **FROM:**, **DATE:**, and **SUBJECT:** or **Re**.
2. The individual sending the memo may or may not use a business title. The sender normally does not use a complete signature. An individual's first name or initials are usually written after the keyed name on the **FROM** line in the heading.
3. The memo is not centered vertically as is a letter.
4. Memos, whether formal or simplified, are normally short and contain only one topic; that topic is indicated in the subject line. If more than one topic is needed, separate memos are sent.
5. The body of the memo is in block style beginning a double space below the heading. The body is single-spaced.
6. Informal writing style is appropriate for memos. First person, I, is commonly used as in letters.

Body

Remember that memos should be concise and easy to read; they should not contain any irrelevant information. Please let me know of any other characteristics of formal memos.

jk

Reference Initials

Figure APA.12
Formal Memo Prepared Using Microsoft Word Memo Template

Stationery

Learning Objective [6]
DISCUSS THE CHARACTERISTICS OF APPROPRIATE STATIONERY FOR LETTERS, MEMOS, AND ENVELOPES.

Stationery used for letters or memos will influence the impression formed by the receiver of the message. The type of stationery that is used will be determined by the purpose of the message. For example, the stationery used for closing a major business transaction should be of a higher quality than the stationery used for announcing an upcoming sale to credit card customers.

Figure APA.13
Simplified Memo Format on Plain Paper

December 29, 2001

All Employees

CHARACTERISTICS OF SIMPLIFIED MEMOS

Many questions have arisen concerning proper construction and use of memos. The following guidelines should answer these questions.

Simplified memos contain several characteristics which are unique. Some of these characteristics follow:

1. Full sheets of either plain paper or letterhead stationery are used to prepare simplified memos.

2. All spacing guidelines for a simplified letter also apply to the simplified memo. The only difference is that no address is used in the simplified memo.

3. Personal titles are not used, but a business title or department name may be used.

4. Memos, whether formal or simplified, are normally short and contain only one topic; that topic is indicated in the subject line. If more than one topic is needed, separate memos are sent.

5. Informal writing style is appropriate for memos. First person, I, is commonly used along with inferences and jargon.

6. Reference initials, enclosure notations, copy notations, and second page headings are used as in letters.

Remember that memos should be concise and easy to read; they should contain only relevant information. Either the formal memo or simplified memo format is acceptable for our interoffice communication.

Herbert Hughes

Herbert Hughes, Office Manager

jk

WEIGHT

The weight of paper plays a part in impressing the receiver of your message. The stationery most commonly used for business letters is 20-pound bond. The weight measurement is determined by the weight of four reams of 8½- by 11-inch paper. One ream usually contains 500 sheets.

SIZE

Most business letters are prepared on **standard size paper**, 8½- by 11-inch. Letters from business executives are sometimes placed on 7¼- by 10-inch high-quality stationery called **executive stationery**. Standard-size paper (8½- by 11-inch) and **half-sheet paper** (8½- by 5½-inch) are the two most common sizes of paper used

Figure APA.14
Round-Trip Memo

To	From
	Sheila Morgan Appel Motors, Inc. Topeka, KS 66605-2531

MESSAGE

SUBJECT ____________________ DATE ____________________

SIGNED ____________________

REPLY

DATE ____________________

SIGNED ____________________

for formal memos. The paper-saving advantage of using half sheets is often outweighed by the disadvantage of locating the smaller sheet when it is filed with standard-size paper. Simplified memos are prepared on standard-size paper.

COLOR

Color is another important consideration in selecting business stationery. White is the most popular color and is acceptable for all correspondence. Recently, there has been a trend toward using other paper colors. Selecting the appropriate stationery color is extremely important to the image of the company. The type of industry certainly must be a determining factor in selecting paper color. For example, Mary Kay Cosmetics uses pink (its theme color) throughout its product line, including its stationery. On the other hand, a lumber company may very effectively use light wood-grained stationery. Some companies use different colored memo forms to identify originating departments.

QUALITY

The quality of stationery is determined by the amount of rag content in the paper. The **rag content** is the amount and type of fiber (usually cotton) used in the composition of the paper. High-quality stationery usually has 25 percent or more rag content. High-quality stationery also has a watermark showing the name of the company that manufactures the paper or the emblem of the organization that uses the stationery. Letters should be prepared on high-quality stationery; all pages should be of the same weight, color, quality, and size. The advantages of using high-quality stationery for letters include superior appearance, excellent texture, and long life without chemical breakdown. Memos should be prepared on less-expensive grades of paper.

ENVELOPE PAPER

Although the previously cited factors are important, they do not represent the end of the stationery selection process. Envelopes, too, must be given consideration. Envelope paper should be of the same weight, color, and quality as the letterhead stationery. Also, envelopes should be in proportion to the size of the stationery. For example, standard 8½- by 11-inch stationery requires No. 10 (9½- by 4⅛-inch) envelopes; executive stationery is 7¼- by 10-inch and requires No. 7 (7½- by 3⅞-inch) envelopes.

An organization may convey a positive or a negative image by its written messages. The stationery selected to carry these messages should share importance with the composition of the messages.

Summary of Learning Objectives

Learning Objective [1]

Describe the seven standard parts of a letter. The seven standard parts of a letter are as follows: (1) heading—consists of a letterhead and the dateline or the return address and a dateline; (2) inside address—includes the receiver's courtesy title, name, street number and name, city, state, and ZIP code; (3) salutation—the greeting that begins the message; (4) body—the message section of the letter; (5) complimentary close—a phrase used to end a message; (6) signature block—contains the writer's signed name, keyed name, and title; and (7) reference initials—the initials of the message originator and/or the keyboard operator.

Learning Objective [2]

Describe the appropriate use of supplementary parts of a letter. Uses for supplementary parts of a letter are as follows: (1) attention line—directs the letter to a person, position title, or department within a company; (2) subject line—identifies the main topic of a letter; (3) company name in signature block—appears when the letter is used as a contract; (4) enclosure notation—indicates the inclusion of material other than the letter in an envelope; (5) copy notation—identifies others receiving the letter; and (6) postscript—used to add personal comment or to emphasize an important point discussed in letter.

Learning Objective [3]

Format business letters using the full block, modified block, and simplified block styles. Letters written in the full block format have the dateline, inside address, salutation, each paragraph of the body, complimentary close, signature block, and reference initials begin at the left margin. Modified block letters have the date, complimentary close, and signature block begin at the horizontal center of the page, whereas everything else begins at the left margin. Paragraphs in modified block letters may be blocked or indented. Simplified block letters are prepared in the block format. The salutation and complimentary close are omitted but the receiver's name appears in the first line of the message. In addition, simplified block letters have keyed in all capital letters the subject line and the writer's name and title. The writer's name and title are both keyed on the same line four spaces below the body of the letter.

Learning Objective [4]

Address an envelope properly. The return address—the sender's address as shown on the letterhead—is keyed in all capital letters in the upper left corner of the envelope. The mailing address, the receiver's name and address as shown in the inside address, is keyed in about ½ inch left of the center and on about line 14 of a No. 10 envelope or line 12 of a No. 6¾ envelope. Mailing instructions for the Postal Service should be placed a double space below the postage stamp. Mailing instructions to individuals handling the receiver's mail should be keyed a double space below the return address.

Learning Objective [5]

Format a memo properly. Memos may be prepared using a formal or a simplified format. A formal memo may be prepared on a preprinted form that contains the headings TO:, FROM:, DATE:, and SUBJECT:, or on letterhead stationery with headings keyed when the memo is prepared. The format of a simplified memo is the same as that of a simplified block letter, except that the address is omitted.

Learning Objective [6]

Discuss the characteristics of appropriate stationery for letters, memos, and envelopes. The most commonly used stationery is 20-pound bond. Most correspondence is prepared on standard-size paper, 8½- by 11-inch, but may be prepared on executive stationery, 7½- by 10-inch, or half-sheet paper, 8½- by 5½-inch. White is the most popular color for stationery, but colored stationery is acceptable. The rag content determines the quality of the stationery. Letters are prepared on higher quality stationery than are memos. The envelopes should be the same quality, color, and size as the stationery.

APPENDIX

B Document Format—APA and MLA

Documentation Format—APA

The American Psychological Association (APA) style uses the author-data method of citation such as (Biggs, 2001) for the in-text citations and a reference list for the bibliography. The APA style is commonly used in the social and physical sciences including business. For detailed information refer to the *Publication Manual of the American Psychological Association,* Fourth Edition, Washington D.C., November 1994, Reference 808.02.

REFERENCE CITATION IN TEXT

As with any style of citation, it is essential that you document your writing throughout the text by citing both the author and date of the material. The APA documentation method uses the author-date method such as (Biggs, 2001). This style of citation briefly identifies the source for readers and enables them to locate the source of information in the alphabetical reference list at the end of the article. It is essential that your paper be well documented in order to avoid plagiarism.

REFERENCE LIST

The reference list included at the end of the document provides the information necessary to identify and retrieve each source. Authors should list only references used in the research and preparation of the document. A reference list cites works that specifically support a particular article. A bibliography cites works for background or for further reading and may include descriptive notes.

The following guidelines will assist you with the development of the APA style reference list.

[1] Make certain that each source referenced in the in-text citation is identical to the listing in the reference list.

[2] Check the dates and spellings of each source carefully. Reference data must be correct and complete to enable readers to retrieve and use the source.

[3] Begin the reference list on a separate page with the title *Reference List* centered at the top of the page. Double space after the heading to begin the list of references.

[4] Indent the first line of each double-spaced entry five spaces. Double space between the entries.

[5] Arrange entries in alphabetical order by the surname of the first author.

[6] Capitalize only the first word of the title and of the subtitles, if any, and any proper name. Do not underline the title or place quotation marks around it. Place nonroutine information that is important in brackets.

[7] Refer to Figure APB.1 for an example of use of the APA documentation.

INTERNET CITATIONS

For electronic reference formats recommended by APA for citing entire Web sites, e-mail communication, articles, and abstracts from electronic databases, visit "Electronic Reference Formats Recommended by the American Psychological Association" at **http://www.apa.org/journals/webref.html**. This Web site gives specific information on citing e-mail communications, citing a Web site, citing specific documents on a Web site, citing articles and abstracts from electronic databases, and Web citations in text. Please refer to Figure APB.1 for example sof how to cite information from a Web site on the Internet, an online magazine article, and an online newspaper article.

Documentation Format—MLA

The MLA style was developed by the Modern Language Association of America. The MLA style is used by writers in government, business, industry, the professions, and the media. The majority of scholarly journals in languages and literature use the MLA manuscript style. For detailed information refer to Joseph Gibaldi, *MLA Handbook for Writers of Research Papers,* Fifth Edition, New York: The Modern Language Association of America, 1999.

Figure ApB.1
APA Reference List

Film, videotape, or audiotape

Book, one author

Newspaper article, one author

Brochure

Book, edited

Book, two authors

Interview

Encyclopedia article, one author

Online magazine article

Internet, Web site

Newspaper article, no author

CD-ROM encyclopedia article, one author

Magazine article

Journal article

Online newspaper article

Government publication

Annual Report

Reference List

A matter of judgment: Conflicts of interest in the workplace. (1997). [Videocassette]. Washington, DC: Ethics Resource Center.

Dent, H. S., Jr. (1999). *The roaring 2000s investor: Strategies for the life you want.* New York: Simon and Schuster.

Earnest, L. (1999, December 15). Y2K eve: priceless party time. *Los Angeles Times,* p. C1.

Ethics Resource Center. (1997). *What is the ethics resource center?* [Brochure] Washington, D.C.: Ethics Resource Center.

Halpern, D. F. (Ed.). (1994). *Changing college classrooms.* San Francisco: Jossey-Bass Publishers.

Kenton, Sherron B. and Valentine, D. (1997). *Crosstalk: Communicating in a multicultural workplace.* Upper Saddle River, NJ: Prentice Hall.

Lin, L., Professor, Cal Poly Pomona. (1999, December 15). Interview by author. Pomona, CA.

Lorenz, J. R. (1999). Commodity exchange. *The World Book Encyclopedia.* Chicago, IL: World Book, Inc.

Lundstrom, M. (1999, December 20). Mommy, do you love your company more than me? Retrieved 21 December 1999 from <http://www.businessweek.com/1999/99_51/b3660167.htm>.

Norway's power to the people. (1999). *Ecotravel.* Retrieved 15 December 1999 from <http://www.goodmoney.com/norway.htm>.

Ousted Romanian premier drops bid to keep job. (1999, December 15). *Los Angeles Times,* p. A4.

Perry, J. (1999). Philosophy of mind. *Microsoft Encarta '99* [CD-ROM]. Redmond, WA: Microsoft.

Sager, I. (1999, December 13). Inside IBM: Internet Business Machines. *Business Week,* 20–38.

Sakamoto, S. (1999). The reality of differences. *The Journal of Interdisciplinary Studies 12,* 125–138.

Soriano, C. G. (1999, December 15). Good grief! Charles Schulz calls it quits. *USA Today.* Retrieved 15 December 1999 from <http://www.usatoday.com/news/acovwed.htm>.

U. S. Bureau of Census. (1998). *Statistical abstract of the United States: 1998.* Washington, DC: Bernam Press.

The Walt Disney Company. (1999). *1999 annual report.* Burbank, CA: The Walt Disney Company.

REFERENCE CITATION IN TEXT

Periodically, you will use primary and secondary sources in writing. Individuals must be given proper credit whenever their works are used by others. When you use the MLA style, you may use parenthetical citations in the text and an alphabetical list of works that appears at the end of the document. The parenthetical citations in the text use the author-page method such as (Biggs 128). This style of citation identifies the source for readers and enables them to locate the source of information in the works cited list at the end of the document.

WORKS CITED LIST

The works cited list at the end of the document provides the information necessary to identify each source and to retrieve the material. This list should contain all the works that are cited in the text.

The following guidelines will assist you with the development of the MLA style works cited list:

[1] The list contains information on all of the works that have been cited in the document.

[2] The most common title for the list is *Works Cited;* however, other titles used for the list include *Bibliography, Literature Cited, Works Consulted,* and *Annotated Bibliography.*

[3] The works cited list is placed at the end of the document.

[4] The works cited list should begin on a separate page and each page should be numbered, continuing with the page numbers of the text.

[5] The title, *Works Cited,* should be centered an inch from the top of the page with a double space between the title and the first reference entry.

[6] Begin each entry flush with the left margin. Indent each subsequent line one-half inch from the left margin.

[7] Arrange entries in alphabetical order by the author's last name.

[8] Refer to Figure APB.2 for an example of the use of the MLA documentation style.

INTERNET CITATIONS

For a summary of the MLA guidelines that cover citing World Wide Web sources, visit "MLA Style" at **http://www.mla.org/style/sources.htm**. Entries for types of Web sources include Scholarly Project, Professional Site, Personal Site, Book, Poem, Article in a Reference Database, Article in a Journal, Article in a Magazine, Work From a Subscription Service, and Posting to a Discussion List. Please refer to Figure APB.2 for examples of how to cite information from a Web site on the Internet, an online magazine article, and an online newspaper article.

Figure APB.2
MLA Works Cited List

Works Cited

Film, videotape, or audiotape

A Matter of Judgment: Conflicts of Interest in the Workplace. Videocassette. Washington, DC: Ethics Resource Center, 1997.

Book, one author

Dent, Henry S., Jr. *The Roaring 2000s Investor: Strategies for the Life You Want.* New York: Simon and Schuster, 1999.

Newspaper article, one author

Earnest, Larry. "Y2K Eve: Priceless Party Time." *Los Angeles Times* 15 Dec. 1999: C1.

Book, edited

Halpern, David F., ed. *Changing College Classrooms.* San Francisco: Jossey-Bass, 1994.

Book, two authors

Kenton, Sherron B., and Darren Valentine. *Crosstalk: Communicating in a Multicultural Workplace.* Upper Saddle River, NJ: Prentice Hall, 1997.

Interview

Lin, Lee. Personal interview. 15 December 1999.

Encyclopedia article, one author

Lorenz, Jerry R. "Commodity Exchange." *The World Book Encyclopedia.* Chicago: World Book, Inc., 1999.

Online magazine article

Lundstrom, Martha. "Mommy, Do You Love Your Company More Than Me?" *Business Week* 21 Dec. 1999 <*http://www.BusinessWeek.com/1999/99_51/b3660167.htm*>.

Internet, Web site

"Norway's Power to the People." *Ecotravel* (1999): n. pag. Online. Internet. Available: <*http://www.goodmoney.com/norway.htm*> 15 Dec. 1999.

Newspaper article, no author

"Ousted Romanian Premier Drops Bid to Keep Job." *Los Angeles Times* 15 Dec. 1999: A4.

CD-ROM encyclopedia article, one author

Perry, James. "Philosophy of Mind." *Microsoft Encarta '99.* CD-ROM. Redmond, WA: Microsoft, 1999.

Magazine article

Sager, Ignacio. "Inside IBM: Internet Business Machines." *Business Week* 13 Dec. 1999: 20–38.

Journal article

Sakamoto, Sam. "The Reality of Differences." *The Journal of Interdisciplinary Studies* 12 (1999): 125–138.

Online newspaper article

Soriano, Csar G. "Good Grief! Charles Schulz Calls It Quits." 15 Dec. 1999. Online posting. *USA Today.* p. 1A. <http://www.usatoday.com/news/acovwed.htm>.

Government publication

U. S. Bureau of Census. *Statistical Abstract of the United States*: 1998. Washington, DC: Bernam Press, 1998.

Annual Report

The Walt Disney Company. *1999 Annual Report.* Burbank, CA: The Walt Disney Company.

Brochure

What Is the Ethics Resource Center? Washington, DC: Ethics Resource Center, 1997.

APPENDIX

C Example Formal Report

States the subject of the report.

CONSUMER PREFERENCES SURVEY FOR HARRISON'S COUNTRY HAMS

Tells to whom it is submitted.

Prepared for

Mr. Phillip Niffen
Director of Marketing
Harrison's Country Hams

Tells who is submitting it.

Prepared by

Sandra Moreno
Consumer Consultant

Gives location of organization.

Market Research, Inc.
5600 West Broadway
Ruder-Fine Building, Suite 21A
St. Louis, MO 63100-2182

Gives the date of submission.

October 15, 2000

A title fly is sometimes used in reports. The title fly may be a blank sheet of paper or may state the title of the report, as in this example. (Note: title flies are not discussed in this text.)

CONSUMER PREFERENCES SURVEY
FOR
HARRISON'S COUNTRY HAMS

Harrison's Country Hams

1000 Pork Lane Kansas City, MO 64100-8462 Tel. (816) 555-1000 Fax (816) 555-2300

June 20, 2000

The letter of authorization.

Ms. Sandra Moreno, Consumer Consultant
Market Research, Inc.
5600 West Broadway
Ruder-Fine Building, Suite 21A
St. Louis, MO 63100-2182

Dear Ms. Moreno:

Subject: Authorization for Consumer Preferences Study

Gives authority for the study.

You are authorized to study consumer preferences for country hams in the Kansas City, Missouri, area. The purposes of your study are

Gives relevant information, such as purposes and procedures.

1. To provide a description of country ham consumers.
2. To analyze consumer perceptions of Harrison's country hams as compared to the competition.
3. To determine if the present Harrison's packaging is satisfactory for consumers.
4. To help Harrison's increase its market share of ham sales by recommending media vehicles and advertising strategy.

I recommend that you survey shoppers who are entering large supermarket chain stores in Kansas City and its suburbs. Your sample should be drawn randomly.

Describes available funding.

As we have agreed, a consulting fee of $7,500 will be paid to Market Research, Inc., on the successful completion of this study and the submission of an acceptable report. Harrison's may authorize additional consumer preference surveys in other geographical areas if the results of this study seem worthwhile.

Your report should be submitted to me by October 30, 2000. Please contact me if you need any further information or guidance from Harrison's.

Gives the date the report is due.

Sincerely,

Phillip Niffen

Phillip Niffen
Director of Marketing

cr

iii

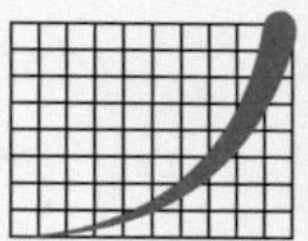

Market Research, Inc.

5600 West Broadway, Ruder-Fine Building, Suite 21A
St. Louis, MO 63100-2182
Tel. (314) 555-5000, Fax (314) 555-7933
mri@SMO.com

October 15, 2000

Mr. Phillip Niffen
Director of Marketing
Harrison's Country Hams
1000 Pork Lane
Kansas City, MO 64100-8462

> The letter of transmittal.

Dear Mr. Niffen:

> Transmits the report.

Here is the report you requested on consumer preferences for country hams in the Kansas City, Missouri, area.

> Describes the procedures and purposes.

We surveyed 100 randomly selected grocery shoppers to determine who buys country hams, how consumers perceive Harrison's hams as compared to the competition, what opinions consumers have on Harrison's packaging, and how Harrison's could increase its market share.

> Gives the highlights of the findings.

The survey results show that Harrison's country hams are purchased predominantly by high school graduates with less than $30,000 in income and who have a preference for country music. Consumers who have tried and liked Harrison's think it is a high-quality ham and a good value. Consumers who disliked Harrison's country ham said that its price is too high. Consumers prefer clear packaging to the present white paper packaging.

Based on these survey findings, we recommend a strengthened marketing strategy directed at a more affluent consumer, increased television and radio advertising with a country music orientation, and a change to clear plastic shrink packaging.

> Summarizes the recommendations.

Thank you for the opportunity to complete this market research for Harrison's. I hope that you find the results valuable and that you will authorize additional, similar studies in other market areas. I am convinced that by doing so you will increase your market share.

> Closes the letter.

Cordially,

Sandra Moreno

Sandra Moreno
Consumer Consultant

kah

iv

The table of contents lists names and page numbers of all major sections.

TABLE OF CONTENTS

The list of illustrations contains the titles and page numbers of all illustrations—figures, charts and graphs, tables, and so forth.

LIST OF ILLUSTRATIONS

FIGURES

TABLES

vi

The executive summary (abstract, synopsis, etc.) summarizes the important parts of the report.

EXECUTIVE SUMMARY

Introductory material.

To increase its market share, Harrison's Country Hams requested that Market Research, Inc., conduct a consumer preferences survey in the Kansas City, Missouri, area. The study was designed to describe the country ham consumer, analyze country ham consumer preferences, determine the adequacy of Harrison's packaging, and recommend improvements in Harrison's media vehicles and advertising strategy. One hundred consumers entering supermarkets were randomly selected and interviewed.

Procedures.

Related literature.

A related literature review showed that household incomes of country ham consumers increased 54 percent between 1989 and 1999, indicating the development of an upscale market. Further, research on packaging found that meat consumers prefer to see meat prior to its purchase.

The survey revealed that country ham consumers predominantly were married high school graduates between 25 and 44 years of age. They had one to two children in a family of three to four. They lived in the suburbs and one-half preferred country music. Approximately one-third of the consumers usually buy Harrison's country hams, and about one-half had eaten Harrison's. Of the consumers who had eaten Harrison's, those who liked it thought it had good taste and was a good value. Those who disliked it thought its price was too high and it had too much salt.

Findings.

In addition, the survey found that Harrison's consumers preferred clear plastic packaging, but a significant number did not like the current pig logo. Only one-third of Harrison's consumers earn more than $30,000, suggesting an untapped upscale market. Most had seen or heard Harrison's advertisements on television or radio. City dwellers were more likely to have seen the ads on television, whereas suburbanites heard them on radio.

Analysis and conclusions.

The analysis of the findings revealed that (1) Harrison's current consumers were from predominantly low-income households, (2) the hams had good taste and value, (3) advertising should target the upscale market, and (4) television and radio were the most successful media.

Based on the conclusions, it is recommended that Harrison's should focus its marketing strategy on the superior taste and quality of its country hams, Harrison's advertising should be directed at the upscale market, the advertising should be primarily on television and radio with a country music orientation, and Harrison's packaging should be clear plastic shrink wrapping with a modified pig logo.

Recommendations.

vii

The introduction assists the reader in understanding the rest of the report.

I. INTRODUCTION

This introductory section includes the background of the problem, statement of the problem, purposes of the study, and scope of the study.

The background describes the problem in general.

Background

Harrison's Country Hams was interested in increasing its market share. In consultation with Market Research, Inc., Harrison's decided to have a consumer preferences survey conducted in the Kansas City, Missouri, area. Other similar studies will be conducted if this study is deemed helpful.

The statement of the problem identifies the specific problem researched.

Statement of the Problem

The focus of this study was to determine (1) selected attributes and preferences of country ham consumers and (2) improvements that could be made in Harrison's product packaging and promotion.

Purposes of the Study

The purposes of the study tell why the study was conducted.

The purposes of this study were as follows:

- To provide a description of country ham consumers.
- To analyze consumer perceptions of Harrison's country hams as compared to the competition.
- To determine if the present Harrison's packaging is adequate for consumers.
- To help Harrison's increase its market share of ham sales by recommending media vehicles and advertising strategy.

The scope defines the boundaries of the study.

Scope

The scope of this study included analyses of country ham consumers, consumer country ham eating habits and preferences, and Harrison's competition. The study was limited to the Kansas City, Missouri, market area.

The related literature reviews research that has been conducted on similar topics.

II. RELATED LITERATURE

The literature on studies of consumer product preferences is extensive. Although this broad expanse of research was generally helpful, two recent studies of consumers were found to be especially valuable for this study.

In a 1999 study by Paula Brockway, it was found that, in constant dollars, the average household income of country ham consumers had increased significantly over the past ten years. In 1989, the average household income of country ham consumers was $15,543. In 1999, that income level had risen to $26,939, a 54 percent increase over the 1989 level. Brockway's conclusion was that country ham merchandisers should target more of their advertising to the upscale market levels.

In 1998, William Seale surveyed consumers' preferences on the packaging of fresh meat and found that consumers wanted to be able to see the meat prior to purchase. Clear plastic shrink wrapping was preferred to unwrapped meat or opaque packaging.

1

The procedures section describes the steps taken in conducting the study.

III. PROCEDURES

A survey was conducted using a sampling technique to ensure randomization in the respondents. It was determined statistically that a sample of 100 grocery shoppers would provide a .05 precision and 95 percent confidence level. The procedures followed included these:

1. A questionnaire was developed that contained simple dichotomous questions, check list questions, open-ended questions, and a semantic differential scale. (See Appendix.)
2. Teams of interviewers were stationed at five large supermarket chain stores located in the Kansas City area.
3. Interviews were conducted over a three-day period—Friday through Sunday—beginning on August 25, 2000.
4. Every 25th adult consumer entering the store was approached for an interview. If the interview was rejected, then the request was repeated of the next available consumer until one was willing to be interviewed.
5. The data were tabulated using a computerized statistical package, SPSS-X.
6. The results were analyzed by a team of Market Research consumer consultants and this report prepared.

IV. FINDINGS

The findings section presents the results of the study in an objective manner.

These findings are presented using the study objectives as a framework. The following sections include information about the demographics of country ham consumers, consumer perceptions of Harrison's compared to the competition, consumer perceptions of packaging, and information on the market and media.

Country Ham Consumers

The demographic information collected for the study—from musical preference to household income—provides a detailed description of country ham consumers. The presentation of these findings is shown in Figures 1 through 8 that follow.

As indicated in Figure 1, 73 percent of the respondents were married. Figure 2 shows that 12 percent of country ham consumers have some high school education, and 40 percent ended their formal education when they graduated from high school. The remaining respondents reported that they had some college (38 percent), or were college graduates (10 percent). A total of 88 percent have at least a high school education.

Figure 1. MARITAL STATUS

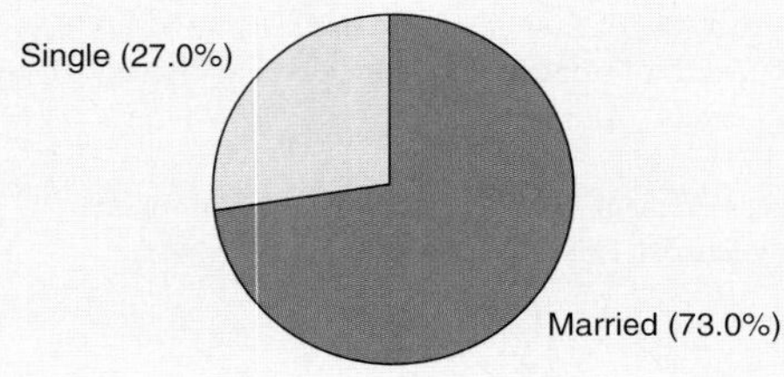

Figure 2. EDUCATION

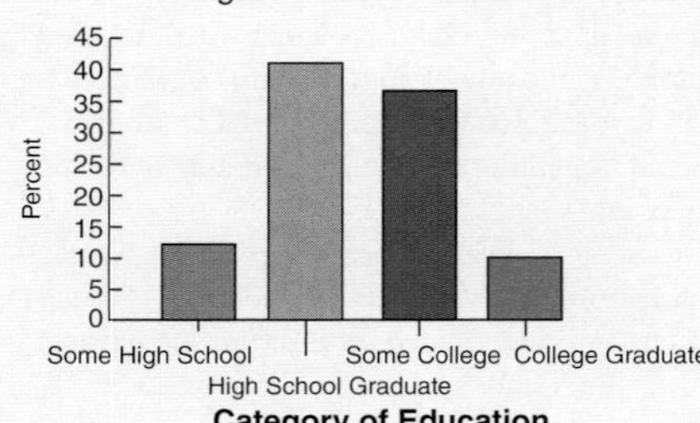

2

Seventy-eight percent were 25 years of age or older, with 56 percent 25 to 44, and 22 percent 45 and over. (See Figure 3.) As shown in Figure 4, most of the respondents (69 percent) had one to two children under the age of 18.

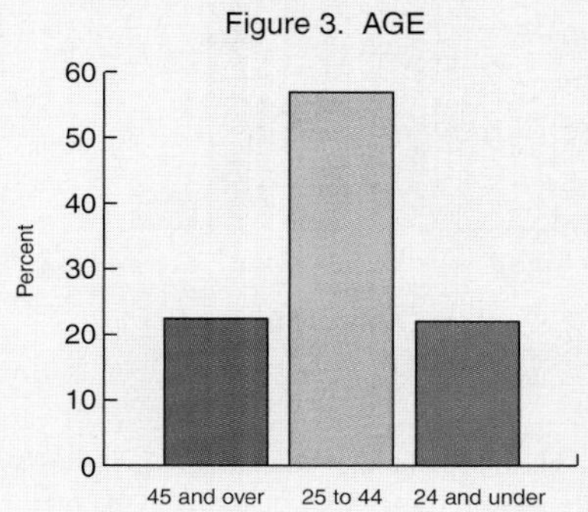

Figure 3. AGE

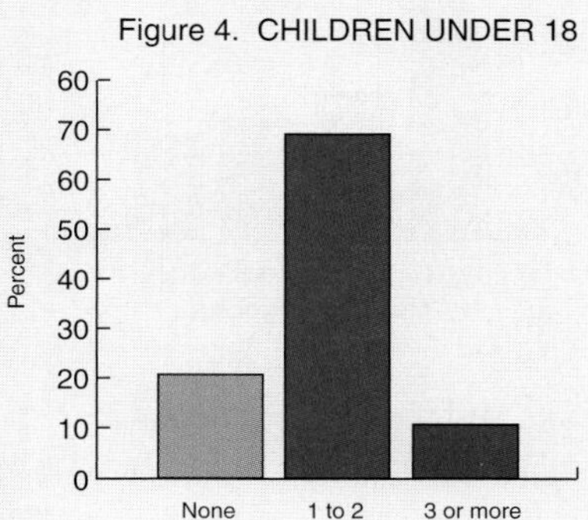

Figure 4. CHILDREN UNDER 18

Figure 5 shows that 65 percent of the respondents' family size was three to four persons. As indicated in Figure 6, most (54 percent) lived in the suburbs.

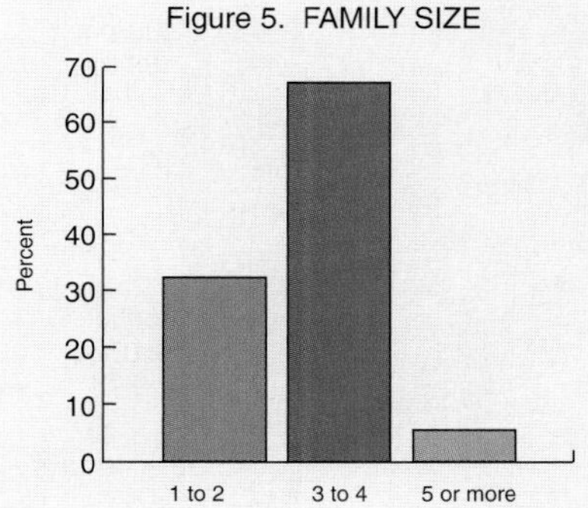

Figure 5. FAMILY SIZE

Figure 6. RESIDENCE LOCATION

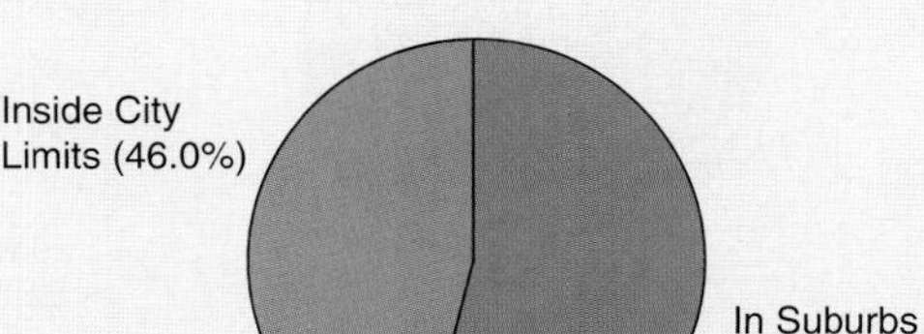

Figure 7 shows that half (50 percent) preferred country music. Seventy-five percent, as shown in Figure 8, had household incomes of less than $30,000.

In summary, those surveyed predominantly were married high school graduates between 25 and 44 years of age. They had one to two children in a family of three to four. They lived in the suburbs and one-half preferred country music. Only one-fourth had household incomes of more than $30,000 per year.

3

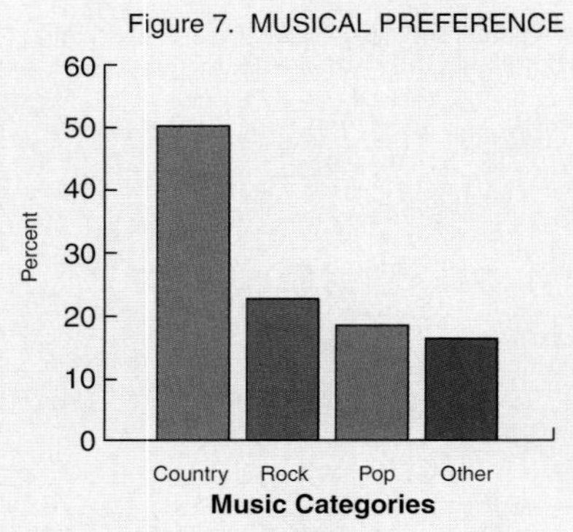

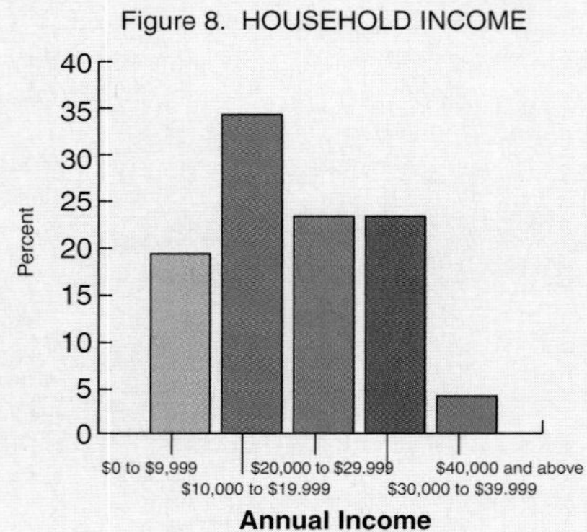

Harrison's and the Competition

As shown in Figure 9, almost half (49 percent) have eaten Harrison's ham, whereas Figure 10 shows that fewer than one-third (32 percent) of the respondents usually choose Harrison's country ham over the competitors' hams.

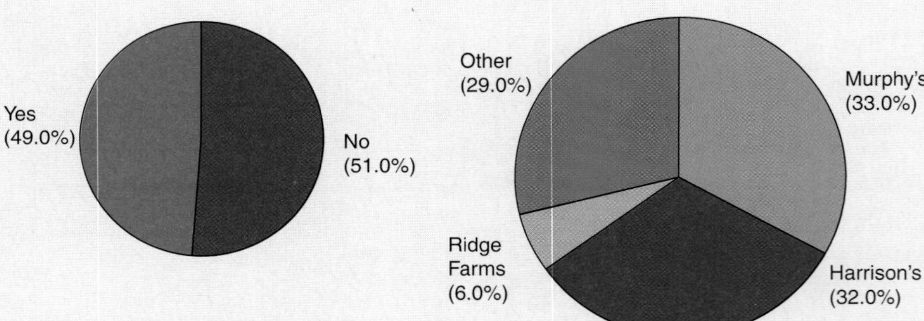

Of the consumers who had eaten Harrison's country hams, we asked what they liked and disliked about the product. As shown in Figure 11, the responses of those who liked it reveal that almost two-thirds (63 percent) thought it had good taste and about one-third (32 percent) thought it was a good value. Figure 12 shows that one-half of the respondents who disliked Harrison's country ham (50 percent) said it was because of high price. Most remaining respondents thought Harrison's had either too much salt (35 percent) or not enough salt (11 percent).

Packaging Preferences

As indicated in Figure 13, 51 percent of the consumers preferred clear plastic packaging. Only 39 percent liked the present Harrison's white paper packaging. Figure 14 shows that over one-third of the respondents (35 percent) did not like Harrison's pig logo.

4

Figure 11. LIKE HARRISON'S HAM

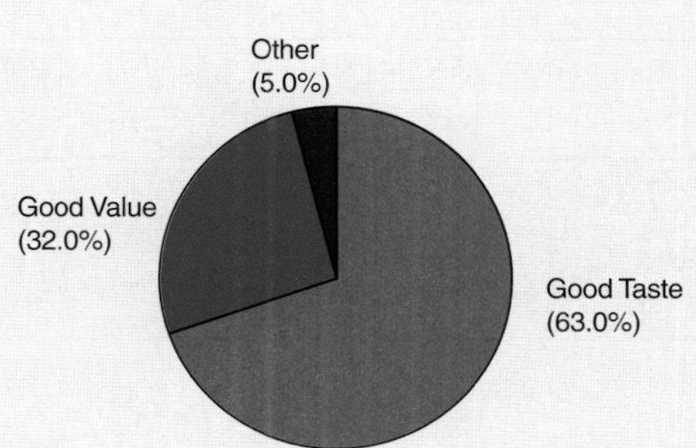

Figure 12. DISLIKE HARRISON'S HAM

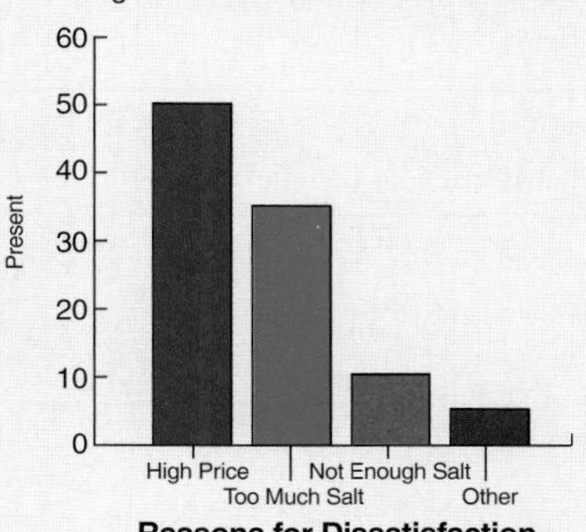

Some of the specific responses of those who said they liked the Harrison pig logo were "OK," "Cute," and "Gets good attention." Those who disliked the logo, however, commented "Could be better," "Offensive," and "Unfavorable association of the food with a pig's rear end."

Figure 13. PACKAGING PREFERRED

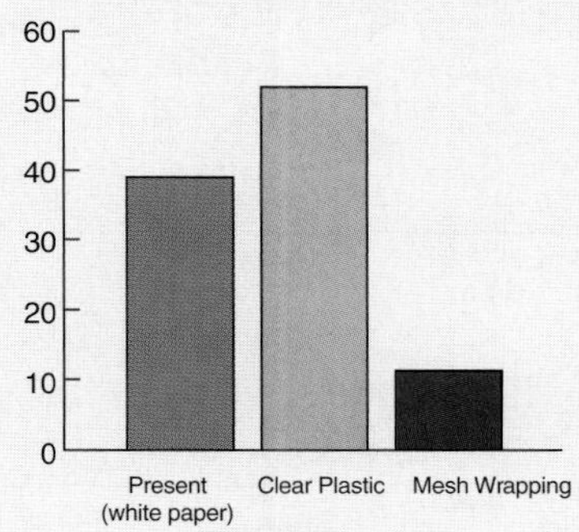

Figure 14. LOGO OPINION

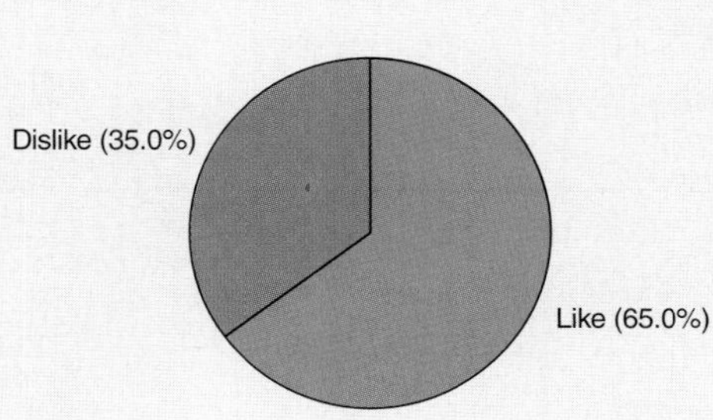

Market and Media

Cross tabulations were run to provide additional market and media information for determining media vehicles and marketing strategy for Harrison's Country Hams.

Market. Table 1 shows a statistically significant difference in the number of consumers who had eaten Harrison's by level of household income.

Of those who had eaten Harrison's country hams, only 33 percent had household incomes of more than $30,000. The less-affluent consumers appeared to constitute the larger current market segment for Harrison's.

Media. A second set of significantly different responses was found in the cross tabulations for advertising media. Table 2 shows that 77 percent of the respondents who had seen or heard a Harrison's advertisement

TABLE 1. THE NUMBER AND PERCENTAGE OF RESPONDENTS WHO HAD EATEN HARRISON'S COUNTRY HAM, BY LEVEL OF INCOME

	Had Eaten Harrison's Ham	
Level of Household Income	**Number**	**Percent**
$0 to $29,999	33	67
$30,000 and above	16	33
TOTAL	49	100

TABLE 2. THE NUMBER AND PERCENTAGE OF RESPONDENTS WHO HAD SEEN OR HEARD HARRISON'S ADVERTISEMENTS, BY TYPE OF ADVERTISEMENT

	Had Seen or Heard Harrison's Ads	
Type of Advertisement	**Number**	**Percent**
Television	21	38
Radio	22	39
Billboard	6	11
Other	7	12
TOTAL	56	100

TABLE 3. THE NUMBER AND PERCENTAGE OF RESPONDENTS WHO HAD SEEN HARRISON'S ADVERTISEMENTS ON TELEVISION, BY RESIDENCE LOCATION

	Saw Harrison's Ads on Television	
Residence Location	**Number**	**Percent**
Inside city limits	13	62
In suburbs	8	38
TOTAL	21	100

had seen it on television (38 percent) or heard it on radio (39 percent). Billboard advertisements were seen by only 11 percent, and other advertisements accounted for only 12 percent. Table 3 shows that 62 percent of those who had seen Harrison's Country Hams' advertisements on television lived within the city limits. As shown in Table 4, however, 77 percent of those who had heard Harrison's advertisements on radio lived in suburbs.

6

TABLE 4. THE NUMBER AND PERCENTAGE OF RESPONDENTS WHO HAD HEARD HARRISON'S ADVERTISEMENTS ON RADIO, BY RESIDENCE LOCATION

	Heard Harrison's Ads on Radio	
Residence Location	**Number**	**Percent**
Inside city limits	5	23
In suburbs	17	77
TOTAL	22	100

Obviously, television was more effective in reaching city dwellers, whereas radio was superior in reaching residents of the suburbs.

The analysis presents relationships that are important.

V. ANALYSIS

Country ham consumers in the Kansas City area tended to be educated and married with established family units. These consumers, however, also tended to have relatively low household incomes—only 25 percent had incomes of $30,000 or more. Brockway, reporting a 54 percent increase in average income of country ham consumers between 1989 and 1999, concluded in her April 1999 article in *The Grocery Retailer* that country ham merchandisers should target more of their advertising at the upscale market levels. Harrison's current market mix (33 percent with over $30,000 income) does not now include its potential share of the upscale market segment.

This study found that most consumers who had eaten Harrison's country ham and liked it thought it had good taste and was a good value. Those who disliked Harrison's, however, did so primarily because of its high price.

Since this study found that most of Harrison's consumers are from the less-affluent segment of the country ham market, a greater effort to reach the untapped higher income households should be profitable. With Harrison's high-quality product, price should not be a sales barrier in this upscale market.

In addition, this study shows clearly that most consumers had seen or heard a Harrison's advertisement on television or radio versus other media. Consumers who live in Kansas City were more likely to have seen Harrison's advertisements on television, and those who lived in the suburbs heard them on radio. Television and radio are obviously the most successful media for Harrison's. A further media consideration is that one-half of the country ham consumers preferred country music over other types of music.

Finally, both this study and Seale's study (as reported in his May 1998 article in *Retail Merchandising*) found that most meat purchasers do not like opaque packaging. The consumers preferred clear plastic packaging of meats, including country hams. Further, a significant number of consumers surveyed for this study—35 percent—disliked the pig logo Harrison's uses on its packaging.

7

VI. CONCLUSIONS AND RECOMMENDATIONS

Conclusions are drawn from the analysis of the findings of the study.

Conclusions

1. Harrison's current consumers in the Kansas City area tend to come predominantly from low-income households.
2. Harrison's country ham is considered to have good taste and to be a good value. Its price is considered high.
3. Harrison's is not reaching its potential share of the upscale market segment.
4. Television and radio are the most successful advertising media for Harrison's.
5. Country ham consumers tend to prefer country music.
6. Harrison's packaging and logo should be changed.

Recommendations are developed from the study's conclusions.

Recommendations

1. Harrison's marketing strategy should advertise its product as superior in both taste and quality in comparison to its competition. Harrison's should promote its product as the "Cadillac" of country hams and aim for a more prestigious image.
2. An increased share of Harrison's advertising content should be directed at appealing to the affluent consumer who is willing and able to pay a higher price for a high-quality product.
3. A greater proportion of Harrison's advertising budget should be spent on television and radio programming with a country music orientation so as to reach more country ham consumers.
4. Harrison's should go to clear plastic shrink packaging as soon as feasible to make its hams more visible. To help reduce consumer dissatisfaction, the pig logo should gradually be changed to show more of a side view of the pig instead of the straight rear view.

8

APPENDIX

STUDY QUESTIONNAIRE

An appendix contains supportive supplementary material that is related to the study.

HARRISON'S CONSUMER PREFERENCES SURVEY

Hello, I am ______________________________ with Market Research, Inc., and I am doing a survey for Harrison's Country Hams. May I ask you a few questions?

1. Are you responsible for most of the grocery shopping for your household?

   ( ) yes ( ) no [if no, terminate]

2. For each of the following characteristics, how would you describe country ham? (Check the space describing how you feel.)

Characteristic		
A. Taste	____ Tasty	____ Not tasty
B. Nutritional value	____ Healthy	____ Not healthy
C. Price	____ Inexpensive	____ Expensive
D. Packaging	____ Important	____ Not important

3. What brand of country ham do you usually buy? (Specify.)

   ____

4. Have you ever eaten a Harrison's country ham?

   ( ) yes ( ) no

5. If your answer to question 4 is yes, please state what you liked or disliked about Harrison's country hams. ____

   ____

6. Harrison's country ham is currently sold in a white paper package like this one (show wrapping to consumer). It could also be sold with a clear plastic cover or a cloth mesh cover. Which would you most prefer?

   ( ) present white paper ( ) clear plastic cover

   ( ) cloth mesh cover ( ) other ______________________________

7. Have you ever seen or heard a Harrison's advertisement?

   ( ) yes ( ) no

8. If your answer to question 7 is yes, where?

   ( ) TV ( ) radio ( ) billboard ( ) other ________________

9. What do you like or dislike about the Harrison's Country Hams logo? (Show them the logo of the pig—a direct rear view of a pig who is looking back and smiling at the viewer.) ______________

   ____

10

10. What type of music do you prefer?
    ( ) country ( ) pop
    ( ) rock ( ) other ______________________

11. Which age category best fits you?
    ( ) 24 and under ( ) 25–44
    ( ) 45–64 ( ) 65 and over

12. Which family size category best fits you?
    ( ) 1 to 2 ( ) 3 to 4 ( ) 5 or more

13. Are you married?
    ( ) yes ( ) no

14. How many of the children in your household are under 18?
    ( ) 0 ( ) 1 to 2 ( ) 3 or more

15. What is the highest level of education you have achieved?
    ( ) attended grade school ( ) attended some high school
    ( ) high school graduate ( ) attended some college
    ( ) college graduate

16. Which household total income category best fits your household?
    ( ) Under $10,000 ( ) $10,000–$19,999
    ( ) $20,000–$29,999 ( ) $30,000–$39,999
    ( ) $40,000 and above

17. Where is your residence located?
    ( ) city ( ) suburbs

BIBLIOGRAPHY

The bibliography is a list of all the references that were used as sources of information in the study.

BIBLIOGRAPHY

Brockway, Paula G., "The Buying Power of Grocery Shoppers," *The Grocery Retailer* 32 (April 1999): 26–32.

Seale, William S., "Meat Packaging: What Does the Consumer Prefer?" *Retail Merchandising* 26 (May 1998): 44–51.

13

Credits

For permission to reproduce the photographs and other copyrighted material on the pages indicated, acknowledgement is made to the following:

page 1: © PhotoDisc, Inc.; page 1: © PhotoDisc, Inc.; page 2: Courtesy of Tara Benson; page 6: © PhotoDisc, Inc.; page 11: Courtesy of Lisa Gutowsky; page 20: BC reprinted by permission of Johnny Hart and Creators Syndicate, Inc.; page 20: Courtesy of Todd Fedora; page 28: Courtesy of Kent Nethery; page 34: Courtesy of Tarja Bentgarde-Childers; page 35: © PhotoDisc, Inc.; page 40: © VCC/FPG International LLC; page 44: Courtesy of Nga Chan; page 45: © 1996 SHOTGUN/The Stock Market; page 60: Courtesy of Michelle Schroer; page 67: Courtesy of Paul Johansen; page 75: DILBERT Reprinted by permission of United Features Syndicate, Inc.; page 77: SALLY FORTH Reprinted with special permission King Features Syndicate; page 81: © Steven Peters/Stone; page 88: Courtesy of Bruce Ray; page 90: © PhotoDisc, Inc.; page 95: © PhotoDisc, Inc.; page 96: Courtesy of Sima Boyahjian; page 110: © AFP/CORBIS; page 120: Courtesy of Andrea Anast Tunks; page 130: © PhotoDisc, Inc.; page 143: Courtesy of Ralph S. Larsen; page 149: © David Young Wolff/Stone; page 156: Courtesy of Brian Delegan; page 159: Courtesy of Brad Fuji; page 173: SALLY FORTH Reprinted with special permission King Features Syndicate; page 176: DILBERT reprinted by permission of United Features Syndicate, Inc.; page 176: Courtesy of Julie Tapp; page 183: © PhotoDisc, Inc.; page 185: Courtesy of Blanca Arellano; page 192: Courtesy of Dick Anderson; page 197: © 2000 Corbis. All rights reserved; page 197: PEANUTS reprinted by permission of United Features Syndicate, Inc.; page 208: © G. Brian Karas/Artville; page 218: Courtesy of Andrea Holle; page 219: © Jose Luis Pelaez, Inc./The Stock Market; page 232: Courtesy of Jim Farmer; page 241: © R.W. Jones/CORBIS; page 246: DUNAGIN'S PEOPLE © Tribune Media Services, Inc. All Rights Reserved. Reprinted with permission; page 264: Courtesy of David Alexander; page 270: FUNKY WINKERBEAN Reprinted with special permission King Features Syndicate; page 295: © PhotoDisc, Inc.; page 296: Courtesy of Connie Cushing; page 298: © PhotoDisc, Inc.; page 299: DILBERT reprinted by permission of United Feature Syndicate, Inc.; page 303: © Dave G. Houser/CORBIS; page 304: Courtesy of Tracy Marks; page 306: © Billy Barnes/Stock, Boston Picture Quest; page 324: Courtesy of Howard W. Kruse; page 352: Courtesy of Bruce Ray; page 377: Courtesy of Steve Schneberger; page 381: Courtesy of Eric Goerdt; page 381: DILBERT reprinted by permission of United Features Syndicate, Inc.; page 385: © R.W. Jones/CORBIS; page 392: Courtesy of Lawana Duncan Sledd; page 394: Courtesy of International Business Machines Corporation; page 408: © 2000 CORBIS. All Rights Reserved; page 409: © PhotoDisc, Inc.; page 411: Source: USDA "The Digital Economy" Seminar, July 2000, Mary Mitchell, GSA. Federal Electronic Commerce Program web site (http://ec.fed.gov/presentations.htm); page 413: Source: USDA "The Digital Economy" Seminar, July 2000, Mary Mitchell, GSA. Federal Electronic Commerce Program web site (http://ec.fed.gov/presentations.htm); page 427: © PhotoDisc, Inc.; page 427: © PhotoDisc, Inc.; page 428: Courtesy of William Ellis; page 431: © 1996 William Taufic/The Stock Market; page 433: FOR BETTER OR FOR WORSE © Lynn Johnston Productions, Inc./Distributed by United Features Syndicate, Inc.; page 433: Courtesy of Erika Ludwig; page 434: Courtesy of Stephen C. Duggan; page 438: © PhotoDisc, Inc.; page 440: © Ken Fisher/Stone; page 446: Courtesy of Amy Brand; page 452: FAMILY CIRCUS Reprinted with special permission King Features Syndicate; page 456: © AFP/CORBIS; page 464: BLONDIE Reprinted with special permission King Features Syndicate; page 469: Courtesy of Colleen Welty; page 477: © PhotoDisc, Inc.; page 477: © PhotoDisc, Inc.; page 478: Courtesy of Lulu Fou; page 482: Courtesy of Mike Wiggins; page 485: © Dennis MacDonald/PhotoEdit/Picture Quest; page 503: Courtesy of Sergio Bautista; page 512: Courtesy of Pam Hay; page 520: Courtesy of Irene Kinoshita; page 523: © Richard Shock/Stone; page 525: © Bob Daemmrich/Stock, Boston/Picture Quest; page 528: Courtesy of Margaret F. Riley Dikel

Index

D

T

U